The Complete Book of
Knitting Crochet & Embroidery

Consultant Editor
PAM DAWSON

Marshall Cavendish London & New York

Published by Marshall Cavendish Books Limited
58 Old Compton Street
London W1V 5PA

© Marshall Cavendish Limited 1972, 1973, 1974, 1975, 1976, 1977
First published and printed in Great Britain 1976
First American edition 1977
Second American edition 1977
Printed in Great Britain

ISBN 0 85685 245 7

Knitting and crochet abbreviations

alt	alternate(ly)	**P-wise**	purlwise, as if to purl
approx	approximate(ly)	**rem**	remain(ing)
beg	begin(ning)	**rep**	repeat
ch	chain(s)	**RS**	right side
cont	continu(e) (ing)	**sc**	single crochet
dec	decrease	**sl**	slip
dc	double crochet	**sl st**	slip stitch
dtr	double treble	**sp**	space(s)
foll	follow(ing)	**st(s)**	stitch(es)
g st	garter stitch, every row knit	**st st**	stockinette stitch, 1 row knit, 1 row purl
grm	gramme(s)	**tbl**	through back of loop
gr(s)	group(s)	**tog**	together
hdc	half double crochet	**tr**	treble
in	inch(es)	**tr tr**	triple treble
inc	increase	**ẂS**	wrong side
K	knit	**yd(s)**	yard(s)
K-wise	knitwise, as if to knit	**yo**	yarn over
No.	number	**ybk**	yarn back
psso	pass slipped stitch over	**yfwd**	yarn forward
patt	pattern	**yrh**	yarn round hook
P	purl	**yrn**	yarn round needle

The list given above contains many of the most commonly used knitting and crochet abbreviations. However, some have been adapted to make them more explicit for the beginner, e.g. "yfwd" and "ybk" (yarn forward and yarn back) often abbreviated solely as "yo". Some knitting pattern companies do, however, have their own style of abbreviating knitting terms so, before starting any pattern, study their list of abbreviations carefully.
Some of the patterns in this book also contain specific instructions for that pattern alone. Where this occurs, the abbreviation will be given in the pattern.

Symbols
An asterisk, *, shown in a pattern row denotes that the stitches shown after this sign must be repeated from that point. Square brackets, [], denote instructions for larger sizes in the pattern. Round brackets, (), denote that this section of the pattern is to be worked for all sizes. Gauge—this is the most important factor in successful knitting or crochet. Unless you obtain the gauge given for each design, you will not obtain satisfactory results.

CONTENTS

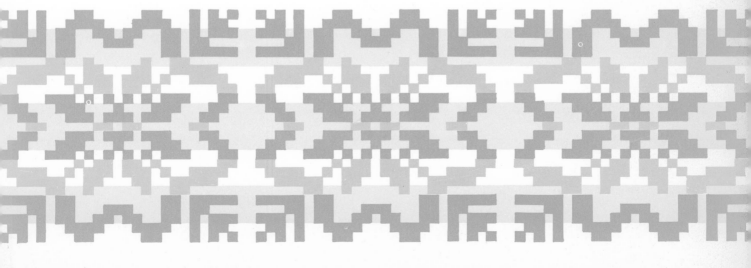

AN INTRODUCTION TO KNITTING

In presenting this book my genuine hope is that I can communicate some of my enthusiasm for this most beautiful craft to the reader and whether you approach it as a complete beginner or knowledgeable knitter, arouse your interest in its almost limitless possibilities.

For the first half of this century, knitting was tagged with the fuddy-duddy image it used to have and suffered an undeserved decline in popularity. Today it has rightly taken its place as a unique and practical way of interpreting fashion but, even now, most knitters are still not aware of its tremendous scope. In no other field of fashion or craft, other than the allied craft of crochet, do you have such complete control not only over the shape of the ultimate design, but the texture and color of the fabric. In this craft, you as the knitter, combine both the skill of a weaver and the practical knowledge of a dressmaker – and all for the price of a pair of needles and a few balls of yarn. Of all the crafts and skills acquired by man – and I use the word 'man' advisedly, in that women's skill in this field is only recent in terms of history – knitting has proved to be one of the most fascinating and enduring. It has survived, sometimes through countless centuries without any record, either written or visual, and has developed and evolved by word of mouth from one generation to the next, as the ideal means of clothing the world's population.

The first steps in knitting are as simple as those required for basic cookery, but its ultimate variety is akin to the art of cordon bleu cooking, where nothing that individual taste, ability and imagination can devise is impossible. The only manufactured materials required are a pair of needles and a ball of spun thread but, with sufficient knowledge and time to experiment, even these are comparatively easy to produce by hand. The simple talents needed to encompass its full range are a willing pair of hands, an eye for color and fabric, some simple mathematical skill and basic dressmaking knowledge. Armed with these attributes the world of knitting is your oyster and you can begin to design garments to suit your own individual shape and taste, without being tied to existing patterns.

The main purpose of this book is to take the technical knowledge it contains and apply this to the basic guide to designing, which is also explained. You can, of course, accept it as it stands and still acquire the necessary skill to become a proficient knitter, but taking the step from knitter to designer is a relatively small one and out of all proportion to the exciting and creative field it opens up for you. With the present necessity to conserve all natural resources and survive an unhealthy economic period, it is even more important to know how to make warm, wearable and fashionable garments for the minimum of outlay, both in costs and materials. Knitting is the most practical and satisfying solution to these problems and has the added bonus of extending your own latent creative talents and the therapeutic benefit of making something beautiful with your own hands.

Pam Dawson

HISTORY OF KNITTING

Knitting is an ancient craft, which developed in the deserts of Arabia among the nomadic tribes who lived there 3,000 years ago. It may even have been a familiar technique in pre-biblical times, for knitting of high quality, well advanced in both technique and design, was certainly being produced in Arabia 1,000 years before the birth of Christ. No one can date the birth of knitting exactly. It has grown up with civilization. The early knitters were the men of the tribes, and they were very skilled at their craft. These people kept straggling herds of sheep and goats, and there was no shortage of material. The women gathered wool from the animals and spun it into yarn for the men, who would sit for hours, tending the flocks and knitting. The articles they produced were simple scarves, robes and socks which could be worn with sandals.

Ancient knitting

Very few examples of really early knitting are still in existence, but a pair of red sandal socks, pre-Christian in origin, still survive. They are beautifully made, with expertly turned heels. It is interesting to note that stitches have been carefully divided for the big toe, so that the socks were comfortable to wear with sandals.

The socks were knitted in the round on a circular frame, probably made of thin wire. Pins were inserted all around the edge of the circle, and loops were made on the pins. When the wool was wound around the outside of the pins and the loops drawn over it, circular knitting of a rather loose gauge was produced.

A spectacular fragment

Twin needles, hooked at the ends rather like today's crochet hooks, were used to make another surviving fragment of Arabic knitting. This piece of work was discovered at Fustat, an ancient ruined city near Cairo, somewhere in Egypt, and it has been dated between the 7th and the 9th centuries. From beneath the sand and dust of centuries a fragile piece of knitted silk fabric was retrieved. Worked with exquisite care on a pair of fine wire needles, to an easily-checked gauge of 36 stitches to the inch, the fragment reveals an elaborate design in maroon and gold.

Between the years 1000 and 1200 little round knitted caps called Coptic caps were being made in Egypt. They were worn by monks and missionaries and it is possible that these men carried the knowledge of knitting with them out of Egypt. Craftsmen in Spain, then in Italy and France and eventually in England and the New World, were fascinated by this new kind of fabric weaving. Knowledge of the craft quickly spread, each nation adding its own ideas and patterns. By the Middle Ages knitting was a common craft all over Europe. Italy and France were the great medieval homes of fine knitting, and there the knitters soon formed themselves, under Church patronage, into organized guilds.

The Knitters' Guilds

The Knitters' Guild of Paris was a typical example. Young boys of intelligence and manual ability were carefully selected as apprentices. They were bound for six years, three of which were spent working with a master-knitter at home and three learning new techniques in a foreign country. At the end of this time the apprentice was required to demonstrate his skill to his elders. The test was prodigious. In only thirteen weeks the apprentice had to knit an elaborate carpet eight feet by twelve, with extremely intricate designs incorporating flowers, birds, foliage and animals in natural colors, using between twenty and thirty different colored wools; a beret, sometimes to be felted and blocked after knitting; a woolen shirt; and a pair of socks with Spanish clocks.

No apprentice was accepted who did not produce masterpieces in all these categories, and when he became a master-knitter he knew that shoddy or skimped work would result in heavy fines and even expulsion from the guild, which meant loss of livelihood. The only women admitted to these guilds were the widows of master-knitters. For the most part, the women still sat at home spinning the wool for the men to knit up.

Apart from the domestic and commercial work being produced in England, much exquisite decorative knitting was done in the seclusion of the monasteries and the nunneries. The religious influence on the knitting of the 16th and 17th centuries is very marked.

The hand knitting tradition continued to be strong in England until the Industrial Revolution in the 19th century, the age of mass production when interest in handcrafts declined.

Individuality still flourished, however, notably in Scotland and the Channel Islands, where traditional sweaters (called 'jumpers') and jerseys were made. The 'guernsey', produced on the Channel Island of Guernsey for centuries, took two forms. The everyday one, in plain stockinette stitch, was the one most often seen, but on special occasions the men wore guernseys in heavy cable and bobble patterns, each family or village having its own distinctive design. They were called 'bridal shirts' because a courting girl would start to knit one for her sweetheart's wedding day.

Knitting in America

The colonists were for the most part English and brought with them English ways. However, knitting and needlecrafts in America became more varied and more colorful as immigration began to add to the eclectic composition of the population. English ways were influenced by German, Scandinavian, Irish and southern European settlers. Today's American knitter therefore has a wide heritage of traditions influencing his work.

The word 'knitting' comes from an old English word meaning 'a knot', and basic techniques have altered little over the centuries. Interest in the craft has revived strongly now after its decline during the Victorian era. Machine knitting techniques have gained popularity, but most knitters still practice the craft using needles very little different from those used by the Arab pioneer knitters. Knitting or Knotting, the ancient craft is more popular now than it has ever been before.

Right: An English apron, knitted in multi-colored yarn in the early nineteenth century.
Below: A sandal sock knitted in wool. It is Egyptian in origin and dates from the fifth century AD. However, it is thought that knitting probably originated centuries before this, possibly as much as 1000 years before the birth of Christ.

BASIC SKILLS
THE FIRST STEPS

Knitting needles

Modern needles are usually made of lightweight coated metal or plastic and are available in a comprehensive range of sizes, both in diameter and length. For American needles, the gauge or diameter of the needle is given as a figure, such as No.11, No.10, No.9 and so on, and the lower the number the smaller the diameter of the needle. The length of the needle is also given and the choice of length will depend on the size and type of garment to be knitted. British needle sizes use the reverse of the American system and the lowest number is used to denote the largest needle.

For 'flat' knitting – that is, working back and forth on two needles in rows – needles are manufactured in pairs and each needle has a knob at one end to prevent the stitches from slipping off.

For 'circular' knitting – that is, working in rounds without a seam – needles are manufactured in sets of four and each needle is pointed at both ends. A flexible circular needle is also manufactured and the effect is the same as dividing the work between three needles and working with the fourth, but a larger number of stitches may be used.

Holding yarn and needles

Until the art of holding both the yarn and needles comfortably has been mastered, it is impossible to begin to knit. For a right handed person the yarn will be looped around the fingers of the right hand to achieve firm, even knitting. The needle which is used to work the stitches is held in the right hand and the left hand holds the needle with the stitches to be worked. The reverse of these positions would be adopted by a left handed person.

To hold the yarn correctly, loop the yarn from the ball across the palm of the right hand between the 4th and 3rd fingers, around the 4th finger and back between the 4th and 3rd fingers, over the 3rd finger, between the 3rd and 2nd fingers, under the 2nd finger then over the index finger, leaving the end of the ball of yarn free, in which a slip loop (see over) will be made to begin casting on.

Casting on

This is the first step in hand knitting and it provides the first row of loops on the needle. Different methods of casting on produce different types of edges, each with its own appropriate use, and it is advisable to practice all these variations at some point or other.

The thumb method is an excellent way to begin most garments where an edge with some elasticity is required, such as the ribbing of a pullover, but the two needle method is necessary where extra stitches need to be made during the actual knitting of a garment, such as for buttonholes and pockets. Beginners should practice these two methods. The invisible method gives the appearance of a machine-made edge and is very flexible and neat. The circular method is required for knitting in rounds to produce seamless garments such as gloves and socks. Experienced knitters will find these methods of interest.

Two needle method of casting on

Make a slip loop (see over) in the end of the ball of yarn and put this loop on to the left hand needle. Holding the yarn in the right hand, insert the point of the right hand needle into the slip loop, wind the yarn under and over the point of the right hand needle and draw a new loop through the slip loop. Put the newly made stitch on to the left hand needle. Place the point of the right hand needle between the 2 loops on the left hand needle and wind the yarn under and over the point of the right hand needle again and draw through a new loop. Put the newly made stitch on to the left hand needle. Place the point of the right hand needle between the last 2 loops on the left hand needle and wind the yarn under and over the point of the right hand needle again and draw through a new loop. Put the newly made stitch on to the left hand needle. Continue in this manner until the required number of stitches are formed on the left hand needle. This method produces a firm edge and is also used as an intermediate stage in increasing.

Two needle method step 1

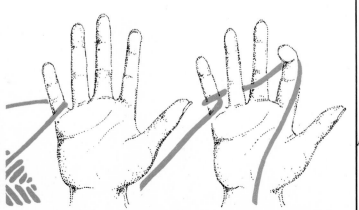

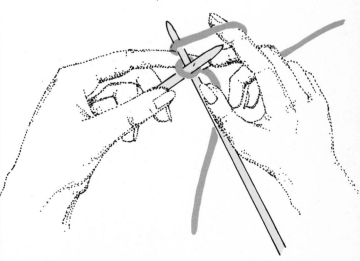

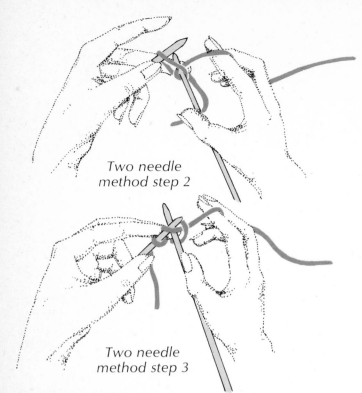

*Two needle
method step 2*

*Two needle
method step 3*

Thumb method of casting on using one needle

Make a slip loop in the ball of yarn about one yard from the end. This length will vary with the number of stitches to be cast on, but one yard will be sufficient for about one hundred stitches.

Put the slip loop on the needle, which should be held in the right hand. Working with the short length of yarn in the left hand, pass this between the index finger and thumb, around the thumb and hold it across the palm of the hand. Insert the point of the needle under the loop on the thumb and bring forward the long end of yarn from the ball. Wind the long end of yarn under and over the point of the needle and draw through a loop on the thumb, leaving the newly formed stitch on the needle. Tighten the stitch on the needle by pulling the short end of yarn, noting that the yarn is then wound around the left thumb ready for the next stitch.

Continue in this way until the required number of stitches are formed on the needle. This method produces a very durable elastic edge.

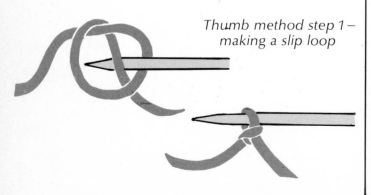

*Thumb method step 1 –
making a slip loop*

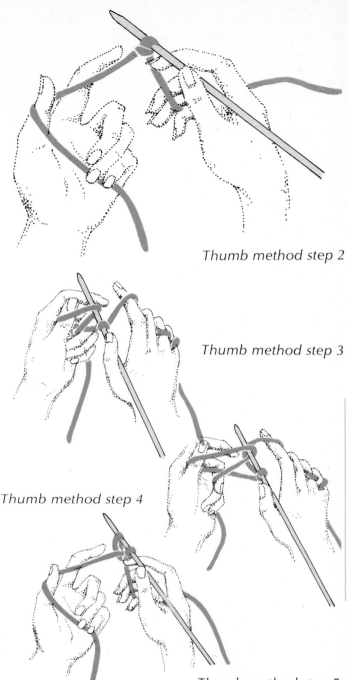

Thumb method step 2

Thumb method step 3

Thumb method step 4

Thumb method step 5

Invisible method of casting on

Using a length of yarn in a contrast color which is later removed, and the thumb method, cast on half the number of stitches required plus one extra. Using the correct yarn and two needles, begin the double fabric which forms the invisible method.

1st row Holding the yarn in the right hand and the needle with the cast on stitches in the left hand, insert the point of the right hand needle into the first stitch from front to back, wind the yarn under and over the point of the right hand needle and draw a loop through which is kept on the right hand needle – this is a knitted stitch and is called 'K1' –, *bring the yarn forward between the two needles and back over the top of the right hand needle to make a stitch on this row only – this is called 'yarn forward' or 'yfwd' –, K1, repeat from the point marked with a * to the end of the row.

2nd row K1, *yfwd and keep at front of work without taking it back over the right hand needle insert the point of the right hand needle into the front of the next stitch on the left hand needle from right to left, and lift it off the left hand needle onto the right hand needle without working it – this is a slipped stitch and is called 'sl 1' –, bring the yarn across in front of the sl 1 and back between the two needles again – this is called 'yarn back' or 'yb' –, K1, repeat from the point marked with a * to the end of the row.

3rd row Sl 1, *ybk, K1, yfwd, sl 1, repeat from the point marked with a * to the end of the row. Repeat the 2nd and 3rd rows once more. Now continue with the single ribbing which completes this method.

6th row K1, *bring the yarn forward between the two needles, insert the point of the right hand needle into the front of the next stitch on the left hand needle from right to left, wind the yarn over the top of the needle around to the front and draw through a loop which is kept on the right hand needle – this is a purled stitch and is called 'P1' –, put the yarn back between the two needles, K1, repeat from the point marked with a * to the end of the row.

7th row P1, *put the yarn back between the two needles, K1, bring the yarn forward between the two needles, P1, repeat from the point marked with a * to the end of the row.

Continue repeating the 6th and 7th rows until the rib is the required length, then pull out the contrast yarn used for casting on. This method gives the appearance of the ribbing running right around the edge with no visible cast on stitches.

Increasing on 1st row of invisible casting on

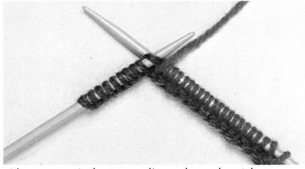

Alternate stitches are slipped on the 4th row

Contrast yarn is pulled out to give a ribbed edge

Circular method of casting on using four needles

When working with sets of four needles, one is used for making the stitches and the total number of stitches required is divided between the remaining three needles. Use the two needle method of casting on and either cast on the total number of stitches on to one needle and then divide them on to the 2nd and 3rd needles, or cast on the required number of stitches on to the first needle, then proceed to the 2nd and 3rd needles, taking care that the stitches do not become twisted. Form the three needles containing the stitches into a triangle shape and the fourth needle is then ready to knit the first stitch on the first needle. This method produces a circular fabric without seams.

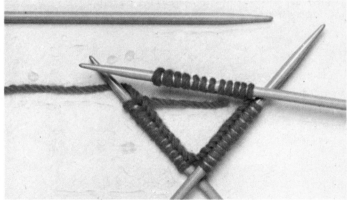

Starting to knit with 4 needles

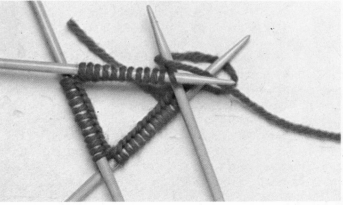

Basic stitches

Once you have cast on your stitches and can hold the yarn and needles comfortably, you can begin to knit – it's as easy as that. All knitting stitches are based on just two methods – knitting and purling – and however complicated patterns may appear, they are all achieved by simple, or intricate, arrangements of these two methods to produce an almost infinite variety of fabrics and textures. Anything from the finest lace to the thickest carpet can be knitted. The advantages of knitted fabrics are almost too numerous to list and they have been used since time immemorial to achieve examples of exquisite beauty.

Tools of the trade
Before beginning to knit it would be useful to know that you have all the tools you will require on hand. Besides yarn and needles you should have:
A rigid metal or wooden ruler
Scissors
Blunt-ended sewing needles
Rustless steel pins required for blocking
Stitch holders to hold stitches not in use
Row gauge for counting rows
Knitting needle gauge to check needle sizes when not marked
Cloth or plastic bag in which to keep work clean
Iron and ironing surface with felt pad or blanket
Cotton cloths suitable for use when pressing

The basic stitches
To work knitted stitches: hold the needle with the cast on stitches in the left hand and the yarn and other needle in the right hand. Insert the point of the right hand needle through the first stitch on the left hand needle from the front to the back. Keeping the yarn at the back of the work pass it under and over the top of the right hand needle and draw this loop through the stitch on the left hand needle. Keep this newly made stitch on the right hand needle and allow the stitch on the left hand needle to slip off. Repeat this step into each stitch on the left hand needle until all the stitches are transferred to the right hand needle. You have now knitted one row. To work the next row, change the needle holding the stitches to your left hand so that the yarn is again in position at the beginning of the row and hold the yarn and free needle in your right hand.

To work purled stitches: hold the needle with the cast on stitches in your left hand and the yarn and other needle in the right hand. Insert the point of the right hand needle through the first stitch on the left hand needle from right to left. Keeping the yarn

at the front of the work pass it over and around the top of the right hand needle and draw this loop through the stitch on the left hand needle. Keep this newly made stitch on the right hand needle and allow the stitch on the left hand needle to slip off. Repeat this step into each stitch on the left hand needle until all the stitches are transferred to the right hand needle. You have now purled one row. To work the next row, change the needle holding the stitches to your left hand so that the yarn is again in position at the beginning of the row and hold the yarn and free needle in your right hand.

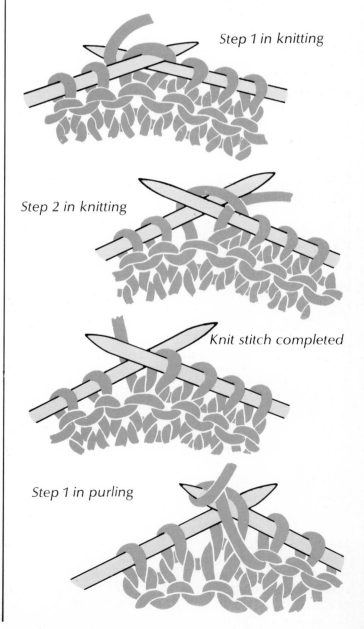

Step 1 in knitting

Step 2 in knitting

Knit stitch completed

Step 1 in purling

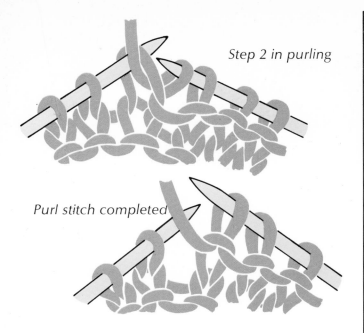

Step 2 in purling

Purl stitch completed

Garter stitch

This is the simplest of all knitted stitches and is formed by working every row in the same stitch, either knit or purl. If you purl every row, however, you will not produce as firm and even a fabric, and unless otherwise stated, wherever you see instructions referring to garter stitch, it is intended that every row should be knitted.

▲ *Purled garter stitch* ▼ *Knitted garter stitch*

Stockinette stitch

This is the smoothest of all knitted stitches and is worked by alternating one row of knitted stitches and one row of purled stitches. The smooth, knitted side of the fabric is usually called the right side of the work, but where a pattern uses the purl side of stockinette

stitch as the fabric, it is referred to as reverse stockinette stitch.

Stockinette stitch

Single rib

This is one of the most useful of all knitted stitches and forms an elastic fabric, ideal for waistbands, cuffs and neckbands, since it always springs back into shape. It is formed by knitting the first stitch of the first row, bringing the yarn forward to the front of the work between the two needles, purling the next stitch, then taking the yarn back between the two needles, ready to knit the next stitch again, and continuing in this way until all the stitches are transferred to the right hand needle. On the next row, all the stitches that were knitted on the first row must be purled and all the stitches that were purled must be knitted. It is important to remember that the yarn must be brought forward after knitting a stitch so that it is in the correct position ready to purl the next stitch, and taken to the back again after purling a stitch so that it is in the correct position ready to knit the next stitch.

Single rib

Useful hints

Before beginning to knit any pattern, study the list of general abbreviations so that you become familiar with them.

Always wash your hands before starting to knit and keep them soft and cool.

A bag pinned over the finished work and moved up as it grows will help to keep your knitting clean.

Never leave your knitting in the middle of a row since you may change the tension of your work when picking it up again.

Never stick knitting needles through a ball of yarn as this can split the yarn.

When measuring knitting, place it on a flat surface and measure it in the center of the work, not at the edges.

Always join in a new ball of yarn at the beginning of a row, never in the center of a row with a knot.

Binding off

Binding off is the final stage in knitting and it securely finishes off any stitches that remain after all the shaping has been completed, or at the end of the work. It is also used as an intermediate step in decreasing, such as binding off the required number of stitches for an underarm or in the center of a row for neck shaping. Where stitches need to be bound off at each end of a row it is customary to do this over two rows, by binding off the given number of stitches at the beginning of the first row then working to the end of the row, turning the work and binding off the same number of stitches at the beginning of the next row and then completing this row. If you bind off stitches at the beginning and end of the same row the yarn must then be broken off and rejoined to start the next row. This is necessary in some designs, but the pattern will always clearly state whether this needs to be done.

Care must be taken in binding off to keep the stitches smooth and even, in this way preventing the edge from becoming too tight or too loose and thus pulling the whole garment out of shape. In some patterns you will come across the phrase 'bind off loosely' and, in this case, it is advisable to use one size larger needle in the right hand and work the stitches with this needle, before binding them off.

The usual method of binding off produces a very firm, neat edge which is not always suitable for some designs such as the toe of a sock where, for example, this type of bound off edge would cause an uncomfortable ridge. In this case, the stitches can be woven together to give an almost invisible seam. Similarly, a ribbed neckband can be bound off by the invisible method to give a very elastic edge with the appearance of a machine-made garment.

Two needle method of binding off

To bind off on a knit row: knit the first two stitches in the regular way and leave them on the right hand needle then *with the point of the left hand needle lift the first stitch on the right hand needle over the top of the second stitch and off the needle, leaving one stitch on the right hand needle, knit the next stitch and leave it on the right hand needle, and repeat from the point marked with a * until the required number of stitches have been bound off and one stitch remains on the right hand needle. If this is at the end of the work, break off the yarn, draw it through the last stitch and pull it up tightly. If stitches have been bound off as a means of shaping, continue working to the end of the row noting that the stitch on the right hand needle will be counted as one of the remaining stitches.

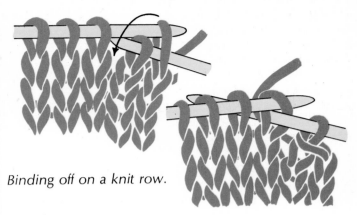

Binding off on a knit row.

To bind off on a purl row: work in exactly the same way but purl each stitch instead of knitting it.

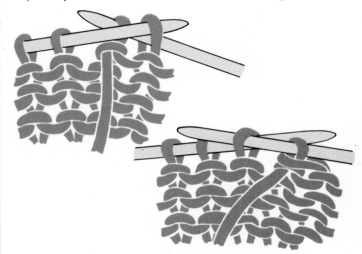

Circular method of binding off using 4 needles
Bind off the stitches on each needle as described for the two needle method of binding off.

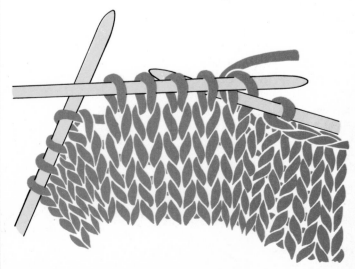

Invisible method of binding off

These instructions are for binding off in single rib when an odd number of stitches has been used and the right side rows begin with K1. Work in ribbing until only two more rows are required to give the finished depth, ending with a wrong side row.

1st row K1, *yfwd, sl 1, ybk, K1, repeat from the point marked with a * to the end of the row.

2nd row Sl 1, *ybk, K1, yfwd, sl 1, repeat from the point marked with a * to the end of the row. Break off the yarn, leaving an end three times the length of the edge to be bound off and thread this into a blunt-ended sewing needle. Hold the sewing needle in the right hand and the stitches to be bound off in the left hand, working from right to left along the row.

1. Insert the sewing needle into the first knit stitch as if to purl it and draw the yarn through, then into the next purl stitch as if to knit it and draw the yarn through leaving both of the stitches on the left hand needle.

2. *Work two of the knit stitches then insert the sewing needle into the first knit stitch as if to knit it, draw the yarn through and slip this stitch off the left hand needle, pass the sewing needle in front of the next purl stitch and into the following knit stitch as if to purl it, and draw the yarn through.

3. Now work two of the purl stitches, then insert the sewing needle into the purl stitch at the end of the row as if to purl it, draw the yarn through and slip this stitch off the left hand needle, pass the sewing needle behind the next knit stitch and into the following purl stitch as if to knit it, draw the yarn through.
Repeat from the point marked with a * until all the stitches have been worked off. Fasten off the end of yarn.

Weaving stitches

To weave two stockinette stitch, or knitted, edges together, have the stitches on two needles, one behind the other, with the same number of stitches on each needle. Break off the yarn, leaving an end three times the length of the edge to be woven and thread this into a blunt-ended sewing needle. Have the wrong sides of each piece facing each other, with the knitting needle points facing to the right.

*Insert the sewing needle through the first stitch on the front needle as if to knit it, draw the yarn through and slip the stitch off the knitting needle, insert the sewing needle through the next stitch on the front needle as if to purl it, draw the yarn through and leave the stitch on the knitting needle, insert the sewing needle through the first stitch on the back needle as if to purl it, draw the yarn through and slip the stitch off the knitting needle, insert the sewing needle through the next stitch on the back needle as if to knit it, draw the yarn through and leave the stitch on the knitting needle, repeat from the point marked with a * until all the stitches have been worked off.

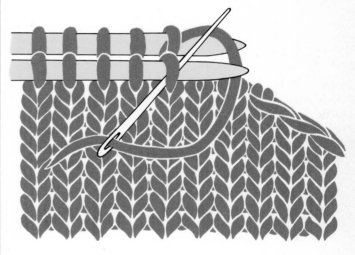

To weave two edges of purl fabric together, work in the same way for the stockinette stitch, reading knit for purl and purl for knit. It is possible, however, to weave purled edges by turning the work to the wrong side and weaving as for the stockinette stitch method, then turn the work to the right side when the weaving is completed.

To weave two garter stitch edges together, work in the same way as for the stockinette stitch method but, making certain that the last row knitted on the front needle leaves a ridge on the right side, or outside, of the work, and that the last row on the back needle leaves a ridge on the wrong side, or inside, of the work.

To weave two ribbed edges together, join each stockinette stitch or knit rib to each stockinette stitch or knit rib, using the stockinette stitch method, and each purl rib to each purl rib, using the purl method described above.

Variations

The ways of using a combination of simple knit and purl stitches to form interesting fabrics are numerous. The following patterns are simple to work and each one gives a different texture. Use knitting worsted yarn and No.5 needles to practice these stitches.

Reverse stockinette stitch

This variation of stockinette stitch uses the wrong side, or purl side, of the work to form the fabric.
Cast on any number of stitches.
1st row (right side) P to end.
2nd row K to end.
These 2 rows form the pattern.

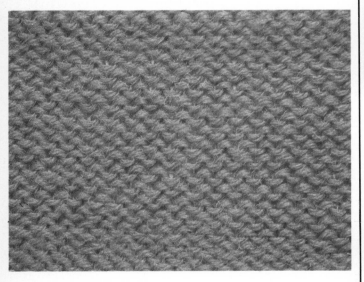

Twisted stockinette stitch

This variation of simple stockinette stitch has a twisted effect added on every knitted row made by working into the back of every stitch.
Cast on any number of stitches.
1st row K into the back of each stitch to end.
2nd row P to end.
These 2 rows form the pattern.

Broken rib

Cast on a number of stitches divisible by 2+1.
1st row K1, *P1, K1, rep from * to end.
2nd row P1, *K1, P1, rep from * to end.
3rd row K to end.
4th row As 3rd
These 4 rows form the pattern.

Rice stitch

Cast on a number of stitches divisible by 2+1.
1st row K to end.
2nd row P1, *K1, P1, rep from * to end.
These 2 rows form the pattern.

Moss stitch

Cast on a number of stitches divisible by 2+1.
1st row K1, *P1, K1, rep from * to end.
This row forms the pattern.
Where an even number of stitches are cast on, moss stitch is worked as follows:
1st row *K1, P1, rep from * to end.
2nd row *P1, K1, rep from * to end.
These 2 rows form the pattern.

Irish moss stitch
Cast on a number of stitches divisible by 2 + 1.
1st row K1, *P1, K1, rep from * to end.
2nd row P1, *K1, P1, rep from * to end.
3rd row As 2nd.
4th row As 1st.
These 4 rows form the pattern.

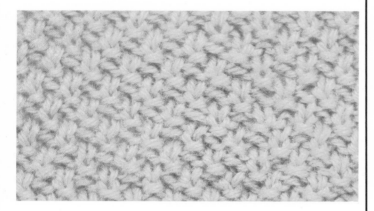

Woven stitch
Cast on a number of stitches divisible by 2 + 1.
1st row K1, *yarn in front (yfwd), sl 1 as if to purl (P-wise), yarn back (ybk), K1, rep from * to end.
2nd row P to end.
3rd row K2, *yfwd, sl 1, P-wise, ybk, K1, rep from * to last st, K1.
4th row As 2nd.
These 4 rows form the pattern.

Honeycomb slip stitch
Cast on a number of stitches divisible by 2 + 1.
1st row P1, *sl 1 P-wise, P1, rep from * to end.
2nd row P to end.
3rd row P2, *sl 1 P-wise, P1, rep from * to last st, P1.
4th row As 2nd.
These 4 rows form the pattern.

Bright and easy knits
For each of these ideas you only need to know how to cast on, how to work the basic stitches and how to bind off!

Muffler
Materials
2 × 4 oz balls of any Knitting Worsted yarn
A pair of No.9 needles

To make
Cast on 60 stitches. Work in garter stitch until scarf measures 70in. Bind off.

Evening belt
Materials
3 × 20grm balls of any glitter yarn
A pair of No.4 needles
A 2in buckle

To make
Cast on 16 stitches. Work in single rib until belt measures desired length to go round waist plus approximately 8in. Bind off. Sew on buckle to one end.

Shoulder bag
Materials
1 × 4oz ball of Knitting Worsted yarn
A pair of No.5 needles

To make
Cast on 50 stitches. Work in stockette stitch until bag measures approximately 24in. Bind off. Fold bag in half with right sides facing and join side edges. Fold over 2in at top edge and sew down. Turn bag right side out. Embroider each side or sew on motifs. Cut remaining yarn into 60in lengths and braid together, knotting each end of braid. Stitch each end of braid along sides of bag, leaving center of braid free as shoulder strap.

GAUGE

Now that you have mastered the basic steps in knitting, the next step is to understand fully the significance of achieving the correct gauge. It is of such vital importance that it cannot be stressed too often and must not be overlooked, either by the beginner or by the more experienced knitter. It is the most important key to success and no amount of careful knitting will produce a perfect garment unless it is observed.

Gauge

Quite simply, the word 'gauge' means the number of rows and stitches to a given measurement, which has been achieved by the designer of the garment, using the yarn and needle size stated. As a beginner, it is vital to keep on practicing and trying to obtain the correct gauge given in a pattern. If it is impossible to hold the yarn and needles comfortably, without pulling the yarn too tight or leaving it too loose and at the same time obtain the correct gauge, then change the needle size. If there are too many stitches to the inch, try using one size larger needles; if there are too few stitches to the inch, try using one size smaller needles. Too many stitches means that the gauge is too tight and too few stitches means that the gauge is too loose and it is vital that your knitting is neither.

This advice applies not only to the beginner but to all knitters starting a new design. It is so often overlooked on the assumption that the knitter's gauge is 'average' and therefore accurate. The point to stress is that although all knitting patterns are carefully checked, the designer of a garment may have produced a tighter or looser gauge than average and all the measurements of the garment will have been based on calculations obtained from her gauge.

With this in mind, it will be readily appreciated that even a quarter of a stitch too many or too few can result in the measurements of the garment being completely inaccurate – through no fault of the designer. It doesn't matter how many times you have to change the needle size – what is important is to obtain the correct gauge given in a pattern, before beginning to knit it. Most instructions give the number of stitches in width, and some also, the number of rows in depth. If you need to choose between obtaining one and not the other, then the width gauge is the most important. Length can usually be adjusted by working more or less rows, as required, being sure to check first that the pattern is not based on an exact number of rows but is measured, rather, in inches.

How to check gauge

Before starting to knit any garment, always work a gauge sample at least 4in square, using the yarn, needle size and stitch quoted. Lay this sample on a flat surface and pin it down. Place a firm ruler over the knitting and mark out 4in in width. Count the number of stitches between the pins very carefully and make sure that you have the same number as given in the gauge. Pin out and count the number of rows in the same way. If there are too many stitches to the given gauge measurement then your gauge is too tight and you need to use needles one, or more sizes larger. If there are too few stitches, then your gauge is too loose and you need to use one size smaller needles.

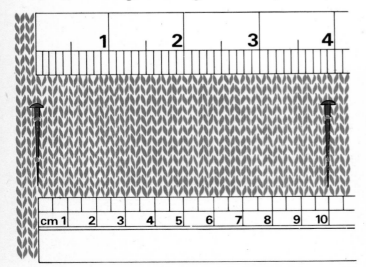

Here the gauge is correct

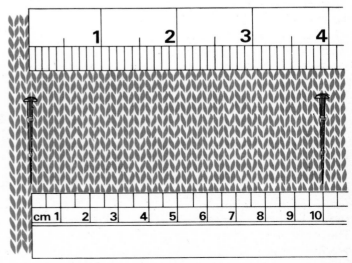

Here the gauge is too tight

A decorative pillow cover

An afghan, made from gauge samples, is a delightful mixture of colors, patterns and textures

Substituting yarns

Each design will have been worked out for the knitting yarn quoted and this is the yarn that should be used, if possible. If for any reason it is not possible to buy the correct yarn, then a substitute may be used but, in this case, it is even more vital to check your gauge before beginning the pattern.

To make an afghan or cushion cover

A few minutes spent in the preparation of a gauge sample need not be wasted. Similarly, samples of the stitches which interest you can be utilized. As each one is finished lay it aside, and when you have collected enough, they can be joined together to make a colorful and original afghan or pillow cover. The only requirement is that each sample must be worked to the same size – 4in square would be an ideal measurement. This way you can keep a lasting record of your progress as a knitter, which is interest-ing and will serve a useful purpose later.

Afghan

You will need a minimum of 120 squares. Join 10 squares together to form one row, and have a total of 12 rows. Bind all the edges with wool braid or work a blanket stitch around all the edges to finish them and give a professional look to your work.

Pillow cover

You will need 32 squares and a pillow form or foam chips for stuffing. Join 4 squares together to form one row, then 4 rows together to form one side of the pillow. Work the second side of the pillow in the same way. Place the right sides of each piece facing each other and join 3 sides together. Turn the cover right side out. Insert the pillow form or stuffing and join the remaining edge, inserting a zipper if you wish.

YARNS

Success in knitting designs is the result of combining two skills in one – those of a weaver and those of a dressmaker – as the fabric and the shape of the garment are produced at the same time. All knitters need to know something about the construction of the many colorful and interesting yarns which are now available. This knowledge, combined with the needle size to be used and the gauge obtained, will enable knitters to understand how the right fabric for any garment is achieved. To produce a durable, textured fabric, using variations of cable stitches, for example, you cannot select a fine baby yarn; similarly, a thick, bulky yarn would not be suitable for a lacy evening top.

Yarns and ply

'Yarn' is the word used to describe any spun thread, fine or thick, in natural fibers such as wool, cotton, linen, silk, angora or mohair, or in man-made fibers such as Acrilan, Orlon or Nylon. These fibers can be blended together, as with wool and Nylon or a Nylon mixture, to produce extra hard-wearing yarns which are not too thick.

The word 'ply' indicates a single spun thread of any thickness. Before this thread can be used it must be twisted together to make two or more plys to produce a specific yarn and this process is called 'doubling'. Because each single thread can be spun to any thickness, reference to the number of plys does not necessarily determine the thickness of the finished yarn. Some Shetland yarns, for instance, use only two ply very lightly twisted together to produce a yarn almost comparable to a knitting worsted quality although, generally speaking, the terms 2 ply, 3 ply, 4 ply and knitting worsted are used to describe yarns of specified thickness.

The following ply classification applies to the majority of hand knitting yarns, whether made from natural fibers, man-made fibers or a blend of both.

Baby yarns are usually made from the highest quality fibers and are available in 2 ply, 3 ply, 4 ply and knitting worsted weights.

Baby Quick-Knit yarns are generally equivalent to a 4 ply but as they are very softly twisted, they are light in weight.

2 ply, 3 ply and 4 ply yarns are available in numerous fibers and are usually produced by twisting two or more single spun threads together.

Knitting worsted yarns are usually made from four single spun threads twisted together to produce durable yarns.

Bulky and Quick-Knit yarns are extra-thick yarns which vary considerably in their construction. They are ideal for outer garments, and some makes are oiled to give a greater amount of warmth and increased protection.

Crepe yarns are rare. However, those that are available are usually in 4 ply qualities, sometimes called 'single crepe' and Knitting Worsted weights – called 'double crepe' – and are more tightly twisted than average yarns. They are used to produce a firm fabric which is particularly hard-wearing.

Weights and measures

Since there is no official standardization, yarns marketed by the various companies often vary in thickness and in yardage. As most yarns are sold by weight, rather than length, even the density of dye used to produce certain colors in each line can result in

more or less yarn in each ball, although the structure of the yarn is exactly the same. Although all knitting designs are carefully checked, it would be impossible to make up a separate garment for each color in the line of yarn quoted and you may sometimes find that you need one ball more or less than given in the instructions because of this difference in dye.

If it is impossible to obtain the correct yarn required in the instructions then another comparable yarn may be used, provided, of course, that it works up to the same gauge as that given in the pattern.

Equivalent yarns can knit up to the right gauge but the quantity of yarn involved will not necessarily be the same.

Always buy sufficient yarn at one time to insure that all the yarn used is from the same dye lot. Yarn from a different dye lot may vary slightly in color, although this variation may not be noticeable until you have started to knit with it.

Yarns and metrication

When purchasing yarn it is advisable to check the weight of each ball as they can now vary considerably due to the proposed introduction of the metric system. Metrication has been adopted in many countries, and others are in the process of changing over. Some American spinners have begun distribution of yarn measured in grams, but large stocks of yarns in ounces will take time to run out, so a confused situation may exist for some time.

Measurements and metrication

Many pattern companies are now giving both Imperial measurements and their metric equivalents. If working from a pattern like this, insure that you work with either one set of measurements or the other. Do not try to combine both sets as this will only lead to inaccuracies in design.

More simple knits

To illustrate how the same stitch worked in a different yarn can produce a variety of fabrics, try making the muffler given earlier in a mohair yarn, to give a lighter, softer version. Or use a yarn which combines a lurex thread to give a glitter effect to work an evening stole. The evening belt also given earlier could be worked equally well in a crisp cotton to make a useful summer accessory. The more you experiment, the more you will be delighted with the fabrics which can be produced.

Shawl

You will need 6oz of a baby or soft 3-ply yarn, and a pair of No.4 needles. You will also need 57in of narrow lace.

Cast on 288 stitches. Work in garter stitch until shawl measures 36in. Bind off loosely. Sew lace on all around the edges, gathering it slightly around the corners.

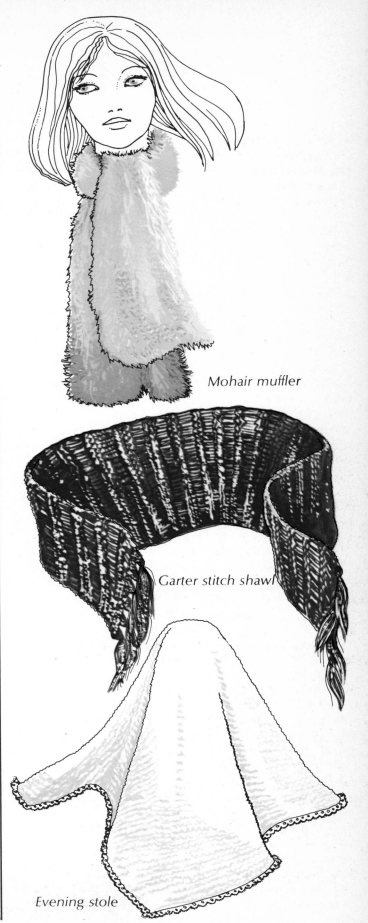

Mohair muffler

Garter stitch shawl

Evening stole

WORKING A PATTERN

A finished knitted garment should look just as attractive and fit just as well as in the illustration. A great deal of care is taken in designing knitting patterns to insure that this is possible. The secret lies in being completely objective about the design you choose, just as you would be when selecting ready-to-wear clothes. The range of knitting patterns which are available cater to every kind of garment in varying sizes. Where a design is only given in smaller sizes, such as a 32 or 34in bust, it is usually because the designer feels that it would not be suitable for a more generous figure. Similarly, if only one size is given it is probably because the pattern used for the design covers a large multiple of stitches and another whole repeat of the pattern, to give a larger size, would not be practical.

When you find a design which incorporates all the details you desire make sure you read through all the instructions before beginning to knit. Beginners and experts alike should pay particular attention to the finishing section – a deceptively simple shape may require a crochet edging to give it that couture look, or an unusual trimming effect such as a twisted cord belt.

Knitting patterns
Knitting publication styles vary considerably, but generally all instructions fall into three sections:
1 Materials required, gauge, finished sizes and abbreviations.
2 Working instructions for each section.
3 Finishing details, edges and trimmings.

Sizes
Check that the size range given in the instructions provides the size you need. If the skirt or sleeve lengths need altering to suit your requirements, read through the working instructions to see if the design allows for these changes. Some designs are based on an exact number of rows which cannot be altered. After the actual measurements of the design are given, take note that the instructions for the smallest size are given as the first set of figures and that the figures for any other sizes follow in order and are usually shown in brackets. Read through the instructions and underline all the figures which are applicable to the size you require, noting that where only one set of figures is given, it applies to all sizes.

Gauge
This section must not be overlooked as it is the vital key to success. Never begin any design without first making sure that you can obtain the correct gauge.

Materials
Each design will have been worked out for the knitting yarn which is quoted and this should be used, if possible. If for any reason it is impossible to obtain the specified yarn, you may select a substitute as long as you gain the correct gauge. But remember though that the quantity given will only apply to the original yarn and, if a substitute is used, you may need more or less yarn.

Abbreviations
All knitting patterns are abbreviated into a form of shorthand and every knitter soon comes to recognize the terms 'K2 tog' or 'sl 1, K1, psso' and their meanings. This book contains a complete list of general knitting abbreviations although the same terms may not be abbreviated in the same way by other publications and this can sometimes lead to confusion. It is therefore essential to read through any list of abbreviations before beginning a pattern to make sure you understand them. This is particularly important when they refer to increasing, as the terms, 'make 1' and 'increase 1' can mean two different things.

In this course, where a specific stitch or technique is given in a pattern, the working method is written out in full for the first time it is used in a row and its abbreviated form given at the end of the working instructions. From that point on, each time the same stitch or technique is used, its abbreviated term will be given.

Working instructions
Each section of a garment being worked will be given separately under an appropriate heading, such as, 'Back', 'Front', 'Sleeves' and so on. Each section should be worked in the correct order as it may be necessary to join parts of the garment together at a given point before you can proceed with the next step. When

measuring knitting it is necessary to lay it on a flat surface and use a firm ruler. Never measure around a curve but, for example, on an armhole or sleeve, measure the depth in a straight line.

Where an asterisk, *, is used in a pattern row it means repeat from that point, as directed. This symbol is also used at the beginning of a section, sometimes as a double asterisk, **, or triple asterisk, ***, to denote a part which is to be repeated later on in the instructions.

When working in rows, always join in a new ball of yarn at the beginning of a row. You can easily gauge whether you have sufficient yarn for another row by spreading out your work and checking whether the remaining yarn will cover its width four times. Any odd pieces of yarn can always be used later for seaming.

If the yarn has to be joined in the middle of the work, which is necessary when working in rounds, then the ends of the old ball of yarn and the new ball should be spliced together. To do this, unravel the end of the new ball and cut away one or two strands from each end. Overlay the two ends from opposite directions and twist them together until they hold. The twisted ends should be of the same thickness as the original yarn. As the join will not be very strong, knit very carefully with the newly twisted yarn for a few rows. Then carefully trim away any odd ends with a pair of sharp scissors.

Never join in new yarn by means of a knot in the middle of your work, whether working in rows or rounds.

Finishing

Most knitters give a sigh of relief when they have bound off the very last stitch and look forward to wearing their new creation. If the finished garment is to be a success, however, the finishing of the separate pieces must be looked upon as an exercise in dressmaking. Details are always given in the instructions as to the order in which the sections are to be assembled, together with any final instructions for edgings or trimmings. Blocking instructions will also be given in this section and if a substitute yarn has been used, it is essential to check whether or not it requires blocking.

Mistakes!

These can happen – a dropped stitch, an interruption, a pattern row which has been misread and then needs ripping – but don't attempt to pull the stitches off the needle until you have tried other ways of rectifying the error.

To pick up a dropped stitch on a knit row: Insert a crochet hook into the dropped stitch from the front to the back, put the hook under the thread which lies between the two stitches above the dropped stitch and draw this thread through the dropped stitch. Continue in this way until the dropped stitch is level with the last row worked and transfer the stitch to the left hand needle. Then continue knitting in the usual way.

To pick up a dropped stitch on a purl row: Insert a crochet hook into the dropped stitch from the back to the front, put the hook over the thread which lies between the two stitches above the dropped stitch and draw this thread through the dropped stitch. Slip the stitch onto a spare needle and remove the hook, ready to insert it into the dropped stitch from the back to the front again. Continue in this way until the dropped stitch is level with the last row worked and transfer the stitch to the left hand needle. Then continue purling in the usual way.

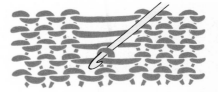

To rip back stitches on a knit row: Insert the left hand needle from the front to the back into the stitch below the next stitch on the right hand needle, then withdraw the right hand needle from the stitch above and pull the yarn with the right hand to unravel this stitch, keeping the yarn at the back of the work. Continue in this way until the required number of stitches have been ripped.

To rip back stitches on a purl row: Insert the left hand needle from the front to the back into the stitch below the next stitch on the right hand needle, then withdraw the right hand needle from the stitch above and pull the yarn with the right hand to unravel this stitch, keeping the yarn at the front of the work. Continue in this way until the required number of stitches have been ripped.

A BETTER FINISH

Shaping stitches

Knitting may be perfectly straight, as in a scarf, or intricately shaped as in a tailored jacket. Shaping is achieved by means of increasing the number of stitches in a row to make the work wider, or decreasing the stitches in a row to make the work narrower. This is usually done by making two stitches out of one, or by working two stitches together to make one stitch at a given point in the pattern. Sometimes the shaping forms an integral part of the design and decorative methods of increasing and decreasing are used to highlight the shaping, such as fully-fashioned seams on a raglan pullover.

By means of an eyelet hole method of increasing stitches, carrying the yarn over or around the needle in a given sequence and compensating for these new stitches later on in the row, beautiful lace patterns are produced.

How to increase

The simplest way is to make an extra stitch at the beginning or end of the row, but a pattern will always give exact details where more intricate shaping is required, such as for skirt darts.

To make a stitch at the beginning of a row, knit or purl the first stitch in the usual way but do not slip it off the left hand needle. Instead, place the point of the right hand needle into the back of the same stitch and purl or knit into the stitch again. One stitch has been increased.

To make a stitch at the end of a row, work until two stitches remain on the left hand needle, increase in the next stitch and work the last stitch in the usual way. One stitch has been increased.

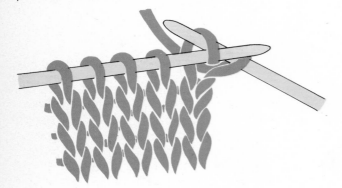

Invisible increasing

Insert the right hand needle into the front of the stitch on the row below the next stitch on the left hand needle and knit a new stitch in the usual way, then knit the next stitch on the left hand needle. One stitch has been increased.

If the increase is on a purl row, insert the right hand needle in the same way and purl a stitch in the usual way, then purl the next stitch on the left hand needle.

Increasing between stitches

With the right hand needle pick up the yarn which lies between the stitch just worked and the next stitch on the left hand needle and place this loop on the left hand needle. Knit into the back of this loop so that the new stitch is twisted and does not leave a hole in the work. Place the new stitch on the right hand needle. One stitch has been increased.

If the increase is on a purl row, pick up the yarn between the stitches in the same way and purl into it from the back, then place the new stitch on the right hand needle.

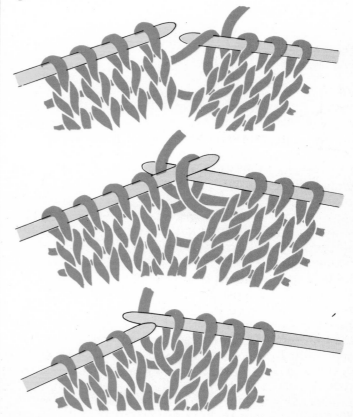

Decorative increasing

To make a stitch between two knit stitches, bring the yarn forward between the needles then back over the top of the right hand needle, ready to knit the next stitch. This is called 'yarn in front' or 'yarn forward' the abbreviation is 'yfwd' or 'yo'. To make a stitch between a purl and a knit stitch, the yarn is already at the front of the work and is carried over the top of the right hand needle ready to knit the next stitch. This is called 'yarn over needle' and the abbreviation is 'yon' or 'yo'.

To make a stitch between two purl stitches, take the yarn over the top of the right hand needle and around between the two needles to the front again ready to purl the next stitch. This is called 'yarn round needle' and the abbreviation is 'yrn' or 'yo'.

To make a stitch between a knit and a purl stitch, bring the yarn forward between the two needles, over the top of the right hand needle then around between the two needles to the front again ready to purl the next stitch. The abbreviation is 'yrn' or 'yo'.

How to decrease

The way to make a simple decrease is by working two stitches together, either at the ends of the row or at any given point. To do this on a knit row, insert the point of the right hand needle through two stitches instead of one and knit them both together in the usual way thus losing one stitch. This is called 'knit 2 together' or 'K2 tog'.

On a purl row, purl the two stitches together. This stitch will slant to the left and the abbreviation is 'P2 tog'.

▲ *Decreasing on a knit row* ▼ *Decreasing on a purl row*

Decreasing by means of a slipped stitch

This method is most commonly used where the decreases are worked in pairs, one slanting to the left and one slanting to the right, as on a raglan sleeve. Slip the stitch to be decreased from the left hand needle on to the right hand needle without working it, then knit the next stitch on the left hand needle. With the point of the left hand needle lift the slipped stitch over the knit stitch and off the needle. This stitch will slant to the left and the abbreviation is 'sl

1, K1, psso'.

On a purl row, purl the two stitches together through the back of the stitches. This stitch will slant to the right and the abbreviation is 'P2 tog through back loop' (tbl).

Decorative decreasing

The decorative use of decreasing can be accentuated by twisting the stitches around the decreased stitches to give them greater emphasis. This example shows a decrease which has been twisted and lies in the opposite direction to the line of the seam. The decrease is worked at the end of the knit row for the left hand side and at the end of a purl row for the right hand side.

Knit to the last six stitches, pass the right hand needle behind the first stitch on the left hand needle and knit the next two stitches together through the back of the stitches, then knit the first skipped stitch and slip both stitches off the left hand needle and knit the last three stitches in the usual way.

On a purl row, purl to the last six stitches, pass the right hand needle across the front of the first stitch on the left hand needle and purl the next two stitches together, then purl the first skipped stitch, slip both stitches off the left hand needle and purl the last three stitches in the usual way.

Decorative decreasing on knit and purl rows

More about shaping

Even the most basic stockinette stitch sweater needs careful shaping at the underarm, back and front neck and shoulders, sleeves and top of the sleeves, if it is to fit together correctly. The correct proportions for all these measurements will have been taken into account in every knitting design and the instructions will clearly state where and when the shaping is to be worked.

Where so many knitters find difficulty is in the accurate measuring of each section, so that when a garment is assembled it all fits together without stretching or easing one piece to fit another. The easiest way to overcome this problem is to use a row counter to insure that the back and front of a garment have exactly the same number of rows before beginning any shaping, and that both sleeves match. Many professional knitters prefer to knit both sleeves at the same time, using two separate balls of yarn, to make sure that the shaping for each sleeve is worked on the same row. Another useful tip is to make a note of the number of rows which have been worked for any section, such as the ribbing on the waist of a sweater, before beginning any pattern rows, so that when you are ready to do the next piece you do not even have to measure the length but can work to the same number of rows.

Whichever method you adopt, it is essential to know how to take accurate measurements if you are to achieve satisfactory results.

Taking measurements

Before taking any measurements it is necessary to lay the section of knitting on a flat surface. If you are sitting comfortably in a chair, it is tempting to try to measure it across your knees, or on the arm of the chair, but this will not give an accurate figure.

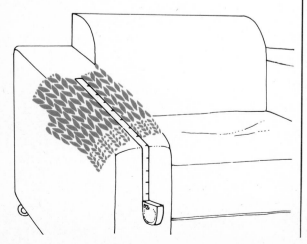

Always measure with a firm ruler and not a tape measure and never be tempted to stretch the section to the required length to avoid working a few extra rows before the next step.

Never measure around a curve but always on the straight of the fabric – a curved measurement is obviously greater and will result in an incorrect depth on armholes or sleeve seams. When measuring an armhole, sleeve or side edge of a section which has been shaped, place the ruler on the fabric in a straight line from the beginning of the section to the point you have reached.

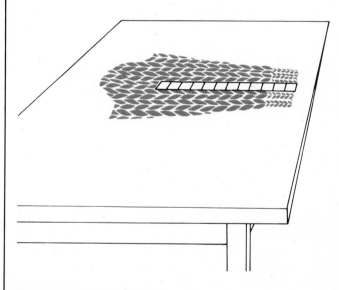

Measurement and gauge

It cannot be stressed too often that every design you knit has been calculated on the gauge achieved by the designer of the garment and based on the correct proportions for each size. The normal ratio of a 2in difference between the bust and hip measurements will have been taken into account, also an allowance of 1in or 2in for movement, or what is known as tolerance. The width gauge, or number of stitches to a given measurement, is vital if you are to obtain an accurate fit. The length gauge, or number of rows to a given measurement, is not so important and can be adjusted where a pattern is not given over an exact number of rows and provided you remember that it is even more essential to measure each section accurately. The designer may have achieved more rows to the inch than you are obtaining and her shaping on the sleeves, for instance, will have been calculated to insure that this is completed well before the point has been reached to shape the cap of the sleep. Where she is increasing on every 6th row in order to complete the shaping within a certain measurement, you may be working to a looser row gauge and will need to increase on every 5th row, in order to end up with the correct number of stitches within the same length. Similarly, if you are working to a tighter row gauge, you may need to adjust the shaping and work it on every 7th row, otherwise all the shaping may well be completed before reaching the elbow level and the whole sleeve will be out of shape.

Shaping in rows

Details of casting on or binding off stitches to achieve the correct shape, such as for the underarm, neck or shoulders, will be given in a pattern in detail.

When shaping is required on both side edges of a section, the pattern may simply say, 'decrease one stitch at each end of the next knitted row' and will leave the knitter to adopt whichever method she prefers. In this case, if you use the slip one, knit one, pass slipped stitch over method at the beginning of the row, producing a decreased stitch which slants to the left when the fabric is facing you, use the knit two together method at the end of the row to make a stitch which slants to the right.

In increasing on a row, whether it is at each end to increase two stitches, or across the row to increase a greater number of stitches, when working twice into a stitch the last stitch made is the increased stitch. If you increase in the first stitch at the beginning of a row, the new stitch will lie inside the first knitted stitch. At the end of the row you should increase in the next to last stitch, so that the increased stitch again lies inside the last stitch, which is then knitted in the usual way. Sometimes a pattern will tell you to increase a given number of stitches across a row, without giving exact instructions. To do this you must first work out the exact position for each increased stitch. As an example, if a pattern has begun with 80

stitches and at a given point you are required to increase 8 stitches evenly across a row, the accurate way to achieve this would be to increase in the 5th stitch and then in every following 10th stitch 7 times more, and then knit the last 5 stitches. In this way, each new stitch would be evenly spaced across the row.

Shaping in rounds

The same principles apply, if you are working in rows or in rounds. A skirt may be worked from the hem to waist in rounds and will need to be shaped by means of decreasing, to lose the extra width at the hem. As an example, if you are working a pattern in wide panels of stockinette stitch and narrow panels of reverse stockinette stitch, the shaping needs to be worked on the stockinette stitch panels to eventually bring them down to the same width as the reverse stockinette stitch panels. The pattern may simply say, 'decrease one stitch at each end of every stockinette stitch panel' and you should use the slip one, knit one, pass slipped stitch over method at the beginning of each panel and the knit two together method at the end of each panel. In this way, each decreased stitch lies in the same direction as the line of the stockinette stitch panels.

Using the same example, when increasing in rounds remember that if you increase in the first stitch of each panel you must increase in the next to the last stitch and not in the last stitch.

Binding off and forming edges

Each piece of knitted fabric has edges which are formed as the work progresses and these must be suitable for the fabric produced. Every section of flat knitting has a cast on edge, the right and left hand side edges and the bound off edge. Round knitting has only a cast on and bound off edge.

Various methods of casting on and binding off have already been given but the following methods are less popular. The ways of forming side edges are also important, as an edge which is too tight or too loose will pull the garment out of shape and present difficulties in finishing.

Double casting on

Two needles are required for this method, which are both held together in the right hand. Make a slip loop in the ball of yarn as for the thumb method and place this on both needles. Take both ends of the yarn, that is, the end of the yarn from the slip loop and the end from the ball and hold them together in the palm of the left hand, putting the slip loop end around the thumb and the ball end around the forefinger. Using both needles put them up under the first loop on the thumb and over and down through the loop on the forefinger, then through the thumb loop. Release the thumb loop and tighten the stitch on the needles with an upward movement of the right hand, without releasing either end of the yarn held in the palm of the hand. Continue in this way until the required number of stitches are formed on the needles, then withdraw the second needle, transfer the needle holding the stitches to the left hand and have the second needle in the right hand, ready to knit. This forms a very strong yet elastic edge.

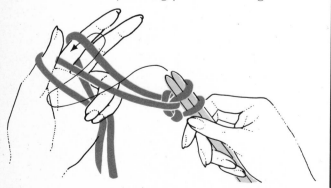

Picot casting on

Two needles are required for this method, one held in each hand. Make a slip loop and place this on the left hand needle, then cast on one stitch by the two needle method. Using these two loops make a strip long enough for the number of stitches required by

placing the yarn over the needle, then slipping the first stitch on the left hand needle as if to purl, knitting the second stitch on the left hand needle and lifting the slipped stitch over the knitted stitch and dropping it off the right hand needle. Turn and repeat this row until the required number of picot loops have been formed by the yarn forward. Pick up these picot loops along one edge with a needle and then continue knitting in the usual way. The other side of the picot edge forms a dainty edge ideal for baby garments.

Suspended binding off

Knit the first two stitches in the usual way, then lift the first stitch over the second stitch but instead of allowing it to drop off the right hand needle, retain it on the point of the left hand needle. Pass the right hand needle in front of the held stitch and knit the next stitch on the left hand needle in the usual way, slipping the stitch and the held stitch off the left hand needle together, leaving two stitches on the right hand needle. Continue in this way until all stitches are bound off. This method avoids any tendency to bind off too tightly.

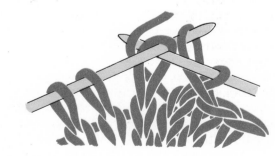

Shaped binding off

Preparation for this method must be made before the final binding off by turning the last few rows of knitting without completing them to form a shaped angle, then binding off all the stitches at one time on the final row. This is an ideal way of working shoulder shaping as it does not produce the stepped effect of normal binding off and makes seaming very much easier. For example, on a right back shoulder edge when the point has been reached for the shoulder shaping, instead of binding off the required number of stitches at the beginning of the next knit row, on the previous purl row work to within this number of stitches then turn the work, slip the first stitch on the left hand needle and knit to the end of the row. Repeat in this manner the required number of times, then purl across all the stitches. Bind them off on the next knit row in the usual way. Reverse this for a left back shoulder edge by beginning the shaping on a knit row.

Three steps of shaped binding off

Side edges
Where side edges are to be joined together in finishing, they need to be firm to allow for a good edge for seaming. When both edges must show, as in a scarf, they need to be neat without pulling the sides out of shape.
To work an edge for seaming: Slip the first stitch purlwise and knit the last stitch on every row, when working in stockinette stitch. On garter stitch, bring the yarn to the front of the work, slip the first stitch on every row purlwise, then put the yarn to the back and knit to the end in the usual way.

To work an open edge: When working in stockinette stitch, slip the first and last stitch on every knit row

to form a chain effect, then purl each stitch on the following row in the usual way.

Slipped stitches
Stitches which are slipped from one needle to the other without being worked are used in various ways – as edge stitches, as a means of decreasing and to form part of a pattern. When a slip stitch forms part of a decrease on a knit row, the stitch must be slipped knitwise, otherwise it will become twisted. On a purl row, the stitch must be slipped purlwise, when decreasing. In working a pattern, however, where the slip stitch is not part of a decrease it must be slipped purlwise on a knit row to prevent it from becoming twisted when it is purled in the following row.

To slip stitch knitwise on a knit row: Hold the yarn behind the work as if to knit the next stitch, insert the point of the right hand needle into the next stitch from front to back as if to knit it and slip it on to the right hand needle without working it.

To slip stitch purlwise on a knit row: Hold the yarn behind the work as if to knit the next stitch, insert the point of the right hand needle into the next stitch from back to front as if to purl it and slip it on to the right hand needle without working it.
To slip stitch purlwise on a purl row: Hold the yarn at the front of the work as if to purl the next stitch, insert the point of the right hand needle into the next stitch from back to front as if to purl it and slip it on to the right hand needle without working it.

FINISHING TOUCHES
Buttonholes

Details for working buttonholes will always be given in the instructions for a garment but unless they are neatly finished they can spoil the appearance of the garment. Various methods may be used, largely depending on the size of the button desired and the overall width of the buttonhole band or border. The buttonholes can be horizontal, vertical or, on a baby garment where a small button is required, simply worked by means of an eyelet hole.

Simple eyelet buttonholes

If the buttonhole is being incorporated in the main fabric, or the buttonhole band, work the front of the garment until the position for the first buttonhole is reached, ending with a wrong side row. On the next row work the first few stitches in the row to the position for the buttonhole, then pass the yarn forward, over or around the needle, depending on the stitch being worked, to make an eyelet hole, work the next two stitches on the left hand needle together to compensate for the made stitch, then work in pattern to the end of the row. On the next row, work across all the stitches in pattern, counting the new stitch as one stitch. Continue in this manner for as many buttonholes as are needed.

Horizontal buttonholes

These can either be worked as part of the main fabric or on a separate buttonhole band.

Buttonholes worked as part of the main fabric: In this case provision will already have been made for a turned under hem and buttonholes will have to be made in the hem and in the main fabric, to form a double buttonhole, which is then finished with a buttonhole stitch on completion. Work until the position for the buttonhole is reached, ending at the center front edge. On the next row work a few

stitches across the hem, bind off the number of stitches required for the buttonhole by the two needle method, then continue across the remainder of the hem. Work the same number of stitches on the main fabric as were worked on the hem, then bind off the same number of buttonhole stitches and work in pattern to the end of the row. On the next row you

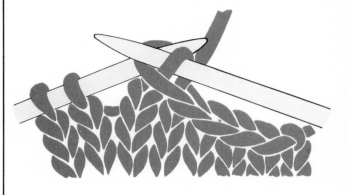

need to replace the same number of stitches as were bound off for each buttonhole on the previous row but need to avoid spoiling the buttonhole with a loose loop of yarn at one end, which would be the result of merely casting on the same number of stitches. To avoid this, work to the last stitch before the bound off stitches and increase in this last stitch by working into the front and back of it, then cast on one stitch less than was bound off on the previous row. Continue in this manner for as many buttonholes as are needed. If a turned under hem is not being worked in one with the main fabric, then only a single buttonhole is required.

Buttonholes worked in a separate border: Where only a single buttonhole is required work the band until the position for the buttonhole is reached, ending at the center front edge. On the next row work a few stitches until the position for the buttonhole is reached, bind off the required number of stitches for the buttonhole and work in pattern to the end of the row. On the next row, cast on the number of stitches needed to complete the buttonhole in the same way as when working buttonholes as part of the main fabric. Continue in this manner for as many buttonholes as are needed.

Vertical buttonholes

This method of working buttonholes is ideal when only a narrow band is required and they can be worked in one with the main fabric. The working instructions are the same for a separate band or when incorporated in the main fabric, remembering to make provision for a double buttonhole if a turned under hem is being worked with the main fabric. Work until the position for the buttonhole is reached, ending at the center front edge. On the next row

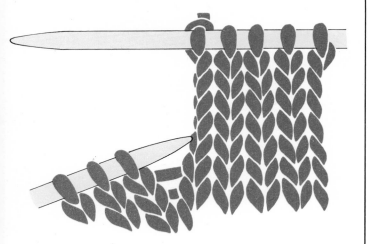

work across a few stitches to the buttonhole opening, then turn the work at this point and continue across these stitches only for the required number of rows to fit the size of the button, ending at the buttonhole opening edge. Break off the yarn and leave these stitches for the time being. Rejoin the yarn to the remaining stitches and work the same number of rows over these stitches, ending at the side edge away from the buttonhole opening. On the next row work across all the stitches to close the buttonhole. Continue in this manner for the number of buttonholes needed.

Finishing buttonholes

All buttonholes need to be finished and reinforced when they are completed. This can either be done by working around them in buttonhole stitch, using the same yarn or a matching silk thread, or by means of a ribbon facing.

Buttonhole stitch: Work along both sides of the buttonhole opening in buttonhole stitch for a horizontal or vertical buttonhole, finishing each end with three straight stitches. Be careful not to take too many stitches around the buttonhole, so that the edges become stretched, or too few stitches, which would make the hole smaller than you intended. Eyelet buttonholes need to be finished with several evenly spaced buttonhole stitches around the hole, keeping the loops lying towards the center.

Ribbon facing: The ribbon should be straight grained and wide enough to cover the buttonholes with an extra $\frac{1}{2}$in on either side and at each end of the band. Take care not to stretch the fabric when measuring the ribbon length and cut the buttonhole and button band facings together so that they match. Fold in the hems on the ribbon and pin in place on the wrong side of the knitting, easing the fabric evenly and checking that the buttonholes are correctly spaced. Pin the ribbon on each side of every buttonhole to hold it in place. Slip stitch neatly around the edges of the ribbon, then cut through the buttonholes in the ribbon making sure that they are exactly the same size as the knitted buttonholes. Work around the knitting and ribbon with buttonhole stitch to finish the edges.

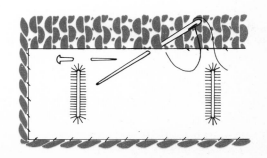

Hems and waistbands

Neat hems and waistbands are very important, particularly on babies' and children's garments where any unnecessary bulk produces an unattractive and uncomfortable edge.

Hems on skirts and dresses may be worked as part of the main fabric, then turned in and slip stitched into place when the garment is completed, or they may be knitted in to avoid seaming. Waistbands should be neatly ribbed and either folded in half to form a casing for the elastic, or the elastic may be directly applied to the wrong side of the fabric by means of a casing, or herringbone stitch.

Turned under stockinette stitch hem

Using one size smaller needles than for the main fabric, cast on the required number of stitches. Beginning with a knitted row work an odd number of rows in stockinette stitch, then change to the correct needle size. On the next row, instead of purling to the end, knit into the back of each stitch to form a ridge which marks the hemline. Beginning with a knitted row again, work one row less in stockinette stitch than was worked for the hem, thus ending with a purl row to complete the hem. **. When the garment is completed and the side seams have been joined, turn the hem to the wrong side of the work at the hemline and slip stitch in place.

Knitted in hem in stockinette stitch

Work as for the turned under hem to **. Before continuing with the pattern, use an extra needle and pick up the loops from the cast on edge from left to right, so that the needle point is facing the same way as the main needle. Hold this needle behind the stitches already on the left hand needle and knit to the end of the row, working one stitch from the left hand needle together with one stitch from the extra needle. When the garment is completed join the side seams, working through the double fabric of the hem.

Picot hem

Using one size smaller needles than used for the main fabric cast on an odd number of stitches. Beginning with a knitted row work an even number of rows in stockinette stitch. Change to the correct needle size.
Next row (eyelet hole row) *K2 tog, yfwd, rep from * to last st, K1.
Beginning with a purl row work one row more in stockinette stitch than was worked for the hem, thus ending with a purl row to complete the hem. When the garment is completed and the side seams have been joined, turn the hem to the wrong side at the eyelet hole row and slip stitch in place.

Ribbed waistband for elastic

Using one size smaller needles than those used for the main fabric, work in K1, P1 rib for twice the width of the elastic to be used, plus a few extra rows. If 1in elastic is being used, work 2in plus 2 extra rows, then bind off in rib. When the garment is completed and the side seams have been joined, turn in the waistband to the wrong side and slip stitch in place, leaving an opening at one side to thread the elastic through. Insert the elastic and sew ends securely, then seam the opening.

Casing stitch waistband

When the garment is completed, join the side seams. Cut the elastic to the necessary length, allowing 1in extra for an overlap, and join the two ends to form a circle.

Using rustless steel pins mark on the waistband and elastic into equal sections. Pin the elastic into place on the wrong side of the fabric. Thread a blunt ended sewing needle with matching yarn and secure to the side seam of the waistband. Hold the waistband and elastic, slightly stretched, over the fingers of the left hand then sew through the elastic and lightly through the top of the waistband from right to left. Sew through the elastic again and lightly through the fabric below the elastic from right to left about 2 stitches along to the right. Return to the top edge again about 2 stitches along to the right, and sew lightly through the fabric from right to left. Continue in this manner around the waistband until the elastic is secured, being very careful to distribute the knitting evenly, then fasten off.

Working casing stitch

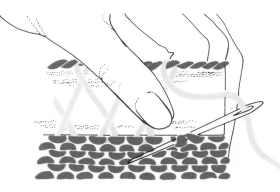

Baby's pants

Size

Directions are to fit 20in hips. Changes for 22 and 24in hips are in brackets [].
Length at side, 7[8:9]in

Gauge

30sts and 40 rows to 4in in stockinette stitch (st st) worked on No.2 needles

Materials

2[2:3] × 1¾oz balls Bucilla Perlette
One pair No.2 needles
One pair No.1 needles
Waist length of 1in wide elastic
Leg lengths of ½in wide elastic

Pants left side

Using No.2 needles cast on 93[99:105]sts. Beg with a K row and work 2 rows st st.

Shape crotch

Cont in st st, bind off 3 sts for back edge at beg of next and foll alt row then dec one st at same edge on every foll 4th row 4 times in all, *at the same time* binding off 2 sts for front edge on foll alt row and dec one st at same edge on every alt row 8 times in all. 73[79:85]sts. Cont without shaping until work measures 6[7:8]in from beg, ending with a P row.

Shape back

Next row K to last 24 sts, turn.
Next row Sl 1, P to end.
Next row K to last 32 sts, turn.
Next row Sl 1, P to end.
Cont working 8 sts less in this way on next and every alt row 4[5:6] times more. Change to No.1 needles.

Waistband

Next row K1, *P1, K1, rep from * to end.
Next row P1, *K1, P1, rep from * to end.
Rep last 2 rows 4 times more. Bind off in rib.

Pants right side

Work as for left side, reversing all shaping.

Leg bands

Using No.1 needles and with RS of work facing, K 93[99:105]sts around leg. Work 1in K1, P1 rib as for waistband.
Bind off in ribbing.

Finishing

Block each piece under a dry cloth with a cool iron. Join front, back and leg seams. Sew elastic inside waistband, using casing st. Fold leg bands in half to WS and sl st down. Thread elastic through leg bands and secure ends. Block seams.

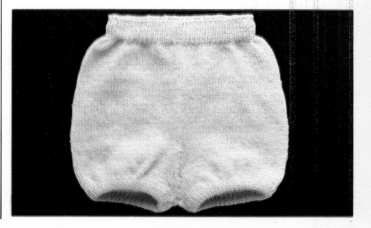

Pockets

Pockets are always a practical addition, particularly on men's and children's garments. They can be easily added to any chosen design, and inserted horizontally or vertically as part of the main fabric, or applied as patch pockets when the garment is finished. In each case a certain amount of planning is required to work out the exact positioning for each pocket before beginning the garment. It must also be remembered that they will use extra yarn, so to be safe, buy an extra ball.

If you have, for example, a favorite cardigan pattern for a man but would like to add inserted horizontal pockets above the waistband, first check the given length to the underarm and work out the depth of pocket desired. About 4in by 4in would be a reasonable size and this should be calculated to allow the pocket lining to come above any ribbed waistband or inside any front edges. The same measurements apply to a patch pocket.

For an inserted vertical pocket the same calculations must be made to insure that the opening is correctly positioned and that the pocket lining has sufficient room to lie flat inside any front edges.

Patch pockets are the simplest to work and easy to apply, see later. They can be used as breast pockets on an otherwise plain sweater, applied to the sleeves above elbow level on a teenage jacket, or on the skirt of a dress at hip level. A straight turned down, buttoned flap can be added, or a plain square pocket can be given a highly individual touch if it is worked in a contrasting stitch or finished with embroidery.

Inserted horizontal pockets

First check the number of stitches you need to make the size of pocket desired – on a gauge of 6 stitches to 1in, a 4in pocket would need 24 stitches. Cast on this number of stitches and make the inside pocket flap first, working in stockinette stitch until it is the desired depth, ending with a wrong side row, then leave these stitches on a holder. Now work the main fabric of the garment until the desired depth for the pocket has been reached, ending with the right side of the work facing you. On the next row work until the position for the pocket opening is reached, slip the required number of stitches for the pocket top on to a holder, then with the right side of the pocket lining stitches facing the wrong side of the main fabric, work across the pocket lining stitches, then work to the end of the row across the main fabric. Complete the section as given in the instructions. With the right side of the work facing, rejoin the yarn to the pocket top stitches on the holder and work $\frac{1}{2}$in to 1in in rib or garter stitch to complete the pocket.

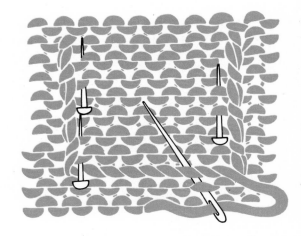

To finish the pocket, stitch the lining in place on the wrong side and slip stitch the side edges of the pocket top to the main fabric.

Inserted vertical pockets

First check the number of rows you need to make the size of pocket desired – if a gauge of 8 rows to 1in is given, a 4in pocket will require 32 stitches. Cast on this number of stitches and make the inside pocket flap first, working in stockinette stitch until it is the required depth, then place these stitches on a holder. Work the main fabric of the garment now until the required position for the pocket opening has been reached, ending with the right side of the work facing you. On the next row work until the position for the pocket opening is reached, turn at this point and work the required number of rows on this piece only, ending with a wrong side row. Break off the yarn.

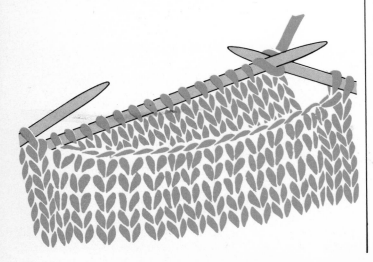

Return to where the work was divided, rejoin the yarn to the remaining stitches, and work the same number of rows on this piece, ending with a wrong side row. Break off the yarn. Return to the first piece, rejoin

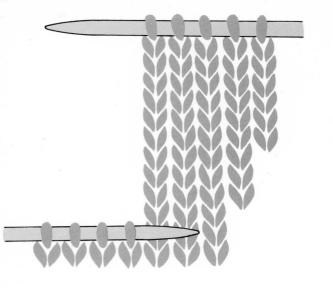

the yarn and work across all the stitches to close the pocket opening, then complete the piece according to the instructions. With the right side of the work facing you, rejoin the yarn along the edge of the first pocket piece worked on the right front of a garment, or along the second pocket piece worked on the left front of a garment, and pick up the required number of stitches.

Work ½ inch to 1 inch ribbing or garter stitch to complete the pocket opening. With the right side of the pocket flap against the wrong side of the main fabric, join the flap to the other edge of the pocket opening and sew around the other 3 edges. Finish the pocket opening by slip stitching the edges to the main fabric.

Patch pocket

Check the number of stitches and rows required to give the correct size for the pocket. If using a patterned stitch, such as cable, make sure that the pattern will work out exactly over the number of stitches and adjust them accordingly – it is better to have a slightly smaller or larger pocket than an incorrect pattern repeat. Cast on the stitches and work the number of rows to give the desired depth, then bind off. With the wrong side of the patch pocket facing the right side of the main fabric, sew around the three sides of the pocket.

Patch pocket with flap

Work as for the patch pocket until the desired depth has been reached but do not bind off. Unless a completely reversible stitch, such as ribbing or garter stitch, has been used for the pocket, the pattern must now be reversed so that when the flap is turned down, the right side of the fabric will be showing. To do this if you have ended with a wrong side row, simply work another wrong side row for the first row of the flap, then continue in pattern for the desired depth of the flap and bind off. Similarly, if you have ended with a right side row, work another right side row and complete in the same way. Sew the pocket on as for patch pockets, then turn the flap over to the right side and trim with one button at each end, if desired.

Patch pockets with cable trim on a slipover and patch pockets with flaps on a basic pullover.

Neckbands and collars

Neckbands and collars

The neck opening on any garment, where the necessary shaping to give a good fit has been worked as part of the main fabric, will require finishing, either by means of a neckband or a collar. The most usual method of working a neckband on a round-necked pullover is to pick up the required number of stitches around the neck opening and work a few rows, or rounds, in single or double rib. This forms a neat edge with sufficient elasticity to hold its shape when it is pulled on or off over the head and to spring back into place when it has been stretched in this way.

Collars may be added to a pullover or cardigan, either by picking up stitches around the neck edge or by making a separate piece which is then sewn around the neck edge to complete the garment. When you are working either a neckband or collar on which the stitches must be picked up (see below), insure that stitches are picked up neatly and evenly round the opening.

Neckbands

To complete a round neck on a pullover, provision for an opening must be made if the neckband is to be worked on two needles. If a back or front neck opening has not been worked as part of the main fabric, only one shoulder seam should be joined, leaving the other seam open until the neckband has been completed. When a round neckband is worked on 4 needles no opening is needed and the stitches are simply picked up and worked in rounds to the desired depth. When working a ribbed neckband the depth can quite easily be adjusted to suit personal taste, to form either a round, crew or turtleneck. If a turtleneck is desired, however, it must be remembered that this will take extra yarn and you must therefore make provision for this when you are purchasing the yarn.

To complete a square neck on a pullover or cardigan, each corner must be mitered to continue the square shape and allow the neckband to lie flat. The best way to do this is to pick up the required number of stitches and mark each corner stitch with colored thread. Keep these marked stitches as knitted stitches on the right side of the work, whether working in rows or rounds, and decrease one stitch on either side of each marked stitch on every row or round, making sure that the decreased stitches slant towards the corner stitch. As an example, when working in rows of garter stitch with the right side of the work facing, work to within 2 stitches of the corner stitch, sl 1, K1, psso, K corner st, K2 tog, then K to within 2 stitches of the next corner. On the following row, the decreased stitches will be worked in the same way but the corner stitch must be purled.

Collars

Collars come in all styles and sizes but, to fit correctly around the neck, they must be carefully shaped. They can be worked in 2 pieces to form a divided collar, where a sweater has a center back neck opening, or in one piece to complete a pullover or a cardigan. Where the fabric used for the collar is reversible, such as garter stitch or ribbing, the stitches should be picked up around the neck in the usual way with the right side of the work facing. Where a fabric such as stockinette stitch is used for a collar, however, the stitches must be picked up with the wrong side of the work facing, to insure that the correct side of the fabric is shown when the collar is turned down.

Pullover with ribbed neckband or shirt collar

Sizes

Directions are to fit 34in bust. Changes for 36 and 38in bust are in brackets [].
Length to shoulder, 23[23½:24]in
Sleeve seam, 17[17½:18]in

Gauge

30sts and 38 rows to 4in in stockinette st (st st) worked on No.2 needles

Materials

12[13:14] × 1oz balls of any 3-ply fingering yarn plus 1 extra ball if collar is desired
One pair No.2 needles
One pair No.1 needles
5 buttons

Back

Using No.1 needles cast on 134[142:150] sts. Work 2in K1, P1 rib. Change to No.2 needles. Beg with a P row cont in reverse st st until work measures 16in from beg, ending with a K row.
Shape armholes
Bind off 5[6:7] sts at beg of next 2 rows. Dec one st at each end of next and every alt row until 102[108:114] sts rem. Cont without shaping until armholes measure 7[7½:8]in from beg, ending with a K row.
Shape shoulders
Bind off at beg of next and every row 12[12:13] sts twice, 12[13:13] sts twice and 12[13:14] sts twice. Place rem 30[32:34] sts on holder.

Front

Work as for back until front measures 15½in from beg, ending with a P row.
Divide for front opening
Next row K62[66:70] sts, bind off 10 sts, K to end. Complete this side first. Cont in reverse st st until work measures same as back to underarm, ending at armhole edge.
Shape armhole
Bind off 5[6:7] sts at beg of next row. Dec one st at armhole edge on every alt row until 46[49:52] sts rem. Cont without shaping until armhole measures 5½in from beg, ending at center front edge.

Shape neck
Bind off 3[4:5] sts at beg of next row. Dec one st at neck edge on every alt row until 36[38:40] sts rem. Cont without shaping until armhole measures same as back to shoulder, ending at armhole edge.

Shape shoulder
Bind off at beg of next and every alt row 12[12:13] sts once, 12[13:13] sts once and 12[13:14] sts once.
With RS of work facing, rejoin yarn to rem sts and complete to correspond to first side, reversing shaping.

Sleeves
Using No.1 needles cast on 64[68:72] sts. Work 3in K1, P1 rib. Change to No.2 needles. Beg with a P row, cont in reverse st st, inc one st at each end of 7th and every foll 8th row, until there are 96[100:104] sts. Cont without shaping until sleeve measures 17[17½:18]in from beg, ending with a K row.

Shape top
Bind off 5[6:7] sts at beg of next 2 rows. Dec one st at each end of next and every alt row until 60 sts rem, ending with a K row. Bind off 4 sts at beg of next 10 rows. Bind off rem 20 sts.

Button band
Using No.1 needles cast on 12 sts. Beg 1st row with P1, work in P1, K1 rib until band fits up left front edge to beg of neck shaping, when slightly stretched. Place sts on holder. Mark position for 4 buttons with 5th to be worked in neckband.

Buttonhole band
Work as for button band, beg 1st row with K1 and making buttonholes as markers are reached, as foll:
Next row (buttonhole row) Rib 5, bind off 2, rib 5.
Next row Rib to end, casting on 2 sts above those bound off on previous row.

Ribbed neckband
Join shoulder seams. Sew on button and buttonhole bands, making sure that next row will beg and end with K1. Using No.1 needles and with RS of work facing, rib across buttonhole band, K 28[30:32] sts up right side of neck, K across back neck sts inc 5 sts evenly spaced across these sts and K 28[30:32] sts down left front neck, then rib across button band. 115[119:123] sts. Work 9 rows K1, P1 rib, making buttonhole as before on 5th and 6th rows. **. Bind off.

Collar
Work as for neckband to **.
Next row Bind off 6 sts, rib 5 sts and place on holder, rib to last 11 sts, rib 5 sts and leave on holder, bind off 6 sts. Break off yarn.
Change to No.2 needles. Using 2 strands of yarn, work 15 more rows rib, inc one st at each end of every row. Dec one st at each end of next 6 rows. Bind off 3 sts at beg of next 6 rows. Bind off rem sts.

Edging
Using No.1 needles and one strand of yarn, rejoin yarn to WS of first set of 5 sts. Work in rib until edging fits around outer edge of collar to center back. Bind off. Work other side in same way. Sew edging around collar, joining at center back.

Finishing
Block. Join side and sleeve seams. Set in sleeves. Sew on buttons.

FINAL FINISHING
BLOCKING AND SEAMS

The finishing of a garment requires as much care and skill as the actual knitting of each part of it. The technical knowledge which has been involved in producing an interesting fabric and the correct shape and proportions of the garment will be of no avail if the pieces are hurriedly assembled, or if scant attention is paid to the specific instructions for handling the yarn used. Some yarns do not require blocking and, in fact, they lose their character if they are blocked and the texture of certain stitches, such as Aran patterns, can be completely ruined by over-blocking. Read the instructions carefully before starting any finishing and if you have not used the yarn specified, check whether or not the substitute requires blocking by referring to the instructions given on the label.

Handling yarns
Each yarn, whether it is made from natural fibers, man-made fibers, or various blends of both, requires a different method of handling in finishing.

Most yarn labels will state the proper care for the yarn you are using. The following list gives a guide to the correct method of handling various qualities but, with so many new and exciting yarns becoming available, it is even more essential to check the specific requirements of each yarn.

Pure wool This quality should be blocked under a damp cloth with a warm iron.

Blends of wool and nylon fibers If the wool content is greater than the nylon content, such as 60% wool and 40% nylon, the yarn should be blocked lightly under a damp cloth with a warm iron.

Blends of wool and acrylic fibers Do not block.

Nylon Block under a dry cloth with a cool iron.

Acrylic fibers Do not block.

Cotton Block under a damp cloth with a fairly hot iron.

Mohair Block very lightly under a damp cloth with a warm iron.

Blends of mohair and acrylic fibers Do not block.

Glitter yarns Do not block, unless otherwise clearly stated on the label.

Angora Using a very damp cloth with a warm iron, steam press by holding the iron over the cloth to make steam but do not apply any pressure.

Embossed stitches Heavy cables, Aran patterns and any fabric with a raised texture should be steam pressed. This will give finish to the fabric without flattening the pattern.

Warning! If in doubt, do not block.

Blocking
As so many yarns now available do not require blocking, it is not always necessary to block out each piece to the correct size and shape. If blocking is required, however, place each piece right side down on an ironing pad and pin it evenly around the edges to the pad.

Always use rustless tailor's pins and never stretch the knitting, for if you do the pins will tend to make a fluted edge.

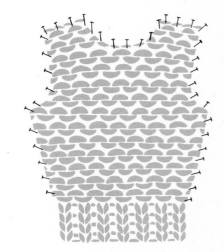

Take care to see that the stitches and rows run in straight lines and that the fabric is not pulled out of shape. Once the pieces are pinned into place, check with a firm ruler to see that the width and length are the same as those given in the instructions.

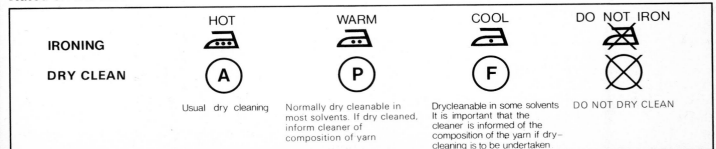

	HOT	WARM	COOL	DO NOT IRON
IRONING				
DRY CLEAN	A	P	F	
	Usual dry cleaning	Normally dry cleanable in most solvents. If dry cleaned, inform cleaner of composition of yarn	Drycleanable in some solvents It is important that the cleaner is informed of the composition of the yarn if dry-cleaning is to be undertaken	DO NOT DRY CLEAN

Use a clean cloth and place it over the piece to be blocked, then place the iron down on top of the cloth and lift it up again, without moving it over the surface of the cloth as you would if you were actually ironing. Each area should be blocked evenly but not too heavily before lifting the iron to go on to the next area.

Ribbed or garter stitch edges on any piece should never be blocked otherwise they will lose their elasticity.

Seams

The choice of a seaming method will largely depend on the type of garment being assembled. A baby's vest needs invisible seams without any hard edges and the flat seam method is normally used to join any ribbed edges where a neat, flat edge is required. Use a blunt ended needle and the yarn from which the garment is made for joining pieces together. If the yarn is not suitable for sewing purposes, as with mohair, use a finer quality such as 3 ply in the same color.

Invisible seam

Fasten the sewing yarn to one side of the pieces to be joined. With the right sides of both the pieces facing you, pass the needle across to the other side of the work, pick up one stitch and draw the yarn through. Pass the needle across the back to the first side of the work, pick up one stitch and draw the yarn through. Continue working in this way, making rungs across from one piece to the other and pulling each stitch up tightly so that it is not seen on the right side of the work when the seam is completed.

Back stitch seam

Place the right sides of each piece to be joined together and work along the wrong side of the fabric about one stitch in from the edge. Keep checking the other side of the seam to make sure that you are working in a straight line. Begin by securing the sewing yarn, making two or three small running stitches one on top of the other, then * with the needle at the back of the work move along to the left and bring the needle through to the front of the work the width of one stitch from the end of the last stitch, and draw the yarn through, take the needle back across the front of the work at the end of the last stitch and draw the yarn through. Continue in this way repeating from * until the seam is completed, taking care to pull each sewing stitch firmly through the knitting without stretching the pieces or drawing up the seaming stitches too tightly.

Flat seam

Place the right sides of each piece to be joined together and place your forefinger between the two pieces. Fasten the sewing yarn to one side of the pieces to be joined, then pass the needle through the edge stitch on the underside piece directly across from the corresponding stitch on the upper side piece and draw the yarn through. Turn the needle and work back through the next stitch on the upper side piece again drawing the yarn through. Continue in this way until the seam is completed.

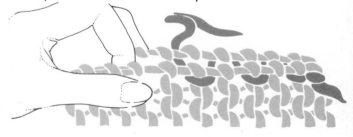

Slip stitch seam

This is used for turning hems and facings to the wrong side of the work. Turn the hem or facing so that the wrong side of the main fabric is toward you. Fasten the sewing yarn at a seam, then insert the needle and lightly pick up one stitch from the main fabric and draw the yarn through. Move along to the left the width of one stitch, insert the needle into the edge stitch of the hem or facing and pick up one stitch, then draw the yarn through. Move along to the left the width of one stitch and continue in this way until the seam is completed.

MORE ABOUT FINISHING

More about finishing! As we have already explained in the previous chapter, the care and attention to detail required in finishing are as essential as in knitting the pieces themselves. The correct seaming method, the correct handling and blocking of yarns, the correct method of finishing hems, applying pockets, completing edgings – all these techniques mean the difference between a handmade garment and a couture design. Here are more tricks of the trade which will enable you to give all your garments the finish and flair of a ready-to-wear design.

Sewn on bands
Where bands are worked separately and are not incorporated into the working instructions for the main sections, such as button and buttonhole bands, use a flat seam to apply the bands. Each band should be slightly less than the finished length of the main fabric and should be slightly stretched and pinned into position before seaming.

Applying the pocket

Shoulder seams
Use a firm back stitch seam, taking the stitches across the steps of shaping in a straight line. On heavy outer garments, such as sports jackets, or any garment where extra strength is needed, reinforce these seams with ribbon or tape.

Set-in sleeves
Mark the center top of the sleeve cap and pin this to the shoulder seam, then pin the bound off underarm stitches to the underarm stitches of the body. Use a back stitch seam, working in a smooth line around the curve of the armhole and taking care not to pull the stitches too tightly.

Sewn on pockets
Use a slip stitch seam to apply the pocket, taking care to keep the line of the pocket and main fabric straight. A useful tip is to use a fine knitting needle, pointed at both ends, to pick up every alternate stitch along the line of the main fabric, then catch one stitch from the edge of the pocket and one stitch from the needle alternately. Make sure that the lower edge of the pocket lies in a straight line across a row of the main fabric.

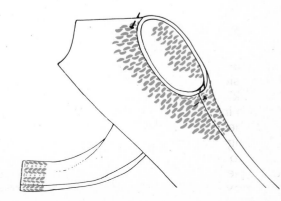

Side and sleeve seams

Use a back stitch seam and join in one piece, working extra stitches across the underarm seam to secure it firmly.

Sewing in a zipper

Pin the zipper into the desired opening, taking care not to stretch the knitting. With the right side of the work facing, sew in the zipper using a back stitch seam and keeping as close to the edge of the knitting as possible. On something like a back neck opening or skirt side seam, work in a straight line down the zipper from top to bottom, then work extra stitches across the end of the zipper to secure it and continue up the other side of the zipper.

When inserting an open-ended zipper, keep the fastener closed and insert it as for an opening from top to lower edge, anchoring it securely at the end. Break off the yarn and work along the other side in the same way. This insures that both sides match and that one side is not pulled out of shape, making it difficult to operate the zipper smoothly.

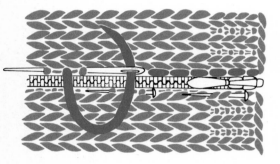

Picking up stitches

You will frequently have to pick up and knit stitches, such as around a neckline or along a front edge or pocket top as a means of finishing an edge. This is usually worked with the right side of the garment facing you. The instructions will always state clearly where stitches are required to be picked up with the wrong side facing you, such as would be needed for a stockinette stitch collar, where the turned down collar fabric must match the main fabric. You can either pick up these stitches directly onto a knitting needle, or use a crochet hook to pick up the stitches and then transfer them to a knitting needle.

Picking up stitches across the line of main fabric

Picking up stitches across the line of main fabric: Have the right side of the fabric facing you and hold the yarn at the back of the work. Use a crochet hook and put this through the work from the right side to the wrong side and pick up a loop of yarn from the back. Bring this loop through to the right side and transfer the stitch to a knitting needle. Continue in this way until the required number of stitches have been picked up.

Picking up stitches around a curved edge: This could apply to a neckband or armhole band. Place the yarn at the back of the work, with the right side of the fabric facing you. Put a knitting needle through from the front to the back of the fabric and pick up a loop of yarn. Bring this loop through to the right side of the work and leave the stitch on the needle. If a crochet hook is used, pick up the loop in the same way with the hook, then transfer the stitch to a knitting needle. Continue in this way until the required number of stitches have been picked up.

An easy way to insure that stitches are picked up evenly is to mark the main section of fabric with pins at regular intervals of about 2in and pick up the same number of stitches between each pin. As a guide, make sure that, where you are picking up stitches across stitches, you pick up one loop for each stitch; and across rows, approximately one stitch for every two rows.

Picking up front bands: Count the number of rows on the main fabric, then check this against the number of stitches to be picked up and make sure that you knit them up evenly. Mark sections as for picking up stitches around a curved edge and pick up the same number of stitches between each pin. Unless otherwise stated in the instructions, always work the button band first so that you can mark the exact position for each button and then work the appropriate buttonhole on the buttonhole band as these markers are reached.

CARE FOR KNITWEAR

The correct after-care of all knitted garments is extremely important if they are to retain their original texture and shape. Many of the yarns available today are machine-washable and the label will clearly indicate where this is applicable. If you are in any doubt at all, however, always hand wash rather than risk ruining the garment. Similarly, check the label to see whether the yarn can be dry cleaned.

Care in washing

Whether you are machine washing or hand washing a garment, it is essential that the minimum amount of handling occurs when the fabric is wet. Before washing, turn the garment inside out. Never lift the garment by the shoulders, thus allowing the weight of the water to pull the design out of shape. Squeeze out any excess moisture very gently but never wring the garment. Always support the whole weight with both hands.

Always rinse two or three times, making sure that all soap or detergent deposits have been thoroughly removed, using a fabric conditioner if desired. Once the garment has been rinsed, gently lift it onto a draining board, again supporting the weight while you prepare a drying area.

Care in drying

Very few yarns react well to contact with direct heat or sunlight and the garment should always be allowed to dry out naturally. You also run the risk of pulling the whole garment out of shape if you pin it to a line while it is still wet, however carefully. The best possible way of drying any garment, whatever the composition of the yarn used, is on a flat surface – a kitchen table top is ideal.

First place 3 or 4 old newspapers over the surface which is to be used for drying. Spread them out well beyond the full extent of the garment. Cover the newspapers completely with one or two clean towels which are color-fast – a white garment placed on a red towel which is not completely color-fast could result in some unsightly pink patches!

Gently place the garment on the center of the towel. Spread it into its original size and shape and gently pat it flat on the towel, smoothing out any creases formed during washing.

Leave the garment until all the excess moisture has been absorbed by the towels and newspapers. Then – and only then – can it be carefully lifted and placed on a clothes line for a final airing, pinning the garment

at the underarms only. Knitted garments should never be hung from the shoulders.

Care in blocking

If the garment has been smoothed out well and allowed to dry in place it should not need blocking. If it does need it, however, check the instructions given on the label, then refer to earlier chapter on handling details.

Care in wear

However careful you are, a garment may become snagged or the yarn may 'pill' into little balls of fluff. It is a simple matter to remedy these faults before the damage has gone too far.

To prevent the risk of snagging, do not put on a garment while you are wearing any jewelry which could catch the yarn and pull a thread. Should you discover a snag in a garment, however, never cut it off or you will risk having the fabric unravel. Using a blunt ended sewing needle, push the snagged end of yarn through to the wrong side of the fabric and gently tighten the yarn until the stitch is the correct size, then knot the end of yarn and leave it on the wrong side.

Where pilling occurs in the yarn, gently pull these

little balls of fluff off, taking care not to snag the yarn. If the pilling is excessive, the fabric should be gently brushed over with a clothes brush to remove the fluff.

Make do and mend

Hand knitting need never be wasted, even if the original garment has outgrown its use. Open the seams of the garment, taking great care not to cut the fabric, and unravel each section, winding the yarn into hanks by passing it around the backs of two chairs. To remove any crinkles from the yarn, either hand wash each hank and hang out to dry, or hold it taut in front of the spout of a gently steaming kettle, moving it back and forth through the steam until the kinks have disappeared. Some spots may wear thin with use, particularly on knitted children's garments. These can easily be reinforced by means of Swiss darning. It doesn't matter if you cannot match the original yarn – a contrasting color darned into a motif will give an interesting new lease of life to the design.

Elbows which are worn through can easily be covered with a patch of leather or suede applied to the right side of the fabric. To disguise the fact that these are patches and add new interest to the garment, make leather patch pockets to match.

KNITTING IN ROUNDS

BASIC TECHNIQUES

Knitting in rounds, as opposed to knitting in rows to produce flat knitting, literally means producing a seamless, tubular piece of fabric. This method may be worked on sets of needles, usually 4, which are pointed at both ends and manufactured in varying lengths and the length of needle used will be determined by

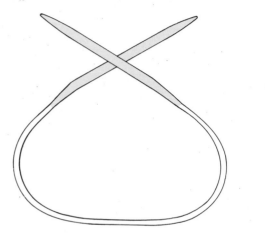

the total number of stitches required.
Circular needles are also available. They are made of two rigid, shaped needle sections pointed at one end, with the other end of each section being joined into one continuous length by a light-weight, flexible strip of nylon. Before using circular needles the twist which the nylon strip may develop through packing may be removed by immersing it in fairly warm water and then drawing it between the fingers until it lies in a gradual curve. These are also manufactured in varying lengths — 16, 24, 29 and 36 inches long. The more stitches you have the longer circular needle you will require. The advantage of circular needles over sets of needles is that they may also be used as an ordinary pair of needles for working in rows.
As knitting in rounds dispenses with seaming, it is the

ideal way of making socks and stockings, gloves and mittens hats, skirts and even sweaters. The minimum of seaming on a sweater is possible simply by working the body in one piece to a point where the work can be divided and then continuing in rows.

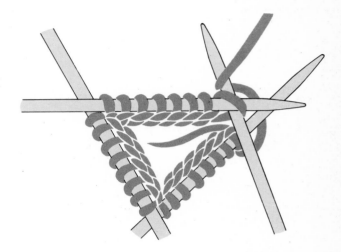

Casting on
Details of casting on with more than two needles have already been given earlier. The total number of stitches required can either be cast on to one needle and then divided between three of the needles, leaving the fourth needle to knit with, or can be cast on to each of the three needles separately.
When casting on with a circular needle, simply use each shaped section as a pair of needles, having one section in the left hand and one in the right.
Whether using sets of needles or a circular needle, the important point to remember is that the cast on stitches must not become twisted before you join them into a round.

Knitting in rounds
Once you have cast on the required number of stitches using sets of needles, form them into a circle by putting the spare needle into the first stitch on the left hand needle and knit this stitch in the usual way. Continue to knit all the stitches on the first needle. Once this is free, use it to knit the stitches on the second needle, then use the second needle to knit the stitches on the third needle. Always pull the yarn tightly across to the first stitch of each needle to avoid a loose stitch.
With a circular needle, simply continue knitting each stitch until you come to the beginning of the round again.

GAUGE	LENGTHS OF CIRCULAR NEEDLES AVAILABLE AND MINIMUM NUMBER OF STITCHES REQUIRED						
Stitches to 1 inch	16"	20"	24"	27"	30"	36"	42"
5	80	100	120	135	150	180	210
5½	88	110	132	148	165	198	230
6	96	120	144	162	180	216	250
6½	104	130	156	175	195	234	270
7	112	140	168	189	210	252	294
7½	120	150	180	202	225	270	315
8	128	160	192	216	240	288	336
8½	136	170	204	220	255	306	357
9	144	180	216	243	270	324	378

As it is easy to lose track of where each round of knitting begins, mark the beginning of the round with a knotted loop of contrast yarn on the needle before the first stitch of every round and slip this loop from the left hand needle to the right hand needle without knitting it.

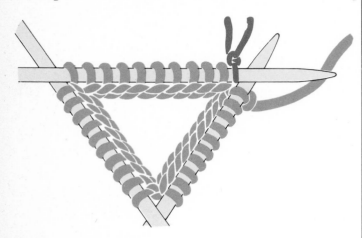

Stockinette stitch in rounds

Since the right side of the fabric is always facing the knitter and the work is not turned at the end of each row as in flat knitting, stockinette stitch (st st) in rounds is produced by knitting every round. This has a great advantage when working complicated, multi-colored patterns.

Garter stitch in rounds

Because the work is not turned, to produce garter stitch in rounds the first round must be knitted and the second round purled, in order to form the ridged effect.

Ribbing in rounds

Here again, the right side of the fabric is facing so each knit stitch must be knitted on every round and each purl stitch purled on every round. When working in rounds of ribbing, remember that if you begin a round with one or more knitted stitches, you must end with one or more purled stitches to complete the round exactly.

Socks without heel shaping

This practical way of producing socks without heel shaping must be worked on sets of needles.

Size

Round top of sock, 8in
Length to toe, 23in, adjustable

Gauge

32 sts and 36 rows to 4in in patt worked on No.1 needles

Materials

5 × 1oz balls of Bucilla 3-ply Fingering Yarn
Set of 4 No.1 double pointed needles

Socks

Using set of 4 No.1 needles cast on 80 sts, 26 each on 1st and 2nd needles and 28 on 3rd needle. Mark beginning of round with colored thread.
1st round *K1, P1, rep from * to end.
Rep 1st round for single ribbing until work measures 4in from beg. Commence patt.
1st patt round *K3, P2, rep from * to end.
Rep 1st patt round 3 times more.
5th patt round P1, *K3, P2, rep from * to last 4 sts, K3, P1.
Rep 5th patt round 3 times more.
9th patt round *P2, K3, rep from * to end.
Rep 9th patt round 3 times more.
13th patt round K1, *P2, K3, rep from * to last 4 sts, P2, K2.
Rep 13th patt round 3 times more.
17th patt round K2, *P2, K3, rep from * to last 3 sts, P2, K1.
Rep 17th patt round 3 times more. These 20 rounds form patt. Cont in patt until piece measures $20\frac{1}{2}$in from beg, or desired length less $2\frac{1}{2}$in. Cont in st st, K each round.

Shape toe

1st round *K8 sts, K2 tog, rep from * to end.
Work 2 rounds st st without shaping.
4th round *K7 sts, K2 tog, rep from * to end.
Work 2 rounds st st without shaping.
7th round *K6 sts, K2 tog, rep from * to end.
Work 2 rounds st st without shaping.
10th round *K5 sts, K2 tog, rep from * to end.
Work 2 rounds st st without shaping.
13th round *K4 sts, K2 tog, rep from * to end.
Work 2 rounds st st without shaping.
16th round *K3 sts, K2 tog, rep from * to end.
Work 2 rounds st st without shaping.
19th round *K2 sts, K2 tog, rep from * to end.
Work 2 rounds st st without shaping.
22nd round *K1 st, K2 tog, rep from * to end.
23rd round *K2 tog, rep from * to end.
Break off yarn, thread through rem sts, draw up and fasten off securely.

DOUBLE FABRICS

A double stockinette stitch fabric can quite easily be produced by working in rounds and using this tube of material as a double sided fabric. Alternatively, double fabric can also be worked in rows on two needles by the simple means of a slipped stitch. This method is most effective when two different yarns, giving the same gauge, are used for each side of the material. The ideas shown here will enable you to practice both these methods to make a warm scarf or a glamorous evening hood.

Scarf

We have made our scarf in stockinette stitch, knitting every round, in wide stripes. You can just as easily work narrow stripes in more than two colors or a simple, all-over patterned stitch in one color, provided you check the multiple of stitches required for the pattern and change the number of stitches and cast on accordingly. The total quantity of yarn given will be a guide to the amount required, but remember that a scarf knitted in a patterned stitch may need more yarn.

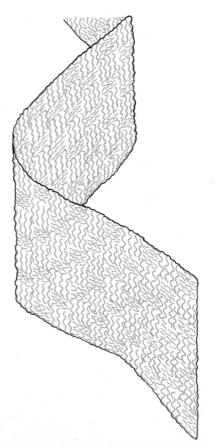

Scarf knitted in all-over patterned stitch.

Size
9in wide by 60in long

Gauge
22 sts and 28 rows to 4in in stockinette stitch (st st) worked on No.5 needles.

Materials
4 × 50 grm balls of Reynolds Classique in main color, A
4 balls of same in contrast color, B
Set of 4 No.5 double-pointed needles *or*
One No.5 circular knitting needle

Scarf
Using set of 4 No.5 needles or No.5 circular needle and A, cast on 100 sts. Work in rounds of st st, every round K, until piece measures 4in from beg. Break off A and join in B. Work a further 4in st st. Cont working stripes in this manner until piece measures 60in from beg. Bind off.

Finishing
Block under a damp cloth with a warm iron. Cut rem yarn into 12in lengths and knot fringe along each short end, knotting the strands through double fabric and using A and B alternately. Trim ends.

Evening hood

We have used a glitter yarn and mohair to make this double sided hood for evening. Using a plain yarn and repeating the first pattern row only, a snug, day-time version can quite easily be made. The total quantity of yarn given will be a guide to the amount required, but make sure that you are getting the exact gauge.

Size
11in wide by 56in long

Gauge
16 sts and 28 rows to 4in in double fabric worked on No.5 needles

Materials
4 × 40 grm balls Reynolds Mohair No. 1 in main color, A
6 × 20 grm balls Reynolds Feu d'Artifice in contrast color, B
One pair No.5 double pointed needles
One pair No.3 needles

Evening hood
Using No.3 needles and A, cast on 88 sts. Change to No.5 needles.

1sr row (RS) Using A, *K1, yarn in front (yfwd), sl 1 as if to purl (P-wise), yarn in back (ybk), rep from * to end. Join in B.
(**Note:** When using one color, turn and rep this row throughout.)

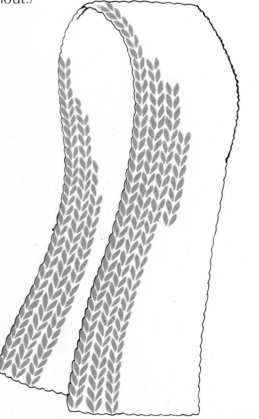

Hood worked in same yarn and color throughout

2nd row Do not turn work but return to beg of row. Using B, *sl 1 P-wise, yfwd, P1, ybk, rep from * to end. 44 sts each in A and B.
3rd row Turn work and cross A and B to close side edge, using B, *K1, yfwd, sl 1 P-wise, ybk, rep from * to end.
4th row Do not turn work but return to beg of row, using A, *sl 1 P-wise, yfwd, P1, ybk, rep from * to end. Turn and cross A and B to close side edge.
These 4 rows form the patt. Cont in patt until work measures 24in from beg, ending with a 2nd or 4th patt row.
Shape top
Next row Dec one st at beg of row in A and B by using both strands tog and (K2 tog) twice, patt to end.
Next 3 rows Patt to end.
Rep last 4 rows 13 times more. 30 sts each in A and B.
Next row Using A and B tog, (inc in next st) twice, patt to end.
Next 3 rows Patt to end.
Rep last 4 rows 13 times more. 44 sts each in A and B. Cont in patt without shaping until work measures 24in from last inc row. Bind off K2 tog across row.

Finishing
Do not block. Join back shaping seam and 6in of straight edges.

GLOVES AND MITTENS

When knitting in rounds to produce gloves, mittens, socks and stockings, the most difficult part to master is the shaping required to give a perfect fit to fingers and thumbs or heels and toes.

At a given point in the pattern some of the stitches will be left unworked and held in abeyance on a stitch holder, while the first section is completed. Then the unworked stitches will be picked up, together with additional stitches in some instances, to complete the work correctly.

All these shaping details should be given out in full in any pattern, and in the sequence in which they are to be worked. This chapter deals with gloves and mittens, which can be worked entirely in rounds without seaming, and includes a pair of mittens for a baby – ideal for a first attempt.

Both the designs given here begin at the wrist, where a firm ribbed edge is needed to give a snug fit, and stockinette stitch has been used for the main sections. They can both be made in one color only but, as a way of using up small amounts of the same quality yarn, we have worked the wrist and thumb of the mittens in a contrasting color, and the wrist, thumb, and each finger of the gloves in a different color, for a fun effect.

Babies' mittens
Size
To fit 9/18 months

Gauge
28 sts and 36 rows to 4in in stockinette stitch (st st) worked on No.3 needles

Materials
1 × 1oz ball of 3 ply yarn in main color, A
Small amount of contrast color, B
Set of 4 No.3 double-pointed needles
Set of 4 No.1 double-pointed needles

Mittens
Using set of 4 No.1 needles and B, cast on 36 sts, 12 on each of 3 needles. Mark beg of round with colored thread.
1st round *K1, P1, rep from * to end.
Rep this round until work measures 1in from beg. Break off B. Join in A. Change to set of 4 No.3 needles. Beg with a K round and work in rounds of st st until work measures 1½in from beg.
Shape thumb
Next round K17, pick up loop lying between sts and K tbl – called inc 1 –, K2, inc 1, K17.
Next round K to end.

Next round K17, inc 1, K4, inc 1, K17. 40 sts.
Next round K to end.
Cont inc in this way on next and every alt round until there are 46 sts.
Divide for thumb
Next round K18, sl next 10 sts on to holder and leave for thumb, turn and cast on 2 sts, turn and K18. 38 sts.
Cont in rounds of st st until work measures 4¼in from beg.
Shape top
Next round K1, sl 1, K1, psso, K13, K2 tog, K2, sl 1, K1, psso, K13, K2 tog, K1. 34 sts.
Next round K to end.
Next round K1, sl 1, K1, psso, K11, K2 tog, K2, sl 1, K1, psso, K11, K2 tog, K1. 30 sts.
Cont dec 4 sts in this way on every alt round until 14 sts rem. Arrange sts on 2 needles and bind off tog or weave them.
Thumb
Using set of 4 No.3 needles, B and with RS of work facing, arrange 10 thumb sts on 3 needles, then K 2 sts from base of cast on sts. 12 sts.
Cont in rounds of st st until thumb measures ¾in from beg.
Shape top
Next round *K2 tog, rep from * to end. 6 sts. Rep last round once more.
Break off yarn, thread through rem sts, draw up and fasten off.

Children's gloves
Size
To fit 6¼in around hand

Gauge
30 sts and 38 rows to 4in in stockinette stitch (st st) worked on No.2 needles.

Materials
1 × 1oz ball of 3 ply yarn in main color, A
1 ball each, or small amounts of contrast colors, B, C, D, E and F
Set of 4 No.2 double-pointed needles
Set of 4 No.1 double-pointed needles

Gloves
Using set of 4 No.1 needles and B, cast on 48 sts and divide on 3 needles.
Mark beg of round with colored thread. Work 2½in rib as for mittens.
Break off B. Join in A. Change to set of 4 No.2 needles. Work 4 rounds st st.
Shape thumb
Next round K23, inc 1 as for mittens, K2, inc 1, K23. Work 3 rounds st st without shaping.
Next round K23, inc 1, K4, inc 1, K23.
Cont inc in this way on every foll 4th round until there are 60 sts, ending with 3 rounds st st after last inc round.

Divide for thumb
Next round K24, sl next 12 sts on to holder and leave for thumb, turn and cast on 2 sts, turn and K24. 50 sts.
Cont in st st until work measures 6in from beg.

First finger
Next round Sl first 18 sts of round on to holder, join C to next st and K14, turn and cast on 2 sts, leave rem 18 sts on 2nd holder.
Cont in st st on these 16 sts until finger measures 2¼in from beg.
Shape top
Next round K1, *K2 tog, K1, rep from * to end. 11 sts.
Next round K to end.
Next round K1, *K2 tog, rep from * to end. 6 sts.
Break off yarn, thread through rem sts, draw up and fasten off.

Second finger
Next round Using D and with RS of work facing, leave first 11 sts on holder and K across last 7 sts on first holder, pick up and K 2 sts from base of first finger, K across next 7 sts on 2nd holder, turn and cast on 2 sts. 18 sts.
Cont in st st until finger measures 2½in from beg.
Shape top
Next round *K1, K2 tog, rep from * to end. 12 sts.
Next round K to end.
Next round *K2 tog, rep from * to end. Complete as for first finger.

Third finger
Next round Using E and with RS of work facing, leave first 6 sts on holder and K across last 5 sts on first holder, pick up and K 2 sts from base of 2nd finger, K across next 5 sts on 2nd holder, turn and cast on 2 sts. 14 sts.
Cont in st st until finger measures 2¼in from beg.
Shape top
Next round K1, *K2 tog, K1, rep from * to last st, K1. 10 sts.
Complete as for 2nd finger.

Fourth finger
Next round Using F and with RS of work facing, K across rem 6 sts on first holder, pick up and K 2 sts from base of 3rd finger, K across rem 6 sts on 2nd holder. 14 sts.
Cont in st st until finger measures 2in from beg.
Shape top
Work as for 3rd finger.

Thumb
Next round Using B and with RS of work facing, K across 12 thumb sts, then pick up and K 4 sts from base of cast on sts. 16 sts.
Cont in st st until thumb measures 1¾in from beg.
Shape top
Work as for first finger.

SOCKS AND STOCKINGS

The previous chapter dealt with knitting in rounds to produce gloves and mittens, where the complete design can be worked without seaming. This chapter shows how simple it is to make socks and stockings, where the leg and foot can be worked in rounds and the stitches are divided at the heel and worked in rows, to produce the heel gusset shaping.

A plain basic sock design can be adapted in a variety of ways, either by using stripes for the leg and instep, keeping the top, heel and sole in a plain color, or by introducing a patterned stitch for the leg and instep but, in this event, making sure that the pattern chosen will divide evenly into the total number of stitches cast on. Alternatively, men's socks look most effective when a small, two-color motif is used as a clock on either side of the leg.

Here we give instructions for a pair of durable socks for children and a fashion accessory for women – a pair of beautiful, lacy stockings.

Socks
Sizes
To fit 7in foot
Length of leg from top of heel, 8in

Gauge
32 sts and 40 rows to 4in in stockinette stitch (st st) worked on No.1 needles

Materials
3 × 1oz balls of Brunswick Fore 'n Aft Sport Yarn
Set of 4 No.1 double-pointed needles

Socks
Using set of 4 No.1 needles cast on 56 sts and arrange on 3 needles. Mark end of round.
1st round *K1, P1, rep from * to end.
Rep this round until work measures 1½in from beg. Beg with a K round cont in rounds of st st until work measures 3in from beg.

Shape leg
Next round K1, sl 1, K1, psso, K to last 3 sts, K2 tog, K1. Work 4 rounds st st without shaping. Rep last 5 rounds until 42 sts rem. Cont without shaping until work measures 8in from beg. Break off yarn.

Divide for heel
Next row Sl first and last 11 sts of round on to one needle, rejoin yarn and P to end. 22 sts.
Beg with a K row work 16 rows st st, ending with a P row.

Turn heel
Next row K14 sts, sl 1, K1, psso, turn.
Next row P7 sts, P2 tog, turn.
Next row K7 sts, sl 1, K1, psso, turn.
Next row P7 sts, P2 tog, turn.
Rep last 2 rows until all sts are on one needle.
Next round K4 sts, using 2nd needle K rem 4 heel sts, K 10 sts down side of heel, using 3rd needle K across 20 sts of instep, using 4th needle K 10 sts up other side of heel then complete heel by knitting the first 4 sts on to this needle.

Shape instep
1st round K to end.
2nd round 1st needle K to last 3 sts, K2 tog, K1; 2nd needle K to end; 3rd needle K1, sl 1, K1, psso, K to end. Rep last 2 rounds until 42 sts rem. Cont without shaping until work measures 4in from where sts were picked up at heel.

Shape toe
1st round 1st needle K to last 3 sts, K2 tog, K1, 2nd needle K1, sl 1, K1, psso, K to last 3 sts, K2 tog, K1; 3rd needle K1, sl 1, K1, psso, K to end.
Work 2 rounds st st without shaping. Rep last 3 rounds until 22 sts rem, then K across sts on 1st needle. Bind off sts tog or weave sts.

Lacy stockings
Sizes
Directions are to fit 8½in foot. Changes for 9½in foot are in brackets [].
Leg length to toe of heel 28in adjustable.

Gauge
28 sts and 30 rows to 4in over patt worked on No.11 needles.

Materials
3 × 1oz balls Reynolds Gleneagles Fingering Yarn
Set of 4 No.8 double-pointed needles
Set of 4 No.6 double-pointed needles
Set of 4 No.4 double-pointed needles
Set of 4 No.3 double-pointed needles

Stockings
Using set of 4 No.8 needles cast on 68 sts very loosely and arrange on 3 needles. Mark beg of round with colored thread. Work 8 rounds K1, P1, rib. Start patt.
1st round *(K2 tog) 3 times, yfwd, (K1, yfwd) 5 times, (K2 tog tbl) 3 times, rep from * to end.
2nd and 3rd rounds K to end.
4th round P to end.
These four rounds form patt being sure that sts are divided on needles as necessary. Rep 4 patt rounds 17 times more, adjusting length at this point and noting that work will stretch to 32in. Change to set of 4 No.6 needles and rep patt rounds 16 times. Change to set of 4 No.4 needles and rep patt rounds 16 times. Change to set of 4 No.3 needles and rep patt rounds 8 times.

Shape heel
Next round K15, K into front and back of next st – called inc 1 –, K1, patt 34 sts, inc 1, K16.
Next round K18, patt 34, K18.
Next round K16, inc 1, K1, patt 34, inc 1, K17.
Next round K19, patt 34, K19.
Keeping heel sts in st st and center 34 sts in patt, cont to inc in this way on next and every alt round until there are 80 sts, then work 4 rounds without shaping.
Next round Still keeping center 34 sts in patt, K21, K2 tog, patt 34, sl 1, K1, psso, K21.
Next round K22, patt 34, K22.
Next round K20, K2 tog, patt 34, sl 1, K1, psso, K20.
Next round K21, patt 34, K21.
Cont dec in this way on next and every alt round until 56 sts rem, then cont without shaping until foot measures 7[8]in from center of heel, or desired length less 1½in.

Shape toe
Next round K12, K2 tog, sl 1, K1, psso, K24, K2 tog, sl 1, K1, psso, K12.
Next round K to end.
Next round K11, K2 tog, sl 1, K1, psso, K22, K2 tog, sl 1, K1, psso, K11.
Next round K to end.
Cont dec in this way on next and every alt round until 20 sts rem. K sts from 3rd needle on to 1st needle and weave sts.

MOTIFS IN ROUNDS

We have already explained how knitting in rounds produces seamless, tubular fabric. This section deals with knitting in rounds using fine cotton yarn to form flat, circular motif shapes with a variety of uses.

Simple hexagonal motif
Using set of 4 double-pointed needles cast on 6 sts, having 2 sts on each of 3 needles. Join needles into a round and K all sts through back loop (tbl) to keep center flat Start patt.

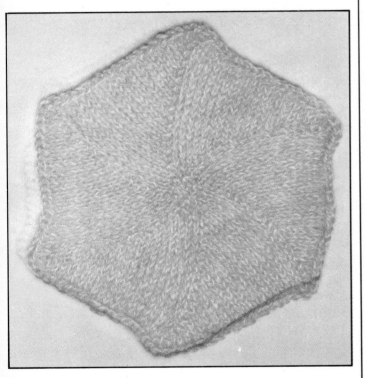

1st round *K into front then into back of next st — called inc 1 —, rep from * to end. 12 sts.
2nd round *Inc 1, K1, rep from * to end. 18 sts.
3rd round *Inc 1, K2, rep from * to end. 24 sts.
4th round *Inc 1, K3, rep from * to end. 30 sts.
5th round *Inc 1, K4, rep from * to end. 36 sts.
6th round *Inc 1, K5, rep from * to end. 42 sts.
Cont inc 6 sts in this way on every round until motif is desired size. Bind off loosely.

To make a throw pillow cover
Size
16in diameter

Gauge
24 sts and 32 rows to 4in in stockinette stitch (st st) worked on No.5 needles

Materials
1 × 50grm ball each of Reynolds Classique in 4 contrast colors, A, B, C and D
Set of 4 No.5 double-pointed needles
One No.5 circular needle
16in diameter circular cushion form
Buttons (optional)

Cover
Work as for hexagonal motif, working 2 rounds each in A, B, C and D throughout and changing to circular needle when required, until work measures 16in diameter. Bind off loosely. Make another hexagonal motif in same way.

Finishing
Block each piece under a damp cloth with a warm iron. With RS facing, join motifs tog leaving an opening to insert pillow form. Turn RS out. Insert form and complete seam. Sew one button to center of each side, if desired.

To make a circular lace table mat
Size
10in in diameter

Materials
1 × 300yd ball Clark's Big Ball Mercerized Crochet Cotton No.20
Set of 4 No.1 double-pointed needles

Table mat
Using set of 4 No.1 needles cast on 8 sts, having 2 sts on 1st needle and 3 sts each on 2nd and 3rd needles. Join needles into a round and K all sts tbl to keep center flat. Commence patt.
1st round *Yfwd, K1, rep from * to end. 16 sts.
2nd and every alt round K to end.
3rd round *Yfwd, K2, rep from * to end. 24 sts.
5th round *Yfwd, K3, rep from * to end. 32 sts.
7th round *Yfwd, K4, rep from * to end. 40 sts.
9th round *Yfwd, K5, rep from * to end. 48 sts.
11th round *Yfwd, K6, rep from * to end. 56 sts.
13th round *Yfwd, K1, K2 tog, yarn round needle twice — called y2rn —, K2 tog, K2, rep from * to end.
Note that on next and subsequent rounds where y2rn has been worked on previous round, you must K1 then P1 into the new stitches.
15th round *Yfwd, K8, rep from * to end.
17th round *Yfwd, K9, rep from * to end.
19th round *Yfwd, K1, K2 tog, y2rn, (K2 tog) twice, y2rn, K2 tog, K1, rep from * to end.

21st round *Yfwd, K11, rep from * to end.

23rd round *Yfwd, K12, rep from * to end.

25th round *Yfwd, K5, K2 tog, y2rn, K2 tog, K4, rep from * to end.

27th round *Yfwd, K4, K2 tog, y2rn, (K2 tog) twice, y2rn, K2 tog, K2, rep from * to end.

29th round *Yfwd, K7, K2 tog, y2rn, K2 tog, K4, rep from * to end.

31st round *Yfwd, K1, yfwd, K2 tog, K3, K2 tog, y2rn, (K2 tog) twice, y2rn, K2 tog, K2, rep from * to end.

33rd round *Yfwd, K1, K2 tog, yfwd, K2 tog, K4, K2 tog, y2rn, K2 tog, K4, rep from * to end.

35th round *Yfwd, K1, yfwd, K2, yfwd, K1, yfwd, K2 tog, K11, rep from * to end.

37th round *Yfwd, K2, yfwd, K1, K2 tog, yfwd, K1, K2 tog, yfwd, K2 tog, K10, rep from * to end.

39th round *Yfwd, K1, yfwd, K2 tog, K1, yfwd, K2 tog, K1, yfwd, K2 tog, yfwd, K1, yfwd, (K2 tog) twice, y2rn, (K2 tog) twice, y2rn, K2 tog, K1, rep from * to end.

41st round *Yfwd, K2 tog, K1, yfwd, K1, K2 tog, yfwd, K2 tog, K1, yfwd, (K2 tog) twice, yfwd, K2 tog, K8, rep from * to end.

43rd round *Yfwd, K1, K2 tog, yfwd, (K2 tog) twice, yfwd, K1, K2 tog, yfwd, K1, K2 tog, yfwd, K2 tog, K7, rep from * to end.

45th round *Yfwd, K1, yfwd, K2 tog, K1, yfwd, K2 tog, K1, yfwd, K2 tog, K1, yfwd, K2 tog, yfwd, K1, yfwd, (K2 tog) twice, y2rn, K2 tog, K2, rep from * to end.

47th round *(Yfwd, K2 tog, K1) 3 times, yfwd, K1, K2 tog, yfwd, K2, yfwd, K2 tog, yfwd, K2 tog, K5, rep from * to end.

49th round *Yfwd, (K2 tog) twice, yfwd, K2 tog, (K1, yfwd, K2 tog) 3 times, K1, yfwd, K2, yfwd, K2 tog, K4, rep from * to end.

51st round *Yfwd, (K2 tog) twice, (yfwd, K2 tog, K1) 5 times, yfwd, K2 tog, K3, rep from * to end.

53rd round *Yfwd, (K2 tog) twice, (yfwd, K2 tog, K1) 5 times, yfwd, K2 tog, K2, rep from * to end.

55th round *Yfwd, K3 tog, K1, (yfwd, K2 tog, K1) 5 times, yfwd, K2 tog, K1, rep from * to end.

57th round *Yfwd, (K2 tog) twice, (yfwd, K2 tog, K1) 5 times, yfwd, K2 tog, rep from * to end.

58th round As 2nd.

Bind off loosely.

Edging

Using 2 No.1 needles cast on 9 sts.

1st row Sl 1, K1, yfwd, K2 tog, K1, yfwd, K2 tog, yfwd, K2.

2nd and every alt row K to end.

3rd row Sl 1, K1, yfwd, K2 tog, K2, yfwd, K2 tog, yfwd, K2.

5th row Sl 1, K1, yfwd, K2 tog, K3, yfwd, K2 tog, yfwd, K2.

7th row Sl 1, K1, yfwd, K2 tog, K1, yfwd, K2 tog, K1, yfwd, K2 tog, yfwd, K2.

9th row Sl 1, K1, yfwd, K2 tog, K2, yfwd, K2 tog, K5.

10th row Bind off 4 sts, K to end.

Rep 1st to 10th rows until edging fits around table mat. Bind off.

Finishing

Block under a damp cloth with a warm iron. Sew cast on edge of edging to bound off edge. Sew around table mat. Block.

More motifs

The same technique which produces flat, circular shapes can be used to form other geometric motifs, such as triangles, squares and octagons. It is simply a matter of working out how many sides you need and spacing the shaping on each side to increase the size of the motif.

Because you are working on 3 needles with numbers of stitches which will not always divide by 3, the number of stitches cast on to each needle will not always be equal. When the number of stitches become too many to hold comfortably on 3 needles, change to a circular needle.

Always mark the beginning of the round with a colored marker and, if you find it easier, cast on the full number of stitches onto one needle and knit each stitch through the back of the loop before dividing them onto 3 needles.

Triangular motif

Using set of 4 needles cast on 6 sts, having 2 sts on each needle.
Join needles into a round and K all sts through back loops (tbl) to keep center flat.

1st round *K into front then into back of next st – called inc 1 –, rep from * to end. 12 sts.
2nd round *Inc 1, K2, inc 1, rep from * to end. 18 sts.
3rd round *Inc 1, K4, inc 1, rep from * to end. 24 sts.
4th round *Inc 1, K6, inc 1, rep from * to end. 30 sts.
5th round *Inc 1, K8, inc 1, rep from * to end. 36 sts.

Cont inc 6 sts in this way on every round until motif is desired size.
Bind off loosely.

Square motif

Using set of 4 needles cast on 8 sts, having 2 sts on 1st needle and 3 sts each on 2nd and 3rd needles.
Join needles into a round and K all sts tbl to keep center flat. Commence patt.
1st round *K into front then into back of next st – called inc 1 –, rep from * to end. 16 sts.

2nd and every alt round K to end.
3rd round *Inc 1, K2, inc 1, rep from * to end. 24 sts.
5th round *Inc 1, K4, inc 1, rep from * to end. 32 sts.
7th round *Inc 1, K6, inc 1, rep from * to end. 40 sts.
8th round K to end.
Cont inc 8 sts in this way on next and every alt round until motif is desired size. Bind off loosely.

Octagonal motif

Cast on and work 1st and 2nd rounds as given for square motif.
3rd round As 1st. 32 sts.
4th and 5th rounds K to end.
6th round *Inc 1, K2, inc 1, rep from * to end. 48 sts.
7th and 8th rounds K to end.
9th round *Inc 1, K4, inc 1, rep from * to end. 64 sts.
10th and 11th rounds K to end.

12th round *Inc 1, K6, inc 1, rep from * to end. 80 sts.
13th and 14th rounds K to end.
Cont inc 16 sts in this way on next and every foll 3rd round until motif is desired size. Bind off loosely.

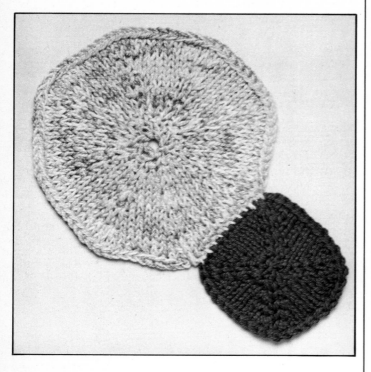

Bath mat
Size
20in wide by 30in long

Gauge
Each octagonal motif measures 5in diameter worked on No.5 needles and using 2 strands of yarn.

Materials
6 × 155yd balls of Lily Sugar 'n Cream Cotton Yarn in main color, A
2 × 155yd balls of contrast color, B
Set of 4 No.5 double-pointed needles

Note
Yarn is used double throughout.

Bath mat
Using set of 4 No.5 needles and A, make 24 octagonal motifs, working 14 rounds only for each one.
Using set of 4 No.5 needles and B, make 15 square motifs, working 8 rounds only for each one.

Finishing
Block each piece under a damp cloth with a warm iron. Join motifs as shown in diagram. When complete, block again.
Another way of using instructions for the bath mat would be to use up left-over pieces of knitting worsted yarn in as many colors as possible to make a cheerful and practical carriage cover.

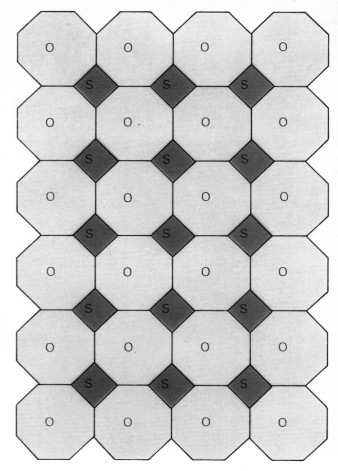

24 octagonal motifs = O
15 square motifs = S

ADJUSTING PATTERNS

Making changes to an existing pattern is quite an easy matter, provided you take the time to work out the correct positioning of your alterations before starting any knitting. A plain cardigan can be given an entirely different look by the addition of picot edgings instead of ribbed edges. Slimming bust darts may be incorporated into a basic pullover to achieve a better fit for the fuller figure. With a little care even the proportions of armholes and shoulders may be altered to suit your own individual requirements. Once you have the know-how, it is a simple matter to apply it and so gain even greater satisfaction from your knitting.

Edges

With knitting, the same basic shape can always be worked in a variety of different stitches (see Bobble stitches). Similarly, an existing pattern for a plain pullover or cardigan does not always need to have ribbed edges. Instead, try a picot edging on the waist, cuffs and neckband of a sweater, or even the front bands of a cardigan. For example, on a straight edge first check the number of stitches for each piece of the original pattern, after the ribbing has been completed. This will be the correct number of stitches to cast on to begin the picot edging. Beginning with a knit row work the desired depth for a turned-under hem, say 1in, ending with a purl row. On the next row make a picot edge by knitting two stitches together, then bring the yarn forward and over the needle to make a stitch and continue in this way to the end of the row, being sure that you end with the correct number of stitches. Beginning with a purl row work one row less than the hemline to complete the edging, then either continue in stockinette stitch or pattern as directed in the instructions, remembering to adjust the total length which will have taken the ribbing into account.

Where picot edges need to be joined at right angles, such as the corner where the hem or neckband meet

the front bands on a cardigan, these edges must be mitered to fit correctly. To do this simply increase one stitch at the joining edge on the 2nd and every following row, work the picot row, then decrease one stitch at the same edge on every row for the completion of the edging until the original number of cast on stitches remains.

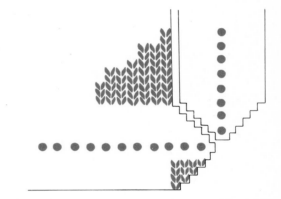

Another alternative is to work turned-under stockinette stitch hems or facing in place of ribbing. To do this on a straight hem, work as for the picot edging but end with a knit row, then instead of working the next row as a picot row, knit each stitch through the back of the loop to form the hemline. From this point you can continue in stockinette stitch or pattern as desired.

To use this method for edges which need to be joined at right angles, you must again miter the corners where the hem or neckband meet the front band.

As an example, say the original number of cast on stitches for the main section is 54 and an additional 8 stitches are needed for the front band, making a total of 62 stitches for the full width. If you are working a turned-under hem of 9 rows and are increasing one stitch at the front edge for the mitered corner on the 2nd and every following row, you will increase

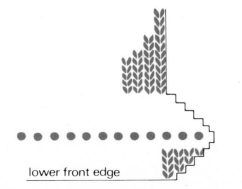

lower front edge

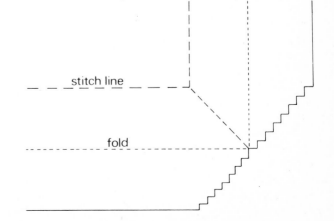

stitch line

fold

8 stitches on this edge and therefore need to cast on 8 stitches less than the total given number, in this case, 54 stitches in place of 62 stitches. Work the turned-under hem and the hemline row, increasing as shown, then continue increasing one stitch at the same edge on every row until you have a total of 70 stitches, which will give 8 extra stitches for the turned-under facing. Slip the last stitch of the main fabric on every right side row to form a fold line. When turned under the increased stitches on the hems and front facing will join into a neat mitered corner.

Bust darts

For the fuller figure, slimming bust darts can be incorporated into a plain stockinette stitch sweater to give extra depth across the bust without altering the underarm length of the garment.

Measure the exact underarm position for the darts, which should start between 1½in and 2½in below the beginning of the armhole shaping. The fuller the figure, the greater the number of rows needed for shaping the darts and the 12 row example given here is suitable for a 38/40in bust size. Work the front of the sweater until the position for the bust darts is reached, ending with a knit row, then start the dart shaping.

1st row P to last 5 sts, turn.
2nd row Sl 1, K to last 5 sts, turn.
3rd row Sl 1, P to last 10 sts, turn.
4th row Sl 1, K to last 10 sts, turn.
5th row Sl 1, P to last 15 sts, turn.
6th row Sl 1, K to last 15 sts, turn.
7th row Sl 1, P to last 20 sts, turn.
8th row Sl 1, K to last 20 sts, turn.
9th row Sl 1, P to last 25 sts, turn.
10th row Sl 1, K to last 25 sts, turn.
11th row Sl 1, P to end of row.
12th row K to end of row, closing holes between groups of 5 sts by picking up loop under the 5th st of each group and K this loop tog with next st on left hand needle.

This completes the dart shaping. Continue until the position for the armhole shaping is reached, remembering to measure on the side seam and not over the bust darts.

Changing proportions of armholes and shoulders
For a narrow shouldered figure it is a simple matter to change underarm and shoulder shaping. If this is desired, first work out the exact number of extra stitches which need to be decreased, based on the gauge given. Mark these alterations on the pattern so that you can work the complete armhole and shoulder section without further calculations.

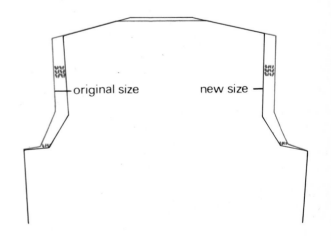

original size — new size

As an example, say you need to lose a further 8 stitches on the back of a sweater to achieve a narrower fit. Decrease half of this total at the underarm point, binding off 2 extra stitches at each side, then work 2 more decreasing rows to lose the remaining 4 stitches, thus arriving at the required total. At the shoulder line bind off 3 stitches less than the given number on the last 2 rows and allow for 2 stitches less than the given number for the remaining center back neck stitches. When working the front remember to make the same adjustments at the underarm and shoulder line and allow for 2 stitches less than the given number for the remaining center front neck stitches. The top of the sleeve shaping must also be changed to correspond to the underarm shaping.

ADJUSTING LENGTHS

With a little care and patience, horizontal hems can quite easily be lengthened or shortened, to contend with fashion changes or a growing family. Skirt, bodice or cuff lengths can be altered in this way and when making children's garments, it is always useful to buy one or two extra balls of yarn in the same dye lot to put aside for the day when such adjustments can be made quickly and inexpensively.

When you shorten a garment no extra yarn is required – in fact, a quantity of the original yarn will become available. Instead of wasting this, wind it into hanks and hand wash it, then hang it up to dry to remove

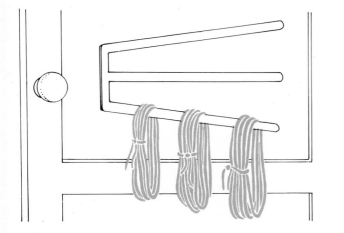

the kinks and lay it aside for some future use.

If a design needs to be lengthened, however, extra yarn is needed but it does not necessarily have to be the original yarn. Odd pieces of the same ply can be used to add a striped hem to a skirt or waist of a sweater and if the neckband is also unraveled and re-knitted in the same stripes, the whole effect will give a

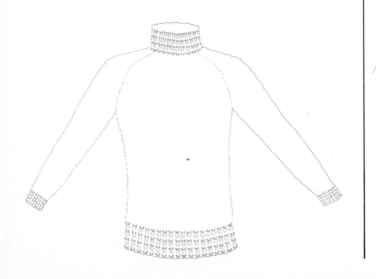

completely new look to the garment. Before beginning any adjustment, check the garment to find the best position for the lengthening or shortening. For example, if the body or sleeves of a sweater need lengthening and it already has a ribbed waistband or cuff 2in long, then the work must be picked up and re-knitted above that waistband or cuff. If a skirt needs shortening and it has a turned under hem, the adjustment must be made above the existing hem-line. It is not advisable to attempt these alterations on a fabric which has used a very complicated stitch unless you are quite certain that you will be able to pick up the original number of stitches in their correct sequence, but stockinette stitch, garter stitch or any simple pattern can be altered quite easily in this way.

Lengthening a garment

Make sure that you have some additional yarn on hand. Check the garment and mark both the position where the garment is to be unraveled and a further point 1in above this, then count the exact number of rows between each point. Prepare the work by

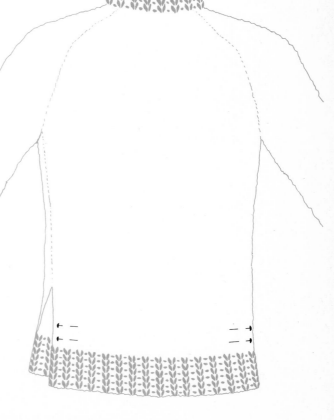

ripping out any hems and side seams to approximately 2in above the last marked point, to allow for freedom in manipulating the needles when re-knitting, taking great care not to cut into the fabric.

With the right side of the fabric facing and the correct needle size, pick up a loop with a needle at the marked row above the required adjustment point, and pull this up tight. Cut through this loop and carefully

pull the fabric apart until two sets of stitches are exposed. Pull the cut end of yarn tight again and cut it, easing the fabric apart. Continue in this way until

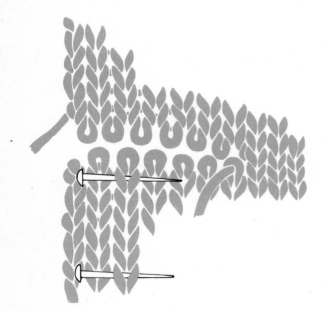

the fabric is in two separate sections, then pick up the stitches of the main section with a knitting needle, making sure that the original number of stitches are on the needle and that each stitch is lying in the correct direction and has not become twisted. Unravel the remaining yarn, winding it into a neat ball ready for use for re-knitting. **. Join the yarn at the

beginning of the row and continue knitting for the required number of rows calculated between the two marked points, then continue knitting to give the extra length desired. Complete the garment by working the original number of rows in ribbing for a waistband or cuff, or by working the exact number of rows used for the original hem on a skirt. Bind off very loosely, then work any other sections in the same way. Re-seam any edges or hems and check whether the new knitting can be blocked, then proceed accordingly.

Shortening a garment

Check and prepare the garment and work as for lengthening to **. Join the yarn at the beginning of the row and continue knitting for the required number of rows calculated between the two marked points.

Bind off very loosely and finish the garment as for lengthening.

Words of caution

When unraveling seams great care must be taken not to cut into the fabric itself only the yarn used for sewing. Never rush this stage, just gently ease the seam apart until you are quite sure which is the exact strand to be cut.

Once the fabric has been divided into two separate sections, check at which end of the work the unraveled yarn finishes, to ascertain whether the next row to be knitted is a right or wrong side row. Only then pick up the stitches with a knitting needle, making sure that each stitch lies in the correct position and that the needle point is facing the correct end, ready to rejoin the yarn. Using a double-pointed needle can help at this stage. Don't panic if a few of the stitches begin to run! These can quite easily be picked up to the correct depth, using a crochet hook. Because the yarn has already been knitted up once, it will not re-knit to the exact even fabric as the original. If the yarn does not require blocking but looks rather uneven, simply wash and dry the garment in the recommended way when it is completed to even out the fabric.

TUCKS AND TRIMS

The more you know about knitting, the more fascinating it becomes. Once you have mastered the basic techniques, it is the small finishing touches that make all the difference in any design.

This chapter deals with four ideas which can be applied to almost any basic design – and they are fun to work. Two of these trimmings are worked in with the actual knitting, one is worked as part of the finishing and the last can be applied when the garment is completed.

Try incorporating one of these suggestions to lift your knitting from the ordinary to the couture class and, at the same time, setting your own individual stamp on any design.

Tucks

Horizontal tucks are easy to work and can be incorporated into the skirt or bodice of almost any plain garment. They look most effective when worked in stockinette stitch with a picot edge – imagine the skirt of a little girl's dress embellished with two or three layers of tucks, or the yoke of a plain sweater finished with two rows of tucking at underarm level. Remember that tucks will use yarn over and above the quantity stated and allow for one or two extra balls before beginning any design.

To work horizontal tucks: Mark the position on the pattern where the tucks are to be incorporated and work to this point, ending with a purl row. Mark each end of the last row with a colored thread. Depending on the depth of tuck required, work a further 5 to 9 rows in stockinette stitch, ending with a knit row. On the next row either knit all the stitches through the back of the loops to mark the foldline of the tuck, or work a row of eyelet holes by knitting 2 together, then bringing the yarn forward to make a stitch, all along the row. Beginning with a knit row work a further 4 to 8 rows stockinette stitch, ending

with a purl row. Using a spare needle, return to the row marked with colored thread and pick up the correct number of stitches all along the row on the wrong side of the work, so that the points of the spare needle and the left hand needle holding the stitches are both facing in the same direction. Hold the spare needle behind the left hand needle and knit to the end of the row, working one stitch from the left hand needle together with one stitch from the spare needle. This forms one tuck and can be repeated as desired.

To work vertical tucks: These can be used to highlight any dart shapings on a design and, again, look their best against a plain stockinette stitch background. The continuity of the tucks must be kept throughout the whole length of the design and an additional 2 stitches should be cast on at the beginning for each tuck required. As an example, if the front of a skirt has two dart shapings which begin below hip level, read through the pattern to ascertain the place in the row where these shapings are first worked and allow 2 extra stitches on the right hand side of the first dart and 2 extra stitches on the left hand side of the second dart. Cast on 4 stitches at the beginning of the skirt and work as follows:

1st row K to within 2 sts of the position for the first dart, sl the next 2 sts P-wise keeping the yarn at the back of the work, work the first dart shaping, K to and then work the second dart shaping, sl the next 2 sts P-wise keeping the yarn at the back of the work, K to end.

2nd row P to end.

These 2 rows form the pattern and are repeated throughout, even after the dart shaping has been completed.

Lapped seams

These are worked at the finishing stage and are referred to in dressmaking as run and fell seams, such as you would see on a man's shirt. To look most effective they should be worked on a smooth fabric, such as stockinette stitch. For example, a plain raglan sleeved sweater on which lapped seams are used to join the side, sleeve and raglan seams would look quite original.

To work lapped seams: Depending on the position of the seam and the yarn being used, cast on an additional 2 or 3 stitches for each vertical seam and work a further 3 or 4 rows for each horizontal seam. When the pieces are completed, block as given in the instructions then place the two pieces to be joined with right sides together, with the underneath piece extending about $\frac{1}{2}$in beyond the edge of the upper piece. Work a firm back stitch seam along this edge. Turn the pieces to the right side and carefully back stitch the loose edge of the seam through both thicknesses of the fabric, about $\frac{1}{2}$in from the first seam. Block seam.

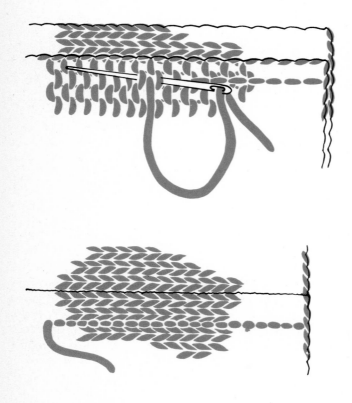

Piping cords

Most knitters will have experimented as children with French knitting, or horse-rein knitting. The round piping produced by this method can be thick or thin, depending on the yarn used and looks most attractive as a straight length of trimming sewn around the neck of a pullover, or on either side of the front bands of a cardigan. Also, separate lengths can be worked, then wound around and stitched to form flat, circular motifs. These motifs could be stitched at random on the bodice of a child's dress or used as a band above the ribbing and cuffs on a plain sweater. Any odd pieces of yarn will do – but think how colorful this piping would look in variegated yarn. The possibilities are endless and fun to work.

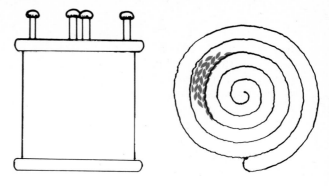

To work piping cord: Either purchase a horse-rein spool or use a wooden spool to make a bobbin, spacing 4 large, round-headed tacks evenly and firmly around the center hole at one end of the spool. Thread the yarn to be used through the center hole of the bobbin or spool, from the opposite end to the tacks, leaving an end free. Working in a clockwise direction throughout, wind the yarn around each of the 4 tacks and work as follows:

1st round Take the yarn once more around all 4 tacks without looping it around the tacks. Placing the yarn above the first round and using a fine crochet hook, lift the first loop over the second strand of yarn from the outside to the center and over the head of the tack. Repeat on all 4 tacks.

Continue repeating this round until the piping is the required length, pulling the cord down through the center hole of the bobbin or spool as it is formed. When the cord is the required length, break off the yarn, leaving an end, thread this end through a blunt ended needle, insert needle through loop on tack and lift loop off tack, repeat on all 4 tacks, pull up yarn and fasten off securely.

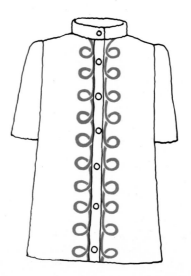

PLEATS

A swirling pleated skirt is a most useful and adaptable knitted garment, which can form the basis of a mix-and-match wardrobe of skirt, pullover, jacket and hat all worked in co-ordinated colors and contrasting patterns or stitch textures.

The method of working the pleats can be a simple, mock version or the inverted type, both of which give such a graceful swing to any skirt. They can be knitted vertically in stripes to form an even more striking variation and this is another ideal way of using up odd pieces of yarn of the same thickness to make a warm and practical skirt for a toddler. Use a yarn which will retain its shape without sagging, for all versions.

Planning pleats

The mock version is the most economical and is based on the width which is required around the hem of the skirt. Use this measurement and the gauge obtained with the yarn chosen to calculate the number of stitches which should be cast on. This number must be divisible by 8, so adjust the total if necessary by adding a few more stitches.

For inverted pleats, work out the required waist measurement and multiply this by three to arrive at the correct hem measurement. Use this measurement to determine the number of stitches to be cast on at the hem, again based on the gauge obtained. This number must be divisible by 12, plus 8, and the total can be adjusted by adding a few more stitches.

For vertical pleats you must measure the length required from waist to hem, plus an allowance of approximately 1in for a turned-under hem. Use this measurement and the gauge obtained to arrive at how many stitches must be cast on, having an even number of stitches, and work from side edge to side edge.

Mock pleats

These can be worked on two needles, either in two separate sections to form the back and the front of the skirt with a seam at each side, or in one piece with a center back seam.

Cast on the required number of stitches.

1st row (RS) *K7, P1, rep from * to end.
2nd row K4, *P1, K7, rep from * to last 4 sts, P1, K3.

These 2 rows form the pattern and are repeated for the required length. Bind off.

To work mock pleats without a seam, use a circular needle and cast on the required number of stitches.

1st round *K7, P1, rep from * to end of round.
2nd round P3, K1, *P7, K1, rep from * to last 4 sts, P4.

These 2 rounds form the pattern and are repeated for

the required length. Bind off.

To complete the skirt, cut a piece of elastic to the

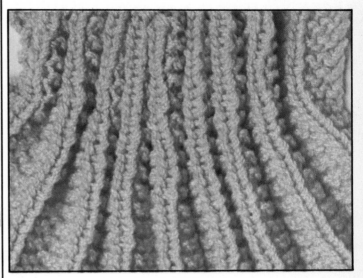

proper waist measurement and sew inside the waist edge, using casing stitch. As an alternative, cast on the number of stitches needed to form a separate waistband, allowing enough extra stitches for ease in pulling the skirt on and off, and work 2¼in st st. Bind off. Sew waistband to waist edge of skirt, fold in half to WS and sew in place. Thread elastic through waistband, sew ends neatly and fasten off.

Inverted pleats

This method requires a set of 4 double-pointed needles to close the pleats. Because the total number of stitches required is high it is easier to work the skirt in two separate sections, with a seam at each side.

Using two of the needles, cast on the required number of stitches.

1st row (RS) *K8, P1, K2, sl 1 as if to purl, rep from * to last 8 sts, K8.

2nd row *P11, K1, rep from * to last 8 sts, P8.

These 2 rows form the pattern and are repeated for the desired length, less 2in for the waistband. To close the pleats you will need to use all 4 needles.

Last row (waist edge) K4, *sl next 4 sts on to first extra needle, sl next 4 sts on to 2nd extra needle, place first extra needle behind 2nd extra needle and hold both extra needles behind the left hand needle, (K tog one st from all 3 needles) 4 times, rep from * to last 4 sts, K4.

Bind off.

To complete the skirt join seams, overlapping 4 sts at beg of row over 4 sts at end of row to complete pleating. Make a separate waistband and complete as you would for mock pleats.

Vertical pleats

This method is worked on two needles to a length that is twice as long as the waist measurement, with one seam at the center back. If you are working in stripes, carry the yarn not in use loosely up the side edge until it is required again. For neatness, this edge will become the waist edge, so that the strands of yarn can be sewn inside the waistband when the skirt is completed.

Cast on the required number of stitches, allowing approximately 1in extra for the hem.

1st row (RS) K to end.

2nd row P to end.

Rep 1st and 2nd rows 5 times more, then 1st row once more.

14th row P across sts for hem, *yo, P2 tog, rep from * to end.

Rep 1st and 2nd rows twice more, then 1st row once more.

20th row P across sts for hem, K tbl all sts to end.

These 20 rows form the pattern. Continue until work measures twice the required waist measurement, ending with a 20th row. Bind off.

To complete the skirt, join cast on edge to bound off edge to form center back seam. Turn hem at lower edge to WS and sew in place. Tack pleats in position along waist edge, folding each pleat at picot row to form inner fold and at knit row to form outer fold. Make separate waistband and complete as you would for mock pleats.

Toddler's striped skirt

Size

To fit 20in waist, adjustable
Length, 10in

Gauge

30 sts and 36 rows to 4in in stockinette stitch (st st) worked on No.3 needles

Materials

4 × 1oz balls 3 ply Fingering Yarn in main color, A
2 balls of contrast color, B
One pair No.3 needles
Waist length of elastic

Skirt

Using No.3 needles and A, cast on 76 sts. Keeping 8 sts at lower edge for hem, work as for vertical pleats, working first 14 patt rows in A and next 6 rows in B throughout, until work measures 40in from beg, or desired length. Bind off.

Waistband

Using No.3 needles and A, cast on 180 sts. Work 2in st st. Bind off.

Finishing

Block as directed on label. Finish as for vertical pleats.

DESIGNING

BASIC TECHNIQUES

Designing your own clothes can be the most rewarding of all aspects of hand knitting. Details have already been given in previous chapters of the important part gauge plays in any designing, together with the compositions of various yarns and the structure of numerous stitches. These three factors form the basis of all successful hand knitted designs.

Before you can begin any design you need to know the exact measurements of the garment you have in mind. Don't tackle anything too complicated for a first attempt – something as simple as the skirt shown here would be ideal, as it does not entail a great deal of shaping.

Each section must be calculated exactly to the required width and length, based on the gauge obtained with any given yarn and needle size. To these measurements you must then add an additional number of stitches which will give sufficient tolerance for ease of movement and also allow for multiples of stitches which will work out correctly in the pattern which has been chosen. An over all tolerance of 2 inches is sufficient for most garments, although something as bulky as a casual jacket which is intended to be worn over another garment will obviously require more tolerance than a sleekly-fitting fine ply pullover.

Measurements

For something as simple as a skirt, five accurate measurements are required.

a The waist measurement in width.
b The hip measurement in width.
c The measurement from waist to hip in depth.
d The measurement from hipline to hemline in depth.
e The width of hemline at lowest point.

The exact shape of the desired skirt must then be determined. It can have almost straight sides, with the hem and hip measurement being about the same, then gently curving from the hipline into the waist. If you want a flared hemline, this must be shaped into the hips, before shaping from the hips to the waist. Whatever the style of skirt you choose, it can be worked in two separate sections, the back and front being exactly the same. To the measurements you now have to add the over all tolerance needed to give an easy-fitting garment, allowing half this additional measurement for the front and half for the back.

At this point, decide whether you want a separate waistband or the waist edge knitted in with the main fabric and finished with casing stitch worked over elastic. If the skirt is to be very slim-fitting you will also need to make provision for a zipper on the side seam. Plan the sort of hem you desire and take this into your calculations – most skirts hang better with a turned up hem, so you will need to add an additional 1 inch to the length.

Gauge

You must now decide on the type of yarn you wish to use. Check the gauge obtained on needles of your choice, which will produce a smooth, even fabric, neither too hard and tight nor too loose and open. Work a sample swatch, using a basic stitch such as stockinette stitch to begin with, and measure this accurately. If you do not measure this sample exactly, or feel that half a stitch difference to 1 inch is unimportant, you will not be able to produce the exact shape you desire. In printed patterns this procedure has already been overcome, as the yarn is specified and a guide to the needle size has been given. When designing for yourself, however, you are no longer limited to the gauge which has been obtained by the original designer but can decide for yourself what gauge will produce the effect you desire.

Making a diagram

Now that you have established the measurements needed and the gauge which will produce the type of fabric you have in mind, you must put all this information down on paper in the form of a diagram.

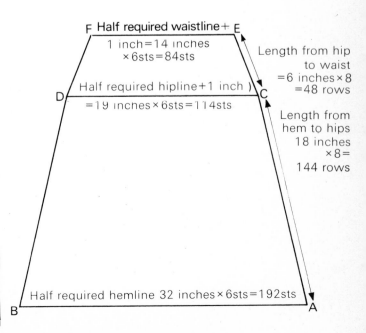

F Half required waistline + E
1 inch = 14 inches
× 6sts = 84sts

Half required hipline + 1 inch)
D = 19 inches × 6sts = 114sts C

Length from hip to waist = 6 inches × 8 = 48 rows

Length from hem to hips 18 inches × 8 = 144 rows

B Half required hemline 32 inches × 6sts = 192sts A

This does not have to be drawn to scale, as with a dressmaking pattern, but is simply used as a guide. The diagram shown here has been based on measurements to give a 36 inch hip size and has been calculated on a gauge of 6 stitches and 8 rows to 1 inch, worked in knitting worsted yarn on No.5 needles. Remember that with most knitted stitches the right side of the work is facing you, therefore your first knitted row will be worked from the right hand edge to the left hand edge. Our example has been worked in rice stitch, where the first, or right side row, is knitted and the second, or wrong side row is worked in single rib. It has also been worked from the hemline to the waist edge, decreasing as required to give the final waist measurement.

Hemline: This is the point marked A–B on the diagram.
Hipline: This is the point marked C–D on the diagram.
Waist: This is the point marked E–F on the diagram.

Calculating the number of stitches and rows

The measurements shown in the diagram given here now have to be multiplied by the number of stitches and rows to 1 inch which have been obtained in your gauge sample. The hemline width is 32 inches and when multiplied by 6 stitches, this gives a total of 192 stitches. Before the hipline point is reached, this width must be decreased to give 18 inches plus 1 inch tolerance, multiplied by 6 stitches to give a total of 114 stitches. Similarly, the depth from the hipline to the waist must be decreased to give 13 inches plus 1 inch tolerance, multiplied by 6 stitches to give a total of 84 stitches.

If you are working a straight skirt, the required number of stitches can be decreased at the side edges only. A flared skirt, however, has considerably more stitches to begin with and these will need to be decreased as carefully spaced darts as well as at the side edges. Calculate the number of rows which will be worked to give the required length from the hemline to the hipline, then work out how many decrease rows are needed to arrive at the correct number of stitches for the hip measurement, then how many rows are required between each set of decreases to give the correct length.

Skirt
Sizes
To fit 36in hips
Length, 25in

Gauge
24 sts and 32 rows to 4in in stockinette stitch (st st) worked on No.5 needles

Materials
10 × 2oz balls Brunswick Pomfret Sport Yarn
One pair No.5 needles
One pair No.4 needles

Waist length of 1in wide elastic

Back
Using No.5 needles cast on 192 sts. Beg with a K row work 7 rows st st.
Next row K all sts tbl to form hemline.
Next row K to end.
Next row *K1, P1, rep from * to end.
The last 2 rows form patt. Cont in patt until work measures 6 inches from hemline, ending with a WS row.

Shape darts
Next row Sl 1, K1, psso, K61, sl 1, K2 tog, psso, K60, sl 1, K2 tog, psso, K61, K2 tog. 186 sts.
Work 7 rows patt without shaping.
Next row Sl 1, K1, psso, K59, sl 1, K2 tog, psso, K58, sl 1, K2 tog, psso, K59, K2 tog. 180 sts.
Work 7 rows patt without shaping.
Cont dec in this way on next and every foll 8th row until 114 sts rem, then on every foll 6th row until 84 sts rem. Cont without shaping until work measures 24in from hemline, ending with a WS row.
Change to No.4 needles. Work 1in K1, P1 rib. Bind off in rib.

Front
Work as given for back.

Finishing
Join side seams. Turn hem at lower edge to WS and sew in place. Sew elastic inside waistband using casing stitch.

MORE ABOUT DESIGNING

This chapter continues with the necessary know-how required for designing your own clothes. As explained in the previous chapter, you need to know the exact measurements plus tolerance allowance for each section of the garment and the gauge obtained with the yarn, pattern stitch and needle size of your choice.

To plan the shape of the garment you can either make a diagram of each section and use this as a guide or, if the design you have in mind is rather complicated, you may find it easier to draft the garment out on squared graph paper, where each square represents one stitch and each line of squares shows a complete row of knitting. Most professional designers use the last method as it forms a detailed record of the design which can be checked against the written instructions.

Neither of these methods will be to the exact scale of the completed garment.

The pullover shown here has been worked to the same gauge as the skirt featured in the previous chapter, that is, 6 stitches and 8 rows to 1in in stockinette stitch worked on No.5 needles. With this knowledge you can make a diagram or knitting chart which will give you the exact measurements you require, but if you alter the yarn or needle size, you must first determine the gauge you will achieve before you can begin your design.

Basic pullover measurements

The diagrams and charts shown here represent the measurements and details of the shaping required for the body and sleeves of a plain, round-necked pullover.

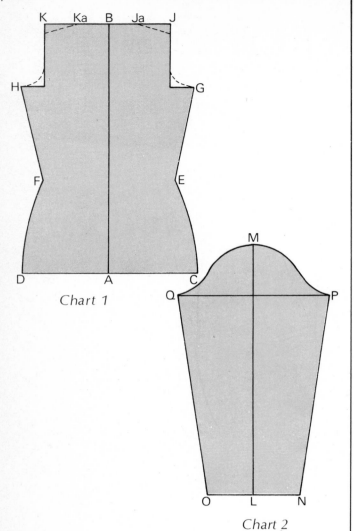

Chart 1

Chart 2

The center line on Chart 1, from the points marked A–B, represents the total length required from the lower edge to the back neck on the back of the pullover. The points marked C–D give the hemline measurements, E–F the waist measurements, G–H the bust measurement before shaping the armholes and J–K the shoulders and back neck width.

The center line on Chart 2, from the points marked L–M, shows the outside sleeve measurement from the wrist to the shoulder line. The points marked N–O represent the total wrist measurement and P–Q, the underarm sleeve width before shaping the cap of the sleeve.

Calculate the number of stitches and rows needed to give these measurements by multiplying the total number of inches from point to point by the number of stitches and rows obtained from your gauge sample.

Using graph paper

Charts 1 and 2 show the basic measurements needed when planning a pullover design, although the waist shaping on the body is not always essential and has been omitted on the pullover shown here. However, it is easier to show details of the graduated shaping required for each section on squared graph paper. The symbols used are a form of shorthand and are in standard use throughout all knitting charts.

Armhole shaping: Where a set in sleeve is required, the shaping takes place in the first 2/3in above the points marked G–H on Chart 1 in a gradual curve,

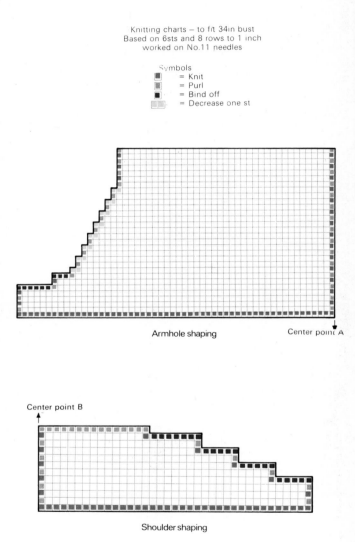

Knitting charts – to fit 34in bust
Based on 6sts and 8 rows to 1 inch
worked on No.11 needles

Symbols

▣ = Knit
▨ = Purl
■ = Bind off
▢▢ = Decrease one st

Armhole shaping   Center point A

Center point B

Shoulder shaping

which is more acute at the beginning to give a neat underarm shape. On a raglan sleeve, the same underarm shaping is required but the remaining stitches are then steadily decreased until only the number needed to form the back neck remain on the needle.

Shoulder shaping: For a set in sleeve, measure the shoulder seam length required from the points marked J–Ja and K–Ka on Chart 1 and start the shoulder shaping approximately 1in below the total length given from points marked A–B on Chart 1.

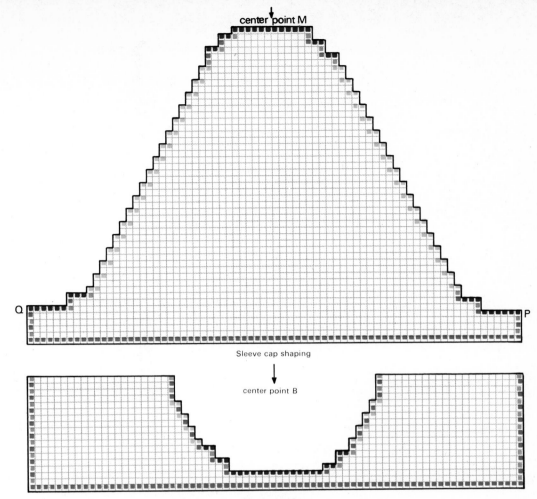

center point M

Sleeve cap shaping

center point B

Neck shaping

A raglan sleeve does not require shoulder shaping, as the cap of the sleeve is continued to form the shoulder line.

Sleeve shaping: All sleeves, whether long, short, set in or raglan, need to be shaped from the lower edge to the underarm to give a good fit. For a set in sleeve the cap must be shaped in a gradual curve, which is always more acute at the beginning to match the underarm shaping on the body. The number of remaining stitches on the last row of the sleeve should be less than 3in in width, to fit well across the shoulder line, and the final shape will depend on how the stitches are decreased to leave the correct number on the last row. After shaping the underarm, one stitch should be decreased at each end of the next 4–8 rows, depending on the row gauge being worked, and then on every other row to soften the curve until the sleeve is approximately 1in less than the total length from points marked L–M on Chart 2. The remaining stitches can then be bound off evenly at the beginning of the last few rows until the correct number remain for the final row.
Raglan sleeves should be shaped at the underarm,

then decreased until sufficient stitches remain to form the side neck edge only.

Neck shaping For a round neck the back and front body sections are exactly the same, except for the shaping of the front neck. This point should be approximately 2in lower than the back neck and the stitches need to be divided at this point and each shoulder worked separately. You will have established how many stitches are required to work each shoulder on the back and this total should be deducted from the stitches which remain after the armhole shaping has been completed. The remaining stitches are used to shape the neck in a gradual curve before the shoulder shaping is started.
A V-neck will be divided at a lower point, either at the same time as the armhole shaping is started or after this section has been completed, depending on the final depth required. Each shoulder is again completed separately, decreasing evenly at the front neck edge until the number of stitches needed to complete the shoulder remain.
The neckband can be completed in a variety of ways, either as a crew neck, turtleneck or ribbed V-neck.

A BASIC DESIGN PROJECT

The two previous chapters have explained how easy it is to design your own basic garments for a desired shape and size. With this knowledge you can begin to combine all the skills and techniques which are given in this course to make the most exciting and original designs – all to your own personal taste.

Once you know how to plan a basic shape, you can begin to experiment with different patterns and textures. If you work with colored patterns, this need not be an expensive trial run as you can use up all sorts of odds and ends of the same thickness of yarn in a variety of ways. Keep to a fairly simple shape to begin with but use as many colors and patterns as you like, so that all the interest of the design is in the fabric and not in the shape. Remember to check the multiple of stitches which are required for each pattern and, if necessary, adjust the row beginnings and endings to insure that each pattern works out correctly over the total number of stitches.

All the stitches, methods and techniques used for the pullover shown here are given in the book.

Rainbow pullover
Sizes
To fit 34/36in bust
Length to shoulder, 25in
Sleeve seam, 17in

Gauge
24 sts and 32 rows to 4in in stockinette stitch (st st) worked on No.5 needles

Materials
Total of 12 × 2oz balls of Brunswick Pomfret Sport Yarn in 12 contrast colors, or as desired
One pair No.5 needles

Note
Colors may be used in any sequence and are not coded.

Pullover body
Using No.5 needles and any color, cast on 112 sts for lower edge. K9 rows garter stitch (g st).
Work 22 rows Greek key pattern, working one extra st at each end of row, see Mosaic patterns later. K6 rows g st.
Work in stripes of 2 rows, 1 row, 3 rows, 1 row, 4 rows, 1 row, 3 rows, 1 row and 2 rows. K6 rows g st.

Bind off loosely. Make another piece in same way, working same color sequence.
Using No.5 needles and any color, cast on 112 sts for main body. K6 rows g st.
Work in diagonal stripes of 2 sts in each of 2 colors for 10 rows, see horizontal stripes later. K6 rows g st.
Work in chevron pattern for 20 rows, having multiples of 11 sts plus 2 instead of 13 stitches plus 2, keeping 3 sts at each side of shaping, see chevron stripes later. K6 rows g stitch.
Work in patchwork pattern across 2nd, 1st, 5th and 3rd patches, or 4 complete patches of 28 sts, for 30 rows, see patchwork later. K6 rows g st.
Work in lattice stitch, omitting 1st row and working one extra st at each end of row for 32 rows, see lattice stitch later.

Shape shoulders
Cont in g st only, bind off at beg of next and every row 10 sts 6 times. K3 rows g st on rem sts.
Bind off loosely. Make another piece in same way, working same color sequence.

Diamond panel
**Using No.5 needles and any color, cast on 2sts. K1 row. Cont in g st, inc one st at each end of next and every alt row until there are 28 sts. K3 rows g st. **.
Dec one st at each end of next and every alt row until 2 sts rem. K1 row. Bind off. Make 7 more diamonds in same way, varying colors.
Make 16 half diamonds working from ** to ** and varying colors. Bind off.

Sleeves
Using No.5 needles and any color, cast on 49 sts. K9 rows g st, inc one st in every st on last row. 98 sts. Omitting diamond panel and chevron pattern, work in body patterns, with 6 rows g st between each pattern and ending with 6 rows g st. Bind off loosely.

Finishing
Block each piece under a damp cloth with a warm iron. Join shoulder seams of main sections and side seams of lower sections. Join side seams of main body leaving 8in open at top for armholes. Join diamonds and half-diamonds as shown in diagram. Sew bound off edge of lower edge of body to lower edge of diamond panel, then sew cast on edge of main body to top edge of diamond panel. Sew in sleeves. Join sleeve seams. Block seams.

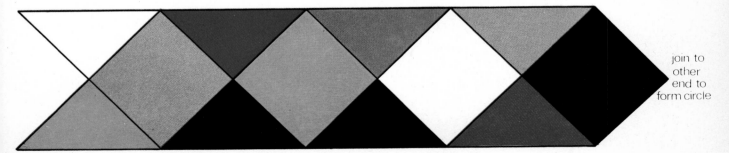

join to other end to form circle

FINISHING TOUCHES

Unusual trimmings and finishing touches on a garment are the easiest way of achieving fashion flair and turning an otherwise simple design into an original which no one else will have. It may just mean the addition of a belt to a dress or tunic, or your own initials embroidered on the shoulder of a plain sweater. These know-how ideas are invaluable and you will have great fun both in trying them out and applying them.

Twisted cords

These are simple to make and have a variety of uses, depending on their thickness and length. They can be used instead of ribbon on a baby garment – saving additional expense as well as using up any odds and ends of left over yarn. Also thick cord trimmed with tassels makes a most attractive belt and avoids the problem of trying to match colors.

The number of strands of yarn required will vary according to the thickness of the cord needed and the yarn being used. As a guide, try using 4 strands for a baby garment and up to 12 strands for a thick belt. Take the required number of strands and cut them into lengths 3 times the length of the finished cord. For example, for a cord 20in long you will need lengths of 60in. Enlist the aid of another person but, if this is not possible, then one end of the strands may be fastened over a convenient hook. Knot each end of the strands together before beginning. If you are working with another person, each should insert a knitting needle into the knot and twist the strands in a clockwise direction, until they are tightly twisted. Do not let go of the strands but, holding them taut, fold them in half at the center and knot the 2 ends together. Holding the knot, let go of the folded end and give the cord a sharp shake, then smooth it down from the knot to the folded end to even out the twists. Make another knot at the folded end, cut through the folded loops, and ease out the ends.

Braided belt

Here is another idea for a highly original belt. In addition to the yarn you will need 12 small wooden beads. Cut 12 lengths of yarn, preferably knitting worsted, 90in long. Take 2 ends together at a time and knot at one end, then slide a bead down to the knot and make 6 strands in this way. Tie these strands together about 10in above the beaded ends. Form into 3 strands having 4 lengths in each strand and braid together, taking the left hand strands over the center strands, then the right hand strands over the center strands and continue in this way to within 16in of the other end. Knot all 12 strands together at this point. Now take 2 ends together and thread a bead on to them, then knot them at the end to hold the bead. Make 5 more strands in this way. Trim ends.

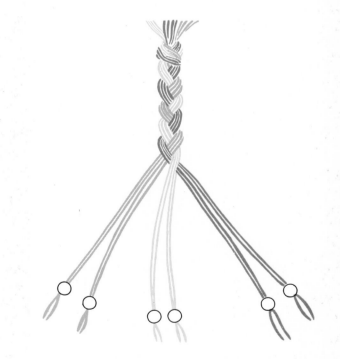

Pompons

These are a most attractive way of trimming a hat, with 2 or more in contrasting colors placed just above the brim, or one enormous loopy pompon placed on the top of a beret.

Round pompon Cut 2 circles of cardboard the size desired for the finished pompon, then cut out a circle from the center of each. Place the 2 pieces of cardboard together and wind the yarn evenly around them and through the center hole until the hole is nearly filled. Break off the yarn, leaving a long end, thread this through a blunt ended needle and use this to thread the last turns through the hole until it is completely filled. Cut through the yarn around the outer edge of the circles, working between the 2 pieces of cardboard. Take a double length of yarn and tie very securely around the center of the pompon, between the 2 pieces of cardboard, leaving an end long enough to sew to the garment. Pull out the cardboard, then fluff the pompon and trim it into shape.

Loopy pompon Cut a strip of very thin cardboard about 8in long by 4in wide, depending on the size of pompon desired. Leave a short end of yarn free, then wind the yarn very loosely along the length of cardboard for the thickness desired. **. Cut the yarn leaving an end about 12in long and thread this into a blunt-ended needle. Insert the needle under the loops at one edge of the cardboard, going under 3 or 4 loops at a time, then bring the needle up and back over these loops to form a firm back stitch. Continue along the length of the cardboard until all the loops are secured in this way, then work another row of back stitch if desired. Bend the cardboard slightly and remove it from the loops, then insert the needle through all the loops at once being careful not to pull up too tightly. Now bring one end of the secured loops around in a circle to meet the other end and fasten off securely, tying the first short end of yarn to secure it and using the remainder of the yarn to sew the pompon onto the garment.

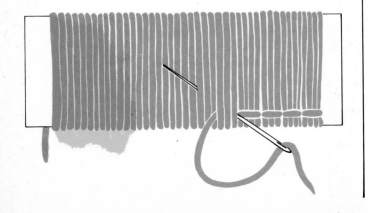

Tassels

Work as for the loopy pompon to **, then cut the yarn. Using a blunt ended wool needle threaded with yarn, insert the needle at one edge of the cardboard under all the strands and fasten off securely. Cut through the strands of yarn at the other untied edge of the cardboard. Finish the tassel by winding an end of yarn several times around the top folded ends, about $\frac{1}{2}$in down and fasten off securely, leaving an end long enough to sew on the tassel.

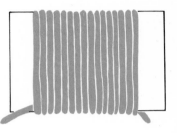

Swiss darning

For this type of embroidery it is advisable to use yarn of the same thickness as the knitted fabric. If the embroidery yarn is too thin the knitting will show through and if it is too thick, it will look clumsy.

Working from the chart, use a blunt ended needle threaded with the embroidery yarn and begin at the lower right hand corner of the design to be applied, working from right to left. Bring the needle through from the back to the front at the base of the first stitch to be embroidered and draw yarn through; insert the needle from right to left under the 2 loops of the same stitch one row above and draw yarn through; insert the needle back into the base of this stitch, along the back of the work, then into the base of the next stitch to the left from the back to the front and draw the yarn through. Taking great care to keep the loops at the same gauge as the knitting continue along the row in this way. At the end of the row, insert the needle into the base of the last stitch worked, then up in the center of this same stitch, which will form the base of the same stitch on the next row above. Now insert the needle from left to right under the 2 loops of this stitch on the row above, and continue working as before from left to right.

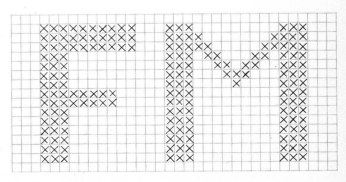

APPLIED EMBROIDERY

Embroidery can quite easily be applied to knitting without the need for charts or transfers. Quite apart from Swiss darning which gives a jacquard effect and is worked from a chart, see previous page, simple embroidery stitches such as cross stitch and chain stitch can be used to highlight a seam, or as a border pattern. Because of the amount of 'give' in most knitted fabrics, smocking, either knitted in as part of the main fabric or applied when the garment is completed, is particularly effective.

The following suggestions can be incorporated in a variety of ways, but a certain amount of planning is needed before beginning any garment. With the exception of smocking, they can all be worked on a plain stockinette stitch background, although care must be taken in working out the exact position for each stitch. Smocking, either applied or as part of the fabric, needs a ribbed background, and the pattern for any garment using this method will give detailed instructions for the correct placing. However, if you wish to try some smocking – perhaps on the bodice of a little girl's dress or around the cuffs of a plain pullover – remember to check and make sure that the number of stitches at the desired point will allow for the correct multiple of stitches.

Knitted-in smocking
Work as part of the main fabric over P3, K1 rib. The background color will be used for the main fabric, coded as A, and a contrast color of the same type will be used to work the smocking, coded as B. Either

cast on or make sure that you have a number of stitches divisible by 8 + 3. This allows for the knit stitches of the rib to be drawn together with the contrast color, alternating the position to give the smocked effect.

1st row (RS) Using A, *P3, K1, rep from * to last 3 sts, P3.
2nd row *K3, P1, rep from * to last 3 sts, K3.
Rep 1st and 2nd rows once more.
5th row Using A, P3, *K1, P3, K1, sl these last 5 sts onto a cable needle and hold at front of work, join in B at back of work, pass B in front of sts on cable needle to back of work then around to front and back again in a counter-clockwise direction, leaving B at back sl 5 sts onto right hand needle – called S5 –, P3 A, rep from * to end. Do not break off B.
6th row As 2nd.
Rep 1st and 2nd rows once, then 1st row once more.
10th row Using A, K3, P1, *K3, S5 by P1, K3, P1, holding cable needle at back of work and winding yarn around in a clockwise direction, rep from * to last 7 sts, K3, P1, K3. Do not break off B.
These 10 rows form the pattern.

Applied smocking
Work the background rib as for knitted-in smocking until the garment or piece to be trimmed is completed. Using a blunt ended needle threaded with B, *insert needle from back to front of the work after the 2nd knitted st of the 5th row, pass the needle across the front of the knit st, the next 3 purl sts and the next knit st, insert it from front to back after this knit st and pull yarn through, carry the yarn across the back of the work through to the front and around the 5 sts again through to the back, carry the yarn across the back of the work, skip (P3, K1) twice, rep from * to end. On the 10th row with the WS of the work facing, * work round the 2nd knit st of the first smocked sts, the next 3 purl sts and the first knit st of next smocked sts, then skip (K3, P1) twice, rep from * to the end. Continue in this way for the desired depth of smocking.

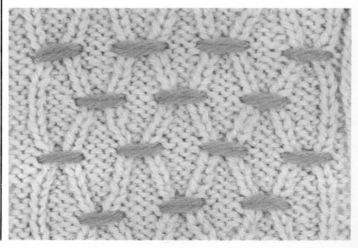

Applied bows

Work the stockinette stitch background and mark the positions for the bows on the RS of the work, allowing 5 sts and 5 rows for each bow and an additional 5 sts between each bow. Using a blunt ended needle threaded with contrast yarn, *insert the needle from back to front at the first marked st of the 1st row and pull yarn through. Working from right to left insert the needle under the 3rd st of the 3rd row and draw yarn through, insert the needle from front to back after the 5th st of the 1st row and draw yarn through; carry yarn across back of work, insert needle from back to front at first marked st of 2nd row and draw yarn through, insert needle under same 3rd st of 3rd row and draw yarn through, insert needle from front to back after 5th st of 2nd row and draw yarn through; carry yarn across back, insert needle from back to front at first marked st of 3rd row and draw yarn through, under the same 3rd st of 3rd row and draw yarn through, insert needle from front to back after 5th st of 3rd row and draw yarn through; carry yarn across back, insert needle from back to front at first marked st of 4th row and draw yarn through, under same 3rd st of 3rd row and draw yarn through, insert needle from front to back after 5th st of 4th row and draw yarn through, carry yarn across back, insert needle from back to front at first marked st of 5th row and draw yarn through, under same 3rd st of 3rd row and draw yarn through, insert needle from front to back after 5th st of 5th row and draw yarn through, carry yarn across back to next position and rep from * to end.

The next time the bows are worked, on 5 rows above, work them over 5 sts in between each bow of previous row.

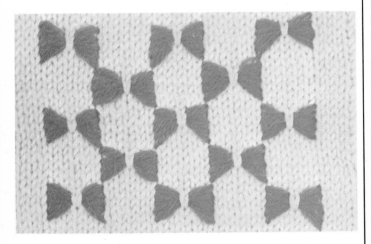

Applied chain stitch

This looks most effective if it is worked in a contrast color on a stockinette stitch background where wide stripes of the main color and narrow stripes of the contrast color have been used to give a checked effect. Mark the positions for vertical chains depending on the size of check desired, allowing one stitch, one above the other, on every row.

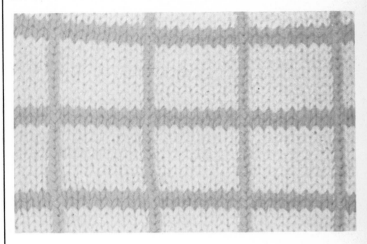

Using a blunt ended needle threaded with contrast color, begin at lower edge of first marked position and insert needle from back to front in center of marked st and draw yarn through, *hold the yarn down with the thumb of the left hand, insert the needle into the same st and up into the next st above, drawing the yarn through. Rep from * to end and fasten off. Repeat on each marked st as desired.

Applied cross stitch

Work the stockinette stitch background and mark positions for the cross sts on the RS of work, allowing 3 sts and 4 rows for each cross st, with an additional 3 sts between each cross st. Using a blunt ended needle threaded with one or two thicknesses of contrast color begin at lower edge, *insert needle from back to front at side of first marked st and draw yarn through, then working from right to left insert needle from front to back after 3rd st on 4th row above and draw yarn through, carry yarn across back of work, insert needle from back to front after first st on 4th row and draw yarn through, insert needle from front to back after 3rd st of 1st row and draw yarn through, carry yarn across back to next position and rep from * to end. The next line of cross sts are worked 4 rows above, working them over 3 sts in between each cross st of previous row.

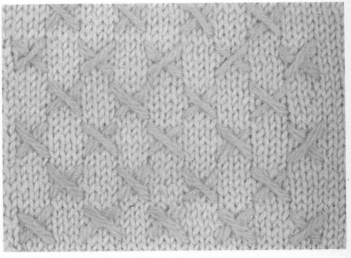

COVERED BUTTONS

Just as untidy buttonholes can mar the effect of an otherwise perfect garment, buttons which do not match exactly or coordinate with the yarn used for a design can spoil the whole appearance.

Sometimes it is impossible to find suitable buttons. The economical and simple answer to this problem is to cover button molds with knitting to achieve a perfect match.

Here we give a selection of buttons to suit all garments.

Bouclé yarn button

Using No.1 needles cast on 4 sts. Working in st st, inc one st at each end of every row until there are 12 sts. Work 6 rows without shaping. Dec one st at each end of every row until 4 sts rem. Bind off. Gather around wooden mold.

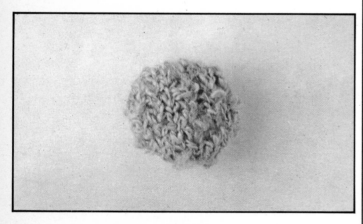

Reverse stockinette stitch button

Using No.1 needles and 3 ply yarn, work as for bouclé yarn button, beg with a P row. This will cover a $\frac{7}{8}$in mold.

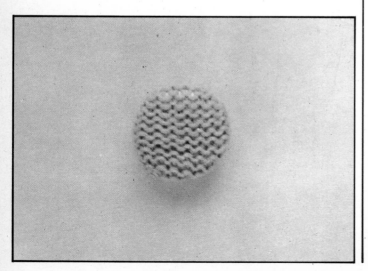

Single rib button

Using No.1 needles and 3 ply yarn, work in K1, P1 rib as for reverse st st button. This will cover a $\frac{7}{8}$in mold.

Bobble button

Using No.1 needles and 3 ply yarn, cast on 3 sts. Working in st st, inc one st at each end of every row until there are 11 sts. Work 3 rows without shaping.

Next row K5, K into front and back of next st 5 times, K5.

Next row P5, K5 tog, P5.

Work 2 rows without shaping. Dec one st at each end of every row until 3 sts rem. Bind off. This will cover $\frac{7}{8}$in mold.

Continental stockinette stitch button

Using No.1 needles and 3 ply yarn, cast on and work as for reverse st st button, working in foll patt:

1st row K into back of each st to end.

2nd row P to end.

Bind off. This will cover a $\frac{7}{8}$in mold.

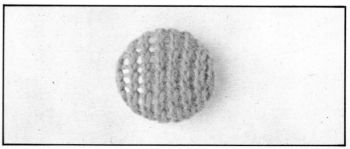

Tweed stitch button

Using No.1 needles and 3 ply yarn, cast on and work as given for reverse st st button, working in foll patt:
1st row *K1, yfwd, sl 1 P-wise, ybk, rep from * to end.
2nd row P to end.
3rd row *Yfwd, sl 1 P-wise, ybk, K1, rep from * to end.
4th row P to end.
Bind off. This will cover a $\frac{7}{8}$in mold.

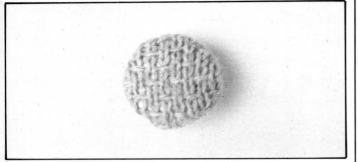

Two-color button

Using No.1 needles and 3 ply yarn in 2 colors, A and B, cast on and work as for reverse st st button, working in foll patt:
1st row (WS) Using A, *P1, sl 1 P-wise, rep from * to end.
2nd row Using A, K to end.
3rd row Using B, as 1st.
4th row Using B, as 2nd.
Bind off. This will cover a $\frac{7}{8}$in mold.

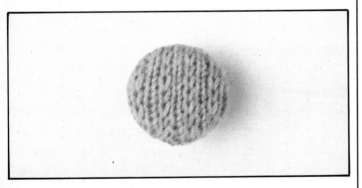

Embroidered button

Using No.1 needles and 3 ply yarn, cast on 6 sts. Work in st st inc one at each end of every row until there are 16 sts. Work 8 rows without shaping.
Dec one st at each end of every row until 6 sts rem. Bind off. Using 3 colors of 6-strand embroidery thread and chain st, work a flower motif in center of button. Gather over wooden mold.

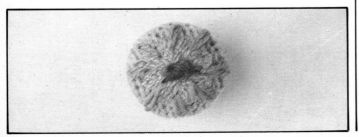

Basket stitch button

Using No.2 needles and knitting worsted, cast on and work as for the bouclé yarn button, working in foll patt:
1st row *K2, P2, rep from * to end.
2nd row As 1st.
3rd row *P2, K2, rep from * to end.
4th row As 3rd.
Bind off. Gather over wooden mold.

Woven basket stitch button

Using No.2 needles and knitting worsted, cast on and work as for the Basket stitch button, working in foll patt:
1st row *Pass right hand needle behind first st on left hand needle and K second st, then K first st in usual way, dropping both sts off needle tog, rep from * to end.
2nd row P1, *P second st on left hand needle then P first st and sl both sts off needle tog, rep from * to last st. P1.
Bind off. Gather over wooden mold.

Beret button

Using No.1 needles and knitting worsted, cast on 11 sts.
1st and every alt row (WS) P to end.
2nd row K1, (K twice into next st, K1) 5 times. 16 sts.
4th row (K2, K twice into next st) 5 times, K1. 21 sts.
6th row (K2, K2 tog) 5 times, K1. 16 sts.
8th row (K1, K2 tog) 5 times, K1. 11 sts.
10th row (K2 tog) 5 times, K1. 5 sts.
Break off yarn, thread through rem sts, insert $1\frac{1}{4}$in wooden mold, draw up and fasten off.

APPLIED EDGINGS

Knitted edgings

Although many beautiful and interesting forms of edgings are given in crochet patterns, reference is seldom made to the equally effective variations of knitted borders. These may be used to trim anything from baby clothes and fashion garments to household linens.

The correct choice of yarn for these borders is very important, depending upon the use to which they will be put. Something as fine as a 2 or 3 ply yarn would produce a delicate edging for a baby dress or shawl, a knitting worsted quality would give a firm, textured border for a fashion garment, or a crisp cotton would be ideal for household linens. All of the examples shown here are worked separately to the desired length, then sewn in place when the item is completed.

Simple lace edging

Cast on a number of stitches divisible by 5 plus 2.
1st row K1, yfwd and over needle to make one st, * K5, turn, lift 2nd, 3rd, 4th and 5th sts over the first st and off the needle, turn, yfwd, rep from * to last st, K1.
2nd row K1, *(P1, yon to make one st, K1 tbl) all into

next st, P1, rep from * to end.
3rd row K2, K1 tbl, *K3, K1 tbl, rep from * to last 2 sts, K2.
Work 3 rows g st. Bind off.

Shell edging

Using thumb method, cast on a number of stitches divisible by 11 plus 2.
1st row P to end.
2nd row K2, *K1, sl this st back on to left hand needle and lift the next 8 sts on left hand needle over this st and off the needle, yfwd and round right hand needle twice to inc 2 sts, then K first st again, K2, rep from * to end.
3rd row K1, *P2 tog, drop extra loop of 2 new sts on previous row, and into this long loop work (K1, K1 tbl) twice, P1, rep from * to last st, K1.
Work 5 rows g st. Bind off.

Leaf edging

Cast on a number of stitches divisible by 13 plus 2.
1st row K1, *K2, sl 1, K1, psso, sl 2, K3 tog, p2sso, K2 tog, K2, rep from * to last st, K1.

2nd row P4, *yrn, P1, yrn, P6, rep from * ending last rep with P4 instead of P6.

3rd row K1, yfwd, *K2, sl 1, K1, psso, K1, K2 tog, K2, yfwd, rep from * to last st, K1.

4th row P2, *yrn, P2, yrn, P3, yrn, P2, yrn, P1, rep from * to last st, P1.

5th row K2, *yfwd, K1, yfwd, sl 1, K1, psso, K1, sl 1, K2 tog, psso, K1, K2 tog, yfwd, K1, yfwd, K1, rep from * to last st, K1.

6th row P to end.

7th row K5, *yfwd, sl 2, K3 tog, p2sso, yfwd, K7, rep from * ending last rep with K5 instead of K7.
Work 4 rows g st. Bind off.

Chain edging

Using 2 needle method and working into each st instead of between sts, cast on a number of stitches divisible by 29.

1st row *K3 tbl, (pick up loop lying between sts and K tbl – called inc 1 –, drop 3 sts off left hand needle, K2 tog tbl) 4 times, inc 1, drop 3 sts off left hand needle, K3, rep from * to end.

2nd row P to end.

3rd row *K2 tbl, (sl 1, K1, psso) twice, sl 1, K2 tog, psso, (K2 tog) twice, K2, rep from * to end.

4th row P to end.
Work 3 rows g st. Bind off.

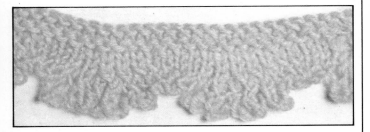

Serrated edging

Cast on 8 sts loosely.

1st row K to last 2 sts, K twice into next st, yfwd and hold at front of work, sl 1 P-wise. 9 sts.

2nd row K1 tbl, K1, (yfwd and over needle – called M1 –, sl 1, K1, psso, K1) twice, yfwd, sl 1 P-wise.

3rd row K1 tbl, K to end, turn and cast on 3 sts.

4th row K1, K twice into next st, K2, (M1, sl 1, K1, psso, K1) twice, M1, K1, yfwd, sl 1 P-wise.

5th row K1 tbl, K to last 2 sts, K twice into next st, yfwd, sl 1 P-wise.

6th row K1 tbl, K twice into next st, K2, (M1, sl 1, K1,

psso, K1) 3 times, K1, yfwd, sl 1 P-wise.

7th row K1 tbl, K to last 2 sts, K2 tog.

8th row Sl 1 P-wise, ybk, K1, psso, sl 1, K1, psso, K4, (M1, sl 1, K1, psso, K1) twice, yfwd, sl 1 P-wise.

9th row K1 tbl, K to last 2 sts, K2 tog.

10th row Cast off 3 sts, K2, M1, sl 1, K1, psso, K1, M1, sl 1, K1, psso, yfwd, sl 1 P-wise, 9 sts.
Rows 3 to 10 inclusive form pattern. Repeat pattern rows until edging is desired length. Bind off.

Fan edging

Cast on 13 sts loosely.

1st row (RS) Sl 1, K1, yfwd, K2 tog, K5, yfwd, K2 tog, yfwd, K2.

2nd and every alt row Yrn to inc 1, K2 tog, K to end.

3rd row Sl 1, K1, yfwd, K2 tog, K4 (yfwd, K2 tog) twice, yfwd, K2.

5th row Sl 1, K1, yfwd, K2 tog, K3, (yfwd, K2 tog) 3 times, yfwd, K2.

7th row Sl 1, K1, yfwd, K2 tog, K2, (yfwd, K2 tog) 4 times, yfwd, K2.

9th row Sl 1, K1, yfwd, K2 tog, K1, (yfwd, K2 tog) 5 times, yfwd, K2.

11th row Sl 1, K1, yfwd, K2 tog, K1, K2 tog, (yfwd, K2 tog) 5 times, K1.

13th row Sl 1, K1, yfwd, K2 tog, K2, K2 tog, (yfwd, K2 tog) 4 times, K1.

15th row Sl 1, K1, yfwd, K2 tog, K3, K2 tog, (yfwd, K2 tog) 3 times, K1.

17th row Sl 1, K1, yfwd, K2 tog, K4, K2 tog, (yfwd, K2 tog) twice, K1.

19th row Sl 1, K1, yfwd, K2 tog, K5, K2 tog, yfwd, K2 tog, K1.

20th row Yrn, K2 tog, K11.
These 20 rows form the pattern. Repeat pattern rows until edging is desired length. Bind off.

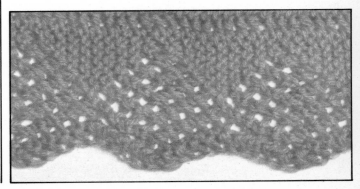

SHAPED EDGINGS

Knitted borders

The last chapter dealt with straight knitted edgings, either worked over a multiple of stitches in rows to give the desired length, or from side edge to side edge on a set number of stitches for the desired length. Where a border is required to fit a rectangular, square or circular shape, however, provision must be made for working corners or shaping the border so that the outer edge is wider than the inner edge. The circular border given here is used to trim a baby's shawl, where the center is knitted in stockinette

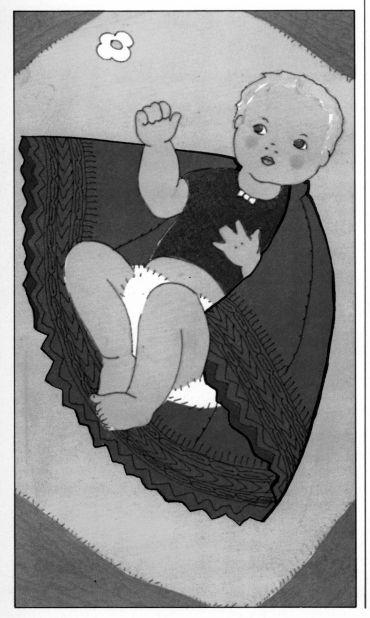

stitch to a circular shape, but if it is worked in a fine cotton yarn, the same border would most effectively trim a circular fabric tablecloth.

The border with corner shaping, used here to trim a fabric place mat, would also be ideal for trimming a pillow case, a tablecloth or a delicate evening stole.

Shawl center

Using set of 4 double-pointed needles, cast on 6 sts.
1st round *K into front then into back of next st, rep from * to end. 12 sts.
2nd round K1, *yfwd to make one, K2, rep from * to last st, yfwd, K1. 18 sts.
3rd round K1, *K into front then into back of yfwd of previous round, K2, rep from * to last 2 sts, K into front then into back of yfwd, K1. 24 sts.
4th round K2, *yfwd, K4, rep from * to last 2 sts, yfwd, K2. 30 sts.
5th round K2, *K into front then into back of yfwd, K4, rep from * to last 3 sts, K into front then into back of yfwd, K2. 36 sts.
6th round K3, *yfwd, K6, rep from * to last 3 sts, yfwd, K3. 42 sts.
7th round K3, *K into front then into back of yfwd, K6, rep from * to last 4 sts, K into front then into back of yfwd, K3.
Cont inc 6 sts on every round in this way until center is desired diameter. Bind off very loosely.

Shawl border

Cast on 52 sts loosely.
1st row K2, (K2 tog, yfwd to inc one – called M1 – K2) 3 times, K2 tog, K11, K2 tog, (K2 tog, M1, K2) 3 times, K2 tog, (M1, K2 tog) 4 times. 49 sts.
2nd row P10, turn and leave 39 sts unworked.
3rd row K2 tog, (M1, K2 tog) 4 times.
4th row P8, (K2 tog, M1, K2) 3 times, P13, (K2 tog, M1, K2) 3 times, K3.
5th row K3, (K2 tog, M1, K2) 3 times, (K2 tog) twice, (M1, K1) 5 times, M1, (K2 tog) twice, (K2 tog, M1, K2) 3 times, K1, (M1, K2 tog) 3 times, M1, K1.
6th row P9, (K2 tog, M1, K2) 3 times, P15, (K2 tog, M1, K2) 3 times, K3.
7th row K3, (K2 tog, M1, K2) 3 times, K2 tog, K11, K2 tog, (K2 tog, M1, K2) 3 times, K2, (M1, K2 tog) 3 times, M1, K1.
8th row P10, (K2 tog, M1, K2) 3 times, P12, turn and leave 16sts unworked.
9th row K1, K2 tog, (M1, K1) 5 times, M1, (K2 tog) twice, (K2 tog, M1, K2) 3 times, K3, (M1, K2 tog) 3 times, M1, K1.
10th row P11, (K2 tog, M1, K2) 3 times, P14, P2 tog, (K2 tog, M1, K2) 3 times, K3.

11th row K3, *K2 tog, M1, K1, sl next 3 sts on to cable needle and hold at back of work, K1, K2 tog from left hand needle, M1, K2 from cable needle, K next st on left hand needle and last st on cable needle tog, M1, K2, *, K2 tog, K11, K2 tog, rep from * to *, K4, (M1, K2 tog) 3 times, M1, K1.

12th row P13, turn and leave 39 sts unworked.

13th row K6, (M1, K2 tog) 3 times, M1, K1.

14th row *P13, (K2 tog, M1, K2) 3 times, rep from * once more, K3.

15th row K3, (K2 tog, M1, K2) 3 times, (K2 tog) twice, (M1, K1) 5 times, M1 (K2 tog) twice, (K2 tog, M1, K2) 3 times, K3, K2 tog, (M1, K2 tog) 4 times.

16th row P12, (K2 tog, M1, K2) 3 times, P15, (K2 tog, M1, K2) 3 times, K3.

17th row K3, (K2 tog, M1, K2) 3 times, K2 tog, K11, K2 tog, (K2 tog, M1, K2) 3 times, K2, K2 tog, (M1, K2 tog) 4 times.

18th row P11, (K2 tog, M1, K2) 3 times, P12, turn and leave 16 sts unworked.

19th row K1, K2 tog, (M1, K1) 5 times, M1, (K2 tog) twice, (K2 tog, M1, K2) 3 times, K1, K2 tog, (M1, K2 tog) 4 times.

20th row P10, (K2 tog, M1, K2) 3 times, P14, P2 tog, (K2 tog, M1, K2) 3 times, K3.

These 20 rows form patt. Cont in patt until inner edge of border fits around outer edge of center. Sew in place around shawl.

Place mat

Cut fabric to required size and hem round all edges.

Border

Cast on 9sts. Start patt.

1st row (RS) K to end.

2nd row K3, K2 tog, yfwd to inc one, K2 tog, yfwd, K1, yfwd, K1. 10 sts.

3rd and every alt row K to end.

4th row K2, K2 tog, yfwd, K2 tog, yfwd, K3, yfwd, K1. 11 sts.

6th row K1, K2 tog, yfwd, K2 tog, yfwd, K5, yfwd, K1. 12 sts.

8th row K3, yfwd, K2 tog, yfwd, K2 tog, K1, K2 tog, yfwd, K2 tog. 11 sts.

10th row K4, yfwd, K2 tog, yfwd, K3 tog, yfwd, K2 tog. 10 sts.

12th row K5, yfwd, K3 tog, yfwd, K2 tog. 9 sts.

These 12 rows form patt. Cont in patt until border is required length to first corner, ending with a 6th row.

Shape corner

1st row K10, turn.

2nd row Sl 1 K-wise, yfwd, K2 tog, yfwd, K2 tog, K1, K2 tog, yfwd, K2 tog. 11 sts.

3rd row K8, turn.

4th row Sl 1 K-wise, yfwd, K2 tog, yfwd, K3 tog, yfwd, K2 tog. 10 sts.

5th row K6, turn.

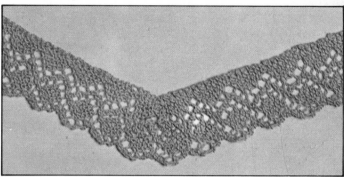

6th row Sl 1 K-wise, yfwd, K3 tog, yfwd, K2 tog. 9 sts.

7th row K6, turn.

8th row K2 tog, yfwd, K2 tog, yfwd, K1, yfwd, K1. 10 sts.

9th row K8, turn.

10th row K2 tog, yfwd, K2 tog, yfwd, K3, yfwd, K1. 11 sts.

11th row K10, turn.

12th row K2 tog, yfwd, K2 tog, yfwd, K5, yfwd, K1. 12 sts.

13th row K to end.

This completes corner shaping. Beg with an 8th patt row, cont in patt to next corner, then rep shaping rows. Cont in this way until border is completed. Sew in place around mat.

EDGINGS AND INSERTIONS

Knitted edgings and insertions can be used most effectively as a trim for fabric garments, or on household linens. They look their best when worked in a fine cotton, such as No.20, which is delicate and will also stand up to laundering without losing its shape.

The insertion pattern given here may be used by itself to form a panel on each side of the front of a fabric blouse, or it could be combined with any one of the edgings to form the yoke of a charming nightgown.

Alternatively, the insertion could be applied across the top of a sheet, which could then be finished off with an edging to transform a plain household linen into a family heirloom.

7th row K4, P2, K1, P4, K2, (yrn, P2 tog) twice, K1.
8th row K3, (yrn, P2 tog) twice, yon, K1 tbl, K1, K1, tbl, yfwd, sl 1, K2 tog, psso, yfwd, K5.
9th row K5, P7, K2, (yrn, P2 tog) twice, K1.
10th row K3, (yrn, P2 tog) twice, yon, K1 tbl, K3, K1 tbl, yfwd, K7.
11th row Bind off 4 sts, K2, P7 K2, (yrn, P2 tog) twice, K1.
The 2nd through 11th rows form the pattern.

Shell edging
Cast on 13 sts.
1st row (WS) P to end.
2nd row Sl 1, K1, yrn, P2 tog, K1, (yfwd, sl 1, K1, psso) 3 times, y2rn, K2 tog.

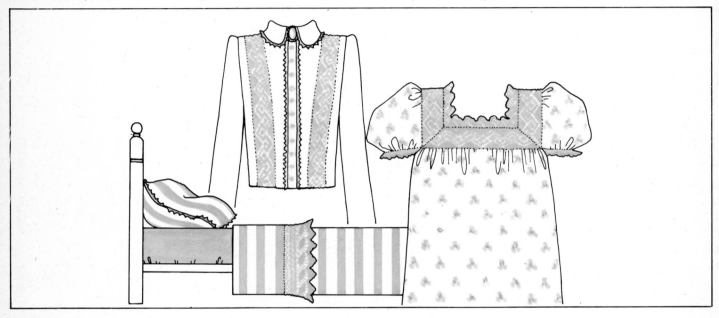

Leaf edging
·Cast on 17 sts.
1st row (WS) K to end.
2nd row K3, (yrn, P2 tog) twice, yon, K1 tbl, K2 tog, P1, sl 1, K1, psso, K1 tbl, yfwd, K3.
3rd row K3, P3, K1, P3, K2, (yrn, P2 tog) twice, K1.
4th row As 2nd.
5th row As 3rd.
6th row K3, (yrn, P2 tog) twice, yon, K1 tbl, yfwd, K2 tog, P1, sl 1, K1, psso, yfwd, K4.

3rd row Yfwd to make 1, K2 tog, P9, yrn, P2 tog, K1, noting that the first K2 tog includes the first loop of

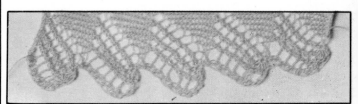

y2rn and the second loop forms the first P st.
4th row Sl 1, K1, yrn, P2 tog, K2, (yfwd, sl 1, K1, psso) 3 times, y2rn, K2 tog.
5th row Yfwd, K2 tog, P10, yrn, P2 tog, K1.
6th row Sl 1, K1, yrn, P2 tog, K3, (yfwd, sl 1, K1, psso) 3 times, y2rn, K2 tog.
7th row Yfwd, K2 tog, P11, yrn, P2 tog, K1.

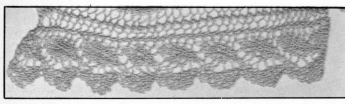

8th row Sl 1, K1, yrn, P2 tog, K4, (yfwd, sl 1, K1, psso) 3 times, y2rn, K2 tog.
9th row Yfwd, K2 tog, P12, yrn, P2 tog, K1.
10th row Sl 1, K1, yrn, P2 tog, K5, (yfwd, sl 1, K1, psso) 3 times, y2rn, K2 tog.
11th row Yfwd, K2 tog, P13, yrn, P2 tog, K1.
12th row Sl 1, K1, yrn, P2 tog, K6, (yfwd, sl 1, K1, psso) 3 times, y2rn, K2 tog.
13th row Yfwd, K2 tog, P14, yrn, P2 tog, K1.
14th row Sl 1, K1, yrn, P2 tog, K7, (yfwd, sl 1, K1, psso) 3 times, y2rn, K2 tog.
15th row Yfwd, K2 tog, P15, yrn, P2 tog, K1.
16th row Sl 1, K1, yrn, P2 tog, K8, yfwd, K1, return last st to left hand needle and with point of right hand needle lift the next 7 sts one at a time over this st and off needle, then sl st back on to right hand needle.
17th row P2 tog, P9, yrn, P2 tog, K1.
The 2nd through 17th rows form the pattern.

Cockleshell edging
Cast on 16 sts.
1st row K to end.
2nd row Yfwd to make 1, K2 tog, K1, yfwd, K10, yfwd, K2 tog, K1.

3rd row K2, yfwd, K2 tog, K12, P1.
4th row Yfwd, K2 tog, K1, yfwd, K2 tog, yfwd, K9, yfwd, K2 tog, K1.
5th row K2, yfwd, K2 tog, K13, P1.
6th row Yfwd, K2 tog, K1, (yfwd, K2 tog) twice, yfwd, K8, yfwd, K2 tog, K1.
7th row K2, yfwd, K2 tog, K14, P1.
8th row Yfwd, K2 tog, K1, (yfwd, K2 tog) 3 times, yfwd, K7, yfwd, K2 tog, K1.
9th row K2, yfwd, K2 tog, K15, P1.
10th row Yfwd, K2 tog, K1, (yfwd, K2 tog) 4 times, yfwd, K6, yfwd, K2 tog, K1.
11th row K2, yfwd, K2 tog, K16, P1.
12th row Yfwd, K2 tog, K1, (yfwd, K2 tog) 5 times, yfwd, K5, yfwd, K2 tog, K1.
13th row K2, yfwd, K2 tog, K17, P1.
14th row Yfwd, K2 tog, K1, (yfwd, K2 tog) 6 times, yfwd, K4, yfwd, K2 tog, K1.
15th row K2, yfwd, K2 tog, K18, P1.
16th row Yfwd, K2 tog, K1, (yfwd, K2 tog) 7 times, yfwd, K3, yfwd, K2 tog, K1.
17th row K2, yfwd, K2 tog, K19, P1.
18th row Yfwd, (K2 tog) twice, (yfwd, K2 tog) 7 times, K3, yfwd, K2 tog, K1.
19th row As 15th.
20th row Yfwd, (K2 tog) twice, (yfwd, K2 tog) 6 times, K4, yfwd, K2 tog, K1.

21st row As 13th.
22nd row Yfwd, (K2 tog) twice, (yfwd, K2 tog) 5 times, K5, yfwd, K2 tog, K1.
23rd row As 11th.
24th row Yfwd, (K2 tog) twice, (yfwd, K2 tog) 4 times, K6, yfwd, K2 tog, K1.
25th row As 9th.
26th row Yfwd, (K2 tog) twice, (yfwd, K2 tog) 3 times, K7, yfwd, K2 tog, K1.
27th row As 7th.
28th row Yfwd, (K2 tog) twice, (yfwd, K2 tog) twice, K8, yfwd, K2 tog, K1.
29th row As 5th.
30th row Yfwd, (K2 tog) twice, yfwd, K2 tog, K9, yfwd, K2 tog, K1.
31st row As 3rd.
32nd row Yfwd, (K2 tog) twice, K10, yfwd, K2 tog, K1.
33rd row K2, yfwd, K2 tog, K11, P1.
The 2nd through 33rd rows form the pattern.

Diamond insertion panel
Cast on 21 sts.
1st and every alt row (WS) P to end.
2nd row K2, yfwd, sl 1, K1, psso, K1, yfwd, sl 1, K1, psso, K3, K2 tog, yfwd, K1, yfwd, sl 1, K1, psso, K6.
4th row K3, (yfwd, sl 1, K1, psso, K1) twice, K2 tog, yfwd, K3, yfwd, sl 1, K1, psso, K5.
6th row K4, yfwd, sl 1, K1, psso, K1, yfwd, K3 tog, yfwd, K2, yfwd, sl 1, K1, psso, K1, yfwd, sl 1, K1, psso, K4.

8th row K5, yfwd, sl 1, K1, psso, (K2 tog, yfwd, K1) twice, yfwd, sl 1, K1, psso, K1, yfwd, sl 1, K1, psso, K3.
10th row K6, yfwd, sl 1, K1, psso, K1, K2 tog, yfwd, K3, yfwd, sl 1, K1, psso, K1, yfwd, sl 1, K1, psso, K2.
12th row K7, yfwd, K3 tog, yfwd, K5, (yfwd, sl 1, K1, psso, K1) twice.
14th row K7, K2 tog, yfwd, K3, yfwd, sl 1, K1, psso, K2, yfwd, sl 1, K1, psso, K1, yfwd, sl 1, K1, psso.
16th row K6, K2 tog, yfwd, K1, yfwd, sl 1, K1, psso, K3, K2 tog, yfwd, K1, K2 tog, yfwd, K2.
18th row K5, K2 tog, yfwd, K3, yfwd, sl 1, K1, psso, (K1, K2 tog, yfwd) twice, K3.
20th row K4, K2 tog, yfwd, K1, K2 tog, yfwd, K2, yfwd, sl 1, K2 tog, psso, yfwd, K1, K2 tog, yfwd, K4.
22nd row K3, (K2 tog, yfwd, K1) twice, yfwd, sl 1, K1, psso, K1, yfwd, sl 1, K1, psso, K2 tog, yfwd, K5.
24th row K2, K2 tog, yfwd, K1, K2 tog, yfwd, K3, yfwd, sl 1, K1, psso, K1, K2 tog, yfwd, K6.
26th row (K1, K2 tog, yfwd) twice, K5, yfwd, sl 1, K2 tog, psso, yfwd, K7.
28th row K2 tog, yfwd, K1, K2 tog, yfwd, K2, K2 tog, yfwd, K3, yfwd, sl 1, K1, psso, K7.
These 28 rows form the pattern.

SEQUINS AND BEADS

Beaded and sequinned tops and jackets make glamorous and dazzling garments for evening wear and the technique is very simple to work. The beads or sequins are knitted in with the fabric and they can be used to form an all-over design, or as a most effective trimming.

Most chain stores sell packets of beads and sequins which will prove suitable for this type of knitting.

If you are using beads, they should not be too large or heavy, so they do not pull the fabric out of shape – small pearl beads are ideal. The hole in the center of the bead must be large enough to thread over the yarn being used.

Sequins also come in various sizes and shapes and must also have a hole large enough to be threaded over the yarn. This hole should be at the top of the sequin and not in the center so that the sequins do not stick out but hang flat against the knitted background.

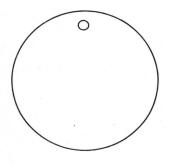

To thread beads or sequins onto a ball of yarn

Cut a 10in length of ordinary sewing thread and fold this in half. Thread both cut ends through a fine sewing needle, leaving a loop of thread as shown in diagram 1.

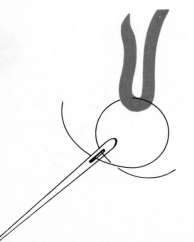

Thread the required number of beads or sequins on to the ball of yarn with which you are going to knit by passing approximately 6in of the end of this ball through the loop of sewing thread. Thread the beads or sequins on to the needle, then slide them down the thread and on to the ball of yarn, as shown in diagram 2.

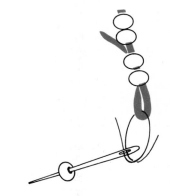

To knit in beads or sequins

Prepare a ball of yarn by threading on the required number of beads or sequins. These should be knitted in on a right side row against a stockinette stitch background, although they can be worked in panels and interspersed with a lace pattern, as shown in the evening top given here.

Knit until the position for the bead or sequin is reached, push one bead or sequin up the ball of yarn close to the back of the work, knit the next stitch through the back of the loop in the usual way, pushing the bead or sequin through to the front of the work with the loop of the stitch, and taking care not to split the yarn. Working this way allows the bead or sequin to lie flat against the fabric.

called y2rn – K2 tog tbl, rep from * to last 3 sts, K3.
2nd row *P4, P into front then into back of y2rn, rep from * to last 4 sts, P4.
3rd row K1, *K1, K sequin in with next st through back loops (tbl) – called K1S –, K2 tog, y2rn, K2 tog tbl, rep from * to last 3 sts, K1, K1S, K1.
4th row As 2nd.
5th row As 1st.
6th row As 2nd.
7th row K1, *K1S, K1, K2 tog, y2rn, K2 tog tbl, rep from * to last 3 sts, K1S, K2.
8th row As 2nd.
These 8 rows form patt. Cont in patt until work measures 12in from beg, ending with a WS row.

Shape armholes
Maintaining patt, bind off 5[6:7:8:9] sts at beg of next 2 rows. Dec one st at each end of next and every alt row 8 times in all, ending with a WS row. 68[72:76:80:84] sts.

Shape neck
Next row Dec one st, patt 20[21:22:23:24] sts, bind off 24[26:28:30:32] sts, patt to last 2 sts, dec one st.
Complete left shoulder first.
Next row Patt to end.
Next row Dec one st, patt to last 2 sts, dec one st.
Rep last 2 rows until 3[2:3:2:3] sts rem K3[2:3:2:3] tog. Fasten off.
With WS of work facing, rejoin yarn to rem sts and complete the right shoulder to correspond to the left shoulder.

Front
Work as for back.

Shoulder straps (make 2)
Using No.3 needles and ball of yarn which has not been threaded with sequins, cast on 11 sts.
1st row K1, *P1, K1, rep from * to end.
2nd row P1, *K1, P1, rep from * to end.
Rep these 2 rows until strap measures 20in from beg, or desired length to fit around armhole to shoulder. Bind off.
Join cast on edge to bound off edge. Join side seams. Pin straps in place around armhole.

Neck edging (make 2)
Work as for shoulder straps until edging fits down side of one shoulder strap, around center neck edge and up side of other shoulder strap.
Bind off.

Finishing
Do not block. Sew shoulder straps in place. Sew neck edging down inner edge of shoulder strap, around neck and along inner edge of other strap, then join shoulder seam. Fold straps and edging in half to WS and sew in place.

ning top

es
ections are to fit 32in bust. Changes for 34, 36, 38
d 40in bust are in brackets [].
gth to center back, 14in

uge
sts and 36 rows to 4in in patt worked on No.4
dles

terials
10oz balls of Bucilla 3-ply Fingering Yarn
prox 700 sequins with hole at top
e pair No.4 needles
e pair No.3 needles

te
read approximately 350 sequins onto each of 2 balls
yarn

ck
ng No.3 needles and ball of yarn which has not
n threaded with sequins, cast on 94[100:106:112:
sts. Work 6in K1, P1 rib. Break off yarn. Change to
4 needles. Join in ball threaded with sequins. Start
t.
row (RS) K1, *K2, K2 tog, yarn round needle twice –

SIMPLE STRIPES

Striped patterns, using simple stitches and subtle combinations of colors, are the easiest way of achieving a colorful knitted fabric. A plain, basic sweater can be changed and given a completely new look by working regular or random stripes in three or four colors. This is, besides, a very useful way of using up odds and ends of yarn of the same thickness.

Twisting yarns to change color

When you work any form of horizontal stripe, there is no problem about joining in different colored yarns. As one color is finished with at the end of a row, the new one is brought in at the beginning of the next row. When each color has been brought into use, it is left until it is needed again, then carried loosely up the side of the work and twisted once around the last color used, before you begin to work with it again.

Vertical or diagonal stripes are a little more difficult to work, as the colors must be changed at several points within the same row. When you knit narrow vertical or diagonal stripes, it is best to twist each yarn with the last color used as it is brought into use, then carry the yarn not in use across the back of the work until it is needed again. For wider stripes however it is not advisable to use this method of carrying the yarn across the back of the work as, apart from the waste of yarn, there is a tendency to pull the yarn too tightly, which results in an unsightly puckering of the fabric and a loss of gauge. It is much better to divide each color into small separate balls before beginning to work and then use one ball of yarn for each stripe, twisting one color to the next at the back of the work when a change is made.

It is important to remember that stripes worked by twisting the yarn in changing colors give a fabric of normal thickness, while stripes worked by carrying the yarn across the back of the work produce a fabric of double thickness.

Horizontal stripes

These are usually worked in stockinette stitch and are achieved by changing color at the beginning of a knit row. This gives an unbroken line of color on the right side of the fabric. An even number of rows must be worked, either two, four, six and so on, and the same number of rows can be used for each color or varied to give a random striped effect.

The purl side of this fabric can also be used as the right side of the work. Where each new color is brought into use, it gives a broken line of color on the purl side which looks most effective.

Ribbed stitches can also be used to produce a striped fabric. If an unbroken line of color is needed on the right side of the fabric, the row where a change of color is made needs to be knitted each time, and the other rows of each stripe worked in ribbing. An interesting fabric is produced by working in ribbing throughout, irrespective of the color change which gives a broken line of color each time.

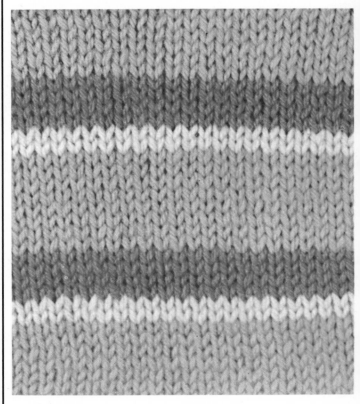

Fancy striped rib

Cast on a number of stitches divisible by 10 plus 5.

1st row P5, *K1, yfwd, sl 1, ybk, K1, yfwd, sl 1, ybk, K1, P5, rep from * to end.

2nd row K1, yfwd, sl 1, ybk, K1, yfwd, sl 1, ybk, K1, *P5, K1, yfwd, sl 1, ybk, K1, yfwd, sl 1, ybk, K1, rep from * to end.

These 2 rows form the pattern, changing colors as you wish.

Chevron stripes

Cast on a number of stitches divisible by 13 plus 2.

1st row *K2, pick up loop lying between needles and place it on the left hand needle then K this loop through the back – called inc 1 –, K4, sl 1 P-wise, K2 tog, psso, K4, inc 1, rep from * to last 2 sts, K2.

2nd row P to end.

These 2 rows form the pattern. Change colors as you wish on any row.

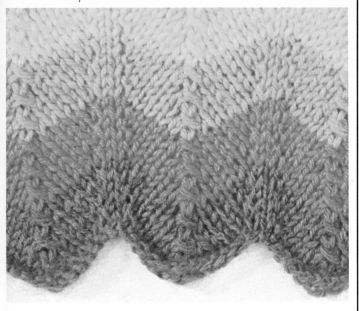

Vertical stripes

To work narrow or wide vertical stripes, the best effect is achieved in stockinette stitch with the knit side of the fabric as the right side. The yarn must be carried across or twisted at the back of the fabric.

To work a wide stripe it is necessary to use a separate ball of yarn for each color. Using two colors, the first color would be referred to as A and the second color as B.

Wide vertical stripe

Cast on 6 stitches with B, 6 with A, 6 with B and 6 with A, making a total of 24 stitches.

1st row *Using A, K6 sts, hold A to the left at the back of the work, pick up B and bring it towards the right at the back of the work and under the A thread no longer in use, K6 B, hold B to the left at the back of the work, pick up A and bring it towards the right at the back of the work and under the B thread no longer in use, rep from * to end.

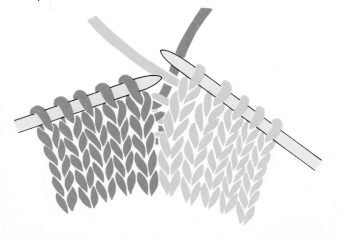

2nd row (WS) *Using B, P6 sts, hold B to the left at the front of the work, pick up A and bring it towards the right at the front of the work and over the B thread no longer in use, P6 A, hold A to the left at the front of the work, pick up B and bring it towards the right at the front of the work and over the A thread no longer in use, rep from * to end.

These 2 rows form the pattern.

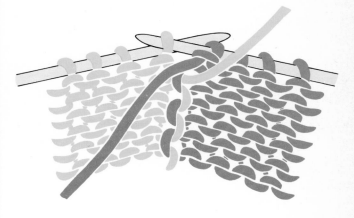

Diagonal stripes

Depending on the width of the stripes, the yarn can either be carried across the back of the work, or separate balls of yarn used for each color as for wide vertical stripes.

Narrow diagonal stripes

Cast on a number of stitches divisible by 5 plus 3, using two colors, A and B.

1st row (RS) K3 A, *pick up B and K2, pick up A and K3, rep from * to end.

2nd row Pick up B and P1, *pick up A and P3, pick up B and P2, rep from * to last 2 sts, pick up A and P2.

3rd row K1 A, *pick up B and K2, pick up A and K3, rep from * to last 2 sts, pick up B and K2.

4th row Pick up A and P1, pick up B and P2, *pick up A and P3, pick up B and P2, rep from * to end.

Continue working in this way, moving the stripes one stitch to the right on K rows and one stitch to the left on P rows.

TWO COLOR PATTERNS

By combining the working method for horizontal stripes with the clever use of slipped stitches colorful tweed fabrics can be quickly and easily made. These stitches can be worked in two or more colors, and on each change of color the yarn is merely carried up the side of the work and does not have to be carried across the back of the fabric as it does for the more difficult jacquard and Fair Isle patterns.

Bird's eye stitch

Using 2 colors coded as A and B, cast on a multiple of 2 stitches.
1st row Using A, *sl 1 P-wise, K1, rep from * to end.
2nd row Using A, P to end.
3rd row Using B, *K1, sl 1 P-wise, rep from * to end.
4th row Using B, P to end.
These 4 rows form the pattern.

Mock houndstooth stitch

Using 2 colors coded as A and B, cast on any multiple of 3 stitches.
1st row Using A, *sl 1 P-wise, K2, rep from * to end.

2nd row Using A, P to end.
3rd row Using B, *K2, sl 1 P-wise, rep from * to end.
4th row Using B, P to end.
These 4 rows form the pattern.

Crossed stitch

Using 2 colors coded as A and B, cast on a multiple of 2 plus 1.
1st row Using A, K to end.
2nd row Using A, K to end.
3rd row Using B, *K1, sl 1 P-wise, rep from * to last st, K1.
4th row Using B, *K1, yfwd, sl 1 P-wise, ybk, rep from * to last st, K1.
5th row Using A, K to end.
6th row Using A, K to end.
7th row Using B, *sl 1 P-wise, K1, rep from * to last st, sl 1 P-wise.
8th row Using B, *sl 1 P-wise, ybk, K1, yfwd, rep from * to last st, sl 1 P-wise.
These 8 rows form the pattern.

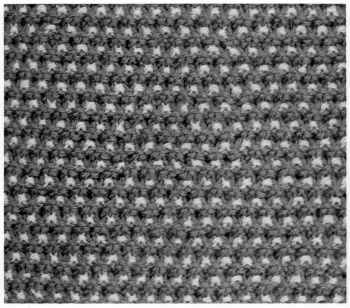

Bee stitch

Using 2 colors coded as A and B, cast any multiple of 2 stitches.
1st row Using A, K to end.
2nd row Using A, K to end.
3rd row Using B, *insert right hand needle into next stitch on the row below and K in usual way – called K1B –, K next st on left hand needle, rep from * to end.
4th row Using B, K to end.
5th row Using A, *K1, K1B, rep from * to end.

6th row Using A, K to end.
Rows 3 through 6 form the pattern.

Two color fuchsia stitch

Using 2 colors coded as A and B, cast on a multiple of 4 stitches.

1st row Using A, K to end.
2nd row Using A, P to end.
Rep 1st and 2nd rows once more.
5th row Using B, *K3, insert right hand needle into next st in first row of A and draw through a loop, K1 and pass the loop over K1, rep from * to end.
6th row Using B, P to end.
7th row Using B, K to end.
8th row Using B, P to end.
9th row Using A, *K1, insert right hand needle into next st in first row of B and draw through a loop, K1 and pass the loop over K1, K2, rep from * to end.
Rows 2 through 9 form the pattern.

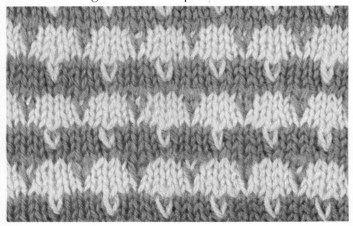

Ladder stitch

Using 2 colors coded as A and B, cast on a multiple of 6 stitches plus 5.

1st row Using A, K2, *sl 1 P-wise, K5, rep from * to last 3 sts, sl 1 P-wise, K2.
2nd row Using A, P2, *sl 1 P-wise, P5, rep from * to last 3 sts, sl 1 P-wise, P2.
3rd row Using B, *K5, sl 1 P-wise, rep from * to last 5 sts, K5.

4th row Using B, *K5, yfwd, sl 1 P-wise, ybk, rep from * to last 5 sts, K5.
These 4 rows form the pattern.

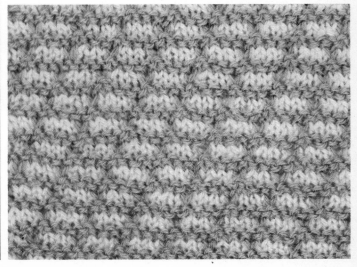

Brick stitch

Using 2 colors coded as A and B, cast on a multiple of 4 stitches.

1st row Using A, K to end.
2nd row Using A, K to end.
3rd row Using B, *K3, sl 1 P-wise, rep from * to end.
4th row Using B, *sl 1 P-wise, P3, rep from * to end.
5th row As 1st.
6th row As 2nd.
7th row Using B, K2, *sl 1 P-wise, K3, rep from * to last 2 sts, sl 1 P-wise, K1.
8th row Using B, P1, *sl 1 P-wise, P3, rep from * to last 3 sts, sl 1 P-wise, P2.
9th row As 1st.
10th row As 2nd.
11th row Using B, K1, *sl 1 P-wise, K3, rep from * to last 3 sts, sl 1 P-wise, K2.
12th row Using B, P2, *sl 1 P-wise, P3, rep from * to last 2 sts, sl 1 P-wise, P1.
13th row As 1st.
14th row As 2nd.
15th row Using B, *sl 1 P-wise, K3, rep from * to end.
16th row Using B, *P3, sl 1 P-wise, rep from * to end.
These 16 rows form the pattern.

TEXTURED PATTERNS

Unlike patterns which produce a plain knitted fabric with colorful designs, such as Fair Isle (see later) patterns worked in stripes which also combine slipped stitches form textured fabrics which are further enhanced by the use of contrasting colors. Because these stitches do not need such careful regulation of the gauge, they do not necessarily need contrasting yarns of the same thickness. A wool yarn can be combined with many different materials, such as macramé cord, cotton, or metallic yarns to give an exciting and colorful effect.

All the stitches illustrated here are produced by working a set number of rows with one or more colors and, however complicated they may appear, the colors are changed at the end of the row just as for more usual striped patterns.

Ridged check stitch

Two colors of the same yarn have been used for this sample, coded as A and B. Cast on a number of stitches divisible by 4 plus 3 in A.

1st row (WS) Using A, P to end.
2nd row Using B, K3, *sl 1 P-wise keeping yarn at back of work – called sl 1B –, K3, rep from * to end.
3rd row Using B, P3, *sl 1 P-wise keeping yarn at front of work – called sl 1F –, P3, rep from * to end.
4th row As 2nd.
5th row Using B, P to end.
6th row Using A, as 2nd.
7th row Using A, as 3rd.
8th row Using A, as 4th.
These 8 rows form the pattern.

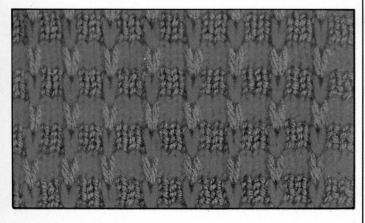

Fancy checked stitch

Two colors of contrasting yarn have been used for this sample, a plain yarn coded as A and a metallic yarn coded as B. Cast on a number of stitches divisible by 6 plus 5 in A.

1st row (RS) Using A, K to end.
2nd row Using A, P to end.
3rd row Using B, K2, *sl 1 P-wise keeping yarn at back of work – called sl 1B –, K1, rep from * to last st, K1.
4th row Using B, K1, *(K1, sl 1 P-wise keeping yarn at front of work – called sl 1F) twice, P1, sl 1F, rep from * to last 4 sts, K1, sl 1F, K2.
5th row Using A, K5, *sl 1B, K5, rep from * to end.
6th row Using A, P5, *sl 1F, P5, rep from * to end.
7th row As 5th.
8th row As 6th.
9th row Using A, as 1 st.
10th row Using A, as 2nd.
11th row Using B, K1, *sl 1B, K1, rep from * to end.
12th row Using B, K1, *sl 1F, P1, (sl 1F, K1) twice, rep from * to last 4 sts, sl 1F, P1, sl 1F, K1.
13th row Using A, K2, *sl 1B, K5, rep from * to last 3 sts, sl 1B, K2.
14th row Using A, P2, *sl 1F, P5, rep from * to last 3 sts, sl 1F, P2.
15th row As 13th.
16th row As 14th.
These 16 rows form the pattern.

Ribbon stitch

Two colors of contrasting yarn have been used for this sample, a plain yarn coded as A and a macramé cord coded as B. Cast on a number of stitches divisible by 4 plus 3 in A.

1st row (WS) Using A, P to end.
2nd row Using B, K1, *sl 1 P-wise keeping yarn at back of work – called sl 1B –, K3, rep from * to last 2 sts, sl 1B, K1.
3rd row Using B, K1, *sl 1 P-wise keeping yarn at front of work – called sl 1F –, K1, K1 winding yarn 3 times around needle, K1, rep from * to last 2 sts, sl 1F, K1.
4th row Using A, K3, *sl 1B dropping extra loops, K3, rep from * to end.
5th row Using A, P3, *sl 1B, P3, rep from * to end.
6th row Using A, K3, *sl 1B, K3, rep from * to end.

7th row Using A, as 5th.
8th row Using A, as 6th.
These 8 rows form the pattern.

Tapestry stitch

Two colors of the same yarn have been used for this sample, coded as A and B. Cast on a number of stitches divisible by 4 plus 3 in A.

1st row (WS) Using A, P to end.
2nd row Using B, K1, sl 1 P-wise keeping yarn at front of work – called sl 1F –, K1, *sl 1 P-wise keeping yarn at back of work – called sl 1B –, K1, sl 1F, K1, rep from * to end.
3rd row Using B, P3, *sl 1F, P3, rep from * to end.
4th row Using A, K1, *sl 1B, K3, rep from * to last 2 sts, sl 1B, K1.
5th row Using A, P to end.
6th row Using B, K1, sl 1B, K1, *sl 1F, K1, sl 1B, K1, rep from * to end.
7th row Using B, P1, *sl 1F, P3, rep from * to last 2 sts, sl 1F, P1.
8th row Using A, K3, *sl 1B, K3, rep from * to end.
These 8 rows form the pattern.

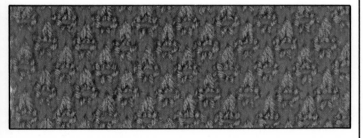

Lattice stitch

Two colors of contrasting yarn have been used for this sample, a plain yarn coded as A and a metallic yarn coded as B. Cast on a number of stitches divisible by 6 plus 2 in A.

1st row (WS) Using A, K to end.
2nd row Using B, K1, sl 1 P-wise keeping yarn at back of work – called sl 1B –, *K4, sl 2B, rep from * to last 6 sts, K4, sl 1B, K1.
3rd row Using B, P1, sl 1 P-wise keeping yarn at front of work – called sl 1F –, *P4, sl 2F, rep from * to last 6 sts, P4, sl 1F, P1.
4th row Using A, as 2nd.
5th row Using A, K1, sl 1F, *K4, sl 2F, rep from * to last 6sts, K4, sl 1F, K1.
6th row Using B, K3, *sl 2B, K4, rep from * to last 5 sts, sl 2B, K3.

7th row Using B, P3, *sl 2F, P4, rep from * to last 5 sts, sl 2F, P3.
8th row Using A, as 6th.
9th row Using A, K3, *sl 2F, K4, rep from * to last 5 sts, sl 2F, K3.
Rows 2 through 9 form the pattern.

Pillow

Size

16in wide by 16in deep

Gauge

26 sts and 32 rows to 4in in patt worked on No.5 needles

Materials

2 × 2oz balls Dawn Wintuk Sport Yarn in main color, A
2 balls of contrast color, B
One pair No.5 needles
16in by 16in pillow form
2yd silk cord, optional
8in zipper

Pillow

Using No.5 needles and A, cast on 103 sts. Work in tapestry st until piece measures 16in from beg. Bind off. Make another piece in same way.

Finishing

Block each piece under a damp cloth with a warm iron. With RS facing, join 3 sides. Turn RS out. Insert pillow form. Join rem seam, inserting zipper in center. Sew cord around edges if desired, looping it at each corner.

MOSAIC PATTERNS

Mosaic patterns are worked in two colors, using the slip-stitch method to form complex and unusual geometric shapes. Although the patterns may appear to be complicated, the working method is very simple and is based on knitting two rows with one color and two rows with the second color.

What makes these designs so interesting is that bands of different patterns which require the same multiples of stitches can be worked together to form an overall fabric, using as many different colors as you like. This is another way of using up odds and ends of yarn which are of the same thickness.

You could use a basic pattern which gives the correct multiple of stitches required for each mosaic pattern to form a colorful and original child's sweater, a throw pillow or a warm and practical afghan or bed throw. Because the yarn is not carried across the back of the work as in Fair Isle knitting, the back of the fabric formed is not untidy and is of a single thickness.

Brick pattern

Two colors are used, coded as A and B. Using A, cast on a number of stitches divisible by 4 plus 3.
1st row (RS) Using A, K to end.
2nd row Using A, P to end.
3rd row Using B, K3, *sl 1, K3, rep from * to end.

4th row Using B, K3, *yfwd, sl 1, ybk, K3, rep from * to end.
5th row Using A, K2, *sl 1, K1, rep from * to last st, K1.
6th row Using A, P2, *sl 1, P1, rep from * to last st, P1.
7th row Using B, K1, *sl 1, K3, rep from * to last 2 sts, sl 1, K1.
8th row Using B, K1, *yfwd, sl 1, ybk, K3, rep from * to last 2 sts, yfwd, sl 1, ybk, K1.
9th and 10th rows As 1st and 2nd.
11th and 12th rows As 7th and 8th.
13th and 14th rows As 5th and 6th.
15th and 16th rows As 3rd and 4th.
These 16 rows form the pattern.

Double brick pattern

Two colors are used, coded as A and B. Using A, cast on a number of stitches divisible by 4 plus 3.
1st row (RS) Using A, K to end.
2nd row Using A, K to end.
3rd row Using B, K3, *sl 1, K3, rep from * to end.
4th row Using B, K3, *yfwd, sl 1, ybk K3, rep from * to end.
5th row Using A, K1, *sl 1, K3, rep from * to last 2 sts, sl 1, K1.
6th row Using A, K1, *yfwd, sl 1, ybk, K3, rep from * to last 2 sts, yfwd, sl 1, ybk, K1.

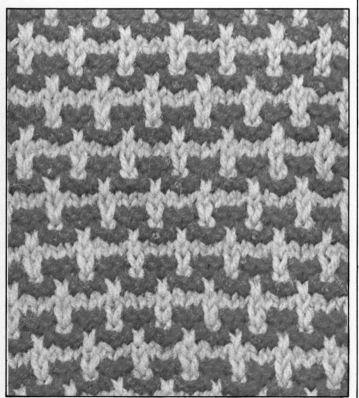

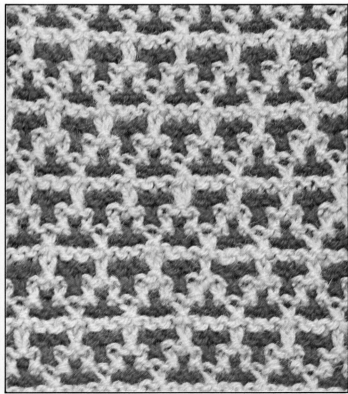

7th row Using B, K2, *sl 1, K1, rep from * to last st, K1.

8th row Using B, K2, *yfwd, sl 1, ybk, K1, rep from * to last st, K1.

9th and 10th rows Using A, as 3rd and 4th.

11th and 12th rows Using B, as 5th and 6th.

13th and 14th rows As 1st and 2nd.

15th and 16th rows As 11th and 12th.

17th and 18th rows As 9th and 10th.

19th and 20th rows As 7th and 8th.

21st and 22nd rows As 5th and 6th.

23rd and 24th rows As 3rd and 4th.

These 24 rows form the pattern.

Vertical chevron pattern

Two colors are used, coded as A and B. Using A, cast on a number of stitches divisible by 6 plus 2.

1st row (RS) Using A, *K5, sl 1, rep from * to last 2 sts, K2.

2nd and every alt row Using same color as previous row, keep yarn at front of work and P all K sts of previous row and sl all sl sts.

3rd row Using B, K2, * sl 1, K3, sl 1, K1, rep from * to end.

5th row Using A, K3, *sl 1, K5, rep from * to last 5 sts, sl 1, K4.

7th row Using B, K4, *sl 1, K1, sl 1, K3, rep from * to last 4 sts, (sl 1, K1) twice.

9th row Using A, K1, *sl 1, K5, rep from * to last st, K1.

11th row Using B, K2, *sl 1, K1, sl 1, K3, rep from * to end.

13th, 15th, 17th, 19th and 21st rows Rep 1st, 3rd, 5th, 7th and 9th rows in that order.

23rd, 25th, 27th and 29th rows Rep 7th, 5th, 3rd and 1st rows in that order.

31st, 33rd, 35th, 37th and 39th rows Rep 11th, 9th, 7th, 5th and 3rd rows in that order.

40th row As 2nd.

These 40 rows form the pattern.

Greek key pattern

Two colors are used, coded as A and B. Using A, cast on a number of stitches divisible by 6 plus 2.

1st row (RS) Using A, K to end.

2nd row Using A, K to end.

3rd row Using B, K1, *sl 1, K5, rep from * to last st, K1.

4th and every alt row Using same color as previous row, keep the yarn at front of work and K all K sts of previous row and sl all sl sts.

5th row Using A, K2, *sl 1, K3, sl 1, K1, rep from * to end.

7th row Using B, K1, *sl 1, K3, sl 1, K1, rep from * to last st, K1.

9th row Using A, K6, *sl 1, K5, rep from * to last 2 sts, sl 1, K1.

11th and 12th rows Using B, as 1st and 2nd.

13th row Using A, K4, *sl 1, K5, rep from * to last 4 sts, sl 1, K3.

15th row Using B, *K3, sl 1, K1, sl 1, rep from * to last 2 sts, K2.

17th row Using A, K2, *sl 1, K1, sl 1, K3, rep from * to end.

19th row Using B, K3, *sl 1, K5, rep from * to last 5 sts, sl 1, K4.

20th row As 4th.

These 20 rows form the pattern.

Maze pattern

Two colors are used, coded as A and B. Using A, cast on a number of stitches divisible by 12 plus 3.

1st row (RS) Using A, K to end.

2nd row Using A, P to end.

3rd row Using B, K1, *sl 1, K11, rep from * to last 2 sts, sl 1, K1.

4th and every alt row Using same color as previous row, keep the yarn at front of work and P all K sts of previous row and sl all sl sts.

5th row Using A, K2, *sl 1, K9, sl 1, K1, rep from * to last st, K1.

7th row Using B, (K1, sl 1) twice, *K7, (sl 1, K1) twice, sl 1, rep from * to end omitting sl 1 at end of last rep.

9th row Using A, K2, sl 1, K1, sl 1, *K5, (sl 1, K1) 3 times, sl 1, rep from * to last 10 sts, K5, sl 1, K1, sl 1, K2.

11th row Using B, (K1, sl 1) 3 times, *K3, (sl 1, K1) 4 times, sl 1, rep from * to last 9 sts, K3, (sl 1, K1) 3 times.

13th row Using A, K2, *sl 1, K1, rep from * to last st, K1.

15th, 17th, 19th, 21st, 23rd and 25th rows Rep 11th, 9th, 7th, 5th, 3rd and 1st rows in that order.

27th row Using B, K7, *sl 1, K11, rep from * to last 8 sts, sl 1, K7.

29th row Using A, K6, *sl 1, K1, sl 1, K9, rep from * to last 9 sts, sl 1, K1, sl 1, K6.

31st row Using B, K5, *(sl 1, K1) twice, sl 1, K7, rep from * to last 10 sts, (sl 1, K1) twice, sl 1, K5.

33rd row Using A, K4, *(sl 1, K1) 3 times, sl 1, K5, rep from * to last 11 sts, (sl 1, K1) 3 times, sl 1, K4.

35th row Using B, K3, *(sl 1, K1) 4 times, sl 1, K3, rep from * to end.

37th row As 13th.

39th, 41st, 43rd, 45th and 47th rows Rep 35th, 33rd, 31st, 29th and 27th rows in that order.

48th row As 4th.

These 48 rows form the pattern.

Lattice window pattern

Two colors are used, coded as A and B. Using A, cast on a number of stitches divisible by 12 plus 3. K 1 row.

1st row (RS) Using B, K1, *sl 1, K11, rep from * to last 2 sts, sl 1, K1.

2nd and every alt row Using same color as previous row, keep the yarn at front of work and K all K sts of previous row and sl all sl sts.

3rd row Using A, K4, *(sl 1, K1) 3 times, sl 1, K5, rep from * to last 11 sts, (sl 1, K1) 3 times, sl 1, K4.

5th row Using B, K3, *sl 1, K7, sl 1, K3, rep from * to end.

7th row Using A, K2, *sl 1, K3, sl 1, K1, rep from * to last st, K1.

9th row Using B, K5, *sl 1, K3, sl 1, K7, rep from * to last 10 sts, sl 1, K3, sl 1, K5.

11th row Using A, K2, *sl 1, K1, sl 1, K5, (sl 1, K1) twice, rep from * to last st, K1.

13th row Using B, K7, *sl 1, K11, rep from * to last 8 sts, sl 1, K7.

15th and 16th rows As 11th and 12th.

17th and 18th rows As 9th and 10th.

19th and 20th rows As 7th and 8th.

21st and 22nd rows As 5th and 6th.

23rd and 24th rows As 3rd and 4th.

These 24 rows form the pattern.

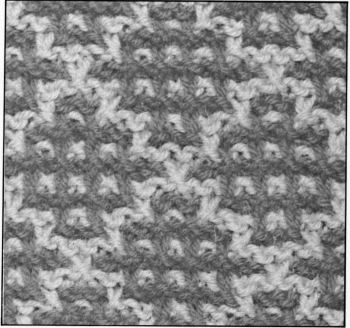

MOCK FAIR ISLE

Although they look rather complicated, Fair Isle patterns are quite simple to work as they rarely use more than two colors in one row at a time. The beautiful, multi-colored effects are achieved by varying the two combinations of colors.

A form of 'mock' Fair Isle, however, is even simpler to work as this only requires two colors throughout – a plain background color and an ombre yarn used for the contrast color.. As the ombre yarn is worked, it changes its color sequence to give a most striking effect.

Unlike horizontal striped patterns, where the color is changed at the end of a row, two yarns will be in use during the course of a row. As only a few stitches are worked in one color, the yarn not in use can be carried loosely across the back of the work until it is required, then twisted around the last color before it is brought into use again.

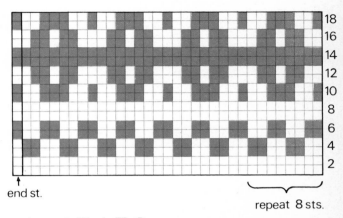

end st.

repeat 8 sts.

color code ☐ = A ■ = B

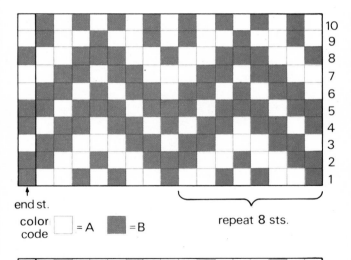

end st.

color code ☐ = A ■ = B

repeat 8 sts.

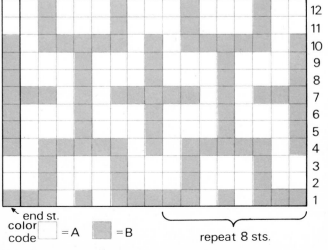

end st.

color code ☐ = A ▨ = B

repeat 8 sts.

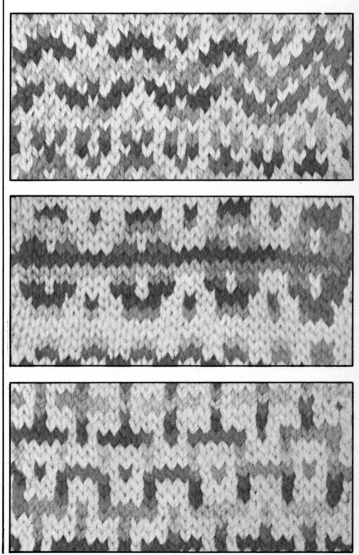

Three 'mock' Fair Isle patterns

We give three samples and charts here, any one of which can be used for the short sleeved pullover, as each pattern requires a multiple of 8 stitches plus one.

Mock Fair Isle pullover

Sizes

Directions are to fit 34in bust. Changes for 36, 38 and 40in bust are in brackets [].
Length to shoulder, 24[24½:26:26½]in
Sleeve seam, 4in

Gauge

26 sts and 32 rows to 4in in patt worked on No.4 needles

Materials

3[3:4:4] × 4oz balls Bucilla Win-Knit in main color, A
2[2:3:3] × 3½oz balls Bucilla Ombre Win-Kit in contrast color, B
One pair of No.4 needles
One pair of No.2 needles

Back

Using No.2 needles and A, cast on 113[121:129:137]sts.
1st row K1, *P1, K1, rep from * to end.
2nd row P1, *K1, P1, rep from * to end.
Rep these 2 rows 11 times more. Change to No.4 needles. Beg with a K row cont in st st, working in any patt from chart, until work measures 17[17:18:18]in from beg, ending with a WS row.

Shape armholes

Maintaining patt, bind off 6[7:8:9] sts at beg of next 2 rows. Dec one st at each end of next 8[9:10:11] rows. 85[89:93:97] sts. Cont in patt without shaping until armholes measure 7[7½:8:8½]in from beg, ending with a WS row.

Shape shoulders

Bind off at beg of next and every row 8[8:9:9] sts twice, 8[9:9:9] sts twice and 9[9:9:10] sts twice. Place rem 35[37:39:41] sts on holder for back neck.

Front

Work as for back until armhole shaping has been completed. 85[89:93:97] sts. Cont without shaping until armholes measure 5½[6:6½:7]in from beg, ending with a WS row.

Shape neck

Next row Work in patt across 32[33:34:35], turn and place rem sts on holder.
Complete this side first. Dec one st at neck edge on next and every row 7 times in all. 25[26:27:28] sts. Cont without shaping until front is same as back to shoulder, ending at armhole edge.

Shape shoulder

Bind off at beg of next and every alt row 8[8:9:9] sts once, 8[9:9:9] sts once and 9[9:9:10] sts once.
With RS of work facing, sl first 21[23:25:27] sts on holder for front neck, rejoin yarn to rem sts and patt to end. Complete to correspond to first side, reversing shaping.

Sleeves

Using No.2 needles and A, cast on 81[89:89:97] sts. Work 12 rows rib as for back. Change to No.4 needles. Beg with a K row cont in st st, working in any patt from chart and inc one st at each end of 3rd and every foll 6th row, until there are 87[95:95:103] sts. Cont without shaping until sleeve measures 4in from beg, ending with a WS row.

Shape top

Bind off 6[7:8:9] sts at beg of next 2 rows. Dec one st at each end of next and every foll alt row until 47[55:47:49] sts rem. Patt one row. Bind off 2 sts at beg of next 16[18:14:14] rows. Bind off rem 15[17:19:21] sts.

Neckband

Join right shoulder seam. Using No.2 needles, A and with RS of work facing, K18 sts down left front neck, K across front neck sts on holder, K19 sts up right front neck and K across back neck sts on holder. 87[91:95:99] sts. Work 12 rows rib as for back. Bind off loosely in rib.

Finishing

Block under a dry cloth with a warm iron. Join left shoulder and neckband seam. Set in sleeves. Join side and sleeve seams. Block seams.

Toddler's robe

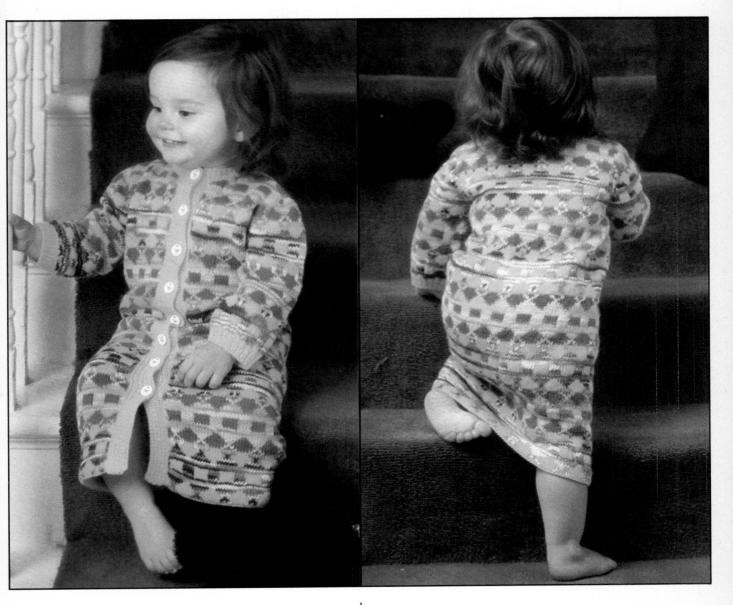

The mock Fair Isle technique has been used for this front-opening toddler's robe. An even more interesting pattern has been achieved, however, by using a plain background with a contrasting ombre yarn for the first pattern repeat, then reversing the pattern by using a second ombre yarn as the background and a second plain color for the contrast for the next repeat.

✳✳ Robe

Sizes
Directions are to fit 22in chest. Changes for 24in chest are in brackets [ ].

Length to shoulder, 22[24]in
Sleeve seam, 6½[8]in

Gauge
28 sts and 36 rows to 4in in patt worked on No.3 needles

Materials
2[3] × 2oz balls Red Heart Wintuk Sport Yarn in 1st contrast, A
2[2] × 1¾oz balls Red Heart Wintuk Ombre Sport yarn in 2nd contrast, B
1[1] × 2oz ball Red Heart Wintuk Sport Yarn in 3rd contrast, C

1[2] × 1¾oz ball Red Heart Wintuk Ombre Sport Yarn in 4th contrast, D
One pair No.3 needles
One pair No.1 needles
8 buttons

Back and fronts
Using No.1 needles and A, cast on 162[175] sts and work in one piece to underarm. Beg with a K row work 9 rows st st.
Next row K all sts tbl to form hemline.
Change to No.3 needles. Beg with a K row cont in st st, join in B and work **22 rows from chart using A and B. Break off A and B. Join in C and D and work 22 rows from chart, using C for A and D for B. **.
Cont in patt from ** to ** until work measures 17[18¾]in from hemline, ending with a WS row.

Divide for armholes
Next row Patt 37[39] sts, bind off 6[8] sts, patt 76[81] sts, bind off 6[8] sts, patt 37[39] sts.
Complete left front first. Maintaining patt, dec one st at armhole edge on every row until 31[32] sts rem. Cont without shaping until armhole measures 3½[3¾]in from beg, ending at neck edge.

Shape neck
Bind off 5 sts at beg of next row. Dec one st at neck edge on every row until 20[20] sts rem. Cont without shaping until armhole measures 4½[4¾]in from beg, ending at armhole edge.

Shape shoulder
Bind off at beg of next and foll alt row 10 sts twice.
With WS of work facing, rejoin yarn to sts for back. Maintaining patt, dec one st at each end of every row until 64[67] sts rem. Cont without shaping until armholes measure same as left front to shoulder, ending with a WS row.

Shape shoulders
Bind off at beg of next and every row 10 sts 4 times and 24[27] sts once.
With WS of work facing, rejoin yarn to rem sts and complete right front to match left front, reversing shaping.

Sleeves
Using No.1 needles and A, cast on 44[48] sts. Work 10 rows K1, P1 rib, inc 19[15] sts evenly across last row. 63[63] sts. Change to No.3 needles. Cont in patt as for back until sleeve measures 6½[8]in from beg, taking care to beg with a patt row and color which will enable sleeve seam to be completed on same row as back and fronts at underarm, ending with a WS row.

Shape top
Bind off 3[4] sts at beg of next 2 rows. Dec one st at each end of next and every alt row until 39[41] sts rem, then at each end of every row until 27 sts rem. Dec 2 sts at each end of every row until 11 sts rem. Bind off.

Button band
Using No.1 needles and A, cast on 12 sts. Work in K1, P1 rib until band is long enough, when slightly stretched, to fit from hemline to beg of neck shaping. Place sts on holder. Sew button band in place on left front for a girl and right front for a boy from hemline to neck. Mark positions for 8 buttons on button band, the first to come in neckband with 7 more evenly spaced at 2in intervals, measured from base of previous buttonhole.

Buttonhole band
Work as for button band, making buttonholes as markers are reached, as foll:
1st row (buttonhole row) Rib 5 sts, bind off 2, rib to end.
2nd row Rib to end, casting on 2 sts above those bound off in previous row.
Place sts on holder.

Neckband
Join shoulder seams. Stitch buttonhole band in place. Using No.1 needles, A and with RS of work facing, sl 12 sts of band on to needle, K 59[63] sts evenly spaced around neck then rib across rem sts on holder. Work 1 row K1, P1 rib. Make buttonhole as before on next 2 rows. Work 3 more rows rib. Bind off in rib.

Finishing
Block each piece under a damp cloth with a warm iron. Join sleeve seams. Set in sleeves. Press seams. Turn hem to WS at lower edge and sew in place. Sew on buttons.

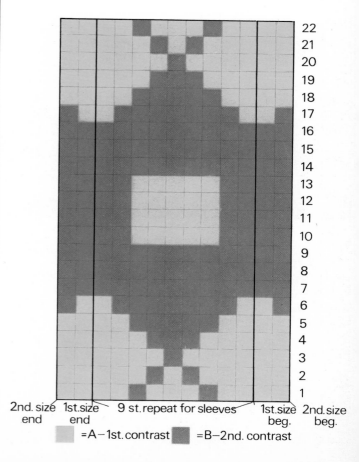

2nd. size end 1st. size end 9 st. repeat for sleeves 1st. size beg. 2nd. size beg.

■ =A−1st. contrast   ■ =B−2nd. contrast

TRADITIONAL FAIR ISLE
Simple patterns

Traditional Fair Isle patterns produce beautiful designs and fabrics which are world-renowned for their subtle color combinations. Ideally, they should be worked in authentic, softly shaded yarns but they look just as effective when worked in bright, contrasting colors. These patterns may be used to form an all-over fabric or as a border to highlight the waist and sleeves of a basic pullover or cardigan. When the pattern is small and is repeated as an all-over design, it is a fairly simple matter to work from a chart, where each color in the pattern is shown as a separate symbol. Some knitters, however, experience difficulty in working from a chart when the pattern is large and fairly complex, particularly where shaping is required. In this event, it is preferable to work from a pattern which gives row-by-row instructions, where each separate color is coded with a letter, such as A, B or C.

To help you decide which of the methods you wish to follow, the patterns here have been given with row by row instructions.

Fair Isle pattern No. 1
Cast on a multiple of 12 stitches plus 6.
1st row *K3 A, 1 B, 5 A, 1 B, 2 A, rep from * to last 6 sts, K3 A, 1 B, 2 A.
2nd row *(P1 A, 1 B) twice, 2 A, rep from * to end.
3rd row *K1 A, 1 B, 3 A, 1 B, rep from * to end.
4th row As 2nd.
5th row *K1 B, 2 A, rep from * to end.
6th row *(P1 B, 1 A) twice, 2 B, rep from * to end.
7th row *K2 B, (1 A, 1 B) twice, rep from * to end.
Rep 6th and 7th rows once more.
10th row *P2 A, 1 B, rep from * to end.
11th row *K2 A, (1 B, 1 A) twice, rep from * to end.

12th row *P1 B, 3 A, 1 B, 1 A, rep from * to end.
13th row As 11th.
14th row *P2 A, 1 B, 5 A, 1 B, 3 A, rep from * to last 6 sts, 2 A, 1 B, 3 A.
15th row *K1 B, 5 A, rep from * to end.
16th row *P1 B, 3 A, 1 B, 1 A, rep from * to end.
17th row *K2 A, (1 B, 1 A) twice, rep from * to end.
18th row As 16th.
19th row *K1 B, 2 A, rep from * to end.
20th row *P1 A, 3 B, 1 A, 1 B, rep from * to end.
21st row *K1 B, 1 A, 3 B, 1 A, rep from * to end. Rep 20th and 21st rows once more.
24th row *P2 A, 1 B, rep from * to end.
25th row *K1 A, 1 B, 3 A, 1 B, rep from * to end.
26th row *(P1 A, 1 B) twice, 2 A, rep from * to end.
27th row As 25th.
28th row *P5 A, 1 B, rep from * to end.
These 28 rows form the pattern.

Fair Isle pattern No. 2
Cast on a multiple of 18 stitches plus 1.
1st row *K1 B, 1 A, rep from * to last st, 1 B.
2nd row Using A, P to end.
3rd row Using A, K to end.
4th row *P1 C, 1 A, 1 C, 6 A, 1 C, 6 A, 1 C, 1 A, rep from * to last st, P1 C.
5th row *K2 C, 1 A, 1 C, 4 A, 3 C, 4 A, 1 C, 1 A, 1 C, rep from * to last st, K1 C.
6th row *P1 C, 3 A, 1 C, 2 A, 2 C, 1 A, 2 C, 2 A, 1 C, 3 A, rep from * to last st, P1 C.
7th row *K1 C, 4 A, 1 C, 1 A, 5 C, 1 A, 1 C, 4 A, rep from * to last st, K1 C.
8th row *P1 A, 1 C, 4 A, 3 C, 1 A, 3 C, 4 A, 1 C, rep from * to last st, P1 A.
9th row *K1 B, 3 A, 3 B, 2 A, 1 B, 2 A, 3 B, 3 A, rep from

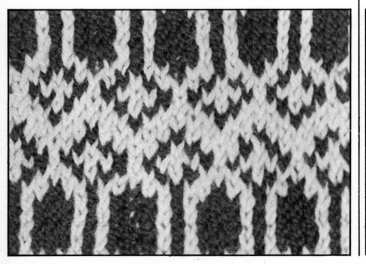

* to last st, 1 B.
10th row *P3 A, 4 B, (1 A, 1 B) twice, 1 A, 4 B, 2 A, rep from * to last st, 1 A.
11th row *K2 A, 2 B, (1 A, 1 B) 5 times, 1 A, 2 B, 1 A, rep from * to last st, 1 A.
Rep 10th to 1st rows. These 21 rows form border pattern, working 22nd row for all-over pattern.

Fair Isle pattern No. 3
Cast on multiples of 18 stitches plus 1.
1st row *K1 B, 1 A, rep from * to last st, 1 B.
2nd row *P1 A, 1 B, rep from * to last st, 1 A.
3rd row Using A, K to end.
4th row Using A, P to end.
5th row As 3rd.
6th row *P3 A, 1 C, 5 A, 1 C, 5 A, 1 C, 2 A, rep from * to last st, 1 A.
7th row *K2 A, 2 C, 4 A, 3 C, 4 A, 2 C, 1 A, rep from * to last st, 1 A.
8th row *P1 A, 3 C, 5 A, 1 C, 5 A, 3 C, rep from * to last st, 1 A.
9th row *K1 D, 2 C, 2 D, 3 C, 3 D, 3 C, 2 D, 2 C, rep from * to last st, 1 D.
10th row *P1 D, 1 C, 2 D, 3 C, 5 D, 3 C, 2 D, 1 C, rep from * to last st, 1 D.
11th row *K1 B, 2 E, 3 B, 3 E, 1 B, 3 E, 3 B, 2 E, rep from * to last st, 1 B.
12th row *P1 F, 2 B, 5 F, 3 B, 5 F, 2 B, rep from * to last st, 1 F.
Rep 11th to 3rd rows.
22nd row *P1 B, 1 A, rep from * to last st, 1 B.
23rd row *K1 A, 1 B, rep from * to last st, 1 A.
These 23 rows form border pattern, repeating 22 rows only for all-over pattern.

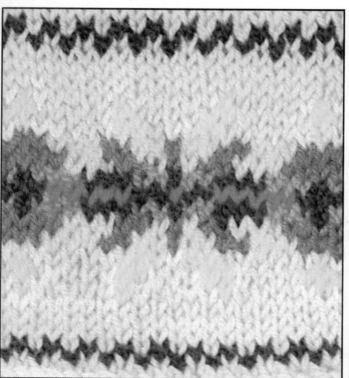

Fair Isle pattern No. 4
Cast on multiples of 28 stitches plus 1.
1st row *K2 B, 1 A, 1 B, rep from * to last st, 1 B.
2nd row *P1 B, 3 A, rep from * to last st, 1 B.
3rd row Using A, K to end.
4th row *P1 A, 2 C, 2 A, 2 C, 2 A, 2 C, 3 A, 1 C, 3 A, 2 C, 2 A, 2 C, 2 A, 2 C, rep from * to last st, 1 A.
5th row *K1 A, 1 C, (2 A, 2 C) twice, 3 A, 1 C, 1 A, 1 C, 3 A, (2 C, 2 A) twice, 1 C, rep from * to last st, 1 A.
6th row *P1 A, 1 C, 1 A, 2 C, 2 A, 2 C, 3 A, (1 C, 1 A) twice, 1 C, 3 A, 2 C, 2 A, 2 C, 1 A, 1 C, rep from * to last st, 1 A.
7th row *K1 A, 3 C, 2 A, 2 C, 3 A, 1 C, 1 A, 3 C, 1 A, 1 C, 3 A, 2 C, 2 A, 3 C, rep from * to last st, 1 A.
8th row *P1 A, 2 C, 2 A, 2 C, 3 A, 1 C, 2 A, 3 C, 2 A, 1 C, 3 A, 2 C, 2 A, 2 C, rep from * to last st, 1 A.
9th row *K1 A, 1 D, 2 A, 2 D, 3 A, 3 D, 2 A, 1 D, 2 A, 3 D, 3 A, 2 D, 2 A, 1 D, rep from * to last st, 1 A.
10th row *P1 A, 1 D, 1 A, 2 D, 3 A, 1 D, 2 A, 2 D, 1 A, 1 D, 1 A, 2 D, 2 A, 1 D, 3 A, 2 D, 1 A, 1 D, rep from *to last st, 1 A.
11th row *K1 A, 3 D, 3 A, 2 D, 3 A, 5 D, 3 A, 2 D, 3 A, 3 D, rep from * to last st, 1 A.
12th row *P1 A, 2 D, 3 A, 1 D, 1 A, 2 D, 3 A, 3 D, 3 A, 2 D, 1 A, 1 D, 3 A, 2 D, rep from * to last st, 1 A.
13th row *K1 A, 1 D, 3 A, 1 D, 3 A, 2 D, 3 A, 1 D, 3 A, 2 D, 3 A, 1 D, 3 A, 1 D, rep from * to last st, 1 A.
14th row *P1 A, 1 D, 2 A, 1 D, 1 A, 2 D, 2 A, 2 D, (1 A, 1 D) twice, 1 A, 2 D, 2 A, 2 D, 1 A, 1 D, 2 A, 1 D, rep from * to last st, 1 A.
15th row *K1 A, (1 B, 1 A) twice, 8 B, 1 A, 1 B, 1 A, 8 B, (1 A, 1 B) twice, rep from * to last st, 1 A.
Rep from 14th through 1st rows. These 29 rows form border pattern, working 30th row for all over pattern.

Snowflake patterns

The Scandinavian countries provide an endless source of what are loosely termed 'Fair Isle' designs, particularly variations of the delightful snowflake pattern. They are worked in the same way as the traditional Shetland designs but the patterns are usually bolder and the choice of color is more distinctive.

From the middle European countries and further east, more intricate and colorful designs are introduced, often involving the use of three or more colors at a time. These beautiful fabrics, often based upon traditional carpet designs, feature floral or symmetrical patterns in rich jewel colors.

To look most effective, the samples given here should not be used as over all patterns but as borders, pockets or cuff motifs.

Border pattern

This can either be worked as a horizontal or vertical

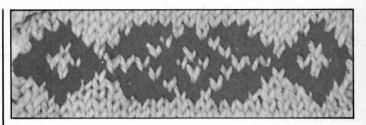

border. For a horizontal border cast on any multiple of 20 stitches plus 7 and work the 7 pattern rows from the chart. To work the border vertically, turn the chart sideways and work over 7 stitches for 20 rows.

Star pattern

This is another motif which can be used singly or as a horizontal border pattern.

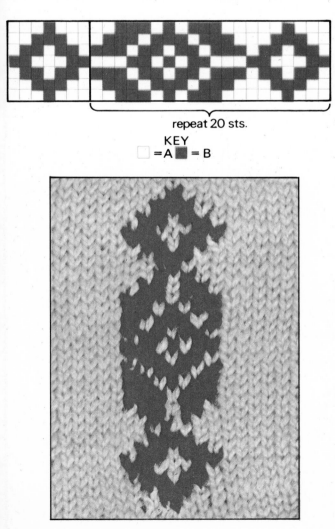

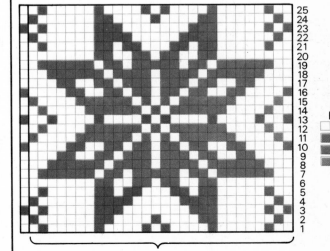

repeat 20 sts.

KEY
☐ = A ■ = B

repeat 28 sts.

KEY
☐ = A
■ = B
■ = C
■ = D

JACQUARD KNITTING

Whereas traditional Fair Isle knitting normally uses only two colors in any one row, jacquard, bobbin and patchwork knitting are all forms of the same technique, where more than two colors are used at a time in any one pattern row. These designs are best worked in stockinette stitch against a stockinette stitch background, although bobbin knitting may also combine many different stitches very effectively.

Unlike Fair Isle knitting this method is a little complicated and difficult to work, since more than one strand has to be carried across the back of the work until it is needed again although it is possible to work a jacquard design with a small repeat in this way, carrying the yarn not in use loosely across the back of the work. This method does, however, inevitably mean a variance in gauge against the main fabric. When using this method, it is therefore advisable to change to one size larger needles to work the pattern, reverting to the original needle size to work the main pattern.

The correct method of working all large multi-colored patterns, motifs, wide vertical stripes and patchwork designs is to use small, separate balls of yarn for each color. In this way a fabric of single thickness is formed, without any strands of yarn across the back of the work. These patterns are usually worked from a chart, just as in Fair Isle knitting, with each different color coded with a symbol.

Use of bobbins

Before beginning to knit, wind all the colors which are to be used into small, separate balls around a bobbin. These are easy to handle and hang at the back of the work, keeping each color free from tangles.

To make a bobbin: Use a stiff piece of cardboard and cut to shape as shown in the diagram with a slit at the top of each bobbin. Wind the yarn around the center of the bobbin with the working end passing through the slit as illustrated.

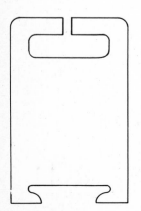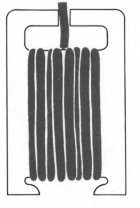

Joining in each new color

The next important point to remember is that knitting patterns of a geometric or random shape, such as diamonds or flower motifs, as opposed to straight vertical stripes, require the color to be changed by means of looping the two yarns around each other when on a right side row, to avoid gaps in the knitting. On the return purl row it is not so essential to loop the yarns around each other as the purl stitch will probably encroach into the pattern sequence and the yarns will automatically be looped. Vertical bands of color, however, must be looped on every row, as there will be no encroaching stitch to form a natural link in either direction.

To loop yarns on a knit row: Keep each ball of yarn at the back of the work until it is required. Knit the last stitch in the first color, then take this end of yarn over the next color to be used and drop it, pick up the next color under this strand of yarn and take it over the strand ready to knit the next stitch.

To loop yarns on a purl row: Keep each ball of yarn at the front of the work until it is required, purl the last stitch in the first color, then take this end of yarn over the next color to be used and drop it, pick up the next color under this strand of yarn and take it over the strand ready to purl the next stitch.

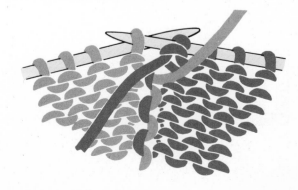

Jacquard borders

Begin by working something as simple as an all-over jacquard border pattern in three colors, carrying each color across the back of the work until it is required again.

In these charts, the background, or main color, is coded as A and shown as a blank square; the first contrast color is coded as B and the second contrast color coded as C.

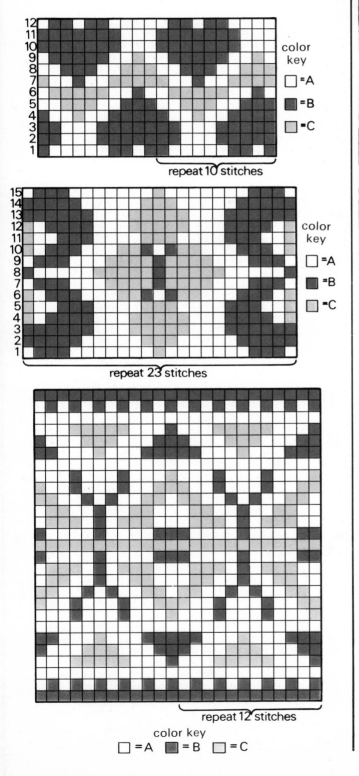

color key

□ = A

■ = B

▨ = C

repeat 10 stitches

color key

□ = A

■ = B

▨ = C

repeat 23 stitches

repeat 12 stitches

color key

□ = A   ■ = B   □ = C

MOTIFS AND COLLAGE

As explained in the previous chapter, jacquard and bobbin knitting provide tremendous scope for interesting all-over patterned fabrics or as a single motif incorporated into an otherwise plain background. Individual motifs can be used very effectively as patch pockets or as decorative panels set into clothes or linens.

The examples shown here should be worked with small, separate balls of yarn, twisting the yarns at the back of the work whenever you change colors.

Motifs

Almost any shape or design can be used as a separate jacquard motif, but if you are working out your own pattern it must be charted out on graph paper first, allowing one square for each stitch and one line of squares for each row. Code each different color with a symbol and make a color key of these symbols. If you do not want to make up your own design, use an embroidery chart, such as given for cross stitch embroidery, and adapt this to suit your own color scheme, again coding each different color with a symbol.

Butterfly motif

This motif is worked in five contrasting colors against a plain background, making six colors in all. Each motif requires a total of 28 stitches and 34 rows to complete.

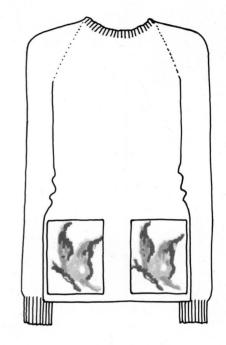

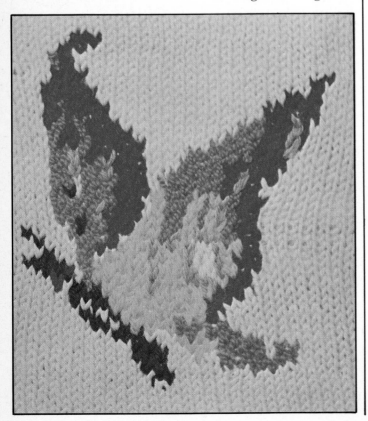

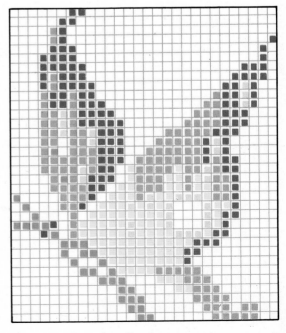

color key

■=B ■=C □=D ■=E ▨=F

Heart motif

Here again, five contrasting colors have been used against a plain background, making a total of six colors. Each motif requires a total of 35 stitches and 32 rows to complete.

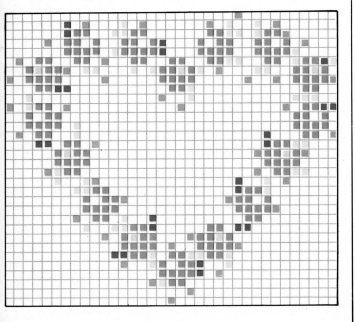

color key

=B =C =D =E =F

Multi-colored bobbin pattern

This design can be worked with as many colors as you like. You should always vary the sequence to insure

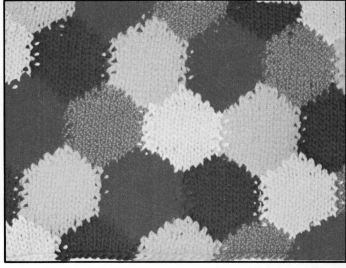

that you do not use the same colors next to each other.

Cast on a number of stitches divisible by 10, using the main color. The sample shown here has been worked on 50 stitches with five colors.

1st row (RS) K10 sts in each of 5 colors.

2nd row Using same colors, P10 sts in each of 5 colors.

Rep 1st and 2nd rows once more.

5th row Varying color sequence as required, K1 with contrast color, K8 with original color, *K2 with next contrast color, K8 with original color, rep from * to last st, K1 with last contrast color.

6th row P2 with same contrast color, *P6 with original color, P4 with same contrast color, rep from * to last 8 sts, P6 with original color, P2 with same contrast color.

7th row K3 with same contrast color, *K4 with original color, K6 with same contrast color, rep from * to last 7 sts, K4 with original color, K3 with same contrast color.

8th row P4 with same contrast color, *P2 with original color, break off original color, P8 with same contrast color, rep from * to last 6 sts, P2 with original color, break off original color, P4 with same contrast color.

9th row K5 with same contrast color, keeping color sequence correct as now set, K10 sts with each color to last 5 sts, K5 sts with same color.

10th row P as 9th row.

Rep 9th and 10th rows 3 times more.

17th row K4 sts with original color as now set, *K2 sts with next contrast color, K8 sts with original color as now set, rep from * to last 6 sts, K2 with next contrast color, K4 with original color as now set.

18th row P3 sts with original color, *P4 with same contrast color, P6 with original color, rep from * to last 7 sts, P4 with same contrast color, P3 with original color.

19th row K2 with original color, *K6 with same contrast color, K4 with original color, rep from * to last 8 sts, K6 with same contrast color, K2 with original color.

20th row P1 with original color, break off original color, *P8 with same contrast color, P2 with original color, break off original color, rep from * to last 9 sts, P8 with same contrast color, P1 with original color, break off original color.

21st row Keeping color sequence as now set, work as for 1st row.

22nd row As 2nd.

23rd row As 1st.

24th row As 2nd.

These 24 rows form the pattern.

Bobbin baby blanket

Size

22in wide by 32in long

Gauge

18 sts and 22 rows to 4in in stockinette stitch (st st) worked on No.7 needles

Materials

5 × 2oz balls of Sirdar Pullman in main shade, A

1 ball each of 7 contrast colors, B, C, D, E, F, G and H
One pair of No.7 needles

Center

Using No.7 needles and A, cast on 80 sts. Work in multi-colored bobbin pattern until work measures 28in from beg, ending with a 12th patt row.
Bind off.

Border

Using No. 7 needles and A, cast on 100 sts. K 16 rows garter st (g st).

Next row K10 sts, bind off 80 sts, K10 sts.

Complete this side first. Cont in g st until band fits along side edge of cover, ending at inside edge. Break off yarn. Place sts on holder.

With WS of work facing, rejoin yarn to rem 10 sts and complete to correspond to first side, ending at outside edge. Do not break off yarn.

Next row K across first 10 sts, turn and cast on 80 sts, K across rem 10 sts on holder. 100 sts.
K16 rows g st. Bind off loosely.

Finishing

Block center only under a damp cloth with a warm iron. With RS facing, sew border around outer edge of center. Block seams.

PATCHWORK KNITTING

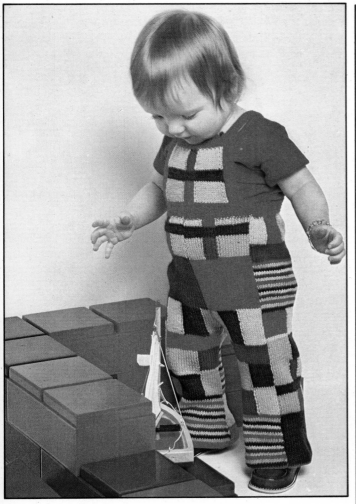

Completely random patchwork fabrics are worked in the same way as bobbin patterns, using separate balls of yarn for each color.

Each patch can be worked on any even number of stitches, and for as many number of rows as desired, and as each patch is completed it is not necessary to bind off, as you simply carry on with the next patch and color sequence. The exciting part of this technique comes in arranging the sequence of patches. Since no two knitters will work either the same color or patch in identical order, each sample has a completely original appearance.

The required number of stitches may be cast on to work two, three, or more patches side by side to give an overall fabric, or single patches can be worked in separate strips to the required length and then sewn together. The latter method means that shaping can be achieved on each side of the strips to achieve a well-fitting skirt, or the delightful patchwork overalls shown here.

Patchwork samples

In all the examples given here the first, or main color, is coded as A, the next color as B, the next as C, and so on and a total of six colors have been used. Once you have decided which colors you would like to use, make a note of the sequence in which you are going to work them so that when you have to pick up contrast color E, for example, you will know immediately to which color this refers.

These samples have been worked over 28 stitches, allowing 30 rows for each patch. Cast on with A.

1st patch
1st row Using A, K to end.
2nd row Using A, P to end.
Rep these 2 rows 14 times more, using each color in turn to form stripes. 30 rows.

2nd patch
1st row K14 B, 14 C.
2nd row P14 C, 14 B.
Rep these 2 rows 6 times more.
15th row Using D, K to end.
16th row Using D, P to end.
17th row K14 E, 14 F.
18th row P14 F, 14 E.
Rep last 2 rows 6 times more. 30 rows.

3rd patch
1st row Using A, K to end.
2nd row Using A, P to end.
Rep these 2 rows 4 times more.
11th row K10 B, 8 C, 10 D.
12th row P10 D, 8 C, 10 B.
Rep last 2 rows 9 times more. 30 rows.

4th patch
1st row Using E, K to end.
2nd row Using E, P to end.
Rep these 2 rows 14 times more. 30 rows.
Each time you work a repeat of this patch, use a different color.

5th patch
1st row K12 F, 4 A, 12 B.
2nd row P12 B, 4 A, 12 F.
Rep these 2 rows 5 times more.
13th row Using C, K to end.
14th row Using C, P to end.
Rep last 2 rows twice more.
19th row K12 D, 4 E, 12 F.
20th row P12 F, 4 E, 12 D.
Rep last 2 rows 5 times more. 30 rows.

Overalls

Size
Length to back waist, 18in
Inside leg, 10in

Gauge
30 sts and 38 rows to 4in in stockinette stitch (st st) worked on No.3 needles

Materials
2 × 2oz balls Bernat Sesame Knitting Worsted in main color, A
1 ball each of 5 contrast colors, B, C, D, E and F
One pair No.3 needles
2 buttons
Waist length of elastic

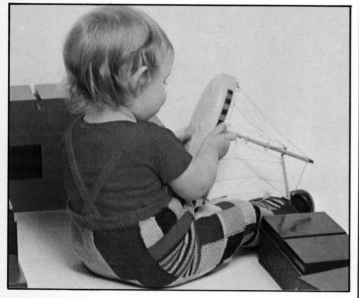

Right front leg
**Using No.3 needles and A, cast on 28 sts. Beg with a K row work 7 rows st st.
Next row Using A, K all sts tbl to form hemline. Work 1st, 2nd, 3rd, 4th and 5th patches, dec one st at beg of 9th and every foll 4th row 4 times in all, noting that less sts will be worked in first block of color. 24 sts. Cont in patt without shaping until 60th patt row has been completed. **. Maintaining patt, inc one st at beg of next and every foll 4th row 6 times in all, noting that extra sts will be worked in first block of color. 30 sts. Cont without shaping until 82nd patt row has been completed.

Shape crotch
Bind off 2 sts at beg of next row. Work 1 row. Dec one st at beg of next and foll alt rows 4 times in all. 24 sts. Cont without shaping until 142nd patt row has been completed. Using A, work 8 rows K1, P1 rib. Bind off loosely in rib.

Right side leg
Using No.3 needles and A, cast on 32 sts. Work hem as given for right front leg. Work 4th, 5th, 2nd, 1st and 3rd patches, shaping dart on 9th row as foll:

1st dec row Patt 14 sts, K2 tog, sl 1, K1, psso, patt 14 sts. Work 3 rows without shaping.
2nd dec row Patt 13 sts, K2 tog, sl 1, K1, psso, patt 13 sts. Work 3 rows without shaping. Cont dec in this way twice more. 24 sts. Cont in patt without shaping until 143rd row has been completed, ending with a K row.

Shape back
***Next 2 rows** Patt to last 8 sts, turn, patt to end.
Next 2 rows Patt to last 16 sts, turn, patt to end.
Next row Patt across all sts.
Using A, work 8 rows K1, P1 rib. Bind off loosely in rib. ***

Right back leg
Work as given for right front leg from ** to **, reversing shaping and working 3rd, 1st, 5th, 2nd and 4th patches in that order. Inc one st at end of next and every alt row, 10 times in all, noting that extra sts will be worked in last block of color. 34 sts. Cont in patt without shaping until 83rd row has been completed, ending with a K row.

Shape crotch
Bind off 2 sts at beg of next row. Work 1 row. Dec one st at beg of next and every alt row 8 times in all. 24 sts. Cont in patt until 149th row has been completed, ending with a K row.

Shape back
Work as given for side from *** to ***, continuing 4th patch.

Left leg
Work 3 pieces as given for right leg, reversing all shaping and sequence of patches, as required.

Bib
Using No.3 needles and A, cast on 44 sts.
1st row Using A, (K1, P1) 4 times, patt 28 sts as 1st row of 5th patch, using separate ball of A, (P1, K1) 4 times.
2nd row Using A, (P1, K1) 4 times, patt 28 sts as given for 2nd row of 5th patch, using A, (K1, P1) 4 times.
Cont in this way until 30th row of patch has been completed. Using A, work 8 rows K1, P1 rib across all sts.
Next row Rib 8, bind off 28 sts, rib to end.
Cont in rib on each set of 8 sts until strap is long enough to reach center back of overalls, making a buttonhole 1in before binding off as foll:
Next row (buttonhole row) Rib 3 sts, yarn in front to make 1, work 2 tog, rib 3 sts.

Finishing
Block each part under a damp cloth with a warm iron. Join 3 right leg sections tog including hem and waistband. Join left leg in same way. Block seams. Join front, back and inner leg seams. Turn hems to WS at lower edge and sew in place. Sew bib in center of front at top of waist ribbing. Sew elastic inside waistband from each side of bib using casing st. Sew on buttons inside back waist.

SIX STITCH PATTERNS

All patterns given here are made up of multiples of six stitches plus two edge stitches. Using the basic pattern which follows, which gives you a gauge of 24 stitches and 32 rows to 4in, you can use any of these stitches providing you make sure you achieve the correct gauge in stockinette stitch.

Cane basket stitch

Cast on a number of stitches divisible by 6 + 2.
1st row K2, *P4, K2, rep from * to end.
2nd row P2, *K4, P2, rep from * to end.
Rep these 2 rows once more.
5th row P3, *K2, P4, rep from * to last 5 sts, K2, P3.
6th row K3, *P2, K4, rep from * to last 5 sts, P2, K3.
Rep last 2 rows once more. These 8 rows form the pattern.

5th row P1, *sl next 2 sts on to cable needle and hold at back of work, K1 then P2 from cable needle – called C3B –, sl next st on to cable needle and hold at front of work, P2 then K1 from cable needle – called C3F –, rep from * to last st, P1.
6th row K1, P1, *K4, P2, rep from * to last 6 sts, K4, P1, K1.
7th row P1, K1, *P4, K2, rep from * to last 6 sts, P4, K1, P1.
Rep 6th and 7th rows once more, then 6th row once.
11th row P1, *C3F, C3B, rep from * to last st, P1.
12th row As 2nd.
These 12 rows form the pattern.

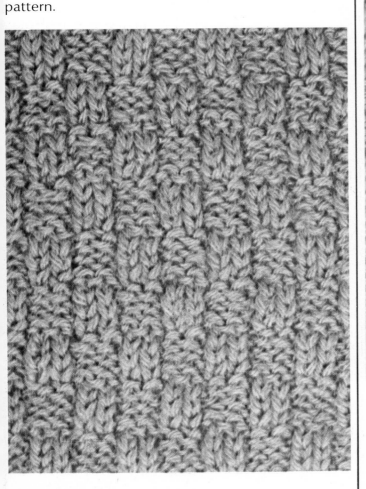

Trellis stitch

Cast on a number of stitches divisible by 6 + 2.
1st row P3, *K2, P4, rep from * to last 5 sts, K2, P3.
2nd row K3, *P2, K4, rep from * to last 5 sts, P2, K3.
Rep these 2 rows once more.

Stepped stitch

Cast on a number of stitches divisible by 6 + 2.
1st row P2, *K4, P2, rep from * to end.
2nd row K2, *P4, K2, rep from * to end.
Rep these 2 rows once more.
5th row P3, *K2, P4, rep from * to last 5 sts, K2, P3.
6th row K3, *P2, K4, rep from * to last 5 sts, P2, K3.
Rep last 2 rows once more.
9th row P to end.
10th row K to end.
These 10 rows form the pattern.

Stepped stitch

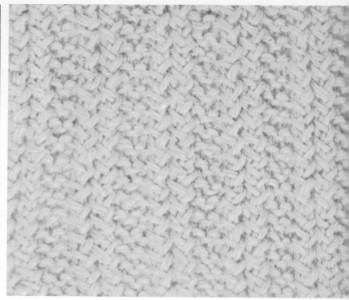

Corded rib

Spiral rib

Cast on a number of stitches divisible by 6 + 2.

1st row P2, *K4, P2, rep from * to end.

2nd and every alt row K2, *P4, K2, rep from * to end.

3rd row P2, *K 2nd st on left hand needle then first st and sl them both off needle tog – called Tw2 –, Tw2, P2, rep from * to end.

5th row P2, *K1, Tw2, K1, P2, rep from * to end.

6th row As 2nd.

The 3rd through 6th rows form the pattern.

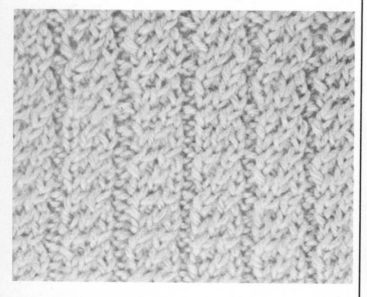

Corded rib

Cast on a number of stitches divisible by 6 + 2.

1st row P2, *K4, P2, rep from * to end.

2nd row P to end.

3rd row P2, *(sl 1, K1, yfwd, pass slip st over K1 and yfwd) twice, P2, rep from * to end.

4th row As 2nd.

The 3rd and 4th rows form the pattern.

Bobble rib

Cast on a number of stitches divisible by 6 + 2.

1st row P2, *K1, P2, rep from * to end.

2nd row K2, *P1, K2, rep from * to end.

3rd row P2, *K1, P2, (P1, K1, P1, K1) all into next st – called K4 from 1 –, P2, rep from * to end.

4th row K2, *P4, K2, P1, K2, rep from * to end.

5th row P2, *K1, P2, P4, turn and K4, turn and P4, P2, rep from * to end.

6th row K2, *P4 tog, K2, P1, K2, rep from * to end.

Rep 1st and 2nd rows once more.

9th row P2, *K4, from 1, P2, K1, P2, rep from * to end.

10th row K2, *P1, K2, P4, K2, rep from * to end.

11th row P2, *P4, turn and K4, turn and P4, P2, K1, P2, rep from * to end.

12th row K2, *P1, K2, P4 tog, K2, rep from * to end.

These 12 rows form the pattern.

A short-sleeved sweater

The pretty bobble stitch sweater shown on the previous page is a marvelous illustration of the versatility of knitting. It can be made from any of the stitches shown on the previous two pages, provided, of course, that you can correctly work the gauge before you start to work the pattern.

Sizes
Directions are to fit 34in bust. Changes for 36 and 38in bust are in brackets [].
Length to shoulder 22[22½:23]in, adjustable
Sleeve seam, 4in

Gauge
24 sts and 32 rows to 4in in stockinette stitch (st st) worked on No.4 needles.

Materials
10[10:11] × 2oz balls Bernat Sesame Knitting Worsted
One pair of No.4 needles
One pair of No.2 needles
Set of 4 No.2 double-pointed needles

Back
Using No.2 needles cast on 109[115:121]sts.
1st row K1, *P1, K1, rep from * to end.
2nd row P1, *K1, P1, rep from * to end.
Rep these 2 rows for 1½in ending with a 2nd row and inc one st in center of last row. 110[116:122]sts. Change to No.4 needles. Work in any desired patt from any of st patts in the previous chapter until piece measures 14½in from beg or desired length to underarm, ending with a WS row.

Shape armholes
Bind off 4 sts at beg of next and every row twice and 2 sts twice. Dec one st at each end of next and foll 5[6:7] alt rows. 86[90:94]sts. Cont without shaping until armholes measure 7½[8:8½]in from beg, ending with a WS row.
Shape neck and shoulders
Next row Bind off 6[7:7]sts, patt 25[25:26]sts, turn and leave rem sts on holder.
Next row Bind off 2 sts, patt to end.
Next row Bind off 6[7:7]sts, patt to end.
Rep last 2 rows once more then the first one once more. Bind off rem 7[5:6] sts.
With RS of work facing, sl first 24[26:28]sts onto holder, rejoin yarn to rem sts and patt to end.
Complete to correspond to first side, reversing shaping.

Front
Work as for back until armhole shaping is completed. Cont without shaping until armholes measure 5½[6:6½]in from beg, ending with a WS row.

Shape neck
Next row Patt 35[36:37]sts, turn and place rem sts on holder.
Bind off 2 sts at beg of next and foll 2 alt rows, then dec one st at neck edge on foll 4 alt rows.
Cont without shaping until armhole measures same as back to shoulder, ending at armhole edge.

Shape shoulder
Bind off at beg of next and every alt row 6[7:7]sts 3 times and 7[5:6]sts once. With RS of work facing, sl first 16[18:20]sts onto a holder, rejoin yarn to rem sts and patt to end. Complete to correspond to first side, reversing shaping.

Sleeves
Using No.2 needles cast on 73[73:79]sts. Work 1in rib as for back, ending with a 2nd row and inc one st in center of last row. 74[74:80]sts. Change to No.4 needles. Cont in patt as for back, inc one st at each end of 3rd and every foll 8th[6th:6th] row until there are 78[82:86]sts. Cont without shaping until sleeve measures 4in from beg, ending with a WS row.

Shape top
Bind off 4 sts at beg of next 2 rows. Dec one st at each end of next and foll 11[12:13] alt rows, ending with a WS row. Bind off at beg of next and every row 2 sts 8[8:10] times, 3 sts 4 times, 4 sts twice and 10[12:10]sts once.

Neckband
Join shoulder seams. Using set of 4 No.2 needles and with RS of work facing, K 8 sts down right back neck, K across back neck sts inc one st in center, K 8 sts up left back neck and 24 sts down left front neck, K across front neck sts inc one st in center and K 24 sts up right front neck. 106[110:114]sts. Cont in rounds of K1, P1 rib for 2½in.
Bind off loosely in rib.

Finishing
Block each piece under a damp cloth with a warm iron. Set in sleeves. Join side and sleeve seams. Block seams. Fold neckband in half to WS and sew in place.

TEXTURED PATTERNS

These fabric stitches are more complicated than the examples given in the previous chapter and use larger multiples of stitches and rows to form the pattern repeat. Each pattern is formed either by stitches which travel from one position to another in a row or by decreased stitches which are then compensated for by an increased stitch, which gives a lacy effect.

Pyramid pattern
Cast on a number of stitches divisible by 15 + 1.
1st row K to end.
2nd row P4, *K8, P7, rep from * to last 12 sts, K8, P4.
3rd row K1, *K up 1, K2, sl 1, K1, psso, P6, K2 tog, K2, K up 1, K1, rep from * to end.
4th row P5, *K6, P9, rep from * to last 11 sts, K6, P5.
5th row K2, *K up 1, K2, sl 1, K1, psso, P4, K2 tog, K2, K up 1, K3, rep from * to last 14 sts, K up 1, K2, sl 1, K1, psso, P4, K2 tog, K2, K up 1, K2.
6th row P6, *K4, P11, rep from * to last 10 sts, K4, P6.
7th row K3, *K up 1, K2, sl 1, K1, psso, P2, K2 tog, K2, K up 1, K5, rep from * to last 13 sts, K up 1, K2, sl 1, K1, psso, P4, K2 tog, K2, K up 1, K2.
8th row P7, *K2, P13, rep from * to last 9 sts, K2, P7.
9th row K4, *K up 1, K2, sl 1, K1, psso, K2 tog, K2, K up 1, K7, rep from * to last 12 sts, K up 1, K2, sl 1, K1, psso, K2 tog, K2, K up 1, K4.
10th row P to end.
These 10 rows form the pattern.

Leaf pattern
Cast on a number of stitches divisible by 24 + 1.
1st row K1, *K up 1, sl 1, K1, psso, K4, K2 tog, K3, K up 1, K1, K up 1, K3, sl 1, K1, psso, K4, K2 tog, K up 1, K1, rep from * to end.

2nd and every alt row P to end.
3rd row K1, *K up 1, K1, sl 1, K1, psso, K2, K2 tog, K4, K up 1, K1, K up 1, K4, sl 1, K1, psso, K2, K2 tog, K1, K up 1, K1, rep from * to end.
5th row K1, *K up 1, K2, sl 1, K1, psso, K2 tog, K5, K up 1, K1, K up 1, K5, sl 1, K1, psso, K2 tog, K2, K up 1, K1, rep from * to end.
7th row K1, *K up 1, K3, sl 1, K1, psso, K4, K2 tog, K up 1, K1, K up 1, sl 1, K1, psso, K4, K2 tog, K3, K up 1, K1, rep from * to end.
9th row K1, *K up 1, K4, sl 1, K1, psso, K2, K2 tog, K1, K up 1, K1, K up 1, K1, sl 1, K1, psso, K2, K2 tog, K4, K up 1, K1, rep from * to end.
11th row K1, *K up 1, K5, sl 1, K1, psso, K2 tog, K2, K up 1, K1, K up 1, K2, sl 1, K1, psso, K2 tog, K5, K up 1, K1, rep from * to end.
12th row P to end.
These 12 rows form the pattern.

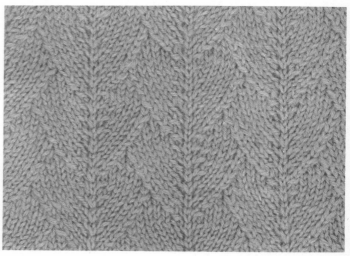

Seeded chevron pattern
Cast on a number of stitches divisible by 14 + 2.
1st row K14, *K second st on left hand needle then K first st and sl both sts off needle tog – called TwR –, K12, rep from * to last 2 sts, K2.
2nd row P1, *sl 1, P12, sl 1, rep from * to last st, P1.
3rd row K1, *put needle behind first st on left hand needle and K into back of second st then K first st and sl both sts off needle tog – called TwL –, K10, TwR, rep from * to last st K1.
4th row P1, K1, *sl 1, P10, sl 1, P1, K1, rep from * to end.
5th row K1, P1, *TwL, K8, TwR, K1, P1, rep from * to end.
6th row P1, K1, *P1, sl 1, P8, sl 1, K1, P1, rep from * to end.
7th row K1, P1, *K1, TwL, K6, TwR, P1, K1, P1, rep from * to end.

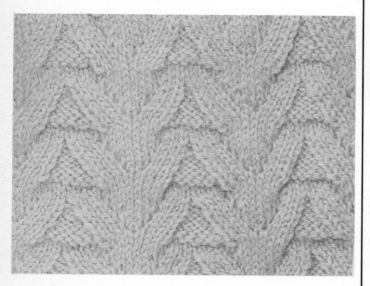

8th row *(P1, K1) twice, sl 1, P6, sl 1, P1, K1, rep from * to last 2 sts, P1, K1.

9th row *(K1, P1) twice, TwL, K4, TwR, K1, P1, rep from * to last 2 sts, K1, P1.

10th row P1, *(K1, P1) twice, sl 1, P4, sl 1, (K1, P1) twice, rep from * to last st, K1.

11th row K1, *(P1, K1) twice, TwL, K2, TwR, (P1, K1) twice, rep from * to last st, P1.

12th row *(P1, K1) 3 times, sl 1, P2, sl 1, (P1, K1) twice, rep from * to last 2 sts, P1, K1.

13th row (K1, P1) 3 times, *TwL, TwR, (K1, P1) twice, TwR, (K1, P1) twice, rep from * to last 10 sts, TwL, TwR, (K1, P1) 3 times.

14th row P1, sl 1, *(P1, K1) 3 times, sl 1, K1, (P1, K1) twice, sl 2, rep from * to last 14 sts, (P1, K1) 3 times, sl 1, K1, (P1, K1) twice, sl 1, P1.

15th row K1, *TwL, (P1, K1) twice, TwL, (P1, K1) twice, TwR, rep from * to last st, K1.

16th row P2, *sl 1, (K1, P1) 5 times, sl 1, P2, rep from * to end.

17th row K2, *TwL, (K1, P1) 4 times, TwR, K2, rep from * to end.

18th row P3, *sl 1, (P1, K1) 4 times, sl 1, P4, rep from * to last 13 sts, sl 1, (P1, K1) 4 times, sl 1, P3.

19th row K3, *TwL, (P1, K1) 3 times, TwR, K4, rep from * to last 13 sts, TwL, (P1, K1) 3 times, TwR, K3.

20th row P4, *sl 1, (K1, P1) 3 times, sl 1, P6, rep from * to last 12 sts, sl 1, (K1, P1) 3 times, sl 1, P4.

21st row K4, *TwL, (K1, P1) twice, TwR, K6, rep from * to last 12 sts, TwL, (K1, P1) twice, TwR, K4.

22nd row P5, *sl 1, (P1, K1) twice, sl 1, P8, rep from * to last 11 sts, sl 1, (P1, K1) twice, sl 1, P5.

23rd row K5, *TwL, P1, K1, TwR, K8, rep from * to last 11 sts, TwL, P1, K1, TwR, K5.

24th row P6, *sl 1, K1, P1, sl 1, P10, rep from * to last 10 sts, sl 1, K1, P1, sl 1, P6.

25th row K6, *TwL, TwR, K10, rep from * to last 10 sts, TwL, TwR, K6.

26th row P8, *sl 1, P13, rep from * to last 8 sts, sl 1, P7.

27th row K7, *TwL, K12, rep from * to last 9 sts, TwL, K7.

28th row P to end.
These 28 rows form the pattern.

Travelling rib pattern

Cast on a number of stitches divisible by 12 + 2.

1st row P6, *K7, P5, rep from * to last 8 sts, K7, P1.

2nd row K1, *P7, K5, rep from * to last st, K1.

3rd row P5, *K second st on left hand needle then K first st and sl both sts off needle tog – called TwR –, K4, TwR, P4, rep from * to last 9 sts, TwR, K4, TwR, P1.

4th row K2, *P7, K5, rep from * to end.

5th row P4, *TwR, K4, TwR, P4, rep from * to last 10 sts, TwR, K4, TwR, P2.

6th row K3, *P7, K5, rep from * to last 11 sts, P7, K4.

7th row P3, *TwR, K4, TwR, P4, rep from * to last 11 sts, TwR, K4, TwR, P3.

8th row K4, *P7, K5, rep from * to last 10 sts, P7, K3.

9th row P2, *TwR, K4, TwR, P4, rep from * to end.

10th row K5, *P7, K5, rep from * to last 9 sts, P7, K2.

11th row P1, *TwR, K4, TwR, P4, rep from * to last st, P1.

12th row K6, *P7, K5, rep from * to last 8 sts, P7, K1.

13th row P1, *put needle behind first st on left hand needle and K into back of second st then K first st and sl both sts off needle tog – called TwL –, K4, TwL, P4, rep from * to last st, P1.

14th row As 10th.

15th row P2, *TwL, K4, TwL, P4, rep from * to end.

16th row As 8th.

17th row P3, *TwL, K4, TwL, P4, rep from * to last 11 sts, TwL, K4, TwL, P3.

18th row As 6th.

19th row P4, *TwL, K4, TwL, P4, rep from * to last 10 sts, TwL, K4, TwL, P2.

20th row As 4th.

21st row P5, *TwL, K4, TwL, P4, rep from * to last 9 sts, TwL, K4, TwL, P1

22nd row As 2nd.
The 3rd through 22nd rows form the pattern.

WOVEN FABRIC STITCHES

Just as the yarn can be carried over the needle in a pattern sequence to form additional stitches, or carried across the back of the work to form stripes or multi-colored patterns, it can also be held in front of a sequence of stitches to form a woven fabric. In many instances, the fabric, as with Fair Isle and jacquard patterns, is double the thickness of ordinary knitting and may be used in a variety of ways.

If you use a very fine yarn and any of the all over stitches shown in this chapter you will produce a very warm but light fabric, suitable for baby garments, bedjackets or lingerie, where you may want extra warmth but not extra weight. Using a knitting worsted quality yarn, the fabric will be firm and virtually windproof and most suitable for heavy outdoor garments, such as windbreakers, ski parkas or bulky jackets.

All these stitches are simple to work as the patterns merely require a given sequence of stitches to be slipped from one needle to the other, carrying the yarn in front of these stitches ready to knit the next stitch. They do not have to be worked to produce an all over fabric but can be worked at given intervals, as with the cluster stitch and the woven butterfly stitch, to add texture to an otherwise plain fabric. To keep the sides of the patterns neat and to avoid any 'fluting' effect, it is advisable to knit the first and last stitch on every row to form a firm, garter stitch edge.

Diagonal woven stitch
Cast on a number of stitches divisible by 4 + 2.
1st row K2, *yfwd, sl 2 P-wise, ybk, K2, rep from * to end.
2nd and every alt row K1, P to last st, K1.
3rd row Yfwd, sl 1 P-wise, ybk, *K2, yfwd, sl 2 P-wise, ybk, rep from * to last st, K1.

5th row Yfwd, sl 2 P-wise, ybk, *K2, yfwd, sl 2 P-wise, ybk, rep from * to end.
7th row K1, yfwd, sl 2 P-wise, ybk, *K2, yfwd, sl 2 P-wise, ybk, rep from * to last 3 sts, K2, yfwd, sl 1 P-wise, ybk.
8th row As 2nd.
These 8 rows form the pattern.

Woven bar stitch
Cast on a number of stitches divisible by 3 + 1.
1st row (RS) K to end.
2nd row *K1, keeping yarn at back of work sl 2 P-wise, rep from * to last st, K1.
These 2 rows form the pattern.

Woven ladder stitch
Cast on a number of stitches divisible by 8 + 1.
1st row *K5, yfwd, sl 3 P-wise, ybk, rep from * to last st, K1.

2nd row K1, *ybk, sl 3 P-wise, yfwd, P5, rep from * to end, ending last rep with K1.
3rd row As 1st.
4th row K1, P to last st, K1.
5th row K1, *yfwd, sl 3 P-wise, ybk, K5, rep from * to end.
6th row K1, *P4, ybk, sl 3 P-wise, yfwd, P1, rep from * to end, ending last rep K1.
7th row As 5th.
8th row As 4th.
These 8 rows form the pattern.

Woven chevron stitch

Cast on a number of stitches divisible by 10.
1st row *K1, yfwd, sl 3 P-wise, ybk, K2, yfwd, sl 3 P-wise, ybk, K1, rep from * to end.
2nd row *Ybk, sl 3 P-wise, yfwd, P2, rep from * to end, ending last rep K1.
3rd row Yfwd, *sl 1 P-wise, ybk, K2, yfwd, sl 3 P-wise, ybk, K2, yfwd, sl 2 P-wise, rep from * to end.
4th row Yfwd, *sl 1 P-wise, yfwd, P2, ybk, sl 3 P-wise, yfwd, P2, ybk, sl 2 P-wise, rep from * to end.
5th row *Yfwd, sl 3 P-wise, ybk, K2, rep from * to end.
6th row *P1, ybk, sl 3 P-wise, yfwd, P1, rep from * to end.
7th row As 5th.
8th row As 4th.
9th row As 3rd.

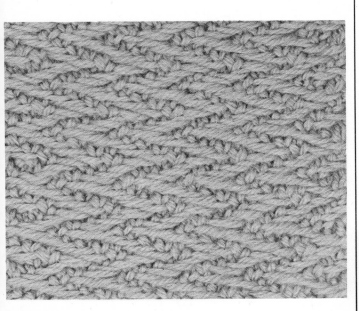

10th row As 2nd.
These 10 rows form the pattern.

Cluster stitch

Cast on a number of stitches divisible by 8 + 5.
1st row K to end.
2nd row P to end.
3rd row *K5, sl next 3 sts on to cable needle and hold at front of work, pass the yarn across the back of these stitches and right around them 6 times in a counter-clockwise direction then K3 sts from cable needle – called 1CL, –, rep from * to last 5 sts, K5.
4th row P to end.
Rep 1st and 2nd rows once more.

7th row *K1, 1CL, K4, rep from * to last 5 sts, K1, 1CL, K1.
8th row P to end.
These 8 rows form the pattern.

Woven butterfly stitch

Cast on a number of stitches divisible by 10 + 7.
1st row K6, *yfwd, sl 5 P-wise, ybk, K5, rep from * to last st, K1.
2nd row P to end.
Rep 1st and 2nd rows 3 times more.
9th row K8, *insert right hand needle under the 4 long loops, yarn around the needle and draw through a stitch, then keeping this st on right hand needle K the next st on the left hand needle and pass the first st over the K1 – called B1 –, K9, rep from * to last 9 sts, B1, K8.
10th row As 2nd.
11th row K1, yfwd, sl 5 P-wise, ybk, *K5, yfwd, sl 5 P-wise, ybk, rep from * to last st, K1.
12th row As 2nd.
Rep 11th and 12th rows 3 times more.
19th row K3, B1, *K9, B1, rep from * to last 3 sts, K3.
20th row As 2nd.
These 20 rows form the pattern.

111

RAISED STITCHES

Bobble and cluster stitches

Although the overall heading refers to a cluster of raised stitches which can be arranged to give an interesting and highly textured fabric, the size of a bobble or cluster can vary considerably.

There are various ways of working bobbles but the basic principle is always the same – working more than once into the stitch where the bobble is required and then decreasing again to the original stitch, either in the same row or several rows later.

Cluster stitches also are worked on this principle but they are not intended to be as dense as bobble stitches and once the cluster is formed, it is decreased more gradually over a number of rows until only the original stitch remains.

Both bobble and cluster stitches may be used very effectively to form an all over pattern but, combined with other stitches such as cables, they produce some of the most beautiful variations of the Aran patterns which are renowned throughout the world.

Bobble patterns

The simplest forms of bobble stitches are small and easy to work. The working methods of the two samples shown here differ slightly, but both produce a small, berry type of stitch. Trinity stitch, which is used in Aran patterns, derives its name from the method of working 'three into one and one into three.'

Blackberry stitch

Cast on a number of stitches divisible by 4.
1st row *(K1, yfwd to make one st, K1) all into next st, P3, rep from * to end.
2nd row *P3 tog, K3, rep from * to end.
3rd row *P3, (K1, yfwd to make one st, K1) all into next st, rep from * to end.
4th row *K3, P3 tog, rep from * to end.
These 4 rows form the pattern.

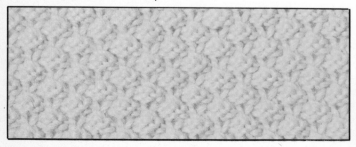

Trinity stitch

Cast on a number of stitches divisible by 4.
1st row *(K1, P1, K1) all into next st, P3 tog, rep from * to end.

2nd row P to end.
3rd row *P3 tog, (K1, P1, K1) all into next st, rep from * to end.
4th row As 2nd.
These 4 rows form the pattern.

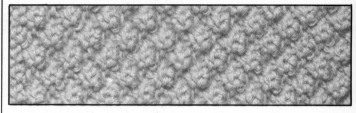

Small bobble stitch

Cast on a number of stitches divisible by 6 plus 5.
1st row (WS) P to end.
2nd row K2, (K1, P1, K1, P1, K1) all into next st then using point of left hand needle lift 2nd, 3rd, 4th and 5th sts over first st and off right hand needle – called B1 –, *K5, B1, rep from * to last 2 sts, K2.
3rd row P to end.
4th row *K5, B1, rep from * to last 5 sts, K5.
These 4 rows form the pattern.

Popcorn stitch

Cast on a number of stitches divisible by 6 plus 5.
1st row (WS) P to end.
2nd row K2, (K1, P1, K1, P1, K1) all into next st, turn and K these 5 sts, turn and P5 then using point of left hand needle lift 2nd, 3rd, 4th and 5th sts over first st and off right hand needle – called B1 –, *K5, B1, rep from * to last 2 sts, K2.
3rd row P to end.
4th row *K5, B1, rep from * to last 5 sts, K5.
These 4 rows form the pattern.

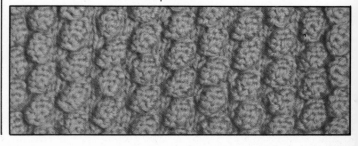

Currant stitch

Cast on a number of stitches divisible by 2 plus 1.

1st row (RS) K to end.

2nd row K1, *(P1, yrn to make one st, P1, yrn, P1) all into next st, K1, rep from * to end.

3rd row P to end.

4th row K1, *sl 2 P-wise keeping yarn at front of work – called sl 2F –, P3 tog, p2sso, K1, rep from * to end.

5th row K to end.

6th row K2, *(P1, yrn, P1, yrn, P1) all into next st, K1, rep from * to last st, K1.

7th row P to end.

8th row K2, *sl 2F, P3 tog, p2sso, K1, rep from * to last st, K1.

These 8 rows form the pattern.

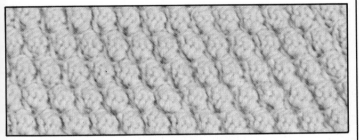

Long bobble stitch

Cast on a number of stitches divisible by 6 plus 3.

1st row (WS) P to end.

2nd row K1, *K3, (K1, yfwd to make one st, K1) all into next st, K1, (turn and P5, turn and K5) twice, K1, rep from * to last 2 sts, K2.

3rd row P1, *P2, P2 tog, P1, P2 tog tbl, P1, rep from * to last 2 sts, P2.

4th row K3, *K4, (K1, yfwd, K1) all into next st, K1, (turn and P5, turn and K5) twice, rep from * to last 6 sts, K6.

5th row P3, *P3, P2 tog, P1, P2 tog tbl, rep from * to last 6sts, P6.

Rows 2 through 5 form the pattern.

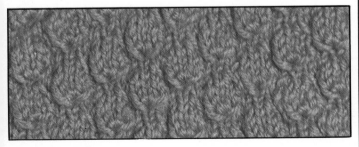

Cluster stitches

These patterns may be worked in two ways – either by increasing and shaping the cluster and working the stitches on either side row by row at the same time, or by working the cluster separately and then continuing to knit the background fabric until it has reached the same height as the cluster.

Bell cluster

Cast on a number of stitches divisible by 4 plus 4.

1st row (WS) K to end.

2nd row P4, *turn and cast on 8 sts – called C1 –, P4, rep from * to end.

3rd row *K4, P8, rep from * to last 4 sts, K4.

4th row P4, *K8, P4, rep from * to end.

5th row As 3rd.

6th row P4, *sl 1, K1, psso, K4, K2 tog, P4, rep from * to end.

7th row *K4, P6, rep from * to last 4 sts, K4.

8th row P4, *sl 1, K1, psso, K2, K2 tog, P4, rep from * to end.

9th row *K4, P4, rep from * to last 4 sts, K4.

10th row P4, *sl 1, K1, psso, K2 tog, P4, rep from * to end.

11th row *K4, P2, rep from * to last 4 sts, K4.

12th row P4, *K2 tog, P4, rep from * to end.

13th row *K4, P1, rep from * to last 4 sts, K4.

14th row P4, *K2 tog, P3, rep from * to end.

These 14 rows form the pattern.

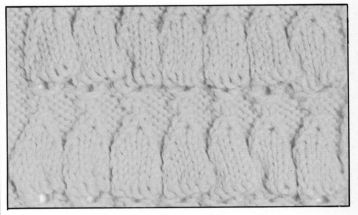

Detached cluster

Cast on a number of stitches divisible by 6 plus 5.

1st row (RS) P to end.

2nd row K to end.

3rd row *P5, (yfwd to make one st, K into next st) 3 times into same st to make 6 out of one, turn and P these 6 sts, turn and sl 1, K5, turn and sl 1, P5, turn and sl 1, K5, turn and (P2 tog) 3 times, turn and sl 1, K2 tog, psso – called C1 –, rep from * to last 5 sts, P5.

4th row K to end.

5th row P to end.

6th row K to end.

7th row P2, *C1, P5, rep from * to last 3 sts, C1, P2.

8th row K to end.

These 8 rows form the pattern.

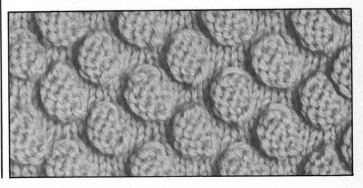

FUR FABRICS

Knitting patterns which have the appearance of fur fabrics are made by looping strands of yarn onto the main background while the row is being knitted.

The usual method is to loop the yarn around fingers or a strip of cardboard for the required number of times, then to secure the loops to the knitted stitch so that they do not unravel. The fabric produced is warm and light and is very suitable for outer garments, and trimmings such as collars and cuffs, baby blankets and washable throw rugs.

Another method shown here combines a knitted background with lengths of crochet chains forming a fur effect which gives a close, astrakan texture to the fabric. The loops made by using this method will not catch or break as easily as those of the first method and this way is therefore most suitable for babies' and children's garments, where frequent washing or rough-and-tumble use is expected. Although it is not as quick or simple to work as the first method, the effect is so attractive that it is well worth a little time and effort spent in practicing it.

Looped patterns

The density of these patterns may be varied as desired, either by the number of times the yarn is looped around, or by the position of each loop on the background fabric. The samples given here have been worked in a knitting worsted yarn, alternating the position of the loops on every 4th row.

Single loop stitch

Here the loops are formed on a right side row when the work is facing you. Cast on a number of stitches divisible by 2 plus 1.

1st row (RS) K to end.
2nd row P to end.
3rd row *K1, K next st without letting it drop off left hand needle, yfwd, pass yarn over left thumb to make a loop approximately 1½in long, ybk and K st rem on left hand needle letting it drop from the needle, return the 2 sts just worked to the left hand needle and K them tog tbl – called L1 –, rep from * to last st, K1.
4th row P to end.
Rep 1st and 2nd rows once more.
7th row K1, *K1, L1, rep from * to last 2 sts, K2.
8th row P to end.
These 8 rows form the pattern.

Double loop stitch

Here the loops are formed on the right side of the fabric when the wrong side of the work is facing you. Cast on a number of stitches divisible by 2 plus 1.

1st row (RS) K to end.
Rep 1st row twice more.
4th row (WS) K1, *insert right hand needle into next st on left hand needle as if to knit it, wind yarn over right hand needle point and round first and 2nd fingers of left hand twice, then over and around right hand needle point once more, draw all 3 loops through st and sl on to left hand needle, insert right hand needle through back of these 3 loops and through the original st and K tog tbl – called L1 –, K1, rep from * to end.

5th 6th and 7th rows K to end.
8th row K1, *K1, L1, rep from * to last 2 sts, K2.
These 8 rows form the pattern.

Chain loop stitch

Here again, the density of the pattern can be changed by the position of each chain loop on the background fabric and by the number of rows worked between each pattern row. To work the sample given here you will need knitting yarn, a pair of No.5 needles and a Size G crochet hook. Cast on a number of stitches divisible by 2 plus 1.
1st row (RS) K to end.

2nd row P to end.
3rd row K1, *K next st without letting it drop off left hand needle, insert crochet hook from front to back through loop on left hand needle, draw a loop through and leave on hook then drop st from left hand needle, wind yarn around left hand and make 12ch in the usual way, then keeping ch at front of work and yarn at back of work sl loop onto right hand needle and remove hook, then lift last K st over loop – called L1 –, K1, rep from * to end.
4th row P to end.
Rep 1st and 2nd rows once more.
7th row K1, *K1, L1, rep from * to last 2 sts, K2.
8th row P to end.
These 8 rows form the pattern.

Tie

7in wide at lower edge by 40in long

Gauge

22 sts and 30 rows to 4in in stockinette stitch (st st) worked on No.5 needles

Materials

4 × 2oz balls of Sports Yarn
One pair No.5 needles

Tie

Using No.5 needles cast on 45 sts. K 3 rows g st. Start patt.
1st row (RS) K2, work in any loop patt over next 41sts, K2.
2nd row K2, patt 41 sts, K2.
Cont in patt, keeping 2 sts at each end in g st throughout, until work measures 5in from beg, ending with a WS row.
Next row K2, sl 1, K1, psso, patt to last 4 sts, K2 tog, K2.
Work 3 rows patt without shaping. Rep last 4 rows 8 times more. 27 sts. Cont without shaping until piece measures 29in from beg, ending with a WS row.
Next row K2, pick up loop lying between sts and K tbl – called inc 1 –, patt to last 2 sts, inc 1, K2.
Work 3 rows patt without shaping. Rep last 4 rows 8 times more. 45 sts. Cont without shaping until work measures 39¾in from beg. K 3 rows g st. Bind off.

Loop fastening

Using No.5 needles cast on 6 sts. Work 4in g st.
Bind off.

Finishing

Do not block. Sew loop fastening across back of one end approximately 7in above bottom edge.
Slot other end through loop to secure.

FISHERMAN KNITTING

Fisherman knitting is the name given to the making of seamless pullovers, knitted in a very closely woven fabric similar to a patterned brocade. Because of the fineness of the needles used for this type of knitting, sometimes to as fine a gauge as Ace 1 knitting pins, the textured patterns do not stand out in relief as they do with Aran stitches. The purpose of this knitting is to make a fabric which is virtually windproof and which will stand up to the constant wear and tear of a fisherman's life.

As with many of the folk crafts which have been handed down to us through countless generations, these pullovers were often knitted by the fishermen themselves, but more often they were lovingly knitted by their womenfolk, in traditional patterns which varied from region to region.

The name 'jersey', originated from the island of that name. Another name in regular use is a 'guernsey', or 'gansey', so called after the sister island in the same group, the Channel Islands, which are situated off the coast of France but are politically a dependency of the United Kingdom.

Each port around the coastline of the British Isles has developed its own regional style of fisherman knitting. Some have patterned yokes, others have vertical panels of patterns and some have horizontal bands of patterns, but the original guernseys, which were made purely as hard-wearing working garments, were nearly always made in stockinette stitch with very little decoration and always in the traditional color, navy blue. The more elaborate examples which evolved were kept for Sunday best and in Cornwall they were often referred to as bridal shirts and were knitted by the young women for their betrothed.

A traditional guernsey is knitted entirely without seams, often worked on sets of 5, 6, or even more double-pointed needles. The body is knitted in rounds to the armholes, then instead of dividing the work for the back and front at this point, the work is continued in rounds with the position of the armholes separated from the main sections of the guernsey by a series of loops wound around the needle on every round. These loops are dropped from the needle on the following round and the process is repeated until the guernsey is the required length. When this section is completed, a series of what look like the rungs of a ladder mark each armhole. These loops are cut in the middle and the ends carefully darned into the main fabric, then the sleeve stitches are picked up round the armholes and the sleeve is knitted in rounds down to the cuff. The shoulder stitches are woven together to finish the garment without a single sewn seam.

The shape of these garments is as distinctive as the patterns. They all feature a dropped shoulder line and crew neckline, with little, if any, shaping. Sometimes buttons and buttonholes would be added to one shoulder for ease in dressing and undressing, a gusset made before the armhole division and carried on into the top of the sleeve, or the neck would be continued to form a small collar, but the simplicity of the basic design has never been bettered, to give the utmost warmth, freedom of movement and protection to the wearer.

Traditional guernsey
Sizes
Directions are to fit 38in chest. Changes for 40, 42 and 44in chest are in brackets [].
Length to shoulder, 23[23½:24:24½]in
Sleeve seam, 18in, adjustable

Gauge
28 sts and 36 rows to 4in over stockinette stitch (st st) worked on No.3 needles

Materials
14[15:16:17] × 2oz balls of Sport Yarn
Set of 4 No.3 double-pointed needles or No.3 circular needle
Set of 4 No.1 double-pointed needles or No.1 circular needle

Guernsey body
Using set of 4 No.1 needles cast on 264[276:288:300] sts. Mark beg of round with colored thread. Cont in rounds of K1, P1 rib for 3in. Change to set of 4 No.3 needles. Cont in rounds of st st until work measures 13in from beg. Commence yoke patt.
**1st round P to end.
2nd round K to end.
Rep these 2 rounds twice more, then 1st round once more. **.
***Work 5 rounds st st.
Divide for armholes
1st round *K132[138:144:150] sts, wind yarn 10 times around right hand needle – called loop 10 –, rep from * once more.
Rep last round once more, dropping extra loops from needle before loop 10.

3rd round *K6[9:0:3], (K6, P1, K11, P1, K5) 5[5:6:6] times, K6[9:0:3], drop extra loops, loop 10, rep from * once more.
4th round *K6[9:0:3], (K4, P1, K1, P1, K9, P1, K1, P1, K5) 5[5:6:6] times, K6[9:0:3], drop extra loops, loop 10, rep from * once more.
5th round *K6[9:0:3], (K4, P1, K3, P1, K7, P1, (K1, P1) twice, K3) 5[5:6:6] times, K6[9:0:3], drop extra loops, loop 10, rep from * once more.
6th round *K6[9:0:3], (K2, P1, (K1, P1) 3 times, (K5, P1) twice, K3) 5[5:6:6] times, K6[9:0:3], drop extra loops, loop 10, rep from * once more.
7th round *K6[9:0:3], (K2, P1, K7, P1, K3, P1, (K1, P1) 4 times, K1) 5[5:6:6] times, K6[9:0:3], drop extra loops, loop 10, rep from * once more.
8th round *K6[9:0:3], (P1, (K1, P1) 6 times, K9, P1, K1) 5 [5:6:6] times, K6[9:0:3], drop extra loops, loop 10, rep from * once more.
9th round *K6[9:0:3], (P1, K11, P12) 5[5:6:6] times, K6[9:0:3], drop extra loops, loop 10, rep from * once more.
10th round *K6[9:0:3], (P11, K1, P1, K9, P1, K1) 5[5:6:6] times, K6[9:0:3], drop extra loops, loop 10, rep from * once more.
11th round *K6[9:0:3], (K2, P1, K7, P1, K13) 5[5:6:6] times, K6[9:0:3], drop extra loops, loop 10, rep from * once more.
12th round *K6[9:0:3], (K14, P1, K5, P1, K3) 5[5:6:6] times, K6[9:0:3], drop extra loops, loop 10, rep from * once more.
13th round *K6[9:0:3], (K4, P1, K3, P1, K15) 5[5:6:6] times, K6[9:0:3], drop extra loops, loop 10, rep from * once more.
14th round *K6[9:0:3], (K16, P1, K1, P1, K5) 5[5:6:6] times, K6[9:0:3], drop extra loops, loop 10, rep from * once more.
15th and 16th rounds As 1st, dropping extra loops.
Keeping armhole loops correct, work 5 rounds st st, then rep from ** to ** once. ***. Rep from *** to *** once more. Beg with a 2nd row, cont working in patt from ** to ** until work measures 8½[9:9½:10]in from beg of loops, omitting loop 10 at end of last round. Break off yarn.
Divide for shoulders
Maintaining patt, sl first and last 35[37:39:41] sts of back and front sections on to holders, knit across each set of 62[64:66:68] sts of neck separately for 6 rows. Bind off loosely. Weave shoulder sts from holders.
Sleeves
Cut loops of armholes and darn in ends. Using set of 4 No.3 needles and with RS of work facing, K 110 [114:118:122] sts round armhole. K 5 rounds st st, then rep from ** to ** as for body.
Cont in rounds of st st, dec one st at beg and end of next and every foll 6th round until 74[80:84:88] sts rem. Cont without shaping until sleeve measures 16in from beg, or required length less 2in. Change to 4 No.1 needles. Work 2in K1, P1 rib. Bind off in rib.

MAXI KNITTING

Working a fabric on very large knitting needles can be both speedy and fun, as even the most basic stitches take on a completely different appearance. This particular type of knitting is often referred to as 'jiffy knitting' and needles for this special gauge are available in varying sizes.

The most popular needles are made from a special lightweight hollow plastic and are graded upwards from the smallest size 11, on to 13, 15 and to the largest size 19. Extra large jumbo sized needles are also available, and graded as sizes 35 and 50.

Great care must be taken in selecting a suitable yarn for this type of knitting, and often two or more strands are used at the same time, producing a very heavy fabric. Any lightweight yarn, such as mohair, is ideal as this gives sufficient bulk to the fabric without being too heavy.

The stitch chosen also plays an important part, as the texture must be firm enough to prevent the knitting from stretching but not so dense that it produces a thick, harsh fabric. Stockinette stitch does not work too well with this method as it is very difficult to keep the smooth, even tension which is the main characteristic of this stitch. On the other hand, garter stitch, moss stitch and small, repeating lace or fabric patterns, such as are shown here, do produce interesting textures which will hold their shape.

When casting on and binding off, the stitches must be worked very loosely to avoid pulling the fabric out of shape.

Indian pillar stitch

Use two or more strands of yarn, depending upon the size of needle chosen. Cast on a number of stitches divisible by 4 plus 2.

1st row P1, *insert needle purlwise into next 3 sts as if to purl them tog but instead (P1, K1, P1) into these 3 sts, K1, rep from * to last st, P1.
2nd row P to end.
These 2 rows form the pattern.

Waffle stitch

Use two or more strands of yarn, depending upon the size of needle chosen, and cast on a number of stitches divisible by 2.

1st row *K1 tbl, P1, rep from * to end.
2nd row *P1 tbl, K1, rep from * to end.
These 2 rows form the pattern.

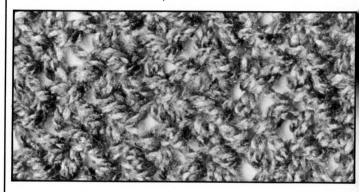

Grecian plait stitch

This stitch requires one small and one large needle, the large needle being twice the size of the small needle. Use two strands of yarn and cast on an even number of stitches with the large needle.

1st row Using the small needle, K to end.
2nd row Using the large needle, P to end.
3rd row Using the small needle, lift the 2nd st over the first st and K it then K the first st, lift the 4th st over the 3rd st and K it then K the 3rd st, cont in this way across the row.
4th row Using the large needle, P to end.
These 4 rows form the pattern.

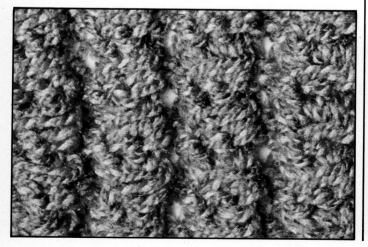

Jiffy-knit scarf

Size
Approximately 9in wide by 66in long, excluding the fringe

Gauge
10 sts to 3in in Indian pillar st worked on No.17 needles

Materials
5 × 2oz balls of Spinnerin Piccadilly in each of 2 contrast colors, A and B
One pair of No.17 needles

Scarf
Using No.17 needles if working in Indian pillar st or waffle st, or one No.11 and one No.17 needle if working in Grecian braid st, and one strand each of A and B, cast on 30 sts loosely. Work in patt as desired until scarf measures 66in from beg.
Bind off very loosely.

Finishing
Do not block. Using 2 strands of A and B tog, make a fringe of desired length along each short end, knotting fringe into every alt st. Trim fringe ends.

TRAVELING STITCHES

Crossed stitches, which have a twisted appearance, are used extensively in Aran patterns and the same methods may be used to create effective miniature and mock cable patterns. Because only two, or at most three, stitches are crossed at any one time, it is not necessary to use a cable needle, therefore these patterns are simple to work.

Crossed stitches should be knitted against a purl background to show to their best advantage, but to produce an even tighter twist on the stitches, it is also necessary to know how to twist them on the wrong side, or on a purl row against a knitted background.

Knitted crossed stitches with back twist

The crossed stitches are worked over two knitted stitches and the twist lies to the left. Pass the right hand needle behind the first stitch on the left hand needle, knit into the back of the next stitch on the left hand needle then knit into the front of the first skipped stitch and slip both stitches off the left hand needle together. The abbreviation for this is 'T2B'.

Mock cable

Cast on a number of stitches divisible by 5 + 3.
1st row P3, *K2, P3, rep from * to end.

2nd row K3, *P2, K3, rep from * to end.
Rep 1st and 2nd rows once more.
5th row P3, *T2B, P3, rep from * to end.
6th row As 2nd.
These 6 rows form the pattern.

Twisted rib

Cast on a number of stitches divisible by 14 + 2.
1st row P2, *T2B, P2, K4, P2, T2B, P2, rep from * to end.
2nd row K2, *P2, K2, P4, K2, P2, K2, rep from * to end.
Rep 1st and 2nd rows once more.
5th row P2, *T2B, P2, into 4th and 3rd sts on left hand needle work T2B leaving sts on needle then work T2B into 2nd and 1st sts and sl all 4 sts off needle tog, P2, T2B, P2, rep from * to end.
6th row As 2nd.
These 6 rows form the pattern.

Knitted crossed stitches with front twist

The crossed stitches are worked over two knitted stitches and the twist lies to the right. Pass the right hand needle in front of the first stitch on the left hand needle, knit into the front of the next stitch on the left hand needle then knit into the front of the first skipped stitch and slip both stitches off the needle together. The abbreviation for this is 'T2F'.

Three stitches can be crossed in the same way by working into the 3rd stitch, then into the 2nd and then into the first, slipping all 3 stitches off the left hand needle together. The abbreviation for this is 'T3F'.

Twisted panels

Cast on a number of stitches divisible by 8 + 2.
1st row P2, *(T2F) 3 times, P2, rep from * to end.
2nd row K2, *P6, K2, rep from * to end.
3rd row P2, *(T3F) twice, P2, rep from * to end.
4th row As 2nd.
These 4 rows form the pattern.

Purled crossed stitches with front twist

The crossed stitches are worked over two purled stitches and form a crossed thread lying to the right on the knitted side of the work. Pass the right hand needle in front of the first stitch on the left hand needle and purl the next stitch on the left hand needle, purl the first skipped stitch and slip both stitches off the left hand needle together. The abbreviation for this is 'T2PF'.

Purled crossed stitches with back twist

The crossed stitches are worked over two purled stitches and form a crossed thread lying to the left on the knitted side of the work. Pass the right hand

needle behind the first stitch on the left hand needle and purl the next stitch on the left hand needle through the back of the loop, purl the first skipped stitch and slip both stitches off the left hand needle together. The abbreviation for this is 'T2PB'.

Crossing two knitted stitches to the right

Pass the right hand needle in front of the first stitch on the left hand needle and knit into the next stitch on the left hand needle, lift this stitch over the first skipped stitch and off the needle then knit the first skipped stitch. The abbreviation for this is 'C2R'.

Crossing two knitted stitches to the left

Slip the first stitch on to the right hand needle without knitting it, knit the next stitch on the left hand needle and slip it on to the right hand needle, using the left hand needle point pass the first slipped stitch over the knitted stitch, knitting into the slipped stitch at the same time. The abbreviation for this is 'C2L'.

Crossed cable

Cast on a number of stitches divisible by 7 + 3.
1st row P3, *K4, P3, rep from * to end.
2nd row K3, *P4, K3, rep from * to end.
3rd row P3, *C2R, C2L, P3, rep from * to end.
4th row As 2nd.
These 4 rows form the pattern.

CABLES
Basic stitches

Cable patterns, using variations of stitches, are among the most popular in knitting, since they are easy to work and give an interesting fabric with many uses – they can be thick and bulky for a sports sweater, or fine and lacy for baby garments. Twisting the cables in opposite directions can produce an all-over fabric, or simple panels of cables against the purl side of stockinette stitch can give a special look to the most basic garment. All cable patterns are based on the method of moving a sequence of stitches from one position to another in a row, giving the effect of the twists you see in a rope – the more stitches moved, the thicker the rope.

The previous chapter dealt with the method of crossing two or three stitches to give a twisted effect, but when altering the position of more than two stitches it is easier to do so by means of a third needle, which is used to hold the stitches being moved until they are ready to be worked. For this purpose a special cable needle is the best, although any short, double pointed needle will do. Cable needles are very short and easy to handle and are made in the same sizes as knitting needles. If the cable needle is not the same thickness as the needles being used for the garment, then it should be finer, not thicker. A thicker needle is more difficult to use and, more important, it will stretch the stitches and spoil the appearance of the finished work.

Cable abbreviations
Although working instructions and abbreviations will usually be found in detail in any cable pattern before you begin to knit, it would be as well to study these, as they do vary considerably. As a general guide, the letter 'C' stands for the word 'cable', followed by the number of stitches to be cabled, then the letter 'B' for back, or 'F' for front, indicating the direction in which the stitches are to be moved. In this way a cable twist from right to left over 6 stitches is abbreviated as 'C6F' and a cable twist from left to right over 6 stitches is abbreviated as 'C6B'.

Cable twist from right to left
This is a simple cable worked over 6 knitted stitches against a purl background. To work this sample cast on 24 stitches.
1st row (RS) P9, K6, P9.
2nd row K9, P6, K9.
Rep 1st and 2nd rows twice more.
7th row P9, sl next 3 sts on to cable needle and hold at front of work, K next 3 sts from left hand needle then K3 sts from cable needle – called C6F –, P9.

8th row As 2nd.
These 8 rows form the pattern. Repeat pattern rows twice more. Bind off.

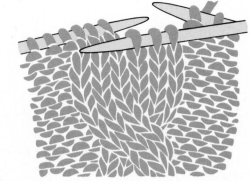

This sample produces a rope-like pattern in the center, consisting of 6 knitted stitches twisted 3 times. Each twist lies in the same direction from the right to the left.

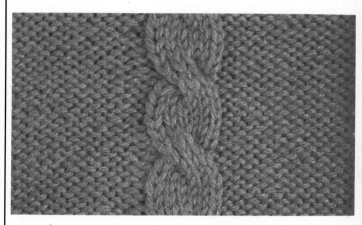

Cable twist from left to right
Cast on and work the first 6 rows as for cable twist from right to left.

7th row P9, sl next 3 sts on to cable needle and hold at back of work, K next 3 sts from left hand needle then K3 sts from cable needle – called C6B –, P9.

8th row As 2nd.

These 8 rows form the pattern. Repeat pattern rows twice more. Bind off.

This sample will be similar to the first, but each twist will lie in the opposite direction from the left to the right.

Cable twist from right to left with row variations

The appearance of each cable twist is altered considerably by the number of rows worked between each twist. Cast on and work the first 4 rows as for cable twist from right to left.

5th row P9, C6F, P9.

6th row As 2nd.

Rep 1st and 2nd rows twice more, then 5th and 6th rows once more.

Rep 1st and 2nd rows 4 times more, then 5th and 6th rows once more.

Rep 1st and 2nd rows 6 times more, then 5th and 6th rows once more.

Rep 1st and 2nd rows once more. Bind off.

This sample shows that the cable twist on every 4th row gives a very close, tight, rope look, whereas twisting on every 8th or 12th row gives a much softer look.

Alternating cables

This combines both the cable twist from right to left and cable twist from left to right, to produce a fabric with a completely different look although the methods used are exactly the same. Cast on and work the first 8 rows as for cable twist from right to left.

9th row As 1st.

10th row As 2nd.

Rep 9th and 10th rows twice more.

15th row P9, C6B, P9.

16th row As 10th.

Rep 9th and 10th rows twice more. Bind off.

This sample shows the same 3 stitches being moved on each twist.

Panels of cable twist from right to left

This pattern is made up of panels of 4 knitted stitches, with one purl stitch between each panel, twisted from right to left on different rows to give a diagonal appearance. Cast on 31 stitches.

1st row P1, *K4, P1, rep from * to end.

2nd row K1, *P4, K1, rep from * to end.

3rd row P1, *K4, P1, sl next 2 sts on to cable needle and hold at front of work, K next 2 sts from left hand needle then K2 sts from cable needle – called C4F –, P1, rep from * to end.

4th row As 2nd.

Rep 1st and 2nd rows once more.

7th row P1, *C4F, P1, K4, P1, rep from * to end.

8th row As 2nd.

These 8 rows form the pattern. Repeat pattern rows 3 times more. Bind off.

More cable stitches

By using combinations of the simple cable twists given in the previous chapter, you can produce numerous patterns. All of the variations given here can be worked as all over patterns or as separate panels against a purl background.

Try incorporating single plaited cable as an all over pattern on a plain sweater design, or use a panel of link cables to highlight the front and center of the sleeves on a basic cardigan. Another simple alternative would be to work two samples of honeycomb cable and use these as patch pockets on a stockinette stitch cardigan, using the reverse side, or purl side, as the right side of the cardigan fabric.

Link cable

The cable pattern is worked on 12 knitted stitches against a purl background. For this sample cast on 24 stitches.

1st row P6, K12, P6.
2nd row K6, P12, K6.
Rep 1st and 2nd rows twice more.
7th row P6, sl next 3 sts on to cable needle and hold at back of work, K next 3 sts from left hand needle then K3 sts from cable needle – called C6B –, sl next 3 sts on to cable needle and hold at front of work, K next 3 sts from left hand needle then K3 sts from cable needle – called C6F –, P6.
8th row As 2nd.
These 8 rows form the pattern. Repeat pattern rows twice more. Bind off.
This pattern gives the appearance of chain links, each link coming up out of the one below.

Inverted link cable

Cast on and work the first 6 rows as for link cable given above.
7th row P6, C6F, C6B, P6.
8th row As 2nd.
These 8 rows form the pattern. Repeat pattern rows twice more. Bind off.
This pattern has the reverse appearance of link cables with each link joining and passing under the link above.

Honeycomb cable

This pattern combines the working methods of link cable and inverted link cable. For this sample cast on 24 stitches.
1st row P6, K12, P6.
2nd row K6, P12, K6.
Rep 1st and 2nd rows once more.

5th row P6, C6B, C6F, P6.
6th row As 2nd.
Rep 1st and 2nd rows twice more.
11th row P6, C6F, C6B, P6.
12th row As 2nd.
These 12 rows form the pattern. Repeat pattern rows twice more. Bind off.
This pattern forms a cable which appears to be superimposed on the fabric beneath.

Single plaited cable
This pattern is achieved by dividing the groups of stitches which are to be cabled into three sections instead of two and cabling each group alternately. For this sample cast on 30 stitches.
1st row P3, *K6, P3, rep from * to end.
2nd row K3, *P6, K3, rep from * to end.
3rd row P3, *sl next 2 sts on to cable needle and hold at back of work, K next 2 sts from left hand needle then K2 from cable needle – called C4B –, K2, P3, rep from * to end.
4th row As 2nd.
5th row P3, *K2, sl next 2 sts on to cable needle and hold at front of work, K next 2 sts from left hand needle then K2 from cable needle – called C4F –, P3, rep from * to end.
6th row As 2nd.
The 3rd through 6th rows from the pattern. Repeat pattern rows 6 times more. Bind off.

Double plaited cable
This pattern is even more textured than single plaited cable and is worked over 18 knitted stitches against a purl background. For this sample cast on 30 stitches.
1st row P6, K18, P6.
2nd row K6, P18, K6.
3rd row P6, (C6B) 3 times, P6.
4th row As 2nd.
Rep 1st and 2nd rows once more.

7th row P6, K3, (C6F) twice, K3, P6.
8th row As 2nd.
These 8 rows form the pattern. Repeat pattern rows twice more. Bind off.

Cable waves
Cable patterns have a completely different appearance when the stitches being moved are worked in knitting against a knitted background, instead of a purl fabric. For this sample cast on 24 stitches.
1st row K to end.
2nd and every alt row P to end.
3rd row *C6F, K6, rep from * to end.
5th row K to end.
7th row *K6, C6B, rep from * to end.
9th row K to end.
10th row As 2nd.
Rows 3 through 10 form the pattern. Repeat pattern rows twice more. Bind off.

Cables in rounds

Cable patterns are just as easy to work in rounds as in rows. Unless the pattern states otherwise, the cable twists are worked on the right side of the fabric and as the right side of the work is always facing you when you knit in rounds, it is a simple matter to use either of these techniques.

This jaunty little hat has been specially designed so that the cable panels can be worked in any one of three variations. This will help you master the method of working cable stitches – while you are making yourself a snug, warm, fashionable accessory!

Size
To fit an average head

Gauge
22 sts and 30 rows to 4in in stockinette stitch (st st) worked on No.8 needles

Materials
1 × 4oz skein of any 4 ply Knitting Worsted Yarn
Set of 4 No.6 double-pointed needles
Set of 4 No.8 double-pointed needles
Cable needle

Hat
Using set of 4 No.6 needles cast on 96 sts and divide on 3 needles.
1st round *P2, K2, rep from * to end.
Rep this round for 4in to form turned back cuff.
Change to set of 4 No.8 needles. Start patt.

Cable patt 1
1st round *P2, K6, rep from * to end.
2nd round As 1st.
3rd round As 1st.
4th round *P2, sl next 3 sts on to cable needle and hold at front of work, K next 3 sts from left hand needle then K3 from cable needle – called C6F –, rep from * to end.
These 4 rounds form the patt.

Cable patt 2
1st round *P2, K6, rep from * to end.
2nd round As 1st.
3rd round As 1st.
4th round *P2, sl next 3 sts on to cable needle and hold at front of work, K next 3 sts from left hand needle then K3 from cable needle – called C6F –, rep from * to end.
5th round As 1st.
6th round As 1st.
7th round As 1st.
8th round *P2, sl next 3 sts on to cable needle and hold at back of work, K next 3 sts from left hand needle then K3 from cable needle – called C6B –, rep from * to end.
These 8 rounds form the patt.

Cable patt 3

1st round *P2, K6, rep from * to end.
2nd round As 1st.
3rd round As 1st.
4th round *P2, sl next 2 sts on to cable needle and hold at back of work, K next 2 sts from left hand needle then K2 from cable needle – called C4B –, K2, rep from * to end.
5th round As 1st.
6th round As 1st.
7th round As 1st.
8th round *P2, K2, sl next 2 sts on to cable needle and hold at front of work, K next 2 sts from left hand needle then K2 from cable needle – called C4F –, rep from * to end.
These 8 rounds form the patt.
Cont in patt until work measures 8in from beg of patt, ending with a 4th or 8th patt round.
Shape top
Next round (dec round) *P2, sl 1, K1, psso, K2, K2 tog, rep from * to end. 72 sts.
Next round *P2, K4, rep from * to end.
Next round *P2, sl 1, K1, psso, K2 tog, rep from * to end. 48 sts.
Next round *P2, K2, rep from * to end.
Next round *P2 tog, K2 tog, rep from * to end. 24 sts.
Next round *P1, K1, rep from * to end.
Next round *Sl 1, K1, psso, rep from * to end. 12 sts.
Break off yarn, thread through rem sts, draw up and fasten off.

Finishing
Blocking on WS is necessary. Omit the ribbing and take care not to flatten the patt. Turn RS out.
Fold cuff in half to outside, then fold back again to form a double cuff.

Cable panels

Panels of cable stitches are a most effective way of highlighting even the most basic pullover or cardigan design. They can be incorporated as separate bands spaced between panels of purl background stitches to form an all over sweater fabric, or a single panel of cable stitches can be used as a border inside the ribbed front bands of a cardigan. Worked lengthwise, they can be used as separate bands which can be sewn onto the lower edge or sleeves of a sweater, or as a headband on a snug little cap, as shown here.

Seeded cable
Cast on 12 stitches.
1st row (WS) K4, P4, K4.
2nd row P4, K4, P4.
3rd row K4, P1, sl next 2 sts keeping yarn at front of work, P1, K4.
4th row P2, sl next 3 sts on to cable needle and hold at back of work, K1 then K1, P1, K1 from cable needle, sl next st on to cable needle and hold at front of work, K1, P1, K1 then K1 from cable needle, P2.
5th row K2, (P1, K1) 3 times, P2, K2.
6th row P2, (K1, P1) 3 times, K2, P2.
Rep 5th and 6th rows twice more.
11th row K2, yfwd, sl 1 keeping yarn at front of work, ybk, (K1, P1) 3 times, sl 1 keeping yarn at front of work, ybk, K2.
12th row P2, sl next st on to cable needle and hold at front of work, P2, K1 then K1 from cable needle, sl next 3 sts on to cable needle and hold at back of work, K1, then K1, P2 from cable needle, P2.
Rep 1st and 2nd rows twice more.
These 16 rows form the pattern.

Round linked cable
Cast on 12 sts.
1st row (WS) K2, yfwd, sl 1 keeping yarn at front of work, P6, sl 1 keeping yarn at front of work, ybk, K2.
2nd row P2, sl next st on to cable needle and hold at front of work, P3 then K1 from cable needle, sl next 3 sts on to cable needle and hold at back of work, K1 then P3 from cable needle, P2.

3rd row K5, P2, K5.
4th row P2, sl next 3 sts on to cable needle and hold at back of work, K1 then K3 from cable needle, sl next st on to cable needle and hold at front of work, K3 then K1 from cable needle, P2.
5th row K2, P8, K2.
6th row P2, K8, P2.
Rep 5th and 6th rows twice more.
These 10 rows form the pattern.

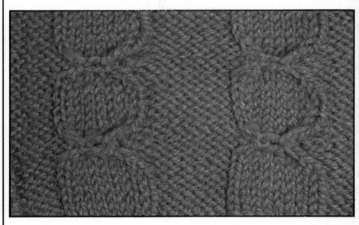

Wishbone cable
Cast on 12 sts.
1st row (RS) P2, sl next 3 sts on to cable needle and hold at back of work, K1 then P1, K1, P1 from cable needle, sl next st on to cable needle and hold at front of work, K1, P1, K1 then K1 from cable needle, P2.
2nd row K2, (P1, K1) 3 times, P2, K2.
3rd row P2, (K1, P1) 3 times, K2, P2.
Rep 2nd and 3rd rows once more.
6th row As 2nd.
7th row P2, K1, P1, K3, P1, K2, P2.
8th row K2, P1, K1, P3, K1, P2, K2.
These 8 rows form the pattern.

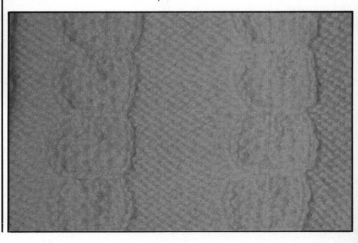

Cross cable

Cast on 12 sts.
1st row (RS) P3, K6, P3.
2nd row K3, P6, K3.
Rep 1st and 2nd rows twice more.
7th row P3, sl next 3 sts on to cable needle and hold at back of work, K3 then K3 from cable needle, P3.
8th row As 2nd.
9th row As 1st.
Rep 8th and 9th rows once more, then 8th row once more.
13th row P5, K2, P5.
14th row K5, P2, K5.
Rep 13th and 14th rows 3 times more.
These 20 rows form the pattern.

Diagonal link cable

Cast on 12 sts.
1st and every alt row (WS) K2, P8, K2.
2nd row P2, K2, sl next 2 sts on to cable needle and hold at front of work, K2 then K2 from cable needle, K2, P2.
4th row P2, K8, P2.
6th row As 2nd.
8th row As 4th.
10th row As 6th.
12th row P2, K2, K2 tog, sl 1, K1, psso, K2, P2.
13th row (WS) K2, P6, K2.
14th row P2, K1, sl 1, K1, psso, K2 tog, K1, K2.
15th row K2, P4, K2.
16th row P2, sl next 2 sts on to cable needle and hold at back of work, K2 then K2 from cable needle, P2.
17th row As 15th.
18th row P2, K1, pick up loop lying between needles and K tbl – called M1 –, K2, M1, K1, P2.
19th row As 13th.
20th row P2, (K2, M1) twice, K2, P2.
These 20 rows form the pattern.

Pull-on cap
Size
To fit an average adult head

Gauge
24 sts and 32 rows to 4in in stockinette st (st st) worked on No.5 needles

Materials
1 × 4oz ball of any Knitting Worsted
One pair No.5 needles
Cable needle

Cap
Using No.5 needles cast on 96 sts. Beg with a P row work in reverse st st until piece measures $4\frac{1}{2}$in from beg, ending with a P row.
Shape top
Next row *K2 tog, K6, rep from * to end. 84 sts.
Next row P to end.
Next row *K2 tog, K5, rep from * to end. 72 sts.
Next row P to end.
Cont dec 12 sts in this way on next and every alt row until 12 sts rem. Break off yarn, thread through rem sts, draw up and fasten off.

Headband
Using No.5 needles cast on 24 sts. Work any cable patt as desired.
1st row Patt 12 sts, K12.
2nd row P12, patt 12 sts.
Rep last 2 rows until band fits round lower edge of cap. Bind off.

Finishing
Block. With RS tog, sew patt edge of head-band to lower edge of cap. Join center back seam. Fold st st edge of headband in half to WS and sew in place.

Experiments with cable stitch

More about cable patterns! There are so many variations of cable stitches and the fabric formed is so effective that it is well worth experimenting to see how they can best be included as, for instance, part of a basic pullover or cardigan design.

As already suggested in the preceding chapters, the cable patterns do not need to be worked as an all-over fabric, but panels can be incorporated in many interesting ways. The patterns shown here required a given number of stitches to form one panel, but if you wish to work more than one panel side by side, intersperse each panel with a few extra stitches, to outline each pattern.

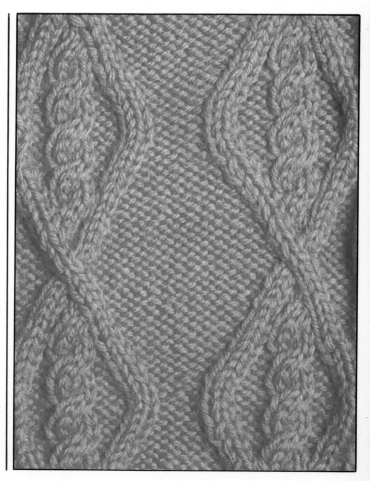

Diamond rope cable

This panel is worked on 18 stitches.

1st row (WS) K7, P4, K7.

2nd row P6, sl next st on to cable needle and hold at back of work, K2, then K1 from cable needle – called Cb3 –, sl next 2 sts on to cable needle and hold at front of work, K1, then K2 from cable needle – called Cf3 –, P6.

3rd and every alt row K all K sts and P all P sts.

4th row P5, Cb3, K2, Cf3, P5.

6th row P4, sl next st on to cable needle and hold at back of work, K2 then P1 from cable needle – called Bc3 –, sl next 2 sts on to cable needle and hold at back of work, K2 then K2 from cable needle – called Cb4 –, sl next 2 sts on to cable needle and hold at front of work, P1 then K2 from cable needle – called Fc3 –, P4.

8th row P3, Bc3, P1, K4, P1, Fc3, P3.
10th row P2, Bc3, P2, Cb4, P2, Fc3, P2.
12th row P1, Bc3, P3, K4, P3, Fc3, P1.
14th row P1, K2, P4, Cb4, P4, K2, P1.
16th row P1, Fc3, P3, K4, P3, Bc3, P1.
18th row P2, Fc3, P2, Cb4, P2, Bc3, P2.
20th row P3, Fc3, P1, K4, P1, Bc3, P3.
22nd row P4, Fc3, Cb4, Bc3, P4.
24th row P5, Fc3, K2, Bc3, P5.
26th row P6, Fc3, Bc3, P6.
28th row P7, sl next 2 sts on to cable needle and hold at front of work, K2 then K2 from cable needle, P7.
These 28 rows form the pattern.

Plaited braid cable
This panel is worked on 16 stitches.

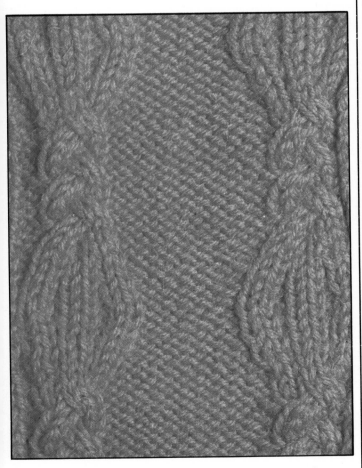

1st row (WS) K5, P6, K5.
2nd row P5, K2, sl next 2 sts on to cable needle and hold at back of work, K2 then K2 from cable needle – called Cb4 –, P5.
3rd and every alt row K all K sts and P all P sts.
4th row P5, sl next 2 sts on to cable needle and hold at front of work, K2 then K2 from cable needle – called Cf4 –, K2, P5.
6th row As 2nd.
8th row As 4th.
10th row As 2nd.
12th row As 4th.

14th row P4, sl next st on to cable needle and hold at back of work, K2 then P1 from cable needle – called Bc3 –, K2, sl next 2 sts on to cable needle and hold at front of work, P1 then K2 from cable needle – called Fc3 –, P4.
16th row P3, Bc3, P1, K2, P1, Fc3, P3.
18th row P2, Bc3, P2, K2, P2, Fc3, P2.
20th row P2, Fc3, P2, K2, P2, Bc3, P2.
22nd row P3, Fc3, P1, K2, P1, Bc3, P3.
24th row P4, Fc3, K2, Bc3, P4.
These 24 rows form the pattern.

Outlined cable
This panel is worked on 18 stitches.

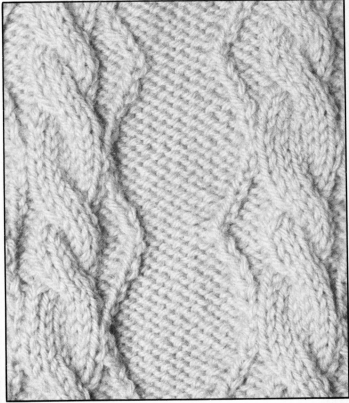

1st row (WS) K5, P8, K5.
2nd row P4, sl next st on to cable needle and hold at back of work, K1 tbl then P1 from cable needle – called Cb2 –, K6, sl next st on to cable needle and hold at front of work, P1 then K1 tbl from cable needle – called Cf2 –, P4.
3rd and every alt row K all K sts and P all P sts.
4th row P3, Cb2, P1, K6, P1, Cf2, P3.
6th row P2, Cb2, P2, sl next 3 sts on to cable needle and hold at front of work, K3 then K3 from cable needle – called Cf6 –, P2, Cf2, P2.
8th row P1, Cb2, P3, K6, P3, Cf2, P1.
10th row P1, Cf2, P3, K6, P3, Cb2, P1.
12th row P2, Cf2, P2, Cf6, P2, Cb2, P2.
14th row P3, Cf2, P1, K6, P1, Cb2, P3.
16th row P4, Cf2, K6, Cb2, P4.
These 16 rows form the pattern.

ARAN KNITTING
Basic stitches

The skilful and imaginative use of such patterns as cables, bobbles and crossed stitches form the basis for a range of intricate and thickly textured fabrics referred to as 'Aran' patterns. Most of the traditional stitches, with their highly evocative names, were originated in the remote Aran islands and derived their inspiration from the daily life of the islanders. The rocks are depicted by chunky bobble stitches, the cliff paths by zig-zag patterns, while the fishermen's ropes inspire a vast number of cable variations. The wealth of the sea around the islands and religious symbols and the ups and downs of married life all play a part in the formation of a rich tapestry of patterns unique in knitting.

The Irish name for the thick, homespun yarn used for Aran knitting is 'bainin', which literally means 'natural'. The traditional stitches are shown to their best advantage in this light-colored natural yarn, although many vivid colors are now used with them, to make fashion garments.

Practice the samples given here, using a knitting worsted yarn and No.5 needles to form separate squares or panels, which can then be joined together to form throw pillows, afghans or even bedspreads.

Ladder of life

This simple design depicts man's eternal desire to climb upwards, the purl ridges forming the rungs of the ladder. Cast on a number of stitches divisible by 6 plus 1.

1st row (RS) P1, *K5, P1, rep from * to end.
2nd row K1, *P5, K1, rep from * to end.
3rd row P to end.
4th row As 2nd.
These 4 rows form the pattern.

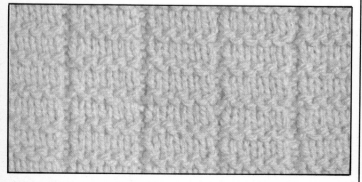

Lobster claw stitch

This represents the bounty of the sea. Cast on a number of stitches divisible by 9.

1st row (RS) *P1, K7, P1, rep from * to end.
2nd row *K1, P7, K1, rep from * to end.
3rd row *P1, sl next 2 sts on to cable needle and hold at back of work, K1 from left hand needle then K2 from cable needle, K1 from left hand needle, sl next st on to cable needle and hold at front of work, K2 from left hand needle, then K1 from cable needle, P1, rep from * to end.
4th row As 2nd.
These 4 rows form the pattern.

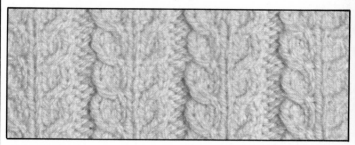

Tree of life

Narrow lines of traveling stitches branching out from a central stem form the basis for this traditional pattern. Cast on a number of stitches divisible by 15.

1st row (RS) *P7, K1, P7, rep from * to end.
2nd row *K7, P1, K7, rep from * to end.
3rd row *P5, sl next st on to cable needle and hold at back of work, K1 from left hand needle then P1 from cable needle – called C2B –, K1 from left hand needle, sl next st on to cable needle and hold at front of work, P1 from left hand needle, then K1 from cable needle – called C2F –, P5, rep from * to end.
4th row *K5, sl 1 P-wise keeping yarn at front of work, K1, P1, K1, sl 1, K5, rep from * to end.
5th row *P4, C2B, P1, K1, P1, C2F, P4, rep from * to end.
6th row *K4, sl 1, K2, P1, K2, sl 1, K4, rep from * to end.
7th row *P3, C2B, P2, K1, P2, C2F, P3, rep from * to end.
8th row *K3, sl 1, K3, P1, K3, sl 1, K3, rep from * to end.

9th row *P2, C2B, P3, K1, P3, C2F, P2, rep from * to end.
10th row *K2, sl 1, K4, P1, K4, sl 1, K2, rep from * to end.
These 10 rows form the pattern.

Aran plaited cable
This simple cable depicts the interweaving of family life. Cast on a number of stitches divisible by 12.
1st row (WS) *K2, P8, K2, rep from * to end.
2nd row *P2, (sl next 2 sts on to cable needle and hold at back of work, K2 from left hand needle then K2 from cable needle) twice, P2, rep from * to end.
3rd row As 1st.
4th row *P2, K2, sl next 2 sts on to cable needle and hold at front of work, K2 from left hand needle then K2 from cable needle, K2, P2, rep from * to end.
These 4 rows form the pattern.

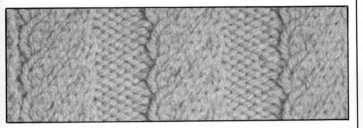

Aran diamond and bobble cable
The small diamond outlined with knitted stitches represents the small walled fields of Ireland and the bobble depicts the stony nature of the ground. Cast on a number of stitches divisible by 17.
1st row (WS) *K6, P2, K1, P2, K6, rep from * to end.
2nd row *P6, sl next 3 sts on to cable needle and hold at back of work, K2 from left hand needle, sl P1 from end of cable needle back on to left hand needle and P1 then K2 from cable needle, P6, rep from * to end.
3rd row As 1st.
4th row *P5, sl next st on to cable needle and hold at back of work, K2 from left hand needle then P1 from cable needle – called C3B –, K1, sl next 2 sts on to cable needle and hold at front of work, P1 from left hand needle then K2 from cable needle – called C3F –, P5, rep from * to end.
5th and every alt row K all K sts and P all P sts.
6th row *P4, C3B, K1, P1, K1, C3F, P4, rep from * to end.

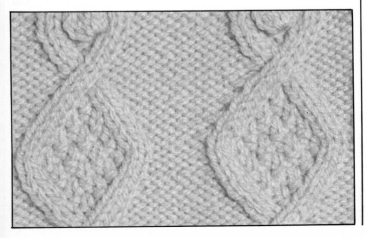

8th row *P3, C3B, (K1, P1) twice, K1, C3F, P3, rep from * to end.
10th row *P2, C3B, (K1, P1) 3 times, K1, C3F, P2, rep from * to end.
12th row *P2, C3F, (P1, K1) 3 times, P1, C3B, P2, rep from * to end.
14th row *P3, C3F, (P1, K1) twice, P1, C3B, P3, rep from * to end.
16th row *P4, C3F, P1, K1, P1, C3B, P4, rep from * to end.
18th row *P5, C3F, P1, C3B, P5, rep from * to end.
20th row As 2nd.
22nd row *P5, C3B, P1, C3F, P5, rep from * to end.
24th row *P4, C3B, P3, C3F, P4, rep from * to end.
26th row *P4, K2, P2, (K1, yfwd to make one st, K1, yfwd, K1) all into next st, turn and P5, turn and K5, turn and P2 tog, P1, P2 tog, turn and sl 1, K2 tog, psso – called B1 –, P2, K2, P4, rep from * to end.
28th row *P4, C3F, P3, C3B, P4, rep from * to end.
30th row As 18th.
These 30 rows form the pattern.

Shoulder bag
Size
12in wide by 12in deep

Gauge
24 sts and 32 rows to 4in in stockinette stitch (st st) worked on No.5 needles

Materials
2 × 4oz balls of any Knitting Worsted
One pair of No.5 needles

Bag
Using No.5 needles cast on 85 sts. Work in Aran diamond and bobble cable patt. Rep 30 patt rows 6 times in all, then first 20 rows once more. Bind off.

Finishing
Fold work in half with RS facing. Join side seams and turns RS out. Turn under ½in hem around top edge and sew in place. Make a braid approx 60in long, leaving a tassel at each end. Sew braid to side seams above tassels, leaving remainder of braid free for strap.

Aran patterns

Aran panels

The variety and complexity of Aran stitches which may be formed give such scope for textured patterns that it is sometimes difficult to know where to begin a design and how best to combine these stitches to produce the most effective fabric. If each stitch is run on into the next, all definition will be lost and none of the stitches will show to their best advantage. Because these stitches nearly always have a raised texture, their beauty is enhanced if they are worked against a purled background. Similarly, if each panel of stitches is enclosed with a rope of twisted stitches and alternated with panels of either purl or moss stitches, each separate Aran panel stands out without detracting in any way from the next panel. The poncho design given here uses these techniques to full effect. It is made from two simple pieces and the size can easily be adjusted by changing the number of stitches in each purl panel.

Poncho
Size
Approx 35in square, without fringe

Gauge
18 sts and 24 rows to 4in in stockinette stitch (st st) worked on No.6 needles

Materials
17 × 2oz balls Bernat Blarney-Spun
One pair No.6 needles
One pair No.5 needles
Set of 4 No.4 double-pointed needles
One No.6 circular needle
One No.5 circular needle
One cable needle

First piece
Using No.5 circular needle cast on 146 sts. K4 rows garter st.
Next row (inc row) K3, pick up loop lying between needles and P tbl – called M1 –, K2, M1, *(K2, M1) twice, (K2, K into front and back of next st – called Kfb –) twice, K3, (M1, K2) twice, *, **(M1, K2) twice, (P1, M1, P1, P into front and back of next st – called Pfb –, P1, M1, P1, K2) twice, M1, K2, M1, **, ***K2, Pfb, K2, Kfb, K3, Pfb, K1, Pfb, K2, Kfb, K3, Pfb, K2, ***, rep from ** to **, then from *** to ***, then from ** to ** again, then rep from * to * once more, M1, K2, M1, K3. 204 sts.
Change to No.6 circular needle. Commence patt.
1st row K2, P1, K1 tbl, P2, K1 tbl, *P2, sl next st on to cable needle and hold at front of work, P1, then K1 tbl from cable needle – called T2L –, P1, T2L, P9, sl next st on to cable needle and hold at back of work, K1 tbl, then P1 from cable needle – called T2R –, P1, T2R, P2, *, K1 tbl, P2, K1 tbl, **(P2, K8) twice, P2, K1 tbl, P2, K1 tbl, P2, K2, P3, into next st (K1, (yfwd, K1) twice, turn, P these 5 sts, turn, K5, turn, P5, turn, sl 2nd, 3rd and 4th sts over first st, then K first and last st tog tbl – called MB –) P3, sl next 3 sts on to cable needle and hold at back of work, K2, sl P st from cable needle onto left hand needle and hold cable needle at front of work, P1 from left hand needle, then K2 from cable needle – called Cr5 –, P3, MB, P3, K2, P2, K1 tbl, P2, K1 tbl, **, rep from ** to ** once more, (P2, K8) twice, P2, K1 tbl, P2, K1 tbl, rep from * to * once more, K1 tbl, P2, K1 tbl, P1, K2.
2nd row K3, *P1 tbl, K2, P1 tbl, K3, P1 tbl, K2, P1 tbl, K9, P1 tbl, K2, P1 tbl, K3, *, P1 tbl, K2, P1 tbl, **(K2, P8) twice, K2, P1 tbl, K2, P1 tbl, K2, (P2, K7, P2, K1) twice, K1, P1 tbl, K2, P1 tbl, **, rep from ** to ** once more, (K2, P8) twice, K2, rep from * to * once more, P1 tbl, K2, P1 tbl, K3.
3rd row K2, P1, *K1 tbl, P2, K1 tbl, P3, T2L, P1, T2L, P7, T2R, P1, T2R, P3, *, K1 tbl, P2, K1 tbl, **(P2, sl next 2 sts on to cable needle and hold at back of work, K2, then K2 from cable needle – called C4B –, sl next 2 sts on to cable needle and hold at front of work, K2, then K2 from cable needle – called C4F –) twice, P2, K1 tbl, P2, K1 tbl, P2, (sl next 2 sts on to cable needle and hold at front of work, P1, then K2 from cable needle – called C3L –, P5, sl next st on to cable needle and hold at back of work, K2, then P1 from cable needle – called C3R –, P1) twice, P1, K1 tbl, P2, K1 tbl, **, rep from ** to ** once more, (P2, C4B, C4F) twice, P2, rep from * to * once more, K1 tbl, P2, K1 tbl, P1, K2.
4th row K3, P1 tbl, K2, *P1 tbl, K4, P1 tbl, K2, P1 tbl, K7, P1 tbl, K2, P1 tbl, K4, *, P1 tbl, K2, P1 tbl, **(K2, P8) twice, K2, P1 tbl, K2, P1 tbl, (K3, P2, K5, P2) twice, K3, P1 tbl, K2, P1 tbl, **, rep from ** to ** once more, (K2, P8) twice, K2, P1 tbl, K2, rep from * to * once more, P1 tbl, K2, P1 tbl, K3.
5th row K2, P1, K1 tbl, *P2, K1 tbl, P4, T2L, P1, T2L, P5, T2R, P1, T2R, P4, *, K1 tbl, P2, K1 tbl, **(P2, K8) twice, P2, K1 tbl, P2, K1 tbl, (P3, C3L, P3, C3R) twice, P3, K1 tbl, P2, K1 tbl, **, rep from ** to ** once more, (P2, K8) twice, P2, K1 tbl, rep from * to * once more, K1 tbl, P2, K1 tbl, P1, K2.
6th row K3, *K2, P1 tbl, (K5, P1 tbl, K2, P1 tbl) twice, K5, *, P1 tbl, K2, P1 tbl, **(K2, P8) twice, K2, P1 tbl, K2, P1 tbl, K4, P2, K3, P2, K5, P2, K3, P2, K4, P1 tbl, K2, P1 tbl, **, rep from ** to ** once more, (K2, P8) twice, K2, P1 tbl, rep from * to * once more, P1 tbl, K2, P1 tbl, K3.

T2L, P1, T2L, P5, *, K1 tbl, P2, K1 tbl, **(P2, K8) twice, P2, K1 tbl, P2, K1 tbl, P5, Cr5, P3, MB, P3, Cr5, P5, K1 tbl, P2, K1 tbl, **, rep from ** to ** once more, (P2, K8) twice, P2, K1 tbl, rep from * to * once more, K1 tbl, P2, K1 tbl, P1, K2.

10th row K3, P1 tbl, *K2, P1 tbl, (K5, P1 tbl, K2, P1 tbl) twice, K5, *, P1 tbl, K2, P1 tbl, **(K2, P8) twice, K2, P1 tbl, K2, P1 tbl, K5, P2, K1, P2, K7, P2, K1, P2, K5, P1 tbl, K2, P1 tbl, **, rep from ** to ** once more, (K2, P8) twice, K2, P1 tbl, rep from * to * once more, P1 tbl, K2, P1 tbl, K3.

11th row K2, P1, K1 tbl, *P2, K1 tbl, P4, T2R, P1, T2R, P5, T2L, P1, T2L, P4, *, K1 tbl, P2, K1 tbl, **(P2, C4F, C4B) twice, P2, K1 tbl, P2, K1 tbl, P4, C3R, P1, C3L, P5, C3R, P1, C3L, P4, K1 tbl, P2, K1 tbl, **, rep from ** to ** once more, (P2, C4F, C4B) twice, P2, K1 tbl, rep from * to * once more, K1 tbl, P2, K1 tbl, P1, K2.

12th row K3, P1 tbl, *K2, P1 tbl, K4, P1 tbl, K2, P1 tbl, K7, P1 tbl, K2, P1 tbl, K4, *, P1 tbl, K2, P1 tbl, **(K2, P8) twice, K2, P1 tbl, K2, P1 tbl, K4, P2, K3, P2, K5, P2, K3, P2, K4, P1 tbl, K2, P1 tbl, **, rep from ** to ** once more, (K2, P8) twice, K2, P1 tbl, rep from * to * once more, P1 tbl, K2, P1 tbl, K3.

13th row K2, P1, K1 tbl, *P2, K1 tbl, P3, T2R, P1, T2R, P7, T2L, P1, T2L, P3, *, K1 tbl, P2, K1 tbl, **(P2, K8) twice, P2, K1 tbl, P2, K1 tbl, (P3, C3R, P3, C3L) twice, P3, K1 tbl, P2, K1 tbl, **, rep from ** to ** once more, (P2, K8) twice, P2, K1 tbl, rep from * to * once more, K1 tbl, P2, K1 tbl, P1, K2.

14th row K3, P1 tbl, *K2, P1 tbl, K3, P1 tbl, K2, P1 tbl, K9, P1 tbl, K2, P1 tbl, K3, *, P1 tbl, K2, P1 tbl, ** (K2, P8) twice, K2, P1 tbl, K2, P1 tbl, (K3, P2, K5) twice, K3, P1 tbl, K2, P1 tbl, **, rep from ** to ** once more, (K2, P8) twice, K2, P1 tbl, rep from * to * once more, P1 tbl, K2, P1 tbl, K3.

15th row K2, P1, K1 tbl, *P2, K1 tbl, P2, T2R, P1, T2R, P9, T2L, P1, T2L, P2, *, K1 tbl, P2, K1 tbl, **(P2, C4F, C4B) twice, P2, K1 tbl, P2, K1 tbl, P2, (C3R, P5, C3L, P1) twice, P1, K1 tbl, P2, K1 tbl, **, rep from ** to ** once more, (P2, C4F, C4B) twice, P2, K1 tbl, rep from * to * once more, K1 tbl, P2, K1 tbl, P1, K2.

16th row K3, P1 tbl, *K2, P1 tbl, (K2, P1 tbl) twice, K11, (P1 tbl, K2) twice, *, P1 tbl, K2, P1 tbl, **(K2, P8) twice, K2, P1 tbl, K2, P1 tbl, K2, (P2, K7, P2, K1) twice, K1, P1 tbl, K2, P1 tbl, **, rep from ** to ** once more, (K2, P8) twice, K2, P1 tbl, rep from * to * once more, P1 tbl, K2, P1 tbl, K3.

These 16 rows form the patt. Cont in patt until 8th row of 6th patt has been completed.

Shape neck
Next row Patt 93 sts, *(K2 tog, K1) twice, K2 tog, P2, (K2 tog, K1) twice, K2 tog, *, (P1, K2 tog) twice, ** P5, K2 tog, P1, K2 tog, (P1, P2 tog) twice, (P1, K2 tog) twice, P5, **, (K2 tog tbl, P1) twice, rep from * to * once more, (P1, K2 tog) twice, P2, P2 tog, (P1, K2 tog) twice, P3, (K2 tog tbl, P1) twice, P2 tog, P2, K2 tog tbl, P1, K2 tog tbl, K2. 172 sts.

Next row Bind off 79 sts, patt to end. 93 sts.

7th row K2, P1, K1 tbl, *P2, K1 tbl, P5, T2L, P1, T2L, P3, T2R, P1, T2R, P5, *, K1 tbl, P2, K1 tbl, **(P2, C4B, C4F) twice, P2, K1 tbl, P2, K1 tbl, P4, C3L, P1, C3R, P5, C3L, P1, C3R, P4, K1 tbl, P2, K1 tbl, **, rep from ** to ** once more, (P2, C4B, C4F) twice, P2, K1 tbl, rep from * to * once more, K1 tbl, P2, K1 tbl, P1, K2.

8th row K3, P1 tbl, *K2, P1 tbl, K6, P1 tbl, K2, P1 tbl, K3, P1 tbl, K2, P1 tbl, K6, *, P1 tbl, K2, P1 tbl, **(K2, P8) twice, K2, P1 tbl, K2, P1 tbl, K5, P2, K1, P2, K7, P2, K1, P2, K5, P1 tbl, K2, P1 tbl, **, rep from ** to ** once more, (K2, P8) twice, K2, P1 tbl, rep from * to * once more, P1 tbl, K2, P1 tbl, K3.

9th row K2, P1, K1 tbl, *P2, K1 tbl, P5, T2R, P1, T2R, P3,

135

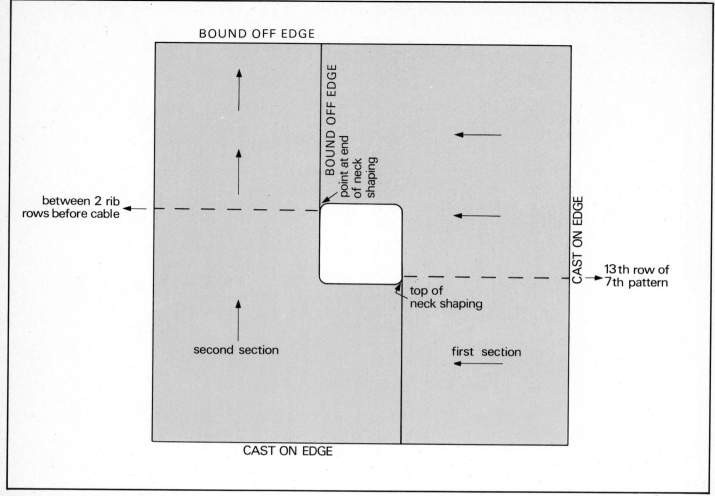

BOUND OFF EDGE

BOUND OFF EDGE

point at end of neck shaping

between 2 rib rows before cable

CAST ON EDGE

13th row of 7th pattern

top of neck shaping

second section

first section

CAST ON EDGE

Next row Patt to last 2 sts, P2 tog.
Maintaining patt, cont dec one st at beg of next and every foll alt row 5 times in all. Work 8 rows without shaping. Inc one st at end of next and every alt row 6 times in all. 93 sts.
Next row K2, K2 tog, P1, K2 tog, P2, P2 tog, (P1, K2 tog tbl) twice, P3 (K2 tog, P1) twice, P2 tog, P2, (K2 tog tbl, P1) twice, rep from * to * of 1st shaping row, (P1, K2 tog) twice, rep from ** to ** of 1st shaping row, patt to end. 69 sts.
Bind off loosely.

Second piece

Using No.5 needles cast on 83 sts. K 4 rows g st.
Next row (inc row) K3, M1, K2, M1, rep from * to * of inc row in first section, then from ** to ** in same row, then from *** to *** in same row, then from ** to ** again, omitting M1 at end of Row. 116 sts.
Change to No.6 needles. Start patt.
1st row K1, P1, K1 tbl, (P2, K8) twice, P2, K1 tbl, P2, K1 tbl, P2, K2, P3, MB, P3, Cr5, P3, MB, P3, K2, P2, K1 tbl, P2, K1 tbl, (P2, K8) twice, P2, K1 tbl, P2, K1 tbl, P2, T2L, P1, T2L, P9, T2R, P1, T2R, P2, K1 tbl, P2, K1 tbl, P1, K2.
2nd row K3, P1 tbl, K2, P1 tbl, patt as now set to last 3 sts, P1 tbl, K2.
Cont in patt as now set until 8th row of 6th patt has been completed.

Shape neck

1st row K1, P1, K1 tbl, P2, (K2 tog, K1) twice, K2 tog, P2, (K2 tog, K1) twice, K2 tog, patt to end.
2nd row Patt 93 sts and leave these sts on a holder, bind off 12 sts, patt to end. 5 sts.
Dec one st at neck edge on foll 3 alt rows. Bind off. With RS of work facing, rejoin yarn to rem sts at neck edge, cont in patt dec one st at neck edge on foll 3 alt rows. 90 sts. Cont without shaping until 13th patt rep has been completed. Change to No.5 needles.
Next row K2, (K2 tog, K2, K2 tog, K1) 12 times, K2 tog, K2. 65 sts.
K 3 rows g st. Bind off.

Finishing

Join both sections as shown in diagram, noting positions of top of neck shaping on second section and point at end of neck shaping on first section. Block seams on wrong side under a damp cloth with a warm iron.
Neckband Using set of 4 No.4 needles, pick up and K 104 sts all around neck edge. Work 5 rounds K1, P1 rib. Bind off in rib, working K2 tog at each corner.
Fringe Cut yarn into lengths of 10in. Using 3 strands folded in half, draw center of threads through edge of poncho and knot. Rep at $\frac{1}{2}$in intervals around entire outer edge.

Aran shaping

Aran shaping

Where each Aran panel is combined with alternate panels of purl or moss stitches, it is simple to make provision for any shaping.

Because Aran stitches are rather complex, it is not advisable to try to combine them with any increasing or decreasing and most designs take this into account. The number of stitches required, for example, for a raglan armhole and sleeve top shaping are carefully calculated to insure that the correct number of stitches are decreased in a plain panel, without interfering with the Aran panels.

The variety of Aran designs available is sometimes restricted by this problem of shaping. This can be overcome, however, by the skillful use of shaping in each alternate plain panel and by the careful choice of a basic stitch, such as garter stitch or ribbing, to complete the shaped sections. The lightweight camisole shell top shown here perfectly illustrates these techniques.

Camisole shell top
Sizes
Directions are to fit 32in bust. Changes for 34 and 36in bust are in brackets [].
Length to shoulder, 18[19$\frac{1}{4}$:20]in

Gauge
32 sts and 40 rows in 4in over reverse stockinette stitch (rev st st) worked on No.2 needles

Materials
3 × 2oz balls Brunswick Pomfret Sport Yarn
One pair No.2 needles
One No.2 circular needle
One No.1 circular needle
7 buttons

Camisole shell fronts and back
Using No.1 circular needle cast on 237[253:269] sts and work in one piece, beg at lower edge.
1st row K1, *P1, K1, rep from * to end.
2nd row P1, *K1, P1, rep from * to end.
Rep last 2 rows 3 times more, then 1st row once more.
Next row P to end.
Next row P to end to form hemline.
Base row Cast on 7 sts for right front band, turn, K8, *P2, K15, P2, K8[10:12], P2, K3, P1, K2, P1, K8, P2, K8 [10:12], rep from * 3 times more, P2, K15, P2, K1, turn and cast on 7 sts for left front band. 251[267:283] sts. Change to No.2 circular needle. Start patt.
1st row (RS) K7, P1, *K 2nd st on left hand needle, then first st − called T2 −, P7, K1, P7, T2, P8[10:12], T2, P7, K 2nd st on left hand needle, then P first st − called C2R −, P1, C2R, P3, T2, P8[10:12], T2, P2, K2, P7, K2, P2, T2, P8[10:12], T2, P7, C2R, P1, C2R, P3, T2, P8[10:12], rep from * once more, T2, P7, K1, P7, T2, P1, K7.
2nd row K8, *P2, K7, P1, K7, P2, K8[10:12], P2, K4, P1, K2, P1, K7, P2, K8[10:12], P2, K2, P3, K5, P3, K2, P2, K8[10:12], P2, K4, P1, K2, P1, K7, P2, K8[10:12], rep from * once more, P2, K7, P1, K7, P2, K8.
3rd row K7, P1, *T2, P6, K1, P1, K1, P6, T2, P8[10:12], T2, P6, C2R, P1, C2R, P4, T2, P8[10:12], T2, (P3, K3) twice, P3, T2, P8[10:12], T2, P6, C2R, P1, C2R, P4, T2, P8[10:12], rep from * once more, T2, P6, K1, P1, K1, P6, T2, P1, K7.
4th row K8, *P2, K6, P1, K1, P1, K6, P2, K8[10:12], P2, K5, P1, K2, P1, K6, P2, K8[10:12], P2, K4, P3, K1, P3, K4, P2, K8[10:12], P2, K5, P1, K2, P1, K6, P2, K8[10:12], rep from * once more, P2, K6, P1, K1, P1, K6, P2, K8.
5th row (buttonhole row) K2, K2 tog, (yrn) twice, sl 1, K1, psso, K1, P1, *T2, P5, (K1, P1) twice, K1, P5, T2, P8[10:12], T2, P5, C2R, P1, C2R, P5, T2, P8[10:12], T2, P5, K5, P5, T2, P8[10:12], T2, P5, C2R, P1, C2R, P5, T2, P8[10:12], rep from * once more, T2, P5, (K1, P1) twice, K1, P5, T2, P1, K7.
6th row K8, *P2, K5, (P1, K1) twice, P1, K5, P2, K8[10:12], P2, K6, P1, K2, P1, K5, P2, K8[10:12], P2, K6, P3, K6, P2, K8[10:12], P2, K6, P1, K2, P1, K5, P2, K8[10:12], rep from * once more, P2, K5, (P1, K1) twice, P1, K5, P2, K3, drop one loop of double loop to make long st and work K1, P1 into same st, K3.
Work 5 more buttonholes in same way with 18[20:22] rows between each buttonhole.
7th row K7, P1, *T2, P4, (K1, P1) 3 times, K1, P4, T2, P8[10:12], T2, P4, C2R, P1, C2R, P6, T2, P8[10:12], T2, P4, C2R, P1, C2R, P6, T2,

P8[10:12], rep from * once more, T2, P4, (K1, P1) 3 times, K1, P4, T2, P1, K7.
8th row K8, *P2, K4, (P1, K1) 3 times, P1, K4, P2, K8[10:12], P2, K7, P1, K2, P1, K4, P2, K8[10:12], P2, K4, P3, K1, P3, K4, P2, K8[10:12], P2, K7, P1, K2, P1, K4, P2, K8[10:12], rep from * once more, P2, K4, (P1, K1) 3 times, P1, K4, P2, K8.
9th row K7, P1, *T2, P3, (K1, P1) 4 times, K1, P3, T2, P8[10:12], T2, P3, C2R, P1, C2R, P7, T2, P8[10:12], T2, (P3, K3) twice, P3, T2, P8[10:12], T2, P3, C2R, P1, C2R, P7, T2, P8[10:12], rep from * once more, T2, P3, (K1, P1) 4 times, K1, P3, T2, P1, K7.
10th row K8, *P2, K3, (P1, K1) 4 times, P1, K3, P2, K8 [10:12], P2, K8, P1, K2, P1, K3, P2, K8[10:12], P2, K2, P3, K5, P3, K2, P2, K8[10:12], P2, K8, ·P1, K2, P1, K3, P2, K8[10:12], rep from * once more, P2, K3, (P1, K1) 4 times, P1, K3, P2, K8.
11th row K7, P1, *T2, P2, (K1, P1) 5 times, K1, P2, T2, P8[10:12], T2, P3, K1, P2, K1, P8, T2, P8[10:12], T2, P2, K2, P7, K2, P2, T2, P8[10:12], T2, P3, K1, P2, K1, P8, T2, P8[10:12], rep from * once more, T2, P2, (K1, P1) 5 times, K1, P2, T2, P1, K7.
12th row K8, *P2, K2, (P1, K1) 5 times, P1, K2, P2, K8 [10:12], P2, K8, P1, K2, P1, K3, P2, K8[10:12], P2, K15, P2, K8[10:12], P2, K8, P1, K2, P1, K3, P2, K8[10:12], rep from * once more, P2, K2, (P1, K1) 5 times, P1, K2, P2, K8.
13th row K7, P1, *T2, P3, (K1, P1) 4 times, K1, P3, T2, P8[10:12], T2, P3, P 2nd st on left hand needle, then K first st − called C2L −, P1, C2L, P7, T2, P8[10:12], T2, P6, K3, P6, T2, P8[10:12], T2, P3, C2L, P1, C2L, P7, T2, P8 [10:12], rep from * once more, T2, P3, (K1, P1) 4 times, K1, P3, T2, P1, K7.

Shape waist
14th row K8, *P2, K3, (P1, K1) 4 times, P1, K3, P2, sl 1, K1, psso, K4[6:8], K2 tog, P2, K7, P1, K2, P1, K4, P2, sl 1, K1, psso, K4[6:8], K2 tog, P2, K5, P5, K5, P2, sl 1, K1, psso, K4[6:8], K2 tog, P2, K7, P1, K2, P1, K4, P2, sl 1, K1, psso, K4[6:8], K2 tog, rep from * once more, P2, K3, (P1, K1) 4 times, P1, K3, P2, K8, 235[251:267] sts.
15th row K7, P1, *T2, P4, (K1, P1) 3 times, K1, P4, T2, P6[8:10], T2, P4, C2L, P1, C2L, P6, T2, P6[8:10], T2, P4, K3, P1, K3, P4, T2, P6[8:10], T2, P4, C2L, P1, C2L, P6, T2, P6[8:10], rep from * once more, T2, P4, (K1, P1) 3 times, K1, P4, T2, P1, K7.
16th row K8, *P2, K4, (P1, K1) 3 times, P1, K4, P2, K6[8:10], P2, K6, P1, K2, P1, K5, P2, K6[8:10], P2, (K3, P3) twice, K3, P2, K6[8:10], P2, K6, P1, K2, P1, K5, P2, K6[8:10], rep from * once more, P2, K4, (P1, K1) 3 times, P1, K4, P2, K8.
17th row K7, P1, *T2, P5, (K1, P1) twice, K1, P5, T2, P6 [8:10], T2, P5, C2L, P1, C2L, P5, T2, P6[8:10], T2, P2, K3, P5, K3, P2, T2, P6[8:10], T2, P5, C2L, P1, C2L, P5, T2, P6[8:10], rep from * once more, T2, P5, (K1, P1) twice, K1, P5, T2, P1, K7.
18th row K8, *P2, K5, (P1, K1) twice, P1, K5, P2, K6[8:10], P2, K5, P1, K2, P1, K6, P2, K6[8:10], P2, K2, P2, K7, P2, K2, P2, K6[8:10], P2, K5, P1, K2, P1, K6, P2, K6[8:10], rep from * once more, P2, K5, (P1, K1) twice, P1, K5, P2, K8.

19th row K7, P1, *T2, P6, K1, P1, K1, P6, T2, P6[8:10], T2, P6, C2L, P1, C2L, P4, T2, P6[8:10], T2, P2, K3, P5, K3, P2, T2, P6[8:10], T2, P6, C2L, P1, C2L, P4, T2, P6[8:10], rep from * once more, T2, P6, K1, P1, K1, P6, T2, P1, K7.

20th row K8, *P2, K6, P1, K1, P1, K6, P2, sl 1, K1, psso, K2[4:6], K2 tog, P2, K4, P1, K2, P1, K7, P2, sl 1, K1, psso, K2[4:6], K2 tog, P2, (K3, P3) twice, K3, P2, sl 1, K1, psso, K2[4:6], K2 tog, P2, K4, P1, K2, P1, K7, P2, sl 1, K1, psso, K2[4:6], K2 tog, rep from * once more, P2, K6, P1, K1, P1, K6, P2, K8. 219[235:251] sts.

21st row K7, P1, *T2, P7, K1, P7, T2, P4[6:8], T2, P7, C2L, P1, C2L, P3, T2, P4[6:8], T2, P4, K3, P1, K3, P4, T2, P4[6:8], T2, P7, C2L, P1, C2L, P3, T2, P4[6:8], rep from * once

more, T2, P7, K1, P7, T2, P1, K7.

22nd row K8, *P2, K7, P1, K7, P2, K4[6:8], P2, K3, P1, K2, P1, K8, P2, K4[6:8], P2, K5, P5, K5, P2, K4[6:8], P2, K3, P1, K2, P1, K8, P2, K4[6:8], rep from * once more, P2, K7, P1, K7, P2, K8.

23rd row K7, P1, *T2, P15, T2, P4[6:8], T2, P8, K1, P2, K1, P3, T2, P4[6:8], T2, P6, K3, P6, T2, P4[6:8], T2, P8, K1, P2, K1, P3, T2, P4[6:8], rep from * once more, T2, P15, T2, P1, K7.

24th row K8, *P2, K15, P2, K4[6:8], P2, K3, P1, K2, P1, K8, P2, K4[6:8], P2, K15, P2, K4[6:8], P2, K3, P1, K2, P1, K8, P2, K4[6:8], rep from * once more, P2, K15, P2, K8.
These 24 rows set patt for Aran panels with rev st st

between each one. Maintaining patt as now set, dec 2 sts as before within each rev st st panel on foll alt row. 203[219:235] sts. Cont in patt until work measures 4½[4¾:5]in from hemline, ending with a RS row.

Next row K8, *P2, patt 15, P2, pick up loop lying between needles and K tbl – called M1 –, K2[4:6], M1, rep from * 7 times more, P2, patt 15, P2, K8.
Maintaining patt, inc 2 sts as before within each rev st st panel on foll 20th row twice more. 251[267:283] sts. Maintain patt without shaping until piece measures 11[11½:12½]in from hemline, ending with a WS row.

Shape yoke
Next row K8, *K2 tog, K6, K2 tog, K7, K2 tog, K8[10:12], rep from * 7 times more, K2 tog, K6, K2 tog, K7, K2 tog, K8. 224[240:256] sts.
Beg with a K row, cont in g st until work measures 12[12½:13]in from hemline, ending with a WS row.

Divide for armholes
Change to No.2 straight needles.
Next row K55[58:61], turn and place rem sts on holder. Complete right front first.

Shape armhole
Bind off at beg of next and every foll alt row 2 sts 3 times and one st 3[4:5] times, *at the same time* work 7th buttonhole 18[20:22] rows above previous buttonhole. K 2 rows, ending at front edge.

Shape neck
Bind off at beg of next and every foll alt row 23[24:25] sts once, 4 sts once, 2 sts 3 times and one st 3 times. 10[11:12] sts. Cont without shaping until piece measures 18[19¼:20]in from hemline. Bind off.
With RS of work facing, rejoin yarn to back sts, bind off first 8[10:12] sts, K until there are 98[104:110] sts on right hand needle, turn and place rem sts on holder for left front. Complete back first.

Shape armholes
Bind off 2 sts at beg of next 5 rows.

Shape back neck
Next row Bind off 2, K until there are 26[28:30] sts on right hand needle, bind off 34[36:38] sts for neck, K to end.
Dec one st at armhole edge on every alt row 3[4:5] times in all, *at the same time* bind off at neck edge on every alt row 4 sts once, 2 sts 3 times and one st 3 times. 10[11:12] sts. Cont without shaping until piece measures 18[19¼:20]in from hemline. Bind off.
With WS of work facing, rejoin yarn to rem back sts and complete as for first side, reversing shaping. With RS of work facing, rejoin yarn to rem left front sts. Bind off 8[10:12] sts, K to end. 55[58:61] sts. Finish to correspond to right front, reversing shaping and omitting buttonhole.

Finishing
Block under a damp cloth with a warm iron. Join shoulder seams. Turn hem to WS at lower edge and sew in place. Block seams. Sew on buttons.

LACE STITCHES
Simple lace

Knitted lace stitches do not need to be complicated in order to produce openwork fabrics. Some of the most effective traditional patterns require only a few stitches and as little as two rows to form the pattern repeat.

The principle used for almost all lace stitches is that of decreasing one or more stitches at a given point in a row and compensating for these decreased stitches, either in the same row or a following row by working more than once into a stitch, or making one or more stitches by taking the yarn over or around the right hand needle the required number of times, as shown on page 25. Use a 3 ply yarn and No.3 needles to practice these simple lace stitches.

Laburnum stitch

Cast on a number of stitches divisible by 5 + 2.
1st row P2, *K3, P2, rep from * to end.
2nd row K2, *P3, K2, rep from * to end.
3rd row P2, *keeping yarn at front of work, sl 1, ybk, K2 tog, psso, bring yarn over top of needle from back to front then around needle again, P2, rep from * to end.
4th row K2, *P into the back of the first made st then into the front of the second made st, P1, K2, rep from * to end.
These 4 rows form the pattern.

Indian pillar stitch

Faggoting rib

Cast on a number of stitches divisible by 5 + 1.
1st row P1, *K2, yfwd, sl 1, K1, psso, P1, rep from * to end.
2nd row K1, *P2, yrn, P2 tog, K1, rep from * to end.
These 2 rows form the pattern.

Lace rib

Cast on a number of stitches divisible by 5 + 2.
1st row P2, *K1, yfwd, sl 1, K1, psso, P2, rep from * to end.
2nd row K2, *P3, K2, rep from * to end.
3rd row P2, *K2 tog, yfwd, K1, P2, rep from * to end.
4th row As 2nd.
These 4 rows form the pattern.

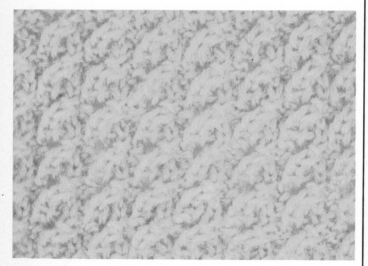

Indian pillar stitch

Cast on a number of stitches divisible by 4 + 3.
1st row (RS) P to end.
2nd row K2, *insert needle P-wise into the next 3 sts as if to P3 tog but instead work (P1, K1, P1) into these 3 sts, K1, rep from * to last st, K1.
These 2 rows form the pattern.

Eyelet cable rib

Cast on a number of stitches divisible by 5 + 2.

1st row P2, *K3, P2, rep from * to end.
2nd row K2, *P3, K2, rep from * to end.
3rd row P2, *sl 1, K2, psso the K2, P2, rep from * to end.
4th row K2, *P1, yrn, P1, K2, rep from * to end.
These 4 rows form the pattern.

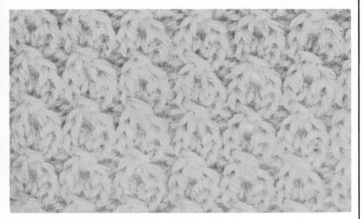

Cat's eye pattern

Cast on a number of stitches divisible by 4.

1st row K4, *yfwd over and round the needle again to make 2 sts, K4, rep from * to end.
2nd row P2, *P2 tog, P the first made st and K the second made st, P2 tog, rep from * to last 2 sts, P2.
3rd row K2, yfwd, *K4, yfwd over and around the needle again, rep from * to last 6sts, K4, yfwd, K2.
4th row P3, *(P2 tog) twice, P the first made st and K the second made st, rep from * to last 7 sts, (P2 tog) twice, P3.
These 4 rows form the pattern.

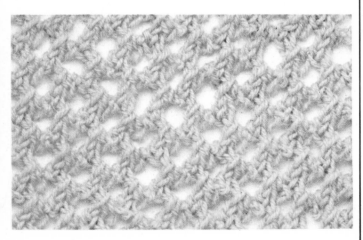

Open star stitch

Cast on a number of stitches divisible by 3.

1st row K2, *yfwd, K3 then pass the first of these 3 sts over the other 2 and off the right hand needle, rep from * to last st, K1.
2nd row P to end.
3rd row K1, *K3 then pass the first of these 3 sts over the other 2, yfwd, rep from * to last 2 sts, K2.
4th row P to end.
These 4 rows form the pattern.

Open star stitch

Hyacinth stitch

Cast on a number of stitches divisible by 6 + 3.

1st, 3rd and 5th rows P to end.
2nd row K1, *(K1, P1, K1, P1, K1) all into next st, K5 tog, rep from * to last 2 sts, (K1, P1, K1, P1, K1) into next st, K1.
4th row K1, *K5 tog, (K1, P1, K1, P1, K1) all into next st, rep from * to last 6 sts, K5 tog, K1.
6th row K to end winding yarn 3 times round right hand needle for each stitch.
7th row P to end dropping the extra loops.
Rows 2 through 7 form the pattern.

Diagonal openwork stitch

Cast on a number of stitches divisible by 2 + 1.

1st row K1, *yfwd, K2 tog, rep from * to end.
2nd row P to end.
3rd row K2, *yfwd, K2 tog, rep from * to last st, K1.
4th row P to end.
These 4 rows form the pattern.

More simple lace

This chapter gives more simple lace patterns which are easy to work and produce most effective fabrics. Use a 3 ply yarn and No.2 or No.3 needles to practice these stitches.

Lace diamond pattern
Cast on a number of stitches divisible by 6 + 1.
1st row P1, *K5, P1, rep from * to end.
2nd row K1, *P5, K1, rep from * to end.
3rd row P1, *yon, sl 1, K1, psso, K1, K2 tog, yrn, P1, rep from * to end.
4th row K1, *K into back of next st – called K1B –, P3, K1B, K1, rep from * to end.
5th row P2, *yon, sl 1, K2, psso the 2 sts, yrn, P3, rep from * to last 5 sts, yon, sl 1, K2, psso the 2 sts, yrn, P2.
6th row K2, *K1B, P2, K1B, K3, rep from * to last 6 sts, K1B, P2, K1B, K2.
7th row P2, *K2 tog, yfwd, sl 1, K1, psso, P3, rep from * to last 6 sts, K2 tog, yfwd, sl 1, K1, psso, P2.
8th row K1, *P2 tog tbl, yrn, P1, yrn, P2 tog, K1, rep from * to end.
These 8 rows form the pattern.

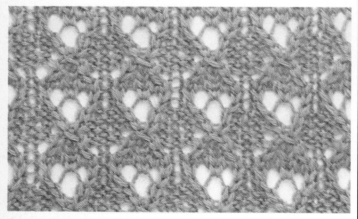

Embossed leaf pattern
Cast on a number of stitches divisible by 7.
1st row P to end.
2nd row K to end.
3rd row P3, *yon, K1, yrn, P6, rep from * to last 4 sts, yon, K1, yrn, P3.
4th row K3, *P3, K6, rep from * to last 6 sts, P3, K3.
5th row P3, *K1, (yfwd, K1) twice, P6, rep from * to last 6 sts, K1, (yfwd, K1) twice, P3.
6th row K3, *P5, K6, rep from * to last 8 sts, P5, K3.
7th row P3, *K2, yfwd, K1, yfwd, K2, P6, rep from * to last 8 sts, K2, yfwd, K1, yfwd, K2, P3.
8th row K3, *P7, K6, rep from * to last 10 sts, P7, K3.
9th row P3, *K3, yfwd, K1, yfwd, K3, P6, rep from * to last 10 sts, K3, yfwd, K1, yfwd, K3, P3.
10th row K3, *P9, K6, rep from * to last 12 sts, P9, K3.

11th row P3, *sl 1, K1, psso, K5, K2 tog, P6, rep from * to last 12 sts, sl 1, K1, psso, K5, K2 tog, P3.
12th row As 8th.
13th row P3, *sl 1, K1, psso, K3, K2 tog, P6, rep from * to last 10 sts, sl 1, K1, psso, K3, K2 tog, P3.
14th row As 6th.
15th row P3, *sl 1, K1, psso, K1, K2 tog, P6, rep from * to last 8 sts, sl 1, K1, psso, K1, K2 tog, P3.
16th row As 4th.
17th row P3, *sl 1, K2 tog, psso, P6, rep from * to last 6 sts, sl 1, K2 tog, psso, P3.
18th row As 2nd.
19th row As 1st.
20th row As 2nd.
These 20 rows form the pattern.

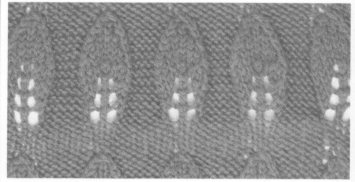

Snowdrop lace pattern
Cast on a number of stitches divisible by 8 + 3.
1st row K1, K2 tog, yfwd, *K5, yfwd, sl 1, K2 tog, psso, yfwd, rep from * to last 8 sts, K5, yfwd, sl 1, K1, psso, K1.
2nd and every alt row P to end.
3rd row As 1st.
5th row K3, *yfwd, sl 1, K1, psso, K1, K2 tog, yfwd, K3, rep from * to end.
7th row K1, K2 tog, yfwd, *K1, yfwd, sl 1, K2 tog, psso, yfwd, rep from * to last 4 sts, K1, yfwd, sl 1, K1, psso, K1.
8th row As 2nd.
These 8 rows form the pattern.

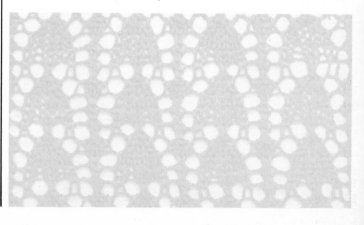

Falling leaf pattern

Cast on a number of stitches divisible by 10 + 1.

1st row K1, *yfwd, K3, sl 1, K2 tog, psso, K3, yfwd, K1, rep from * to end.

2nd and every alt row P to end.

3rd row K1, *K1, yfwd, K2, sl 1, K2 tog, psso, K2, yfwd, K2, rep from * to end.

5th row K1, *K2, yfwd, K1, sl 1, K2 tog, psso, K1, yfwd, K3, rep from * to end.

7th row K1, *K3, yfwd, sl 1, K2 tog, psso, yfwd, K4, rep from * to end.

9th row K2 tog, *K3, yfwd, K1, yfwd, K3, sl 1, K2 tog, psso, rep from * to last 9 sts, K3, yfwd, K1, yfwd, K3, sl 1, K1, psso.

11th row K2 tog, *K2, yfwd, K3, yfwd, K2, sl 1, K2 tog, psso, rep from * to last 9 sts, K2, yfwd, K3, yfwd, K2, sl 1, K1, psso.

13th row K2 tog, *K1, yfwd, K5, yfwd, K1, sl 1, K2 tog, psso, rep from * to last 9 sts, K1, yfwd, K5, yfwd, K1, sl 1, K1, psso.

15th row K2 tog, *yfwd, K7, yfwd, sl 1, K2 tog, psso, rep from * to last 9 sts, yfwd, K7, yfwd, sl 1, K1, psso.

16th row As 2nd.

These 16 rows form the pattern.

Cat's paw pattern

Cast on a number of stitches divisible by 12 + 1.

1st row K5, *yfwd, sl 1, K2 tog, psso, yfwd, K9, rep from * to last 8 sts, yfwd, sl 1, K2 tog, psso, yfwd, K5.

2nd and every alt row P to end.

3rd row K3, *K2 tog, yfwd, K3, yfwd, sl 1, K1, psso, K5, rep from * to last 10 sts, K2 tog, yfwd, K3, yfwd, sl 1, K1, psso, K3.

5th row As 1st.

7th row K to end.

9th row K2 tog, *yfwd, K9, yfwd, sl 1, K2 tog, psso, rep from * to last 11 sts, yfwd, K9, yfwd, sl 1, K1, psso.

11th row K2, *yfwd, sl 1, K1, psso, K5, K2 tog, yfwd, K3, rep from * to last 11 sts, yfwd, sl 1, K1, psso, K5, K2 tog, yfwd, K2.

13th row As 9th.

15th row As 7th.

16th row As 2nd.

These 16 rows form the pattern.

Gothic Pattern

Cast on a number of stitches divisible by 10 + 1.

1st row K1, *yfwd, sl 1, K1, psso, K5, K2 tog, yfwd, K1, rep from * to end.

2nd and every alt row P to end.

3rd row K2, *yfwd, sl 1, K1, psso, K3, K2 tog, yfwd, K3, rep from * to last 9 sts, yfwd, sl 1, K1, psso, K3, K2 tog, yfwd, K2.

5th row K3, *yfwd, sl 1, K1, psso, K1, K2 tog, yfwd, K5, rep from * to last 8 sts, yfwd, sl 1, K1, psso, K1, K2 tog, yfwd, K3.

7th row K4, *yfwd, sl 1, K2 tog, psso, yfwd, K7, rep from * to last 7 sts, yfwd, sl 1, K2 tog, psso, yfwd, K4.

9th row K1, *yfwd, sl 1, K1, psso, K2 tog, yfwd, K1, rep from * to end.

10th row As 2nd.

11th-18th rows Rep the 9th and 10th rows 4 times more.

19th row K2, *yfwd, sl 1, K1, psso, K3, K2 tog, yfwd, K3, rep from * to last 9 sts, yfwd, sl 1, K1, psso, K3, K2 tog, yfwd, K2.

21st row K3, *yfwd, sl 1, K1, psso, K1, K2 tog, yfwd, K5, rep from * to last 8 sts, yfwd, sl 1, K1, psso, K1, K2 tog, yfwd, K3.

23rd row K4, *yfwd, sl 1, K2 tog, psso, yfwd, K7, rep from * to last 7 sts, yfwd, sl 1, K2 tog, psso, yfwd, K4.

24th row As 2nd.

These 24 rows form the pattern.

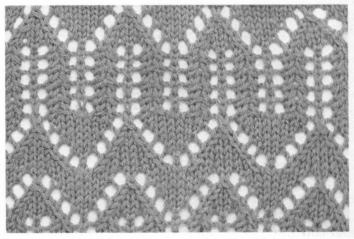

Traditional lace patterns

The history of lace stitches spans several centuries; many of the stitches, like those described in this chapter, have traditional names which are both beautiful and descriptive.

Shell and shower
Cast on a number of stitches divisible by 12 + 3.
1st row K2, *yfwd, K4, sl 1, K2 tog, psso, K4, yfwd, K1, rep from * to last st, K1.
2nd and every alt row P to end.
3rd row K3, *yfwd, K3, sl 1, K2 tog, psso, K3, yfwd, K3, rep from * to end.
5th row K1, K2 tog, *yfwd, K1, yfwd, K2, sl 1, K2 tog, psso, K2, yfwd, K1, yfwd, sl 1, K2 tog, psso, rep from * to last 12 sts, yfwd, K1, yfwd, K2, sl 1, K2 tog, psso, K2, yfwd, K1, yfwd, sl 1, K1, psso, K1.
7th row K1, *yfwd, sl 1, K1, psso, K2, yfwd, K1, sl 1, K2 tog, psso, K1, yfwd, K3, rep from * to last 2 sts, yfwd, K2 tog.
9th row K2, *yfwd, sl 1, K2 tog, psso, yfwd, K1, rep from * to last st, K1.
10th row As 2nd
These 10 rows form the pattern.

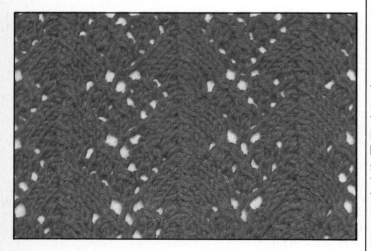

Ogee lace
Cast on a number of stitches divisible by 24 + 1.
1st row *K2, yfwd, K2 tog, K1, K2 tog, K3, yfwd, sl 1, K1, psso, yrn, P1, yon, K2, yfwd, sl 1, K1, psso, K1, sl 1, K1, psso, K1, sl 1, K1, psso, yfwd, K1, rep from * to last st, K1.
2nd row P1, *P7, yrn, P2 tog, P5, yrn, P2 tog, P8, rep from * to end.
3rd row *K1, yfwd, K2 tog, K1, K2 tog, K3, yfwd, sl 1, K1, psso, yfwd, K1, yfwd, K3, yfwd, sl 1, K1, psso, K1, sl 1, K1, psso, K1, sl 1, K1, psso, yfwd, rep from * to last st, K1.

4th row P1, *P6, yrn, P2 tog, P7, yrn, P2 tog, P7, rep from * to end.
5th row *K3, K2 tog, K3, yfwd, sl 1, K1, psso, K1, yfwd, K3, yfwd, K3, yfwd, sl 1, K1, psso, K1, sl 1, K1, psso, K2, rep from * to last st, K1.
6th row P1, *P5, yrn, P2 tog, P9, yrn, P2 tog, P6, rep from * to end.
7th row *K2, K2 tog, K3, yfwd, sl 1, K1, psso, K3, yfwd, K1, yfwd, K5, yfwd, sl 1, K1, psso, K1, sl 1, K1, psso, K1, rep from * to last st, K1.
8th row P1, *P4, yrn, P2 tog, P11, yrn, P2 tog, P5, rep from * to end.
9th row *K1, K2 tog, K3, yfwd, sl 1, K1, psso, K3, yfwd, K3, yfwd, K5, yfwd, sl 1, K1, psso, K1, sl 1, K1, psso, rep from * to last st, K1.
10th row P1, *P3, yrn, P2 tog, P13, yrn, P2 tog, P4, rep from * to end.
11th row Sl 1, K1, psso, *K3, yfwd, sl 1, K1, psso, K1, sl 1, K1, psso, yfwd, K2, yfwd, K1, yfwd, K2, yfwd, K2 tog, K3, yfwd, sl 1, K1, psso, K1, sl 1, K2 tog, psso, rep from * to last 23 sts, K3, yfwd, sl 1, K1, psso, K1, sl 1, K1, psso, yfwd, K2, yfwd, K1, yfwd, K2, yfwd, K2 tog, K3, yfwd, sl 1, K1, psso, K1, sl 1, K1, psso.
12th row P1, *P2, yrn, P2 tog, P15, yrn, P2 tog, P3, rep from * to end.
13th row Sl 1, K1, psso, *K2, yfwd, sl 1, K1, psso, K5, yfwd, K3, yfwd, K7, yfwd, sl 1, K1, psso, sl 1, K2 tog, psso, rep from * to last 23 sts, K2, yfwd, sl 1, K1, psso, K5, yfwd, K3, yfwd, K7, yfwd, sl 1, K1, psso, sl 1, K1, psso.
14th row K1, *P1, yrn, P2 tog, P17, yrn, P2 tog, P1, K1, rep from * to end.
15th row *P1, yon, K2, yfwd, sl 1, K1, psso, K1, sl 1, K1, psso, K1, sl 1, K1, psso, yfwd, K3, yfwd, K2 tog, K1, K2 tog, K3, yfwd, sl 1, K1, psso, yrn, rep from * to last st, P1.
16th row As 12th.
17th row *K1, yfwd, K3, yfwd, sl 1, K1, psso, K1, sl 1, K1, psso, K1, sl 1, K1, psso, yfwd, K1, yfwd, K2 tog, K1, K2 tog, K3, yfwd, sl 1, K1, psso, K1, yfwd, rep from * to last st, K1.
18th row As 10th.
19th row *K2, yfwd, K3, yfwd, sl 1, K1, psso, K1, sl 1, K1, psso, K5, K2 tog, K3, yfwd, sl 1, K1, psso, K1, yfwd, K1, rep from * to last st, K1.
20th row As 8th.
21st row *K1, yfwd, K5, yfwd, sl 1, K1, psso, K1, sl 1, K1, psso, K3, K2 tog, K3, yfwd, sl 1, K1, psso, K3, yfwd, rep from * to last st, K1.
22nd row As 6th.
23rd row *K2, yfwd, K5, yfwd, sl 1, K1, psso, K1, sl 1, K1, psso, K1, K2 tog, K3, yfwd, sl 1, K1, psso, K3, yfwd, K1, rep from * to last st, K1.

24th row As 4th.
25th row *K1, yfwd, K2, yfwd, K2 tog, K3, yfwd, sl 1, K1, psso, K1, sl 1, K2 tog, psso, K3, yfwd, sl 1, K1, psso, K1, sl 1, K1, psso, yfwd, K2, yfwd, rep from * to last st, K1.
26th row As 2nd.
27th row *K2, yfwd, K7, yfwd, sl 1, K1, psso, sl 1, K2 tog, psso, K2, yfwd, sl 1, K1, psso, K5, yfwd, K1, rep from * to last st, K1.
28th row P1, *P8, yrn, P2 tog, P1, K1, P1, yrn, P2 tog, P9, rep from * to end.
These 28 rows form the pattern.

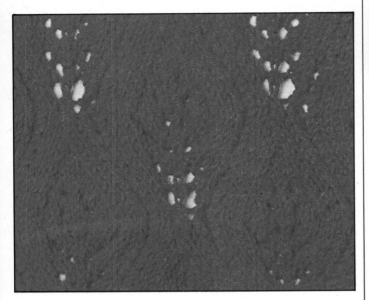

Spanish lace

Cast on a number of stitches divisible by 34 + 4.
1st row K2, *K3, K2 tog, K4, yrn, P2, (K2, yfwd, sl 1, K1, psso) 3 times, P2, yon, K4, sl 1, K1, psso, K3, rep from * to last 2 sts, K2.
2nd row P4, *P2 tog tbl, P4, yrn, P1, K2, (P2, yrn, P2 tog) 3 times, K2, P1, yrn, P4, P2 tog, P4, rep from * to end.
3rd row K3, *K2 tog, K4, yfwd, K2, P2, (K2, yfwd, sl 1, K1, psso) 3 times, P2, K2, yfwd, K4, sl 1, K1, psso, K2, rep from * to last st, K1.
4th row P2, *P2 tog tbl, P4, yrn, P3, K2, (P2, yrn, P2 tog) 3 times, K2, P3, yrn, P4, P2 tog, rep from * to last 2 sts, P2.
Rep the 1st through 4th rows twice more.
13th row *(K2, yfwd, sl 1, K1, psso) twice, P2, yon, K4, sl 1, K1, psso, K6, K2 tog, K4, yrn, P2, K2, yfwd, sl 1, K1, psso, rep from * to last 4 sts, K2, yfwd, sl 1, K1, psso.
14th row *(P2, yrn, P2 tog) twice, K2, P1, yrn, P4, P2 tog, P4, P2 tog tbl, P4, yrn, P1, K2, P2, yrn, P2 tog, rep from * to last 4 sts, P2, yrn, P2 tog.
15th row *(K2, yfwd, sl 1, K1, psso) twice, P2, K2, yfwd, K4, sl 1, K1, psso, K2, K2 tog, K4, yfwd, K2, P2, K2, yfwd, sl 1, K1, psso, rep from * to last 4 sts, K2, yfwd, sl 1, K1, psso.
16th row *(P2, yrn, P2 tog) twice, K2, P3, yrn, P4, P2 tog, P2 tog tbl, P4, yrn, P3, K2, P2, yrn, P2 tog, rep from * to last 4 sts, P2, yrn, P2 tog.

Rep the 13th through 16th rows twice more.
These 24 rows form the pattern.

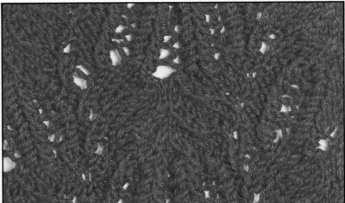

Candlelight lace

Cast on a number of stitches divisible by 12 + 1.
1st row K1, *yfwd, sl 1, K1, psso, K7, K2 tog, yfwd, K1, rep from * to end.
2nd and every alt row P to end.
3rd row K1, *yfwd, K1, sl 1, K1, psso, K5, K2 tog, K1, yfwd, K1, rep from * to end.
5th row K1, * yfwd, K2, sl 1, K1, psso, K3, K2 tog, K2, yfwd, K1, rep from * to end.
7th row K1, *yfwd, K3, sl 1, K1, psso, K1, K2 tog, K3, yfwd, K1, rep from * to end.
9th row K1, *yfwd, K4, sl 1, K2 tog, psso, K4, yfwd, K1, rep from * to end.
11th row *K4, K2 tog, yfwd, K1, yfwd, sl 1, K1, psso, K3, rep from * to last st, K1.
13th row *K3, K2 tog, K1, (yfwd, K1) twice, sl 1, K1, psso, K2, rep from * to last st, K1.
15th row *K2, K2 tog, K2, yfwd, K1, yfwd, K2, sl 1, K1, psso, K1, rep from * to last st, K1.
17th row *K1, K2 tog, K3, yfwd, K1, yfwd, K3, sl 1, K1, psso, rep from * to last st, K1.
19th row K2 tog, *K4, yfwd, K1, yfwd, K4, sl 1, K2 tog, psso, rep from * to last 11 sts, K4, yfwd, K1, yfwd, K4, sl 1, K1, psso.
20th row As 2nd.
These 20 rows form the pattern.

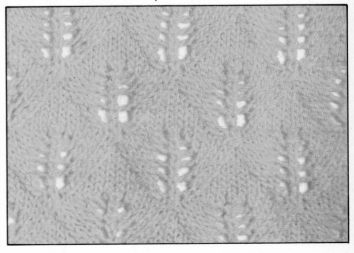

Larger lace patterns

The traditional lace stitches described here vary in complexity but each of them can be used to form a fabric of delicate beauty.

Wheat ear pattern

Cast on a number of stitches divisible by 11.

1st row (RS) *K1, (K1, yfwd to make a st, K1, yfwd, K1) all into same st, turn and K5, turn and P5, turn and K1, sl 1, K2 tog, psso, K1, turn and P3 tog – called B1 –, K2, yfwd, K1, yfwd, K4, K2 tog, rep from * to end, noting that one extra st is inc in each rep on this and every RS row.

2nd, 4th, 6th, 8th and 10th rows *P2 tog, P10, rep from * to end.

3rd row *K5, yfwd, K1, yfwd, K3, K2 tog, rep from * to end.

5th row *K6, yfwd, K1, yfwd, K2, K2 tog, rep from * to end.

7th row *K7, (yfwd, K1) twice, K2 tog, rep from * to end.

9th row *K8, yfwd, K1, yfwd, K2 tog, rep from * to end.

11th row *Sl 1, K1, psso, K4, yfwd, K1, yfwd, K2, B1, K1, rep from * to end.

12th, 14th, 16th and 18th rows *P10, P2 tog tbl, rep from * to end.

13th row *Sl 1, K1, psso, K3, yfwd, K1, yfwd, K5, rep from * to end.

15th row *Sl 1, K1, psso, K2, yfwd, K1, yfwd, K6, rep from * to end.

17th row *Sl 1, K1, psso, (K1, yfwd) twice, K7, rep from * to end.

19th row *Sl 1, K1, psso, yfwd, K1, yfwd, K8, rep from * to end.

20th row As 12th.

These 20 rows form the pattern.

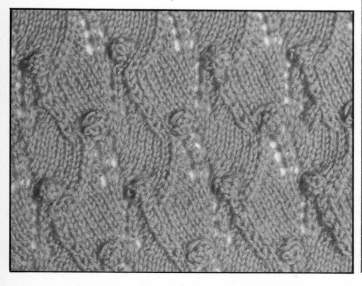

Fountain pattern

Cast on a number of stitches divisible by 16 plus 1.

1st row (WS) P to end.

2nd row Sl 1, K1, psso, *yfwd, K2, K2 tog, yfwd, K1, yfwd, sl 1, K2 tog, psso, yfwd, K1, yfwd, sl 1, K1, psso, K2, yfwd, sl 1, K2 tog, psso, rep from * ending last rep K2 tog instead of sl 1, K2 tog, psso.

3rd and every alt row P to end.

4th row Sl 1, K1, psso, *K3, yfwd, K2 tog, yfwd, K3, yfwd, sl 1, K1, psso, yfwd, K3, sl 1, K2 tog, psso, rep from * ending last rep as 2nd row.

6th row Sl 1, K1, psso, *(K2, yfwd) twice, K2 tog, K1, sl 1, K1, psso, (yfwd, K2) twice, sl 1, K2 tog, psso, rep from * ending last rep as 2nd row.

8th row Sl 1, K1, psso, *K1, yfwd, K3, yfwd, K2 tog, K1, sl 1, K1, psso, yfwd, K3, yfwd, K1, sl 1, K2 tog, psso, rep from * ending last rep as 2nd row.

These 8 rows form the pattern.

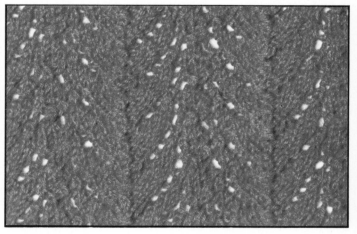

Oriel pattern

Cast on a number of stitches divisible by 12 plus 1.

1st row (RS) P1, *sl 1, K1, psso, K3, yrn, P1, yon, K3, K2 tog, P1, rep from * to end.

2nd row K1, *P5, K1, rep from * to end.

Rep 1st and 2nd rows twice more.

7th row P1, *yon, K3, K2 tog, P1, sl 1, K1, psso, K3, yrn, P1, rep from * to end.

8th row As 2nd.

9th row P2, *yon, K2, K2 tog, P1, sl 1, K1, psso, K2, yrn, P3, rep from * ending last rep P2 instead of P3.

10th row K2, *P4, K1, P4, K3, rep from * ending last rep K2 instead of K3.

11th row P3, *yon, K1, K2 tog, P1, sl 1, K1, psso, K1, yrn, P5, rep from * ending last rep P3 instead of P5.

12th row K3, *P3, K1, P3, K5, rep from * ending last rep K3 instead of K5.

13th row P4, *yon, K2 tog, P1, sl 1, K1, psso, yrn, P7, rep from * ending last rep P4 instead of P7.

14th row K4, *P2, K1, P2, K7, rep from * ending last rep K4 instead of K7.

15th row As 7th.

16th row As 2nd.

Rep 15th and 16th rows twice more.

21st row As 1st.

22nd row As 2nd.

23rd row P1, *sl 1, K1, psso, K2, yrn, P3, yon, K2, K2 tog, P1, rep from * to end.

24th row K1, *P4, K3, P4, K1, rep from * to end.

25th row P1, *sl 1, K1, psso, K1, yrn, P5, yon, K1, K2 tog, P1, rep from * to end.

26th row K1, *P3, K5, P3, K1, rep from * to end.

27th row P1, *sl 1, K1, psso, yrn, P7, yon, K2 tog, P1, rep from * to end.

28th row K1, *P2, K7, P2, K1, rep from * to end.

These 28 rows form the pattern.

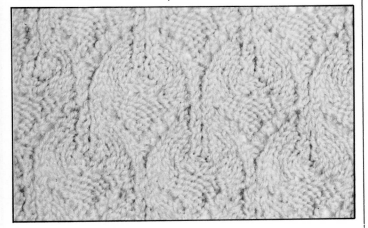

Bell pattern

Cast on a number of stitches divisible by 18 plus 1, noting that the number of stitches do not remain the same on every row but will revert to the original number on the 12th, 14th, 26th and 28th rows.

1st row (RS) K1, *(P2, K1) twice, yfwd, K2 tog, yfwd, K1, yfwd, sl 1, K1, psso, yfwd, (K1, P2) twice, K1, rep from * to end.

2nd row *(P1, K2) twice, P9, K2, P1, K2, rep from * to last st, P1.

3rd row K1, *(P2, K1) twice, yfwd, K2 tog, yfwd, K3, yfwd, sl 1, K1, psso, yfwd, (K1, P2) twice, K1, rep from * to end.

4th row *(P1, K2) twice, P11, K2, P1, K2, rep from * to last st, P1.

5th row K1, *(P2 tog, K1) twice, yfwd, K2 tog, yfwd, sl 1, K1, psso, K1, K2 tog, yfwd, sl 1, K1, psso, yfwd, (K1, P2 tog) twice, K1, rep from * to end.

6th row *(P1, K1) twice, P11, K1, P1, K1, rep from * to last st, P1.

7th row K1, *(P1, K1) twice, yfwd, K2 tog, yfwd, K1 tbl, yfwd, sl 1, K2 tog, psso, yfwd, K1, tbl, yfwd, sl 1, K1, psso, yfwd, (K1, P1) twice, K1, rep from * to end.

8th row *(P1, K1) twice, P13, K1, P1, K1, rep from * to last st, P1.

9th row K1, *(K2 tog) twice, yfwd, K2 tog, yfwd, K3,

yfwd, K1, yfwd, K3, yfwd, sl 1, K1, psso, yfwd, (sl 1, K1, psso) twice, K1, rep from * to end.

10th, 12th and 14th rows P to end.

11th row K1, *(K2 tog, yfwd) twice, sl 1, K1, psso, K1, K2 tog, yfwd, K1, yfwd, sl 1, K1, psso, K1, K2 tog, (yfwd, sl 1, K1, psso) twice, K1, rep from * to end.

13th row K2 tog, *yfwd, K2 tog, yfwd, K1 tbl, yfwd, sl 1, K2 tog, psso, yfwd, K3, yfwd, sl 1, K2 tog, psso, yfwd, K1 tbl, yfwd, sl 1, K1, psso, yfwd, sl 1, K2 tog, psso, rep from * ending last rep sl 1, K1, psso, instead of sl 1, K2 tog, psso.

15th row K1, *yfwd, sl 1, K1, psso, yfwd, (K1, P2) 4 times, K1, yfwd, K2 tog, yfwd, K1, rep from * to end.

16th row P5, *(K2, P1) 3 times, K2, P9, rep from * ending last rep P5 instead of P9.

17th row K2, *yfwd, sl 1, K1, psso, yfwd, (K1, P2) 4 times, K1, yfwd, K2 tog, yfwd, K3, rep from * ending last rep K2 instead of K3.

18th row P6, *(K2, P1) 3 times, K2, P11, rep from * ending last rep P6 instead of P11.

19th row K1, *K2 tog, yfwd, sl 1, K1, psso, yfwd, (K1, P2 tog) 4 times, K1, yfwd, K2 tog, yfwd, sl 1, K1, psso, K1, rep from * to end.

20th row P6, *(K1, P1) 3 times, K1, P11, rep from * ending last rep P6 instead of P11.

21st row K2 tog, *yfwd, K1 tbl, yfwd, sl 1, K1, psso, yfwd, (K1, P1) 4 times, K1, yfwd, K2 tog, yfwd, K1 tbl, yfwd, sl 1, K2 tog, psso, rep from * ending last rep sl 1, K1, psso, instead of sl 1, K2 tog, psso.

22nd row P7, *(K1, P1) 3 times, K1, P13, rep from * ending last rep P7 instead of P13.

23rd row K1, *yfwd, K3, yfwd, sl 1, K1, psso, yfwd, (sl 1, K1, psso) twice, K1, (K2 tog) twice, yfwd, K2 tog, yfwd, K3, yfwd, K1, rep from * to end.

24th and 26th rows P to end.

25th row K1, *yfwd, sl 1, K1, psso, K1, K2 tog, (yfwd, sl 1, K1, psso) twice, K1, (K2 tog, yfwd) twice, sl 1, K1, psso, K1, K2 tog, yfwd, K1, rep from * to end.

27th row K2, *yfwd, sl 1, K2 tog, psso, yfwd, K1 tbl, yfwd, sl 1, K1, psso, yfwd, sl 1, K2 tog, psso, yfwd, K2 tog, yfwd, K1 tbl, yfwd, sl 1, K2 tog, psso, yfwd, K3, rep from * ending last rep K2 instead of K3.

28th row P to end.

These 28 rows form the pattern.

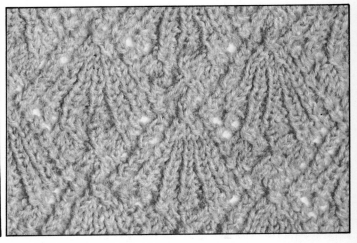

PATTERN SHAPES AND PICTURES

Patterned shapes and pictures can be achieved in knitting by means of different textures and stitches, using a single, overall color. This technique can be incorporated into any plain, basic garment most effectively, either as a repeating border such as the fir trees and tulip stitches shown here, or as a single motif, such as the house pattern, in the middle or placed on the front of a sweater.

Before you begin to knit, work out the position for the border or motif, making sure that you have the correct multiple of stitches for the design repeat or that a single motif is correctly placed.

Fir tree border

This pattern requires a multiple of 12 stitches plus 1 and is worked against a reverse stockinette stitch background.

1st row (RS) K1, *P1, K1, rep from * to end.
2nd row P1, *K1, P1, rep from * to end.
3rd row P6, *K1, P11, rep from * to last 7 sts, K1, P6.
4th row K6, *P1, K11, rep from * to last 7 sts, P1, K6.
Rep last 2 rows 3 times more.
11th row P2, *K1, P3, rep from * to last 3 sts, K1, P2.
12th row K2, *P1, K3, rep from * to last 3 sts, P1, K2.
13th row P2, *K2, P2, K1, P2, K2, P3, rep from * to last 11 sts, K2, P2, K1, P2, K2, P2.
14th row K2, *P2, K2, P1, K2, P2, K3, rep from * to last 11 sts, P2, K2, P1, K2, P2, K2.
15th row P2, *K3, P3, rep from * to last 5 sts, K3, P2.
16th row K2, *P3, K3, rep from * to last 5 sts, P3, K2.
17th row P2, *K4, P1, K4, P3, rep from * to last 11 sts, K4, P1, K4, P2.
18th row K2, *P4, K1, P4, K3, rep from * to last 11 sts, P4, K1, P4, K2.
19th row P3, *K7, P5, rep from * to last 10 sts, K7, P3.
20th row K3, *P7, K5, rep from * to last 10 sts, P7, K3.
21st row P4, *K5, P7, rep from * to last 9 sts, K5, P4.
22nd row K4, *P5, K7, rep from * to last 9 sts, P5, K4.
23rd row P5, *K3, P9, rep from * to last 8 sts, K3, P5.
24th row K5, *P3, K9, rep from * to last 8 sts, P3, K5.
25th row P6, *K1, P11, rep from * to last 7 sts, K1, P6.
26th row K6, *P1, K11, rep from * to last 7 sts, P1, K6.
These 26 rows complete the border pattern.

Tulip bed border

This pattern requires a multiple of 20 stitches plus 1 and is worked against a stockinette stitch background.
1st row (RS) K5, *K2 tog, yfwd, K1, yfwd, K2 tog, P1, sl 1, K1, psso, yfwd, K1, yfwd, sl 1, K1, psso, K9, rep from * ending last rep K5 instead of K9.

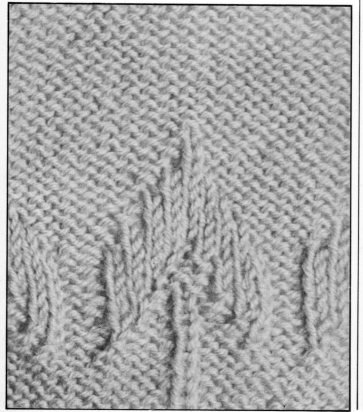

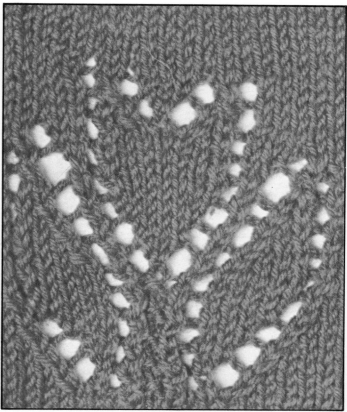

2nd and every alt row P to end.

3rd row K4, *K2 tog, yfwd, K2, yfwd, K2 tog, P1, sl 1, K1, psso, yfwd, K2, yfwd, sl 1, K1, psso, K7, rep from * ending last rep K4.

5th row K3, *K2 tog, yfwd, K3, yfwd, K2 tog, P1, sl 1, K1, psso, yfwd, K3, yfwd, sl 1, K1, psso, K5, rep from * ending last rep K3.

7th row K2, *K2 tog, yfwd, K4, yfwd, K2 tog, P1, sl 1, K1, psso, yfwd, K4, yfwd, sl 1, K1, psso, K3, rep from * ending last rep K2.

9th row K1, *K2 tog, yfwd, K5, yfwd, K2 tog, P1, sl 1, K1, psso, yfwd, K5, yfwd, sl 1, K1, psso, K1, rep from * to end.

11th row K2, *yfwd, K2 tog, K2, (K2 tog, yfwd) twice, K1, (yfwd, sl 1, K1, psso) twice, K2, sl 1, K1, psso, yfwd, K3, rep from * ending last rep K2.

13th row K2, *yfwd, K2 tog, K1, (K2 tog, yfwd) twice, K3, (yfwd, sl 1, K1, psso) twice, K1, sl 1, K1, psso, yfwd, K3, rep from * ending last rep K2.

15th row K2, *yfwd, (K2 tog) twice, yfwd, K2 tog, yfwd, K5, yfwd, sl 1, K1, psso, yfwd, (sl 1, K1, psso) twice, yfwd, K3, rep from * ending last rep K2.

17th row K2, *yfwd, sl 2, K1, p2sso, yfwd, K2 tog, yfwd, K7, yfwd, sl 1, K1, psso, yfwd, sl 2, K1, p2sso, yfwd, K3, rep from * ending last rep K2.

19th row K2, *K2 tog, yfwd, K2, yfwd, K2 tog, K5, sl 1, K1, psso, yfwd, K2, yfwd, sl 1, K1, psso, K3, rep from * ending last rep K2.

21st row K6, *yfwd, K2 tog, K5, sl 1, K1, psso, yfwd, K11, rep from * ending last rep K6.

23rd row K6, *yfwd, (K2 tog) twice, yfwd, K1, yfwd, (sl 1, K1, psso) twice, yfwd, K11, rep from * ending last rep K6.

25th row K6, *yfwd, sl 2, K1, p2sso, yfwd, K3, yfwd, sl 2, K1, p2sso, yfwd, K11, rep from * ending last rep K6.

26th row As 2nd.

These 26 rows complete the border pattern.

House motif

This pattern is worked on 28 stitches in all against a reverse stockinette stitch background.

1st row (RS) P2, K7, K into front of 2nd st on left hand needle then into front of first st – called T2R –, P6, K into back of 2nd st on left hand needle then into front of first st – called T2L –, K7, P2.

2nd row K2, P9, K6, P9, K2.

Rep 1st and 2nd rows once more.

5th row P2, K2, (K2, yfwd, K2 tog for window), K1, T2R, P6, T2L, K1, (K2, yfwd, K2 tog), K2, P2.

6th row K2, P2, (P2, yrn, P2 tog), P3, K6, P3, (P2, yrn, P2 tog) P2, K2.

Rep 5th and 6th rows twice more.

11th row P2, K2, (K2, yfwd, K2 tog), K1, T2R, P1, (P1, K1, P1) all into next st, turn and K3, turn and P3 then lift 2nd and 3rd sts over first st to form door knob, P4, T2L, K1, (K2, yfwd, K2 tog), K2, P2.

12th row As 6th.

Rep 5th and 6th rows twice more.

17th row As 1st.

18th row As 2nd.

19th row P2, K8, T2R, P4, T2L, K8, P2.

20th row K2, P10, K4, P10, K2.

21st row P2, K9, T2R, P2, T2L, K9, P2.

22nd row K2, P11, K2, P11, K2.

23rd row P2, K10, T2R, T2L, K10, P2.

24th row K2, P24, K2.

25th row P2, K24, P2.

26th row As 24th.

27th row P2, K2, (K2, yfwd, K2 tog for window), K4, (K2, yfwd, K2 tog), K4, (K2, yfwd, K2 tog), K2, P2.

28th row K2, P2, (P2, yrn, P2 tog), P4, (P2, yrn, P2 tog), P4, (P2, yrn, P2 tog), P2, K2.

Rep 27th and 28th rows twice more, then 25th and 26th rows twice more.

37th row K to end.

38th row K to end.

39th row P1, K26, P1.

40th row K to end.

41st row P2, K24, P2.

42nd row K to end.

43rd row P3, K22, P3.

44th row K to end.

45th row P4, K20, P4.

46th row K to end.

47th row P5, K18, P5.

48th row K to end.

49th row P10, (K1, P1) twice, K1, P13.

50th row K13, (P1, K1) twice, P1, K10.

Rep 49th and 50th rows 3 times more.

These 56 rows complete the motif.

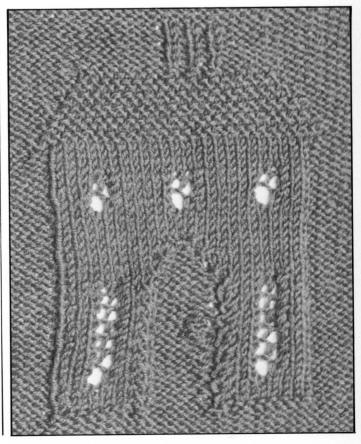

A simple patterned pullover

Here is a simple pullover pattern which incorporates the house motif given in the previous chapter on patterned shapes and motifs. The motifs are positioned in rows across front and back of the sweater, and a single motif has been incorporated into each of the short set-in sleeves.

Pullover
Sizes
Directions are to fit 34in bust. Changes for 36 and 38in bust are in brackets [].
Length to shoulder, 23[$23\frac{1}{4}$:$23\frac{1}{2}$]in
Sleeve seam, 7in

Gauge

28 sts and 36 rows to 4in in stockinette stitch (st st) worked on No.3 needles

Materials

12[13:14] × 1oz balls 3 ply fingering yarn
One pair No.3 needles
One pair No.2 needles

Back

Using No.2 needles cast on 120[124:128] sts. Work 2in K1, P1 rib. Change to No.3 needles. Beg with a P row work 4 rows reverse st st.
Next row P2, (patt 28 sts as for 1st row of house motif, P16 [18:20] sts) twice, patt 28 sts as shown for 1st row of house motif, P2.
Next row K2, (patt 28 sts as for 2nd row of house motif, K16 [18:20] sts) twice, patt 28 sts as for 2nd row of house motif, K2.
Cont in patt as now set until 56 patt rows have been completed. Beg with a P row work 4 rows reverse st st.
Next row P24 [25:26] sts, patt 28 sts as for 1st row of house motif, P16 [18:20] sts, patt 28 sts as for 1st row of house motif, P24 [25:26].
Next row K24 [25:26] sts, patt 28 sts as for 2nd row of house motif, K16 [18:20] sts, patt 28 sts as for 2nd row of house motif, K24 [25:26].
Cont in patt as now set until second 56 patt rows have been completed. Beg with a P row work 4 rows reverse st st.
Next row P46 [48:50] sts, patt 28 sts as for 1st row of house motif, P46 [48:50].
Next row K46 [48:50] sts, patt 28 sts as for 2nd row of house motif, K46 [48:50].
Cont in patt as now set until work measures 16in from beg, ending with a K row.

Shape armholes

Maintaining patt until third 56 patt rows have been completed, then cont in reverse st st across all sts, bind off at beg of next and every row 5 sts twice and 2 sts 4 times. Dec one st at each end of next and foll 5 alt rows 90[94:98] sts. Cont without shaping until armholes measure 7[7¼:7½]in from beg, ending with a K row.

Shape shoulders

Bind off at beg of next and every row 7 sts 4 times and 11[12:13] sts twice. Place rem 40[42:44] sts on holder for center back neck.

Front

Work as for back until armhole shaping is completed and third 56 patt rows have been worked. Cont without shaping in reverse st st until armholes measure 5[5¼:5½]in from beg, ending with a K row.

Shape neck

Next row P35[36:37] sts, bind off 20[22:24] sts, P to end. Complete this side first. K 1 row. Bind off at beg of next and every alt row 2 sts 3 times, then dec one st at neck edge on every alt row 4 times. 25[26:27] sts.

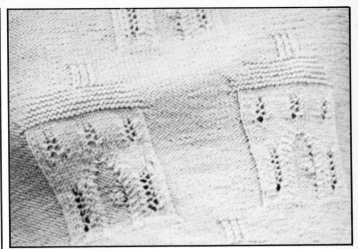

Cont without shaping until armhole measures same as back to shoulder, ending at armhole edge.

Shape shoulder

Bind off at beg of next and every alt row 7 sts twice and 11[12:13] sts once.
With WS of work facing, rejoin yarn to rem sts and complete to correspond to first side, reversing shaping.

Sleeves

Using No.2 needles cast on 76[78:80] sts. Work 1in K1, P1 rib. Change to No.3 needles. Beg with a P row work 4 rows reverse st st.
Next row P2, patt 28 sts as given for 1st row of house motif, P16[18:20] sts, patt 28 sts as for 1st row of house motif, P2.
Next row K2, patt 28 sts as for 2nd row of house motif, K16[18:20] sts, patt 28 sts as given for 2nd row of house motif, K2.
Cont in patt as now set, inc one st at each end of next and every foll 6th row until there are 86[90:94] sts, working extra sts in reverse st st, until 56 patt rows have been completed. Cont in reverse st st across all sts.

Shape top

Bind off 5 sts at beg of next 2 rows. Dec one st at each end of next and foll 10[11:12] alt rows, ending with a K row. Bind off at beg of next and every row 2 sts 6 times, 3 sts 6 times and 4 sts 4 times. Bind off rem 8[10:12] sts.

Neckband

Join right shoulder seam. Using No.2 needles and with RS of work facing, K 20[21:22] sts down left front neck, K 20[22:24] sts across front neck, K 20[21:22] sts up right front neck and K across 40[42:44] back neck sts on holder. 100[106:112] sts. Work 2in K1, P1 rib. Bind off in rib.

Finishing

Block as suggested on label. Join rem shoulder and neckband seam. Set in sleeves. Join side and sleeve seams. Fold neckbands in half to WS and sew in place. Block seams.

SHETLAND LACE

Of all the traditional knitting techniques which have flourished in Britain, such as Aran and Fair Isle patterns, typical Shetland Isle lace stitches are among the most beautiful.

The finest examples come from Unst, the most northerly of all the Shetland Islands, where a few skilled knitters have carried on the tradition for many generations.

The stitches are few in number, only ten being truly native, and were inspired by examples of fine Spanish lace brought to the Shetland Isles as part of an exhibition in the early nineteenth century. Each stitch has been adapted to represent the natural beauty of the islands and they carry such evocative names as 'Ears o' Grain', 'Print o' the Wave' and 'Fir Cones'.

Even today, the yarn used for the superb examples of this craft is hand spun to a single ply of such delicate fineness that few knitters would be able to work with it. However, a 3 ply yarn worked on No.1 needles can produce a reasonable facsimile of this most beautiful and rewarding method of knitting.

Casting on and binding off for lace knitting

Thick, harsh lines caused by casting on and binding off, or seaming, must be avoided or they will immediately detract from the delicate appearance of the lace.

Use the 2 needle method of casting on but instead of inserting the right hand needle between the last

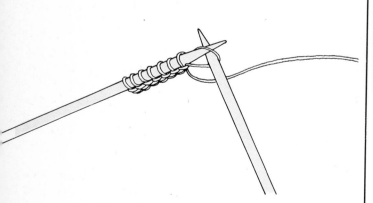

2 stitches on the left hand needle, insert it from front to back into the last stitch on the left hand needle and then draw a loop through to form the next stitch, transferring this to the left hand needle. This forms a loose, open edge.

Binding off should be worked in the usual way, using a needle 2 times larger to work the binding off than the size used for the main fabric.

Where the fabric has to be joined, it is best to use a spare length of yarn for casting on which can later be withdrawn, to allow the first and last rows to be woven together for an invisible join.

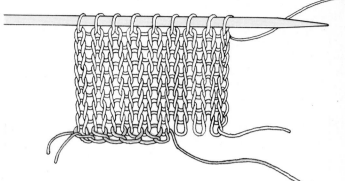

Crown of Glory pattern

This stitch is also known by the descriptive name of 'Cat's paw'. Cast on a number of stitches divisible by 14 plus 5.

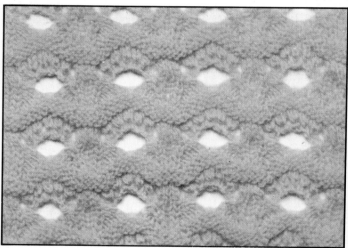

1st row (RS) K3, *sl 1, K1, psso, K9, K2 tog, K1, rep from * to last 2 sts, K2.

2nd row P2, *P1, P2 tog, P7, P2 tog tbl, rep from * to last 3 sts, P3.

3rd row K3, *sl 1, K1, psso, K2, yrn 3 times, K3, K2 tog, K1, rep from * to last 2 sts, K2.

4th row P2, *P1, P2 tog, P2, (K1, P1, K1, P1, K1) all into yrn 3 times making 5 sts, P1, P2 tog tbl, rep from * to last 3 sts, P3.

5th row K3, *sl 1, K1, psso, K6, K2 tog, K1, rep from * to last 2 sts, K2.

6th row P2, *P1, P2 tog, P6, rep from * ending last rep P3.

7th row K3, *K1, (yfwd, K1) 6 times, K1, rep from * to last 2 sts, K2.

8th row P to end.

9th and 10th rows K to end.

11th row P to end.

12th row K to end.

These 12 rows form the pattern.

Razor shell pattern

This stitch takes its name from the shells on the beach. It can be worked in multiples of 4, 6, 8, 10 or 12 stitches. For the sample shown here, cast on a number of stitches divisible by 6 plus 1.

1st row (WS) P to end.

2nd row K1, *yfwd, K1, sl 1, K2 tog, psso, K1, yfwd, K1, rep from * to end.

These 2 rows form the pattern.

Horseshoe print pattern

Derived from the imprint of horseshoes on wet sand, this sample requires a number of stitches divisible by 10 plus 1.

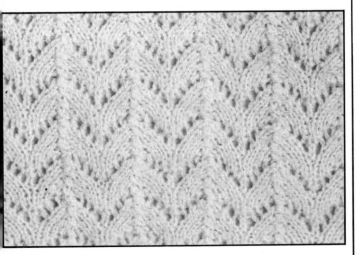

1st row (WS) P to end.

2nd row K1, *yfwd, K3, sl 1, K2 tog, psso, K3, yfwd, K1, rep from * to end.

3rd row As 1st.

4th row P1, *K1, yfwd, K2, sl 1, K2 tog, psso, K2, yfwd, K1, P1, rep from * to end.

5th row K1, *P9, K1, rep from * to end.

6th row P1, *K2, yfwd, K1, sl 1, K2 tog, psso, K1, yfwd, K2, P1, rep from * to end.

7th row As 5th.

8th row P1, *K3, yfwd, sl 1, K2 tog, psso, yfwd, K3, P1, rep from * to end.

These 8 rows form the pattern.

Fern pattern

This stitch is often used as a shawl border since the shape of the motif allows for easy corner shaping. The size of the lace motif can vary but the working method remains the same. For the sample shown here, cast on a number of stitches divisible by 15.

1st row (RS) *K7, yfwd, sl 1 K-wise, K1, psso, K6, rep from * to end.

2nd row P to end.

3rd row *K5, K2 tog, yfwd, K1, yfwd, sl 1 K-wise, K1, psso, K5, rep from * to end.

4th row P to end.

5th row *K4, K2 tog, yfwd, K3, yfwd, sl 1 K-wise, K1, psso, K4, rep from * to end.

6th row P to end.

7th row *K4, yfwd, sl 1 K-wise, K1, psso, yfwd, sl 1, K2 tog, psso yfwd, K2 tog, yfwd, K4, and rep from * to end.

8th row P to end.

9th row *K2, K2 tog, yfwd, K1, yfwd, sl 1 K-wise, K1, psso, K1, K2 tog, yfwd, K1, yfwd, sl 1 K-wise, K1, psso, K2, rep from * to end.

10th row P to end.

11th row *K2, (yfwd, sl 1 K-wise, K1, psso) twice, K3, (K2 tog, yfwd) twice, K2, rep from * to end.

12th row *P3, (yrn, P2 tog) twice, P1, (P2 tog tbl, yrn) twice, P3, rep from * to end.

13th row *K4, yfwd, sl 1 K-wise, K1, psso, yfwd, sl 1, K2 tog, psso, yfwd, K2 tog, yfwd, K4, and rep from * to end.

14th row *P5, yrn, P2 tog, P1, P2 tog tbl, yrn, P5, rep from * to end.

15th row *K6, yfwd, sl 1, K2 tog, psso, yfwd, K6, rep from * to end.

16th row P to end.

These 16 rows form the pattern.

A Shetland lace shawl

The gossamer Shetland lace shawl shown here is a superb example of what is known as a 'wedding ring' shawl. It is so fine that it can easily be pulled through a wedding ring, hence its name, and it can be likened to a spider's web, having no beginning and no end.

This particular shawl is reproduced by kind permission of Highland Home Industries of Edinburgh, who still employ a few highly skilled Shetland Islanders to make these garments in their own homes. Traditionally this would be made as a christening shawl, but it could also be used as a beautiful winter wedding veil. As you can imagine, these shawls are in great demand but take so long to knit that they are literally worth their weight in gold. The yarn used has been homespun and is so fine that two strands together have been used to knit this shawl. It has been spun from the fine, soft wool which grows around the sheep's neck.

The needles used to knit this shawl are still called by their traditional name of 'wires' and, in all probability, the pattern has been passed from one generation to another by word of mouth and the instructions have never been written down.

Once a shawl of this delicacy has been completed, it will be washed and then 'dressed' or stretched into shape. To dress the shawl in the traditional manner, special wooden frames as large as a bed are needed. The shawl is tied to this frame with lacing through every point along the edges of the border and left to dry naturally. In this way it is kept taut and square and each point or scallop of the border is stretched out to its correct shape.

In this chapter we give two other traditional lace stitches to inspire you to experiment with this most beautiful craft.

Fir cone pattern

As its name implies, this pattern represents the cones of fir trees and the number of times the pattern rows are repeated can be varied. For the sample shown here cast on a number of stitches divisible by 10 plus 1.

1st row (RS) K1, *yfwd, K3, sl 1, K2 tog, psso, K3, yfwd, K1, rep from * to end.

2nd row P to end.

Rep these 2 rows 3 times more.

9th row K2 tog, *K3, yfwd, K1, yfwd, K3, sl 1, K2 tog, psso, rep from * to last 9 sts, K3, yfwd, K1, yfwd, K3, sl 1, K1, psso.

10th row P to end.

Rep 9th and 10th rows 3 times more.

These 16 rows form the pattern.

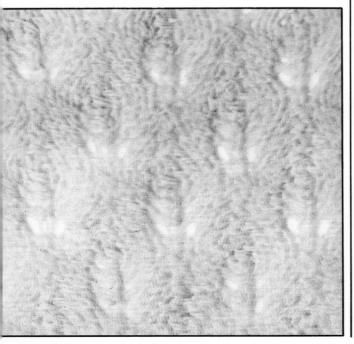

Point o' the wave pattern

This beautiful undulating pattern is a reminder that the sea is a constant part of life in the islands. To work this sample, cast on a number of stitches divisible by 22 plus 3 *very* loosely.

1st row (RS) K4, *K2 tog, K3, (yfwd, K2 tog) twice, yfwd, K13, rep from * to end, ending last rep with K12 instead of K13.

2nd and every alt row P to end.

3rd row K3, *K2 tog, K3, yfwd, K1, yfwd, (sl 1, K1, psso, yfwd) twice, K3, sl 1, K1, psso, K7, rep from * to end.

5th row K2, *K2 tog, (K3, yfwd) twice, (sl 1, K1, psso, yfwd) twice, K3, sl 1, K1, psso, K5, rep from * to last st, K1.

7th row K1, *K2 tog, K3, yfwd, K5, yfwd, (sl 1, K1, psso, yfwd) twice, K3, sl 1, K1, psso, K3, rep from * to last 2 sts, K2.

9th row *K12, yfwd, (sl 1, K1, psso, yfwd) twice, K3, sl 1, K1, psso, K1, rep from * to last 3 sts, K3.

11th row *K7, K2 tog, K3, (yfwd, K2 tog) twice, yfwd, K1, yfwd, K3, sl 1, K1, psso, rep from * to last 3 sts, K3.

13th row K6, *K2 tog, K3, (yfwd, K2 tog) twice, (yfwd, K3) twice, sl 1, K1, psso, K5, rep from * to end, ending last rep with K2 instead of K5.

15th row K5, *K2 tog, K3, (yfwd, K2 tog) twice, yfwd, K5, yfwd, K3, sl 1, K1, psso, K3, rep from * to end, ending last rep with K1 instead of K3.

16th row As 2nd.

These 16 rows form the pattern.

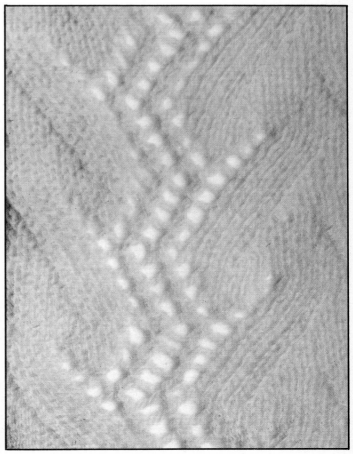

PICOT KNITTING

Picot knitting is an unusual technique which imitates Irish crochet, worked with a pair of knitting needles instead of a crochet hook. It looks its best when it is worked in a very fine cotton, such as No.20, and on fine needles.

It has many applications and can be used as edgings, insertions, motifs or as an all-over background fabric. The dainty baby bonnet shown here is an example of how the various methods can be combined to form a garment.

To make a picot point

Make a slip loop in the usual way and place this on the left hand needle, *cast on 2 stitches, making 3 in all. Knit and bind off 2 of these 3 stitches, leaving one stitch on the needle. This forms one picot point. Transfer the remaining stitch to the left hand needle and repeat from * until the required length of picot points is completed. Fasten off.

The size of these picot points may be varied by casting on and binding off 3 stitches, 4 stitches or as many as required. This strip forms the basis of picot work and can be used to join motifs such as flower centers, or as a simple edging.

It can also be used to form a dainty bound off edge on a garment as follows:

Binding off row Insert the needle through the first st of the row to be bound off, *cast on 2 sts, knit and bind off 2 sts, knit the next st of the row, knit and bind off one st, transfer the rem st to the left hand needle, rep from * to end of row.
Fasten off.

Picot point crown

This method is worked across a number of stitches to give the width of edging required. Once this first section has been completed, it forms the basis for what is termed a 'lacis', or openwork fabric, and is referred to as a 'strip' and not a row. To continue working strips to build up a lacis, the last stitch is not fastened off.

Cast on a number of stitches divisible by 5 plus one.
1st row K to end.
2nd row Insert needle into the first st, *cast on 2 sts, bind off 2 sts, transfer rem st to left hand needle, *, rep from * to * 3 times more, (4 picot points formed), knit and bind off next 5 sts, transfer rem st to left hand needle, rep from * to end.
This completes first strip.
Next strip *Transfer rem st to left hand needle, make 4 picot points as in 2nd row of first strip, join to center of next picot crown in first strip by picking up and knitting a st between the 2 center picot points, bind off one st, rep from * to end of strip.
Cont in this way until lacis is required depth. Fasten off.

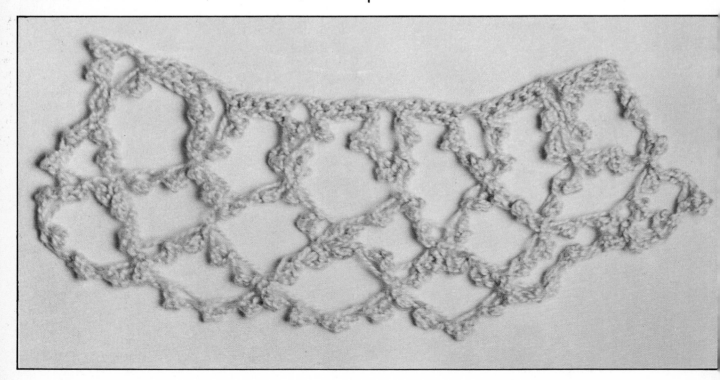

Picot point motif

This simple motif can be used separately or to form the center of a flower. Each separate motif can be stitched from the top of one point to the corresponding point of the next motif to form a daisy edging, and a number of rows can be joined in the same way to form delicate shawls, or interesting table linen, such as place mats and coasters.

However you wish to use these motifs, you can make as many picot points as you like, varying the size of each picot point as already explained. The example shown here has 6 picot points, using 3 stitches instead of 2 for each point.

Make a slip loop and place on left hand needle, *cast on 3 sts, making 4 in all, bind off 3 of these sts, transfer rem sts to left hand needle, rep from * 5 times more. To join into a circle, insert needle into the first loop and draw up a st, bind off one st. Fasten off.

To continue making a flower motif, do not fasten off but transfer remaining stitch to left hand needle, ready to begin the first petal.

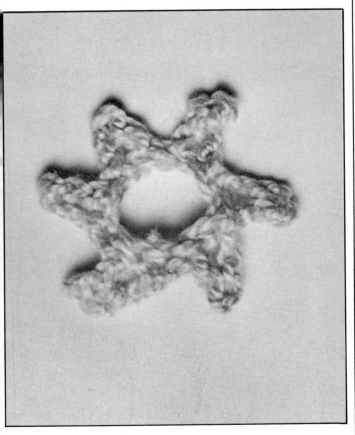

Picot point flower

Make a motif as above. Cast on one st, making 2 stitches on left hand needle.

1st row K1, K into front then into back of next st — called M1. 3 sts.
2nd and 4th rows K to end.
3rd row K2, M1.
5th row K3, M1. 5sts.
K4 rows g st.

10th row Bind off one st, K to end. 4sts.
11th row K to end.
Rep last 2 rows twice more.
16th row Cast off one st, pick up and knit a loop between next 2 picot points, cast off one st, transfer rem st to left hand needle.
Cont in this way making 6 petals in all, or desired number, joining last petal to same place as first petal, as shown for picot point.

Picot flower and lacis motif

Make a picot point flower and fasten off. Rejoin yarn to center of any petal tip.

1st round Make 4 picot points casting on and binding off sts for each point, K up one st at tip of next petal, bind off one st, transfer rem st to left hand needle, rep from * all around flower.

2nd round Make 4 picot points and join between 2nd and 3rd picots of 1st round, make another 4 picot points and skip 2 picot points of 1st round, join between next 2 picot points of 1st round, cont in this way to end of round joining last stitch to same place as first stitch. Fasten off.

3rd round Rejoin yarn between 2nd and 3rd of any picot points, *make 4 picot points and join between 2nd and 3rd of next 4 picot points, rep from * to end of round, joining as before. 12 loops. Fasten off.

4th round Rejoin yarn between 2nd and 3rd of any picot points, *make 3 picot points and join into same place to form a picot crest, make 4 picot points and join between 2nd and 3rd of next 4 picot points, rep from * to end of round, joining as before. Fasten off. Make as many more motifs as required, joining picot crests of each motif where they touch to form a row.

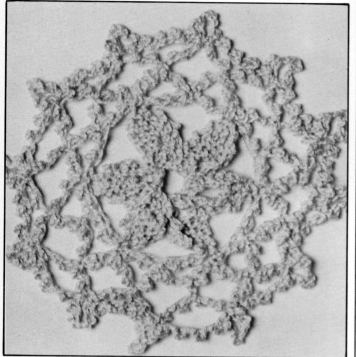

Baby bonnet

Size
To fit newborn to 3 months.

Gauge
32sts and 60 rows to 3·9 inches over garter stitch (g st) worked on No.1 needles.

Materials
1 1oz ball 3 ply baby yarn
One pair No.1 needles
1 yard ribbon for ties

Bonnet
Make one flower and lacis motif, omitting 4th round, to form center of crown.

Make 11 picot point motifs and join into a row, joining the center picots on each side and leaving 2 free at top and bottom. Sew around edge of center motif, joining 2 free points of each motif to the center 2 picots of each loop and leaving one loop free for bottom edge of bonnet.

Make a strip of 42 picots, mark the last picot with contrast thread and turn.

Next row Make 4 picots, join between 3rd and 4th picots after marker, *make 4 picots, skip 4 picots, join between 4th and 5th picots, rep from * to last 3 picots, make 4 picots, join to end of strip after last picot. Fasten off and turn.

Next row Rejoin yarn between 2nd and 3rd picots of first loop, make 4 picots, join between 2nd and 3rd picots of next loop, rep from * to end. Do not fasten off but turn.

Next row Make 4 picots, join between 2nd and 3rd picots of first loop, *make 4 picots, join between 2nd and 3rd picots of next loop, rep from * to end, make 4 picots, join to beg of previous row where yarn was rejoined.

Rep last 2 rows once more. Fasten off.

Join the cast on edge of this strip to the center piece, joining the first 2 picots to the 2 picots of first motif, *skip 2 picots, join next 2 picots to 2 points of next motif, rep from * to end.

Finishing
Pin out and block under a damp cloth with a warm iron. Sew ribbon to each corner to tie at front.

FILET KNITTING

The word 'filet' means 'net', and this type of square mesh fabric can be produced in both knitting and crochet. Just as with crochet, patterns can be introduced into the knitted mesh background, consisting of solid parts of the pattern, which are referred to as 'blocks', and open parts of the pattern which are called 'spaces'. The stitch used to produce filet lace fabric is garter stitch throughout, so it is a very simple method to work.

This fabric looks best when it is worked in a fine cotton on small size needles to give a lace effect. It has many uses but is better used for insertions and edgings, rather than as an all over fabric.

To knit filet lace

Working a block: These comprise solid sections of garter stitch and each block consists of three knitted stitches in width and four rows in depth. Whether working an insertion or an edging, a number of extra stitches are required at the beginning and end of the rows and these are knitted throughout in the usual way.

Working a space: These are the open sections of a design and each space is worked on three stitches. The third stitch of each space is knitted in the usual way and is either used as an edge stitch, or as a bridging stitch between spaces or between spaces and blocks. Each space is worked over two rows in depth.

After completing a block of three knitted stitches or the edge stitches, as the case may be, bring the yarn forward between the needles, take it over the right hand needle and to the front again – called y2rn. Over the next three stitches, slip the first stitch knitwise, then slip the 2nd stitch knitwise, using the point of the left hand needle lift the first stitch over the 2nd stitch and off the right hand needle.

Slip the 3rd stitch knitwise, using the point of the left hand needle lift the 2nd stitch over the 3rd stitch and off the right hand needle, return the 3rd stitch to the left hand needle and knit this in the usual way.

This working method is referred to as making a space. There are now three loops on the right hand needle again, composed of the yarn twice around the needle and one knitted stitch. On the following row the first yarn around the needle is knitted and the 2nd yarn around the needle is purled, then the 3rd stitch is knitted, to complete the space.

Working basic filet net

This is worked entirely in spaces, plus one edge stitch at the beginning of the row. The 3rd stitch of each space forms the bridging stitch between each space.

Working blocks and spaces

As each block requires four rows to complete it and a space only requires two rows, the pattern rows must be worked twice to give the necessary square shape to each block.

When a block changes to a space in a pattern, treat the three stitches of the block as a space, or when changing a space to a block, work the three stitches of the space as a block.

Filet lace insertion

This simple pattern can be used in many ways, either as center front panels on a fabric or knitted blouse, as

an insertion on a dainty slip or on household linens. It is worked over a total of five squares, each consisting of three stitches, plus three edge stitches at the beginning of the rows and two edge stitches at the end of the rows. Only two stitches are needed to balance the end of the rows, as the last stitch of the last space is taken into this edge. The chart given here does not show the edge stitches.

Cast on a total of 20 stitches to work the insertion.

1st row (RS) K3 edge sts, work 2 spaces, K3 sts for a block, work 2 spaces, K2 edge sts.

2nd and every alt row K to end, purling the 2nd yarn around needle of every space.

Rep 1st and 2nd rows once more to complete the center block.

5th row K3 edge sts, work 1 space, (K3 sts for a block, work 1 space) twice, K2 edge sts.

6th row As 2nd.

Rep 5th and 6th rows once more to complete the

blocks, then rep them twice more to complete another block.

13th row As 1st.

Chart for lace insertion

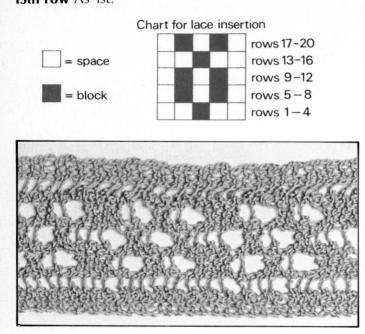

☐ = space

■ = block

	■		■		rows 17–20
	■	■			rows 13–16
		■			rows 9–12
	■	■			rows 5–8
		■			rows 1–4

14th row As 2nd.

Rep 13th and 14th rows once more to complete the center block.

17th row As 5th.

18th row As 6th.

Rep 17th and 18th rows once more to complete the blocks.

These 20 rows form the pattern and are repeated for the required length of the insertion.

Filet lace edging

This pattern has a notched edge along one side and

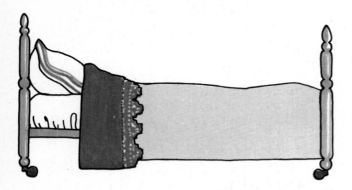

forms an ideal trimming for all types of household linens. The serrated edge is formed by casting on additional stitches two rows before they are taken into the pattern.

The pattern consists of three squares at the beginning, each comprising three stitches, plus one edge stitch at the beginning of the row only, the last edge stitch being formed by the last stitch of the last space. The chart given here does not show the edge stitch.

Cast on a total of 10 stitches to begin the edging.

1st row (RS) K1 edge st, work 1 space, K3 sts for a block, work 1 space.

2nd and every alt row K to end, purling the 2nd yarn around needle of every space.

3rd row As 1st, then turn and cast on 6 sts to form 2 extra spaces on the 5th row.

5th row K1 edge st, work 1 space, K3 sts for a block, work 3 spaces.

7th row As 5th, then turn and cast on 3 sts to form 1 extra space on the 9th row.

9th row K1 edge st, work 1 space, K3 sts for a block,

Chart for lace edging

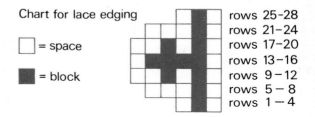

☐ = space

■ = block

		■			rows 25–28
		■			rows 21–24
		■			rows 17–20
	■	■	■		rows 13–16
		■			rows 9–12
		■			rows 5–8
		■			rows 1–4

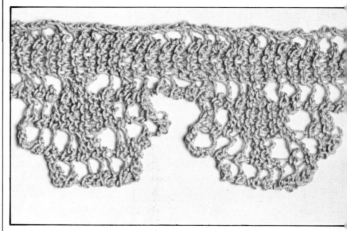

work 1 space, K3 sts for a block, work 2 spaces.

10th row As 2nd.

Rep 9th and 10th rows once more to complete blocks.

13th row K1 edge st, work 1 space, K12 sts to form 4 blocks, work 1 space.

14th row As 2nd.

Rep 13th and 14th rows once more to complete blocks.

17th row As 9th.

18th row As 2nd.

19th row As 17th.

20th row Bind off 3 sts to reduce one space, then work as 2nd row to end.

21st row As 5th.

22nd row As 2nd.

23rd row As 21st.

24th row Bind off 6 sts to reduce 2 spaces, then work as 2nd row to end.

25th row As 1st.

26th row As 2nd.

Rep 25th and 26th rows once more to complete block. These 28 rows form the pattern and are repeated for the desired length of the edging.

AN INTRODUCTION TO CROCHET

This publication provides a new and completely different approach to crochet which will be of interest both to beginners and experts. It guides the reader clearly and carefully through the very early stages onto the more complicated techniques, and it adds a new dimension to the many ways in which crochet can be applied.

Very little is known about the early history of crochet. For many centuries it was worked mostly by nuns, and to that extent it was often referred to as "nuns work". During the mid-nineteenth century, the beautiful fabric formed by Irish crochet became popular, and throughout Queen Victoria's reign was applied to everything from antimacassars to camisole tops. However, some of the pieces produced at that time were terribly unattractive and did little to enhance the natural beauty of this delicate craft.

Gradually the art did decline in popularity and for almost fifty years after that it remained virtually unknown and unpracticed in many areas with the exception of Ireland, where it was fortunately kept alive. During the 1950's, however, a tremendous revival of interest in all crafts began in America, and the impetus spread rapidly to Britain and the European continent. One of the first of these to reappear was the art of crochet and its popularity was so phenomenal that designers and publishers were inundated with requests for patterns.

It was realized for the first time that crochet could be used to make things to wear and that it was not limited merely to the making of trimmings or insertions. Interest quickly gathered momentum and all aspects of the craft were eagerly researched to cope with the demand for fashionable garments and also for items of home decor.

Today crochet is appreciated as a unique way of interpreting fashion. The craftsman has complete control over the texture and color of the fabric and over the ultimate shape of the design. And, as in knitting, both the skills of weaving and dressmaking are combined. The fabric can be tough and sturdy; or gossamer light and lacy. The shape can be casual and practical, or softly romantic.

Almost any kind of spun thread can be used in crochet, from very fine cotton to chunky machine-washable yarns. Apart from its fashion appeal, crochet remains one of the most popular of all crafts for making things for the home too. Nothing else lends itself quite so successfully to the delicate lace fabric which can be used to produce heirloom bedspreads and tablecloths, or to edgings and insertions on sheets and pillow cases.

All you really need to begin exploring the exciting possibilities which this craft has to offer are a crochet hook, a ball of yarn and a willing pair of hands. With surprisingly little effort even a beginner can make simple "granny" squares, which can soon build up into a complete garment, and the more experienced crochet worker will be delighted to discover ways in which to extend his or her knowledge to combine leather with crochet, or to apply crochet to net material for a most original and attractive fabric.

Pam Dawson

HISTORY OF CROCHET

Nobody can really pinpoint the day or year when someone picked up a bone or stick and some yarn and started knotting chains of fabric into what is now known as crochet. If you were to ask any number of the millions of people all over the world who practice this simple, yet very creative craft, you would not find many who could tell you much about its history. That, however, is not quite as surprising as it sounds. Its origins are very obscure, although archaeological finds do lead us to believe that Arabia may have been the original area where wool was first worked with just one needle or hook. Ancient crochet specimens have been found in Egypt, and it can be presumed that the craft is of an age parallel with knitting, its sister craft. We know that it does go back at least as far as the days of Solomon (around 950 BC), and some biblical historians credit its use even earlier—1200 BC—when the Israelites fled Egypt during the Exodus. They were said to have worked with wool in this way during their long trek across the Sinai desert. Actually, the evidence of this early use is quite substantial. The start of modern civilization usually dates from the time (about 5500 BC) when the Sumerians left central Asia and settled in the plains of Babylon—now Iraq. Babylon was the center for wool crafts, just as Egypt was known as the home of fine linen weaving. Babylon's pleasant climate made sheep-rearing a good prospect there, although that was not the only reason for the growth of the wool crafts in that area. Unlike the Egyptians, who appeared to have loved clarity of line in everything, the Babylonians were fond of ornate designs, made of heavy woolen fabric covered with elaborate decoration. It is almost certain that crochet work was used early in time there for this purpose, although later in Babylonian history, there was a revolt against the luxury of over-ornate clothes and the people needed to resort to the simple wool "sack" again, often knitted or worked in crochet.

Also, crochet and other wool crafts had a very profound place in the philosophy of the time. Creating fabric without any artificial aid was seen as a declaration of man's kinship with a god. It was an acknowledgement of the fact that he owed his skill and intellect to some greater being.

Crochet patterns in use in India are very similar to Moslem patterns found in North Africa, this again giving strength to the theory that crochet has been a continuously used craft in the Middle East for thousands of years; and although it never quite died out over the centuries, the art did suffer an almost total eclipse when more mechanical fabric-making methods were developed, and did not begin to flourish again until the time of the Renaissance. Then, ecclesiastical crochet, along with other fabrics of the time, acquired a high standard of technique and beauty. Much crochet work during that period was imitative of the more expensive lace or embroidery, such as needlepoint, Richelieu, Guipure, Honiton and filet.

It is no wonder, however, that the art of crochet earned the nickname of "nuns' work". At that time, wool crafts, such as crochet or knitting, were common occupations in convents. They remained the almost exclusive domain of the clergy (unlike weaving which lay people practised in their own homes) until a later time, when crochet was thought to be suitable for the more comfortable young ladies of the parish to learn. Nuns established it as one of the main crafts to be taught in the "finishing courses" of the day.

The word "crochet" is probably derived from the French word "croc", meaning hook—but has only really been in popular use since the early 1800s, when the production of fine cotton thread in the newly established English mills made it easy to carry out the craft. Paradoxically enough, it took a disaster to make the craft a really widespread and popular pastime. It was the Irish potato famines of the 1840s and '50s which revived an almost forgotten skill and made it into a major cottage industry. Crop failures forced millions of farming families to look for an alternative method of earning much-needed cash. Making crochet collars, ruffles and other adornments was a simple, though time-consuming way, and crochet work was much in demand by the well-to-do ladies of the time. There had been a history of crochet in Ireland since the end of the eighteenth century. The craft had probably been introduced from France by a young Irish woman, Honoria Nagle, who was lucky enough to have been sent to Paris to be educated. There, she became aware of the vast difference between the rich and the poor. The squalor of the poor compared with the ludicrous extravagance of the court made her determined to do something worthwhile in her homeland when she returned. She recruited four other young women who were sympathetic to her cause, and they, too, went to learn the craft from the Carmelite nuns in France. The five determined women passed the basic skills on to any one of the poor of County Cork who were willing to learn. Whoever had a spare hour or two among these hard-working people could be found busy with the crochet hook. And it was not just woman's work.

Irishmen and boys tending sheep or goats on the hills were expected to contribute their share of hours and income.

Irish crochet became a craft in its own right. Its workers incorporated beautiful designs taken from their rural backgrounds. Motifs included farmyard animals, roses, wheels and, of course, the legendary shamrock leaf. The art became a widespread cottage industry and was also included in the syllabus of the educational system in Ireland.

The main crochet centers were Cork and its surrounding district in the south, and Monaghan in the north. County Cork became a principal center of the industry and by the 1870s it is estimated that there were from 12,000 to 20,000 women in the area producing crochet, using continental patterns adapted from original lace designs from France, Italy and Greece.

Many Irish men and women saved the extra money which they earned by creating Irish crochet for their passage to America, taking their skills with them. Eventually there were many immigrants in the prosperous Midwest who could thank the humble crochet hook for their deliverance from the starvation which had killed thousands in their homeland.

In England, Prince Albert's inspired Great Exhibition of 1851 did much to promote the craft by bringing it to the attention of designers and manufacturers all over the world. In fact, the Victorians at that time almost smothered the art with their enthusiasm for it. Ladies became addicted to the crochet hook and made coverings to decorate everything imaginable. Nothing escaped them. Antimacassars, bedspreads, tablecloths, coasters were all produced with an almost feverish addiction. One wonders now whether these objects were made as useful household items or merely to indulge their passion for crochet. Even piano legs were discreetly covered with crochet frills!

Unfortunately, Victorian over-indulgence helped to dampen the enthusiasm of following generations for the craft, and it ceased to be fashionable for several decades. Luckily it did not disappear completely. It has a remarkable survival record and was revived in the 1950s along with a new appreciation of all the well-known handcrafts. Crochet has become widely popular, partly as a reaction to mass-production, and it is probably used more creatively now than at any time in its long history.

Below An exquisite example of Irish crochet

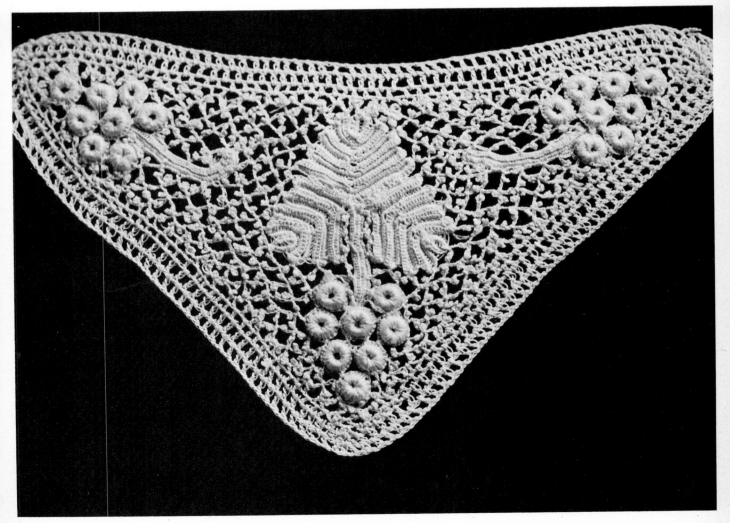

BASIC STITCHES

The crochet hook

There are a variety of hook sizes to choose from and these range from very fine to very thick. Aluminum or plastic hooks are graded from size A up to K. An appropriately sized hook should be selected for working each thickness of yarn. For example, use a size K hook for thick rug yarn, a size H hook for knitting worsted weight yarn, a size F for sport weight yarn and a fine steel hook ranging anywhere from No.1 through No. 14. For cotton thread, the size of the hook depends on the fineness of the cotton. A beginner will find it much easier to work with a fairly large hook such as an H and a knitting worsted weight yarn.

Unlike knitting, all crochet is made up from one working loop on the hook at any time. This first working loop begins as a slip loop. To make a slip loop, hold the cut end of yarn in the left hand and wrap the yarn around the first and second fingers. Place the hook under the first finger and draw yarn through loop on the fingers, removing loop from left hand. Draw the yarn tightly onto the hook to keep it in place. This first slip loop does not count as a stitch, but is merely a starting loop for any pattern, and is the last loop fastened off at the end of the work. The left hand holds the yarn to feed it towards the hook, and there are several ways of holding it to control the flow of yarn important for achieving an even fabric. Try to remember always to keep the thumb and first finger of the left hand as close to the hook as possible and to move up the work as each new stitch is completed.

To work chain stitches

Hold the hook in the right hand between the thumb and first finger, letting the hook rest against the second finger, and place the hook under the yarn between the first and second fingers of the left hand from front to back. Let the hook catch the yarn and draw through a loop on the hook, thus replacing the stitch. One chain has now been completed and the abbreviation for this is "ch". Repeat this action to make the necessary number of chains.

An alternative to this method of making a foundation chain is the double chain. To work this, make 2 chain in the usual way, insert hook into the 2nd chain from hook, * yarn around hook and draw through a loop, yarn around hook and draw through both loops on hook, *, continue to make a length of double chain by inserting the hook into the 2nd or left hand loop of the 2 loops which have just been dropped from the hook and repeat from * to *. This method gives a firm foundation and is easy to work.

Left hand workers should reverse the instructions, reading left for right and right for left. To follow the illustrations, prop up the book in front of a mirror where the reversed image can be clearly seen.

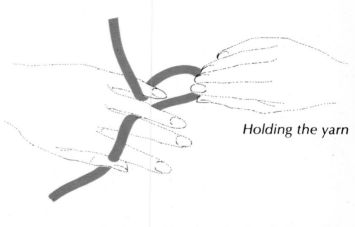

Holding the yarn

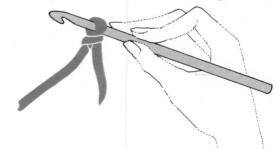

Position of hook to begin chain stitches

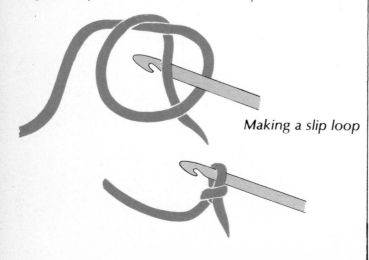

Making a slip loop

Basic stitches

Various stitches can now be worked into the foundation chain to form a crochet fabric. Each stitch gives a different texture and varies in depth, and every row gives a new chain line into which the next row is worked. When stitches are worked back and forth in rows, there is no right or wrong side of the fabric, and the work is turned at the end of each row ready to begin the next row.

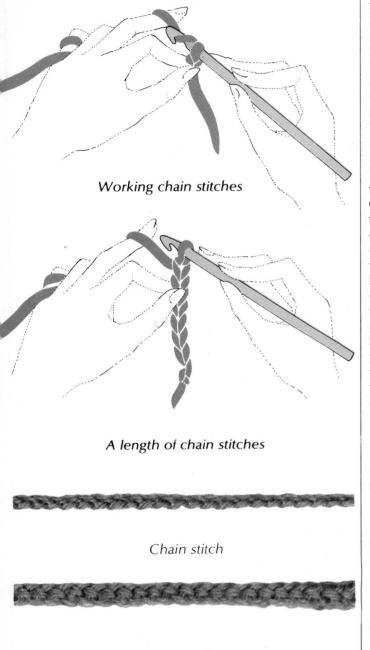

Working chain stitches

A length of chain stitches

Chain stitch

Single chain

Slip stitch The first stitch with the smallest depth is the slip stitch and this is abbreviated as "sl st". To work slip stitch into the foundation chain work the desired length, say 10 chain, and place the hook into the last chain, then place hook under the yarn in the left hand – this is called "yarn around hook" and is abbreviated as "yrh" or "yo" –, and draw yarn through the chain and the loop on the hook. Continue in this manner to the end of the chain.

Single crochet The second stitch, which has a greater depth than slip stitch, is single crochet and this is abbreviated as "sc". To work this stitch make 10 foundation chain, but remember that this stitch is deeper than slip stitch. Therefore, before you work this row, provision must be made to lift the working loop on the hook to the height of the single crochet stitches. For single crochet, work one chain more than the required number of stitches, in this case 11 chain in all, and work the first single crochet into the 2nd chain from the hook. These extra chains are called "turning chains" and the number of chains vary according to the depth of the stitch being worked. To work single crochet, place the hook under both loops of the chain or just under one loop of the chain, place yarn around hook and draw yarn through both loops on hook. One single crochet has now been worked and this is repeated to the end of the row. Check that 10 single crochet have been worked, noting that the turning chain counts as the first single crochet on this row only. Turn the piece, work one chain to count as the first single crochet of the next row, skip the first single crochet of the previous row which has been replaced by a turning chain then work one single crochet into each stitch of the previous row including the first turning chain at the beginning of the previous row.

Fastening off When you have worked the fabric to the necessary length, cut the yarn about 6 inches from the work, thread the end through the one loop on the hook and pull tight. The remaining end can be darned in later.

Chain with slip stitch

Single crochet worked into two loops

Single crochet worked into a single loop

Sample worked in single crochet

FABRIC STITCHES

There are numerous crochet stitches and, by experimenting with different types of yarn, you can achieve many effects. Here we give instructions for working some of the basic stitches and several variations that may be formed from them. Work each sample on 10 stitches. Each stitch has a given depth and it is important that provision is made for this depth at the start of each row with "turning chains".

Half double crochet

Work 10ch plus 1ch to be the turning chain. Place yarn around hook – this is abbreviated as "yo" –, insert hook into 3rd ch from hook, yo and draw through a loop (3 loops on hook), yo and draw through all 3 loops. One half double has now been completed and this is abbreviated as "hdc". Continue in this way into each ch to the end of the row. Turn work. Start a new row with 2ch to count as the first hdc and work 1hdc into each stitch to end, including the turning chain at the beginning of the previous row.

Double crochet

Work 10ch plus 2ch to be the turning chain. Yo and insert hook into 4th ch from hook, yo and draw through a loop (3 loops on hook), yo and draw through first 2 loops on hook, yo and draw through remaining 2 loops. One double crochet has now been completed. This is abbreviated as "dc". Work 1dc into each ch to the end of the row. Turn work. Start a new row with 3ch to count as the first dc and work 1dc into each stitch to the end of the row, including the 3rd of the turning chain 3 of the previous row.

Treble crochet

Work 10ch plus 3ch to be the turning chain. Yo twice, insert hook into the 5th ch from hook, yo and draw through a loop (4 loops on hook), (yo and draw through first 2 loops on hook) twice, yo and draw through remaining 2 loops. One treble has now been completed and this is abbreviated as "tr". Work 1tr into each ch to the end of the row. Turn work. Start a new row with 4ch to count as first tr and work 1tr into each stitch to the end of the row, including the 4th ch of the turning chain 4 of the previous row.

Double trebles

Work 10ch plus 4ch to be the turning chain. Yo three times, insert hook into 6th ch from hook, yo and draw through a loop (5 loops on hook), (yo and draw through first 2 loops on hook) four times. One double treble has now been completed and this is abbreviated as "dtr". Start new rows with 5ch to count as first dtr and work 1dtr into each stitch to the end of the row, including the 5th ch of the 5 turning chain.

Ridged single crochet

This is produced by working in sc, but the hook is inserted into the back loop only of each stitch of every row. The unworked front loops of the stitches produce a pronounced ridged effect.

Russian stitch

This is another stitch that is formed by working in single crochet, but not turning the work at the end of each row. Instead, the yarn is fastened off and cut when each row has been completed and the cut ends are darned in later. There is a definite right and wrong side to this stitch.

Raised treble crochet

These are worked on the surface of a basic single crochet fabric to give a vertical ridged effect. Make 21ch and work 1sc into 3rd ch from hook, then work 1sc into each ch to the end of the row. Turn work. Start the pattern row with 1ch and 1sc into next sc, *yo twice and insert hook into the horizontal loop of next sc on the third row below, yo and complete the tr in the usual way, 1sc into each of next 3sc, rep from * to the end of the row. Always working 3 rows of single crochet between the pattern rows, work subsequent pattern rows by inserting the hook under the vertical bar of the previous tr and completing the tr in the usual way.

Counterpane stitch

As the name implies, "counterpanes" or bedspreads, were made in this stitch. The fabric produced is soft and elastic. Work 11ch. Yo, insert hook into 3rd ch from hook, yo and draw a loop through this stitch and the first loop on the hook, yo and draw through the remaining 2 loops. Repeat into each stitch throughout, always working 2ch for the first stitch at the beginning of every row.

Double crochet in relief

This is a more decorative stitch with a ridged effect. Make 12ch and work 1dc into 4th ch from hook, then work 1dc into each ch to the end of the row. Turn work. Start a new row with 3ch to count as the first dc and work across the row in dc by placing the hook between the first and second dc of the previous row horizontally, yo and draw through a loop, yo and complete the stitch. At the end of the row work 1dc into the 3rd of the 3 turning chain.

A selection of squares worked in the various stitches learned so far may be made in Knitting Worsted yarn and a size H crochet hook. Each will have a different texture and, made in a variety of colors, the squares will look most attractive. They then can be sewn together to make an attractive area rug.

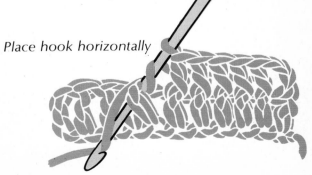

Place hook horizontally

First projects

One of the most convenient ways of trying out new crochet stitches is to combine learning with the making of practical items. These two projects not only afford the beginner the opportunity of trying out her new skills, but also show the versatility of crochet when worked with unusual materials.

Mini pillows

These pillows, about 9 inches square, are worked in half double crochet but can be made in either double or single crochet.

Materials

4oz of tubular rayon macramé cord, straw, or very narrow ribbon
One size K crochet hook
9in square pillow pad

Working the crochet

Using size K hook make enough ch to measure 9in, about 22ch, including one extra chain to count as turning ch.
1st row Into third ch from hook work 1hdc, then 1hdc into each ch to end. Turn. If you had 22ch to start with you should now have 21hdc.
2nd row 2ch to count as first hdc, skip first hdc, 1hdc into each hdc to end, working the last hdc under the turning ch of the previous row. Rep second row until work measures 18in from beg. Fasten off.

Finishing

Fold work in half WS tog and join 2 side edges with a sl st. Insert cushion pad and join the remaining edge.

Rag rug

This rug, measuring 8ft 8in by 4ft 4in, is another example of using materials other than crochet wools. If you have a lot of scrap cotton fabric in a rag-bag, you can tear it up into strips about $\frac{3}{4}$ inch wide. Wind up the strips into balls, separating the colors. Work two or three rows with one color then change

to another to build up an interesting pattern. Because the rug is worked in strips it is easy to handle while you work. If you don't feel like tackling a rug, use slightly thinner strips of fabric – about $\frac{1}{2}$ inch wide – to make country-style table mats.

Materials

Lengths of cotton fabric in 4 colors. (The total amount of material will depend on the length of rug desired and the way in which stripes of colors are arranged: 6yds of 36in wide fabric will work out to about 30in in length.)

One size K crochet hook
Button thread

To work the crochet

1st strip Using size K hook and any color, make enough ch to measure 13 inches in width, about 27ch should be the correct amount and this includes one ch for turning.
1st row Into third ch from hook work 1sc, then 1sc into each ch to end. Turn. If you had 27ch to start with you should now have 26sc.
2nd row 1ch to count as first sc, 1sc into each sc to end, working the last sc under the turning ch of the previous row. Turn. Rep second row for desired length, changing colors as desired and working over the ends each time a new strip is joined in to secure them.
2nd strip Make enough ch (about 19 should be right including 1ch for turning) to measure 9 inches in width.
3rd strip Make enough ch (about 35 should be right including 1ch for turning) to measure 17 inches in width.
4th strip Work as given for first strip to make 13 inches in width.

Finishing

Sew strips together with button thread.

SHAPING
Increasing and decreasing

Crochet patterns can be increased or decreased in two ways – either at the side edges or in the course of a row. More than one stitch may be increased or decreased at a time and is usually worked at the beginning and end of a row. To increase several stitches, extra chains are added, and to decrease several stitches at the beginning of a row, the necessary number to be decreased are worked across in slip stitch and then remain unworked on subsequent rows; and at the end of a row, the required number of stitches are simply left unworked.

In most designs the shaping required either to insure a properly fitting garment or to make provision for essential openings, such as armholes and neckbands, is achieved by increasing or decreasing at a given point in the pattern. Because of the depth of most crochet stitches, unless this shaping is worked neatly and evenly, a noticeable gap will be left in the pattern, and this can spoil the appearance of the finished garment. The methods given here will overcome this problem, and wherever you are instructed to increase or decrease in a pattern without being given specific details, choose the method which will give the best results.

Increasing
To increase one stitch in the course of a row, simply work twice into the same stitch. For example, when working in double crochet continue along the row in the usual way until you reach the position for the increase, put yarn over hook, insert hook into next stitch and draw through yarn (three loops on the hook), yarn over hook and draw through two loops on hook, yarn over hook and draw through last two loops on hook, yarn over hook and insert hook into the same stitch again and draw through yarn (three loops on the hook), yarn over hook and draw through two loops on hook, yarn over hook and draw through last two loops on hook. One loop is now left on the hook and one double crochet has been increased. This method applies to all stitches.

To increase one stitch at each end of row, work twice into the first and last stitch of the previous row. When using thick yarns, however, a smoother edge is formed if the increase is worked into the second stitch at the beginning of the row and into the next to last stitch at the end of the row. This method applies to all stitches.

To increase several stitches at the beginning of a row, make a chain equivalent to one less than the number of extra stitches required plus the required number of turning chains. If six stitches are to be increased when working in double crochet, for example, make five chains plus three turning chains, the next double crochet for the new row being worked into the fourth chain from the hook. The three turning chains count as the first stitch.

To increase several double crochet at the end of a row, the best way is to make provision for these extra stitches at the beginning of the previous row. To do this make three chain to count as the turning chain, then make the exact number of chains required for the increased stitches, say six. Work in slip stitch along these first six chains, then complete the row by working one double crochet into each stitch of the previous row, noting that the three turning chains have already been worked to count as the first stitch.

To increase several stitches at the beginning and end of the same row, combine the two previous methods, noting that the increase row will end by working one double crochet into the turning chain and in each of the six slip stitches of the previous row.

Decreasing
To decrease one stitch in the course of a row when working in single crochet, simply skip one stitch of the previous row at the given point. Because single crochet is a short stitch, this skipped stitch will not leave a noticeable hole.

To decrease one stitch when working in half double crochet, work along the row until the position for the decrease is reached, yarn over hook and insert hook into next stitch, yarn over hook and draw through loop, yarn over hook and insert hook into next stitch, yarn over hook and draw through loop (five loops on hook), yarn over hook and draw through all loops on hook. One half double crochet has now been decreased by making one stitch out of two.

To decrease one stitch when working in double crochet, work along the row until the position for the decrease is reached, yarn over hook and insert hook into next stitch, yarn over hook and draw through loop, yarn over hook and draw through two loops on hook, yarn over hook and insert hook into next stitch, yarn over hook and draw through loop, yarn over hook and draw through two loops on hook, yarn over hook and draw through remaining three loops on hook. One double crochet has now been decreased by making one stitch out of two.

To decrease one stitch when working in treble crochet, work along the row until the position for the decrease is reached, yarn over hook twice and insert hook into next stitch, yarn over hook and draw through loop, yarn over hook and draw through two loops on hook, yarn over hook and draw through two loops on hook (two loops on hook), yarn over hook twice, insert hook into next stitch, yarn over hook and draw through loop, yarn over hook and draw through two loops on hook, yarn over hook and draw through two loops on hook (three loops

on hook), yarn over hook and draw through all loops on hook. One treble crochet has now been decreased by making one stitch out of two.

To decrease one stitch at each end of a row when working in single crochet, make two turning chains at the beginning of the row, skip the first two single crochet of the previous row, noting that the turning chain forms the first stitch, work one single crochet into the next stitch, continue in single crochet along the row until only one single crochet and the turning chain of the previous row remain, skip the last single crochet and work one single crochet into the turning chain.

To decrease one stitch at each end of a row when working in half double crochet, make one turning chain at the beginning of the row instead of two, skip the first half double crochet of the previous row, noting that the turning chain forms this stitch, work in half double crochet across the row until only one half double crochet and the turning chain of the previous row remain, work the last half double crochet and the turning chain together to make one stitch. At the end of the next row, work one half double crochet into the last half double crochet and skip the turning chain.

To decrease one stitch at each end of a row when working in double crochet and treble crochet, work as for half double crochet, noting that only two and three turning chains respectively are worked at the beginning of the decrease row.

To decrease several stitches at the beginning of a row, slip stitch over the required number of stitches, make the required number of turning chains for the stitch being used and continue along the row.

To decrease several stitches at the end of a row, continue along the row to within the number of stitches to be decreased and turn the work, noting that the turning chain of the previous row must be counted as one of the stitches.

How to make a belt or pillow

To practice the methods of increasing and decreasing, you can make attractive triangle shapes using odds and ends of Knitting Worsted and a size 1 crochet hook. To make a belt, begin with three chain and work in single crochet, increasing one stitch at the beginning and end of every row until the desired size is reached, then fasten off. Continue making triangles in this way for the desired length of the belt, then sew them together as shown. Finish one end of the belt with a buckle.

To make a pillow you will need eight large triangles, four for each side. Begin with 70 chain for each triangle and work in half double crochet, decreasing one stitch at each end of every row until two stitches remain, then work these two stitches together to form a point. Sew four triangles together for each side, points to center, then sew outside edges together, inserting a zipper in center of the last edge. Insert a pillow pad to complete the project.

A pretty pull-on hat

Size
To fit an average head

Gauge
24 sts and 16 rows to 4in in patt worked
with size E crochet hook

Materials
2 × 2oz balls sport yarn
One size E crochet hook
1yd narrow ribbon

Hat
Using size E hook make 5ch. Join with
a sl st to first ch to form a ring.
1st round 3ch to count as first hdc and
1ch sp, (work 1hdc into ring, 1ch) 7 times.
Join with a sl st to 2nd of first 3ch. 8 sps.
2nd round 3ch to count as first hdc and
1ch sp, work 1hdc into first ch sp, 1ch,
*work 1hdc, 1ch, 1hdc all into next ch sp—
called inc 1—, 1ch, rep from * to end.
Join with a sl st to 2nd of first 3ch. 16 sps.
3rd round 3ch, work 1hdc into first ch sp,
1ch, work 1hdc into sp between hdc
groups, 1ch, *inc 1 into next inc 1, 1ch,
1hdc into sp between hdc groups, 1ch,
rep from * to end. Join with a sl st to 2nd
of first 3ch. 24 sps.
4th round 3ch, skip first 1ch sp, *work
1hdc into next 1ch sp, 1ch, rep from *
to end. Join with a sl st to 2nd of first 3ch.
The 4th round forms the patt and is rep
throughout.
5th round 3ch, work 1hdc into first ch
sp, 1ch, (1hdc into next 1ch sp, 1ch) twice,
*inc 1, 1ch, (1hdc into next 1ch sp, 1ch)
twice, rep from * to end. Join with a sl st
to 2nd of first 3ch. 32 sps.
6th round As 4th.
7th round 3ch, work 1hdc into first ch sp,
1ch, (1hdc into next 1ch sp, 1ch) 3 times,
*inc 1, 1ch, (1hdc into next 1ch sp, 1ch)
3 times, rep from * to end. Join with a sl
st to 2nd of first 3ch. 40 sps.
8th round As 4th.
Cont inc 8 sps in this way on next and
every alt round until there are 64 sps.
Mark end of last round with colored
thread to show beg of rounds. Work 4th
patt round 16 times more, without inc
and without joining rounds.
Shape brim
Next round *Patt 7 sps, inc 1, rep from *
to end.
Next round *Patt 8 sps, inc 1, rep from *
to end.
Rep 4th patt round 4 times more, without
inc and without joining rounds. Fasten
off.

Finishing
Do not block. Thread ribbon through
lower edge of crown to tie at back.

DECORATIVE FABRIC STITCHES

This chapter is about decorative fabric stitches, telling you how to work them and how they might be used. They are all variations of the basic stitches already described. Included with them are examples of cluster and bobble stitches, which look very effective when used with basic stitches such as double crochet and single crochet, since they form a raised surface and add texture to the work.

Aligned stitch

Using size H hook and Knitting Worsted, make 22ch.
1st row (Yo and insert hook into 4th ch from hook, yo and draw through a loop, yo and draw through first 2 loops on hook) twice, yo and draw through remaining 3 loops – one aligned st has now been formed –, rep into every ch to the end of the row. Turn.
2nd row 3ch to count as first st, skip first aligned st, * yo and insert hook into next aligned st, (yo and draw through a loop, yo and draw through first 2 loops on hook), yo and rep this step once more into the same st, yo and draw through 3 remaining loops on hook, rep from * to the end of the row, working last aligned st into 3rd of the 3ch. Turn.
The last row is repeated throughout to form the pattern.

Crossed half double crochet

Using size H hook and Knitting Worsted, make 21ch.
1st row Yo and insert hook into 3rd ch from hook, yo and draw through a loop, yo and insert hook into next ch, yo and draw through a loop, yo and draw through all 5 loops on hook, 1ch, * yo and insert hook into next ch, yo and draw through a loop, yo and insert hook into next ch, yo and draw through a loop, yo and draw through all 5 loops on hook, 1ch, rep from * to last ch, 1hdc into last ch. Turn.

2nd row 3ch, yo and insert hook into first 1ch space, yo and draw through a loop, yo and insert hook into next 1ch space, yo and draw through a loop, yo and draw through all 5 loops on hook, 1ch, * yo and insert hook into same 1ch space, yo and draw through a loop, yo and insert hook into next 1ch space, yo and draw through a loop, yo and draw through all 5 loops on hook, 1ch, rep from * to end, 1hdc into 2nd of the 3ch. Turn.
The last row is repeated throughout to form the pattern.

Granite stitch

Using size H hook and Knitting Worsted, make 22ch.
1st row Into 3rd ch from hook work (1sc, 1ch and 1sc), skip next ch, * (1sc, 1ch and 1sc) into next ch, skip next ch, rep from * to last ch, 1sc into last ch. Turn.
2nd row 1ch, * (1sc, 1ch and 1sc) into 1ch space of next group, rep from * end, 1sc into the turning ch. Turn.
The last row is repeated throughout to form the pattern.

Palm leaves

Using size H hook and Knitting Worsted, make 22ch.

1st row Into 4th ch from hook work 1sc, * 2ch, skip next 2ch, 1sc into next ch, rep from * to end. Turn.

2nd row 3ch to count as first dc, 1dc into first sc, * 3dc into next sc, rep from * to end, working 2dc into first of the 3ch. Turn.

3rd row 3ch, 1sc into 2nd dc of the first 3dc group, * 2ch, 1sc into 2nd dc of next 3dc group, rep from * to end, working last sc into 3rd of the 3ch. Turn.

Repeat the 2nd and 3rd rows throughout to form the pattern.

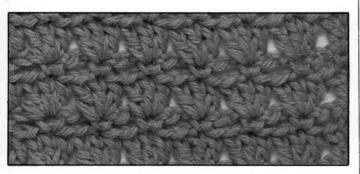

Cock's head doubles

Using size H hook and Knitting Worsted, make 22ch.

1st row Into 4th ch from hook work 1dc, * (yo and insert hook into next ch, yo and draw through a loop, yo and draw through first 2 loops on hook) twice, yo and draw through all 3 loops, 1ch, rep from * to end, omitting the 1ch at the end of the last rep.

2nd row 4ch, yo and insert hook into first st, yo and draw through a loop, yo and draw through first 2 loops, skip next st, yo and insert hook into next st, yo and draw through a loop, yo and draw through first 2 loops, yo and draw through all 3 loops, * 1ch, yo and insert hook into same st that last st was worked into, yo and draw through a loop, yo and draw through first 2 loops, skip next st, yo and insert hook into next st, yo and draw through a loop, yo and draw through first 2 loops, yo and draw through all 3 loops, rep from * to end, 1ch, 1dc into 3rd of the 3ch. Turn.

3rd row As 2nd, but note that the last st is worked into the 3rd of the 4ch. Turn.

The last row is repeated throughout to form the pattern.

Forget-me-not stitch

Using size H hook and Knitting Worsted, make 25ch.

1st row Into 4th ch from hook work (1dc, 2ch and 1sc), * skip next 2ch, (2dc, 2ch and 1sc) into next ch, rep from * to end. Turn.

2nd row 3ch, (1dc, 2ch and 1sc) into first 2ch space, * (2dc, 2ch and 1sc) into next 2ch space, rep from * to end. Turn.

The last row is repeated throughout to form the pattern. This stitch looks very attractive when two colors are used on alternate rows.

To design a dirndl skirt

Any one of these attractive stitches that you have just learned, together with a knowledge of checking gauge are all you will need to design a lovely dirndl skirt.

For example, if you are a 36 inch hip size, you will need one inch ease. This means that each piece of your skirt will measure $18\frac{1}{2}$ inches across. If your gauge is 4 sts to one inch, then you will require $18\frac{1}{2} \times 4 = 74$ stitches for the basic pattern.

No shaping is required. You just work to the desired length and gather the waist with rows of shirring elastic.

Wall hanging

Another use for the various stitches learned thus far is to make them into a wall hanging. This will look particularly attractive if you choose one color and work each stitch in a different shade of this color. A very good finishing touch to this would be to mount the hanging on a brass pole.

CLUSTER AND BOBBLE STITCHES

Cluster and bobble stitches

Edgings using either the bobble or cluster stitch make ideal trimmings for the neckline or hemline of a dress and also edgings for jackets, vests and household linens. The same stitches can also be used to make square or circular motifs for a bedspread or evening stole, and they can replace stitches on a basic design, adding a great deal of interest to a simple fabric.

Here three examples of the many variations of cluster stitch are illustrated and explained in detail. For these samples a size G crochet hook and Knitting Worsted were used, although the hook size and type of yarn will vary depending on the purpose of the work.

Cluster or pine stitch

Make 26ch.

1st row Into 3rd ch from hook work 1sc, 1sc into each ch to end. Turn.

2nd row 1ch to count as first sc, skip first sc, 1sc into each sc, ending with 1sc into the turning chain. Turn.

3rd row (cluster row) 4ch, skip first 2sc, ** yo and insert hook into next sc, yo and draw through a loop extending it for $\frac{3}{8}$ inch, * yo and insert hook into same sc, yo and draw through a loop, extending it for $\frac{3}{8}$ inch, rep from * 3 times, yo and draw through all 11 loops on hook – called 1cl –, 1ch, skip next sc, rep from ** ending with 1dc into the turning chain. Turn.

4th and 5th rows Work in sc. Fasten off.

Using the cluster stitch, practice making square motifs. Worked in one color and a cotton yarn, they are ideal for making quilts or tablecloths, or worked in fine, multi-colored yarns they are lovely for attractive evening stoles.

In the instructions for the square motif given here we

used 4 colors which are referred to as A, B, C and D.

Square motif

With A, make 5ch. Join into ring with a slip stitch.

1st round 1ch to count as first sc, 15sc into ring, ending with a sl st into first ch. 16sc. Fasten off A and join in B.

2nd round 4 ch to count as first dc and linking ch, * 1dc into next sc, 1ch, rep from * ending with a sl st into 3rd of the 4 starting ch. Fasten off B and join in C.

3rd round Sl st into next 1ch space, * 3ch, 1cl into same 1ch space, rep from * ending with 3ch, sl st into top of first cl. Fasten off C and join in D.

4th round Sl st into next 3ch space, 1ch, 2sc into same space, 3sc into each of next 2 spaces, * (1hdc, 1dc, 2ch, 1dc, 1hdc) into next space for corner, 3sc into each of the next 3 spaces, rep from * twice more, 1 corner into next space, sl st into first ch. Fasten off.

Raised clusters

By using the method of raising clusters on a basic fabric, many designs such as diagonals and zigzags may be incorporated.

The instructions given below are for raised clusters on a single crochet background.

Make 25ch.

1st to 3rd rows Work in sc as for the basic cluster sample.

4th row 1ch to count as first sc, skip first sc, 1sc into each of next 3sc, * insert hook into next sc, yo and draw through a loop, (yo and insert hook into space on the 3rd row directly below this stitch, yo and draw through a loop, yo and draw through first 2 loops on hook) 5 times, yo and draw through all 6 loops on hook – called 1 raised cl – , 1sc into each of next 4sc, rep from * to end.

5th to 7th rows Work in sc.

8th row Repeat the raised cluster on every 5th stitch depending on the effect that you want to create.

You will see that diagonals or alternating clusters have been formed in our illustrations. Repeat rows 1 through 8 to achieve this effect.

Two more raised stitches are the bobble and the

popcorn stitch. The instructions given here are for an allover bobble design and a popcorn stitch that is worked into a braid.

Bobble stitch

Make 26ch.

1st row Into 3rd ch from hook work 1sc, 1sc into each ch to end. Turn.

2nd row 1ch to count as first sc, * 4ch, skip 2sc, leaving the last loop of each st on hook work 6dtr into next sc, yo and draw through all 7 loops on hook – called B1 – , 4ch, skip next 2sc, 1sc into next sc, rep from * ending with 1sc into turning chain. Turn.

3rd row 5ch to count as first dc and linking ch, 1sc into first B1, * 5ch, 1sc into next B1, rep from * ending with 2ch, 1dc into the turning chain. Turn.

4th row 5ch to count as first dc and linking ch, 1sc into next sc, * 4ch, B1 into next 5ch space, 4ch, 1sc into next sc, rep from * ending with 2ch, 1dc into 3rd of the turning chain. Turn.

5th row 1ch to count as first sc, * 5ch, 1sc into next B1, rep from * ending with 5ch, 1sc into 3rd of the turning chain. Turn.

6th row 1ch to count as first sc, * 4ch, B1 into next 5ch space, 4ch, 1sc into next sc, rep from * ending with 1sc into the turning chain. Turn.

The 3rd through 6th rows are repeated throughout to form the pattern.

Bobble stitch

Popcorn stitch

Make 25ch.

1st row Into 4th ch from hook work 1dc, 1dc into each ch to end. Turn.

2nd row 3ch to count as first dc, skip first dc, 1dc into each dc, ending with 1dc into the turning chain.

3rd row 3ch to count as first dc, skip first dc, 1dc into next dc, * 1ch, 5dc into next dc, slip working st off the hook and pick up the ch st worked before the 5dc, pick up working loop and draw through the ch st – 1 popcorn st has now been worked – , 1dc into each of next 2dc, rep from * ending with 1dc into the turning chain. Turn.

4th and 5th rows Work in dc. Fasten off.

BLOCKING AND FINISHING

In the previous chapters, many stitches and some ways of working them have been explained, using a variety of materials. This chapter is designed to give you some useful hints on the blocking and finishing of your work and on how to apply these and various other interesting techniques to the making of many useful decorative things such as the bags we show here.

Gauge

Before starting a piece of work that has a definite size requirement, for example, a sweater to fit a 34 inch bust, it is important to make sure that the garment will measure the correct size when it is completed. A gauge sample must be worked before you start. Follow the gauge guide at the beginning of the pattern and, using the suggested yarn and hook, make a small square approximately 4in in width and depth. Place a ruler on the work and count how many stitches and rows there are to the inch. If there are too many stitches, then your gauge is too tight and you must practice with a larger hook until you gain the correct gauge. Too few stitches mean that you are working too loosely and need to use a smaller hook.

Blocking

Part of the pleasing appearance of crochet is its textured surface. Many people prefer not to block the work as they fear the effect of a warm iron and damp cloth will spoil this texture. Also, with so many new and different kinds of yarn on the market, blocking could quite well be unnecessary. Always read the manufacturer's instructions on the yarn label to check if this final finish is recommended and also the way in which it should be done.

As a general rule, most yarns containing a high percentage of natural fibers such as wool and cotton can be blocked under a damp cloth with a warm iron. Man-made yarns such as nylon and acrylics need a cool iron and dry cloth.

Most crochet, especially when it is very open in texture, does need blocking out on completion. When you are blocking the individual pieces before finishing use a clean, flat covered surface onto which you pin the pieces out to the correct measurements with rustless dressmaking pins.

When done cover the work with a damp cloth and leave until the cloth is absolutely dry.

Cotton crochet items such as delicate edgings or table cloths and place mats often look better for a light starching.

For this use a starch solution (about two teaspoonfuls to a pint of hot water), or a gum arabic solution. Dab the solution over the article while it is being blocked out.

Joining in new yarn

In crochet, it is better to avoid tying knots when joining in new yarn. Work until about 3 inches of the yarn is left, lay this across the top of the previous row to the left, lay the beginning of the new yarn with it and work over both ends with the second ball of yarn.

If the join comes when chain is being worked, lay the new thread alongside the first one, the ends pointing

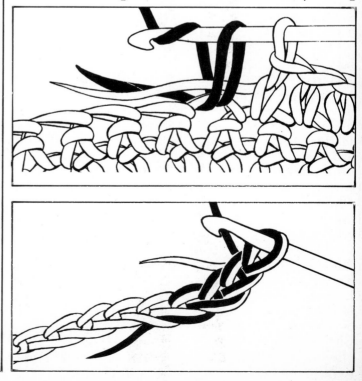

in opposite directions, and work with the double thickness until the first thread runs out.

Joining two pieces of crochet work

There are two methods of doing this – either by sewing the pieces together or by using crochet stitches to make a seam.

Sewing Place the two pieces of work with right sides together and pin firmly. Overcast the edge using a matching yarn. When the seam is completed it may be necessary to block it.

When joining stripes or patterns take care to see that the seams match exactly to insure a professional finish.

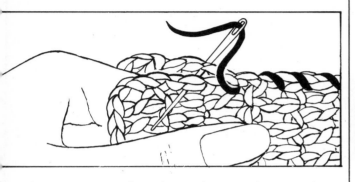

Crochet Joining work with crochet stitches can form part of the design and look very attractive. In the illustration you will see a section of a bag where the gusset has been joined to the main part with single crochet.

Methods of making a handbag

Generally there are two types of handbags, one with a gusset and one without. The gusset is a narrow piece of fabric between the two main sections used to give the bag a three-dimensional effect.

Commercial handles for bags may be purchased from the needlework counters of most large stores. The traditional wooden frames illustrated do not require a

gusset. Simply work two pieces of crochet to the required size and join together either by sewing or crocheting, leaving an opening in the top edge of the handles to be inserted and hemmed into place.

If you have used crochet stitches to join your bag, then you could insert tassels through the joining stitches along the lower edge at whatever spacing you like. Our sample illustration has been worked in different colors to clarify the various stages of finishing and the method of adding the tassels is shown clearly.

Other types of commercial handles available are the bamboo rings and various metal frames which have a screw-in bar and clasp fastening.

A firm handle may not be required and a gusset strip can be made to fit around the bag with an extension which is left free for a handle as shown in our illustration.

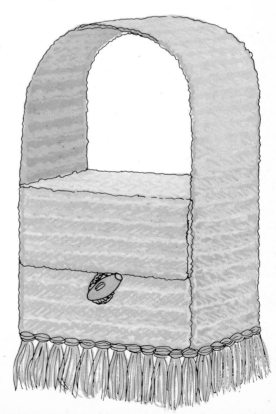

FIRST SIMPLE GARMENTS
Smart dress set

A simple dress to crochet with a cardigan and beret to match.

Sizes
Directions are to fit 32in bust. Changes for 34:36:38 and 40in bust are in brackets [ ].
34[36:38:40:42]in hips
Dress length to shoulder, 39[39:39¼:39¼:39½]in
Jacket length to shoulder, 23½[23½:23½:24:24]in
Sleeve seam 17½in

Gauge
Dress and beret 19 sts and 24 rows to 4in in patt worked with size F crochet hook
Jacket 21 sts and 13 rows to 4in in patt worked with size F crochet hook

Materials
Dress 9[10:11:12:13] × 2oz balls Brunswick Pomfret Sport yarn
One size F crochet hook
One 20 in zipper

Jacket 7[7:8:8:9] × 2 oz balls Brunswick Pomfret Sport yarn
One size F crochet hook
3 buttons

Beret 2 × 2oz balls Brunswick Pomfret Sport yarn
One size F crochet hook

Dress front
**Using size F hook make 111[115:121:125:131]ch.
Base row (WS) Into 2nd ch from hook work 1sc, 1sc into each ch to end. Turn. 110[114:120:124:130] sts.
Start patt.
1st row 1ch, 1sc into each st to end. Turn.
This row forms patt. Work 7 more rows in patt.
Shape sides
Cont in patt, dec one st at each end of next and every foll 8th row until 88[92:98:102:108] sts rem. Work 7 rows without shaping. **
Shape waist darts
1st row Dec one st, 1sc into each of next 21[22:25:26:28] sts, dec one st, 1sc into each of next 38[40:40:42:44] sts, dec one st, 1sc into each st to last 2 sts, dec one st. Turn.
Work 7 rows without shaping.
9th row Dec one st by working 2sc tog, 1sc into each of next 20[21:24:25:27] sts, dec one st, 1sc into each of next 36[38:38:40:42] sts, dec one st, 1sc into each st to last 2 sts, dec one st. Turn.
Work 7 rows without shaping. Cont dec

in this way on next and every foll 8th row until 68[72:78:82:88] sts rem. Cont without shaping until work measures 24½in from beg, ending with a WS row.
Shape bust darts
1st row 1ch, 1sc into same st, 1sc into each of next 17[18:21:22:24] sts, 2sc into next st, 1sc into each of next 30[32:32:34:36] sts, 2sc into next st, 1sc into each st to last st, 2sc into last st. Turn.
Work 7 rows without shaping.
9th row 1ch, 1sc into same st, 1sc into each of next 18[19:22:23:25] sts, 2sc into next st, 1sc into each of next 32[34:34:36:38] sts, 2sc into next st, 1sc into each st to last st, 2sc into last st. Turn.
Work 7 rows without shaping. Cont inc in this way on next row and foll 8th rows. 84[88:94:98:104] sts. Cont without shaping until front measures 31½[31½:31½:32½:32½]in from beg, ending with a WS row.
Shape armholes
1st row Sl st over first 5[5:6:7:8] sts, 1ch, patt to last 5[5:6:7:8] sts, turn.
Dec one st at each end of next and every foll alt row until 62[66:70:70:74] sts rem. Cont without shaping until armholes measure 5¾[5¾:6:6:6¼]in from beg, ending with a WS row.
Shape neck
Next row Patt 25[27:28:28:30] sts, turn. Complete this side first. Keeping armhole edge straight, dec one st at neck edge on each of next 7 rows, ending at armhole edge.
Shape shoulder
1st row Sl st across first 3[4:5:5:4] sts, 1ch, patt to end. Turn.
2nd row Patt to last 4[4:4:4:5] sts, turn.
3rd row Sl st over first 4[4:4:4:5] sts, 1ch, patt to end. Turn.
4th row Patt 3[4:4:4:4] sts. Fasten off.
With RS of work facing, skip first 12[12:14:14:14] sts for center front neck, rejoin yarn to next st, 1ch, 1sc into each st to end. Turn.
Dec one st at neck edge on each of next 7 rows, ending at neck edge.
Shape shoulder
1st row Patt to last 3[4:5:5:4] sts, turn.
2nd row Sl st over first 4[4:4:4:5] sts, 1ch, patt to end. Turn.
3rd row Patt 7[8:8:8:9] sts. Turn.
4th row Sl st across first 4[4:4:4:5] sts, 1ch, patt to end. Fasten off.

Dress back
Work as given for front from ** to **
Shape waist darts
1st row Dec one st, 1sc into each of next 21[22:25:26:28] sts, 1sc into each of next 38[40:40:42:44] sts, dec

one st, 1sc into each st to last 2 sts, dec one st. Turn.
Work 3 rows without shaping.
5th row 1ch, 1sc into each of next 21[22:25:26:28] sts, dec one st, 1sc into each of next 36[38:38:40:42] sts, dec one st, 1sc into each st to end. Turn.
Work 3 rows without shaping.
9th row Dec one st, 1sc into each of next 20[21:24:25:27] sts, dec one st, 1sc into each of next 34[36:36:38:40] sts, dec one st, 1sc into each st to last 2 sts, dec one st. Turn.
Work 3 rows without shaping.
13th row 1ch, 1sc into each of next 20[21:24:25:27] sts, dec one st, 1sc into each of next 32[34:34:36:38] sts, dec one st, 1sc into each st to end. Turn. 76[80:86:90:96] sts.
Work one row without shaping.
Divide for back opening
Next row 1ch, 1sc into each of next 37[39:42:44:47] sts, turn.
Complete this side first.
1st row 1ch, 1sc into each st to end. Turn.
2nd row Dec one st, 1sc into each of next 19[20:23:24:26] sts, dec one st, 1sc into each st to end. Turn.
Work 3 rows without shaping.
6th row 1ch, 1sc into each of first 19[20:23:24:26] sts, dec one st, 1sc into each st to end. Turn.
Work 3 rows without shaping.
10th row Dec one st, 1sc into each of next 18[19:22:23:25] sts, dec one st, 1sc into each st to end. Turn.
Work 3 rows without shaping.
14th row 1ch, 1sc into each of first 18[19:22:23:25] sts, dec one st, 1sc into each st to end. Turn.
Work 3 rows without shaping.
18th row Dec one st, 1sc into each of next 17[18:21:22:24] sts, dec one st, 1sc into each st to end. Turn.
Work 3 rows without shaping.
22nd row 1ch, 1sc into each of first 17[18:21:22:24] sts, dec one st, 1sc into each st to end. Turn 29[31:34:36:39] sts.
Cont without shaping until back measures 24½in from beg, ending with a WS row.
Shape side edge and dart
1st row 1ch, 1sc into same st, 1sc into each of next 17[18:21:22:24] sts, 2sc into next st, 1sc into each st to end. Turn.
Work 3 rows without shaping.
5th row 1ch, 1sc into each of next 18[19:22:23:25] sts, 2sc into next st, 1sc into each st to end. Turn.
Work 3 rows without shaping.
9th row 1ch, 1sc into same st, 1sc into each of next 18[19:22:23:25] sts, 2sc into next st, 1sc into each st to end. Turn.
Cont inc at side edge in this way on every foll 8th row and for dart on every

179

4th row until there are 41[43:46:48:51] sts. Cont without shaping until back measures same as front to underarm, ending at side edge.

Shape armhole
1st row Sl st over first 5[5:6:7:8] sts, 1ch, patt to end. Turn.
Dec one st at armhole edge on next and every alt row until 31[33:35:35:37] sts rem. Cont without shaping until armhole measures same as front to shoulder, ending at armhole edge.

Shape shoulder
1st row Sl st across first 3[4:5:5:4] sts, 1ch, patt to end. Turn.
2nd row Patt to last 4[4:4:4:5] sts, turn.
3rd row Sl st across first 4[4:4:4:5] sts, 1ch, patt 7[8:8:8:9] sts, turn.
4th row Work in patt 3[4:4:4:4] sts. Fasten off. With RS of work facing, rejoin yarn to rem sts at back opening and complete to correspond to first side, reversing shaping.

Finishing
Block each piece lightly under a damp cloth with a warm iron.
Join shoulder and side seams.
Neck and back opening edging Using size F hook and with RS of work facing, rejoin yarn to left back neck edge at opening edge. Work one row sc round neck, down right back opening and up left back opening. Do not turn, but work one row in sc from left to right instead of from right to left.
Armhole edging Using size F hook and with RS of work facing, work as given for neck and back edging.
Block seams lightly. Sew zipper into back opening.

Jacket right front
**Using size F hook make 44[47:50:53:56] ch.
Base row (WS) Into 2nd ch from hook work 1sc, *2ch, skip 2ch, 1sc into next ch, rep from * to end. Turn.
43[46:49:52:55] sts.
Start patt.
1st row 2ch, 1dc into first sc, *skip 2ch, 3dc into next sc, rep from * ending with skip 2ch, 2dc into last sc. Turn.
2nd row 1ch, 1sc into first dc, *2ch, skip 2dc, 1sc into next dc, rep from * to end. Turn.
The last 2 rows form patt. Work 7 more rows in patt, ending with a RS row.
Shape side edge
Maintaining patt, dec one st at beg of next row and at same edge on every foll 3rd row until 37[40:43:46:49] sts rem. Cont without shaping until front measures 10in from beg, ending with a RS row. **

Shape side and front edges
1st row Inc in first st, patt to last 2 sts, dec one st. Turn.
2nd and 3rd rows Patt to end. Turn.
4th row Dec one st, patt to end. Turn.
5th and 6th rows Patt to end. Turn.
Rep last 6 rows twice more. 34[37:40:43:46] sts.

Shape armhole
Next row Sl st over first 4[5:5:6:6] sts, 1ch, patt to last 2 sts, dec one st. Turn.
Cont dec at front edge as before, *at the*

same time dec one st at armhole edge on next 4[5:7:7:8] rows. Keeping armhole edge straight, cont dec at front edge on every 3rd row until 19[20:21:23:25] sts rem. Cont without shaping until armhole measures 7[7:7:7½:7½]in from beg, ending at armhole edge.

Shape shoulder
1st row Sl st over first 4[5:5:5:7] sts, 1ch, patt to end. Turn.
2nd row Patt to last 5[5:5:6:6] sts, turn.
3rd row Sl st over first 5[5:5:6:6] sts, 1ch,

patt to end. Fasten off.

Left front
Work as given for right front from ** to **, reversing shaping.
Shape front and side edges
1st row Dec one st, patt to last st, inc in last st. Turn.
2nd and 3rd rows Patt to end. Turn.
4th row Patt to last 2 sts, dec one st. Turn.
5th and 6th rows Patt to end. Turn.

Rep last 6 rows twice more. Turn.
Shape armhole
Next row Dec one st, patt to last 4[5:5:6:6] sts, turn.
Complete armhole and front edge shaping as given for right front, reversing shaping. Cont without shaping until armhole measures 7[7:7:7½:7½]in from beg, ending at neck edge. Turn.
Shape shoulder
1st row Patt to last 4[5:5:5:7] sts, turn.
2nd row Sl st over first 5[5:5:6:6] sts, 2ch, patt to end. Turn.
3rd row Patt 5[5:6:6:6] sts.
Fasten off.

Back
Using size F hook make 92[98:104: 110:116] ch. Work base row as given for right front. 91[97:103:109:115] sts. Work 9 rows patt as given for right front.
Shape sides
Dec one st at each end of next and every foll 3rd row until 79[85:91:97:103] sts rem. Cont without shaping until piece measures 10in from beg, ending with a RS row. Inc one st at each end of next and every foll 6th row 3 times in all. 85[91:97:103:109] sts.
Work 5 rows without shaping.
Shape armholes
Next row Sl st over first 4[5:5:6:6] sts, 1ch, patt to last 4[5:5:6:6] sts, turn.
Dec one st at each end of next 4[5:7:7:8] rows. 69[71:73:77:81] sts.
Cont working in patt without shaping until armholes measure same as front to shoulder, ending with a RS row.
Shape shoulders
1st row Sl st over first 4[5:5:5:7] sts, 1ch, patt to last 4[5:5:5:7] sts, turn.
2nd row Sl st over first 5[5:5:6:6] sts, 2ch, patt to last 5[5:5:6:6] sts, turn.
3rd row Sl st over first 5[5:5:6:6] sts, 1ch, patt over next 5[5:6:6:6] sts, sl st over next 31 sts, patt over next 5[5:6:6:6] sts.
Fasten off.

Sleeves
Using size F hook make 41[44:44: 47:47] ch. Work base row as given for right front. 40[43:43:46:46] sts. Work 3 rows patt as given for right front. Maintaining patt, inc one st at each end of next and every foll 3rd row until there are 50[53:55:62:64] sts, then inc one st at each end of every foll 4th row until there are 64[67:69:72:74] sts. Cont without shaping until sleeve measures 17½in from beg, ending with a RS row.
Shape top
Next row Sl st over first 4[5:5:6:6] sts, 1ch, patt to last 4[5:5:6:6] sts, turn.
Dec one st at each end of every row until

34[35:37:34:36] sts rem. Dec 2 sts at each end of next 4 rows. 18[19:21:18:20] sts. Fasten off.

Finishing
Block each piece under a damp cloth with a warm iron. Join shoulder seams. Set in sleeves. Join side and sleeve seams.
Border Using size F hook and with RS of work facing, rejoin yarn to right front at lower edge. Work one row sc up right front edge, working 3sc into each 2 row ends, cont across back neck, working into each st, then work down left front as given for right front. Turn.
Next row 1ch 1sc into each st to end. Turn. Rep last row once more. Mark position for 3 buttonholes on right front, the first ½in below first row of front edge shaping and the last to come 2½in from lower edge with the third spaced evenly between.
Next row (buttonhole row) Work in sc to end, making 3 buttonholes when markers are reached by working 3ch and skipping 3 sts. Work 3 rows sc, working 3sc into 3ch buttonhole loop on first row. Fasten off. Block seams and border lightly. Sew on buttons.

Beret
Using size F hook make 6ch. Join with a sl st to first ch to form a ring.
1st round 1ch, work 11sc into a ring. Join with a sl st to first ch. 12 sts.
2nd round 1ch, 1sc into same st, 1sc into next st, *2sc into next st, 1sc into next st, rep from * to end. Join with a sl st to first 1ch. 18 sts.
3rd round 1ch, 1sc into same st, 1sc into each of next 2 sts, *2sc into next st, 1sc into each of next 2 sts, rep from * to end. Join with a sl st to first 1ch. 24 sts.
4th round 1ch, 1sc into same st, 1sc into each of next 3 sts, * 2sc into next st, 1sc into each of next 3 sts, rep from * to end. Join with a sl st to first 1ch. 30 sts.
Cont inc in this way on every round until there are 132 sts. Work 10 rounds without shaping.
Shape headband
Next round *Dec one st, 1sc into each of next 20 sts, rep from * to end. Join with a sl st to first st.
Next round *Dec one st, 1sc into each of next 19 sts, rep from * to end. Join with a sl st to first st.
Cont dec in this way on every round until 84 sts rem. Turn.
Next round 1ch, 1sc into each sc to end. Join with a sl st to first 1ch. Turn.
Rep last round 3 times more. Fasten off.

Finishing
Block lightly as for dress.

A simple lightweight dress

**

Short and simple, here's a light-weight dress that will look good day or evening.

Size
Directions are to fit 34in bust, changes for 36, 38 and 40in bust sizes are in brackets [ ].
Length to shoulder, 36[36¼:36½:36¾]in
Sleeve seam, 5in

Gauge
20 sts and 9 rows to 4in in dc worked with size E crochet hook;
22 sts and 20 rows to 4in in sc worked with size E crochet hook

Materials
17[20:23:25] 125yd balls Lily Sugar 'n Cream Yarn in main color, A
1 ball each of contrast colors, B and C
One size E crochet hook
20in zipper

Skirt
Using size E hook and A, make 111ch

and start at waist, working from top to lower edge.

1st row (RS) Into 3rd ch from hook work 1sc, 1sc into each of next 18ch, 1hdc into each of next 20ch, 1dc into each of next 70ch. Turn. 110 sts.

2nd row 3ch to count as first dc, 1dc into front loop only of next 69dc, 1hdc into front loop only of next 20hdc, 1sc into front loop only of next 19sc, 1sc into turning ch. Turn.

3rd row 1ch to count as first sc, 1sc into front loop only of next 19sc, 1hdc into front loop only of next 20hdc, 1dc into front loop only of next dc, 1dc into turning ch. Turn.

The 2nd and 3rd rows form the patt and are rep throughout. Cont in patt until work measures 25[27:29:31]in from beg, measured across the waist edge. Fasten off.

Hem

Using size E hook, B and with RS of work facing, rejoin yarn to lower edge of skirt.

Next row 2ch to count as first sc, (1dc, 1ch, 1dc, 1sc) into first row end, *1ch, 1sc into next row end, 1ch, (1sc, 1dc, 1ch, 1dc, 1sc) into next row end, rep from * to end. Break off B. Join in C. Do not turn.

Next row Rejoin yarn at beg of row, 2ch, (1dc, 1ch, 1dc, 1sc) into first ch sp between dc's, *1ch, 1sc into next sc, 3ch, 1sc into same sc, 1ch (1sc, 1dc, 1ch, 1dc, 1sc) into next 1ch sp between dc's, rep from * to end. Fasten off.

Bodice

Using size E hook, A and with RS of work facing, rejoin yarn and work 150[162:174:186]sc across waist edge. Work 3 rows sc, working into front loop only of each sc throughout.

Shape darts

Next row 1ch, work 1sc into each of next 40[43:46:49]sc, (2sc into next sc) twice, 1sc into each of next 19[22:25:28]sc, (2sc into next sc) twice, 1sc into each of next 22sc, (2sc into next sc) twice, 1sc into each of next 19[22:25:28]sc, (2sc into next sc) twice, 1sc into each of next 41[44:47:50]sc. Turn. 158[170:182:194]sc.

Work 3 rows without shaping.

Next row 1ch, work 1sc into each of next 41[44:47:50]sc, (2sc into next sc) twice, 1sc into each of next 21[24:27:30]sc, (2sc into next sc) twice, 1sc into each of next 24sc, (2sc into next sc) twice, 1sc into each of next 21[24:27:30]sc, (2sc into next sc) twice, 1sc into each of next 42[45:48:51]sc. Turn. 166[178:190:202]sc.

Work 3 rows without shaping. Cont inc 8 sts in this way on next and every foll 4th row until there are 198[210:230:242]sts. Cont without shaping until work measures 8in from waist, or desired length to underarm, ending with a WS row.

Divide for armholes

Next row Patt across 45[48:52:55] sts, turn.

Complete left back first. Dec one st at beg of next and at same edge on every row until 35[38:42:45] sts rem. Cont without shaping until armhole measures 5½[5¾:6:6¼]in from beg, ending at armhole edge.

Shape neck

Next row Patt across 20[22:24:26] sts, turn.

Dec one st at beg of next and at same edge on every row until 16[18:20:22] sts rem. Cont without shaping until armhole measures 7[7¼:7½:7¾]in from beg, ending at neck edge.

Shape shoulder

Next row Patt across 8[9:10:11] sts, turn and fasten off.

With RS of work facing, skip first 8[8:10:10] sts for underarm, rejoin yarn to next st and patt across 92[98:106:112] sts for front, turn.

Dec one st at each end of next 10 rows. 72[78:86:92] sts. Cont without shaping until armholes measure 3½[3¾:4:4¼]in from beg, ending with a WS row.

Shape neck

Next row Patt across 26[28:30:32] sts, turn.

Complete this side first. Dec one st at beg of next and at same edge on every row until 16[18:20:22] sts rem. Cont without shaping until armhole measures same as back to shoulder, ending at neck edge.

Shape shoulder

Next row Patt across 8[9:10:11] sts, turn and fasten off.

With RS of work facing, skip first 20[22:26:28] sts for center neck, rejoin yarn to rem sts and patt to end. Complete to match first side, reversing shaping.

With RS of work facing, skip first 8[8:10:10] sts for underarm, rejoin yarn to rem sts and patt to end. Complete right back to correspond to left back, reversing shaping.

Sleeves

Using size E hook and A, make 22ch and work from side edge to side edge.

1st row (RS) Into 4th ch from hook work 1dc, 1dc into each ch to end. Turn. 20dc.

2nd row 3ch to count as first dc, *1dc into front loop only of next dc, rep from * ending with 1dc into turning ch. Turn.

Shape top

Next row 3ch, 1hdc, into 3rd of these 3 ch, *1dc into front loop only of next dc, rep from * ending with 1dc into turning ch. Turn. 22 sts.

Next row 3ch to count as first dc, 1dc into front loop only of next 19dc, 1hdc into front loop only of next hdc, 1hdc into turning ch. Turn.

Next row 3ch, 1hdc into 3rd of these 3 ch, 1hdc into front loop only of next 2hdc, 1dc into front loop only of each dc to end. Turn. 24 sts.

Next row 3ch to count as first dc, 1dc into front loop only of next 19dc, 1hdc into front loop only of next 3hdc, 1hdc into turning ch. Turn.

Cont inc in this way, rep last 2 rows 4[5:6:7] times more. 32[34:36:38] sts.

Next row 5ch, 1sc into 3rd of these 5ch, 1sc into each of next 2ch, 1hdc into front loop only of each of next 14[16:18:20] hdc, 1dc into front loop only of each dc to end. Turn. 36[38:40:42] sts.

Next row 3ch, 1dc into front loop only of next 19dc, 1hdc into front loop only of next 14[16:18:20] hdc, 1sc into front loop only of next 3sc, 1sc into turning ch. Turn.

Rep last 2 rows 2[3:4:5] times more. 44[50:56:62] sts. Work 12 rows patt as now set without shaping, ending at top edge.

Next row Sl st across first 4sc and into next sc, 1ch to count as first sc, patt to end. Turn. 40[46:52:58] sts.

Next row Patt to end. Turn.

Rep last 2 rows 2[3:4:5] times more. 32[34:36:38] sts.

Next row Sl st across first 2hdc and into next hdc, 2ch to count as first hdc, patt to end. Turn. 30[32:34:36] sts.

Next row Patt to end. Turn.

Rep last 2 rows until 20dc rem. Work 1 row dc. Fasten off.

Cuff

Using size E hook, B and with RS of work facing, work along lower edge of sleeve as given for hem. Fasten off.

Neckband

Join shoulder seams. Using size E hook, B and with RS of work facing, work evenly round neck edge as given for hem. Fasten off.

Finishing

Block each piece under a damp cloth with a warm iron. Join sleeve seams. Set in sleeves, easing in fullness at top. Join center back seam leaving an opening for zipper to reach to top of neckband. Sew in zipper. Press seams.

Using rem yarn make a twisted cord or braided belt.

CROCHET IN ROUNDS
CIRCULAR MOTIFS

Crochet may very easily and effectively be worked into circles or squares instead of back and forth in rows. Each piece is worked from the same side. This means that there is a definite right and wrong side to the work.

Circular shapes are an important technique in crochet. Sun hats, berets, bags and doilys are among the many articles worked in this way.

Attractive shapes may be joined together to give a patchwork fabric that works well for shawls, rugs, vests, boleros and evening skirts.

Again, try experimenting in various yarns to see the many effects that may be achieved.

To work a circle in crochet

Using size H hook and Knitting Worsted make 6ch. Join together to form a ring with a sl st into the first ch.

1st round 3ch to count as the first dc, then work 15dc into the ring. Join with a sl st to the 3rd of the first 3ch. 16dc.

2nd round 3ch, 2dc into each dc of the previous round, 1dc into the base of the turning ch. Join with a sl st to the 3rd of the first 3 ch. 32dc.

3rd round 3ch, (1dc into next stitch, 2dc into next stitch) 15 times, 1dc into next stitch, 1dc into base of the turning ch. Join with a sl st to the 3rd of the first 3ch. 48dc.

4th round 3ch, (1dc into each of next 2 stitches, 2dc into next stitch) 15 times, 1dc into each of next 2 stitches, 1dc into base of the turning ch. Join with a sl st to the 3rd of the first 3ch. 64dc.

Continue in this way, working 1 extra dc on each round until the circle is the desired size. To practice this method of making a circle and produce a useful item for the home at the same time, make two circles to any desired size and use them to cover a pillow pad or, using three thicknesses of Speed-Cro-Sheen Cotton and a size K hook, make a bath mat. A fringed edging would add the final touch to either of these items.

Another way to make a circular motif

Make 6ch. Join with a sl st to first ch to form a ring.

1st round 2ch to count as first sc, work 7sc into ring. Do not join, but cont working rounds, working next 2sc into second of first 2 ch.

2nd round Work 2sc into each sc to end. 16sc.

3rd round Work 1sc into each sc to end.

4th round Work 2sc into each sc to end. 32sc.

5th round Work 1sc into each sc to end.

6th round 2sc into first sc, 1sc into next sc,*2sc into next sc, 1sc into next sc, rep from * to end. 48sc.

7th round Work 1 round without shaping.

8th round 2sc into first sc, 1sc into each of next 2sc, *2sc into next sc, 1sc into each of next 2sc, rep from * to end. 64sc.

Cont inc 1sc on every other round until the motif is the desired size.

To do this, the space between each 2sc into 1sc increases by one stitch every increasing round so that on round 10, work 2sc into next sc, 1sc into next 3sc; and on round 12, work 2sc into next sc, 1sc into next 4sc. Cont increasing 16sc on every alternate round in this way until the circle is desired size. Sl st into first st of previous round and fasten off.

String place mat (page 24)
Size
12in in diameter

Materials
1 ball of garden twine

One size H crochet hook

Place mat
Work as given for circular motif until 14 rounds have been completed and total 112sc. Do not fasten off.

To make a scallop edging
Next round 3ch to count as first sc and 1ch sp, skip first 2sc, 1sc into each of the next 3sc, *1ch, skip 1sc, 1sc into each of next 3sc, rep from * to last 2sc, 1sc into each of last 2sc. Join with sl st to second of first 3ch.
Next round Into each 1ch sp work (1sc, 3dc, 1sc). Join with sl st to first sc. Fasten off.

Using circles to make a clown
This toy is made up of circles in various sizes. Odds and ends of Knitting Worsted in red, yellow, orange and black and size G crochet hook are used. For the main part, make a total of 95 circles by working the first and second rounds of the circle motif. The black cuffs and ankle ruffles have the third round added, while the neck ruffle has the fourth round worked and the skirt has an additional fifth round. Make 2 small black circles for each hand and foot, joining each pair of circles and stuffing them with cotton batting. For the head work 3 rounds of the circle motif and include a circle of stiff cardboard with the stuffing.
Thread elastic through the center of each circle and join them together in this way: each arm consists of 17 small circles and a cuff which is inserted 1 circle before the hand; the body has 11 circles plus the skirt, and the legs have 25 circles each plus a ruffle which again is inserted 1 circle before the foot.

Straw belt
Size
To fit 23[25:27]in waist
(Each motif measures $2\frac{1}{4}$in in diameter)
Figures in [ ] refer to 25 and 27in sizes respectively

Materials
3[3:4] hanks of straw in 1 color or in odds and ends of different colors
1 size F crochet hook

Belt
With size F hook and any color work first 3 rounds as for the circular motif.
Join next color and work 2 more rounds as for the circular motif. Fasten off.
Make 9[10:11] more motifs in the same way.

Finishing
Join motifs tog where edges touch to form one row. Make 3 separate ch, each to measure 48[50:52]in long. Working on wrong side, stitch one ch across the back of top

WORKING WITH SQUARES

To work a square in crochet

Either make this square entirely in one color or use a different color for each round.

Using size H crochet hook and Knitting Worsted, make 6ch. Join to form a ring with a sl st into the first ch.

1st round 6ch, work (1dc and 3ch) 7 times into the ring. Join with a sl st to the 3rd of the first 6ch.

2nd round Sl st into the first 2ch space, so that the next group of dc will be worked into a space and not into a stitch, work 3ch to count as the first dc, 3dc into this same space, (2ch and 4dc into the next space) 7 times, 2ch. Join with a sl st to the 3rd of the first 3ch.

3rd round Sl st into each of next 4 stitches to insure that the next group of dc's will be worked into a 2ch space, 3ch, 5dc into this same space, 1ch, (6dc and 3ch into next space, 6dc and 1ch into next space) 3 times, 6dc into next space, 3ch. Join with a sl st to the 3rd of the first 3ch.

4th round Sl st into each of next 6 stitches to insure that the hook is over the next 1ch space, 4ch, (1sc into space between the 3rd and 4th dc of next 6dc group, 3ch, 2dc, 3ch, 2dc all into next space, 3ch, 1sc into space between 3rd and 4th dc of next 6dc group, 3ch, 1sc into next 1ch space, 3ch) 3 times, 1sc into space between 3rd and 4th dc of next 6dc group, 3ch, 2dc, 3ch, 2dc all into next 3ch space, 3ch, 1sc into space

between 3rd and 4th dc of next 6dc group, 3ch. Join with a sl st to 2nd of the first 4ch. Fasten off.

Granny squares using 2 or more colors

(Breaking off yarn at end of each round.) Make starting ch and work first round as for motif in one color. Break off yarn and fasten off.

2nd round Join next color to any 2ch sp with a sl st, 3ch to count as first dc, work 2dc into same ch sp, *1ch, work (3dc, 2ch, 3dc) into next 2ch sp to form corner, rep from * twice more, 1ch, 3dc into same 2ch sp, as at beginning of round, 2ch. Join with a sl st to third of first 3ch. Break off yarn and fasten off.

3rd round Join next color to any 2ch sp with a sl st, 3ch to count as first dc, work 2dc into same ch sp, *1ch, 3dc into 1ch sp, 1ch, work (3dc, 2ch, 3dc) into 2ch sp, rep from * twice more, 1ch, 3dc into 1ch sp, 1ch, 3dc into same 2ch sp as at beginning of round, 2ch. Join with a sl st to third of first 3ch. Break off yarn and fasten off.

4th round Join next color to any 2ch sp with a sl st, 3ch to count as first dc, work 2dc into same ch sp, *(1ch, 3dc into next 1ch sp) twice, 1ch, work (3dc, 2ch, 3dc) into 2ch sp, rep from * twice more, (1ch, 3dc into next 1ch sp) twice, 1ch, 3dc into same 2ch sp as at beginning of round, 2ch. Join with a sl st to third of first 3ch. Break off yarn and fasten off. Darn in ends of yarn where colors were joined.

To make a half-square

Using one or more colors Each row must be started with a fresh strand of yarn at the same side at which the row was first started.

Make 5ch. Join with sl st to first ch to form a ring.

1st row Using same color, 4ch to count as first dc and 1ch sp, work (3dc, 2ch, 3dc) into a ring, 1ch, 1dc into a ring. Fasten off.

2nd row Join next color to third of first 4ch with sl st, 4ch, 3dc into first 1ch sp, 1ch, work (3dc, 2ch, 3dc) into 2ch sp, 1ch, 3dc into last 1ch sp, 1ch, 1dc into top of last dc on previous row. Fasten off.

3rd row Join next color to third of first 4ch with sl st, 4ch, 3dc into first 1ch sp, 1ch, 3dc into next 1ch sp, 1ch, work (3dc, 2ch, 3dc) into 2ch sp, (1ch, 3dc into next 1ch sp) twice, 1ch, 1dc into top of last dc on previous row. Fasten off.

4th row Join next color to third of first 4ch with sl st, 4ch, 3dc into first 1ch sp, 1ch, (3dc into next 1ch sp, 1ch) twice, work (3dc, 2ch, 3dc) into 2ch sp, (1ch, 3dc into next 1ch sp) 3 times, 1ch, 1dc into last dc. Fasten off.

Square pillow

A pillow 16in square

Materials

$8\frac{3}{4}$oz of Knitting Worsted in one color; $1\frac{3}{4}$oz in each of 7 contrasting colors, A, B, C, D, E, F and G.
One size H crochet hook
Pillow pad 16in square
8in zipper

Large square

Using size H crochet hook and any color, work first 4 rounds as for square motif, changing color on each round.

5th round Join in any color with sl st to corner 2ch sp, 3ch to count as first dc, 2dc into same sp, *(1ch, 3dc into next 1ch sp) 3 times, 1ch, (3dc, 2ch, 3dc) into corner 2ch sp, rep from * twice more, (1ch, 3dc into next 1ch sp) 3 times, 1ch, 3dc into same sp as beg of round, 2ch. Join with sl st to third of first 3ch. Fasten off.

Cont in this way, changing the color as shown, and working one more group of 3dc and 1ch on each side of every round until work measures 16in across. Fasten off. Darn in all ends. Make another square in the same manner

Finishing

With RS of squares tog, join 3 edges.

Turn RS out. Insert pillow pad. Join rem seam, leaving sp to insert zipper in center.

Edging Using size H hook and any color, rejoin yarn with sl st to any corner sp through both thicknesses. Into each ch sp round all edges work (1 sl st, 4dc, 1 sl st) working through both thicknesses, except across the zipper opening, where you work through only one thickness. Join with sl st to first sl st. Fasten off. Sew in zipper.

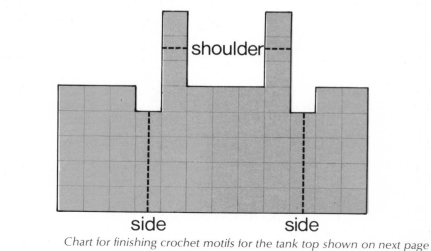

Chart for finishing crochet motifs for the tank top shown on next page

Tank top

Sizes

34[36/38:39/40]in bust
Length to shoulder 19½[21:22½]in
The figures in brackets [ ] refer to 36/38 and 39/40in bust respectively.

Gauge

One square motif for first size measures 3in × 3in worked with size C hook; for second size measures 3¼in × 3¼in worked with size D hook; for third size measures 3½ × 3½in worked with size E hook.

Materials

Brunswick Fore'n Aft Sport Yarn
3[4:4] × 2oz balls in main color, A
3[4:4] balls of contrast color, B
One size C[D:E] crochet hook 8in zipper

1st square motif (make 10)
Using size C[D:E] hook and B, make 4ch. Join with a sl st into first ch to form a ring.
1st round 3ch to count as first dc, 2dc into ring, *1ch, 3dc into ring, rep from * twice more, 1ch. Join with a sl st into 3rd of 3ch.
2nd round Sl st into next ch sp, 3ch to count as first dc, 2dc into same sp, 1ch, 3dc into same sp, *1ch, into next ch sp work 3dc, 1ch and 3dc, rep from * twice more, 1ch. Join with a sl st into 3rd of 3ch. Break off B.
3rd round Join in A. Sl st into next ch sp, 3ch to count as first dc, 3dc into same sp, 1ch, 4dc into same sp, 1sc into next ch sp, *into next ch sp work 4dc, 1ch and 4dc, 1sc into next ch sp, rep from * twice more. Join with a sl st into 3rd of 3ch.
4th round Sl st into next ch sp, 3ch to count as first dc, 2dc into same sp, 1ch, 3dc into same sp, into next ch sp 2 rounds below work 3tr, 1ch and 3tr, *into next ch sp of previous round work 3dc, 1ch 3dc, into next ch sp 2 rounds below work 3tr, 1ch and 3tr, rep from * twice more. Join with a sl st to 3rd of 3ch. Fasten off.

2nd square motif (make 10)
As 1st square motif in color sequence of 2 rounds A and 2 rounds B.

3rd square motif (make 11)
As 1st square motif in color sequence of 1 round B, 2 rounds A and 1 round B.

4th square motif (make 10)
As 1st square motif in color sequence of 1 round B, 1 round A, 1 round B and 1 round A.

5th square motif (make 11)
As 1st square motif in color sequence of 1 round A, 2 rounds B and 1 round A.

6th square motif (make 12)

As 1st square motif in color sequence of 1 round A, 1 round B, 1 round A and 1 round B.
There are now 64 square motifs in all.

Finishing

Block each square under a damp cloth with a warm iron. Using A, join squares as shown opposite, making a patchwork with the different color combinations.
Edging Using size C[D:E] hook and A, work 1 row sc around each armhole, neck and around shoulder edges and lower edge. Block seams.

A bright bag made of Granny squares

Chart for finishing bag

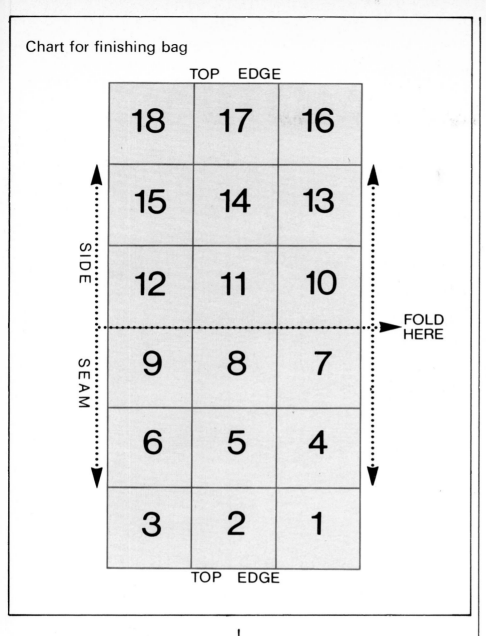

TOP EDGE

18	17	16
15	14	13
12	11	10
9	8	7
6	5	4
3	2	1

SIDE SEAM

FOLD HERE

TOP EDGE

5th round Using C, 1ch, *4ch, into 4ch sp work (3dc, 3ch, 3dc) to form corner, 4ch, 1sc into hdc, 1sc into 3ch sp, 1sc into hdc, rep from * twice more, 4ch, work corner, 4ch, 1sc into hdc, 1sc into 3ch sp. Join with a sl st to first ch. Break off C. Join in D.

6th round Using D, 1ch, *5ch, 1dc into each of next 3dc, 5ch, insert hook into 3rd ch from hook and work 1dc to form a picot – called 5ch picot –, 2ch, 1dc into each of next 3dc, 5ch, sl st into next sc, 4ch, insert hook into 3rd ch from hook and work 1sc to form picot – called 4ch picot –, 1ch, skip 1sc, sl st into next sc, rep from * twice more, 5ch, 1dc into each of next 3dc, 5ch picot, 2ch, 1dc into each of next 3dc, 5ch sl st into next sc, 4ch picot, 1ch. Join with a sl st to first ch. Fasten off.

Second motif

Using colors as desired, work as given for 1st motif until 5th round has been completed.

6th round (joining) Using any color, 1ch, *5ch, 1dc into each of next 3dc, 2ch, with RS of 1st motif facing RS of 2nd motif, work 1sc into 5ch picot at corner of 1st motif, 2ch, 1dc into each of next 3dc of 2nd motif, sl st into first of 5ch after last dc on 1st motif, 4ch, sl st into next sc of 2nd motif, 1ch, 1sc into 4ch picot of 1st motif, 1ch, skip 1sc on 2nd motif, sl st into next sc on 2nd motif, 4ch, sl st into last ch before next 3dc on 1st motif, 1dc into each of next 3dc on 2nd motif, 2ch, 1sc into 5ch picot at corner of 1st motif, 2ch, then complete round as given for 1st motif.

Work 16 more motifs in same way, using colors as desired and joining each motif where edges touch, as shown on chart.

Finishing

Darn in all ends. Press on WS under a dry cloth with a cool iron.

Top edges Using size I hook, A and with RS of work facing, rejoin yarn to corner picot at end of motif, 3ch to count as first dc, work 14 more dc evenly across first motif, work (15dc across next motif) twice. Turn. 45dc. Work 2 more rows dc. Fasten off. Work along other end in same way.

With RS facing fold motifs in half and join side seams as shown on chart. Seam lining in same way. Turn bag RS out and insert loose lining. Fold top edge over handle to WS and sew in place. Work other handle in same way. Sew top of lining to WS of top edge, easing in fullness. Sew lining to side edges of opening.

Size
18in wide by 18in deep

Gauge
Each motif measures 6in × 6in worked with size I crochet hook

Materials
6 ounces Knitting Worsted in main color, A
1 ounce each of 5 contrast colors, B, C, D, E and F
One size I crochet hook
2 round wooden handles
Lining material 18in wide × 36in long

First motif
Using size I hook and A, make 6ch. Join with a sl st to first ch to form a ring.
1st round Using A, 2ch to count as first sc, work 15sc into ring. Join with a sl st to 2nd of first 2ch.

2nd round Using A, 5ch to count as first hdc and 3ch, *skip 1sc, 1hdc into next sc, 3ch, rep from * 6 times more. Join with a sl st to 2nd of first 5ch. Break off A. Join in B.

3rd round Using B, work (1sc, 1hdc, 1dc, 1hdc, 1sc, 1ch) into each ch sp to end. Join with a sl st to first sc. 8 petals. Break off B. Join in C.

4th round Using C, 2ch to count as first hdc, *3ch, 1sc into dc of next petal, 4ch, 1sc into dc of next petal, 3ch, 1hdc into 1ch sp before next petal, 3ch, 1hdc into same ch sp, rep from * twice more, 3ch, 1sc in dc of next petal, 4ch, 1sc in dc of next petal, 3ch, 1hdc into last 1ch sp after last petal, 3ch. Join with a sl st to 2nd of first 2ch.

SQUARE AND WHEEL MOTIFS

The simple stitches you have learned can be used for all kinds of motifs, including these two completely different lacy ones. The motifs can be worked in fine or thick yarns, depending on the project in work or on personal choice.

Square lace motif

Make 6ch. Join with sl st to first ch to form a ring.

1st round 2ch to count as first sc, work 15sc into ring. Join with sl st to second of first 2ch.

2nd round 4ch to count as first hdc and 2ch, *skip 1sc, 1hdc into next sc, 2ch, rep from * 6 times more. Join with sl st to second of first 4ch.

3rd round Work (1sc, 1hdc, 1dc, 1hdc, 1ch) into each ch sp to end. Join with sl st to first sc. 8 petals.

4th round 2ch to count as first hdc, *3sc, 1sc into dc of next petal, 4ch, 1sc into dc of next petal, 3ch, 1hdc into 1ch sp before next petal, 2ch, 1hdc into same ch sp, rep from * twice more, 3ch, 1sc into dc of next petal, 4ch, 1sc into dc of next petal, 3ch, 1hdc into last 1ch sp after last petal, 2ch. Join with sl st to second of first 2ch.

5th round 1ch, *4ch, into 4ch sp, work (3dc, 3ch, 3dc) to form corner, 4ch, 1sc into hdc, 1sc into 2ch sp, 1sc into hdc, rep from * twice more, 4ch, into 4ch sp work (3dc, 3ch, 3dc), 4ch, 1sc into hdc, 1sc into 2ch sp. Join with sl st to first ch.

6th round 1c, *5ch, 1dc into each of next 3dc, 5ch, insert hook into third ch from hook to form a loop (see diagram) and work 1sc to form picot – called 5ch picot – 2ch, 1dc into each of next 3dc, 5ch, sl st into next sc, 4ch, insert hook into third ch from hook and

Forming a picot loop

work 1sc to form picot – called 4ch picot – 1ch, skip 1sc, sl st into next sc, rep from * twice more, 5ch, 1dc into each of next 3dc, 5ch picot, 2ch, 1dc into each of next 3dc, 5ch, sl st into next sc, 4ch picot, 1ch. Join in with sl st to first ch. Fasten off.

Catherine wheel motif

Make 8ch. Join with sl st to first ch to form a ring.

1st round 1ch to count as first sc, work 15sc into a ring. Join with sl st to first ch. 16 sts. Do not break off yarn.

First spoke

1st row Make 14ch, work 1sc into third ch from hook, 1sc into next ch, work 10sc around the chain, 1sc into each of last 3ch, sl st into next sc along the ring, turn.

2nd row Work 1sc into each of first 3sc, (4ch, skip 1sc, 1sc into next sc) 5 times, 1sc into each of next 2sc, 1sc into second of first 2ch. Turn.

3rd row 1ch to count as first sc, 1sc into each of next 3sc, (4sc into 4ch loop, 1sc into next sc) 5 times, 1sc into each of last 2sc, sl st into next sc. Turn.

Second spoke

1st row Make 13ch, sl st into center st of third loop along first spoke, turn, work 1sc into each of next 3ch, work 10sc along the ch, 1sc into each of last 3ch, sl st into next sc, turn and complete as for first spoke, but on next row end with 1sc into each of last 3sc instead of last 2sc and turning ch.

Work 6 more spokes in the same way and when working the last one, join the center of the 3rd loop to the tip of the first spoke. Fasten off. 8 spokes.

Last round Rejoin yarn with sl st to top of any spoke. 1ch to count as first sc, work 1sc into each st around outside edge of motif. Join with sl st to first ch. Fasten off.

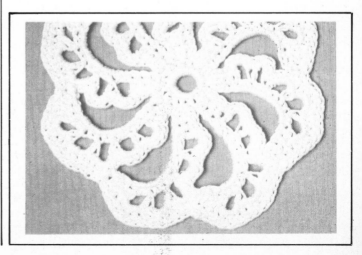

Cafe curtains

Size

55in wide × 55in long, excluding tabs.
Each motif measures 5in in diameter

Materials

9 × 100yd balls of Speed-Cro-Sheen in main color, A, 10 balls of contrast color, B, 9 balls of contrast color, C and 7 balls each of contrast colors, D and E
1 ball makes 2 motifs

One steel crochet hook No.0
Length of wooden curtain rod

Curtain

Make 22 Catherine wheel motifs in A, 20 in B, 18 in C, 14 in D and 13 in E.

Finishing

Join motifs tog as shown in illustration on opposite page.
Tabs Using size 0 hook, over color and with RS of first top motif facing, rejoin yarn with sl st to fifth sc along edge, 3ch to count as first dc, work 1dc into each of next 5sc, turn. 6 sts. Cont working rows of dc across these 6 sts until tab is long enough to fit over top of curtain rod and down to top of motif. Fasten off.
Work 10 more tabs in same way. Sew tabs in place to back of each motif, as shown in illustration on opposite page.

Place mat and coaster
Size
Place mat 11¼in wide × 9in long and coaster 4½in square.
Each motif measures 2¼in square

Materials
300yd ball of No.20 mercerized cotton (1 ball makes approximately 36 motifs)
One steel crochet hook No.7.

Place mat
Work as given for square lace motif, joining 5 motifs to form one row and 4 rows in all, a total of 20 motifs.

Coaster
Work as given for square lace motif, joining 2 motifs to form one row and, 2 rows in all, a total of 4 motifs.

Below: Crochet place mat and coaster

To join square lace motifs
Work first 5 rounds as given on previous page.

6th round (joining round) 1ch, *5ch, 1dc into each of next 3dc, 2ch. With RS of completed motif A facing RS of motif B which is to be joined, work 1sc into 5ch picot at corner of motif A, 2ch, 1dc, into each of next 3dc of motif B, sl st into first of 5ch after last dc on motif A, 4ch, sl st into next sc of motif B, 1ch, 1sc into 4ch picot of motif A, 1ch, skip 1sc on motif B, sl st into next sc on motif B, 4ch, sl st into last ch before next 3dc on motif B, 2ch, 1sc into 4ch picot at corner of motif A, 2ch. One side has been joined. Complete around motif B as for square lace motif A. Fasten off.
Work in the same way where the squares have to be joined on two sides.

Above: Diagram to show how Catherine wheel motifs are joined for a cafe curtain

Catherine wheel motifs used in a circular tablecloth

USING COLOR
PATCHWORK EFFECTS

This chapter explains how to work crochet with various colors to form a patchwork effect. Several samples are shown and explained in detail to help you follow the methods involved in this technique. As with patchwork crochet using separate shapes (see later) it is best to use the same weight of yarn throughout the work to make sure that your fabric will have an even tension. Multicolored fabrics can be worked in straight lines, or in circles and other shapes in the same manner as solid colored crochet. The most popular stitch to give a good fabric is single crochet.

Sample 1

Two colors of Knitting Worsted, A and B, have been used to work this basic patchwork design which is formed from checked squares. The techniques covered in this sample show how to join in a new color and how to carry the color not in use along with the work.

To help you make this first sample, we are giving both written instructions and a chart.

Using size G hook and A, make a length of chain with multiples of 5 + 1 stitches.

Note: Practice the method of joining in a new color, given in the 1st row, since it is important that the new color is joined right into the stitch preceding the stitches to be worked with that new color. Further

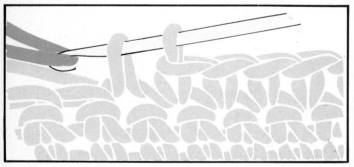
Joining in a new color in the middle of a row

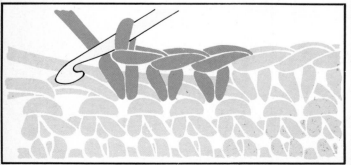
Working over the color which is not in use

instructions for joining in new colors will not be given in detail, and this method should be used throughout. The color not in use is held along the row of work and kept in place by the crochet stitch being worked over the yarn in order to avoid unnecessary or unattractive loops appearing on the work. It also insures that the work is completely reversible.

1st row Using color A, into 3rd ch from hook work 1sc, 1sc into each of next 2ch, insert hook into next ch, yo and draw through a loop, yo with color B and draw through both loops on hook, then using color B, work 1sc into each of next 5ch, using color A, work 1sc into each of next 5ch, cont in this way working 5 sts alternately in A and B to end of row. Turn.

2nd row Using same color as last 5sc of previous row and working new color over color not used on that row, work 1ch to count as first sc, 1sc into each of next 4sc, change color, 1sc into each of next 5sc, cont in this way to end of row, working last sc into turning ch. Turn.

3rd to 5th rows As 2nd.

6th to 10th rows As 2nd, working a square of color A over color B and a square of color B over color A. The 1st through 10th rows form the color sequence for this sample. When you have completed this piece you will see how your work compares with the photograph above and you will then be able to make up your own designs with this technique.

Sample 2

Here we have used the same techniques as explained in sample 1, but a much more varied effect has been achieved with the use of three colors and random shapes. As there is no definite pattern of colors, odd pieces of yarn can quite easily be used. A further technique is employed here, where the yarn not in use is left on the wrong side of the work, ready for taking into the work again on the next row. This method is used when a colored yarn is being used on one block only. Remember that if a color of yarn which is already in use is needed further along the row, then this yarn must be carried along the row until needed. Using size G hook and 3 colors of Knitting Worsted make 24ch. Work in single crochet and follow the chart to make our sample.

Sample 3

This is a lovely patchwork fabric made up of traditional church window shapes worked in many different colors. The effect of these colors and shapes is very interesting when they are made into such garments as long skirts, jackets or tank tops. Household items such as pillow covers and afghans also look very attractive when they are worked in this way.

As so many colors are used it is a good idea to work a single church window shape to estimate how much yarn is required for each individual shape. Then, when you are deciding on your colors, wind each one into a ball of the correct length.

Using size G hook and Knitting Worsted, make a chain with multiples of 8 + 1 stitches and follow our diagram, changing color for each shape. There is no need to work over the color not in use. This should be left behind the work until the next row where it is needed. When a shape in one color is finished, leave the end of yarn hanging free and darn in all ends on the wrong side of the work for a neat finish when the work is completed.

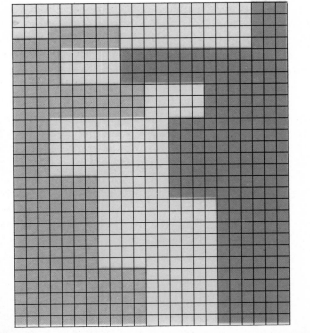

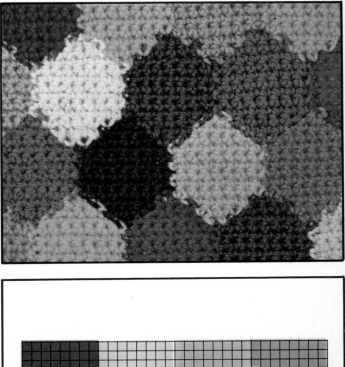

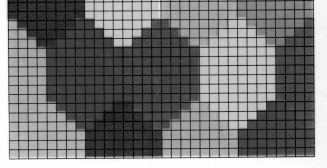

COLOR DESIGNS

Here we continue with our chapters on the use of different colored yarns within a single piece of crochet work, showing how rows of color can be incorporated into a design. This type of design would be ideal for border patterns on a plain piece of work such as a scarf, skirt or bedspread. In some of the samples shown here the lines of color are raised from the background by applying a technique known as blistering, which is described in detail.

Sample 1
This is a double sided fabric, worked in two colors of Knitting Worsted, A and B. Using size G hook and A, make 21ch.

1st row Into 3rd ch from hook work 1sc, 1sc into next ch, join in B as shown in previous chapter, using B and working over A, also see previous chapter, work 1sc into each of next 2ch, using A and working over B work 1sc into each of next 10ch, using B and working over A work 1sc into each of next 2ch, using A and working over B work 1sc into each of next 3ch. Turn. Continue in this way, working in pattern from the chart.

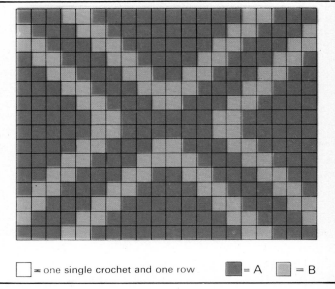

☐ = one single crochet and one row   ▨ = A   ▨ = B

Sample 2
Here two colors of Knitting Worsted A and B, have been used to give a raised, or blistered, effect to the work. When working individual narrow rows of color which follow through a design, it is not always necessary to carry the yarn not in use in with the work. Just leave this yarn behind the work ready to be worked into the crochet on the next row. There is a definite right and wrong side to the work when this technique is used. Using size E hook and A, make 21ch.

1st row Into 3rd ch from hook work 1sc, 1sc into each of next 5ch, join in B as shown in previous chapter, leaving A free on WS of work. Using B work 1sc into each of next 6ch joining in A on the last st, pull A taut to form a blister. Using A work 1sc into each of next 7ch. Turn.

2nd row Using A work 1ch to count as first sc, skip first st, 1sc into each of next 6sc joining in B on the last st and keeping A towards you while you work, work 1sc into each of next 6sc using B and joining in A on the last st worked. Leave B on WS of work (towards you) and pull A taut to form a blister. Using A work 1sc into each of next 7sc. Turn.

3rd row Using A work 1ch to count as first sc, skip

first st, 1sc into each of next 6sc joining in B on the last st. Leave A on WS of work (away from you), work 1sc into each of next 6sc using B and joining in A on the last st. Leave B on WS of work and pull A taut to form a blister. Using A work 1sc into each of next 7sc. Turn.

The 2nd and 3rd rows are repeated throughout.

Sample 3

In this sample both the techniques of working over the yarn not in use or leaving it free at the back of the work are used. The background color, A, is carried throughout, while the other colors in the design, B, C and D, are left free at the back of the work when not in use. Using size E hook and A, make 17ch.

1st row Join in color B as shown in previous chapter. Using B work 1sc into 3rd ch from hook, 1sc into each of next 2ch working over A, using A work 1sc into each of next 2ch, using C work 1sc into each of next

2ch, using A work 1sc into each of next 2ch, using D work 1sc into each of next 4ch, using A work 1sc into next ch. Turn.

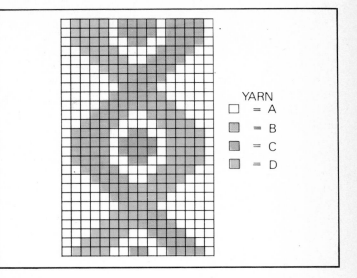

YARN
☐ = A
▨ = B
▨ = C
▨ = D

2nd row Using A, work 1ch to count as first sc, skip first st, 1sc into next sc, using D work 1sc into each of next 4sc, using A work 1sc into each of next 4sc, using B work 1sc into each of next 4sc, using A work 1sc into each of next 2sc. Turn.

Continue working in this way following the chart, noting that yarn C covers only a small area of color so that the yarn may be cut after each motif is finished to avoid unnecessary strands hanging behind the work.

Sample 4

Our belt has been worked in 3 colors of Knitting Worsted, using a size E hook. Follow the chart given for sample 3, omitting color C, and form a blistered or raised effect on the crossover lines by applying the technique used in sample 2, and keeping A taut while it is not in use. A large bead has been added as trim in the center of each diamond.

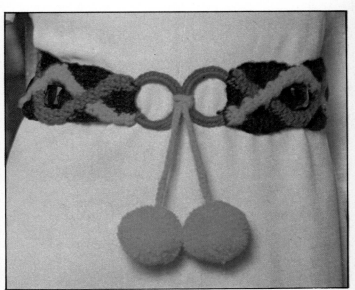

A hat of many colors

Size
To fit an average head

Gauge
12 hdc and 9 rows to 2in in patt worked with size E crochet hook

Materials
1 × one oz ball 3-ply fingering yarn in each of 5 colors, A, B, C, D and E
One size E crochet hook

Note
When using two different colored yarns in the same round, always work over the color not in use and, when changing color, draw the new color through all the loops on the hook of the last st in the old color.

Hat
Using size E hook and A, make 6ch. Join with a sl st to first ch to form a ring.

1st round Using A, 2ch to count as first hdc, 7hdc into ring. Join with a sl st into 2nd of 2ch. 8hdc. Break off A.

2nd round Using B, 2ch to count as first hdc, 1hdc into st at base of ch, *2hdc into next hdc, rep from * to end. Join with a sl st into 2nd of 2ch. 16hdc.

3rd round Working 4 sts each of B and C around, work 2ch to count as first hdc, 2hdc into next hdc, *1hdc into next hdc, 2hdc into next hdc, rep from * to end. Join with a sl st into 2nd of 2ch. 24hdc. Break off B and C.

4th round Using D, 2ch, 1hdc into next hdc, 2hdc into next hdc, *1hdc into each of next 2hdc, 2hdc into next hdc, rep from * to end. Join with a sl st into 2nd of 2ch. 32hdc.

5th round Using 5 sts each of D and E around, work 2ch, 1hdc into each of next 2hdc, 2hdc into next hdc, *1hdc into each of next 3hdc, 2hdc into next hdc, rep from * to end. Join with a sl st into 2nd of 2ch. 40hdc. Break off E.

6th round Using D, 2ch, 1hdc into each of next 3hdc, 2hdc into next hdc, *1hdc into each of next 4hdc, 2hdc into next hdc, rep

into each of next 7 hdc, 2hdc into next hdc, rep from * to end. Join with a sl st into 2nd of 2ch. 72hdc. Break off A.

10th round Using E, 2ch, 1hdc into each of next 7 hdc, 2hdc into next hdc, *1hdc into each of next 8 hdc, 2hdc into next hdc, rep from * to end. Join with a sl st into 2nd of 2ch. 80hdc. Break off E.

11th round Using 4 sts each of B and D all around, 2ch, 1hdc into each of next 8 hdc, 2hdc into next hdc, *1hdc into each of next 9 hdc, 2hdc into next hdc, rep from * to end. Join with a sl st into 2nd of 2ch. 88hdc.

12th round Using 4 sts each of B and D and working into same colors as on previous round, 2ch, 1hdc into each hdc to end. Join with a sl st into 2nd of 2ch. Break off B and D.

13th round Using E, as 12th. Break off E.
14th round Using C, as 12th. Break off C.
15th round Using B, as 12th. Break off B.
16th round Using one st of A and 7 sts of D all around, as 12th.
17th round Using 3 sts of A and 5 sts of D all round, as 12th. Break off A and D.
18th round Using E, as 12th. Break off E.
19th round Using A, as 12th.
20th round Using 4 sts of A and 4 sts of C all round, as 12th.
21st round As 20th. Break off A and C.
22nd round Using B, as 12th. Break off B.
23rd round Using A, as 12th.
24th round Using C, as 12th.
25th round Using 3 sts of B and 5 sts of E all around, as 12th. Break off B and E.
26th round Using D, as 12th.
27th round As 26th.

Shape brim
28th round Using E, 2ch, 2hdc into next hdc, *1hdc into next hdc, 2hdc into next hdc, rep from * to end. Join with a sl st into 2nd of 2ch. 132hdc. Break off E.
29th round Using B, as 12th. Break off B.
30th round Using C, as 12th. Break off C.
31st round Using 8 sts of A and 4 sts of E all round, as 12th. Break off A and E.
32nd round Using D, 2ch, 1hdc into each of next 4 hdc, 2hdc into next hdc, *1hdc into each of next 5 hdc, 2hdc into next hdc, rep from * to end. Join with a sl st into 2nd of 2ch. 154hdc. Break off D.
33rd round Using A, as 12th.
34th round Using 4 sts of A and 3 sts of B all around, as 12th. Break off A and B.
35th round Using E, 2ch, 1hdc into each of next 5 hdc, 2hdc into next hdc, *1hdc into each of next 6 hdc, 2hdc into next hdc, rep from * to end. Join with a sl st into 2nd of 2ch. 176hdc. Break off E.
36th round Using D, as 12th. Break off D.
37th round Using C and working from left to right (in a backwards direction), work 1sc into each hdc to end. Join with a sl st into first sc. Fasten off.

from * to end. Join with a sl st into 2nd of 2ch. 48hdc. Break off D.
7th round Using C, 2ch, 1hdc into each of next 4 hdc, 2hdc into next hdc, *1hdc into each of next 5 hdc, 2hdc into next hdc, rep from * to end. Join with a sl st into 2nd of 2ch. 56hdc. Break off C.

8th round Using A, 2ch, 1hdc into each of next 5 hdc, 2hdc into next hdc, *1hdc into each of next 6 hdc, 2hdc into next hdc, rep from * to end. Join with a sl st into 2nd of 2ch. 64hdc.
9th round Using A, 2ch, 1hdc into each of next 6 hdc, 2hdc into next hdc, *1hdc

PATCHWORK CROCHET

Patchwork crochet

Traditionally we think of patchwork as a means of using odds and ends of fabric to make a quilt or piece of clothing. Today there is a great revival of interest in the art, and fabrics are carefully selected and co-ordinated to create colorful and exciting designs.

The same designs may be worked in crochet too, again working with odd pieces of yarn to use up scraps, or choosing a selection of colors to produce a desired effect. A pleasing choice of colors is an important part of patchwork, for this really makes a design. Closely related colors are usually a satisfactory choice, so that if you choose red, you can use all the various shades of red from deep ruby to oranges and yellows. Our samples have been worked in blues and greens to illustrate a variation of the same grading of colors. Patchwork crochet can be used in many ways for both fashion items and household accessories such as quilts, pillow covers, afghans, wall hangings and room dividers. The most suitable fashion items are ones which require little or no shaping, such as straight skirts, jerkins and belts.

In order to achieve a high standard of work, it is necessary to use the same weight of yarn throughout, although to add interest they may be of different textures. As the yarn should be of one weight, then the same size crochet hook should also be used for each. Firm, even stitches, such as single crochet or half doubles, should be used. These will help to give body to the shape.

The shapes described in this chapter are all geometric and include the square, rectangle, diamond, triangle and hexagon. They are all worked in a Knitting Worsted using a size G crochet hook.

To join the separate shapes, place the right sides together and sew them with a firm overcast stitch in the same yarn. The seam should be blocked on the wrong side under a damp cloth with a warm iron as part of the finishing. Where there is more than one color used in the same shape, such as samples 5 and 6, these are fitted into the work as desired.

Sample 1

To work the diamond shape Make 3ch.

1st row Into 3rd ch from hook work 1sc. Turn. 2 sts.

2nd row 1ch to count as first st, 1sc into st at base of ch, 1sc into turning ch. Turn. One st increased.

3rd row 1ch to count as first st, 1sc into st at base of ch, 1sc into next st, 1sc into turning ch. Turn. One st increased.

Cont in this way, inc one st at beg of every row, until there are 20 sts.

Next row 1ch to count as first st, skip next st, 1sc into next st, 1sc into each st to end, ending with 1sc into turning ch. Turn. One st decreased.

Cont in this way, dec one st at beg of every row, until 2 sts rem. Fasten off.

Sample 2

To work the church window shape Work as for sample 1, but when the required size or width is reached (20 sts, for example), work 14 rows without shaping. Then work the decrease shaping as before.

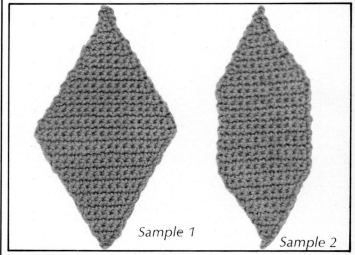

Sample 1

Sample 2

Sample 3

To work the triangle Make 3ch.

1st row Into 3rd ch from hook work 1hdc. Turn. 2 sts.

2nd row 2ch to count as first hdc, 1hdc into st at base of ch, 2hdc into 2nd of 2ch. Turn. 2 sts increased.

3rd row 2ch to count as first hdc, 1hdc into st at base of ch, 1hdc into each of next 2 sts, 2hdc into 2nd of 2ch. Turn. 2 sts increased.

Cont in this way, inc one st at each end of every row, until there are 24 sts or the triangle is the desired size. Fasten off.

Sample 4

To work the hexagon Make 5ch. Join with a sl st into first ch to form a ring.

1st round 4ch, *1dc into ring, 1ch, rep from * 10 times more. Join with a sl st into 3rd of 4ch.

2nd round 3ch to count as first dc, 2dc into next 1ch sp, 1dc into next dc, 1ch, *1dc into next dc, 2dc into next 1ch sp, 1dc into next dc, 1ch, rep from * 4 times more. Join with a sl st into 3rd of 3ch.

3rd round 3ch to count as first dc, 1dc into st at base of ch, 1dc into each of next 2dc, 2dc into next dc, 2ch,

*2dc into next dc, 1dc into each of next 2dc, 2dc into next dc, 2ch, rep from * 4 times more. Join with a sl st into 3rd of 3ch. Fasten off.
This completes the sample illustrated, but a smaller or larger shape can be made by working in the same way, inc one st at each end of every block of dc and one ch between blocks on every round, until the shape is the desired size.

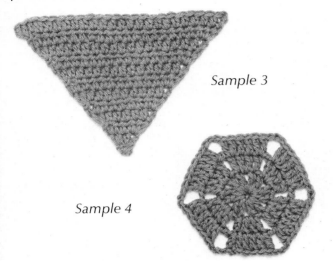

Sample 3

Sample 4

Sample 5
Four colors, A, B, C and D, are used for this sample square. Note the effect of the colors when four squares are joined together. Using A, make 17ch.
1st row Into 3rd ch from hook work 1sc, 1sc into each ch to end. Turn. 16 sts.
2nd row 1ch to count as first sc, 1sc into each sc to end, ending with 1sc into turning ch. Turn.
Rep last row twice more. Break off A. Join in B.

Note: Care should be taken when joining in a new color. It is better to work 2 turning chains instead of 1 and then pull up the old color tightly. Work 4 rows in sc with each of B, C and D. Fasten off. Sew or weave in the cut ends. Place squares to give the desired pattern and sew together.

Sample 6
Here four triangular shapes, as in sample 3, have been worked with four colors shown in each, and then joined together.
Work 2 triangles with 4 rows each in A, B, C and D, and then 2 more triangles using the color sequence of D, C, B and A. Arrange with alternate colors meeting and then sew them together. Finish the cut ends by weaving them back into the work on the wrong side.

Sample 7
This sample is made up of brick shapes. There are 16 in all, 4 in each color.
To work the brick shape Make 11ch.
1st row Into 3rd ch from hook work 1sc, 1sc into each ch to end. Turn. 10 sts.
2nd row 1ch to count as first sc, 1sc into each sc to end, ending with 1sc into turning ch. Turn.
Rep last row 3 times more. Fasten off.
Work the desired number of bricks in each color and place them carefully in rows of one color before sewing into place. When finished, sew or weave in all the cut ends on the wrong side of the work.

A patchwork jacket

Sizes

Directions are to fit 34in bust. Changes for 36, 38 and 40in bust are in brackets [ ].
Length to shoulder, 27[27:30:30]in
Sleeve seam, 18[18:20:20]in

Gauge

18 sts and 9 rows to 4in in dc worked with size E crochet hook

Materials

5[5:6:6] × 4oz balls Bucilla Knitting Worsted in main color, A 1[1:1:1] ball each of contrast colors, B, C and D 1[1:1:2] balls of contrast color, E
One size E crochet hook
26[26:28:28]in open ended zipper

Back

Using size E hook and A, make 82 [88:94:86]ch.

1st row Into 4th ch from hook work 1dc, 1dc into each ch to end. Turn. 80[86:92: 94]dc.

2nd row 3ch to count as first dc, skip first dc, 1dc into each dc to end. Turn. Rep 2nd row 40[40:49:49] times more.

Shape raglan armholes

Next row Sl st across first 6[6:7:7]dc, 1dc into each dc to last 6[6:7:7]dc, turn.

Next row 3ch to count as first dc, yo insert hook into next dc, yo and draw through loop, yo and draw through 2 loops on hook, yo and insert hook into next dc, yo and draw through loop, yo and draw through 2 loops on hook, yo and draw through 3 loops on hook — called dec 1 —, 1dc into each dc to last 3dc, dec 1, 1dc into last dc.
Turn. Rep last row 19[19:21:21] times more.
Fasten off.

Sleeves

Using size E hook and A, make 40 [40:49:49]ch. Work 1st row as given for back. 38[38:47:47]dc.

1st and 2nd sizes only

Work 2 rows dc.

4th row 3ch, 2dc into next dc — called inc 1 —, 1dc into each dc to last 2dc, inc 1, 1dc into last dc.
Turn.
Work 2 rows dc without shaping. Cont inc in this way on next and every foll 3rd row until 34 rows have been worked from beg, then inc in same way on every foll 2nd row 5 times in all. 70[70]dc.

3rd and 4th sizes only

Work 4 rows dc. Inc as given for 1st and 2nd sizes on next and every foll 4th row until 21 rows have been worked, then inc in same way on every foll 3rd row

until there are 77[77]dc.

All sizes

Shape raglans

Next row Sl st across first 6[6:7:7]dc, 3ch, 1dc into each dc to last 6[6:7:7] dc, 3ch, 1dc into each dc to last 6[6:7:7]dc, turn. Dec one st at each end of every row until 30[30:31:31]dc rem.

Next row 3ch, dec 1, 1dc into each of next 9dc, dec 1, 1dc into each of next 2[2:3:3]dc, dec 1, 1dc into each of next 9dc, dec 1, dc into last dc. Turn.

Next row 3ch, dec 1, 1dc into each of next 7dc, dec 1, 1dc into each of next 2[2:3:3]dc, dec 1, 1dc into each of next 7dc, dec 1, 1dc into last dc. Turn.
Cont dec in this way on next 4 rows. 6[6:7:7]dc.
Fasten off.

Left and right fronts

Work motifs for fronts, noting that colors may be varied as desired and should be twisted at back of work when being changed.

1st motif

Using A, make 16[16:18:18]ch.

1st row Into 4th ch from hook work 1dc, 1dc into each ch to end. Turn. 14[14:16:16] dc.

2nd row 3ch to count as first dc, skip 1dc, 1dc into each dc to end. Turn. Rep 2nd row 5[5:6:6] more times.
Fasten off and sew or weave in ends. Work 1 more motif in same way using A, then 2 motifs each in B, C, D and E. 10 motifs, 5 for each front.

2nd motif

Using A, work first 2 rows as given for 1st motif. Break off A. Join in E. Complete as given for 1st motif. Work 1 more motif in same way, then 2 more using D and C and 2 more using E and B. 6 motifs, 3 for each front.

3rd motif

Using B, make 7[7:8:8] ch, join in D and make 9[9:10:10] ch.

1st row Using D, into 4th ch from hook work 1dc, 1dc into each of next 5[5:6:6] ch working last 2 loops of last dc with B — called 1dcNc —, using B, work 1dc into each ch to end. Turn. 7[7:8:8]dc each in D and B.

2nd row Using B, 3ch to count as first dc, 1dc into each of next 6[6:7:7]dc, keeping B to front of work and D to back under hook to work 1dcNc with D in last dc, using D, work 1dc into each dc to end. Turn.

3rd row Using D, 3ch, work 1dc into each of next 6[6:7:7]dc, keeping yarn at back of work and working 1dcNc with B in last dc, using B, work 1dc into each dc to end. Turn.
Rep 2nd and 3rd rows twice more, then

2nd row 0[0:1:1] times more. Fasten off and sew or weave in ends. Work 1 more motif in same way, then 2 motifs using A and D and 2 using C and E. 6 motifs, 3 for each front.

4th motif
Using B and C, work first 3 rows as given for 3rd motif.

4th row Using B, 3ch, 1dc into each dc to end. Turn.

5th row Using B, 3ch, 1dc into each of next 6[6:7:7]dc, keeping yarn at back of work, join in C and work 1dcNc on last dc, 1dc into each dc to end. Turn.

6th row Using C, 3ch, 1dc into each of next 6[6:7:7]dc, keeping C to front of work and B back under hook, work 1dc Nc with B in last dc, 1dc into each dc to end. Turn.

7th row As 5th

Rep 6th row 0[0:1:1] times more. Fasten off and sew or weave in ends. Work 1 more motif.

5th motif
Using B, work first 3 rows as for 1st motif, joining in E and working 1dcNc in last dc. Break off B.

4th row Using E, 3ch, work 1dc into each of next 6[6:7:7]dc, join in C and work 1dcNc in last dc, 1dc into each dc to end. Turn.

5th row Using C, 3ch, work 1dc into each of next 6[6:7:7]dc, 1dcNc with C in last dc using E, 1dc into each dc to end. Turn.
Rep 4th and 5th rows once more, then 4th row 0[0:1:1] times more. Fasten off and sew or weave in ends. Work 1 more motif in same way, then 2 more using C, E and D and 2 more using A, B and E. 6 motifs, 3 for each front.

6th motif
Using E, make 7[7:8:8] ch, join in D and make 9[9:10:10] ch.

1st row Using D, into 4th ch from hook work 1dc, 1dc into each of next 4[4:5:5] ch, keeping yarn at back of work join in C and work 1dcNc in last dc, using C, 1dc into each of next 2ch. Keeping yarn at back of work join in E and work 1dcNc in last dc, 1dc into each of next 6[6:7:7] ch. Turn.

2nd row Using E, 3ch, 1dc into each of next 4[4:5:5]dc, keeping E to front of work and C to back under hook and working 1dcNc with C in last dc, using C, 1dc into each of next 4dc, keeping C to front of work and D to back under hook and working 1dcNc with D on last dc, using D, 1dc into each dc to end. Turn.

3rd row Changing colors as for 1st row, using D, 3ch, 1dc into each of next 3[3:4:4]dc, using C, 1dc into each of next 6dc, using E, 1dc into each dc to end. Turn.

4th row Changing colors as for 2nd row,

using E, 3ch, 1dc into each of next 2[2:3:3]dc, using C, 1dc into each of next 8dc, using D, 1dc into each dc to end. Turn.

5th row Changing colors as for 1st row, using D, 3ch, 1dc into next dc, using C, 1dc into each of next 10dc, using E, 1dc into each dc to end. Turn.

6th row Changing colors as for 2nd row, using E, 3ch, 1dc into each of next 0[0:1:1]dc, using C, 1dc into each of next 12dc, using D, 1dc into each dc to end. Turn.

7th row Using C, 3ch 1dc into each dc to end. Turn.
Rep 7th row 0[0:1:1] times more. Fasten off and sew or weave in ends. Work 1 more motif in same way, then 2 using B, A and C, 2 using E, C and B, 2 using A, D and B, 2 using B, C and E and 2 using D, A and E. 12 motifs making 6 diamond shapes, 3 for each front.

Quarter raglan motif
Using D, make 10[10:12:12] ch. Work 1st row as given for 1st motif. 8[8:9:9]dc.

2nd row 3ch, dec 1, 1dc into each dc to end. Turn.

3rd row 3ch, 1dc into each dc to last 3dc,

dec 1, 1dc into last dc. Turn.
Rep 2nd and 3rd rows twice more, then 2nd row 0[:1:1] times more. Fasten off. Make another quarter motif in same way.

Three-quarter raglan motif
Using C, make 16[16:18:18] ch. Work 1st row as given for 1st motif. 14[14:16:16]dc.

2nd row 3ch, 1dc into next dc, dec 1, 1dc into each dc to end. Turn.

3rd row 3ch, 1dc into each dc to last 4dc, dec 1, 1dc into each of last 2 dc. Turn.
Rep 2nd and 3rd rows twice more, then 2nd row 0[0:1:1] times more. 8[8:9:9]dc. Fasten off.

Neck motif
Using E, make 16[16:18:18] ch.

1st row Into 4th ch from hook work 1dc, 1dc into each ch to last 4ch, dec 2 working over next 3ch as given for dec 1, 1dc into last ch. Turn.

2nd row 3ch, dec 2, 1dc into each dc to end. Turn.

3rd row 3ch, 1dc into each dc to last 4dc, dec 2, 1dc into last dc. Turn.
Rep 2nd and 3rd rows once more, then 2nd row once more. Fasten off.

Finishing

Block each piece under a damp cloth with a warm iron. Sew motifs tog with bound off edge to cast on edge, with the exception of 6th motif which must be sewn cast on edges tog to form diamond shape. Join 3 motifs, arranging as desired or as shown in diagram, to form one row. Join 5 more rows in same way, then join these 6 rows tog to form one front to underarm. Join 2 motifs working from front edge for 7th row then join quarter raglan motif for armhole edge. Join one motif for front edge with three-quarter raglan motif for armhole edge for 8th row, then join neck motif to raglan edge of armhole, leaving 9dc at neck edge free for 9th row. Join other front in same way, reversing motifs.

Collar Using size E hook, A and with RS of work facing, work 86[86:90:90] sc around neck edge. Work 1 row dc, dec one st at each side of sleeve, (4 dec). Cont dec in same way, work 1 row sc and 1 row dc. Work 2[2:3:3] rows sc without shaping. Fasten off.

Lower edge Using size E hook, A and with RS of front facing, work 2[2:3:3] rows dc along the lower edge for hem. Fasten off. Work other front in same way.

Front edges Using size E hook, A and with RS of work facing, work 3 rows sc along each front edge. Fasten off. Join raglan, side and sleeve seams. Turn up hem at lower edge and sew in place. Turn up 2[2:3:3] rows dc at cuffs and sew in place. Sew in zipper. Block seams.

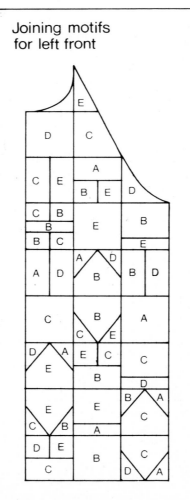

Joining motifs
for left front

FREE SHAPING

This chapter illustrates a creative and individual way of crocheting, this being a breakaway from the accepted traditional methods of working in straight rows back and forth.

Here the method of making free and unusual lines and shapes, which are then worked around to form a flat fabric, is explained. To achieve this type of work, increased and decreased stitches must be introduced at certain points on the piece, so our samples are explained in detail to help you understand the technique and encourage you to try out your own ideas.

You will see that color is very important since the fabric is formed by using different colors of yarn for each new row or part of a design thus creating somewhat of a patchwork effect.

Start by making a square or rectangular shape which could be used as a pillow cover or enlarged to make a rug. Later fashion garments can be attempted or, possibly before that, a border design on a plain skirt.

Sample 1

The basic shape here consists of two circles. By using the same method of work and varying the number of stitches between increases and decreases, you can use several circles in a row, three to form a triangle or four to form a square. The sample has been worked in five colors of Knitting Worsted, A, B, C, D and E.

To work the basic circles (make 2) Using size F hook and A, make 3ch. Join with a sl st into first ch to form a ring.

1st round 1ch to count as first sc, 7sc into ring. Join with a sl st into first ch.

2nd round 1ch, 1sc into st at base of ch, *2sc into next sc, rep from * to end. Join with a sl st into first ch. 16sc.

3rd round 1ch, 1sc into st at base of ch, 1sc into next sc, *2sc into next sc, 1sc into next sc, rep from * to end. Join with a sl st into first ch. 24sc.

4th round 1ch, 1sc into st at base of ch, 1sc into each of next 2sc, *2sc into next sc, 1sc into each of next 2sc, rep from * to end. Join with a sl st into first ch. 32sc.

5th round 1ch, 1sc into st at base of ch, 1sc into each of next 3sc, *2sc into next sc, 1sc into each of next 3sc, rep from * to end. Join with a sl st into first ch. 40sc. Break off A, and leave working st on a holder.

Join in B to either circle. **Replace working st onto hook, 1ch, 1sc into st at base of ch, 1sc into each of next 4sc, *2sc into next sc, 1sc into each of next 4sc, rep from * to end of round. Join with a sl st into first ch. **. Turn work.

1st row 1ch to count as first sc, skip first sc, 1sc into each of next 5sc. Turn work.

2nd–6th rows As 1st.

Join in 2nd circle Place circle to be joined behind the present work with RS tog and rep from ** to ** as for 1st circle, working through double fabric for first 7 sts. Break off yarn, thread cut end through working st and pull up tightly.

Join in C With RS of work facing, join C to first increased sc of left hand circle (as shown in diagram) and working in a counter-clockwise direction around the circle, 1ch, 1sc into st at base of ch, 1sc into each of next 5 sts, (2sc into next sc, 1sc into each of next 5 sts) 5 times, cont along row ends of straight strip with B by working 2sc tog, 1sc into each of next 4 sts, work 2sc tog, then cont around right hand circle by working (1sc into each of next 5sc, 2sc into next sc) 6 times, 1sc into each of next 5sc and then cont along 2nd side of straight strip and with B work 2sc tog, 1sc into each of next 4 sts, work 2sc tog, 1sc into each of next

5 sts. Join with a sl st into first ch. Break off yarn, thread cut end through working st and pull up tightly.

Join in D With RS of work facing, join in D by inserting hook into first ch of last round and cont in a counter-clockwise direction around entire piece by working 1ch, 1sc into st at base of ch, (1sc into each of next 6 sts, 2sc into next st) 5 times, 1sc into each of next 5 sts, work 2sc tog, 1sc into each of next 3sts, work 2sc tog, 1sc into each of next 5 sts, (2sc into next st, 1sc into each of next 6 sts) 5 times, 2sc into next st, 1sc into each of next 5 sts, work 2sc tog, 1sc into each of next 3 sts, work 2sc tog, 1sc into each of next 5 sts. Join with a sl st into first ch. Break off yarn, thread cut end through working st and pull up tightly.

Join in E With RS of work facing, join in E by inserting hook into first ch of last round and cont around piece by working 1ch, 1sc into st at base of ch, (1sc into each of next 7 sts, 2sc into next st) 5 times, 1sc into each of next 4 sts, work 3 sts tog using dc instead of sc, 1dc into each of next 2 sts, work 3dc tog, 1sc into each of next 4 sts, (2sc into next st, 1sc into each of next 7 sts) 5 times, 2sc into next st, 1sc into each of next 4 sts, work 3dc tog, 1dc into each of next 2 sts, work 3dc tog, 1sc into each of next 4 sts. Join with a sl st into first ch. Break off yarn, thread cut end through working st and pull up tightly.

Join in B With RS of work facing, join in B by inserting hook into first ch of last round and cont around piece by working 1ch, 1sc into st at base of ch, (1sc into each of next 8 sts, 2sc into next st) 5 times, 1sc into each of next 2 sts, work 3dc tog, 1dc into each of next 3 sts, work 3dc tog, 1sc into each of next 2 sts, (2sc into next st, 1sc into each of next 8 sts) 5 times, 2sc into next st, 1sc into each of next 2 sts, work 3dc tog, 1dc into each of next 3 sts, work 3dc tog, 1sc into each of next 2 sts. Join with a sl st into first ch. Break off yarn, thread cut end through working st and pull up tightly.

Join in A Cont as before by working 1ch, 1sc into st at base of ch, (1sc into each of next 9 sts, 2sc into next st) 5 times, work 3dc tog, 1dc into each of next 4 sts, work 3dc tog, 2sc into next st, (1sc into each of next 9 sts, 2sc into next st) 5 times, work 3dc tog, 1dc into each of next 4 sts, work 3dc tog. Join with a sl st into first ch.

Final round Using A, 1ch, 1sc into st at base of ch, (1sc into each of next 10 sts, 2sc into next st) 4 times, 1sc into each of next 29 sts, (2sc into next st, 1sc into each of next 10 sts) 4 times, 1sc into each of next 8 sts. Join with a sl st into first ch. Fasten off.

Sample 2

Five colors of Knitting Worsted A, B, C, D and E have been used for this sample. Using size F hook and A, make a chain with multiples of 6 +1 stitches.

1st row Into 3rd ch from hook work 1sc, 1sc into each ch to end. Turn.

2nd row 1ch to count as first sc, skip first st, 1sc into each of next 5ch, *10ch, into 3rd ch from hook work 1sc, 1sc into each of next 7ch, 1sc into each of next 6sc, rep from * to end. Turn.

3rd row Join in B, 1ch, skip first st, 1sc into each of next 4sc, *work 2sc tog, 1sc into each of next 7sc, 3sc into tip of chain length, 1sc into each of next 7 sts, work 2sc tog, 1sc into each of next 4 sts, rep from * ending with 1sc into turning ch. Turn.

4th row Join in C, 1ch, skip first st, 1sc into each of next 3 sts, *work 2sc tog, 1sc into each of next 7 sts, (2sc into next st) twice, 1sc into each of next 7 sts, work 2sc tog, 1sc into each of next 3 sts, rep from * ending with 1sc into turning ch. Turn.

5th row Join in D, 1ch, skip first st, 1sc into each of next 2sc, *work 2sc tog, 1sc into each of next 7 sts, (2sc into next st) 3 times, 1sc into each of next 7 sts, work 2sc tog, 1sc into each of next 2 sts, rep from * ending with 1sc into turning ch. Turn.

6th row Join in E, 1ch, skip first st, 1sc into next sc, work 2sc tog, 1sc into each of next 7 sts, *(2sc into next st, 1sc into next st) twice, 2sc into next st, 1sc into each of next 7 sts, work 2sc tog, skip next st, work 2sc tog, insert hook into next to last sc just worked, yo and draw a loop through st on hook, (insert hook into next sc on right, yo and draw through a loop, insert hook into next sc on left, yrh and draw through a loop, yrh and draw through all loops on hook) 7 times to join shapes tog, rep from * omitting joining on last rep, working in sc to end. Fasten off.

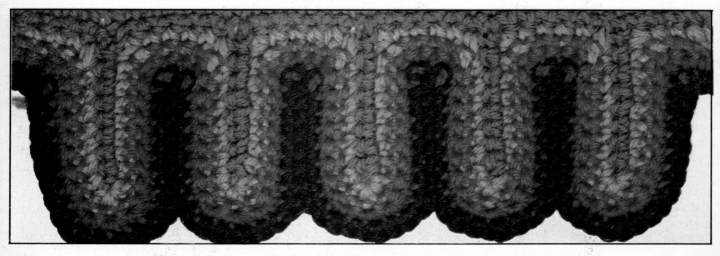

Bedspread in color

Size
To fit average single bed, 36in wide

Gauge
Motifs 1, 2 and 3 measure 8½in square

Materials
Brunswick Fore 'n Aft Sport Yarn
4 × 2oz balls Mint, A
3 balls Turquoise, B
3 balls Pansy, C
4 balls Dark Lime, D
4 balls Dark Green, E
4 balls Black, F
3 balls Purple, G
3 balls Pastel Ombre, H
3 balls Seaspray Ombre, I
One size H crochet hook

Bedspread
The bedspread is made of 8 square motifs using variations of 9 colors which are sewn together. Borders and more motifs are then worked onto the basic design.

Square motif (1)
Using size H hook and A, work 4ch. Join with a sl st into first ch to form a ring.

1st round 3ch, 11dc into circle. Join with a sl st into 3rd of the 3ch.

2nd round Sl st into first sp between dc, 3ch, 1dc in same sp, *2dc into next sp between dc, rep from * around. Join with a sl st into 3rd of the 3ch. Break off A and join in B.

3rd round Sl st into first sp between dc, 3ch, 2dc into same sp, skip next sp, * 3dc into next sp, skip next sp, rep from * around. Join with a sl st into 3rd of the 3ch. Break off B and join in G.

4th round Sl st into first sp between groups of 3dc, (3ch, 2dc, 1ch – to form corner sp, 3dc) into same sp, skip next 2 sp between dc, 1dc into each of next 4 sp, skip next 2 sp, *(3dc, 1ch, 3dc) into next sp, skip next 2 sp, 1dc into each of next 4 sp, skip next 2 sp, rep from * around. Join with a sl st into 3rd of the 3ch. Break off G and join in E.

5th round Sl st into corner sp, (3ch, 2dc, 1ch, 3dc) into same sp, *skip next 2 sp between dc, 1dc into each of next 5 sp, skip next 2 sp, (3dc, 1ch, 3dc) into corner sp, rep from * around. Join with a sl st into 3rd of the 3ch. Break off E and join in A.

6th round Sl st into corner sp, (3ch, 2dc, 1ch, 3dc) into same sp, *skip next 2 sp between dc, 1dc into each of next 6 sp, skip next 2 sp, (3dc, 1ch, 3dc) into corner sp, rep from * around. Join with a sl st into 3rd of the 3ch.
Break off A and join in G.

7th round Sl st into corner sp, (3ch, 2dc, 1ch, 3dc) into same sp, *(skip next 2 sp between dc, 3dc into next sp – thus forming 1sh) 3 times, (3dc, 1ch, 3dc) into corner sp, rep from * around. Join with a sl st into 3rd of the 3ch. Fasten off G and join in C.

8th round Sl st into corner sp, (3ch, 2dc, 1ch, 3dc) into same sp, *(skip next sh, 3dc into sp between next 2 shs) 4 times, skip next sh, (3dc, 1ch, 3dc) into corner sp, rep from * around. Join with a sl st into 3rd of the 3ch. Break off C. Make another motif in the same way.

Square motif (2)
Make 3 motifs in the same way as above, but work in color sequence as follows:
1st and 2nd rounds Work with H.
3rd round Work with A.
4th round Work with D.
5th round Work with E.
6th round Work with B.
7th round Work with H.
8th round Work with C.

Square motif (3)
Make 3 motifs using color sequence as follows:
1st and 2nd rounds Work with B.
3rd round Work with I.
4th round Work with B.
5th round Work with F.
6th round Work with G.
7th round Work with D.
8th round Work with C.
Using C, join these 8 motifs tog as shown in diagram.

Next round Join E to corner sp marked (a) on diagram, (3ch, 2dc, 1ch, 3dc) into corner, *work a 4dc sh into each sp between shs to (b) on diagram, 2dc into (b), (4dc sh into each sp to next corner, (3ch, 1ch, 3dc) into corner) twice, rep from *around motifs. Join with a sl st into 3rd of the 3ch. Break off E and join in D.

Next round Sl st into corner sp, (3ch, 2dc, 1ch, 3dc) into same sp, *4dc sh into each sp between shs to within one sp of point (b), 1dc into next sp, skip 2dc at (b), 1dc into next sp, (4dc sh into each sp to corner, (3dc, 1ch, 3dc) into corner) twice, rep from * around. Join with a sl st into 3rd of the 3ch. Break off D.

Semi-circular motif (4)
Using size H hook and A, work 4ch. Join with a sl st into first ch to form a ring.

1st row 3ch, 6dc into ring. Turn.
2nd row Sl st into first sp, 3ch, 1dc into same sp, 2dc into each sp to end. Turn. Break off A and join in B.
3rd row As 2nd row.
Break off B and join in E.

4th row Sl st into first sp, 3ch, 1dc into same sp, skip next sp, *3dc sh into next sp, skip next sp, rep from * to last sp, 2dc into last sp. Turn. Break off E and join in H.
5th row 3ch, 3dc sh into each sp between shs, 1dc into 3rd of the 3ch. Turn.
6th row Sl st into first sp, 3ch, 1dc into same sp, *4dc sh into next sp between shs, rep from * to last sp, 2dc into last sp. Turn. Break off H and join in E.
7th row 3ch, 4dc sh into first sp between shs, *5dc sh into next sp, rep from * to last sp, 4dc into last sp, 1dc into 3rd of the 3ch. Turn. Break off E.
Make 3 more motifs in the same way and join the main section as shown in the diagram. Cont working a border around the main piece as foll:

1st round With RS of work facing join A to point (*) on diagram and work 4dc shs into each sp between shs to point (b), dec at (b) by working 1dc into sp at either side of previous dec, cont in shs to next corner, 4dc into corner, *3dc sh into 3rd dc of previous 5dc sh, 3dc sh into next sp between shs, rep from * around semicircular motif and cont around piece dec at each point (b), working (3dc, 1ch, 3dc) into each corner and working around motifs as shown above. Break off A and joint in G.

2nd round As 1st round, but work 3dc shs into each sp between shs around motif 4. Break off G and join in F.

3rd round As 2nd round. Break off F and join in G.

4th round Working all around work 1dc into each dc and 1dc into each sp, 1dc into each of 3 sp at point (b), (3dc, 1ch, 3dc) into each corner, skipping 3dc before and after each corner sp. Break off G and join in F.

5th round Working all around work 1dc into each dc, (3dc, 1ch, 3dc) into each corner, and at point (b) dec over 3dc by working 1dc into each of the 3dc and leaving the last lp of each on hook, yo and draw through all 4 lps on hook. Break off F and join in D.

6th round As 4th round, but dec over 5dc at each point (b). Break off D and join in F.

7th round As 5th round, but dec over 5dc at each point (b). Break off F and join in C.

8th round As 7th round, but work 2dc into every 10th dc around motif 4. Break off C and join in D.

9th round As 7th round. Break off D and join in F.

10th round As 7th round, but at each point (b) dec over 2dc, 1tr into next dc, dec over next 2dc. Break off F and join in G.

11th round As 7th round, but dec over

2dc only at each point (b).
Break off G and join in H.
12th round As 7th round, but do not dec at point (b) and work 5dc shs into each corner sp. Break off H and join in B.
13th round As 12th round, but work 5dc into 3rd dc of previous 5dc sh at corners. Break off B and join in E.
14th round As 12th round.

Motif (5)

Work as for semi-circular motif (4) until 2nd row has been completed. Break off A and join in B.
3rd row 3ch, skip first sp, 1dc into next sp, 1dc into each sp to last 2 sp, 1dc into each of last 2 sp. Turn. Break off B and join in E.
4th row 3ch, 1dc into first sp, *skip next sp, 3dc into next sp, skip next sp, 2dc into next sp, rep from * to end. Turn.

Break off E and join in H.
5th row 3ch, *2dc into next sp, 3dc into next sp, rep from * to end, 1dc into 3rd of the 3ch. Turn.
6th row 3ch, 1dc into first sp, *3dc into next sp, 2dc into next sp, rep from * to end. Turn. Break off H and join in E.
7th row 3ch, 3dc into each sp to end, 1dc into 3rd of the 3ch. Turn. Break off E and join in H.
8th row 3ch, 2dc into first sp, *3dc into next sp, rep from * to last sp, 2dc into last sp, 1dc into 3rd of the 3ch. Turn. Break off H and join in E.
9th row 4ch, 1tr between 1st and 2nd dc (4tr into next sp) twice, *4dc into next sp, rep from * to last 2 sp, 4tr into each of next 2 sp, 1tr between last 2dc, 1tr into 4th of the 4ch. Turn.
10th row 4ch, 2tr into first sp, 5tr into next sp, *5dc into next sp, rep from * to

last 2 sp, 5tr into next sp, 2tr into last sp, 1tr into 4th of the 4ch. Turn. Break off E and join in H.
11th row 4ch, 5tr into first sp, *5dc into next sp, rep from * to last sp, 5tr into last sp, 1tr into 4th of the 4ch. Break off H.
Make one more motif in the same way and join to the main part as shown in the diagram. Cont with the border as foll:
15th round Join in A and work 1dc into each dc around and (3dc, 1ch, 3dc) into 3rd dc of every·5dc sh. Break off A and join in D.
16th round *3dc sh into next sp, skip next 2 sp, rep from * around, but work (3dc, 1ch, 3dc) into each corner. Break off D and join in A.
17round Work 3dc shs into each sp and over motif (5), 4dc shs over the curves and (3dc, 1ch, 3dc) into each corner. Break off A and join in F.
18th round As 17th round. Break off F and join in C.
19th round As 17th round. Break off C and join in I.
20th round As 17th round. Break off I.
Complete the piece by working the following extensions:
1st row Join I to point marked (c) on diagram, 3ch and 3dc into same sp, 4dc sh into each sp between shs to point marked (d) on diagram. Turn. Break off I and join in B.
2nd row Sl st into first sp between shs, 3ch and 3dc into same sp, 4dc sh into each sp to end. Turn. Break off B and join in E.
3rd row As 2nd row. Break off E and join in H.
4th row As 2nd row. Break off H and join in D.
5th row As 2nd row. Break off D and join in A.
6th row As 2nd row. Break off A.
Work a similar extension at the opposite end of the cover, then work around the cover as follows:
Join E to any sp between shs, 3ch and 3dc into same sp, 4dc sh into each sp between shs around, sl st into 3rd of the 3ch. Break off E. Finish off all ends.

Finishing

Tassels (make 6)
Cut 20in lengths of each color. Using 40 strands tog, tie them in the middle, fold in half and tie again 2in from the top Attach the tassels as shown.

Fringe

Cut lengths of each color as for tassels. Using 8 strands tog, draw center of threads through each sp between shs around outer edge and knot into place.

LACE CROCHET
FILET CROCHET

Filet is the French name for "net" and you will recognize this type of crochet by its simple lacy quality. It is made up of two simple stitches, already learned, the chain and the double crochet. The doubles are worked in groups to form a solid block and the space between each block is covered with a length of chain which corresponds in number to the group of doubles over which it is worked.

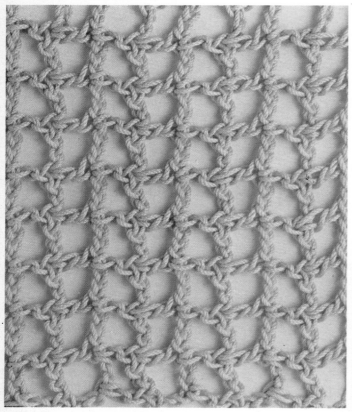

The composition of filet crochet forms the basis of the work and this is usually made up of single doubles with two chain separating them. However, when, for the purpose of design, various spaces are filled in with doubles, a block is formed and from the basic net many different patterns can be made.

An easy way of designing your own pattern is to use squared graph paper. Presuming that each square across represents a stitch and each square up equals a row, then block in squares accordingly to create your own individual design.

Instructions are given for working the basic net and for one of the many variations on this theme. Most yarns are suitable for filet crochet, although cotton or finer yarns are more popular since they add to the lightness and airiness of the work.

Basic filet crochet

Using size B hook and a cotton yarn, make 32ch.
1st row Into 8th ch from hook work 1dc, *2ch, skip next 2ch, 1dc into next ch, rep from * to end. Turn.
2nd row 5ch to count as first dc plus linking ch, skip first 2ch space, 1dc into next dc, *2ch, skip next 2ch space, 1dc into next dc, ending with 1dc into 3rd of the turning chain. Turn.
The last row is repeated throughout.

Filet crochet using blocks and spaces

Using size B hook and a cotton yarn, make 32ch.
1st row Work as given for 1st row of basic filet crochet.
2nd row 5ch to count as first dc plus linking ch, skip first 2ch space, 1dc into next dc, *2ch, skip next 2ch space, (1dc into next dc, 2dc into next 2ch space) twice, 1dc into next dc, rep from * once more, 2ch, skip next 2ch space, 1dc into next dc, 2ch, 1dc into 3rd of the turning chain. Turn.
3rd row 5ch, skip first 2ch space, 1dc into next dc, *2ch, skip next 2ch space, 1dc into each of next 7dc, rep from * once more, 2ch, skip next 2ch space, 1dc into next dc, 2ch, 1dc into 3rd of the turning chain. Turn.
4th row 5ch, skip first space, 1dc into next dc, 2ch,

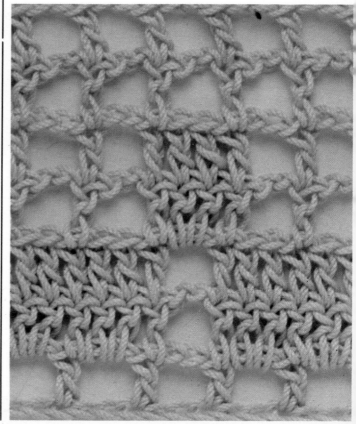

skip next space, 1dc into next dc, (2ch, skip next 2dc, 1dc into next dc) twice, 2dc into next space, (1dc into next dc, 2ch, skip next 2dc) twice, 1dc into next dc, 2ch, skip next space, 1dc into next dc, 2ch, 1dc into 3rd of the turning chain. Turn.

5th row 5ch, skip first space, 1dc into next dc, (2ch, skip next space, 1dc into next dc) twice, 2ch, skip next space, 1dc into each of next 4dc, (2ch, skip next space, 1dc into next dc) 3 times, 2ch, 1dc into 3rd of the turning chain. Turn.

6th row 3ch, (2dc into next space, 1dc into next dc) twice, (2ch, skip next space, 1dc into next dc) 5 times, 2dc into next space, 1dc into next dc, 2dc into last space, 1dc into 3rd of the turning chain. Turn.

7th row 3ch, skip first dc, 1dc into each of next 6dc, (2ch, skip next space, 1dc into next dc) 5 times, 1dc into each of next 5dc, 1dc into 3rd of the turning chain. Fasten off.

If you have managed to work this sample successfully, then you are ready to make up a design of your own using the method described above.

Very fine cotton used for this work produces a beautiful filet crochet lace. Worked into strips the piece you make can be used for a lace insertion or edging or you can make the strips a bit wider and cover the cuffs of a favorite blouse. The instructions below are for making two simple lace edgings.

Lace edging 1

Make a chain the length that you desire, using a multiple of 3 stitches plus 2.

1st row Into 4th ch from hook work 1dc, 1dc into each ch to end. Turn.

2nd row 5ch to count as first dc plus 2 linking ch, skip first 3dc, 1dc into next dc, *2ch, skip 2dc, 1dc into next dc, rep from * ending with 1dc into 3rd of the turning chain. Turn.

3rd row 3ch, *2dc into next space, 1dc into next dc, rep from * to end. Fasten off.

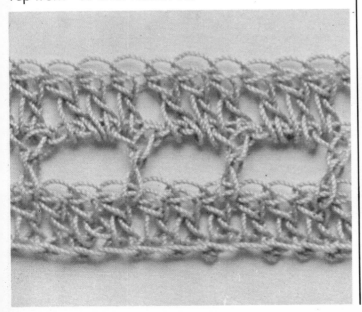

Lace edging 2

Make a chain the length that you desire, using a multiple of 6 stitches plus 5.

1st row Into 8th ch from hook work 1dc, 1dc into each of next 3ch, * 2ch, skip next 2ch, 1dc into each of next 4ch, rep from * to end. Turn.

2nd row 5ch, skip first 3dc, *1dc into next dc, 2dc into next space, 1dc into next dc, 2ch, skip 2dc, rep from * ending with last dc into 3rd of the turning chain. Turn.

3rd row As 2nd. Fasten off.

Using the same technique, and still working with very

fine yarns, you can make other lovely things for your home, such as pillow covers, tablecloths, placemats and even wall hangings.

Similar strips to those described above, if worked in thicker yarn, can make attractive braids and belts. Plastic strips threaded between the double crochets of the middle row would add interest and firmness to a belt.

Belt with plastic strip threaded between double crochets

213

FILET LACE TRIMMINGS

This chapter continues our previous work on filet lace crochet, which is made up of blocks and spaces, and offers different and more advanced techniques. Here we deal particularly with finer yarns used for a more traditional type of work. Filet lace, or crochet lace as it is sometimes called, is in its finest form a popular trimming for underclothes and for many types of household linen. Today it is also fashionable for decorating window shades, Tiffany lampshades and tablecloths—although probably for these latter you will want to use a slightly thicker yarn.

There are fine cotton yarns available in a wide range of colors and thicknesses, varying from No.3 which is the thickest to No.100, the finest. The average range of steel crochet hooks to use with fine cotton varies in size from No.00 hook to No.14.

Traditionally, filet lace crochet is produced in white or ecru, although more contemporary designs sometimes call for colored yarns. It is particularly important, however, if you are trimming underclothes that you have the right color lace. If it should not be available, you can dye the yarn you have with a water dye, first rewinding the ball of cotton into a skein and then, following the dye manufacturer's instructions. Contrast colors can also be used very effectively.

When the lace trimming has been completed, it should be washed and blocked before it is applied to a garment. This will prevent any shrinkage later on. Sew the lace on to the garment with hemming or embroidery stitches.

There are two methods of working the lace trimming—in narrow strips, beginning with the number of stitches required for the depth of the lace and working until the desired length has been completed, or working the number of stitches to give the required length of work and then working in rows to give the correct depth.

Our photograph shows a sample of filet lace crochet where blocks and spaces have been increased and decreased. You will also see a chart of this design. Earlier we showed you a simple way of charting a design, but now we would like to teach you the professional way of doing it.

In our chart here, one space across represents either a block of double crochets or a space and each space up represents a row. To help you follow the chart, the techniques of increasing and decreasing are explained in detail below, and then there are instructions of how to work our sample.

To increase a block at the beginning of a row. Work 5 ch. Into 4th ch from hook work 1dc, 1dc into next ch,

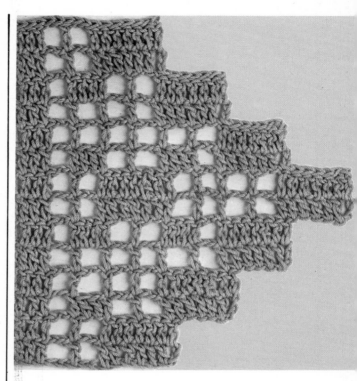

Use this chart to work the sample

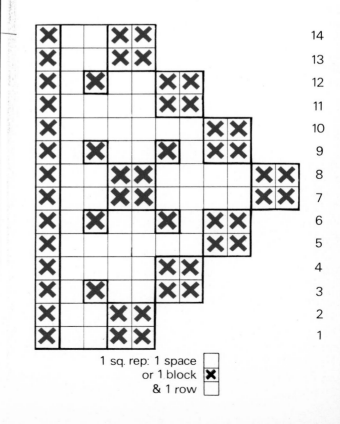

14
13
12
11
10
9
8
7
6
5
4
3
2
1

1 sq. rep: 1 space or 1 block & 1 row

1dc into next st (i.e. the last st of the previous row), continue across the row in pattern. To increase two blocks as in our chart, work 8ch. Into 4th ch from hook work 1dc, 1dc into each of next 4ch, 1dc into next st.

To increase a space at the beginning of a row Work 7ch which will represent a 2ch space at the end of the last row, 3ch to count as the first dc of the new row and another 2ch between the first dc and the next st, then work 1dc into last st of the previous row.

To decrease a block or space at the beginning of a row Skip the first st, sl st loosely into each of the next 3 sts, then work 3ch to count as the first dc and continue in pattern.

To increase a block at the end of a row Provision has to be made for this increase by working 7ch at the beginning of the previous row, skip the first ch, sl st into each of next 3ch, leaving 3ch which count as the first dc of the new row. Complete the row in pattern. At the end of the following row work 1dc into each of the 3 sl st, thus increasing one block.

To increase a space at the end of a row Work as for increasing a block at the end of a row, but when the increasing is reached, work 2ch, skip next 2 sts, 1dc into the last st.

To decrease a block or space at the end of a row Work to within the last block or space, then turn the work and proceed in pattern.

To work the sample
Make 18ch.
1st row Into 4th ch from hook work 1dc, 1dc into each of next 5 sts, (2ch, skip next 2ch, 1dc into next ch) twice, 1dc into each of next 3ch. Turn.
2nd row 3ch to count as first dc, 1dc into each of next 3dc, (2ch, 1dc into next dc) twice, 1dc into each of next 5dc, 1dc into 3rd of the 3ch. Turn.
3rd row Increase 2 blocks by working 8ch, 1dc into 4th ch from hook, 1dc into each of next 5 sts, (2ch, skip next 2 sts, 1dc into next st) twice, 1dc into each of next 3 sts, 2ch, skip next 2 sts, 1dc into each of next 3 sts, 1dc into 3rd of the 3ch. Turn.
Continue working in pattern from the chart, increasing 2 blocks at the beginning of the 5th and 7th rows and decreasing 2 blocks at the beginning of the 9th, 11th and 13th rows. The 13 rows worked may be repeated to whatever length you desire.
Following here are the instructions and chart for a simple edging which would make an ideal tasselled trimming for a window shade. You will notice that this sample is worked in the width and until the piece is the desired length.

Trimming with tassels
Make 17ch.
1st row Into 8th ch from hook work 1dc, 1dc into each of next 3ch, (2ch, skip 2ch, 1dc into next ch) twice. Turn.
2nd row 5ch, 1dc into 2nd dc, 1dc into each of next 3 sts, 2ch, skip next 2 sts, 1dc into next st. Turn. One

space has been decreased.
3rd row 7ch (thus increasing one space), 1dc into first dc, 1dc into each of next 3 sts, 2ch, skip next 2 sts, 1dc into next dc, 2ch, 1dc into 3rd of the 5ch. Turn.
The 2nd and 3rd rows are repeated throughout. When finished thread two tassels through each increased space.

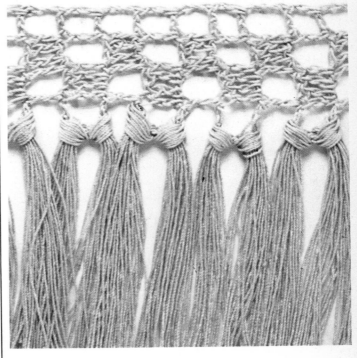

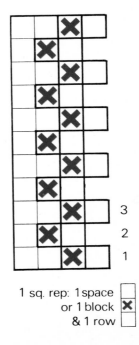

3
2
1

1 sq. rep: 1 space
or 1 block ✗
& 1 row

215

DESIGNING AND WORKING CORNERS

The technique of designing and working corners in filet crochet may present problems, but here we shall explain these two procedures in detail. If you follow our charts and instructions, you should not have any difficulty in producing a beautiful mitered corner suitable for use on a fitted couch cover, or details such as a square neckline on clothing.

In the last chapter you were taught how to create your own designs in filet crochet by using squared graph paper; each square across represents either a block or a space and each square up represents a row. Our basic filet chart in the samples here is formed by working single double crochets with two chains between each. You can, however, make the design of the chart to your specifications.

When designing a corner, first draw a diagram and then a line through the corner at an angle of 45 degrees from the outer edge of the design. On one side of the corner sketch in your pattern as you would like it to appear, stopping at the corner line, then mirror your design exactly over this line.

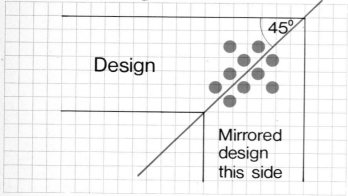

To work sample 1

In our photograph of a mitered corner two colors have been used to clarify the working process. There

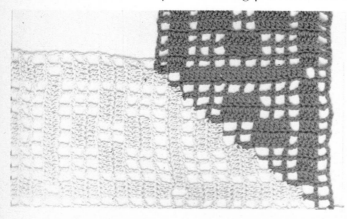

is also a chart of the design which you can follow. Make 41ch.

1st row Into 8th ch from hook work 1dc, 2ch, skip next 2ch, 1dc into each of next 25ch – thus forming 8 blocks –, (2ch, skip next 2ch, 1dc into next ch) twice. Turn.

2nd through 9th row Work in patt from the chart.

10th row Dec one square by skipping first st, sl st into each of next 3 sts, 5ch, skip 2dc, 1dc into each of next 25 sts, 2ch, skip 2dc, 1dc into next dc, 2ch, 1dc into 3rd of the 5ch. Turn.

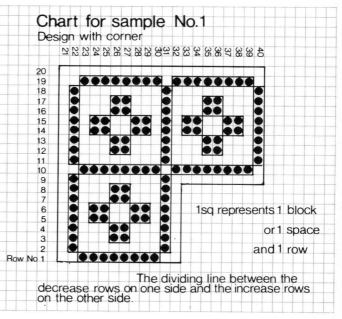

Chart for sample No.1
Design with corner

1sq represents 1 block
or 1 space
and 1 row

Row No 1

The dividing line between the decrease rows on one side and the increase rows on the other side.

11th row 5ch, skip 2ch, 1dc into each of next 4 sts, (2ch, skip 2dc, 1dc into next dc) 8 times, turn. One square has been decreased.

12th row Dec one square by skipping first st, sl st into each of next 3 sts, 5ch, skip 2ch, 1dc into next dc, 2ch, skip 2ch, 1dc into each of next 7 sts, (2ch, skip 2ch, 1dc into next dc) 3 times, 1dc into each of next 3dc, 2ch, 1dc into 3rd of the 5ch. Turn.

13th row 5ch, skip 2ch, 1dc into each of next 4dc, (2ch, skip 2ch, 1dc into next dc) 3 times, 1dc into each of next 6dc, 2ch, skip 2ch, 1dc into next dc, turn. One square has been decreased.

14th row Dec one square by skipping first st, sl st into each of next 3 sts, 5ch, skip 2dc, 1dc into next dc, 2ch, skip 2dc, 1dc into each of next 7 sts, 2ch, skip 2ch, 1dc into each of next 4dc, 2ch, 1dc into 3rd of the 5ch. Turn.

15th row 5ch, skip 2ch, 1dc into each of next 4dc, 2ch, skip 2ch, 1dc into each of next 7dc, 2ch, skip 2ch, 1dc into next dc, turn. One space has been decreased.

16th row Dec one square by skipping first st, sl st into each of next 3 sts, 5ch, skip 2dc, 1dc into next dc, 2ch, skip 2dc, 1dc into next dc, 2ch, skip 2ch, 1dc into each of next 4dc, 2ch, 1dc into 3rd of the 5ch. Turn.

17th row 5ch, skip 2ch, 1dc into each of next 4dc, (2ch, skip 2ch, 1dc into next dc) twice, turn. One space has been decreased.

18th row Dec one square by skipping first st, sl st into each of next 3 sts, 5ch, skip 2ch, 1dc into each of next 4dc, 2ch, 1dc into 3rd of the 5ch. Turn.

19th row 5ch, skip 2ch, 1dc into next dc, 2ch, skip 2dc, 1dc into next dc, turn. One space has been decreased.

20th row Decrease one space by skipping first st, sl st into each of next 3 sts, 5ch, 1dc into 3rd of the 5ch of previous row. Turn the work and sl st into each of the sts across the top of last space worked.

21st row 5ch, sl st into corner of last space on left of the previous row. Do not turn.

22nd row 3ch, 1dc into each of next 2ch, (i.e. down side of space), sl st into corner of last space on left of the previous row, turn, skip first st, sl st into each of next 3 sts, 2ch, skip 2ch, 1dc into 3rd of the 5ch. Turn.

23rd row 5ch, skip 2ch, 1dc into each of next 4dc, 2ch, sl st into corner of last space of the row on the left. Do not turn.

24th row 5ch, sl st into corner of last space of the row on the left, turn, skip first st, sl st in to each of next 3 sts, 2ch, skip 2ch, 1dc into each of next 4dc, 2ch, 1dc into 3rd of the 5ch. Turn.

25th row 5ch, skip 2ch, 1dc into each of next 4dc, 2ch, skip 2ch, 1dc into each of next 6 sts, sl st into corner of last space of the row on the left. Do not turn.

26th row 5ch, sl st into corner of last space of the row on the left, turn, skip first st, sl st into each of next 3 sts, 1dc into each of next 6dc, 2ch, skip 2ch, 1dc into each of next 4dc, 2ch, 1dc into 3rd of the 5ch. Turn.

27th row 5ch, skip 2ch, 1dc into each of next 4dc, 2ch, skip 2ch, 1dc into next dc, (2ch, skip 2dc, 1dc into next dc) twice, 1dc into each of next 5 sts, sl st into corner of last space of the row on the left. Do not turn.

28th row 5ch, sl st into corner of last space of the row on the left, turn, skip first st, sl st into each of next 3 sts, 1dc into each of next 6dc, (2ch, skip 2ch, 1dc into next dc) 3 times, 1dc into each of next 3dc, 2ch, 1dc into 3rd of the 5ch. Turn.

29th row 5ch, skip 2ch, 1dc into each of next 4dc, (2ch, skip 2 sts, 1dc into next st) 6 times, 2ch, sl st into corner of the last space of the row on the left. Do not turn.

30th row 2ch, 1dc into each of next 2 sts, sl st into corner of last space of the row on the left, turn, skip first st, sl st into each of next 3 sts, 1dc into each of next 21 sts, 2ch, skip 2dc, 1dc into next dc, 2ch, 1dc into 3rd of the 5ch. Turn.

31st row 5ch, skip 2ch, 1dc into each of next 4 sts, (2ch, skip 2dc, 1dc into next dc) 8 times, 1dc into each of next 2 sts, sl st into corner of last space of the row on the left. Do not turn.

32nd row 5ch, skip 2 sts (i.e. the side of last space on 10th row), 1dc into next st, turn, skip first st, sl st into

each of next 3 sts, 1dc into each of next 4dc, (2ch, skip 2dc, 1dc into next dc) 3 times, 1dc into each of next 6 sts, (2ch, skip 2ch, 1dc into next dc) 3 times, 1dc into each of next 3dc, 2ch, 1dc into 3rd of the 5ch. Turn.

33rd through 39th row Work in patt from the chart.

To work sample 2

Above we gave details on how to work sample 1, but actually it is possible to work entirely from a chart without written directions. Practice working sample 2 from the chart. This illustrates the same technique, but it should be worked in a very fine yarn and it is shown in one color only to show the actual working of the technique.

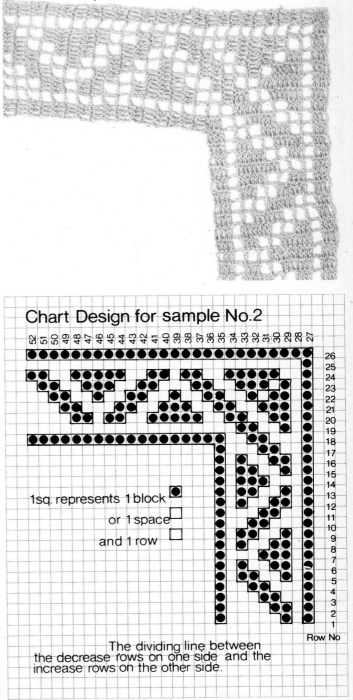

Chart Design for sample No.2

1sq. represents 1 block
or 1 space
and 1 row

Row No

The dividing line between the decrease rows on one side and the increase rows on the other side.

A butterfly top

Sizes
Directions are to fit 32in bust. Changes for 34 and 36in bust are in brackets [ ]. Side seam, 14[14 :14½]in

Gauge
8 sps and 12 rows to 4in in patt worked with size C crochet hook

Materials
3 × 20grm balls Reynolds Feu d'Artifice
One size C crochet hook
3 snaps
2 glass beads for trim

Back
Using size C hook make 83[89:95]ch.
Base row Into 8th ch from hook work 1dc, *2ch, skip 2ch, 1dc into next ch, rep from * to end. Turn.
1st row 5ch to count as first dc and 2ch, 1dc into next dc, * 2ch, 1dc into next dc, rep from * to end, working last dc into 3rd of 7ch. Turn. 26[28:30] sp. Rep last row 4[4:6] times more, noting that on subsequent rows the last dc will be worked into 3rd of 5 turning ch.
Shape sides
1st row 3ch to count as first dc, 1dc into first dc, patt to end, working 2dc into 3rd of 5ch. Turn.
2nd row 3ch, 1dc into first dc, 1dc into next dc, patt to end, working 2dc into 3rd of 3ch. Turn.
3rd row 3ch, 1dc into first dc, 1dc into each of next 2dc, patt to last 2dc, 1dc into each of next 2dc, 2dc into 3rd of 3ch. Turn.
4th row 5ch, skip 2dc, 1dc into next dc, patt to last 3dc, 2ch, skip 2dc, 1dc into 3rd of 3ch. Turn. 2 sp inc.
Rep last 4 rows twice more. 32[34:36] sp. Cont without shaping until 31[31:33] rows in all have been worked.
Next row 3ch, *2dc into next sp, 1dc into next dc, rep from * to end. Fasten off.

Front
Work as for back until 2[2:4] rows have been completed. Start butterfly patt.
1st row Patt 7[8:9] sp, 1ch, 1dc into next sp, 1dc into next dc, patt 10 sp, 1dc into next sp, 1ch, 1dc into next dc, patt to end. Turn.
2nd row Patt 7[8:9] sp, 1dc into next 1ch sp, 1dc into each of next 2dc (1 block of 4dc has been worked), patt 4 sp, 1ch, 1dc into next sp, 1dc into next dc, 1dc into next sp, 1ch, 1dc into next dc, patt 4 sp, 1dc into next dc, 1dc into next 1ch sp, 1dc into next dc, patt to end. Turn.
3rd row Patt 6[7:8] sp, 2dc into next sp, 1dc into each of next 4dc, patt 4 sp, 1dc into next 1ch sp, 1dc into each of next 3dc, 1dc into next 1ch sp, 1dc into next dc, patt 4sp, 1dc into each of next 3dc, 2dc into sp, 1dc into next dc, patt to end. Turn.
Cont working butterfly in this way from chart, *at the same time* shaping sides as for back, until 28 rows of patt have been completed.

Note The chart represents a filet crochet of blocks, spaces, half blocks and half spaces. Spaces are formed by working single doubles with 2ch between them and blocks are spaces which have been filled in by working 2dc into the appropriate 2ch sp. Here spaces have been subdivided into half block/half space by working 1dc and 1ch into a 2ch sp. Patt one more row in sp. Work last row as for back.
Fasten off.

Straps (make 2).
Using size C hook make 8ch.
1st row Into 4th ch from hook work 1dc, 1dc into each ch to end. Turn. 6dc.
2nd row 3ch to count as first dc, 1dc into each dc to end. Turn.
Rep 2nd row until strap measures 14in from beg, or desired length. Fasten off.

Finishing
Do not block. Join right side seam. Join left side seam to within 3in of lower edge.

Edging Using size C hook and with WS of work facing, rejoin yarn to first ch at lower edge, 3ch, *2dc into first sp, 1dc into next dc, rep from * around lower edge, Turn.
Next row 3ch, *1dc into next dc, rep from * to end.
Cont working in dc up side of opening, working 1dc into each dc and 2dc into each sp, turn and work down other side in same way. Fasten off.
Turn edging to WS on front edge of side opening and sew into place to form overlap. Sew snaps along opening.
Sew straps in position. Sew on beads for butterfly eyes.

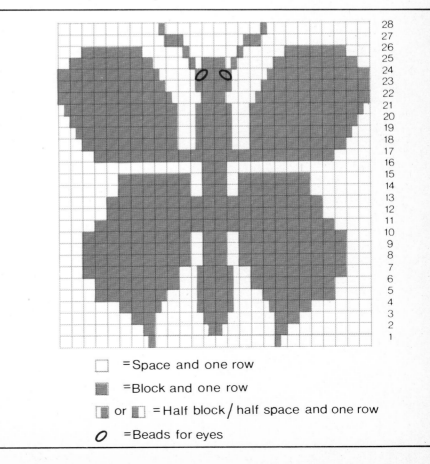

□ = Space and one row

▨ = Block and one row

▨ or ▨ = Half block / half space and one row

O = Beads for eyes

Filet crochet smock

Sizes

Directions are to fit 32in bust. Changes for 34 and 36in bust sizes are in brackets [].

Length to shoulder, 28[28½:29]in
Sleeve seam, 19in

Gauge

24 sts and 12 rows to 4in in dc worked with size D crochet hook

Materials

15[16:17] × 1oz balls Bucilla Fingering yarn
One size B crochet hook
One size D crochet hook
11 small buttons

Back

Using size B hook make 200[212:224]ch for lower edge.
1st row (WS) Into 3rd ch from hook work 1sc, 1sc into each ch to end. Turn. 199[211:223] sts.
Change to size D hook. Start patt.
2nd row 5ch to count as first dc and 2ch, skip first 3 sts, 1dc into next st, *2ch, skip 2 sts, 1dc into next st, rep from * to end. Turn.
3rd row 5ch, skip first dc, 1dc into next dc, *2ch, 1dc into next dc, rep from * ending with last dc into 3rd of 5ch. Turn.
The last row forms the main patt. Cont in patt until work measures 2in from beg, ending with a WS row. Cont in patt, placing rose motifs as foll:
Next row 5ch, skip first dc, (1dc into next dc, 2ch) 1[2:3] times, work across next 85 sts as given for 1st row of rose motif from chart, (2ch, 1dc into next dc) 5[7:9] times, 2ch, work across next 85 sts as for 1st row of rose motif from chart, (2ch, 1dc into next dc) 1[2:3] times 2ch, 1dc into 3rd of 5ch. Turn.
Next row 5ch, skip first dc, (1dc into next dc, 2ch) 1[2:3] times, work across next 85 sts as given for 2nd row of rose motif from chart, (2ch, 1dc into next dc) 5[7:9] times, 2ch, work across next 85 sts as for 2nd row of rose motif from chart, (2ch, 1dc into next dc) 1[2:3] times, 2ch, 1dc into 3rd of 5ch. Turn.
Cont working in this way until 30 rows of rose motif from chart have been completed. Cont in patt as before until work measures 20in from beg, ending with a RS row.
Shape yoke
Next row 3ch, (1dc into next 2ch sp, 1dc into each of next 2dc) 13[14:15] times, 1dc into next 2ch sp, 1dc into next dc, 1dc into next 2ch sp, 1dc into each of next 3dc, 1dc into each of next three 2ch sp, 1dc into each of next 3dc, 1dc into next 2ch sp, 1dc into next dc, 1dc into next 2ch sp, (1dc into next 2ch

sp, 1dc into each of next 2dc) 13[14:15] times, 1dc into last ch sp, 1dc into 3rd of 5ch. Turn. 98[104:110] sts.
Next row 3ch, skip first st, 1dc into each st, ending with last dc into 3rd of 3ch. Turn.
Rep last row once more. **
Shape armholes
1st row Sl st across first 3 sts then 3ch, (yo, insert hook into next st, yo and draw through a loop, yo and draw through first 2 loops on hook) 3 times, yo and draw through all 4 loops on hook – called dec 2 –, 1dc into each st to last 7 sts, dec 2, 1dc into next st, turn. 88[94:100] sts.
2nd row 3ch, skip first st, dec 2, 1dc into each st to last 4 sts, dec 2, 1dc into 3rd of 3ch. Turn.
3rd row 3ch, skip first st, (yo, insert hook into next st, yo and draw through a loop, yo and draw through first 2 loops on hook) twice, yo and draw through all 3 loops on hook – called dec 1 –, 1dc into each st to last 3 sts, dec 1, 1dc into 3rd of 3ch. Turn.
Rep last row 5[6:7] times more. 72[76:80] sts. Cont in dc without shaping until armholes measure 7[7½:8]in from beg, ending with a WS row.
Shape shoulders
Next row Sl st across first 4[5:5] sts, 1sc into each of next 5 sts, 1hdc into each of next 5 sts, 1dc into each st to last 14[15:15] sts, 1hdc into each of next 5sts, 1sc into each of next 5 sts. Fasten off.

Front

Work as given for back to **.
Shape armholes and divide for opening
1st row Sl st across first 3 sts and 3ch, dec 2 into next st, 1dc into each of next 40[43:46] sts, turn. Cont on these 42[45:48] sts for first side as foll:
2nd row 3ch, skip first st, 1dc into each st to last 4 sts, dec 2, 1dc into 3rd of 3ch. Turn.
3rd row 3ch, skip first st, dec 1, 1dc into each st to end. Turn.
4th row 3ch, skip first st, 1dc into each st to last 3 sts, dec 1, 1dc into 3rd of 3ch. Turn.
Rep 3rd and 4th rows 2[2:3] times more. 34[37:38] sts.
2nd size only
Rep 3rd row once more. 36 sts.
All sizes
Cont in dc without shaping until armhole measures 4½[5:5½]in from beg, ending at armhole edge.
Shape neck
1st row 3ch, skip first st, 1dc into each st to last 9[10:11] sts, dec 2, 1dc into next st, turn.

2nd row 3ch, skip first st, dec 2, 1dc into each st to end. Turn.
3rd row 3ch, skip first st, 1dc into each st to last 4 sts, dec 2, 1dc into 3rd of 3ch. Turn.
Rep 2nd and 3rd rows once more. 19[20:21] sts. Cont without shaping until front measures same as back to shoulder, ending at armhole edge.
Shape shoulder
Next row Sl st across first 4[5:5] sts, 1sc into each of next 5 sts, 1hdc into each of next 5 sts, 1dc into each of next 5[5:6] sts. Fasten off.
With RS of work facing, return to start of neck shaping and leaving center 4sts unworked, rejoin yarn to next st, 3ch, 1dc into each st to last 7 sts, dec 2, 1dc into next st, turn. Complete to correspond to first side reversing shaping.

Left sleeve

1st piece Using size B hook make 23[25:27]ch.
1st row (WS) Into 3rd ch from hook work 1sc, 1sc into each ch to end. Turn. 22[24:26] sts.
2nd row 1ch to count as first sc, skip first st, 1sc into each st to end. Turn.
Rep last row until cuff measures 2in from beg, ending with a WS row. Change to size D hook.
Next row 5ch, skip first st, 1dc into next st, *2ch, 1dc into next st, rep from * to end. 64[70:76] sts.
Cont in main patt as given for back until 1st piece measures 4in from beg, ending with a WS row. Fasten off.
2nd piece Using size B hook make 14ch.
1st row (WS) Into 3rd ch from hook work 1sc, 1sc into each ch to end. Turn. 13sts.
2nd row 1ch to count as first sc, skip first st, 1sc into each st to end. Turn.
Rep last row until cuff measures 2in, ending with a WS row. Change to size D hook.
Next row 5ch, skip first st, 1dc into next st, *2ch, 1dc into next st. Rep from * to end. Turn. 37 sts. Cont in patt as for back until 2nd piece measures same as 1st piece, ending with a WS row.
Next row Work in patt across 37 sts of 2nd piece, 2ch, then with RS of work facing, patt across 64[70:76] sts of 1st piece. 103[109:115] sts. Turn.
** Cont in patt until sleeve measures 18in from beg, measured at center, ending with a RS row.
Next row 3ch, (1dc into next 2ch sp, 1dc into next dc) 16[17:18] times, 1dc into each of next two 2ch sp, (1dc into next dc, 1dc into next 2ch sp) 16[17:18] times, 1dc into 3rd of 5ch. Turn. 68[72:76] sts.
Work 2 rows in dc.

Chart for rose motif

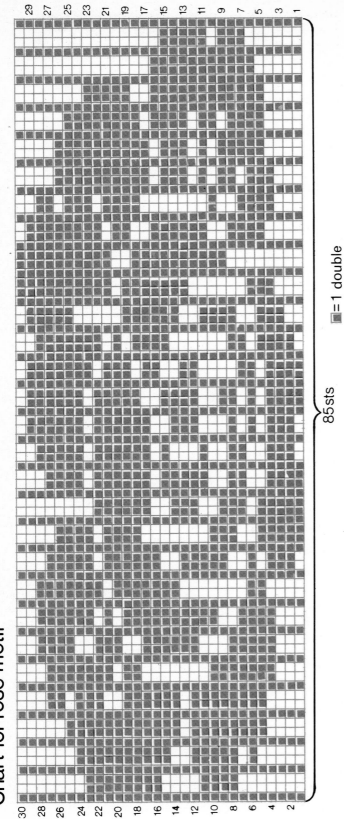

29 27 25 23 21 19 17 15 13 11 9 7 5 3 1

30 28 26 24 22 20 18 16 14 12 10 8 6 4 2

85 sts

■ = 1 double
□ = 1 chain

Shape top

1st row Sl st over first 3 sts and into next st, 3ch, dec 1, 1dc into each st to last 6 sts, dec 1, 1dc into next st, turn.

2nd row 3ch, skip first st, dec 1, 1dc into each st to last 3 sts, dec 1, 1dc into 3rd of 3ch. Turn.

Rep last row 9[9:11] times more. 40[44:44] sts.

Next row 3ch, skip first st, dec 2, 1dc into each st to last 4 sts, dec 2, 1dc into 3rd of 3ch. Turn.

Rep last row 4[5:5] times more. 20 sts. Fasten off.

Right sleeve

1st piece Work as given for 2nd piece of left sleeve and fasten off.

2nd piece Work as given for 1st piece of left sleeve, but do not fasten off.

Next row Work in patt across 64[70:76] sts of 2nd piece, 2ch, then with RS of work facing, patt across 37 sts of 1st piece. Turn. 103[109:115] sts.

Complete as given for left sleeve from ** to end.

Finishing

Block lightly under a damp cloth with a warm iron. Join shoulder seams. Set in sleeves. Join side and sleeve seams.

Neck edging Using size B hook and with RS of work facing, rejoin yarn to top of right front neck and work 3 rows sc around neck edge. Fasten off.

Left front border Using size B hook and with RS of work facing, work 5 rows sc down left side of opening.

Mark position for 5 buttonholes on this border, the first ½in from base of opening, the last 2 sts below top of neck and the others evenly spaced between.

Right front border Work as for left front border, making buttonholes on 3rd row to correspond with markers by working 2ch and skipping 2sc.

Tack down ends of borders to base of opening, the right border over the left one.

Sleeve opening border Using size B hook and with RS of work facing, work 2 rows sc around opening, working 3 button loops evenly spaced along cuff part of larger piece on 2nd row by making 3ch and skipping 2sc.

Lower edging Using size B hook and with RS of work facing, work 1sc into each of first 3 sts, *(sl st, 5ch, sl st, 5ch, sl st, 5ch, sl st) all into next st, 1sc into each of next 5sts, *, rep from * to * 32[34:36] times more, 1sc into next st, rep from * to * 32[34:36] times more, (sl st, 5ch, sl st, 5ch, sl st, 5ch, sl st) all into next st, 1sc into each of last 3 sts. Join with a sl st into first st. Fasten off. Press seams. Sew on buttons.

OPEN LACE DESIGNS

Open lace designs

Open lace is quick and easy to work in crochet since it is formed with large spaces between the stitches, consequently the pattern grows rapidly. Any type of yarn may be used and should be determined by the nature of the work.

There are many uses for the kind of crochet in which an open effect is desired. It can be used for entire garments, which naturally will need to be lined. More commonly, strips of open lace work are used as inserts, especially on evening clothes where the laciness of the crochet looks most effective.

Openwork designs do however serve many more functions as well. String bags, onion bags or simple cotton lace curtains for the windows in your home are examples of a few of the things that you can make once you have practiced some of the samples of open lace work that are given below.

String stitch used as an insert on a bodice

Solomon stitch

Using size C crochet hook and a fine yarn make 35ch loosely.

1st row Extend loop on hook for $\frac{3}{4}$ inch, placing thumb of left hand on loop to keep it extended, yo and draw through a loop, place hook from front to back under left hand vertical loop of stitch just worked, yo and draw through a loop, yo and draw through both loops on hook – called one Solomon st –, sl st into 10th ch from last Solomon st, * 1ch, work 2 Solomon sts, sl st into 5th ch from last Solomon st, rep from * to end. Turn.

2nd row 6ch, work 1 Solomon st, sl st into st between first pair of Solomon sts on previous row, 1ch, * work 2 Solomon sts, sl st into st between next pair of Solomon sts, rep from * ending with last sl st into last of the turning ch of the previous row. Turn.

The last row is repeated throughout to create a very attractive lacy stitch with a 3-dimensional effect.

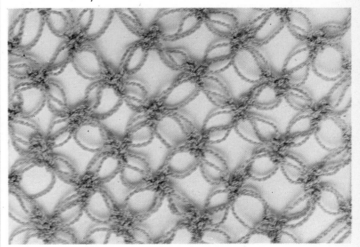

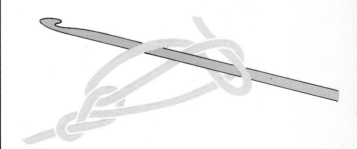

Working a Solomon stitch

Chain lace

Using size C crochet hook and a fine yarn make 44ch.

1st row Into 12th ch from hook work 1sc, *8ch, skip next 3ch, 1sc into next ch, rep from * to end. Turn.

2nd row 8ch, 1sc into first 8ch loop, *8ch, 1sc into next loop, rep from * to end. Turn.

The last row is repeated throughout to form a very simple diamond shaped mesh.

This stitch is ideal for an evening snood or a string bag like the one in our illustration.

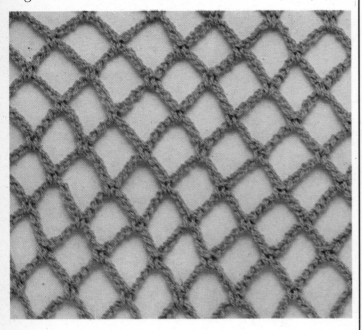

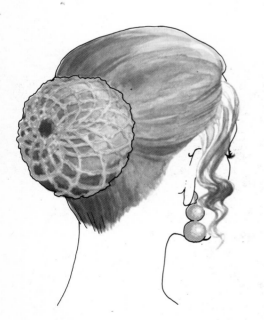

Chain lace used for a snood

To make a string bag

You will need one ball of household string, a brass curtain ring 1¼ inch in diameter and a size F crochet hook.

1st round Form a slip loop on the hook, 1sc into brass ring, *9ch, 1sc into ring, rep from * 21 times more, sl st into first sc.

Next and all following rounds Sl st into first 4ch of next 9ch loop, 1sc into this loop, *9ch, 1sc into next loop, rep from * around ending with 9ch, sl st into first sc of the round. Turn.

When the bag is the desired depth, fasten off and slot drawstrings through the spaces.

String stitch

Using No.0 crochet hook and a fine yarn, make 43ch.

1st row Sl st into 5th ch from hook, skip next ch, 1sc into next ch, *5ch, skip next 5ch, 1sc into next ch, 5ch, sl st into last sc worked, 1sc into same ch as last sc, rep from * to end. Turn.

2nd row Sl st to top of first 5ch loop, 6ch, sl st into 5th ch from hook, 1sc into first loop, *5ch, 1sc into next 5ch loop, 5ch, sl st into last sc worked, 1sc into same loop, rep from * to end. Turn.

The last row is repeated throughout to form the pattern.

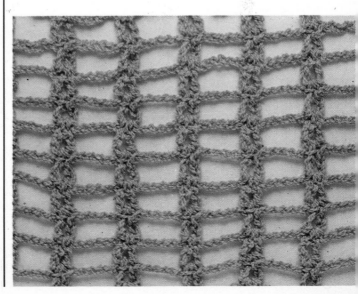

Mohair muffler

Size

12in wide by 96in long

Materials

5 × 40grm balls variegated mohair
One size H crochet hook

The muffler

Using the crochet hook make 20
Solomon's knots, drawing each loop up
to a height of 1 inch.
Continue working in pattern until the
work measures 96in from the beginning.
Fasten off.

Solomon's knot worked in mohair

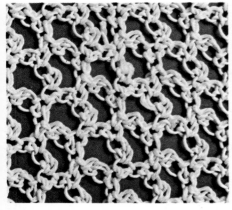

Solomon's knot worked in fine string

Shopping bag

Size

A bag about 14in wide by 16in deep

Materials

2 balls of fine household string
One size E crochet hook

Bag

Using the crochet hook make 40
Solomon's knots, drawing each loop up
to a height of ½in.
Continue in pattern until the work
measures 32in from the beginning.
Fasten off.

Finishing

Make up the bag by folding in half
lengthwise. Join the side seams by
overcasting them, from the lower edge
to within 6in of the top edge.

Handle

Cut 12 lengths of string, each 36in long
for the handle.
Divide the string into 3 groups with 4
lengths in each and braid them together,

knotting each end.
Thread each braid through the last row at the top of the bag from the outer edge to the center and tie the ends together to form a handle.
Complete the other handle in the same way.

Wool shawl

Size

A shawl measuring about 66in across the top edge, excluding the fringe

Materials

3½oz of Fingering Yarn plus 1oz extra for fringe
One size D crochet hook

Shawl

Using the crochet hook make 140 Solomon's knots, drawing each loop to a height of ½in, then shape the sides by working as follows:
Next row Skip knot on hook and next 4 knots, insert hook into center of next knot and work 1sc, *make 2 knots, skip 1 knot along 1st row, 1sc into center of next knot on 1st row, rep from * to end, working last sc into first ch.
Next row Make 3 knots, skip first knot, next unjoined knot and joined knot of last row, 1sc into center of next unjoined knot of last row, *make 2 knots, skip next joined knot of last row, 1sc into center of next unjoined knot of last row, rep from * to end.
Repeat the last row until 2 knots remain. Fasten off.
Cut lengths of yarn, each 16in long. Take 6 strands together at a time and knot into each space along side edges only.
Work 2 rows of fringing (see chapters on Trimmings and Braids later), each row 1in below previous knots. Trim the fringe.

Solomon's knot worked in fingering yarn

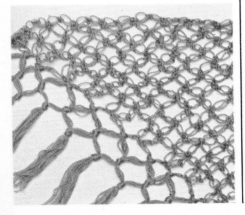

Solomon's knot stitch worked in fingering yarn makes a gossamer shawl.

FUR FABRICS AND LOOP STITCHES

Recently it has become very popular to simulate fur fashions with "fun fur" fabrics. In crochet this is done with the use of loop stitches. Here we tell you how to work three basic loop stitches and in the next chapter we will continue with more advanced techniques. Loop stitches produce an attractive raised effect and form a solid, virtually windproof fabric which is ideal for cooler days. It is important in this work not to underestimate the amount of yarn you will need for any particular garment worked in this stitch, since it does consume a considerable amount.

Vests, jackets and hats made entirely in loop stitch in bright paintbox colors are perfect for children's wear. Or, using the same stitches, create a "fur" trimming effect. Besides using this stitch for clothes, you can also make very attractive bathroom sets and area rugs, particularly if you are using a machine-washable, quick-drying yarn.

Loop stitch

This is loop stitch in its most common form, worked right into the fabric as you proceed in rows.

Using size H crochet hook and Knitting Worsted make 22ch.

1st row 1sc into 3rd ch from hook, work 1sc into every ch to end. Turn.

2nd row 1ch to count as first sc, skip first st of previous row, work a loop by inserting hook into next stitch, place yarn over 1st and 2nd fingers and draw it up

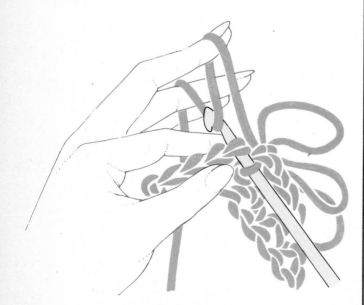

by lifting 2nd finger. Draw through a loop as shown in illustration, then draw loop through st, yo and draw

through both loops on hook, remove 2nd finger from loop and continue making loops in this manner into every st to the end of the row. 1sc into the turning chain. Turn.

Repeat the 2nd and 3rd rows throughout to form the pattern.

Note You will see, as you are working, that the loops are on the back of the fabric. This occurs since you are making the loops on the wrong side of the work. The density of the loops can be changed by working them across the rows in alternate stitches or into the stitches between loops on every other row.

Chain fur stitches

Again these chain loops are formed as part of the fabric, which has a close, curly fur effect, resembling the look of many popular furs.

Using size H crochet hook and a Knitting Worsted make 25ch.

1st row 1dc into 4th ch from hook, work 1dc into every ch to end. Turn.

2nd row 1ch to count as first sc, skip first st of previous row, * 1sc into back loop only of next st, 10ch, rep from * to end of row, working last sc into the turning chain. Turn.

3rd row 3ch to count as first dc, skipping the first st, work 1dc into each st of the last row worked in dc,

inserting the hook into the loop skipped in the previous row of sc, 1dc into the turning chain. Turn.
Repeat the 2nd and 3rd rows throughout to form the pattern.

Cut fur stitch
Here the loops are added after the basic background – a mesh – has been worked.
Using size H crochet hook and a Knitting Worsted, make 25ch.

1st row 1sc into 3rd ch from hook, *1ch, skip next ch, 1sc into next ch, rep from * to end. Turn.
2nd row 1ch to count as first sc, 1sc into first 1ch sp, *1ch, 1sc into next 1ch sp, rep from * to last sp, 1ch, 1sc into the turning chain. Turn.
The 2nd row is repeated throughout.

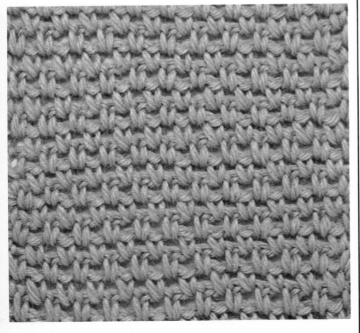

To add the loops Cut several lengths of yarn each to measure 5 inches.
Using two strands together fold them in half, and with right side of work facing, insert the crochet hook horizontally through the first sc in the mesh, place the two loops of yarn over the hook and draw through the work, place the four cut ends of yarn over the hook. Pull up tightly to secure. Repeat this process into each sc throughout the mesh.
Note As with loop stitch, you can vary the amount of cut loops and their position on the fabric. Also experiment to see how attractive these loops can look and the different designs you can create if you work them in various colors, or in shades of one color, as on our sample.

▼ *Hat in loop stitch and chain fur stitch on jacket*

'Fun fur' carriage cover

Color chart for cover

1 Square =1DC

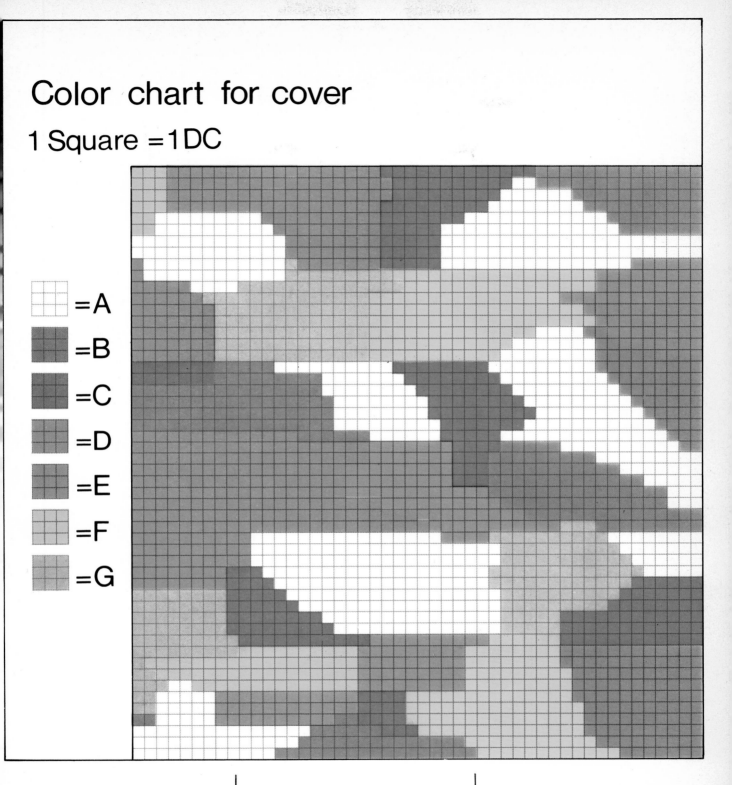

=A
=B
=C
=D
=E
=F
=G

Size
Crochet base measures 23in × 13½in

Gauge
13dc and 9 rows to 4in worked on size F hook

Materials
4 × 2oz balls Dawn Wintuk Sport Yarn in main color, A and 2 balls each of

contrast colors B, C, D, E, F and G
One size F crochet hook

Crochet base
Using size F hook and A, make 50 ch.
1st row Into 4th ch from hook work 1dc, 1dc into each ch to end. Turn. 48dc.
2nd row 3ch to count as first dc, skip first dc, 1dc into each dc, ending with 1dc

into 3rd of 3ch. Turn.
Rep last row 50 times more. Fasten off.

Finishing
Cut rem balls, of all colors into 5in lengths.
Following chart knot 2 strands together around every dc on the piece. Trim strands to desired length or leave shaggy.

231

LOOPED BRAIDS AND EDGINGS

In this chapter we shall continue with more variations of the looped stitches you learned in the last chapter. More advanced techniques are illustrated, including working with beads, and suggestions are made as to how you might use these stitches.

Here the methods, because they are so decorative, are used as a trim rather than an all-over design. To get the greatest contrast when using these trimmings on a crochet garment, you should use very basic stitches, such as single or double crochet.

Accordion braid

This is formed by working many double crochets into a small space on a background fabric of treble crochet to give a fluted effect.

Using size H crochet hook and Knitting Worsted, make 23ch.

1st row 1tr into 5th ch from hook, work 1tr into every ch to end. Turn.

2nd row 4ch to count as first tr, skip first st on previous row, 1tr into each st to end, 1tr into the turning chain. Do not turn.

3rd row 3ch, work 6dc down side of first tr, 1dc into st at base of this tr, *work 7dc up side of next tr on row, 1dc into st at top of this tr, work 7dc down side of next tr on row, 1dc into st at base of this tr, rep from * to end of row. Fasten off.

Work in this manner along the first row of tr that was made.

This braid can be incorporated into a garment or applied to one that has been completed. It looks very effective around the outer edges of a long, simple evening coat, its bulkiness counteracting the length of the coat.

Accordion braid used to trim an evening coat

Triple loops worked over a bar

This is an unusual technique for making very thick loops. To be most effective it should be worked into the garment you are making as single rows or no more than three rows at the most. You might also try spacing single rows at varying distances, as in our illustrations.

Work up to the point in your garment where you wish to include triple loops, ending with a right side row.

Take a separate ball of yarn and wind it in a single strand several times over a ruler or a rug wool gauge used for cutting yarns for rug making and which has a groove down one side.

Next row Holding the yarn-covered ruler or gauge behind your work, and beginning at opposite end to the ball of yarn, *insert hook into next st, then insert hook behind first 3 loops on ruler, yo and draw beneath the 3 loops of yarn and through the st of the previous row, yo and draw through both loops on hook, rep from * to end of row, taking care to remove the yarn from the ruler in consecutive order. Remove the ruler from the loops now and cut the loop yarn at the end of the row. Work one row in single crochet before starting another triple loop row.

Vertical beaded loops
These are ideal for working a jabot around the front opening of an evening top.

Make sure that you buy beads that have the correct size hole for the yarn that you are using. Usually the beads will already be threaded on a coarse string when you purchase them, but you will need to transfer them onto the crochet yarn with which you will be working before you start to work. To do this, make an overhand knot in one end of the bead thread, place the crochet yarn through this knot as in the diagram and carefully slide the beads from the thread on to the crochet yarn. Work to the position where a beaded row is desired, ending with a right side row.

Next row Sl st into the first st, *yo and draw through a loop extending it for 6 inches, push up the required number of beads on the yarn and draw through the extended stitch, draw the enlarged st over the beaded loop and pull yarn tightly to secure (there is now no loop on the hook), insert hook into next st, yo and draw through a st, sl st into next st, *, rep from * to * until the desired number of beaded loops have been worked. Use this same method to work beaded fringes, varying the number of beads used in a loop to give different depths.

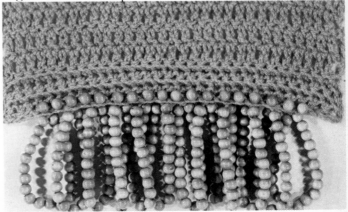

ARAN CROCHET
BASIC STITCHES

Aran is usually considered to be a knitting technique, but in this and following chapters we explain how you can achieve a similar effect working in crochet. It is a satisfying technique for those who prefer to crochet, for it gives quicker results, and the same range of garments and items for the home can be made as with the knitted patterns.

Traditional Aran work is usually seen in natural or off-white shades of yarn, although today many wool manufacturers make a special, very thick Aran yarn, in a variety of shades. The samples here explain how to work those basic patterns in crochet, which resemble the knitted versions quite closely.

Sample 1
Rib stitch This is the crochet version of the knitted rib. The fabric is used from side to side across a garment, so that the foundation chain forms the side seam rather than the hem. If you are making a garment, this stitch is suitable for the waistband. Using a smaller hook size than that used for the rest of the garment, say size H, make a length of chain to give the required depth of rib.

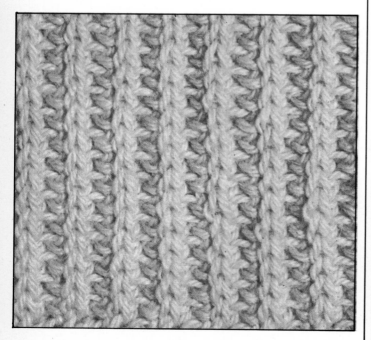

1st row Into 3rd ch from hook work 1sc, 1sc into each ch to end. Turn.
2nd row 1 ch to count as first sc, skip first st, 1sc into each st to end, placing the hook into the horizontal loop under the normal ch loop of the sc, 1sc into turning ch. Turn.

Repeat the 2nd row throughout until the rib is the width of the garment.

To begin work on the main part of the garment, the ribbed fabric is then turned so that the ridges run vertically. The loops formed by the row ends are now used as a base for the first row of the main fabric. A larger hook, size 1, is used for the main part and it may

be necessary to increase the number of stitches by working 2sc into some loops. In the following photograph the rib stitch is shown complete, followed by several rows of single crochet. This forms the base of many Aran styles.

Even moss stitch

The following attractive stitches could be used as an over all pattern or as a panel within an Aran design. Make a length of chain with multiples of 2 stitches.

1st row Skip first ch, sl st into next ch, * 1hdc into next ch, sl st into next ch, rep from * to end. Turn.

2nd row 1ch, skip first st, 1 hdc into next st, sl st into next st, rep from *, ending with last sl st worked into turning ch. Turn.

The 2nd row is repeated throughout.

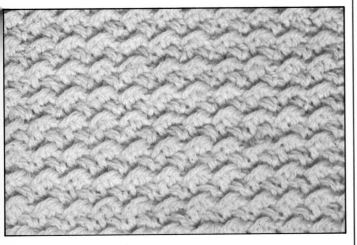

Uneven moss stitch

Make a length of chain and work 1st and 2nd rows as given for even moss stitch.

3rd row 2ch to count as first hdc, skip first st, sl st into next st, * 1hdc into next st, sl st into next st, rep from * to end, 1hdc into turning ch. Turn.

4th row As 3rd.

5th row As 2nd.

6th row As 2nd.

The 3rd through 6th rows are repeated throughout.

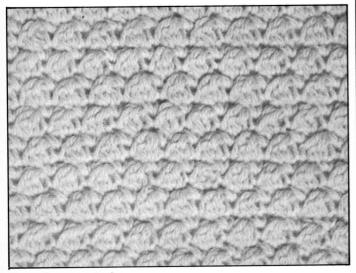

Even berry stitch

Make a length of chain with multiples of 2 stitches.

1st row Into 3rd ch from hook work 1sc, 1sc into each ch to end. Turn.

2nd row 1ch to count as first sl st, skip first st, *yo and insert hook into next st, yo and draw through a loop, yo and draw through first loop on hook, yo and insert hook into same st, yo and draw through a loop, yo and draw through all 5 loops on hook, 1ch to secure st—called berry st—, sl st into next st, rep from *

ending with last sl st worked into turning ch. Turn.

3rd row 1ch to count as first sc, skip first st, *sl st into next berry st, 1sc into next sl st, rep from * to end. Turn.

4th row 1ch to count as first sl st, * 1 berry st into next sl st, sl st into next sc, rep from * to end. Turn. The 3rd and 4th rows are repeated throughout.

Uneven berry stitch

Make a length of chain and work 1st to 3rd rows as given for even berry stitch.

4th row 1ch to count as first sl st, 1 berry stitch into first sc, sl st into next sl st, * 1 berry st into next sc, sl st into next sl st, rep from * to end. Turn.

5th row As 3rd.

The 2nd through 5th rows are repeated throughout.

RAISED DESIGNS

We have already shown you how to work the basic background effects necessary for Aran crochet, where the single crochet or double crochet stitches are very important. Here you will see how the background can be decorated with raised designs which are added after the main fabric has been completed.

Practice our samples first on a piece of double crochet fabric before attempting to start your own designs.

Sample 1

Raised lines may run horizontally, vertically or diagonally. For all samples of raised work begin at the lower edge and hold the crochet hook on top of the crochet (right side of work) with the yarn to be used held in the usual way, under the work. Using size I hook, make a slip loop on the hook, insert hook into first hole on the foundation chain, yo and draw through a loop, drawing it through loop on hook, * insert hook into same hole as last st, yo and draw through a loop (2 loops on hook), insert hook into next hole above lost insertion, yo and draw through a loop, drawing it through both loops on hook— called one raised double crochet—, rep from * to end of the row.

Other crochet stitches, such as slip stitch or double crochet may be substituted for the raised single crochet, depending on the depth of stitch required.

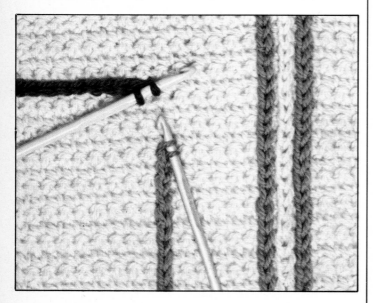

Sample 2

This sample depicts a variety of designs worked on a single crochet background. From left to right across the design there are 2 vertical rows of single crochet, then, looking at the illustration, there is a row of twisted raised single crochet (work black line first),

2 lines of twisted single crochet which form a diamond pattern, another line of twisted raised single crochet and finally 2 more vertical lines of crochet.

These designs can be used as a pattern panel on a garment, or on household articles such as the pillow cover given in the instructions.

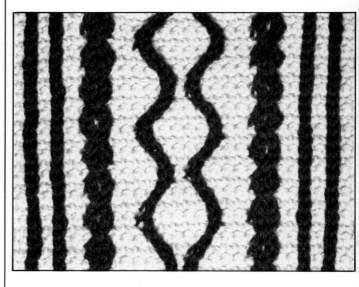

Aran pillow cover

Size

22inches × 15inches, excluding fringe

Gauge

13sts and 8 rows to 4in in dc worked on size F crochet hook

Materials

One size F crochet hook
One size I crochet hook
$\frac{3}{4}$ yard cotton lining material
Material for filling
1 × 20in zipper

Pillow cover (make 2)

Using size F crochet hook, make 72ch loosely.

1st row Into 4th ch from hook work 1dc, 1dc into each ch to end. Turn. 70dc.

2nd row 3ch to count as first dc, skip first dc, 1dc into each dc ending with last dc into 3rd of 3ch. Turn. Rep last row 28 times more. Fasten off.

Surface crochet This can be worked on either one or both sides as desired. Using size I hook and double yarn throughout, follow the chart and work in raised slip stitch following the direction of the arrows throughout, and noting that in row C the

cable patt should be worked first by following the arrows, then in the opposite direction indicated by the dots.

Finishing

With WS tog and using size I hook and double yarn, join 2 short sides and 1 long side by working a row of sc through both thicknesses, working 1sc into each dc, 1sc into each row end and 3sc into each corner. On 4th side, work in sc along one side only, leaving an opening for the zipper. Sew in zipper. Finish pillow pad to required size using lining material and stuffing. Insert into pillow cover.

Fringe Cut yarn into 12-inch lengths and, using 3 strands tog, knot through each sc along both short edges.

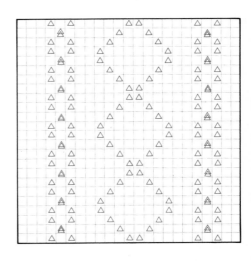

☐ = one space between single crochet

△ = one raised single crochet

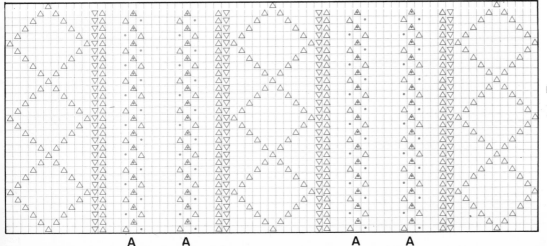

☐ one space between doubles

△ =one raised slip stitch

· =one raised slip stitch in opposite direction to arrows

A   A   A   A

BERRY STITCH MOTIFS

This chapter shows in detail how berry stitch, which was previously explained as an all-over design, can be worked into motifs on a single crochet background. The motifs are then outlined with raised single crochet to form a panel which could be incorporated into an Aran style garment.

Sample 1
This illustrates one method of grouping berry stitches. Using size I hook and an Aran yarn, make a length of chain with multiples of 8 +4 stitches.

1st row Into 3rd ch from hook work 1sc, 1sc into each ch to end. Turn.

2nd row 1ch to count as first sc, skip first st, 1sc into each st to end. Turn.

3rd row 1ch, skip first st, 1sc into each of next 3 sts, *sl st into next st, yo and insert hook into next st, yo and draw through a loop, yo and draw through first loop on hook, yo and insert hook into same st, yo and draw through a loop, yo and draw through all loops on hook, 1ch to secure st – called berry st –, sl st into next st, 1sc into each of next 5 sts, rep from * ending last rep with 1sc into each of next 4 sts. Turn.

4th row 1ch, skip first st, 1sc into each of next 3 sts, *1sc into next sl st, sl st into next berry st, 1sc into next sl st, 1sc into each of next 5 sts, rep from * ending last rep with 1sc into each of next 4 sts. Turn.

5th row 1ch, skip first st, 1sc into each of next 2 sts, * sl st into next sc, berry st into next sc, sl st into next sl st, berry st into next sc, sl st into next sc, 1sc into each of next 3 sts, rep from * to end. Turn.

6th row 1ch, skip first st, 1sc into each of next 3 sts, *sl st into next berry st, 1sc into next sl st, sl st into next berry st, 1sc into each of next 5 sts, rep from * ending last rep with 1sc into each of next 4 sts. Turn.

7th–8th rows As 3rd and 4th rows.

9th row 1ch, skip first st, berry st into next sc, sl st into next sc, *sc into each of next 5 sts, sl st into next sc, berry st into next sc, sl st into next sc, rep from * to end. Turn.

10th row 1ch, skip first st, sl st into next berry st, *1sc into each of next 7 sts, sl st into next berry st, rep from * ending with 1sc into last st. Turn.

11th row 1ch, skip first st, *sl st into next sl st, berry st into next sc, sl st into next sc, 1sc into each of next 3 sts, sl st into next sc, berry st into next sc, rep from * to last 2 sts, sl st into next sl st, 1sc into last st. Turn.

12th row 1ch, skip first st, 1sc into next sl st, sl st into next berry st, *1sc into each of next 5 sts, sl st into next berry st, 1sc into next sl st, sl st into next berry st, rep from * to last 3 sts, sl st into next berry st, 1sc into next sl st, 1sc into last st. Turn.

13th–14th rows As 9th and 10th rows.

The 3rd through 14th rows are repeated to form the pattern.

Sample 2
This is a sample design where berry stitches in a diamond pattern have been included in a single crochet background and then the entire design has been outlined with lines of raised single crochet. The technique of working raised single crochet was explained in detail previously and in our sample the rows are worked in varying colors to give them definition.

Using size I hook and an Aran yarn, make 23ch.

1st row Into 3rd ch from hook work 1sc, 1sc into each ch to end. Turn.

Continue working in single crochet until one row before the position for starting the berry stitch motif

Next row Work across first 7 sts marking last st with a colored thread, work across next 7 sts – this is the pattern area for the berry st motif, work across last 8 sts marking first st with a colored thread. Turn.

1st patt row Work to marked position, 1sc into each of next 2 sts, sl st into next st, berry st into next st, sl st into next st, 1sc into each of next 2 sts, work to end. Turn.

Note From this point the instructions refer only to the center 7 sts involved in the berry st design.

2nd patt row 1sc into each of next 3 sts, sl st into next st, 1sc into each of next 3 sts.

3rd patt row 1sc into next st, (sl st into next st, berry st into next st) twice, sl st into next st, 1sc into next st.

4th patt row 1sc into each of next 2 sts, (sl st into next st, 1sc into next st) twice, 1sc into next st.

5th patt row Sl st into next st, (berry st into next st, sl st into next st) 3 times.

6th patt row 1sc into next st, (sl st into next st, 1sc into next st) 3 times.

7th–8th patt rows As 3rd–4th rows.

9th–10th rows As 1st–2nd rows.

Continue working in single crochet for the desired depth, making more motifs if required. Complete the design by working the lines in raised single crochet from the chart.

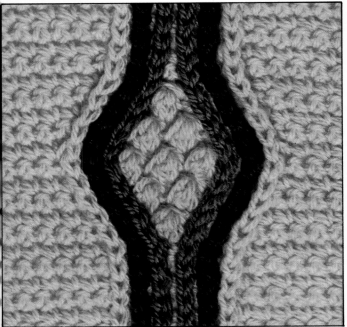

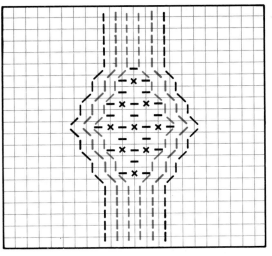

KEY

Each vertical line on each square = 1 single crochet
Each horizontal line on each square = one row

 = one berry stitch in place of a single crochet stitch
= one slip stitch in place of a single crochet stitch
= one raised single crochet worked vertically
= one raised single crochet worked diagonally

Sample 3

This is a variation of the previous sample with an enlarged berry stitch motif and double lines of raised single crochet crossing each other.

Work in same way as for sample 2, marking a center panel to cover 7 sts. Repeat 1st through 6th patt rows, 3rd through 6th, 3rd through 4th and then 1st through 2nd rows. Following the chart in that order work the rows of raised single crochet.

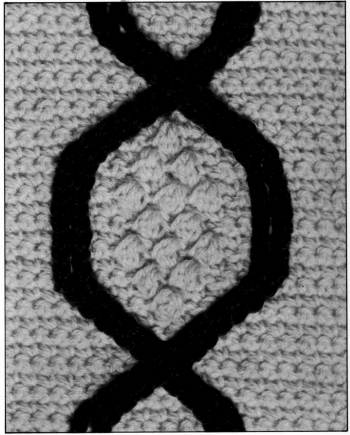

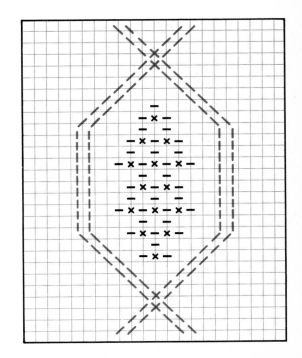

IRISH CROCHET
BASIC TECHNIQUES

Irish crochet, also known as Honiton crochet, is a form of lace which originated as a copy of the Guipure laces of Spain. The lace background and various motifs, such as the rose, leaf, shamrock and other flowers and curves, are both major characteristics of this work.

This introductory chapter to the craft will cover some of the techniques used for working the background, and also a selection of some of the more simple motifs. In this work, the motifs may either be applied directly on to the background, or the lace mesh may be worked around the finished motifs.

The samples shown here were worked with a No.5 cotton yarn with a No.1 crochet hook. Once you understand the basic techniques, try experimenting with some more unusual yarns and see what different effects can be achieved. Any of the net backgrounds seen here, for example, would make an attractive evening shawl, if you worked with one of the new mohair yarns.

Sample 1
To work the net background Make 50ch loosely.
1st row Into 10th ch from hook work 1sc, *6ch, skip 3ch, 1sc into next ch, rep from * to end of row. Turn.
2nd row 9ch, 1sc into first ch sp, *6ch, 1sc into next ch sp, rep from * to end of row. Turn.
The 2nd row is repeated throughout.

To work the rose motif Wrap the yarn 20 times around a pencil.
1st round Remove yarn carefully from the pencil, work 18sc into the ring. Join with a sl st into first sc.
2nd round 6ch, skip 2sc, 1hdc into next sc, *4ch, skip 2sc, 1hdc into next sc, rep from * 3 times more, 4ch. Join with a sl st into 2nd of 6ch.
3rd round Into each 4ch sp work 1sc, 1hdc, 3dc, 1hdc and 1sc to form a petal. Join with a sl st into first sc.
4th round Sl st into back of nearest hdc of 2nd round, *5ch, passing chain behind petal of previous round, sl st into next hdc of 2nd round, rep from * 5 times.
5th round Into each 5ch sp work 1sc, 1hdc, 5dc, 1hdc and 1sc. Join with a sl st into first sc.
6th round Sl st into back of sl st of 4th round, *6ch, passing chain behind petal of previous round, sl st into next sl st of 4th round, rep from * 5 times more.
7th round Into each 6ch sp work 1sc, 1hdc, 6dc, 1hdc and 1sc. Join with a sl st into first sc. Fasten off.

Sample 2
To work the net background Make 58ch loosely.
1st row Into 16th ch from hook work 1sc, 3ch, 1sc into same ch as last sc, *9ch, skip 5ch, 1sc into next ch, 3ch, 1sc into same ch as last sc, rep from * to end of row. Turn.
2nd row 13ch, 1sc into first ch sp, 3ch, 1sc into same sp, *9ch, 1sc into next ch sp, 3ch, 1sc into same sp,

240

rep from * to end of row. Turn.
The 2nd row is repeated throughout.
To work the motif Wrap yarn 12 times around a pencil.
1st round Remove yarn carefully from the pencil, work 18sc into the ring. Join with a sl st into first sc.
2nd round 8ch, skip 4sc, sl st into next sc, 10ch, skip 4sc, sl st into next sc, 8ch, skip 4sc, sl st into next sc, work 12ch for stem, into 3rd ch from hook work 1sc, 1sc into each of next 9ch, turn.
3rd row Into first ch sp work 16sc, 20sc into next ch sp and 16sc into next ch sp. Turn.
4th row 3ch to count as first dc, skip first sc, 1dc into each sc to end of row. Fasten off.

Sample 3

To work the net background This background incorporates an attractive picot design. Make 47ch loosely.
1st row Work 4ch, sl st into 4th ch from hook – called a picot –, 2ch, into 12th ch from picot work 1sc, *4ch, work a picot, 2ch, skip 4ch, 1sc into next ch, rep from * to end of row. Turn.
2nd row 6ch, work a picot, 2ch, 1sc into first ch sp, *4ch, work a picot, 2ch, 1sc into next ch sp, rep from * to end of row. Turn.
The 2nd row is repeated throughout.
To work the motif Wrap yarn 14 times around the little finger of your left hand.
1st round Remove yarn carefully from finger, work 38sc into the ring. Join with a sl st into first sc.
2nd round *9ch, skip 6sc, sl st into next sc, rep from * 4 times more, sl st into each of next 3sc.
3rd round Into each 9ch sp work 12sc, work 14ch for stem, into 3rd ch from hook work 1sc, 1sc into each of next 11ch. Join with a sl st into first sc.
4th round 3ch to count as first dc, skip first sc, 1dc into each sc on all 5 loops. Fasten off.

Sample 4

Here our sample has the same net background as sample 2, but it is worked with ordinary household string and the raffia motif is made in the same way as the motif on sample 3. Use different colored motifs to decorate a string tote bag.

Sample 5

Use the rose motif described in sample 1 to decorate a wedding veil. This rose is worked in an extremely fine yarn and has beads sewn on to the motif over the background. The net shown here is a commercial one, but you could, with time and patience, make a valuable family heirloom if you worked the veil itself in a crochet net.

ADVANCED DESIGNS

To continue our series about Irish crochet we here provide ideas for a more complicated background net, and for several different motifs.

The crochet lace background could be used for a scarf or evening shawl, made either into a straight stole shape or a large triangle trimmed with a fringe. Instead of the traditional cotton used for Irish crochet, try working with mohair, lurex or a novelty cotton for an unusual effect. By working the motifs illustrated here you will learn the two techniques which are most common in this type of work. They both give a raised look to the work, each in a different way. One is worked over several thicknesses of yarn, and the other is made by inserting the hook into the horizontal loop under the two loops where it is usually placed.

1st row Into 4th ch from hook work a sl st – one picot formed –, 8ch, sl st into 4th ch from hook, 2ch, 1sc into 8th ch from first picot worked, *6ch, sl st into 4th ch from hook, 8ch, sl st into 4th ch from hook, 2ch, skip 4ch, 1sc into next ch, rep from * to end. Turn.

2nd row 9ch, sl st into 4th ch from hook, 8ch, sl st into 4th ch from hook, 2ch, 1sc into first ch sp (between the 2 picots), *6ch, sl st into 4th ch from hook, 8ch, sl st into 4th ch from hook, 2ch, 1sc into next ch sp, rep from * to end. Turn.

The 2nd row is repeated throughout.

To work the rose motif Repeat the instructions given for the rose in the last chapter, but do not fasten off. Continue as follows:

Next round *7ch, passing chain behind petal of

Shawl incorporating net background, rose and leaf motifs

The samples in this chapter were worked with a very fine No.30 cotton yarn and a fine crochet hook, although the size of the hook will vary with the type of yarn you decide to use.

Sample 1
To work the net background Make 57ch loosely.

previous round sl st between the 2sc of next adjoining petals, rep from * 5 times more.

Next round Into each 7ch sp work 1sc, 1hdc, 8dc, 1hdc, 1sc. Join with a sl st into first sc. Turn work.

Next round Into each 7ch sp work 1sc, 1hdc, 8dc, 1hdc, 1sc into each st around placing the hook each time into the horizontal loop of the st on the previous row –

this st gives a raised effect on the right side of the work. Fasten off.

To work the leaf motif All the single crochet stitches from a given point in the pattern are worked over four thicknesses of yarn to give a ridged effect. Cut four lengths of yarn, each 16 inches long, and when the first sc to be worked in this way is indicated, place the yarn behind the work on a level with the stitch into which the hook is to be placed.

Make 16ch. Into 3rd ch from hook work 1sc, 1sc into each ch to last ch, 5sc into last ch to form tip of leaf, then work 1sc into each st along the other side of chain. Work 3sc over the 4 thicknesses of yarn, still working over the yarn and continuing towards tip of leaf, work 1sc into each of next 12sc, working into back loop only of each st. Turn work, 1ch, skip first sc, working down one side of leaf and up the other side, work 1sc into each sc to within 4sc of tip of leaf. Turn work, *1ch, skip first st, 1sc into each sc of previous row to last 4sc of row and working 3sc into sc at base of leaf. Turn work. *. Repeat from * to * until the leaf is the desired size.

Sample 2
Wrap yarn 14 times around a pencil.

1st round Remove yarn carefully from pencil, work 21sc into ring. Join with a sl st into first sc.

2nd round 1ch to count as first sc, skip first st, 1sc into each sc around. Join with a sl st into first ch.

3rd round 1ch to count as first sc, skip first sc, 1sc into each of next 6 sts, (12ch, 1sc into each of next 7 sts) twice, 14ch. Join with a sl st into first ch.

4th round 1ch to count as first sc, skip first sc, 1sc into each of next 4 sts, (22sc into next 12ch sp, 1sc into each of next 5 sts) twice, 24sc into next 14ch sp. Join with a sl st into first ch.

5th round Sl st into each of next 4 sts, *4ch, skip 2 sts, sl st into next st, * rep from * to * 6 times more, skip next 3 sts, sl st into each of next 3 sts, rep from * to * 7 times, skip next 3 sts, sl st into each of next 3 sts, rep from * to * 8 times. Join with a sl st into first sl st.

6th round 1ch to count as first sc, skip first st, 1sc into each of next 2 sts, (6sc into next 4ch sp) 7 times, sl st into next st, work 18ch for stem, into 3rd ch from hook work 1sc, 1sc into each of next 15ch, sl st into next st on main motif, (6sc into next 4ch sp) 7 times,

1sc into each of next 3 sts, (6sc into next 4ch sp) 8 times. Join with a sl st into first ch. Fasten off.

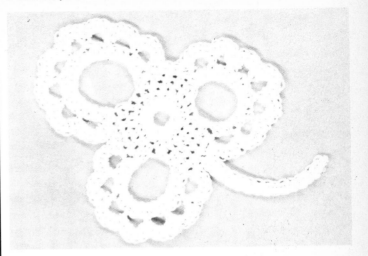

Sample 3
Make 40ch.

1st row Into 3rd ch from hook work 1sc, 1sc into each ch to last ch, 5sc into last ch. Do not turn.

2nd row 1sc into each ch along opposite side of 1st row. Turn.

3rd row The petals are worked individually down each side of the stem beginning from the tip where the last sc was worked as follows: *12ch, sl st into st at base of ch, 3ch, skip 2sc, sl st into next sc, turn, work 25dc into 12ch sp, sl st into first sc on row 1, turn, 1ch to count as first sc, skip first dc, 1sc into each dc around petal, sl st into same sl st as last sl st – one petal has been completed –, rep from * to give the desired number of petals noting that when the 25dc have been worked, the sl st is placed in front of the previous petal by inserting the hook into the 3rd sc up from the base of the petal being worked. Fasten off.

To complete the other side, rejoin yarn at the tip and work the petals in the same way, joining the last of the 25dc behind the previous petal.

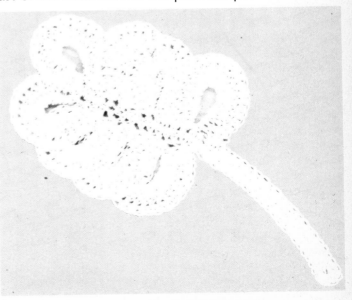

COMBINING MOTIFS AND BACKGROUNDS

In our previous chapters on Irish crochet instructions have been given for working the background and motifs separately. This chapter will deal with the alternative techniques of producing the background and motifs together.

Sample 1

This is a six-sided figure where the net background has been worked around the central motif. The shapes may eventually be joined together to form a large piece of fabric (see the chapter on joining square and circular motifs) which would serve as an attractive bedcover of tablecloth.

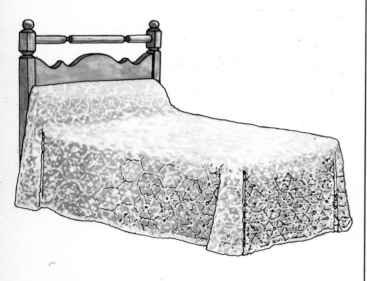

To work the sample Using a No.1 crochet hook and a No.30 cotton yarn, make a rose motif in the same way as that explained earlier.

Next round Sl st into each of next 3 sts of first petal, *(5ch, skip 2 sts, sl st into next st) twice, 5ch, skip 3 sts, sl st into next st, rep from * 5 times more.

Next round Sl st into each of next 2 sts, 6ch, *1sc into next 5ch sp, 5ch, rep from * 16 times more. Join with a sl st into 2nd of 6ch.

Next round *Into next 5ch sp work 1sc, 1hdc, 5dc, 1hdc and 1sc, (5ch, 1sc into next 5ch sp) twice, 5ch, rep from * 5 times more. Join with a sl st into first sc.

Next round Sl st into each of next 5 sts, 6ch, (1sc into next 5ch sp, 5ch) 3 times, *1sc into center dc of next petal gr, (5ch, 1sc into next 5ch sp) 3 times, 5ch, rep from * 4 times more. Join with a sl st into 2nd of 6ch.

Next round Sl st into each of next 2 sts, 6ch, *1sc into next 5ch sp, 5ch, rep from * 22 times more. Join with a sl st into 2nd of 6ch.

Next round Sl st into each of next 2 sts, 6ch, (1sc into next 5ch, sp, 5ch) twice, into next 5ch sp work 1sc, 1hdc, 5dc, 1hdc and 1sc, *(5ch, 1sc into next 5ch sp) 3 times, 5ch, into next 5ch sp work 1sc, 1hdc, 5dc, 1hdc and 1sc, rep from * 4 times more, 5ch. Join with a sl st into 2nd of 4ch.

Next round Sl st into each of next 2 sts, 6ch, 1sc into next ch sp, 5ch, 1sc into next ch sp, 5ch, 1sc into center dc of next petal gr, *(5ch, 1sc into next ch sp) 4 times, 5ch, 1sc into center dc of next petal gr, rep from * 4 times more, 5ch, 1sc into next ch sp, 5ch. Join with a sl st into 2nd of 6ch.

Next round Sl st into each of next 2 sts, 6ch, *1sc into next ch sp, 5ch, rep from * 28 times more. Join with a sl st into 2nd of 6ch.

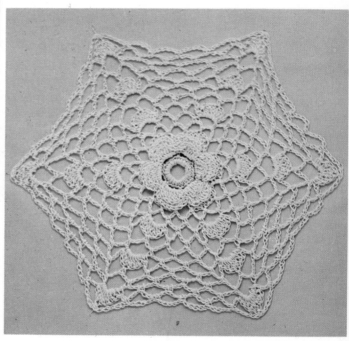

Next round Sl st into each of next 2 sts, 6ch, 1sc into next ch sp, 5ch, into next ch sp work 1sc, 1hdc, 5dc, 1hdc, and 1sc, *(5ch, 1sc into next ch sp) 4 times, 5ch, into next ch sp work 1sc, 1hdc, 5dc, 1hdc and 1sc, rep from * 4 times more, (5ch, 1sc into next ch sp) twice, 5ch. Join with a sl st into 2nd of 6ch.

Next round Sl st into each of next 2 sts, 6ch, 1sc into next ch sp, 5ch, 1sc into center dc of next petal gr, *(5ch, 1sc into next 5ch sp) 5 times, 5ch, 1sc into center dc of next petal gr, rep from * 4 times more, (5ch, 1sc into next ch sp) 3 times, 5ch. Join with a sl st into 2nd of 6ch. Fasten off.

Sample 2

The technique shown here is the method of working motifs and placing them onto paper so that a chain stitch may be worked to join the motifs together to form a fabric.

To work the ring Wrap yarn 20 times around a pencil.

1st round Remove yarn carefully from pencil, work 24sc into ring. Join with a sl st into first sc.

2nd round 8ch, skip 2sc, *1dc into next sc, 5ch, skip 2sc, rep from * 6 times more. Join with a sl st into 3rd of 8ch.

3rd round 3ch to count as first dc, 3dc into first ch sp, 4ch, sl st into 4th ch from hook – called 1 picot –, 4dc into same ch sp, 1 picot, *(4dc, 1 picot) twice into next ch sp, rep from * 6 times more. Join with a sl st into 3rd of 3ch. Fasten off.

To work the curve Cut ten lengths of yarn, each 7 inches long. Work 60sc over cut yarn. Turn work and leave extra yarn to hang freely.

Next row 1ch, sl st into 2nd sc, 3ch, skip 3sc, 1hdc into next sc, (3ch, skip 3sc, 1dc into next sc) 5 times, (3ch, skip 2sc, 1dc into next sc) 8 times, (3ch, skip 2sc, 1hdc into next sc) 3 times, 3ch, sl st into last sc. Join with a sl st into sc below 3rd dc worked at beg of row to make a ring plus a small length of work. Turn.

Next row Into ch sp work 5sc, (4sc into next ch sp, 1 picot) 16 times, 4sc into next ch sp, double back the extra 10 lengths of yarn and work 4sc very tightly over the double length, 1sc into end loop, 1ch. Fasten off working yarn. Pull ten lengths of yarn tight to finish, then cut away.

To join the motifs Make the desired number of motifs and tack on to a firm paper background. The green tacking stitches may be seen in the illustration and further tacks, rather than pins which tend to fall out, should be used as the filling-in progresses.

Our sample shows a ring and four curves, but any of the previous motifs which you have learned could be incorporated into this method of working. Only half of the filling-in has been completed so that the working method may be clearly seen.

A dress pattern of an evening bodice could be used as the paper backing and the various motifs would then be joined together to give the appearance of lace. It would be necessary to make a lining for this lace.

Chain stitches are used for filling-in which starts at the top right hand corner of the work. At random intervals a picot is worked by making four chain and slip stitching into the first of these. It is easiest to work back and forth in rows, joining the motifs together and slip stitching back across a few chain stitches where necessary, or even breaking off the yarn and re-joining it at a new position on the work. When all the motifs are joined, the tacks may be removed and all the cut ends of yarn should be woven in on the wrong side of the work.

IRISH MOTIFS ON SQUARES

Our illustration shows a long evening skirt which is made up of simple crochet squares, some of which are decorated with Irish crochet motifs. To make the skirt, which has no side seams or opening, work 80 squares with a Knitting Worsted weight and a size H crochet hook, making the squares as described later in this chapter. When done, they are to be joined, by the same method described in the chapter on Square and Wheel motifs, into ten lines of eight squares each.

Use the crochet motifs, also described in this chapter to decorate squares, using a matching yarn and tiny stitches. Finish the waist with a round of loosely worked double treble crochets and then thread elastic, dyed to a matching shade if necessary, through the trebles. Two motifs may be placed at the center front of the waistband to be used as buckles.

To work the square motif Make 6ch. Join with a sl st into first ch to form a ring.

1st round 3ch to count as first dc, work 19dc into the ring. Join with a sl st into 3rd of 3ch.

2nd round 1ch to count as first sc, 1hdc into next st, 1dc, 3ch, and 1dc into next st, 1hdc into next st, 1sc into next st, *1sc into next st, 1hdc into next st, 1dc, 3ch and 1dc into next st, 1hdc into next st, 1sc into next st, rep from * twice more. Join with a sl st into first ch.

3rd round 3ch to count as first dc, 1dc into each of next 2 sts, into corner 3ch sp work 2dc, 3ch and 2dc, *1dc into each of next 6 sts, into corner 3ch sp work 2dc, 3ch and 2dc, rep from * twice more, 1dc into each of next 3 sts. Join with a sl st into 3rd of 3ch.

4th round 3ch to count as first dc, 1dc into each of next 4 sts, into corner 3ch sp work 2dc, 3ch and 2dc, *1dc into each of next 10 sts, into corner 3ch sp work 2dc, 3ch and 2dc, rep from * twice more, 1dc into each of next 5 sts. Join with a sl st into 3rd of 3ch.

5th round 3ch to count as first dc, 1dc into each of next 6 sts, into corner 3ch sp work 2dc, 3ch and 2dc, *1dc into each of next 14 sts, into corner 3ch sp work 2dc, 3ch and 2dc, rep from * twice more, 1dc into each of next 7 sts. Join with a sl st into 3rd of 3ch. Fasten off. You now have a firm crochet square, as used in samples 1 and 2, where the corners are emphasized by the diagonal line of holes. Samples 3 and 4 have the same square as a base, but are made more solid by replacing the 3ch at each corner with 1ch.

Sample 1

To work the wheel motif Wrap yarn 20 times around first finger of left hand.

1st round Remove yarn carefully from finger, work 20sc into ring. Join with a sl st into first sc.

2nd round 12ch, into 3rd ch from hook work 1sc, work 11sc over complete length of chain instead of into each ch, skip next sc on ring, sl st into next sc, *10ch, join with a sl st into 6th sc up from circle of last "petal", 1ch, work 12sc over the complete chain, skip next sc on ring, sl st into next sc, rep from * 7 times

more, 10ch, join with a sl st into 6th ch up from ring of last "petal," 1ch, work 6sc over the complete chain, join with a sl st into free end of first "petal", work 6 more sc over complete chain. Join with a sl st into a ring. Fasten off.

Sample 2

This is known as the Clones knot and it is often seen in Irish lace. Here we use a very different yarn from the traditional since it is easier to work with, but you will need to practice to achieve a perfect knot.

To work the knots Make 10ch. Hold the length of chain firmly between thumb and first finger of left hand, *yo, bring hook towards you, under the length of chain and draw through a loop, rep from * approx 18 times, being careful that the yarn passing over the hook and length of chain is loosely but evenly placed to give a good looped knot. When the required number of loops have been worked, yo and draw through all the loops on the hook, sl st into the ch just behind the looped knot. Continue by making as many lengths of chain and knots as desired.

A stem may be added to complete the motif by working 14ch after the last knot has been completed, into 3rd ch from hook work 1sc, work 14sc over complete length of chain, sl st into last knot. Fasten off. Arrange the knots in position on the square and sew in place.

Sample 3

This is a simple design achieved by making several small rings.

To work the rings Wrap yarn 12 times around first finger of left hand.

Next round Remove yarn carefully from finger, work 14sc into ring. Join with a sl st into first sc. Fasten off. Make as many rings as desired, then work a stem to complete the design.

To work a stem Make 14ch. Into 3rd ch from hook work 1sc, work 14sc over the complete length of chain. Fasten off.

Arrange the rings and stem on the square to give the desired effect and sew in place.

Sample 4

This is known as coiled work. Take 8 thicknesses of yarn, approx 20 inches long, to form a filling core. We worked approximately 25sc over the entire core, but you can experiment with any number you desire, then take the beginning of the work, twist it behind the hook to form a ring, sl st into 5th sc worked, continue by working another 25sc over the core, forming it into a ring as before.

Continue in this way until the desired shape is achieved. Fasten off yarn and arrange in place on the square.

247

Glittering Irish crochet bolero

Sizes
Directions are to fit 32/36in bust
Changes for 37/40in bust are in brackets []
Length to center back, 16[17]in
Sleeve seam, 12in

Gauge
4½ shells and 16 rows to 4in in patt worked with size B crochet hook

Materials
10[11] × 20grm balls Reynolds Feu d'Artifice
One size B crochet hook
One button

Note
It is easier to work with Feu d'Artifice if the ball of yarn is first placed on a central spool. This can be done by rolling up a piece of cardboard, about 5in square, and anchoring the end with Scotch tape.

Jacket
Using size B crochet hook make 90[99]ch and start at neck edge.
Base row Into 3rd ch from hook work 1sc, 1sc into each ch to end. Turn. 89[98]sc.
1st inc row 1ch to count as first sc, 1sc into each of next 7sc, *2sc into next sc, 1sc into each of next 8sc, rep from * to end, working last sc into turning ch. Turn. 98[107]sc.
Next row 1ch, *1sc into next sc, rep from * to end. Turn.
2nd inc row (buttonhole row) 1ch, 1sc into each of next 2sc, 3ch, skip 3sc, 1sc into each of next 2sc, *2sc into next sc, 1sc into each of next 9[10]sc, rep from * to end. Turn. 107[116]sc.
Next row 1ch, 1sc into each sc to end, working 3sc into 3ch loop of previous row. Turn.
3rd inc row 1ch to count as first sc, 1sc into each of next 7sc, *2sc into next sc, 1sc into each of next 10[11]sc, rep from * to end. Turn. 116[125]sc.
Next row 1ch, 1sc into each sc to end.

Turn.
Start lace patt.
Base row 1ch to count as first sc, 1sc into each of next 6sc for right front border, *5ch, skip 2sc, 1sc into next sc, rep from * to last 7sc, turn and leave these 7sc for left front border. 34[37] 5ch loops.
1st row 1ch, *into next 5ch loop work (2sc, 3ch, sl st into last sc to form picot, 3sc, 1 picot, 2sc) – called 1 shell –, sl st into next sc, rep from * to end, working 1sc into last sc. Turn.
2nd row 7ch, 1sc into center sc between first 2 picots, *5ch, 1sc into center sc between 2 picots on next shell, rep from * to end, 3ch, 1tr into last sc. Turn.
3rd row 1ch to count as first sc, into next 3ch loop work (1sc, 1 picot, 2sc), sl st into next sc, *1 shell into next 5ch loop, sl st into next sc, rep from * to end, ending with 2sc, 1 picot, 2sc into 7ch loop, 1sc into 4th of 7ch. Turn.
4th row 1ch to count as first sc, *5ch, 1sc into center sc between 2 picots on next shell, rep from * to end, 3ch, 1tr into last sc. Turn.
These 4 rows form patt, noting that on subsequent 1st patt rows the first shell will be worked into 3ch loop and last sc will be worked into 3rd of 5ch loop. Rep the four rows once more, then first one again.
Shape yoke
**1st inc row Patt 6[7] loops, (always counting ½ loops at ends of rows as 1 loop), (5ch, skip next picot and 2sc, 1sc into sl st between shells, 5ch, 1sc between next 2 picots – called inc 1), patt 6[6] loops, inc 1, patt 7[8] loops, inc 1, patt 6[6] loops, inc 1, patt to end. 39[42] loops.
Patt 3 rows without shaping.
2nd inc row Work as given for 1st inc row, working 11[12] loops in center-back instead of 7[8] loops. 43[46] loops.
Patt 3 rows without shaping.
3rd inc row Patt 3[4] loops, *inc 1, patt 5 loops, rep from * ending last rep with 3[5] loops.
Patt 3 rows without shaping.
4th inc row Patt 3[5] loops, *inc 1, patt 5

loops, rep from * ending last rep with 3[5] loops.
Patt 3 rows without shaping.
5th inc row Patt 2[3] loops, *inc 1, patt 5 loops, rep from * ending last rep with 1[3] loops. 68[71] loops.
Patt 3 rows without shaping.
Divide for underarm
Next row Patt 12[13] loops, *work 15[18]ch, skip 11[12] shells, 1sc between next 2 picots, *, patt 19[20] loops, rep from * to * once more, patt to end. Turn.
Next row Patt 12[13] loops, *1sc into each of next 15[18]ch, *, patt 19[20] loops, rep from * to * once more, patt to end. Turn.
Next row Patt 12[13] loops, *5ch, skip first of 15[18]sc at underarm, 1sc into next sc, (5ch, skip 3sc, 1sc into next sc) 3[4] times, 5ch, 1sc between next 2 picots, *, patt 18[19] loops, rep from * to * once more, patt to end. Turn. 51[56] loops.
Maintaining patt, cont without shaping until 13[15] picot rows in all have been worked from underarm. Fasten off.
Sleeves
Using size B hook and with WS of work facing, rejoin yarn to center sc at 15 underarm sc for 1st size and between 2 center sc of 18sc for 2nd size.
Next row (5ch, skip 3sc, 1sc into next sc) once[twice], 5ch, 1sc into next sc, (5ch, 1sc between next 2 picots) 11[12] times, 5ch, 1sc into next sc before underarm, (5ch, skip 3sc, 1sc into next sc) twice. Turn. 16[18] loops.
Cont in patt until 14 picot rows in all have been worked from underarm, ending with a picot row.
New row (inc) Patt 1 loop, inc 1 as given for yoke, patt 5[6] loops, inc 1, patt 6[7] loops, inc 1, patt to end. Turn. 19[21] loops.
Patt 7[9] more rows without shaping. Fasten off.

Finishing
Do not block. Join sleeve seams.
Edging Using size B hook and with WS of left front facing, rejoin yarn to 7sc at neck, 1ch, 1sc into each sc to end. Turn.
Next row 1ch, 1sc into each sc to end. Turn.
Rep this row until border, slightly stretched, fits down left front to lower edge. Fasten off.
Work other side in same way. Sew borders into place.
With RS of work facing, rejoin yarn to right front at neck edge and work 1 row around neck edge. Fasten off.
Sl st around neck edge. Fasten off.
Sew on button to correspond to buttonhole.

Irish motif pillows

**

Sizes
Each pillow measures 16in square

Gauge
Brown and orange motif measures 3in square, worked with No.1 crochet hook

Turquoise and lemon motif measures 4½in between widest points worked with No.1 crochet hook

Materials
Both pillows 3 × 53yd balls DMC No.5 Pearl Cotton in each of two colors, A and B
One No.1 steel crochet hook
½yd of 36in wide gingham material
16in square pillow form

Brown and orange motifs
1st motif
Using No.1 hook and A, make 8ch. Join with a sl st into first ch to form a ring.
1st round 4ch, leaving last loop of each st on hook work 2tr into ring, yo and draw through all loops on hook – called 1st cluster –, *4ch, leaving last loop of each st on hook work 3tr into ring, yo and draw through all loops on hook – called 1 cluster –, rep from * 6 times more, 4ch. Join with a sl st to top of 1st cluster. Break off A.
2nd round Join B with a sl st into any 4ch loop, work 1st cluster into this loop, (4ch and 1 cluster) twice into same loop, *3ch, 1sc into next 4ch loop, 3ch, 1 cluster into next 4ch loop, (4ch and 1 cluster) twice into same loop, rep from * twice more, 3ch, 1sc into next 4ch loop, 3ch. Join with a sl st to top of first cluster. Break off B.
3rd round Join A with a sl st to next 4ch loop, 1sc into same loop, *9ch, 1sc into next 4ch loop, (5ch, 1sc into next 3ch loop) twice, 5ch, 1sc into next 4ch loop,

rep from * 3 times, omitting last sc. Join with a sl st into first sc.
4th round Using A work *7dc, 5ch and 7dc into 9ch loop, 1sc into next 5ch loop, 3sc, 3ch and 3sc into next 5ch loop, 1sc into next 5ch loop, rep from * 3 times more. Join with a sl st into top of first dc. Fasten off.

2nd motif
Work as given for 1st motif until 3rd round has been completed.
4th round Work 7dc into first 9ch loop, 2ch, sl st into corresponding 5ch loop on 1st motif, 2ch, 7dc into same 9ch loop on 2nd motif, 1sc into next 5ch loop, 3sc into next 5ch loop, 1ch, sl st into corresponding 3ch loop on 1st motif, 1ch, 3sc into same 5ch loop on 2nd motif, 1sc

into next 5ch loop, 7dc into next 9ch loop, 2ch, sl st into corresponding 5ch loop on 1st motif, 2ch, 7dc into same 9ch loop on 2nd motif, complete as given for 1st motif. Fasten off.
Make and join the 3rd and 4th motifs in the same way so that they form a square.
5th motif
Work as given for 1st motif, using B instead of A and A instead of B and joining to one free side of 1st motif on 4th round.
6th motif
Work as given for 5th motif and join on the 4th round to other free side of 1st motif, also joining to 5th motif at one corner.
7th and 8th motifs

around.

3rd round 5ch, *working across back work 1sc round stem of next dc on 1st round, 5ch, rep from * 4 times more. Join with a sl st around last stem, taking in first 5ch.

4th round *Into next 5ch loop work 1sc, 1hdc, 5dc, 1hdc and 1sc, rep from * to end.

5th round *7ch, 1sc into back of sc between petals of previous round, rep from * around, ending with 7ch, 1sc into back of next sc between petals, taking in the base of the 7ch.

6th round *Into next 7ch loop work 1sc, 1hdc, 7dc, 1hdc and 1sc, rep from * all round. Join with a sl st into first sc. Break off A.

7th round Join in B to sc between petals, 1sc into same place, *8ch, 1sc into 4th of 7dc of next petal, 8ch, 1sc between petals, rep from * around. Join with a sl st into first sc.

8th round Sl st into first 4ch, 1sc into 8ch loop, *12ch, 1sc into next 8ch loop, 1sc into next 8ch loop, rep from * omitting sc at end of last rep. Join with a sl st into first sc.

9th round *1sc into each of next 6ch, 3ch, 1sc into each of next 6ch, 1sc between 2sc of previous round, rep from * to end. Join with a sl st into first sc. Fasten off.

2nd motif

Work as given for 1st motif until 8th round has been completed.

9th round 1sc into each of first 6ch, 1ch, sl st into 3ch loop on 1st motif, 1ch, 1sc into each of next 6ch on 2nd motif, work as given for 1st motif, joining as before in the next 3ch loop, complete as given for 1st motif. Fasten off.

Make 7 more motifs, joining as before into 3 rows with 3 motifs on each.

Small motif

Using No.1 hook and A, make 5ch. Join with a sl st into first ch to form a ring.

1st round 3ch, 11dc into ring. Join with a sl st into 3rd of 3ch.

2nd round 1sc into sp between 3ch and next dc, *8ch, skip next 2 sp between dc, 1sc into sp between next 2dc, rep from * to end. Join with a sl st into same sp as first sc.

3rd round Sl st into first 4ch, 1sc into 8ch loop, *6ch, 1sc into join of large motif, 6ch, 1sc into next 8ch loop on small motif, rep from * 3 times more, working last sc into first sc.

Fasten off. Make 3 more small motifs and join to large motifs in the same way.

Finishing

Complete as given for other pillow.

Work as given for 5th motif, but join to the two free sides of 3rd motif and to each other at one corner.

Small flowers

Using A only, work as given for 1st motif until 1st round has been completed.

2nd round Work 3sc, 3ch and 3sc into each 4ch loop to last loop, 3sc into last loop, 1ch, sl st to free 5ch loop of motif of opposite color, 1ch, 3sc into same 4ch loop. Join with a sl st to first sc. Fasten off. Make 3 more motifs in A and 2 in B.

Finishing

Cut a piece of gingham 34in square, fold in half and seam along 3 edges, leaving $\frac{1}{2}$in turnings. Turn to RS and insert a piece of cardboard into the case to make pinning the motifs easier. Pin crochet in position on cover, then sew in place using a matching color. Place pad in cover, turn in raw edges and sew together with an overcast st.

Turquoise and lemon motifs
1st motif

Using No1 hook and A, make 8ch. Join with a sl st into first ch to form a ring.

1st round 6ch to count as first dc and 3ch, 1dc into ring, *3ch, 1dc into ring, rep from * 3 times more, 3ch. Join with a sl st into 3rd of 6ch.

2nd round *Into next 3ch loop work 1sc, 1hdc, 3dc, 1hdc and 1sc, rep from *

COLORED PATTERNS

ZIGZAG STRIPES

Zigzag crochet designs

The technique of working this very attractive form of patterning is very different from those learned in previous chapters. Crochet formed in this way with a knitting worsted yarn gives a very decorative, thick fabric which is suitable for jackets and vests. The same technique could be worked in Lurex for evening bags and belts, or in straw yarns for more casual accessories. Instructions for working the technique and several variations of the design are given here.

Sample 1

Two colors of knitting worsted yarn, A and B, have been used for this sample. Using size F hook and A, make a chain with multiples of 10 + 2 stitches.

1st row Into 3rd ch from hook work 1sc, 1sc into each ch to end. Turn.

2nd row 1ch to count as first sc, skip first st, 1sc into each st, ending with last sc into turning ch. Turn.

3rd–6th rows As 2nd. Do not break off A.

7th row Using B, 1ch to count as first sc, *1sc into next st skipping 1 row, noting that each time the hook is inserted into a stitch skipping a row the yarn forming the loop on the hook must be extended to meet the

previous st of the working row, 1sc into next st skipping 2 rows, 1sc into next st skipping 3 rows, 1sc into next st skipping 4 rows,1sc into next st skipping 5 rows , 1sc into next st skipping 4 rows, 1sc into next st skipping 3 rows, 1sc into next st skipping 2 rows, 1sc into next st skipping 1 row, 1sc into next st, rep from * to end. Turn.

8th–12th rows Using B, as 2nd.

13th row 1ch (this does not count as first st), 1sc into first st skipping 5 rows, .1sc into next st skipping 4 rows, 1sc into next st skipping 3 rows, 1sc into next st skipping 2 rows, 1sc into next st skipping 1 row, 1sc into next st, 1sc into next st skipping 1 row, 1sc into next st skipping 2 rows, 1sc into next st skipping 3 rows, 1sc into next st skipping 4 rows, 1sc into next st skipping 5 rows, rep from * to end. Turn.

14th–18th rows Using A, as 2nd.

The 7th through 18th rows inclusive are repeated throughout.

Note At the beginning of a row when changing color it is a good adea to wind the working color around the yarn not in use in order to give a neat edge.

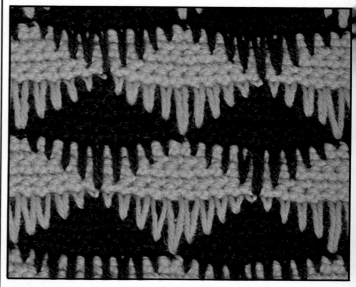

Sample 2

Here we have used three colors of Knitting Worsted A, B and C. Using size F hook and A, make a chain with multiples of 14 + 4 stitches.

1st–6th rows As 1st–6th rows of sample 1. Do not break off A.

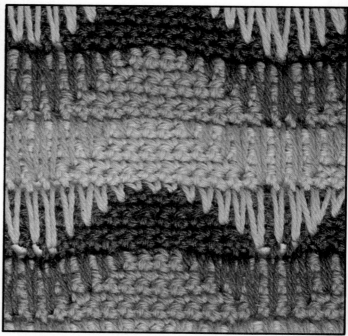

7th row Using B, 1ch to count as first sc, 1sc into each of next 2 sts, * 1sc into next st skipping 1 row, 1sc into next st skipping 2 rows, 1sc into next st skipping 3 rows, 1sc into next st skipping 4 rows, 1sc into each of next 3 sts skipping 5 rows, 1sc into next st skipping 4 rows, 1sc into next st skipping 3 rows, 1sc into next st skipping 2 rows, 1sc into next st skipping 1 row, 1sc into each of next 3 sts, rep from * to end. Turn.

8th–12th rows Using B, as 2nd row of sample 1. Do not break off B.

13th–18th rows Using C, as 7th–12th rows. Do not break off C.

19th–24th rows Using A, as 7th–12th rows. The 7th through 24th rows are repeated throughout.

Sample 3

The four colors of knitting worsted yarn used here are noted as A, B, C and D. Using size G hook and A, make a chain with multiples of 6 + 1 stitches.

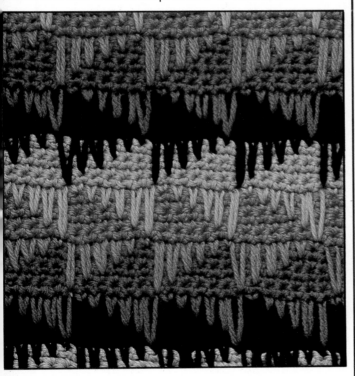

1st–6th rows As 1st–6th rows of sample 1. Do not break off A.

7th row 1ch to count as first sc, *1sc into next st skipping 1 row, 1sc into next st skipping 2 rows, 1sc into next st skipping 3 rows, 1sc into next st skipping 4 rows, 1sc into next st skipping 5 rows, 1sc into next st, rep from * to end, omitting 1sc at end of last rep. Turn.

8th–12th rows Using B, as 2nd row of sample 1. Do not break off B.

13th row Using C, 1ch (this does not count as first st), *1sc into first st skipping 5 rows, 1sc into next st skipping 4 rows, 1sc into next st skipping 3 rows, 1sc into next st skipping 2 rows, 1sc into next st skipping 1 row, 1sc into next st, rep from * to end. Turn.

14th–18th rows Using C, as 2nd row of sample 1. Do not break off C.

19th–24th rows Using D, as 7th–12th rows. Do not break off D.

25th–30th rows Using A, as 13th–18th rows.
The 7th through 30th rows inclusive form the pattern and color sequence for this design.

Sample 4

Shiny and mat straw in four colors, A, B, C and D have been used for this sample. Using size F hook and A, make a chain with multiples of 6 + 2 stitches.

1st–4th rows As 1st–4th rows of sample 1. Do not break off A.

5th row Using B, 1ch (this does not count as first st),

1sc into first st, *1sc into next st skipping 1 row, 1sc into next st skipping 2 rows, 1sc into next st skipping 3 rows, 1sc into next st skipping 2 rows, 1sc into next st skipping 1 row, 1sc into next st, rep from * to end. Turn.

6th–8th rows Using B, as 2nd row of sample 1. Do not break off B.

9th row Using C, 1ch (this does not count as first st), 1sc into first st skipping 3 rows, *1sc into next st skipping 2 rows, 1sc into next st skipping 1 row, 1sc into next st, 1sc into next st skipping 1 row, 1sc into next st skipping 2 rows, 1sc into next st skipping 3 rows, rep from * to end. Turn.

10th–12th rows Using C, as 2nd row of sample 1. Do not break off C.

13th–16th rows Using D, as 5th–8th rows. Do not break off D.

17th–20th rows Using A, as 9th–12th rows.
The 5th through 20th rows inclusive are repeated throughout.

CHEVRON DESIGNS AND BRAIDS

More zigzag designs in crochet

A different kind of zigzag design which is very simple to work is illustrated in this chapter. Both wavy lines and pronounced zigzags are formed by this method, either an over-all patterned fabric or a strip of crochet braid.

If knitting worsted yarn is used, this crochet work makes beautiful bed covers, afghans and pillow covers or could be used as a pattern on a fashion garment such as a jacket where a scalloped edge is desired as a design feature. More unusual yarns, like string and straw in particular, could be used to make bags, belts and slippers.

Our samples show different stitches for you to experiment with before starting a design of your choice.

Sample 1

Using size G hook and Knitting Worsted in various colors, make a length of chain with multiples of 17 + 4 stitches.

1st row Into 4th ch from hook work 3dc, **1dc into each of next 5ch, *yo and insert hook into next ch, yo and draw through a loop, yo and draw through first 2 loops on hook, yo and insert hook into next ch, yo and draw through a loop, yo and draw through first 2 loops on hook, yo and draw through all 3 loops on hook − called dec 1dc −, *, rep from * to * twice more, 1dc into each of next 5ch, 4dc into next ch, rep from ** to end. Turn.

2nd row 3ch to count as first dc, skip first 2 sts, 3dc into next st, *1dc into each of next 5 sts, dec 3dc over next 6 sts, 1dc into each of next 5 sts, 4dc into next st, rep from * ending last rep with 4dc into 3rd of 3ch. Turn.

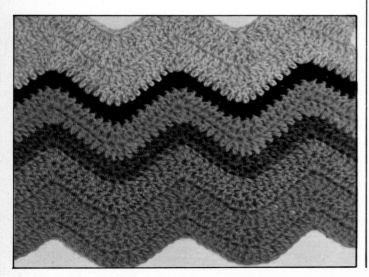

Repeat 2nd row throughout, alternating the colors as desired. You will see that the pattern gives a flowing, wavy line.

Sample 2

This design, which gives a very ribbed zigzag pattern, has been worked throughout in four rows each of two colors of Knitted Worsted, A and B. Using size G hook and A, make a length of chain with multiples of 16 + 4 stitches.

1st row Insert hook into 3rd ch from hook, yo and draw through a loop, insert hook into next ch, yo and draw through a loop, yo and draw through all 3 loops on hook, **1sc into each of next 6ch, 3sc

into next ch, 1sc into each of next 6ch, *insert hook into next ch, yo and draw through a loop, *, rep from * to * twice more, yo and draw through all 4 loops on hook − called dec 2sc −, rep from ** to end. Turn.

Note From this point, insert hook into back loop only of each st throughout.

2nd row 2ch, insert hook into st at base of ch, yo and draw through a loop, insert hook into next st, yo and draw through a loop, yo and draw through all loops on hook, *1sc into each of next 6 sts, 3sc into next sc, 1sc into each of next 6 sts, dec 2sc over next 3 sts, rep from * ending last rep by working into 2nd of 2ch. Turn. The 2nd row is repeated throughout the design.

Sample 3

Two colors of Knitting Worsted, A and B, have been used for this sample. Using size G hook and A, make a length of chain with multiples of 13 + 6 stitches.

1st row Yo and insert hook into 4th ch from hook, yo and draw through a loop, yo and draw through first 2 loops on hook, *yo and insert hook into next ch, yo and draw through a loop, yo and draw through first 2 loops on hook, *, rep from * to *, yo and draw through 4 loops on hook, **1dc into each of next 4ch, 4ch into next ch, 1dc into each of next 4ch, rep from * to * 4 times, yo and draw through all 5 loops on hook – called dec 3dc –, rep from ** to end, 2ch. Fasten off A. Do not turn.

2nd row Join B to 3rd of 3ch at beg of previous row, 1ch to count as first sc, 1sc into front loop of each st to end. Fasten off B. Do not turn.

3rd row Join A to first ch at beg of previous row, 3ch, working into back loop only of each st in previous alternate row, *yo and insert into next st, yo and draw through a loop, yo and draw through first 2 loops on hook, *, rep from * to * twice more, yo and draw through all loops on hook, **1dc into each of next 4 sts, 4dc into next st, 1dc into each of next 4 sts, dec 3dc over next 4 sts, rep from ** to end, 2ch. Fasten off A. Do not turn.

The 2nd and 3rd rows complete the design and are repeated throughout.

Sample 4

Sometimes zigzag designs require at least one straight edge, as on a belt. Here our sample illustrates this method of work with two zigzag lines between the straight edges. Two colors of Knitting Worsted, A and B, have been used so that it is easy to distinguish between the straight lines and the zigzag.

Using size G hook and A, make a length of chain with multiples of 13 + 4 stitches. The 4 extra chains are not turning chains but are for the 4 slip stitches

at each end of the pattern repreat.

1st row Skip first ch, sl st into each of next 3ch, *1sc into next ch, 1hdc into next ch, 1dc into next ch, 1 tr into next ch, 1dtr into next ch, 1tr into next ch, 1dc into next ch, 1hdc into next ch, 1sc into next ch, sl st into each of next 4ch, rep from * to end. Turn. Break off A.

2nd row Join B to first st, 3ch, *yo and insert hook into next st, yo and draw through a loop, yo and draw through first 2 loops on hook, *, rep from * to * twice more, yo and draw through all loops on hook, **1dc into each of next 4 sts, 4dc into next st, 1dc into each of next 4 sts, rep from * to * 4 times, yo and draw through all loops on hook, rep from ** to end. Turn.

3rd row As 2nd, working a 4dc group between 2nd and 3rd dc of 4dc group of previous row. Fasten off B.

4th row This shows how to end a zigzag design with a straight edge. Join A to last st worked on previous row, 4ch to count as first dtr, *tr into next st, 1dc into next st, 1hdc into next st, 1sc into next st, sl st into each of next 4 sts, 1sc into next st, 1hdc into next st, 1dc into next st, 1tr into next st, 1dtr into next st, rep from * to end. Fasten off.

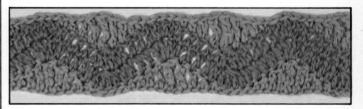

Sample 5

Here is one of the many interesting effects that can be achieved by using the techniques given here. Make two lengths of crochet by working the first two rows as given for sample 2, using only 4sc between each increase and decrease, then twist the lengths around each other to give this braided effect which could be used as trim or as a belt.

Crochet dress with chevron skirt

Sizes
Directions are to fit 32in bust. Changes for 34, 36, 38 and 40in bust are in brackets [ ].
Length to shoulder, 37½[38:38½:39:39½]in
Long sleeve seam, 16[16½:16½:17:17]in
Short sleeve seam, 4in

Gauge
20 sts and 24 rows to 4in in sc worked with size E crochet hook

Materials
Dress with long sleeves 16[17:18:19:20] × 1oz balls Brunswick Fairhaven Fingering Yarn in main color, A
4[4:4:5:5] × 1oz balls of contrast color, B
Dress with short sleeves 14[15:16:17:18] × 1oz balls Brunswick Fairhaven Fingering Yarn in main color, A
3[3:4:4:5] × 1oz balls of contrast color, B
One size D crochet hook
One size E crochet hook
One size F crochet hook
One 22in zipper

Dress
(worked in one piece to underarm)
Using size F hook and A, make 224[260:276:292:308] ch for entire lower edge.
1st row (RS) Into 4th ch from hook work 1dc, *1dc into each of next 6ch, skip 3ch, 1dc into each of next 6ch, 3dc into next ch, rep from * ending last rep with 2dc into last ch instead of 3. Turn.
2nd row 3ch to count as first dc, 1dc into st at base of ch, *dc into each of next 6dc, skip 2dc, 1dc into each of next 6dc, 3dc into next dc, rep from * ending last rep with 2dc into 3rd of 3ch instead of 3. Turn.
The 2nd row forms the patt. Cont in patt until work measures 6in from beg.
Next row 3ch, skip first dc, 1dc into each of next 6dc, *skip 2dc, 1dc into each of next 13dc, rep from * to last 9dc, skip 2dc, 1dc into each of next 6dc, 1dc into 3rd of 3ch. Turn.
Next row 3ch, 1dc into st at base of ch,

*1dc into each of next 5dc, skip 2dc, 1dc into each of next 5dc, 3dc into next dc, rep from * ending last rep with 2dc into 3rd of 3ch. Turn.
The last row forms the patt. Cont in patt until work measures 12in from beg.
Next row 3ch, skip first dc, 1dc into each of next 5dc, *skip 2dc, 1dc into each of next 11dc, rep from * to last 8dc, skip 2dc, 1dc into each of next 5dc, 1dc into 3rd of 3ch. Turn.
Next row 3ch, 1dc into st at base of ch, *1dc into each of next 4dc, skip 2dc, 1dc into each of next 4dc, 3dc into next dc, rep from * ending last rep with 2dc into 3rd of 3ch. Turn.
Cont in patt as now set until work measures 18in from beg.
Next row 3ch, skip first dc, 1dc into each of next 4dc, *skip 2dc, 1dc into each of next 9dc, rep from * to last 7dc, skip 2dc, 1dc into each of last 4dc, 1dc into 3rd of 3ch. Turn.
Next row 3ch, 1dc into st at base of ch, *1dc into each of next 3dc, skip 2dc, 1dc into each of next 3dc, 3dc into next dc, rep from * ending last rep with 2dc into 3rd of 3ch. Turn.
Cont in patt as now set until work measures 21in from beg, ending with a WS row. Change to size E hook.

Shape waist
1st row 1ch to count as first sc, skip first st, *1sc into next dc, 1hdc into next dc, 1dc into next dc, 1tr into each of next 2dc, 1dc into next dc, 1hdc into next dc, 1sc into next dc, skip next dc, rep from * to end working 1sc into 3rd of 3ch. Turn. 122[130:138:146:154] sts.
2nd row (eyelet hole row) 3ch to count as first dc, skip first st, 1dc into next st, *1ch, skip next st, 1dc into each of next 3 sts, rep from * to end. Turn.
3rd row 1ch to count as first sc, skip first st, work 1sc into each dc and ch sp to end. Turn.
4th row 1ch to count as first sc, skip first st, 1sc into each sc to end. Turn.
Join in B. Using B, rep 4th row twice.

Using A, rep 4th row twice. The last 4 rows form the stripe patt for the bodice which is repeated throughout.

Shape bodice
Next row 1ch, skip first st, 1sc into each of next 28[30:32:34:36]sc, 2sc into each of next 2sc, 1sc into each of next 60[64:68:72:76]sc, 2sc into each of next 2sc, 1sc into each of next 29[31:33:35:37]sc. Turn.
Next row Work in sc.
Next row 1ch, skip first st, 1sc into each of next 29[31:33:35:37] sts, 2sc into each of next 2sc, 1sc into each of next 62[66:70:74:78]sc, 2sc into each of next 2sc, 1sc into each of next 30[32:34:36:38]sc. Turn.
Cont inc 4sc in this way on foll alt rows until there are 138[146:158:166:178] sts, then on every foll 4th row until there are 166[174:186:194:206] sts. Cont without shaping until work measures 31in from beg, ending with a WS row.

Divide for back and front armholes
Next row 1ch, skip first st, 1sc into each of next 38[40:43:45:48]sc, turn.
Cont on these 39[41:44:46:49] sts for left back.
Next row 1ch, skip first 2 sts, 1sc into each sc to end. Turn.
Next row 1ch, skip first st, 1sc into each sc to last 2sc, skip next sc, 1sc into last st. Turn.
Rep last 2 rows 3[3:4:4:5] times more. 31[33:34:36:37] sts. Cont without shaping until armhole measures 6½[7:7½:8:8½]in from beg, ending at back edge.

Shape shoulder
Next row Patt to last 8 sts, turn.
Next row Sl st into each of next 8[10:11:13:14] sts, patt to end. Fasten off.
With RS of work facing, return to part where stitches were divided, skip 5sts for underarm, rejoin yarn to next st and work 1ch, 1sc into each of next 77[81:87:91:97]sc, turn. Cont on these 78[82:88:92:98] sts for front.
Next row 1ch, skip first 2 sts, 1sc into each sc to last 2sc, skip next sc, 1sc into last st. Turn.

Rep last row 7[7:9:9:11] times more. 62[66:68:72:74] sts. Cont without shaping until work measures 14 rows less than back to shoulder shaping.

Shape Neck

Next row Patt across 23[25:26:28:29] sts. Turn.

Next row 1ch, skip first 2 sts, patt to end. Turn.

Next row Patt to last 2 sts, skip next sc, 1sc into last st. Turn.

Rep last 2 rows twice more, then first row again. 16[18:19:21:22] sts. Cont without shaping until work measures same as back to shoulder, ending at armhole edge.

Shape shoulder

Next row Sl st into each of next 8 sts, patt to end. Fasten off.

With RS of work facing return to rem sts at front, skip center 16 sts for front neck, rejoin yarn to next st, 1ch, patt to end. Turn. Complete to correspond to first side of neck, reversing shapings.

With RS of work facing return to part where sts were divided, skip 5sts for underarm, rejoin yarn to next st, 1ch, patt to end for right back. Complete to correspond to left back, reversing shaping.

Long sleeves

Using size D hook and A, make 39 [41:43:45:47]ch.

1st row Into 3rd ch from hook work 1sc, 1sc into each ch to end. Turn. 38[40:42:44:46] sts.

2nd row 1ch to count as first sc, skip first st, 1sc into each sc to end, ending with last sc into turning ch. Turn.

Join in B. Using B, rep 2nd row twice. Using A, rep 2nd row twice more. These 4 rows form the striped patt which is repeated throughout. Cont in patt until work measures 2in from beg.

Change to size E hook. Cont in patt, inc one sc at each end of next and every foll 6th row until there are 60[64:68:72:76] sts. Cont without shaping until work measures 16[16½:16½:17:17]in from beg.

Shape top

1st row Sl st into each of next 4 sts, 1ch, patt to last 3 sts, turn.

2nd row Patt to end. Turn.

3rd row 1ch, skip 2 sts, 1sc into each st to last 2 sts, skip next sc, 1sc into last st. Turn.

Rep 2nd and 3rd rows until 36[36:40:40:44] sts rem, then rep 3rd row until 14 sts rem. Fasten off.

Short sleeves

Using size E hook and A, make 53[57:61:65:69]ch.

1st row Into 3rd ch from hook work 1sc, 1sc into each ch to end. Turn. 52[56:60:64:68] sts.

2nd row As 2nd row of long sleeves.

Join in B and working in stripe sequence as given for bodice, inc one sc at each end of next and every foll 6th row until there are 60[64:68:72:76] sts. Cont without shaping until work measures 4in from beg.

Shape top

Work as given for long sleeves.

Finishing

Block each piece under a damp cloth with a warm iron. Join shoulder and sleeve seams. Set in sleeves.

Neck edging Using size D hook and A, work 5 rows sc evenly around neck edge.

Sew in zipper, joining rem back seam. Using 6 strands of A tog, make a twisted cord approx 60in long and thread through eyelet holes at waist. Block seams.

CHECK PATTERNS

Checked pattern in crochet

Effective checked crochet patterns in one or more colors may be worked, and they, because of the method used, form a thick fabric suitable for warm outer garments such as coats, jackets and skirts. The stitches used to form the checks pass over previous rows thus forming a double fabric in some designs. Many of these can be reversible, and this should be taken into account when deciding on the kind of garment which you are going to make.

Knitting Worsted and a size G crochet hook are recommended for the samples you see illustrated. Samples 2 and 3 are worked from one side, therefore the crochet could be worked in continuous rounds without turning the work or breaking the yarn at the end of each row. This technique would be ideal for making a skirt, since it avoids side seams.

Sample 1

Make 26ch.

1st row Into 4th ch from hook work 1dc, 1dc into each ch to end. Turn. 24dc.

2nd row 3ch to count as first dc, skip first dc (1dc into next dc, inserting hook from the front of the work horizontally from right to left under the vertical bar of the dc on the previous row so that the hook is on the front of the work) 3 times, (1dc into next dc inserting the hook from the back of the work from right to left over the vertical bar of the dc on the

previous row so that the hook is on the back of the work) 4 times. Cont in this way, working 4dc to the front and 4dc to the back of the work to the end of the row, working last dc in 3rd of the 3ch. Turn.

3rd row As 2nd.

4th row 3ch to count as first dc, skip first dc, work 1dc to the back of each of the next 3dc, work 1dc to the front of each of the next 4dc. Cont in this way, reversing the checked effect to the end of the row, working the last dc into 3rd of the 3ch. Turn.

5th row As 4th.

Rows 2 through 5 form the pattern.

Sample 2

This is worked in 2 colors, A and B. With A, make 26ch.

1st row Into 3rd ch from hook work 1sc, 1sc into each ch to end. 25sc. Fasten off yarn. Do not turn.

Note Unless otherwise stated, work into the back loop only of each st to end of design.

2nd row Join B to beg of previous row, 1ch to count as first sc, skip first st, 1sc into each st to end. Fasten off yarn. Do not turn work.

3rd and 4th rows As 2nd.

5th row Join A to beg of previous row, 1ch to count as first sc, skip first st, insert hook under horizontal front loop of next st, yo and draw through a loop, (insert hook under horizontal front loop of st immediately below st just worked into, yo, and draw

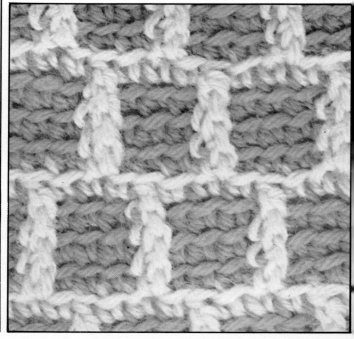

through a loop) 3 times, (yo and draw through first 2 loops on hook) 4 times – 1 connected quad dc has been worked –, *1sc into each of next 3 sts, 1 connected quad dc into next st, rep from * to last 2 sts, 1sc into each of next 2 sts. Fasten off yarn. Do not turn work.

6th to 8th rows As 2nd.

9th row Join A to beg of previous row, 1ch to count as first sc, skip first st, 1sc into each of next 3 sts, *1 connected quad dc into next st, 1sc into each of next 3 sts, rep from * to last st, 1sc into last st. Fasten off yarn. Do not turn.

Rows 2 through 9 form the pattern and are repeated throughout.

Sample 3

Three colors are used for this sample, A, B and C. Unless otherwise stated, insert the hook into the back loop only of each st. With A, make 26ch.

1st row Into 3rd ch from hook work 1sc, 1sc into each ch to end. 25sc. Fasten off yarn. Do not turn.

2nd row Join A to beg of previous row. 1ch to count as first sc, skip first st, 1sc into each st to end. Fasten off yarn. Do not turn.

3rd row As 2nd.

4th row Join B to beg of previous row. 1ch to count as first sc, skip first st, 1sc into next st, yo 3 times, insert hook under horizontal front loop of next st in 4th row below, yo and draw through a loop, (yo and draw through first 2 loops on hook) 4 times – 1 surface dtr has been worked –, 1 surface dtr into each of next 2 sts, *1sc into each of next 3 sts, 1 surface dtr into each of next 3 sts, rep from * to last 2 sts, 1sc into each of next 2 sts. Fasten off yarn. Do not turn.

5th and 6th rows With B, as 2nd.

7th row Join C to beg of previous row. 1ch to count as first sc, skip first st, 1sc into each of next 4 sts, *1 surface dtr into each of next 3 sts, 1sc into each of next 3 sts, rep from * to last 2 sts, 1sc into each of last 2 sts.

Fasten off yarn. Do not turn.

8th and 9th rows With C, as 2nd.

10th to 12th rows With A, as 4th to 6th rows.

13th to 15th rows With B, as 7th to 9th rows.

16th to 18th rows With C, as 4th to 6th rows.

Rows 1 through 18 form the pattern and color sequence for this sample.

Sample 4

Two colors, A and B, are used for this sample. With A, make 22ch.

1st row Into 3rd ch from hook work 1sc, 1sc into each ch to end. Turn. 21sc.

2nd row 1ch to count as first sc, skip first sc, 1sc into front loop only of each st to end. Turn. Fasten off yarn.

3rd row Join in B. 2ch to count as first hdc, skip first st, 1hdc into each st to end placing hook each time under both loops. Fasten off yarn. Do not turn.

4th row Join A to beg of previous row. 1ch to count as first sc, (1tr into front loop only of next st in 3rd row below) twice, 1sc into back loop only of next 3 sts, *1tr into each of next 3 sts placing the hook as before, 1sc into back loop only of next 3 sts, rep from * to last 3 sts, 1tr into each of next 2 sts, 1sc into last st. Fasten off yarn. Do not turn work.

5th row As 3rd.

6th row Join A to beg of previous row. 1ch to count as first sc, 1sc into back loop only of next 2 sts, *(1tr into front loop only of next st in 3rd row below) 3 times, 1sc into back loop only of next 3 sts, rep from * to end. Fasten off. Do not turn.

7th row As 3rd.

Rows 4 through 7 form the pattern.

CROCHET WITH LEATHER AND SUEDE

In this chapter we have used circular leather motifs and crochet stitches together to give some interesting results. This type of work lends itself especially to the making of belts, bags and vests. A firm, good quality leather, suede or grain skin should be chosen to withstand the pull of the crochet work. Most local handicraft shops will sell off-cut leather pieces suitable for this purpose. First mark the shape on the wrong side of the skin by drawing around a circular object with a pencil. Cut out the circles with a sharp pair of scissors to avoid making a rough edge. You will need a special tool, called a leather punch, to make the holes, which must be evenly spaced around the circle, but not too near the edge. Also make sure that the holes are the correct size to accommodate the yarn and crochet hook you are using.

We have worked with various sized circles decorated with a Knitting Worsted, string and a lurex yarn, and a No.1 steel crochet hook. We show a number of methods for working crochet around leather circles here, along with instructions for joining the circles.

Sample 1
This illustrates a 1½ inch leather circle with the holes cut out ready to start work.

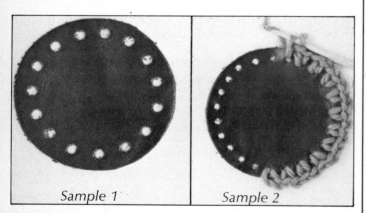

Sample 1   *Sample 2*

Sample 2
This is a 2¼ inch circle with the surrounding crochet in progress.
To work the crochet Hold the leather circle so that the right side is facing you and place the working yarn behind the circle, insert hook through any hole, yo and draw through hole, yo and draw through loop on hook, 2ch, *insert hook into next hole, yo and draw yarn through hole, yo and draw yarn through both loops on hook – 1sc has been worked into the hole–, 1ch, rep from * until you have crocheted around the circle. Join with a sl st into first ch to finish. Fasten off.

Sample 3
The single crochet edging around this circle is now complete.

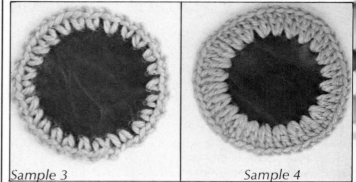

Sample 3   *Sample 4*

Sample 4
Using the same technique as described in sample 2, work 3ch at the beginning of the edging and work 1dc into the same hole, *2dc into next hole, rep from * to the end of the circle. Join with a sl st into 3rd of 3ch. Fasten off.

Sample 5
Here is a grouping of circles ranging in sizes from 1 inch to 2¼ inches. The surrounding stitches vary in depth to give a "clam" appearance.
Begin by working 2ch into the first hole, 1sc into each of next 2 holes with 1ch between them, then continue by working 2 sts into each hole and increase the stitch depth by working into the same number of holes with hdc, dc and hdc, then decrease the st size in the same way. The number of sts in each group will have to be varied according to the size of the circle and number of holes.
Samples 6, 7, 8 and 9 show a more experimental way to edge the leather. These would make ideal edgings for a plain leather vest.

Sample 6

1st round Begin with 2ch and 1sc into first hole, 2sc into each hole around. Join with a sl st into 2nd of 2ch.

2nd round 2ch (yo and insert hook into st at base of ch, yo and draw through a loop extending it for $\frac{3}{8}$ inch) twice, yo and draw through all 5 loops on hook, 1ch, skip next st, *yo and insert hook into next st, yo and draw through a loop extending it for $\frac{3}{8}$ inch, (yo and insert hook into same st as last, yo and draw through an extended loop) twice, yo and draw through all 7 loops on hook, 1ch, skip next st, rep from * to end of circle. Join with a sl st into 2nd of 2ch.

3rd round 1ch to count as first sc, *2sc into next sp between bobbles, 1sc into top of next bobble, rep from * to end, 2sc into next sp. Join with a sl st into first ch. Fasten off.

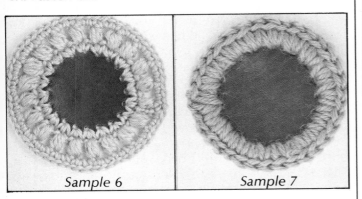

Sample 6   *Sample 7*

Sample 7

Cut 8 thicknesses of yarn to fit around the outer edge of the circle.

Next round Working over 8 thicknesses of yarn to produce a rounded effect, begin with 2ch and 1sc into first hole, 2sc into each hole to end of round. Join with a sl st into 2nd of 2ch. Fasten off.

Sample 8

Two colors, A and B, were used for this sample.

1st round Using A, beg with 3ch and 1dc into first hole, 2dc into each hole to end of round. Join with a sl st into 3rd of 3ch.

2nd round Join in B. Work 1sc into each st, working from left to right (working backwards around circle) instead of from right to left. Fasten off.

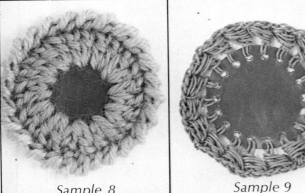

Sample 8   *Sample 9*

Sample 9

Green parcel string was used for this sample.

1st round Begin with 4ch into first hole, (yo and take hook in front of chain, around to the back and yo) 3 times, yo and draw through all 7 loops on hook, 1ch, *1dc into next hole, (yo and take hook in front of dc, around to the back and yo) 3 times, yo and draw through all 7 loops on hook, 1ch, rep from * to end of round. Join with a sl st into 3rd of 4ch. Fasten off.

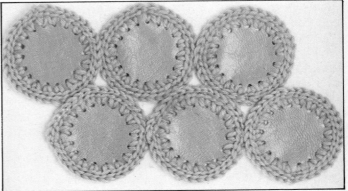

Sample 10

1st round Begin with 2ch, then work 1sc and 1ch into each hole to end of round. Join with a sl st into 2nd of 2ch.

2nd round Sl st into back loop only of each st to end of round.

To join the circles At the point where two circles are to be joined on the 2nd round, insert the hook into the next st of the circle on which you are working and then into any stitch of the circle to be joined, yo and draw through all loops on hook. In our sample three stitches were used at each joining point. Our circles were all the same size, but even if there were a variety of sizes they could be joined in the same way.

Sample 11

This gold belt illustrates the method of edging used in sample 7. Twelve circles, each 2 inches in diameter were used to fit a 27-inch waist. Work around half the circle in crochet before joining onto the next circle, and when the complete length has been worked, the return crochet is worked on the second half of each circle.

Brass rings are used as a fastening with a cord worked in double chain threaded through to link them.

PROJECTS WITH LEATHER AND VINYL

The technique of working crochet around leather circles was dealt with in the last chapter, and now we shall show you more ideas for using this technique with a variety of shapes and different materials.

Vinyl is an interesting fabric to work with as it has a very glossy surface which is a good contrast to most crochet yarns. Also it has the additional advantage of being able to be cut without the edges fraying in the same way as they do with leather. There are two types of vinyl available, one with a light backing fabric and one without. Both are suitable to use.

To make the suitcase
You will need four pieces of vinyl, two measuring 8 inches by 10½ inches for the outer piece and lining and another two measuring 16 inches by 10½ inches. The two larger pieces are for the back allowing for a fold-over flap, and the corners of these pieces should be rounded. Only the corners of the lower edge on the smaller front piece need to be rounded.

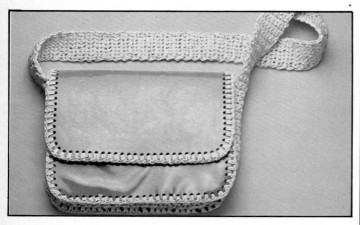

A middle layer of thick bonded interfacing is attached with a suitable fabric adhesive between the outer vinyl and the lining. The three layers are then treated as one. Holes are punched evenly around the vinyl pieces about ¼ inch in from the edge.

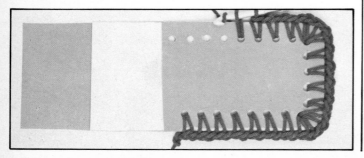

The back and front are then linked with a crochet gusset which extends to form the handle.

To work the gusset Using size F crochet hook and a very strong knitting yarn or string make 9ch.

Next row Into 3rd ch from hook work 1sc, 1sc into each ch to end. Turn.

Next row 1ch to count as first sc, 1sc into each st to end. Turn.

Rep last row until work measures 57 inches from beg. Fasten off. Join 2 short ends to form a circle.

To work the edging and join the sections together
Begin with a slip loop on the hook and hold the bag section with RS towards you, insert hook from front to back into first hole at right hand side of flap, yo and draw through a loop, yo and draw through both loops on hook – 1sc has been worked into the hole –, *1ch, work 1sc into next hole, rep from * to halfway down first long side (where back begins), then join bag onto gusset by placing hook through next hole as before and also through edge of gusset and complete the st in the usual way. Cont in this way until all the back and flap section has been worked. Work around the front section and join to the gusset in the same way.

To make the leather belt
The same techniques have been incorporated into the making of a belt. Depending on the size needed, you will need approximately ten rectangles of leather each 1¾ inches by 2½ inches. To these a strong bonded interfacing is again adhered to the wrong side of each shape.

To work the crochet Using a size E hook, a lurex yarn and with the RS of the work facing you, insert the hook from front to back into a hole, yo and draw through hole, yo and draw through a loop – 1ch has been worked –, *insert hook into next hole, yo and draw through hole, yo and draw through first loop on hook, yo and draw through both loops on hook, rep from * around shape, working 3 sts into each corner hole. Fasten off and finish ends.

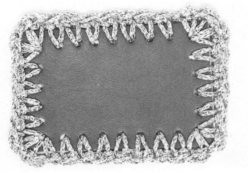

To join the parts Place two pieces with right sides together so that the chain of each stitch is uppermost on the right side thus giving a pronounced ridge effect. Sew together.

To fasten the belt Two large eyelets, available at most chain stores, are placed at either side of the center front opening. A double chain tie is then made to lace through the eyelets; this needs to be long enough to allow the belt to open enough for the wearer to slip the belt over her hips. Four loops of beads are then added to each end of the tie for trim.

To make the slippers
Another use for this form of work is for attractive slippers which are easy to make. Our size fits a size 5–6 foot. The pattern for the upper portion is divided into five pieces and each piece is cut out in both suede and a heavy bonded interfacing, which is then adhered to the suede. Holes are then punched around each piece.

To work the crochet Using size E crochet hook, a chenille yarn (or any other type of heavy yarn) and with the RS of the work facing you, insert hook into hole from front to back, yo and draw through hole, yo and insert hook into same hole, yo and draw through a loop, yo and draw through all 4 loops on hook, cont in this way around work, working 3 sts into each corner hole.

To join the parts together When the 5 pieces are completed, sew them firmly together on the wrong side. A lining fabric can also be sewn into place at this point, if desired.
The insole is cut from a plastic fabric and has a bonded interfacing backing adhered to it. Holes are punched around the sole. The stitches described for the suede shapes are then worked into the holes, noting that 1ch should be worked between the stitches at the heels and toes and also that the upper portions should be joined to the insoles between the marked positions by inserting the hook into the upper part and then into the insole, completing the stitch in the usual way. At this point the completed work is then adhered to a main rubber sole with a suitable adhesive. These instructions are repeated for the second slipper, making sure that the pattern pieces are reversed.

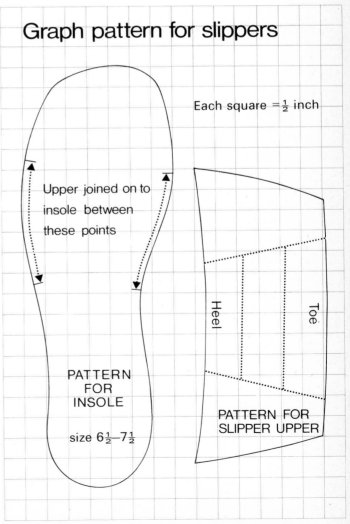

Graph pattern for slippers

Each square = ½ inch

Upper joined on to insole between these points

Heel

Toe

PATTERN FOR INSOLE

size 6½–7½

PATTERN FOR SLIPPER UPPER

COVERED RINGS
BASIC TECHNIQUES

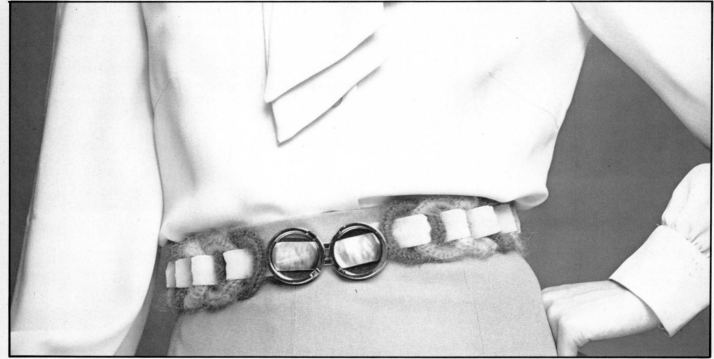

Crochet covered rings can be used in a variety of ways, ranging from belt fastenings to window hangings. There are several different methods of covering rings, some of which have already been illustrated, as, for example, covering them with a looped or buttonhole stitch or with simple crochet stitches.

This chapter develops the technique further and shows what can be done by using several rings on a belt. Any kind of curtain ring, obtainable from the drapery counters of your local department or large store, may be used. The type of yarn depends on the item being made, although this is largely a question of choice. The crochet hook should be one size smaller than usual in order to obtain a close stitch which will cover the ring completely.

To make the belt

For a belt which is approximately 28 inches long, you will need 23 rings each 1½ inches in diameter, five different shades of mohair yarn, a length of 1 inch wide velvet ribbon, a clasp and a size C crochet hook.

Before starting work on covering the ring note that the cut end of yarn at the beginning can be laid along the ring and worked over in order to finish it. Remember to keep the stitches close together so that the ring will be completely covered. Hold the yarn

in the left hand in the usual way and place the ring over the yarn and, holding it between the thumb and first finger of left hand, insert the hook from front to back into the center of the ring, yo and draw through a loop, place the hook over the top of the ring, yo and draw yarn through loop on hook, *insert hook from front to back into the center of the ring, yo and draw through a loop, place hook over top of the ring, yo and draw through both loops on hook, rep from * until the ring is completely covered. Join with a sl st into first st. Break off the yarn and darn in the cut end.

Slot ribbon through the rings as shown in the illustration to form a continuous belt and attach a clasp at either end.

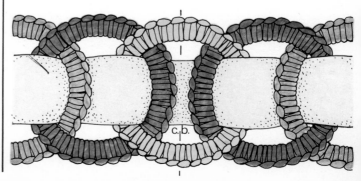

Alternative methods of working and joining rings suitable for belts

(a) Here the method of work is the same as that used for the belt rings, except that the rings are covered and joined continuously in one operation. Using size C hook, Knitting Worsted and 1¼-inch in diameter rings, work 14 stitches as previously shown to cover half the ring, then work the same number of stitches in a semi-circle around the next ring. Continue in this way until the required number of rings are joined and half covered in crochet. Work completely around the last ring and continue back along the other side of the rings.

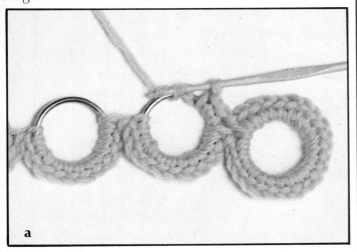

a

(b) Using size C crochet hook, a cotton yarn and 1¼-inch rings, work in the same way as given for

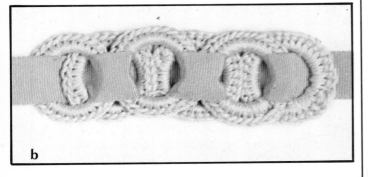

b

the belt and cover each ring individually. Thread grosgrain ribbon through the rings as shown in the illustration.

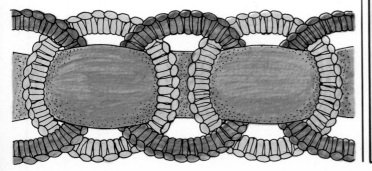

Alternative methods of covering individual rings

Each ring here is 2 inches in diameter and a size C hook is used for all the work.

(a) Here 34 stitches worked in straw yarn are needed to cover the ring. The straw gives a distinct chain edging to the circumference.

(b) Chenille yarn gives a softer appearance to this ring. You will need to work 46 stitches to cover the ring completely. The reverse side of the work is illustrated since this shows more of a looped effect.

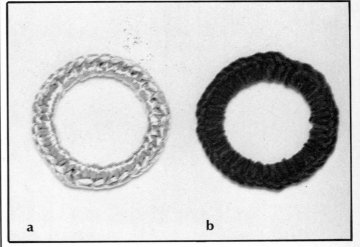

a   b

(c) Two rounds in two different yarns are worked over this ring. Using Knitting Worsted, work 50 stitches into the ring as given for the belt. Lurex yarn is used for the 2nd round where single crochet is worked into each stitch on the 1st round, working from left to right instead of from right to left.

(d) Work in the same way as for the previous sample until the 1st round has been completed. For the 2nd round, instead of working into all the stitches of the previous round, the hook is inserted into the center of the ring at various intervals. In this sample, using lurex yarn, work *1sc into each of next 3 sts, 1sc inserting hook into center of ring, 1sc into each of next 3 sts, 3sc inserting hook into center of ring, repeat from * to end of round. Join with a sl st into first st. Fasten off.

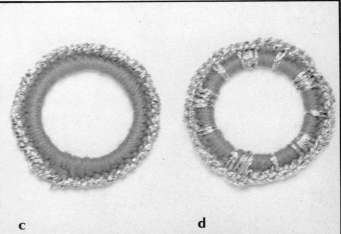

c   d

LARGE CIRCULAR MOTIFS

In this chapter, by telling you how to work our attractive window hanging, we hope to increase your knowledge of working circular motifs and to combine it now with two new techniques which we will give in these instructions. One is the method of covering a large ring and making loops so that crochet work may be attached to the ring; and the other is the method of making small circles by wrapping yarn around the fingers to form the base of the ring.

Window hangings are a popular continental form of decoration. Usually white yarn is used for this kind of work, this making more effective the many designs which are based on snowflake patterns. Once you know the new methods of working described in this chapter, use them with the various techniques and stitches with which we have dealt in previous chapters, and in this way you will be able to enjoy designing your own circular motifs.

To cover the ring

The most suitable ring to use is a plastic covered lampshade ring. Ours is 12 inches in diameter and the use of the plastic is practical, since it is rust proof and the white yarn will not stain.

Work eleven pair of reserve half hitch knots, making a picot between each group of eleven knots by leaving ½ inch of yarn free before working the next knot. Continue in this way until 24 picots have been made, join to first knot and fasten off. The covered ring will next be used in the final round of the crochet work.

To work the window hanging

Using size B crochet hook and a cotton yarn, wrap yarn 20 times around first two fingers of your left hand, insert hook under all the strands of yarn, yo and draw through a loop which now becomes your working st.

1st round 1ch to count as first sc, work 47sc into the circle of yarn. Join with a sl st into first ch.

2nd round 3ch, 1dc into same place as sl st, * 11ch, skip 5sc, leaving the last loop of each on hook, work 2dc into next sc, yo and draw through all 3 loops on hook, rep from * 6 times more. 11ch. Join with a sl st into 3rd of the 3ch.

3rd round * 13sc into next 11ch sp, sl st into top of pair of dc in previous round, rep from * 7 times more.

4th round ** Sl st into each of next 5sc, 5ch, skip 3sc, yo 4 times and insert hook into next sc, yo and draw through a loop, (yo and draw through first 2 loops on hook) 5 times—called a quad dc—, * 8ch, work a ring as foll: wrap yarn 10 times around second finger of left hand, insert hook under all the strands of yarn, yo and draw a loop through the working st on the hook, remove yarn from finger, work 23sc into the ring, join with a sl st into first st, (10ch, skip next 5sc on ring, sl st into next sc) twice, 8ch, sl st into top of pair of quad dc's at base of previous 8ch, * , 17ch, 1 quad dc into 5th sc of next sp, skip 3sc, 1 quad dc into next sc, rep from * to * , work 5 sl st down side of

next quad dc, sl st into each of next 5sc of sp, 21ch and now work 1sc into 3ch from hook, 1sc into each ch just worked, **. Rep from ** to ** 3 times more. Join with a sl st into first sl st of round. Fasten off.

5th round * Rejoin yarn into the top of the length of ch just worked, 6ch, 6sc into first 10ch sp above next ring, 6sc into next 10ch sp above same ring, 5ch, leaving the last loop of each st on hook work 3dc into next 17ch sp, yo and draw through all 4 loops on hook, 5ch, (6sc into next 10ch sp above ring) twice, 6ch, sl st into top of next length of 20ch, rep from * 3 times more.

6th round * 1ch, 6sc into next 6ch sp, sl st into each of next 12sc, (6sc into next 5ch sp) twice, sl st into each of next 12sc, 7sc into next 6ch sp, rep from * 3 times more working 7sc at beg of each rep instead of 1ch, 6sc. Join with a sl st into first ch.

7th round 3ch to count as first dc, 1dc into same place, * 5ch, skip next 4 sts, leaving the last loop of each st on hook, work 2dc into next st, yo and draw through all 3 loops on hook, rep from * around, ending with 5ch. Join with a sl st into 3rd of the 3ch.

8th round This is the round where the crochet motif is joined into the circle. Work 1ch, 5sc into first 5ch sp, 6sc into each sp to end of round, *at the same time* after every 10th st, remove hook from working loop, insert it into the picot on ring from front to back, reinsert it into the working loop and draw through picot. Join with a sl st into first ch.

A window hanging

Our last chapter dealt with the basic techniques involved in working large circular motifs which are popularly used as window hangings. The intricate design shown here involves three more complicated techniques in crochet. These show how to cover a narrow tube, enclose spheres with crochet, and one more way of covering and joining a center motif into a ring.

Follow our step by step instructions for making the window hanging and learn these new methods. You will enjoy making the pieces and will also find them useful for other forms of crochet work. The spheres, for example, could be very handsomely used as a decorative fringe on a lampshade. Once again, a plastic covered lampshade ring 12 inches in diameter was used for the large circle. Also used were a fine cotton yarn and a size B crochet hook.

To cover the tube
Make a slip loop on the hook, * holding the tube between thumb and first finger of left hand and having the yarn behind the tube, insert hook inside tube

from top to lower edge, yo and draw through tube, taking hook behind tube, yo and draw through both loops on hook, rep from * 47 times more. Join with a sl st into first st. Fasten off.

Move the chain ridge formed by the previous row to give a zig-zag pattern with 3 points at each edge of the tube.

To work the center motif
1st round Join yarn into one of the zig-zag points, * 6ch, sl st into next point at same edge, rep from * twice more.

2nd round 12dc into first 6ch sp, 12ch into each of next 2 sps.

3rd round * 6ch, skip 5 sts, sl st into next st, rep from * 5 times more.

4th round Work 1sc into each sc worked on 2nd round. 36sc. Join with a sl st into first sc.

5th round * 4ch, sl st into next 6ch sp, 4ch, sl st into 6th sc of previous round (behind the joining point of two 6ch sp), rep from * 5 times more.

6th round Work 5sc into each 4ch sp around. Join

with a sl st to first sc.

7th round 9ch, skip 4sc, sl st into next sc, sl st into next to last ch just worked, *7ch, skip 4sc, sl st into next sc, sl st into next to last ch just worked, rep from * 9 times more, 5ch. Join with a sl st into 2nd of first 9ch.

8th round Work 7sc into each 5ch sp around. Join with a sl st into first sc.

9th round 3ch to count as first dc, 2dc into st at base of ch, *7ch, skip 6sc, 2tr into next sc, 7ch, skip 6sc, 3dc into next sc, rep from * 4 times more, 7ch, skip 6sc, 2tr into next sc, 7ch, skip 6sc. Join with a sl st into 3rd of first 3ch.

10th round 1ch to count as first sc, 1sc into each of next 6 sts, 10ch, skip 8 sts, *1sc into each of next 11 sts, 10ch, skip 8 sts, rep from * 4 times more, 1 sc into each of next 4 sts. Join with a sl st into first ch. Fasten off. Rejoin yarn into one of the zig-zag points at the other end of the tube and repeat the 1st through 10th rounds, thus giving a 3-dimensional effect to the work.

To cover the small spheres

These are made from a crochet casing filled with cotton wool which forms a firm ball shape approximately 1½in in diameter. You will need six balls for our window hanging.

Using the same yarn and crochet hook, leave a length of yarn 14in long and then make 3ch. Join with a sl st into the first ch to form a ring.

1st round 1 ch to count as first sc, work 9sc into ring. Join with a sl st into first ch.

2nd round 1ch to count as first sc, 2sc into next sc, *1sc into next sc, 2sc into next sc, rep from * to end. Join with a sl st into first ch. 15sc.

3rd round 2ch to count as first cluster st, *yo and insert hook into next sc, (yo and draw through a loop extending it for ⅜in) 4 times, yo and draw through all loops on hook—called 1 cluster st —, 1ch to secure the st, rep from * into each sc around. Join with a sl st into 2nd of the 2ch.

4th round 2ch to count as first cluster st, work 1 cluster st and 1ch into each cluster st around. Join with a sl st into 2nd of the 2ch.

Keeping the right side of the work on the outside, insert the cotton wool into the ball at this point.

5th round 1ch, (yo and insert hook into next cluster st, yo and draw through a loop) twice, yo and draw through all 5 loops on hook—thus dec 1sc. Rep from * around. Join with a sl st into first ch.

6th round 1ch to count as first sc, 1sc into each st of previous round. Join with a sl st into first ch. Thread yarn carefully through each st of last round and draw through the last st on the hook. Leave a length of yarn 14in long for attaching the sphere on to the work.

To cover the ring and join in the center motif

To work the covering of our lampshade ring, we used a size D crochet hook and a slightly thicker cotton. First place a slip loop on to the crochet hook, keeping the yarn behind the ring, insert the hook into the ring, from top to lower edge, yo and draw through both loops on hook. Repeat this stitch until the ring is completely covered. You will need 258 stitches if you are using the same size ring as in our directions. Fasten off.

Next round Rejoin yarn into any st and draw through, thus making a st. Work 1sc into each st around. Join with a sl st into first st.

Next round *36ch, skip 42sc, sl st into next sc, rep from * 5 times more.

Next round Sl st into each of next 2ch, 3ch, 1dc into st at base of 3ch, (2ch, skip next 2ch, leaving the last loop of each st on hook, work 2ch into next ch, yo and draw through all 3 loops on hook—called a joint dc—, 5 times, 1ch, remove hook from working loop and insert it from back to front into any of the 10ch sp of 10th round of either section of center motif, *pick up the working loop and work 1ch, skip 2ch, (a joint dc into next ch, 2ch, skip 2ch) 5 times, a joint dc into next ch, skip 2ch, a joint dc into next ch, (2ch, skip 2ch, a joint dc into next ch) 5 times, remove hook from working loop and insert it into next 10ch sp of *same* section as before*. Repeat from * to * 4 times more, pick up the working loop and work 1ch, skip 2ch, (a joint dc into next ch, 2ch, skip 2ch) 5 times, a joint dc into next ch. Join with a sl st into 3rd of the 3ch.

To join the spheres

Using the 10ch sp of the other part of the center motif, attach one end of the sphere firmly to the center of the space. At the other end of the sphere, crochet 4ch and attach to the point where two joint double crochet meet at the point of a star on the ring.

CROCHET ON MESH
CROCHET ON NET

This is an unusual and unexpected use for crochet—working on to net to create a design, which can eventually be completed to give the appearance of lace. The samples in this chapter demonstrate the basic techniques and are worked in straight rows. These need to be practiced first, however, before attempting anything more complicated.

Several types of net are available, usually made from nylon, silk or rayon. Although colored nets are easy to obtain, white still is the most popular, one reason being that it is available in very wide yardages which makes it ideal for wedding veils.

For beginners the usual commercial net is rather fine to work with at first, consequently for our samples we have used one with a larger hole. Work with a size B hook and Knitting Worsted when practicing. If you cannot obtain net with the larger holes, we suggest that you use the plastic net often found in supermarkets for covering oranges and other fruits. You may find it easier to work the crochet if the net is placed in an embroidery ring, holding it taut in this way to ease the insertion of the hook.

Sample 1

The chain on net is the first basic stitch, and all the other designs are variations of this, therefore it is important to master this technique first. Place the net firmly in the ring. Begin working from the outer edge of the ring and plan to work in an upward direction. This is the easiest way to start, but when you are more familiar with this technique you will be able to work in any chosen direction. Holding the yarn under the net or the ring and the hook over the net on the ring, insert the hook into one hole, yo and draw through a loop, * insert the hook into the next hole above (as shown in the illustration), yo and draw

through a loop, drawing it through the loop already on the hook—one chain st has been worked over one hole in the net. Repeat from * for the desired length.
Note It is important to keep your chain stitches fairly loose, otherwise the net will pucker.

Sample 2

Chain stitch is used again, but the hook is placed into alternate holes.

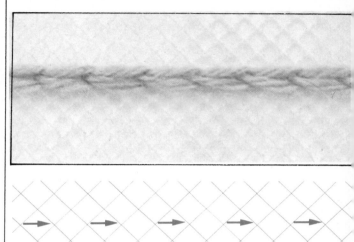

Sample 3

This is worked in the same way as for sample 2, but in 8 rows of 4 colors to give a striped effect. The chain is worked back and forth, and you turn the ring for each new row and cut the yarn only when changing colors.

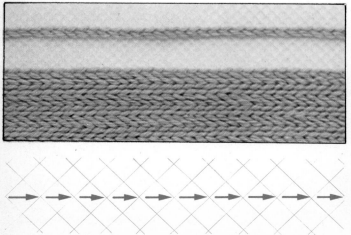

Sample 4

Straight lines have been used again here, but a zigzag effect has been achieved by, *working 8 sts into alternate diagonal holes in a left to right direction, then another 8 sts into alternate diagonal holes in a right to left direction, rep from * for the required length. Two rows have been worked in a variety of colors, leaving a space of two rows of holes between each new color.

Sample 5

Here a variety of stitches has been worked using the same technique. First place the net in the ring as given for sample 1.

(a) Insert hook into one hole on the edge of the ring,

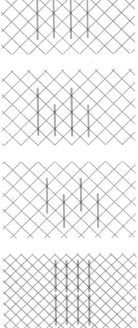

and again working upward, yo and draw through a loop extending it to reach 3rd hole on right, insert hook into this hole, yo and draw through a loop drawing it through loop on hook, *insert hook into adjacent hole above last st on left, yo and draw through a loop extending it as before, insert hook into 3rd hole on the right, yo and draw through all loops on hook, rep from * to end of the row.

(b) Following the illustration work in a similar way to previous sample, but extend the stitches alternately two and three spaces to the right.

(c) You will see from the illustration that this sample has been worked over 3 sts in a zigzag direction.

(d) Two rows of sts as given for sample (a) have been worked side by side (work one row as on sample (a), then turn the ring so that the completed row is on the right and work a second row as the first thus working the chain sts in adjacent rows).

Sample 6

These stitches are all a zigzag variation of chain stitch.

(a) Place net in ring as given for sample 1. Working upward as before, insert hook into hole at left edge, yo and draw through a loop, skip one hole on the right, insert hook into next hole on the right, yo and draw through a loop drawing it through loop on hook, *insert hook into next hole above last st on the left, yo and draw through a loop drawing it through loop on hook, skip one hole on the right, insert hook into next hole above last st on the right, yo and draw through a loop drawing it through loop on hook, rep from * to end of row.

(b) This is worked in the same way as sample (a), but slightly more spaced (there is one hole skipped between each st worked on the left and on the right).

(c) Here is another variation where the hook is inserted to give a diamond effect.

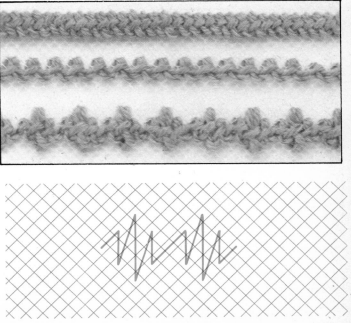

CROCHET ON RUG CANVAS

Crochet on rug canvas

Most stitches on canvas are worked with a needle, but many interesting effects will be illustrated in this chapter where crochet techniques are used.

In the last chapter we demonstrated how crochet is worked onto net where the holes do not come immediately one above the other, but rather to either side on each new row. With canvas, however, the holes are immediately next to and above each other, consequently your designs can easily be worked out on ordinary squared graph paper.

Both double and single weave canvas can be used for this technique, and very delicate work can be achieved by using a finer canvas with more holes to the square inch. Choose a hook which will easily enter the holes in the canvas and a yarn which will completely cover the weave when the stitches are worked. Too fine a yarn used with a thick canvas will result in gaps in the finished work.

No frame is necessary if you are using a stiff canvas. If a large amount of work is being done and a finer canvas is being used, an embroidery frame is recommended, which can be obtained from any good crafts supplier or shop. For our samples we have used an ordinary rug canvas, a bulky knitting yarn and a size E crochet hook. This combination of materials is suitable for making shoulder bags, carryalls and chair seat covers.

Sample 1

At the top of the sample a straight line of chain stitch has been worked in every adjacent hole. This was worked upward from the lower edge of the canvas and then turned to give a horizontal row of stitches. Two rows have been completed and the third is in the process of being worked.

To work the stitches Holding the yarn under the canvas in the usual way and the hook above the right side of the canvas, insert hook into one hole on the line of canvas to be worked, yo and draw loop through hole, *insert hook into next hole upwards, yo and draw through a loop drawing it through loop on hook, rep from * for the desired length of chain.

To the left of the photograph the same chain stitches have been worked vertically. The canvas is turned at the end of every row in order to keep working in an upward direction.

The remaining sample shows chain stitches worked into a zigzag design. Again work up the canvas and follow the chart which shows where to insert the hook.

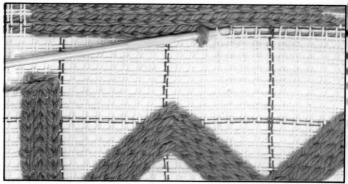

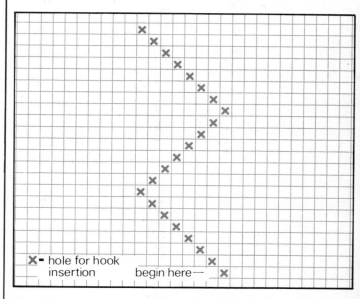

✕ = hole for hook insertion   begin here—

Sample 2

This is a square design worked in chain stitch which can be either enlarged to form one pattern, or on a smaller gauge, used together as motifs.

Each new round of our sample has been worked in a different color and a different yarn, including straw. Follow the diagram for the order of working, beginning with the 1st round which is to be worked over the four holes at the center.

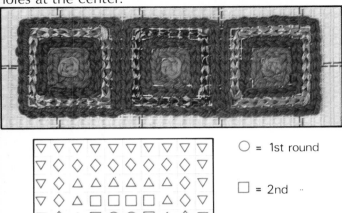

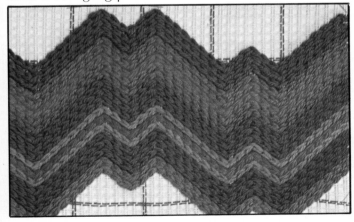

○ = 1st round

□ = 2nd ''

△ = 3rd ''

◇ = 4th ''

▽ = 5th ''

Sample 3

This is a copy of Florentine embroidery, the zigzag stitchery which is often seen on canvas. Careful color selection is necessary for this and the work can be made much more effective by varying the number of rows worked in each color. The chart illustrates our design, but it is quite easy to adapt your own ideas into zigzag patterns.

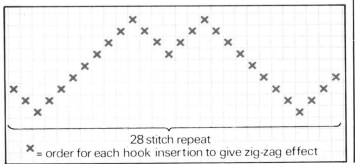

28 stitch repeat
✕ = order for each hook insertion to give zig-zag effect

Sample 4

This illustrates three stitches which can be used on rug canvas in place of chain stitch. Follow the instructions given here to learn how to work these stitches.

(a) Holding the yarn and hook as given for sample 1 and working in an upward direction, insert hook into one hole on the row of work, yo and draw through a loop, insert hook into next hole up, yo and draw through a loop, drawing it through loop on hook, *insert hook into next hole up on 2nd row to the left, yo and draw through a loop extending it to meet the next hole above last st worked on the right, insert hook into that hole, yo and draw through a loop drawing it through both loops on hook. Rep from * for the desired length.

(b) Holding the yarn and hook as given for sample 1 and working in an upward direction, insert hook into one hole on the row of work, yo and draw through a loop, insert hook into next hole up, yo and draw through a loop drawing it through loop on hook, insert hook into next hole up on 2nd row to the left, *yo and draw through a loop extending it to meet the next hole above last st worked on the right, insert hook into that hole, yo and draw through a loop drawing it through both loops on hook, *, – one long st has been worked. Insert hook into next hole up on the next row to the left and rep from * to * to form a short st. Cont working a long and a short st alternately to end of the line. Turn work and repeat a second row of crochet opposite the first, working a long st next to a short st and a short st next to a long st.

(c) Holding the yarn and hook as given for sample 1 and working in an upward direction, insert hook into one hole on row of work, *insert hook into next hole up to the left, yo and draw through a loop drawing it through loop on hook, insert hook into next hole to the right, yo and draw through a loop drawing it through loop on hook, rep from * for the desired length.

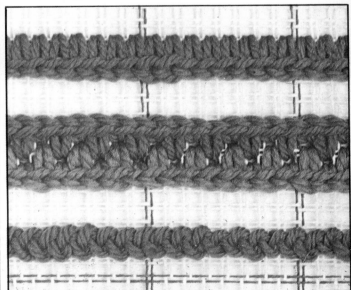

EMBROIDERY ON CROCHET

Crochet plus stitchery
A background of simple crochet lends itself attractively to decorative stitchery and many of the traditional embroidery stitches can be worked onto crochet fabrics.

To work the crochet background This is a basic mesh which is quick and simple to work. Vary the size of the mesh by working a smaller or larger crochet stitch with additional or fewer chain stitches between as desired. Any yarn may be used but for these samples we have used a size E crochet hook and Knitting Worsted. Make a length of chain with multiples of 4 plus 11 stitches.

1st row Into 11th ch from hook work 1tr, *3ch, skip next 3ch, 1tr into next ch, rep from * to end. Turn.
2nd row 7ch to count as first tr and 3ch, skip first tr, 1tr into next tr, *3ch, 1tr into next tr, rep from * ending with last tr into 4th of turning ch. Turn.

Rep the 2nd row for the required depth of work. Throughout these samples we have used an embroidery stitch which is a form of darning. Again any yarn can be used, but choose it carefully and work a trial piece before beginning work since different yarns make stitches which can look entirely different. Many varied and attractive designs can be made with this basic stitch technique including table linen, bedcovers and curtains. A more delicate effect can be made by using a finer cotton yarn and a smaller sized crochet hook.

Sample 1
Here is a design which is suitable for an over-all pattern. Certain squares on the background have been filled in with the darning or weaving stitch as shown on the illustration. The chart shows which squares are to be filled in.

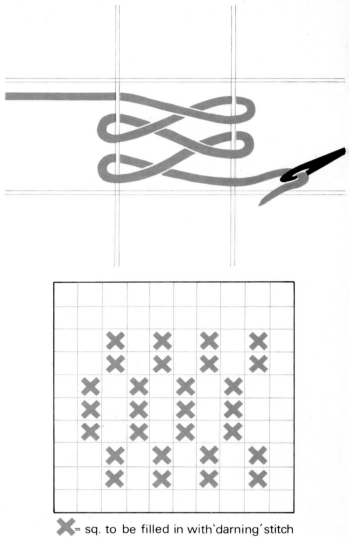

✖ = sq. to be filled in with 'darning' stitch

Sample 2
This basic background has a shaped edge and the finished piece of work could be used as a window valance or as an edging on a window shade.
To work the background Work 3 rows as given for the basic background.
4th row Sl st across first 4 sts to dec one square, 7ch, patt to end. Turn.
5th row Patt to last square, turn to dec one square.
6th row 8ch to count as first tr of this row and space at end of next row, sl st into each of first 4ch, 3ch, patt to end. Turn.

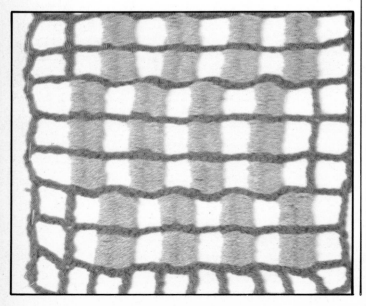

7th row Patt to end, working last tr into last sl st of previous row to inc one square. Turn.

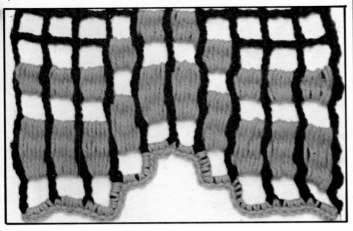

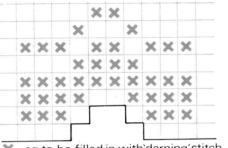

✕ = sq. to be filled in with 'darning' stitch

8th row 10ch to inc one square, 1tr into first tr, patt to end. Turn.

9th–10th row Patt to end. Turn.

These 10 rows form the basic pattern which can be repeated for the desired length.

Darn the appropriate squares as shown in the chart and then, using the same yarn as for the darning, complete the shaped edge by working 3sc into each square and 1sc into each tr or corner of a square.

Sample 3

Circular motifs have been added to the basic background. Using two strands of a 4 ply yarn together,

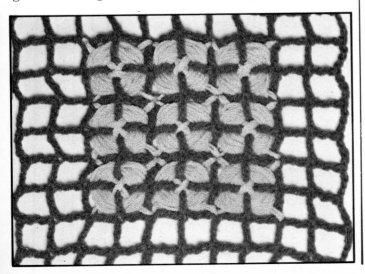

thread the motifs over four squares as shown in the illustration. The photograph shows the motifs worked over adjacent groups of four squares.

Sample 4

Here a single flower motif has been worked onto a basic background using a bulky yarn. After working the four basic lines as shown in the illustration twice, weave the thread around the center by passing the needle (under the blue line, over the green, under the red and over the brown) six times in all. All the cut ends of yarn should then be finished on the wrong side of the work.

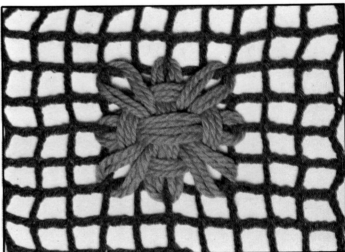

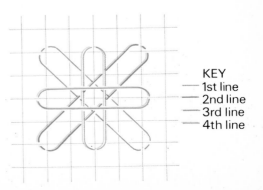

KEY
— 1st line
— 2nd line
— 3rd line
— 4th line

MORE EMBROIDERY DESIGNS

This is a continuation of our chapter about weaving designs onto a crochet mesh background. We also give instructions for working an unusual and decorative shawl, which is simple to make and employs the techniques shown in recent chapters. Practice the samples shown here before starting to work on the shawl.

Sample 1

To work the background Using size D crochet hook and a 4 ply yarn, make a length of chain with multiples of 4 + 11 stitches.
1st row Into 11th ch from hook work 1tr, *3ch, skip 3ch, 1tr into next ch, rep from * to end. Turn.
2nd row 7ch to count as first tr and 3ch, skip first sp, 1tr into next tr, *3ch, 1tr into next tr, rep from * to end with last tr into 4th of turning ch. Turn.
The 2nd row is repeated throughout.

Sample 2

Work the mesh as given for sample 1, then weave the flower with a double thickness of contrasting yarn as in the illustration for sample 4 of previous chapter.

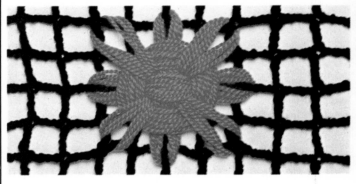

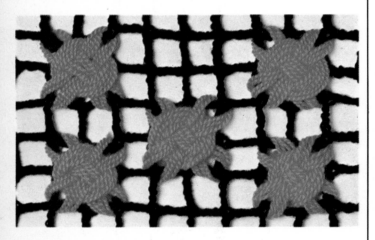

To work the flower Using double thickness of a contrasting yarn and a large blunt-ended needle, follow the diagram and work the yarn through the crochet mesh.

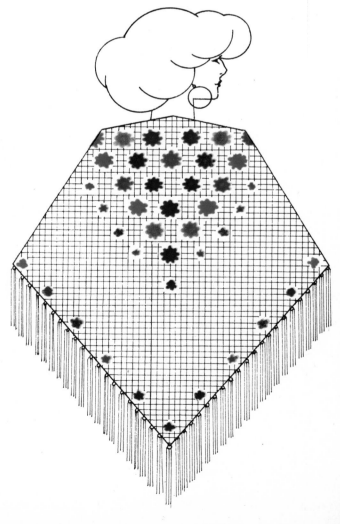

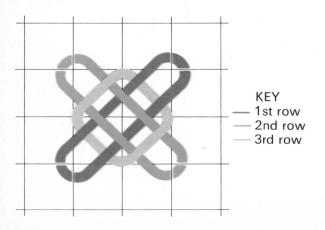

KEY
— 1st row
— 2nd row
— 3rd row

Crochet shawl

Size

Triangle measures approximately 45 inches across top and 30 inches from center of top edge to point

Gauge

5ch sp and 6 rows to 3 inches in patt worked with size C crochet hook

Materials

10 × 30grm balls Reynolds Parfait
Small amounts of six contrasting colors
One size C crochet hook

Shawl

Using size C hook and A, make 327ch loosely.

1st row Into 11th ch from hook work 1tr, *3ch, skip 3ch, 1tr into next ch, rep from * to end. Turn. Eighty 3ch sp.

2nd row 7ch to count as first tr and 3ch, skip first sp, 1tr into next tr, *3ch, 1tr into next tr, rep from * ending with last tr into 4th of turning ch. Turn.

3rd and 4th rows As 2nd.

5th row (dec row) 7ch to count as first tr and 3ch, skip first sp, (1tr into next tr) twice – i.e. skip the 3ch between tr, so dec one sp –, *3ch, 1tr into next tr, rep from * to last 2 sp, 1tr into next tr, 3ch, 1tr into 4th of turning ch. Turn. 2 sp decreased.

6th and 7th rows As 2nd.

8th row As 5th.

Cont in this way, dec 2 sp on every foll alt row, until 46 sp rem, then on every row until 2 sp rem. Fasten off.

Finishing

Using the contrasting colors, apply motifs as shown in the illustration. Care should be taken to finish all the cut ends neatly on the wrong side of the work.

Fringe Cut 10 strands of yarn each 13 inches long, fold in half and using crochet hook pull folded end through first space at side of shawl, pull cut ends through loop thus made and pull tight to form a knot. Rep these knots into each space along 2 sides of the triangle. Trim fringe ends evenly.

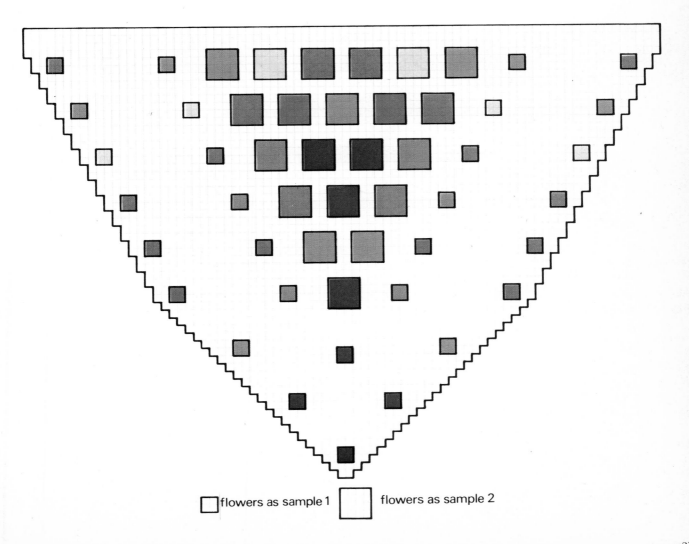

□ flowers as sample 1   □ flowers as sample 2

BEADED DESIGNS

Beaded designs may easily be incorporated into crochet work during the process of making an article. There are numerous types of beads, normally made of glass, china or wood, available in most large department or chain stores.

The size of beads varies considerably, but any type can be used for this kind of work providing that the hole in the bead is large enough to take the yarn which is being used. To thread the beads onto the yarn, see the second chapter on Loopy Stitches. Each bead is positioned so that it forms part of a design and care must be taken to see that the beads are placed on the right side of the work.

It should be remembered too that beads are quite heavy if they are used in large quantities. Therefore small articles are really the most suitable, or border pattern areas. Even these articles will need to be lined to strengthen the work and to accomodate the weight of the beads.

Beads are particularly popular for evening wear. Very attractive patterns using beads may be designed and applied to evening jackets and bags, or used as a border around the hem of a long evening coat or skirt. There are two distinct methods of applying the beads. One way is to thread the beads onto the yarn which you will be using, before you start working. The bead is then pushed up and positioned as it is needed and the next stitch is then worked in the usual way. This technique is illustrated in samples 1 and 2. Another method, used in sample 3, is to thread the beads onto a separate ball of yarn. When a bead row is being worked, the yarn on either side of the bead is caught into place during the working of the crochet by looping the working yarn around the yarn holding the beads. Our samples show some simple designs which follow the two methods described above. If you practice these samples from our instructions you will soon become familiar with the art of beaded crochet.

Sample 1

Using a fine yarn and No.0 crochet hook, make 40ch.

1st row Into 3rd ch from hook work 1sc, 1sc into each ch to end. Turn.

2nd–7th rows 1ch to count as first sc, 1sc into each sc to end. Turn.

8th row 1ch to count as first sc, 1sc into each of next 6 sts, *push up one bead, placing it at back of the work which will be the right side, 1sc into next st – called 1 Bsc –, 1sc into each of next 7 sts, rep from * 3 times more. Turn.

9th row 1ch to count as first sc, 1sc into each of next 6 sts, *noting that beads are placed at the front of the work, 1Bsc into each of next 2 sts, 1sc into each of next 6 sts, rep from * 3 times more. Turn.

10th row 1ch to count as first sc, 1sc into each of next 5 sts, *1Bsc into each of next 3 sts, 1sc into each of next 5 sts, rep from * 3 times more, ending last rep 1sc with each of next 6 sts. Turn.

11th row 1ch to count as first sc, 1sc into each of next 5 sts, *1Bsc into each of next 4 sts, 1sc into each of next 4 sts, rep from * 3 times more, ending last rep 1sc with each of next 5 sts. Turn.

12th row 1ch to count as first sc, 1sc into each of next 4 sts, *1Bsc into each of next 5 sts, 1sc into each of next 3 sts, rep from * twice more, 1Bsc into each of next 5 sts, 1sc into each of next 5 sts. Turn.

13th row As 11th.

14th row As 10th.

15th row As 9th.

16th row 1ch to count as first sc, 1sc into each of next 2 sts, *1Bsc into next st, 1sc into each of next 3 sts, rep from * 8 times more. Turn.

17th row 1ch to count as first sc, 1sc into each of next 2 sts, *1Bsc into each of next 2 sts, 1sc into each of next 6 sts, rep from * 3 times more, 1Bsc into each of next 2 sts, 1sc into each of next 2 sts. Turn.

18th row 1ch to count as first sc, 1sc into next st, *1Bsc into each of next 3 sts, 1sc into each of next 5 sts, rep from * 3 times more, 1Bsc into each of next 3 sts, 1sc into each of next 2 sts. Turn.

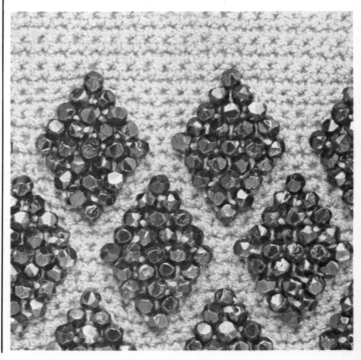

19th row 1ch to count as first sc, 1sc into next st, *1Bsc into each of next 4 sts, 1sc into each of next 4sc, rep from * 3 times more, 1Bsc into each of next 4 sts, 1sc into last st. Turn.

20th row 1ch to count as first sc, *1Bsc into each of next 5 sts, 1sc into each of next 3 sts, rep from * 3 times more, 1Bsc into each of next 5 sts, 1sc into last st. Turn.

21st–24th rows As 19th–16th rows, in that order. The 9th row is then repeated to complete the pattern and to start the next diamond shape.

Sample 2

Using a cotton yarn and No.0 crochet hook, make 40ch.

1st row Into 3rd ch from hook work 1hdc, 1hdc into each ch to end. Turn.

2nd row 2ch to count as first hdc, 1hdc into each of next 6 sts, *push up one bead, placing it at back of work which will be the right side, 1hdc in the next st – called 1Bhdc –, 1hdc into each of next 7 sts, rep from * 3 times more. Turn.

3rd row 2ch to count as first hdc, *1hdc into each of next 5 sts, 1Bhdc into next st, 1hdc into next st, 1Bhdc into next st, rep from * 3 times more, 1hdc into each of next 6 sts. Turn.

4th row 2ch to count as first hdc, 1hdc into each of next 4 sts, *1Bhdc into next st, 1hdc into each of next 3 sts, rep from * 7 times more, 1Bhdc into next st, 1hdc into each of next 2 sts. Turn.

5th row 2ch to count as first hdc, 1hdc into each of next 3 sts, *1Bhdc into next st, 1hdc into each of next 5 sts, 1Bhdc into next st, 1hdc into next st, rep from * 3 times more, 1hdc into each of next 3 sts. Turn.

6th row 2ch to count as first hdc, 1hdc into each of next 2 sts, *1Bhdc into next st, 1hdc into each of next 7

sts, rep from * 3 times more, 1 Bhdc into next st, 1hdc into each of next 3 sts. Turn.

7th–10th rows As 5th–2nd rows, in that order. The 2nd through 10th rows form the pattern.

Sample 3

Wooden beads, approximately $\frac{3}{4}$ inch long, were used for this sample. Thread them on to a separate ball of yarn.

Using a cotton yarn and size C crochet hook, make 33ch.

1st row Into 3rd ch from hook work 1sc, 1sc into each ch to end. Turn.

2nd–8th rows 1ch to count as first sc, 1sc into each sc to end. Turn.

9th row 1ch to count as first sc, 1sc into next st, *hold the yarn with the beads behind the work, place the working yarn round the yarn holding the beads, work 1sc into next st, work 1sc into each of next 3 sts using the main yarn, push up one bead into position behind the work, *, rep from * to * 9 times more, ending last rep with 1sc into each of next 2 sts. Turn. Cut off yarn holding beads.

10th row Work in sc.

11th row 1ch to count as first sc, 1sc into each of next 3 sts, rep from * to * of 9th row to complete the row. The 9th and 11th rows show the sequence of working the beads so that they lie in alternate spaces. You may make your own designs by using this sequence, but remember that the beads are always placed from the opposite side of the work, so that you will have to cut the yarn after each bead row.

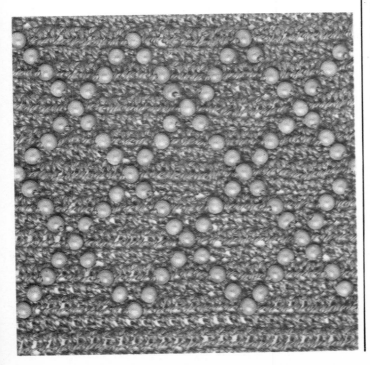

NEEDLEWEAVING
BASIC DESIGNS

Crochet with needleweaving
This chapter gives instructions for working a crochet background into which various materials may be woven to produce a solid fabric. The background is formed by working in double crochets with one chain separating each one, and on subsequent rows the double crochets are worked into those on the previous row to give a straight vertical line. The chains of each space or the double crochets worked between the spaces, form bars over or under which the weaving threads may pass, according to the design.

A crochet hook or blunt-ended needle is used to pass the threads vertically, horizontally or diagonally across the fabric, breaking off the yarn after each row. It is interesting to experiment with different yarns and ribbons for weaving. We have used four thicknesses of the same yarn, rug wool, various ribbons and strips of plastic. Strips of fur could also be used to produce a very expensive-looking fabric.

The weaving threads help to keep the crochet in position and, as the fabric formed is thick and warm, it is especially suitable for outer garments such as jackets, coats, scarves and skirts. The fabric made by this technique is also ideal for pillows and rugs.

Follow the instructions for our samples before experimenting with your own designs and yarns.

Sample 1
This is the basic open background for needle weaving. Using size F hook and Knitting Worsted, make 30ch.
1st row Into 6th ch from hook work 1dc, *1ch, skip next ch, 1dc into next ch, rep from * to end. Turn.

Note A firmer fabric is produced by placing the hook under three loops of each dc, instead of the usual one or two loops.
2nd row 4ch to count as first dc and 1ch, skip first ch sp, 1dc into next dc, *1ch, skip next ch sp, 1dc into next dc, rep from * to end, working last dc into 4th of 5ch. Turn.

The 2nd row is repeated throughout, noting that each subsequent row will end with last dc worked into 3rd of 4ch.

One attractive item to make entirely in this stitch is a bag. It is quick and easy to work in one piece which is folded in half and seamed at the sides. A row of crochet chain gathers the top edges and at the same time joins them to wooden handles.

Sample 2
Work a basic background as given for sample 1. Ribbon, $\frac{1}{4}$ inch wide, is then woven vertically through the spaces.
1st weaving row Draw the ribbon under the ch of the foundation row and up into the first space, *skip the next space and insert ribbon from front to back into the next space, draw ribbon from back to front into the next space, *, rep from * to * to end of fabric.
2nd weaving row Insert ribbon from front to back into first space of next row, then draw ribbon from back to front into second space, rep from * to * of 1st weaving row to end of fabric.
3rd weaving row Insert ribbon from front to back into second space of next row, then draw ribbon from back to front into third space, rep from * to * of 1st weaving row to end of fabric.

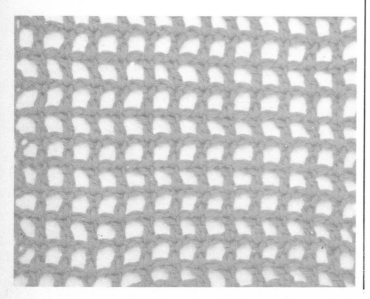

The 3 weaving rows are repeated vertically across the fabric.

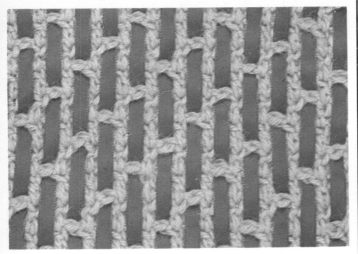

Sample 3
Green household string has been used for the background of this sample. Using size H hook make 31ch.

1st row Into 7th ch from hook work 1tr, *1ch, skip next ch, 1tr into next ch, rep from * to end. Turn.

2nd row 5ch, skip next sp, 1tr into next tr, *1ch, 1tr into next tr, ending with last tr into 5th of 6ch. Turn.

The 2nd row is repeated throughout, noting that each subsequent row will end with last tr worked into 4th of 5ch.

$\frac{3}{4}$ inch wide grosgrain ribbon is woven horizontally through each space on the first row, and then through alternate spaces on the next row.

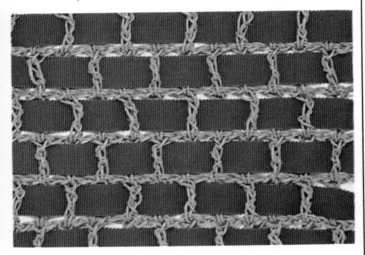

Sample 4
Work a basic background as given for sample 1.
There are two types of weaving involved in this design. First, thick rug wool is placed vertically around each treble crochet working up the fabric. Instead of working in and out of the crochet fabric, the rug wool is placed under each treble from left to right working upwards on the first row and on

alternate rows. On the remaining rows the rug wool is threaded in the same way, but it is passed from right to left.

Strips of plastic $\frac{1}{4}$ inch wide, matching the background color, and ribbon $\frac{1}{4}$ inch wide, matching the rug wool are then woven alternately between each row of treble crochets. The plastic is threaded so that on the right side the strip passes completely over one space, while the ribbon goes into alternate spaces.

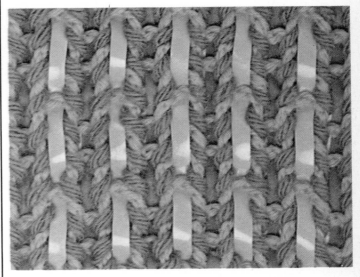

Sample 5
Work a basic background as given for sample 1.
The weaving is worked in two different colors, A and B, of Knitting Worsted, using four thicknesses together each time. With A work into alternate horizontal spaces on the first row. Continue with A into each horizontal row throughout the fabric, alternating the spaces worked into with those on the previous row. Color B is woven vertically into each row in the same way as A, weaving in and out of the strands of A as well as the bars of the background fabric.

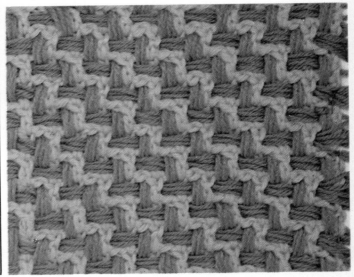

EXPERIMENTAL TECHNIQUES

The basic methods of needle weaving were dealt with in the last chapter, and now we shall illustrate some more experimental uses of this technique with different yarns and with other methods of weaving. Two of the samples are checked fabrics worked onto the basic background and they are thick and warm because of the way in which they are worked. Other samples are worked in different crochet stitches to form a background. Most of these samples of needle weaving are suitable for an over-all fabric, but some (such as sample 4) can be adapted very well to the making of an attractive border for a jacket or long skirt.

Sample 1
To work the background This is worked in two colors of Knitting Worsted, A and B. Using size H hook and A, make 30ch.

1st row Into 6th ch from hook work 1dc, *1ch, skip 1ch, 1dc into next ch, rep from * to end. Turn.

2nd row 4ch to count as first dc and 1ch, skip 1ch sp, 1dc into next dc, *1ch, skip 1ch sp, 1dc into next dc, rep from * finishing with last dc into 5th of 6ch. Turn.

Join in B and rep 2nd row twice more, noting that on subsequent rows the last dc is worked into 3rd of 4ch. Continue in this way, working 2 rows in each color, for the desired length.

To work the weaving Using 4 thicknesses of A together, weave in and out of each vertical space on the first row. Then using A again, work into each space on the next row alternating where the yarn passes over or under a bar. Alternating A and B, repeat this process in two row stripes throughout the fabric.

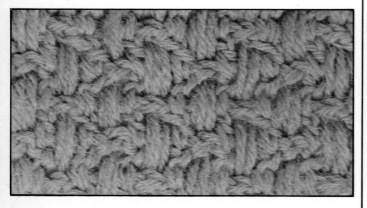

Sample 2
To work the background This is worked in three colors of Knitting Worsted, A, B and C. Using size H hook make a background as given for sample 1, but work one row in A, two rows in B and three rows in

C. Note also that colors A and C will have to be cut at the end of the row so that the yarn will be in the correct position for the repeat of color sequence.

To work the weaving This is worked in the same way as sample 1, but with one vertical row in A, two rows in B and three rows in C.

Sample 3
Two colors of Knitting Worsted are used for this sample, color A for the background and B for the needle weaving.

To work the background Using size H hook and A, make 27ch.

1st row Into 5th ch from hook work 4dc leaving last loop of each st on hook, yo and draw through all loops on hook, 1ch, skip 1ch, 1sc into next ch, *1ch, skip 1ch, into next ch work 4dc leaving last loop of each on hook, yo and draw through all loops on hook, 1ch, skip 1ch, 1sc into next ch, rep from * to end. Turn.

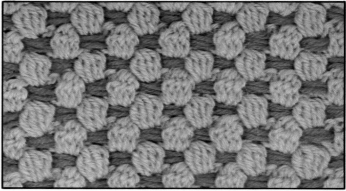

2nd row 3ch, into first sc work 3dc leaving last loop of each on hook, yo and draw through all loops on hook, 1ch, *1dc into top of next 4dc gr, 1ch, into next sc work 4dc leaving last loop of each on hook, yo and draw through all loops on hook, 1ch, rep from *

finishing with last 4dc gr into turning ch. Turn.

3rd row 2ch, *into next sc work 4dc leaving last loop of each on hook, yo and draw through all loops on hook, 1ch, 1sc into top of next 4dc gr, 1ch, rep from * to end, omitting 1ch at end of last rep. Turn. The 2nd and 3rd rows are repeated throughout.

To work the weaving Four thicknesses of color B are placed horizontally across every row by weaving them under each four double crochet group, and over each single crochet.

Sample 4

This crochet background illustrates an attractive stitch made up of blocks and spaces.

To work the background Using size G hook and Knitting Worsted, make 29ch.

1st row Into 5th ch from hook work 2tr, skip 2ch, 1sc into next ch, *3ch, skip 3ch, 3tr into next ch, skip 2ch, 1sc into next ch, rep from * to end. Turn.

2nd row 4ch, 2tr into first sc, 1sc into next 3ch sp, *3ch, 3tr into next sc, 1 sc into next 3ch sp, rep from * ending with last sc into turning ch. Turn.

The 2nd row is repeated throughout.

To work the weaving Following the illustration, thread the ribbon and four thicknesses of yarn in alternate strips over the vertical bars formed by the three chain in the background.

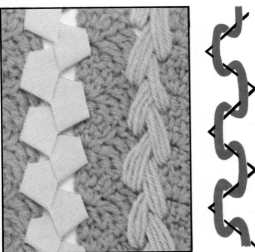 

Sample 5

To work the background Using size G hook and a mohair yarn, make 29ch.

1st row Into 7th ch from hook, work 1sc, 2ch, skip next ch, 1dc into next ch, *2ch, skip next ch, 1sc into next ch, 2ch, skip next ch, 1dc into next ch, rep from * to end. Turn.

2nd row 3ch to count as first sc and 2ch, *1dc into next sc, 2ch, 1sc into next dc, 2ch, rep from * to end, working last sc into 3rd of turning ch. Turn.

3rd row 5ch to count as first dc and 2ch, 1sc into first dc, 2ch, 1dc into next sc, 2ch, rep from * to end, working last dc into 2nd of 3rd ch. Turn.

The 2nd and 3rd rows are repeated throughout.

To work the weaving Diagonal lines of alternate strips of velvet ribbon and four thicknesses of a contrasting shade of mohair are worked over the diagonal chain bars and under the double crochet stitches in each row.

This fabric is very light, warm and luxurious and would be very suitable for a long evening skirt, straight evening stole or an area rug.

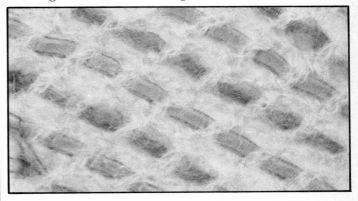

Sample 6

This beautiful evening belt is simple to make by following the needle weaving techniques. Using Size E hook and a lurex yarn, make a length of chain long enough to fit around your waist or hips less the combined diameters of the two rings used for fastening. Into the chain work 6 rows as given for the basic needle weaving background. Two colors of

soutache are threaded through the background to give a raised effect. Secure the ends of the belt over the fastening rings (ours are large brass rings, 2in in diameter) and crochet a length of cord to bind the rings together.

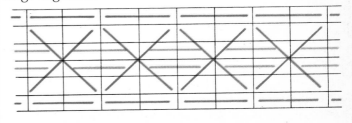

A woven crochet rug

rep from * to end. Turn. 95 sps.
1st row 3ch to count as first dc, *1dc into next dc, 1ch, rep from * to last sp, skip 1ch, 1dc into 4th of first 5ch. Turn.
The last row forms the patt. Rep last row 3 times more. Break off A. Continuing in patt work a striped sequence of 5 rows B, 5 rows C and 5 rows A throughout.
Rep this striped sequence 6 times more. Fasten off.

Finishing
Sew in ends. Block lightly with a cool iron under a dry cloth.
Weaving Cut 70 lengths of A, 60 lengths of B and 60 lengths of C, all 88in long. Take 2 strands of A and, being careful not to twist the strands, weave vertically over and under 1ch bars separating the dc, beg with 1st row of sps and leaving 6in hanging free.
A firmer edge will be obtained if the needle is passed through the first ch on the lower edge rather than into sp, and also through the final ch in the top edge. Do not pull yarn too tightly, but weave at a tension that will leave 6in hanging free at the top edge. Work another 4 rows in A, weaving over alternate bars from those woven on the preceding row.

Continue in same way as for striped sequence on rug.
Fringe Cut two 13in lengths of color required for each sp along both short ends of rug. Fold strands to form a loop. Insert hook into first sp at lower edge, draw loop through, draw woven ends through loop then draw fringe ends through loop and draw up tightly.
Rep along lower edge and upper edge, taking care to keep same side of rug uppermost while knotting fringe.
Trim fringe ends evenly.

Size
60in × 52in excluding fringe

Gauge
10dc and 10 sps and 10 rows to 6½in patt worked on size J crochet hook

Materials
15 × 1 oz balls Dawn Sayelle Knitting Worsted in main color, A
13 balls each of contrast colors, B and C
One size J crochet hook
Large tapestry needle

Note
To obtain an even background always insert the hook under 3 top strands of the dc of previous row working into body of st

Rug
Using size J hook and A make 194ch.

Base row Into 6th ch from hook work 1dc, *1ch, skip 1ch, 1dc into next ch,

CROCHET TRIMMINGS
INSERTIONS

Crochet as an insertion

An insertion is usually thought of as a decorative open work strip which joins two pieces of fabric together, often used to add a pretty, patterned panel to a dress, or along the side seams of slacks. In this chapter we deal with making straight insertions which are applied directly onto straight pieces of fabric, working the crochet and joining the pieces together in one easy stage. Dress patterns with simple seams could easily employ this method, remembering though that the crochet has a certain depth and therefore the appropriate amount of the fabric should first be cut away from your pattern (half the width of the total insertion could be removed from both pattern pieces being joined), before starting work. When working on a sample, turn under a 2 inch seam allowance, or for a garment, press back the seam on the fitting line, then follow our instructions to learn the techniques and some interesting new designs.

Sample 1

This sample shows the seam pressed back and ready for work to begin. As a crochet hook cannot be inserted directly into the majority of dress fabrics, an even back stitch has been worked along the

fitting line (this has been emphasized in our sample by the use of green yarn). The size of the sewing stitch should be large enough to allow the crochet hook to pass through it.

Sample 2

Here the first row of crochet is being worked. Make a slip loop on the hook, then working from right to left, with the right side of the work facing, remove hook from loop and insert it into first st on fabric, replace the loop on the hook and draw through the st on the fabric, 2ch, *insert hook into next sewing stitch, yo and draw through a loop, yo and draw through both loops (1sc has been worked), 1ch, rep from * to end of work. Fasten off.

Note Our sample illustrates 1sc followed by 1ch, but if the back stitches are smaller there is no need for 1ch between stitches.

Sample 3

This is the completed insertion. First work along the edges of fabrics, A and B, as described in sample 2. With RS of work facing and working from right to left, insert hook into first ch of fabric A, work 5ch, slip hook out of st and insert into first ch of fabric B again with RS facing, *replace st on the hook and draw through the st on B, yo 3 times, insert hook into next ch of fabric A, yo and draw through a loop, (yo and draw through first 2 loops on hook), 4 times – 1dtr has been worked –, remove hook from st and insert into next ch on fabric B, rep from * to end. Fasten off yarn by replacing st and draw through the ch sp on fabric B, then yo and draw through cutting the end.

Note When joining two pieces of fabric together in this way, it is important that the two rows of back stitches are exactly the same in size and number.

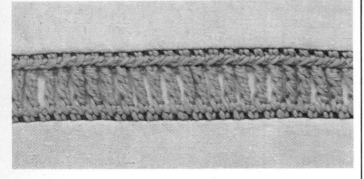

Sample 4

This sample has been made in the same way as sample 3, with one more addition to its design. A cord has been worked through pairs of dtr's – denoted as A and B. To do this, follow our diagram and place first dtr – A over second dtr – B and then take the cord under B and over A. Repeat over each pair of dtr's. Here the insertion has been used vertically as it would be on a pants seam.

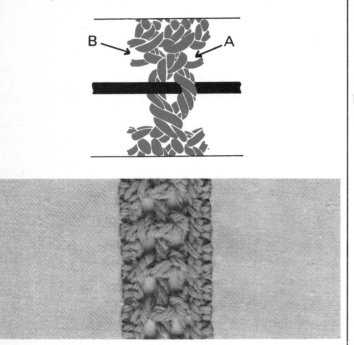

Sample 5

Work a row of sc along two pieces of fabric, A and B, as given for sample 2. To work the crochet joining the two pieces together, with RS of work facing and working from right to left, join yarn to first st on fabric A, work 9ch, slip hook out of st and insert it into first st on fabric B, then still with RS of work facing, *replace the st on the hook and draw through the st on fabric B, yo 8 times, insert hook into next st on fabric A, yo and draw through a loop, (yo and draw through first 2 loops on hook) 9 times – called 1dc8 –, remove st from hook and insert hook into next ch on

fabric B, rep from * to end. Fasten off yarn by replacing st on hook, then draw through the st on fabric B, yo and draw through yarn, then cut off the end. The illustration shows the method of threading the cord through the stitches.

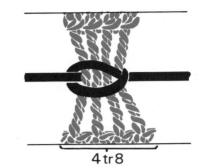

4 tr 8

Sample 6

Work as given for sample 5, working 10ch at the beginning and working a 1dc9 by placing yarn over the hook 9 times and (yo and draw through first 2 loops on hook) 10 times.

4 tr 9

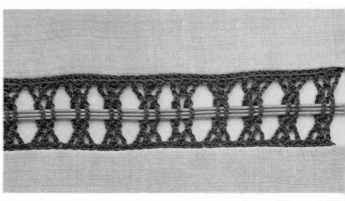

The illustration shows the method of working three rows of cord through the stitches.

EDGINGS

One of the neatest and most attractive ways of finishing off the outer edges of a garment, whether it is knitted or worked in crochet, is with the use of a crochet edging.

The edging may be worked in rounds or rows. It normally consists of only one row or round of crochet, but it is sometimes necessary to work a foundation row or round of single crochet before the actual edging in order to give a firmer edge to it. Our edgings are worked into the stitches around the outer edges of a garment or piece of crochet work after the main part has been completed and sewn together. Edgings can either be a subtle finishing or an important feature of the design, depending on the piece that is to be trimmed. A decorative edging can liven up a plain jacket, while a very simple edging may be all that is needed to finish a heavily patterned piece of work. Choose a yarn that is applicable to the type of work you are doing. You will probably want to use the same yarn as you used for the rest of the garment, perhaps in a different color to add contrast. Should you want to make more of a feature of the edging however and decide to use an entirely different yarn, remember the type of yarn being used for the rest of the work, and do not, for instance, pick a thick, heavy yarn to be worked on a piece of delicate baby's clothing.

There are an infinite number of edgings and below we give instructions for some of the most unusual ones including basic picots, shells and clusters.

Edging 1 Into first st work 1sc, *3ch, skip next st, 1sc into next st, rep from * to end.

Edging 2 This is called cord stitch. It is worked with just a single crochet into every stitch, working, however, from left to right instead of the usual right to left.

Edging 3 This is the most usual way of working a picot. Work 1sc into each of first 3 sts, *4ch, remove hook from st and insert it into first ch worked from front to back, pick up the st that was left and draw through the loop on the hook — 1 picot has been made —, 1sc into each of next 3 sts, rep from * to end.

Edging 4 Here is a more decorative picot edging. Work 1sc into each of first 3 sts, *4ch, 1sc into 3rd ch from hook, 1ch, skip next st, 1sc into each of next 3 sts, rep from * to end.

Edging 5 The picots worked here form a very thick edge. Sl st into first st, *4ch and work a picot into 4th ch from hook as described in edging 3, sl st into next st, rep from * to end.

Edging 6 This is an easy way of making a looped edging. *Work 1sc into first st, extend loop on hook and transfer it to a No.11 knitting needle, keeping the needle at the back of the work, reinsert hook into last sc worked, yo and draw through a loop, 1sc into next st, rep from * to end.

Edging 7 Sl st into each of first 2 sts, *1sc into next st, 3ch, sl st into same st where last sc was worked, sl st into each of next 2 sts, rep from * to end.

Edging 8 The group of stitches in this edging form a decorative scallop shape. Work 3ch, into st at base of ch work (1hdc, 1ch, 1dc, 1ch and 1tr), *skip next 2 sts, sl st into next st, (1hdc, 1ch, 1dc, 1ch and 1tr) into same st as sl st, rep from * to end.

Edging 9 More loops, but this time formed by chain stitches. Work 1sc into first st, *3ch, sl st into same st where last sc was worked, skip next st, 1sc into next st, rep from * to end.

Edging 10 The stitches in each group form a shell. Join in yarn and into 3rd st from hook work (2dc, 1ch, 1tr, 1ch, 2dc), *skip next 2 sts, sl st into next st, skip 2 sts, (2dc, 1ch, 1tr, 1ch, 2dc) into next st, rep from * to end.

Edging 11 This edging gives an unusual geometric outline. *Work 7ch, into 3rd ch from hook work 1sc, 1hdc into next ch, 1dc into next ch, 1tr into next ch, 1dtr into next ch, skip next 3 sts, sl st into next st, rep from * to end.

Edging 12 Here a cluster of stitches gives an interesting variation. Work 2ch, skip first st, 1hdc into next st, *(yo and insert hook into the ch sp at right of hdc just worked from front to back, yo and draw through a loop) 3 times, yo and draw through all 7 loops on hook, 1ch, skip next st, 1hdc into next st, rep from * to end.

SIMPLE BRAIDS AND CORDS

Decoration plays an important part in style today, both for the fashions we wear and for our home decor. Interesting types of decoration are braids and cords. Here we shall tell you how to work a number of different kinds of this type of trim, any of them suitable for any type of garment.

A braid is usually considered to be a narrow piece of work made in a chosen yarn to complement that used on the main fabric, and applied either as a binding to cover or finish a raw edge, or as a trim on the fabric. The color, texture and width of the braid should be chosen carefully to coordinate it with the fabric with which it is to be used and the trimming design used should be worked out with thought to the appearance of the total garment.

The cords illustrated in this chapter can be used for any form of tie lacing or decoration and several strips of cord can be applied one alongside of the other to produce an interesting trim of wider proportion.

Sample 1

This is a simple cord made with a size G hook and Knitting Worsted. Work a length of chain, and then slip stitch back along the length by placing the hook into the loop on the reverse side of each chain.
chain.

Sample 2

Make a length of chain in the same way as sample 1 and then slip stitch back along the length by placing the hook into the single top loop on the front of each chain. The reverse side of this chain has been illustrated here and shows an attractive knotted effect.

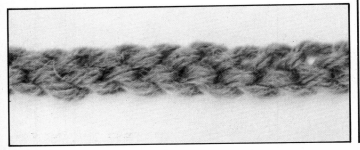

Sample 3

Using size G hook and Knitting Worsted, make a length of chain, working very loosely. When the chain is the desired length, draw four thicknesses of a chenille yarn through the chain stitches.

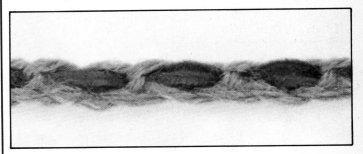

Sample 4

In this sample four thicknesses of chenille yarn are threaded into the cord as you are working it. Using size G hook and Knitting Worsted, make a length of chain, passing the chenille back and forth over the incoming yarn behind the hook between every two stitches worked. The reverse side of this chain has been illustrated.

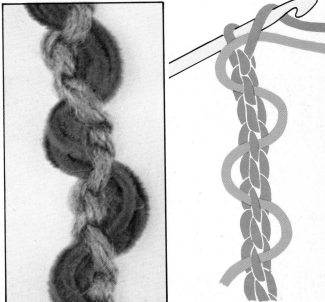

Sample 5

This attractive beaded cord has been worked in a similar way to sample 4. Thread small wooden beads onto a separate length of yarn. Using a size G hook and Knitting Worsted, make a length of chain and while you are working, pass a doubled length of beaded yarn back and forth between every four chain stitches. In the illustrated sample below the beads have been positioned in groups of five followed by groups of three on either side of the chain.

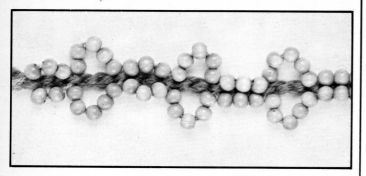

Sample 6

This sample has been worked with a modern interpretation of a "lucet" which is an old-fashioned tool for making a chain type cord. It is usually in the shape of a lyre, and is also known as a "chain fork". However, two crochet hooks placed together, as shown in our illustration, can be used to make this cord.

Rug wool has been used for this particular cord and two size K crochet hooks and one in size B. Place a slip loop on the left hand hook, and then hold the two hooks together. Wrap the yarn behind the right hook and in front of the left hook. Hold the yarn behind the hooks and using the smaller hook slip the loop on the left hook over the yarn. *Place yarn behind the right hook in front of both loops, holding it behind the hooks, then slip the under loop over the top loop on both hooks. *. Repeat from * to * for the required length.

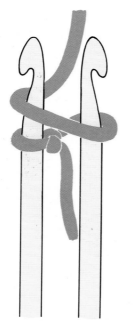

Sample 7

Here the same method as sample 6 is illustrated

using two size H hooks in place of the lucet, Knitting Worsted and a size B hook for working the chain.

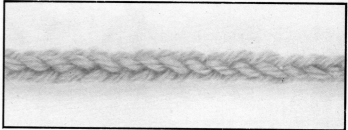

Sample 8

Using two size J hooks in place of the lucet, two thicknesses of Knitting Worsted together and a size B hook, place a slip loop on the left hook behind and then around the left hook from behind as in the illustration. Slip the under loop over the top loop on both hooks. *. Repeat from * to * for the desired length. This forms a very firm cord suitable for a tie belt.

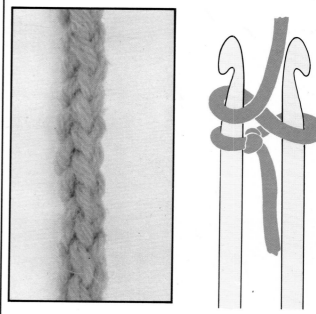

Sample 9

After the completion of a braid made with a lucet, a narrow ribbon has been threaded in and out of the chain, and then it has been drawn through tightly, thus producing a zigzag effect.

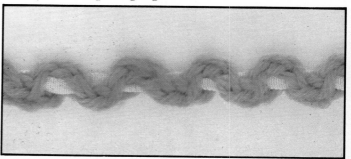

INTRICATE BRAIDS

Here are some braids and trimmings more intricate than the simple cords suitable for lacing and ties described in the last chapter. The samples in this chapter are worked in a different way and produce slightly wider trimmings which are suitable for clothes, as well as lampshades and window blind hems. Again, remember that the choice of yarn you use for working the trimming is very important and that it should complement the fabric on which it will be used.

Sample 1

A very attractive braid is formed by a new technique where the work is turned after each individual stitch has been made. Using a size G hook and Knitting Worsted, make a slip loop on the hook. Yo and draw through loop, insert hook into first loop made, yo and draw through loop, yo and draw through both loops on hook. Turn work. Insert hook from right to left into the small loop on the left hand side, yo and draw through a loop, yo and draw through both loops on hook. Turn work. *Insert hook from right to left into the two loops on the left hand side, yo and draw through a loop, yo and draw through both loops on hook. Turn work. *. Repeat from * to * for required length of braid.

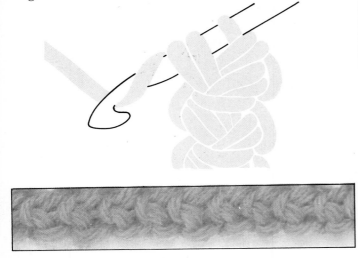

Sample 2

Both sides of this unusual braid are illustrated here, since each has a completely different appearance. Using two thicknesses of Knitting Worsted and a size

H hook, make a slip loop on the hook. Yo and draw through loop, insert hook into first loop made, yo and draw through loop, yo and draw through both loops on hook. Turn work. Insert hook from right to left into the small loop on the left hand side, yo and draw through a loop, yo and draw through both loops on hook. Turn work. *Insert hook from right to left into the two loops on the left hand side as given for sample 1, yo and draw through a loop, yo and draw through both loops on hook. *. Turn work from right to left. Repeat from * to *. Turn work from left to right. Continue in this way, turning work alternately from right to left and then from left to right for the desired length of the cord. One good way of using this braid is for trimming a pocket as shown in our illustration.

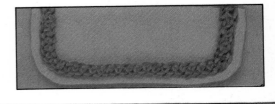

Sample 3

This is worked in the same way as sample 1, but in double instead of single crochet. When finished, a double length of mohair yarn has been threaded through the vertical loops on the surface.

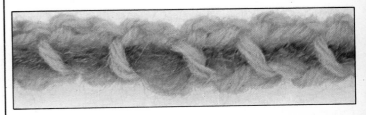

Sample 4

Using a very thick embroidery yarn and a size H hook, work in the same way as sample 1, using half double crochets instead of single crochets.

Sample 5

Here is a very pretty shell design which is very easy to make. Using a size G hook and Knitting Worsted, make 8ch. Join with a sl st into first ch to form a ring. 3ch to count as first dc, work 7dc into ring, 6ch, work 1sc into ring. Turn work. *3ch to count as first sc, work 7dc into 6ch sp, 6ch, 1sc into 6ch sp. Turn work. *. Repeat from * to * for the desired length.

Sample 6

Using two thicknesses of Knitting Worsted and a size H hook, make 4ch. Into 4th ch from hook work 1dtr and 1sc. Turn work. *3ch, into sc work 1dtr and 1sc. Turn work. *. Repeat from * to * for the desired length. This produces a thick, chunky accordion type braid.

Sample 7

Straw has been used for this braid to give a shiny and crinkly texture. Using a size H hook work in the same way as sample 1, but instead of single crochet make a 7 loop double by placing (yo insert hook into stitch, yo and draw through a loop) 3 times, yo and draw through all 7 loops.

Sample 8

Bobble stitches give an interesting chunky look to this braid. Using size H hook and two thicknesses of Knitting Worsted, make 2ch. (Yo and insert into first ch worked, yo and draw through a loop) 3 times, yo and draw through all loops on hook, 3ch, 1sc into first ch worked. Turn work. *(Yo and insert into 3ch sp, yo and draw through a loop) 3 times, yo and draw through all loops on hook, 3ch, 1sc into 3ch sp. Turn work. *. Continue in this way for the required length. You will note that the bobbles lie in an alternating

pattern with the outer edges forming gently scalloped lines on either side of the braid.

Sample 9

An interesting frieze has been created by working crochet stitches within a border. Using size G hook and Knitting Worsted, make a chain the desired length with multiples of 4 stitches.

1st row Into 3rd ch from hook work 1sc, 1sc into each ch to end. Turn.

2nd row 4ch, skip first 2sc, *leaving last loop of each on hook work 2tr into next sc, yo and draw through all 3 loops – called a joint tr –, 3ch, work a joint tr into same sc as before, skip next 3sc, rep from * finishing with 1tr into last sc. Turn.

3rd row Work 1sc into each st to end of row. Fasten off.

Sample 10

Two colors of Knitting Worsted, A and B, create an unusual effect in this braid. Using a size G hook and A, make 5ch.

1st row Into 2nd ch from hook work 1sc, 1hdc into next ch, 1dc into next ch, leaving the last loop of each on hook work 3tr into next ch, yo and draw through all loops on hook. Turn.

2nd row Join in B. *Work 1sc into first st, 1tr into next st, 1dc into next st, leaving the last loop of each on hook work 3tr into next st, yo and draw through all loops on hook. Turn. *.

3rd row Join in A. Rep from * to * of 2nd row.
Repeat 2nd and 3rd rows for the desired length.

Note Always work over the color not in use to keep the loose ends of yarn behind the work.

BRAIDS USING RIBBON

Braids using ribbons

Most of the braids illustrated here can be used for either a trimming added to a garment, or a chosen sample could be incorporated as part of the design of a garment and worked in with the regular crochet stitches. They can be used as trimmings around the hemline of a plain skirt, pants or vests. If the braid is placed on the waistline of a garment, then the ribbon can act as a drawstring at the waist.

Sample 1

This demonstrates the basic technique used in this chapter, and the samples following show developments of this method of work.
Using size F hook and a cotton yarn, make a length of chain with multiples of 2 stitches.
1st row Into 3rd ch from hook work 1hdc, 1hdc into each ch to end. Turn.
2nd row 4ch to count as first dc and ch sp, skip first 2 sts, 1dc into next st, *1ch, skip next st, 1dc into next st, rep from * to end. Turn.
3rd row 2ch to count as first hdc, 1hdc into each ch sp and dc, ending with 1hdc into 4ch sp, 1hdc into 3rd of 4ch. Fasten off.
The ribbon has been threaded through alternate double crochet in the 2nd row.

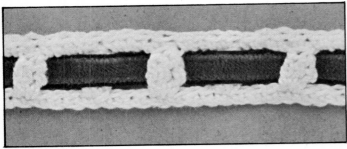

Sample 2

Using size C hook and a cotton yarn, make a chain with multiples of 4 +2 stitches.
1st row Into 3rd ch from hook work 1sc, 1sc into each ch to end. Turn.

2nd row 4ch to count as first tr, 2tr leaving last loop of each st on hook into st at base of ch, yo and draw through all loops on hook, *ch, skip next 3 sts, 3tr leaving last loop of each on hook into next st, yo and draw through all loops on hook rep from * to end. Turn.
3rd row 1ch to count as first sc, 1sc into each st to end. Fasten off.
Velvet ribbon has been threaded in and out of alternate treble groups.

Sample 3

Using size C hook and a cotton yarn, make a length of chain with multiples of 6 +3 stitches.
1st row Into 3rd ch from hook work 1sc, 1sc into each ch to end. Turn.
2nd row 1ch to count as first sc, 1sc into each st to end. Turn.
3rd row As 2nd.
4th row 1ch to count as first sc, 1sc into each st working into same sts as for 3rd row — this gives a very firm ridge. Turn.
5th row 6ch to count as first st and ch sp, skip first 2 sts, *yo 5 times, insert hook into next st, yo and draw through a loop, (yo and draw through first 2 loops on hook) 6 times — called 1dc5 —, (1ch, skip next st, 1dc5 into next st) twice, 1ch, yo twice, take hook in front of last 3 vertical bars worked to the back, yo and draw through a loop, yo and draw through one loop, yo twice, skip next st, insert hook into next st, yo and draw through a loop, (yo and draw through first 2 loops on hook) 6 times, rep from * to end, beg each new rep with first 1dc5 into same st as last 1dc5. Turn.
6th row 1ch to count as first sc, 1sc into each st to end. Turn.
7th row 1ch to count as first sc, 1sc into each st working into same sts as for 6th row. Turn.
8th and 9th rows As 2nd. Fasten off.
Ribbon has been threaded through alternate groups of crossed stitches.

Sample 4

Using size C hook and a cotton yarn, make a length of chain with multiples of 6 + 2 stitches.

1st to 3rd rows As 1st to 3rd rows of sample 3.

4th row 9ch, skip first 6 sts, sl st into next st, *9ch, skip next 5 sts, sl st into next st, rep from * to end. Turn.

5th row 1ch to count as first sc, 10sc into first 9ch sp, 11sc into each 9ch sp to end. Turn. Fasten off.

6th row Join yarn into 3rd st of first sp between half circles, *9ch, sl st into 3rd ch of next sp passing ch length in front of work, rep from * taking the ch length behind and in front of work alternately. Turn.

7th row As 5th.

8th row Make a slip loop on the hook, 2ch, ss into 6th sc of first half circle, *2ch, sl st into 6th sc of next half circle, rep from * to end, 2ch. Turn.

9th row 1ch to count as first sc, 1sc into each st to end. Turn.

10th and 11th rows As 9th.

This braid is reversible and grosgrain ribbon has been threaded through as illustrated.

Sample 5

Using size E hook and Knitting Worsted, make 2ch. (Yo and insert hook into first ch worked, yo and draw through a loop) 3 times, yo and draw through all loops on hook, 3ch, 1sc into first ch worked. Turn. *(Yo and insert hook into ch sp, yo and draw through a loop) 3 times, yo and draw through all loops on hook, 3ch, 1sc into same ch sp. Turn. * Rep from * to * for required length.

Double cord has been threaded in and out of the chain spaces.

Sample 6

Using size E hook and Knitting Worsted, make a length of chain with multiples of 4 + 3 stitches.

1st row Into 5th ch from hook work 1sc, *1ch, skip next ch, 1sc into next ch, rep from * to end. Turn.

2nd row *5ch, 3tr into 4th ch from hook, skip next ch sp, 1sc into next ch sp, rep from * to end. Break off yarn.

3rd row Rejoin yarn to other side of foundation ch and rep 2nd row, working the sc into the sp skipped on that row.

A narrow velvet ribbon has been threaded in a spiral over the center core, working in and out of the spaces below the trebles.

Sample 7

This sample is worked with a size E hook and Knitting Worsted.

1st line *6ch, (yo and insert hook into first ch, yo and draw through a loop) 3 times, yo and draw through all loops on hook, rep from * for required length.

2nd line *3ch, sl working loop off hook and insert into next 6ch sp of first line, pick up working loop and draw through to front of work, 3ch, (yo and insert hook into first ch worked, yo and draw through a loop) 3 times, yo and draw through all loops on hook, rep from * joining each 6ch length to the next 6ch sp of the 1st row. Fasten off. Narrow velvet ribbon has been threaded in and out between the 6 chain spaces.

Hatband with leather trim

Size
1in wide by 23in long

Gauge
12sts to 3.9in and 1 row to 1in worked on size F crochet hook.

Materials
Approximately 9yds of garden twine

Approximately 4yds of leather thonging for trimming
Size F crochet hook

Hatband
Using size F hook and twine, make 72ch.
1st row Into 6th ch from hook work 1dc, 1ch, skip 1ch, 1dc into next ch, rep from * to end.

Fasten off.

To finish
Block with a warm iron under a damp cloth. Darn in ends.
Leather thonging Cut leather thonging into 3 lengths. Thread through holes on hatband, leaving ends to tie at center back.

EDGINGS FOR LINEN

Crochet trimmings for household linens

The theme of this chapter centers around trims on household linens. The samples illustrated are worked in white since traditionally these "laces" would have been used on white linen sheets and pillowcases. Even though the trend today is for colored and patterned bed linen, however, the white trimmings can still make attractive decoration or colored yarn can be used.

Before starting to work you must first decide where the trim is to be placed, and whether it is to be on the edge of the work or within the main fabric. This will determine if you should use a trim with a definite straight edge (the other edge being curved, scalloped, pointed or fringed) which can be sewn onto the edge of an article or a double sided trim (the two edges being exactly the same) which is suitable for an insertion on the main fabric and is usually placed within a border of the hem.

All the designs illustrated may be used as an edging, or can be made into a double sided trim by repeating the design on the opposite side of the foundation chain, as in sample 7. Always remember to wash and block all trimmings before sewing them to the linen to prevent them from shrinking during laundering.

Sample 1

Using size E hook and a cotton yarn, make a length of chain with multiples of 4 + 3 stitches.
1st row Into 3rd ch from hook work 1hdc, 1hdc into each ch to end. Turn.
2nd row 2ch to count as first hdc, 1hdc into next hdc, *6ch, into 4th ch from hook work 1dc, 1dc into each of next 2ch, skip 2hdc, 1hdc into each of next 2hdc, rep from * ending with last hdc into top of turning ch. Fasten off.

Sample 2

Using size E hook and a cotton yarn, make a length of chain with multiples of 6 + 8 stitches.

1st row Into 8th ch from hook work 1dc, *2ch, skip next 2ch, 1dc into next ch, rep from * to end. Turn.
2nd row *3ch, 3tr into next ch sp, 3ch, 3sc into next ch sp, rep from * to last ch sp, 3ch, 3tr into last ch sp, 3ch, sl st into ch sp. Fasten off.

Sample 3

Using size E hook and a cotton yarn, make a length of chain with multiples of 6 + 4 stitches.
1st row Into 6th ch from hook work 1dc, *1ch, skip next ch, 1dc into next ch, rep from * to end. Turn.
2nd row Sl st into first ch sp and into next dc, *5ch, skip next ch sp, (sl st into each of next dc and ch sp) twice, sl st into next dc, rep from * finishing with 3 sl st instead of 5 at end of last rep. Turn.
3rd row *Into next 5ch sp work 5dc, 5ch, sl st into 4th ch from hook, 1ch and 5dc, sl st into 3rd of next 5 sl st, rep from * to end. Fasten off.

Sample 4

Using size E hook and a cotton yarn, make a length of chain with multiples of 5 + 1 stitches.
1st row Into 3rd ch from hook work 1sc, 1sc into each ch to end. Turn.
2nd row 1ch to count as first sc, skip first st, 1sc into each st to end. Turn.
3rd row As 2nd.
4th row 4ch to count as first tr, 1tr into first st, *skip next 3 sts, leaving last loop of each st on hook work 2tr into next st, yo and draw through all 3 loops on hook – called a joint tr –, 3ch, a joint tr into next st, rep from * to last 4 sts, skip next 3 sts, a joint tr into last st. Turn.
5th row 4ch to count as first tr, 1tr into first st, *3ch, a joint tr into top of next joint tr on previous row, skip next 3 sts, a joint tr into top of next joint tr on previous row, rep from * to last 2tr, 3ch, a joint tr into last 2tr. Turn.
6th–8th rows 1ch to count as first sc, 1sc into each st to end. Turn.
9th row 6ch, skip first 4 sts, sl st into each of next 2 sts, *6ch, skip next 3 sts, sl st into each of next 2 sts, rep from * finishing with a sl st into last st. Turn.

10th row Into each 6ch sp work 3sc, 3ch, 1dc, 3ch and 3sc. Fasten off.

Sample 5

Using size E hook and a cotton yarn, make 13ch.

1st row Into 4th ch from hook work 1dc, 1dc into each of next 3ch, 2ch, skip next 2ch, 1dc into each of next 4ch, 2ch, 1dc into last ch. Turn.

2nd row 3ch, skip ch sp, 1dc into each of next 4dc, 2ch, 1dc into each of next 4dc. Turn.

3rd row 3ch to count as first dc, 1dc into each of next 3dc, 2dc into next 2ch sp, 1dc into each of next 4dc, 5dc into next ch sp at beg of 2nd row, 5dc into next ch sp at end of 1st row. Do not turn.

4th row 1 ch to count as first sc, work 1sc into front loop only of each st to end of row working from left to right instead of right to left. Do not turn.

5th row 3ch to count as first dc, 1dc into each of next 3 sts placing hook into back loop only of each st, 2ch, skip next 2 sts, 1dc into back loop only of next 4 sts, 2ch, 1dc into next st. Turn.

Repeat 2nd through 5th rows for desired length.

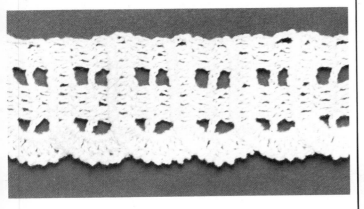

Sample 6

Using size E hook and a cotton yarn, make a length of chain with multiples of 10 + 9 stitches.

1st row Into 5th ch from hook work 1dc, *1ch, skip next ch, 1dc into next ch, rep from * to end. Turn.

2nd row 3ch to count as first dc, 1dc into first ch sp, 3ch, skip next ch sp, *2dc into next ch sp, 3ch, skip next ch sp, rep from * ending with 1dc into last ch sp, 1dc into 4th of 5ch. Turn.

3rd row 4ch, 1dc into first ch sp, *1ch, 1dc into next ch sp, 1ch, 1dc into same ch sp, rep from * to last ch sp, 1ch, 1dc into last ch sp, 1ch, 1dc into 3rd of 3ch. Turn.

4th row 1ch to count as first sc, 2sc into first ch sp, 8ch, *3sc into each of next 3 ch sp, 8ch, rep from * to last ch sp, 2sc into last ch sp, 1sc into 3rd of 4ch. Turn.

5th row Sl st into each sc worked and into each 8ch loop work 2sc, 2hdc, 9dc, 2hdc and 2sc. Fasten off.

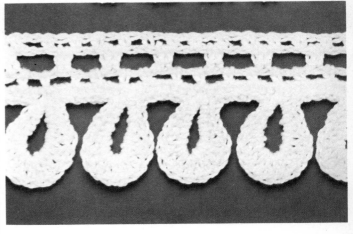

Sample 7

Using size E hook and a cotton yarn, make a length of chain with multiples of 8 stitches.

1st row Into 6th ch from hook work 1dc, *1ch, skip next ch, 1dc into next ch, rep from * to end. Turn.

2nd row 4ch, 1dc into first sp, 1ch, 1dc into next sp, *6ch, skip next sp, 1dc into next sp, 1ch, 1dc into next sp, 1ch, 1dc into next sp, rep from * to end. Turn.

3rd row Sl st into each of next sp, dc and foll sp, * into 6ch sp work 2sc, 2hdc, 5dc, 2hdc and 2sc, sl st into each of next 3 sts, rep from * to end. Turn.

4th row *3ch, 1dc into first dc of 5dc gr, 3ch, 1tr into center dc of gr, 3ch, 1tr into same dc, 3ch, 1dc into last dc of gr, 3ch, 1dc into center sl st, rep from * to end. Turn.

5th row *3sc into each of next 2 sp, into next sp work 3sc, 4ch, sl st into first ch worked so forming a picot and 3sc, 3sc into each of next 2 sp, rep from * to end. Fasten off. This forms a trim with one straight edge, although the crochet design may be worked on the other side of the foundation chain to produce a double sided trim as in our illustration.

EDGINGS FOR SOFT FURNISHINGS

Trimmings for soft furnishings

In the last chapter we showed samples of edgings and double sided braids suitable for trim on household articles. Here we extend the theme to include more decorative and elaborate trimmings, such as deep shaped edgings and crochet braids with long tassels and pompons. This work is ideal for trim on lampshades, both hanging from the ceiling and table lamps, window shades, curtains and valances.

Our samples have been worked in white cotton yarns, although certain other colors and types of yarn are quite suitable for most of the designs. One word of caution in this work is to choose a yarn that will not fray since tassels and pompons have cut edges that might easily shred with the use of the wrong yarn.

Sample 1

Using size E hook and a cotton yarn, make a length of chain with multiples of 2 stitches.

1st row Into 3rd ch from hook work 1sc, 1sc into each ch to end. Turn.

2nd row 1ch to count as first sc, skip 1sc, 1sc into each sc to end. Turn.

3rd row 4ch to count as first dc and sp, skip first 2sc, 1dc into next sc, *1ch, skip next sc, 1dc into next sc, rep from * to end. Turn.

4th row 3ch to count as first dc, *(yo and insert hook into next ch sp, yo and draw through a loop) 4 times, yo and draw through all loops on hook, 1ch, rep from * omitting 1ch at end of last rep and ending with 1dc into 3rd of 4ch. Turn.

5th row 4ch to count as first dc and sp, *skip next bobble, 1dc into next ch, 1ch, rep from * omitting 1ch at end of last rep and ending with last dc into 3rd of 3ch. Fasten off.

Fringe Cut 5 lengths of yarn each 5in long and fold in half lengthwise. Insert folded end through ch sp in the 5th row, then pull the cut ends through the loop. Pull up tightly. Repeat into each ch sp along the row. Trim ends to an equal length.

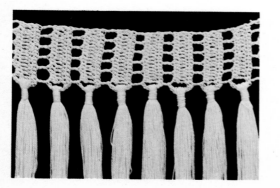

Sample 2

Using size E hook and a cotton yarn, make a length of chain with multiples of 4 +1 stitches.

1st–2nd rows As 1st–2nd rows of sample 1.

3rd row (crossed double trebles) Sl st into each of first 4 sts, 5ch to count as first dtr, yo 3 times, insert hook behind ch length into next st at right of ch just worked, yo and draw through a loop, (yo and draw through first 2 loops on hook) 4 times − called 1dtr −, work 1dtr into each of next 2 sts to the right of last dtr, *skip 3 sts to left of first dtr, 1dtr into next st, 1dtr into each of next 3 sts to the right of last dtr always placing hook behind the last st worked, rep from * to end. Turn.

4th row 1ch to count as first sc, 1sc into each st to end. Turn.

5th row As 4th.

6th row 6ch, skip first 2 sts, sl st into next st, *3ch, skip next st, sl st into next st, 6ch, skip next st, sl st into next st, rep from * to end. Fasten off.

Fringe Work as given for sample 1, and thread through each 6ch loop on 6th row.

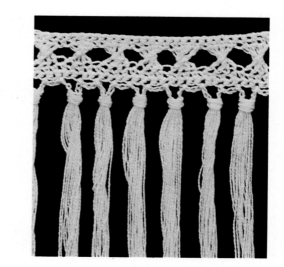

Sample 3

Using size E hook and a cotton yarn, make 20ch.

1st row Into 8th ch from hook work 1dc, *2ch, skip 2ch, 1dc into next ch, rep from * to end. Turn.

2nd row 1ch to count as first sc, skip first st, 1sc into each st to last ch sp, 2sc into ch sp, 1sc into 5th of 7ch. Turn.

3rd row 3ch to count as first dc, skip first st, 1dc into each st to end of row. Turn.

4th row As 2nd row, working last sc into 3rd of 3ch, but do not turn, 5ch, sl st into base of first sc in 2nd row, 7ch, sl st into top of last sc worked. Turn.

5th row 5ch, skip first 3 sts, 1dc into next st, *2ch, skip next 2 sts, 1dc into next st, rep from * to end. Fasten off. The 2nd through 5th rows inclusive form the pattern and are repeated for the desired length.

Fringe Cut yarn into 12in lengths and using 34 of these lengths together place over a length of double chain. Tie very securely in place below the chain. Repeat into each length of double chain along the row, and then trim the ends.

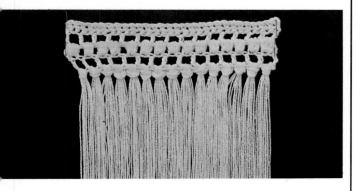

Sample 4

Using size F hook and a thick cotton yarn, make a chain the desired length with multiples of 4+3 stitches.

1st row Into 3rd ch from hook work 1sc, 1sc into each ch to end. Turn.

2nd row (crossed double crochet) Sl st into each of first 2 sts, 3ch to count as first dc, placing the hook behind the length of chain work 1dc into next st to the right of the chain, * skip next stitch to left of first dc, 1dc into next st, placing the hook in front of the last dc worked, 1dc into next st to the right, skip next st, 1sc into next st, placing the hook behind the last dc worked, 1dc into next st to the right, rep from * to end. Turn.

3rd row 1ch to count as first sc, 1sc into each st to end. Turn.

4th row 6ch, skip first 4sts, 1sc into next st, * 5ch, skip 3 sts, 1sc into next st, rep from * to end. Fasten off.

Pompons Cut two circular pieces of cardboard both 2 inches in diameter and make a hole, 1 inch in diameter in the centers of each piece. Use the circles to make pompons in the usual manner, then work a length of chain for attaching them on to the 5ch loops of the 4th row.

Sample 5

This is a variation of the traditional filet crochet known as filet guipure. The techniques of working filet crochet are described in detail earlier. Here we give you a chart comprising blocks and spaces for you to follow. Our spaces are formed by one double crochet at either side of two chain, and blocks are spaces filled in with two trebles. Also in this design a double space has been worked in an unusual way by making three chain, then working one single crochet where the usual double crochet would be, three more chain and the next dc in its usual position. On the following row five chain will be worked above this particular group. This variation is shown on the chart below by the symbols on the diagram.

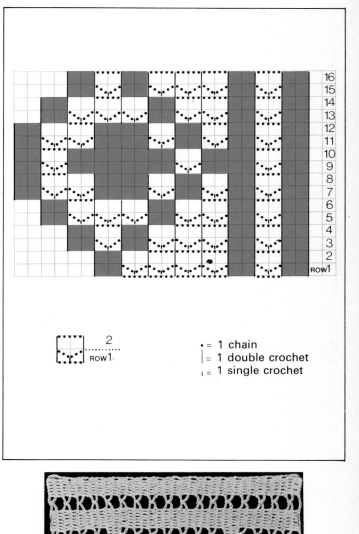

• = 1 chain
| = 1 double crochet
ı = 1 single crochet

FRINGES

Continuing our chapters on trimmings and braids, we now give you instructions for making more of them, this time using fringes as the focal point. These are formed during the working of the crochet by the unusual technique of twisting the yarn to form the fringe. It is a method which requires some practice in order to master the work. Depending on the yarn chosen, the fringes are suitable for both household and dress trimmings.

Sample 1

Using size F hook and a rayon yarn, make a chain the desired length.

1st row Into 3rd ch from hook work 1hdc and 1hdc in each ch to end. Turn.

2nd row (loop row); 1ch to count as first st, skip first st, insert hook into next st, yo and draw through a loop, yo and draw through both loops on hook extending loop on hook for 6in, hold work over st with thumb and first finger of left hand, and with the hook in the extended loop, twist in a clockwise direction approx 24 times, halve the twisted yarn, placing the hook into the last st worked, the extended st will twist

firmly in an anti-clockwise direction, yo and draw through both loops on hook, rep from * to end of row. Fasten off. This completes the fringe.

Note The depth of fringe will depend on the length of the extended stitch and the number of times that it is twisted. You must practice this stitch to obtain perfect results.

Sample 2

Using size F hook and a rayon yarn, make a chain the desired length.

1st row Into 4th ch from hook work 1hdc, 1dc into each ch to end. Turn.

2nd row Work loop row as for sample 1. Fasten off. Velvet ribbon, $\frac{1}{2}$in wide, is drawn through between every other double crochet in the 1st row.

Sample 3

Using size F hook and a Knitting Worsted yarn, make a chain the desired length.

1st row Work a length of braid as for sample 1 of Chapter on "Intricate braids". Fasten off. Join in a different color of rayon yarn and work the loop row as foll:

2nd row Insert the hook into the loop at the top right hand edge of the braid and work a twisted loop as for sample 1, extending the loop for 5in, then insert the hook into the next loop, this time at the lower edge of the braid and make a twisted loop thus forming a stitch over the braid. Continue in this way, working a twisted loop into every other stitch along the top and bottom edges of the braid.

Fasten off.

Sample 4

Using a size F hook and Knitting Worsted, make a length of chain with multiples of 4+2 stitches.

1st row Into 3rd ch from hook work 1sc, 1sc into each st to end. Turn.

2nd row 1ch to count as first sc, skip first st, 1sc into next st, *1dtr into next st, 1sc into each of next 3 sts, rep from * to last 3 sts, 1dtr into next st, 1sc into each of next 2 sts. Turn.

3rd row 1ch to count as first sc, skip first st, 1sc into each st to end. Fasten off.

Join in a different color of rayon yarn and work a loop row as foll:

4th row Work as for loop row of sample 1, placing hook first into (a) next st of last row, then (b) into next st of row below, then (c) into next st of row below that and rep in the order of (b), (a), (b), (c), (b) and (a) for the required length. Fasten off.

Sample 5

Using size F hook and a rayon yarn make a chain of the desired length.

1st row In 4th ch from hook work 1dc, 1dc into each ch to end. Turn.

2nd row 1ch to count as first sc, skip first st, work 1sc into each st to end placing hook from back to front into sp between the regular chain st and the horizontal loop below it, thus giving a raised chain effect on the right side of the work. Turn.

3rd row (loop row): This is slightly different from the loop row of sample 1. Work 4ch to count as first

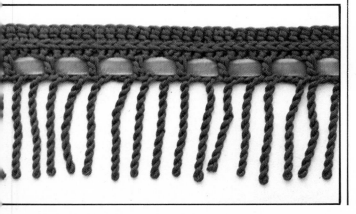

dc and sp, skip first 2 sts, *yo and insert hook in next st, yo and draw through a loop, (yo and draw through first 2 loops on hook) twice, extend loop on hook, twisting it as before, insert hook into last st worked, yo and draw through both loops on hook, 1ch, skip next st, rep from * ending with last dc into turning chain. Fasten off. Velvet ribbon has been drawn through every other double crochet on the loop row.

Sample 6

Using size D hook and a cotton yarn, make a chain of the desired length.

1st row Into 4th ch from hook work 1dc, 1dc in each ch to end. Turn.

2nd row 1ch to count as first sc, 1sc into each st to end. Turn.

3rd row 1ch to count as first sc, 1sc into back loop only of each st to end. Turn.

4th row 2ch to count as first dc, 1dc into each single loop rem from last row—now to the back of the work —to end of row. Turn.

5th row (loop row): Work as given for loop row of sample 1. Fasten off.

6th row (loop row): Rejoin yarn to sts of row 3 on front of braid and work as for loop row of sample 1.

Velvet ribbon has been drawn through every other double crochet in the 1st row.

DECORATIVE FRINGES

Exciting fringes may be worked in many ways and in this chapter we cover a variety of very decorative ones which are most suitable for fashion garments. The fringes illustrated could be used on vests, long scarves, stoles and dresses. Master the techniques described here and when you feel competent, try experimenting with different yarns, beads and threads.

Sample 1

This has been worked in two yarns, a gold ribbon— A and a tubular rayon—B. Using size F hook and B, make 6ch.

1st row Place yarn A between the incoming yarn B and the hook, placing the cut end to the right hand side of the work, 1ch with B, *take yarn A from left to right, placing it between incoming yarn B and the hook, leaving a 3in folded loop, 1ch with B, take yarn A now on the right and place it between the incoming yarn B and the hook leaving no loop, 1ch with B, rep from * for the desired length of fringe, then work 12ch with B. Break off A and reverse work.

2nd row Fold the 12ch length just worked in half and hold in the left hand with the loops to the right, the incoming yarn should be under or behind the work and the hook on top or towards you, *place hook over single thickness of next loop, yo and draw through st on hook, place hook over next single thickness of same loop, yo and draw through st on hook, rep from * to end of loops, then work 12ch and reverse work.

3rd row Fold the 12ch length just worked in half and hold in the right hand with the loops to the left, rep from * of 2nd row to end.

The 2nd and 3rd rows are repeated to give the required proportion of heading to the looped fringe.

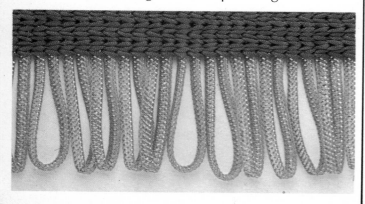

Sample 2

Two types of yarn have been used for this sample,

A for the working yarn and 4 thicknesses of B together for the fringe. Using size E hook and A, make 6ch.

1st row Place yarn B (all 4 thicknesses) between the incoming yarn A and the hook, placing the cut ends to the right hand side of the work, 1ch with A,* take yarn B from left to right placing it between incoming yarn A and the hook, leaving a 3in folded loop, 1ch with A, take yarn B now on the right and place it between the incoming yarn A and the hook leaving no loop, 1ch with A, rep from * for the desired length of fringe, then work 12ch with A. Break off B and reverse work.

2nd row Fold the 12ch length just worked in half and hold in the left hand with the loops to the right, the incoming yarn should be under or behind the work and the hook on top or toward you, * place hook over 4 thicknesses of next loop, yo and draw through st on hook, place hook over next 4 thicknesses of same loop, yo and draw through st on hook, rep from * to end of loops, then work 12ch and reverse work.

3rd row Fold the 12ch length just worked in half and hold in the right hand with the loops to the left, rep from * of 2nd row to end.

The 2nd and 3rd rows are repeated to give the required proportion of heading to the fringe. The loops can either be cut as in our sample or left uncut.

Sample 3

Here is an attractive method of making a beaded fringe. A lurex yarn has been used for the crochet while the beads have been threaded on to a separate length of yarn. The number of beads will of course depend on the amount of fringing required. Using size E hook and lurex yarn, make 6 ch.

1st row With cut end to the right, place yarn with beads between incoming yarn and the hook, 1ch with lurex yarn, *place yarn with beads from left to right, placing 21 beads on a loop plus 1 inch of free yarn, between incoming yarn and hook, 2ch with lurex yarn, place yarn with beads from right to left, leaving no loop between incoming yarn and hook, work 1ch with lurex yarn, rep from * to give desired length of fringe, then work 12ch with lurex yarn. Break off yarn with beads and reverse work.

2nd row Hold the work with the chain heading to the left and beaded loops to the right, work 1ch over next length of yarn with beads, having one bead on the left, *1ch, 1ch over next length of yarn with beads having one bead on the left, rep from * to end of fringe, work 12ch. Reverse work.

3rd row Hold the work with the chain heading to the right and beaded loops to the left, work as for 2nd row. Fasten off.

Note The yarn with beads will require tightening in order to give an all-beaded loop with no yarn showing between the beads.

Sample 4

Using size F hook and Knitting Worsted, make 6ch.

1st row Into 3rd ch from hook work 1sc, 1sc into each ch to end. Turn. 4sts.

2nd row 1ch to count as first sc, skip first st, 1sc into each of next 3 sts. Turn.

3rd row As 2nd.

4th row As 2nd, but do not turn. Work 24ch. Turn.

5th row Into 4th ch from hook work 3dc, 4dc into each of the next 20ch, 1dc into each of next 4 sts. Turn.

The 2nd through 5th rows inclusive are repeated for the length of trimming desired.

Sample 5

To work the braid: Using size F hook and Knitting Worsted make a chain with multiples of 4+2 stitches.

1st row Into 3rd ch from hook work 1sc, 1sc into each ch to end. Turn.

2nd row 1ch to count as first sc, skip first st, 1sc in each st to end. Turn.

3rd row 4ch to count as first dc and sp, skip first 2 sts, *(yo and insert hook into next st, yo and draw through a loop, yo and draw through first 2 loops on hook) 9 times, always inserting hook into same st, yo and draw through all 10 loops on hook, work 1ch very tightly to hold bobble, 1ch, skip next st, 1dc into next st, 1ch, skip next st, rep from * ending with 1dc into last st. Turn.

4th row 1ch to count as first sc, *1sc into next ch sp, 1sc in top of next bobble, 1sc into next ch sp, 1sc into next dc, rep from * to end. Turn.

5th row As 2nd. Fasten off.

To work the crochet balls: Using same yarn and hook, place the cut end of yarn in the palm of left hand and wrap yarn once around first finger, insert hook into loop around finger from underneath, yo and draw through a loop, slip loop off finger and hold between finger and thumb of left hand, *insert hook into ring, yo and draw through a loop, yo and draw through both loops on hook, rep from * 7 times more. Tighten ring by pulling the cut end of yarn. Mark beg of each round with a colored thread.

Next round Work 2sc into each of 8 sts. Do not join.

Next 2 rounds Work 1sc into each of 16 sts. Do not join. Place cotton batting into ball.

Next round (Work 2sc tog) 8 times. Do not join.

Next round Work 1sc into each of 8 sts. Draw sts tog by threading working st through each free st to make a neat end, do not break off yarn, 9ch, sl st to braid below bobble, sl st back along chain to ball, 9ch, skip next bobble on braid, sl st to braid below next bobble, sl st back along chain and fasten to ball. Continue in this way, first fastening each new ball below the bobble omitted in the previous joining, thus forming a cross-over design.

RUFFLES

Crochet ruffles are easy to work and make effective trimmings for a variety of garments. When working a ruffle, choose a yarn which is appropriate for the design and fabric of the main garment, such as a lurex yarn for evening wear or a fine cotton yarn for lingerie. Our samples in the photographs are worked with a size G crochet hook and Knitting Worsted.

Here we explain two methods of making ruffles. One way is to work more than one stitch into each stitch of the previous row, and this is illustrated in samples 1, 2, 4 and 5. Sample 3 demonstrates the method of gathering crochet to form a ruffle. This is simple to work and produces a very attractive trim. Crochet ruffles can be starched before being applied to the garment, if desired.

Sample 1

Make 31ch. This can be made longer by adding multiples of 4 stitches.

1st row Into 3rd ch from hook work 1sc, 1sc into each ch to end. Turn.

2nd row 5ch, skip first 4sc, sl st into next sc, *(5ch, skip 3sc, sl st into next sc), rep from * 5 times more. Turn. Seven 5ch sps.

3rd row 1ch to count as first sc, 7sc into first 5ch sp, 8sc into each 5ch sp to end.

Rep 2nd and 3rd rows now along the opposite side of the foundation chain. Turn.

4th row 4ch to count as first dc and ch, *1dc, 1ch into next sc, rep from * around both sides of foundation chain. Turn.

5th row Using a contrast color, join yarn into first 1ch sp, sl st into same sp, *3ch, sl st into next ch sp, rep from * to end. Fasten off.

This ruffle can be used to trim the center front of a long evening gown.

Sample 2

This ruffle is ideal for a decorative cuff. To work the fabric shown in our sample make 26ch.

1st row Leaving the last loop of each st on hook, work 1dc into each of 4th and 5ch from hook, yo and draw through all 3 loops on hook, 1ch, then * leaving the last loop of each st on hook, work 1dc into each of next 2ch, yo and draw through all 3 loops on hook, 1ch, rep from * to last ch, 1dc into last ch. Turn.

2nd row 3ch to count as first dc, *leaving the last loop of each st on hook, work 2dc into next 1ch sp, yo and draw through all 3 loops on hook, 1ch, rep from * ending with 1dc into 3rd of the turning ch. Turn. The 2nd row is repeated throughout.

To work the ruffle:

1st row 5ch, sl st into top of first pair of dc, *5ch, sl st into top of next pair of dc, rep from * to end. Turn.

2nd row 3ch to count as first dc, 2dc into first sp, 3ch, 3dc into same sp, *2ch, sl st into next sp, 2ch, (3dc, 3ch, 3dc) into next sp, rep from * to end. Turn.

3rd row 1ch to count as first sc, 1sc into each st to end, working 5sc into each 3ch sp. Turn.

4th row 3ch to count as first dc, 1dc in each of next 4 sts, *2dc into each of next 3 sts, 1dc into each of next 13 sts, rep from * ending last rep with 1dc into each of next 3 sts, 1dc into the turning ch. Fasten off.

Sample 3

This sample would also be very effective as a cuff trimming. Using the first color, make a foundation chain to fit the desired measurement; we worked on 30 chain.

1st row Work 1dc by placing the hook under the complete ch so that the st will move freely over the chain when done, *3ch, work 1dc in the same way, rep from * 8 times more. Turn.

2nd row *3ch, sl st into next ch sp, rep from * to end. Turn.

3rd row *5ch, sl st into next ch sp, rep from * to end. Turn.

4th row *7ch, sl st into next ch sp, rep from * to end. Turn.

5th row *9ch, sl st into next ch sp, rep from * to end.

Turn.

6th row *11ch, sl st into next ch sp, rep from * to end. Turn.

7th row Into each 11ch sp work 12sc. Fasten off.

Next row Using second color, join yarn into right hand sp at base of first dc worked on the foundation ch, 6ch to count as first dc and 3ch, 1dc into next sp between dc working over foundation ch as before, *3ch, 1dc into next sp between dc, rep from * to end. Turn.

Next 4 rows Rep 2nd through 5th rows as given for first color.

Next row Into each 9ch sp work 11sc. Fasten off.

Note When using the second color, if the same side of the sc row is to appear on both ruffles then the yarn should be cut and rejoined between the 5th and 6th rows in order to work from the correct side. The double crochets are arranged along the foundation chain to give the desired amount of ruffling.

Sample 4

Worked in a fine yarn, this ruffle would look lovely on a nightgown, or in a thicker yarn, it could be added for trim to a circular hat, such as a beret. The basic fabric in our sample is worked in double crochet with a repeat of 5 stitches plus one. Work your design until the position for the ruffle is reached, then continue as follows:

Next row *5ch, skip next 4 sts, sl st into next st, rep from * to end. Turn.

Next row Into each ch sp work 1sc, 1hdc, 1dc, 3ch, 1dc, 1hdc, 1sc. Turn.

Continue in double crochet until the position for the next ruffle is reached.

Sample 5

This is a narrow ruffle which could be used for any type of trimming. Make a foundation chain the required length of the ruffle.

1st row Into 3rd ch from hook work 1sc, 1sc into each ch to end. Turn.

2nd row *5ch, skip next st, sl st into next st, rep from * to end. Turn.

3rd row Into each ch sp work 1sc, (3ch, 1sc) 5 times. Fasten off.

FINISHING TOUCHES
BUTTONS

Sample 1　　　　　Sample 2　　　　　Sample 3

Covered buttons

So often it is difficult to purchase the right button for a garment that you are making. Sometimes the size is wrong and sometimes you are unable to match the color; there are also times when you would like an unusual button at a reasonable price to be used as an important trim on a simple garment. Crochet covered buttons can be very decorative and can add a great deal to a design.

The wooden or metal forms for covered buttons are available on most notions counters and they come in a variety of shapes and sizes. The method of work is simple, but before starting try a sample piece of crochet with the yarn and hook you are going to use. This sample should look right on the garment for which the buttons are being made, and the crochet fabric should be firm enough entirely to cover the form beneath it. We recommend a smaller size hook than usual in order to achieve a close stitch.

Sample 1

6 yards of Soutache braid is required to cover this large round button which is 1¾in in diameter.

1st round Form a ring with the braid in the left hand, using size D hook, work 8sc into the ring, draw the short end tight to close it. Join with a sl st into first sc.
2nd round 1ch to count as first sc, 1sc into st at base of ch, *2sc into next sc, rep from * to end. Join with a sl st into first sc.
3rd round 1ch, 1sc into st at base of ch, 1sc into next sc, *2sc into next sc, 1sc into next sc, rep from * to end. Join with a sl st into first sc.
4th round 1ch, 1sc into each sc to end. Join with a sl st into first sc.
5th round As 4th.

In this sample the back of the crochet work is the most effective, and we have placed it on the button mold as the right side. Lace the edge of the crochet circle now on to the wrong side of the mold and secure it very firmly in several places around the edges, then place the metal covering disc over the back, or neatly hem a circle of lining fabric to cover the edges. All the following methods of covering buttons should be finished in this way.

Sample 2

This is a more unusual method of working the crochet covering for a 1¾in button. Five shades of yarn and a size E crochet hook are used. Using A, make 7ch.
1st row In 3rd ch from hook work 1sc, 1sc into each ch to end. Turn.
2nd row 1ch to count as first sc, 1sc into st at base of ch, 2sc into each st, ending with 2sc into turning ch. Turn. 12sc.
3rd row 1ch, 1sc into st at base of ch, 1sc into next st, *2sc into next st, 1sc into next st, rep from * ending with 1sc into turning ch. Turn. 18sc.
4th row 1ch, 1sc into st at base of ch, 1sc into each of next 2 sts, *2sc into next st, 1sc into each of next 2 sts, rep from * ending with last sc into turning ch. Turn. Break off A.
5th row Using B, 1ch, skip first st, 1sc into each of next 8 sts, then using C, 1sc into same st as last sc, 1sc into each of next 4 sts, using D, 1sc into same st as last sc, 1sc into each of next 4 sts, using E, 1sc into same st as last sc, 1sc into each of next 7 sts. Turn.
Note When joining in new colors, follow the instructions given earlier.
6th row As 5th, dec one st at each end of row and omitting increased sts between colors.

7th row As 5th, dec one st at each end of row and inc between colors as before.

Dec one st at each end of every row now and, omitting increased sts, continue in this color sequence until there are no sts left. Fasten off.

Sample 3
Eight colors of cotton and a size D hook have been used here to give a subtly shaded look to another 1¾in diameter button. Using a new color for each round, follow the instructions given for 1st–3rd rounds of sample 1. Continue in rounds of sc, working 1 more sc between the increased stitches on each round.

Sample 4
This tiny, ½in diameter button has been delicately covered with a very fine Lurex embroidery thread. Using No. 12 steel hook, work as for sample 3.

Sample 5
Using a Lurex yarn and size D hook, work as for sample 3.

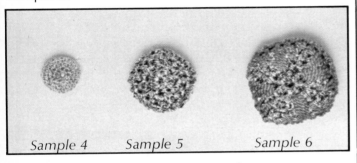

Sample 4   *Sample 5*   *Sample 6*

Sample 6
Lurex and cotton yarns are combined in this design to cover a 1in diameter button. Using size D hook and the Lurex yarn, work as given for 1st–3rd rounds of sample 1.
Break off yarn.
4th round Using cotton yarn, 2ch, *1sc into next st, 1sc into next st inserting hook into 2nd round, 2sc into next st on 1st round, 1sc into next st on 2nd round, 1sc into next st, 1ch, rep from *, omitting 1ch at end of last rep. Join with a sl st into first ch.
5th round 1ch to count as first sc, 1sc into each st to end. Join with a sl st into first ch. Fasten off.

Sample 7
Seven colors of a cotton yarn have been used to cover this square button with varying widths of diagonal stripes. You can change the colors in any way you desire. Using Size D hook make 3ch.
1st row Into 3rd ch from hook work 1sc. Turn.
2nd row 1ch to count as first sc, 1sc into st at base of ch, 2sc into next st. Turn.
3rd row 1ch, 1sc into st at base of ch, 1sc into each st to turning ch, 2sc into turning ch. Turn.
Continue to inc one st at each end of every row in this way until the crochet is the required diagonal width for the button mold, then dec one st at each end of every row until there are no sts left. Fasten off.

Sample 8
This button cover consists of 2 triangular shapes joined together, then decorated with chain stitch. Three colors of cotton yarn, A, B and C and a size D crochet hook are required. Using A, make 15ch.
1st row Into 3rd ch from hook work 1sc, 1sc into each of next 5sts, join in B, 1sc into each of next 7 sts. Turn.
2nd row Using B, 1ch to count as first sc, 1sc into each of next 6 sts, using A, 1sc into each of next 7 sts. Turn. Working in colors as above, dec one st at each end of every row until there are no sts left. Make another triangle in the same way, then crochet the shapes together and, using C, work a chain st over the color join.

Sample 9
Work in the same way as sample 8, using 3 colors for each triangle and begin by working 7sc in A, 3sc in B and 4sc in C. When 2 triangles have been completed, place the alternate color sequence side by side and crochet together.

Sample 7   *Sample 8*   *Sample 9*

FASTENINGS

Crochet fastenings

This chapter illustrates some decorative fastenings achieved by various crochet techniques. These fastenings are useful when working with fabrics where it is difficult to use the more traditional types of fastening, such as fabric or machine-made button-holes.

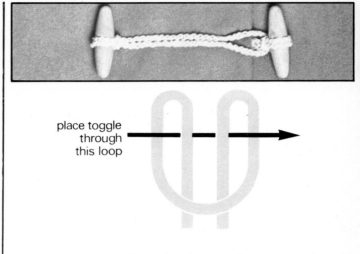

place toggle through this loop ➜

The longer piece of cord is fastened into a circle and looped over a traditional wooden toggle. The cord and toggle are then sewn on to the right hand side of a garment, leaving a loop extension over the outer edge. The shorter piece of cord is not joined into a circle, but is looped over another toggle which is then sewn in position on the left hand side of the garment.

Sample 2

The finished effect of these loops and buttons can be very decorative, this depending on the buttons and yarn you choose to use. To make the loops in our sample you will need a Lurex yarn, a string of medium thickness and a size D crochet hook. Hold the string in the left hand with the cut end to the right and the incoming string to the left. Holding the yarn in the usual way, place the hook under the string, and catch the yarn to form a loop on the hook, place the hook over the string, yo and draw yarn through loop on hook, *place cut end of string in the right hand and continuing to hold incoming yarn in the left hand, place the hook under the string, yo, place the hook

The crochet stitches which have been used are all simple, and have been explained in previous chapters. The important thing to bear in mind when making your fastening for the type of garment you are trimming is just how decorative you want the fastening to be.

Sample 1

This toggle fastening is most suitable for a casual garment. Using string make two lengths of cord, one 7in and the other 12in long, as described in sample 10.

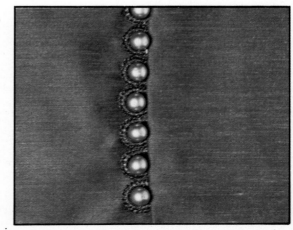

over the string, yo and draw through both loops on hook, rep from * for the required length. (Our sample took approx 2½in of string for each loop.) Position the loops one below another so that the chain extends over the outer edge, on the right side of the fabric, and making all loops an even size, tack them firmly in place as shown in the diagram. With right sides of the fabric together, now tack the facing over the cording and machine stitch it firmly along the stitching line. Line up the extended loop with the left hand side of the garment and attach buttons.

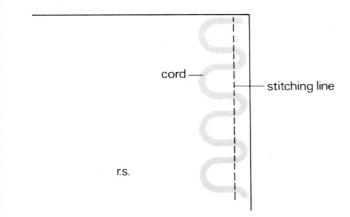

Sample 3

This single frog fastening is still more decorative and could probably be used on its own as trim on an evening cape. Using size D hook and Lurex yarn, work

over piping cord, 15 inches to 20 inches long as explained in sample 2. Then work the second row by turning the work so that you crochet back along the first row, *(yo, insert hook into next st, yo and draw through a loop) 3 times into same st, yo and draw through all loops on hook, sl st into each of next 2 sts, rep from * to end of cord.

Form the cord into the required shape for four loops on the right hand side of the garment, with one loop extending over the outer edge, and sew it firmly in place. Line up the extended loop with the left hand side of the garment and attach button.

Sample 4

For the cord here you will require two lengths of piping cord, one approx 20 inches long and the other approx 17 inches long, a size E crochet hook and a chenille yarn.

Make 4ch. Join with a sl st in first ch to form a ring. Thread piping cord through the ring. Tie an overhand knot about 6 inches from the end of the cord and place the knot behind the ring so that the free-cord is coming towards you.

To work the crochet Insert the hook into the back loop of the first ch, yo and draw through the loop and the st on hook—one sl st has been worked—, *insert the hook into the back or lower single loop of the next st and work one sl st. rep from * working around the cord until the required length has been covered.

Position the longer piece of cord on the right hand side of the garment, forming the desired size of loops, with one loop extending over the outer edge. Sew in place. Line up the extended loop with the left hand side of the garment and position the shorter length of cord to make three loops equal in size to those at the opposite side. A covered button has been sewn on to the join of the loops on both the right and left hand side.

To cover the button shape You will need a 1 inch ball button, some chenille yarn and a size E crochet hook. Form a ring with the yarn in the left hand, work 8sc into the ring, draw the cut end of yarn tightly to close the ring and sl st into the first sc worked.

2nd round 1ch to count as first sc, 1sc into st at base of ch, *2sc into next st, rep from * to end. Join with a sl st to first ch.

3rd round 1ch, 1sc into st at base of ch, 1sc into next st, *2sc into next st, 1sc into next st, rep from * to end. Join with a sl st into first ch.

4th round 1 ch, 1sc into each st to end. Join with a sl st into first ch.

5th round As 4th.

6th round 1ch, work 2sc tog in next 2 sts, *1sc into next st, work 2sc tog in next 2 sts, rep from * to end. Join with a sl st into first ch.

7th round 1ch, *work 2sc tog in next 2 sts, rep from * to last st, 1sc into last st. Join with a sl st into first ch. Fasten off.

FLOWERS

Fluted crochet

Flowers for trim are very much a part of the fashion scene. They are used on day and evening dresses, and on hats and other accessories. Most commercial flowers are made of fabric, but here we illustrate how you can make your own by using the technique of fluted crochet.

The type of yarn you choose for making your flower will depend on the type of garment you want to trim, and might be a crisp cotton for a hatband or a glitter yarn for an evening outfit. A selection of centers for different flowers are shown.

5th round Sl st into each of first 3ch of next loop, sl st into center of same loop, 7ch, *sl st into center of next ch loop, 7ch, rep from * to end. Join with a sl st into sl st at center of first loop. Fasten off.

2nd circle Using size F hook and a 4 ply yarn make 5ch. Join with a sl st into first ch to form a ring.

1st round 1ch to count as first sc, 20sc into ring. Complete as given for 1st circle.

Finishing: Place the larger, more fluted circle over the first circle and sew the centers together. In our sample wooden beads in groups of three, five and seven on a loop have been used as additional decoration.

1st flower

This flower consists of two circles.

1st circle Using size F hook and a 4 ply yarn, make 5ch. Join with a sl st into first ch to form a ring.

1st round 1ch to count as first sc, 15sc into ring. Join with a sl st into first ch.

2nd round *4ch, sl st into next sc, rep from * to end. 16ch loops.

3rd round Sl st into each of first 2ch of next loop, sl st into center of same loop, 5ch, *sl st into center of next ch loop, 5ch, rep from * to end. Join with sl st into sl st at center of first loop.

4th round Sl st into each of first 3ch of next loop, sl st into center of same loop, 6ch, *sl st into center of next ch loop, 6ch, rep from * to end. Join with a sl st into sl st at center of first loop.

2nd flower

Using size F hook and a 4 ply yarn, make 6ch. Join with a sl st into first ch to form a ring.

1st round 1ch to count as first sc, 20sc into ring. Join with a sl st into first ch.

2nd round 3ch to count as first dc, 1dc into st at base of ch, *2dc into next sc, rep from * to end. Join with a sl st into 3rd of 3ch. 42 sts.

3rd round 3ch to count as first dc, 1dc into st at base of ch, *2dc into next dc, rep from * to end. Join with a sl st into 3rd of 3ch. 84 sts.

4th round As 3rd. 168 sts.

5th round 1ch to count as first sc, 1sc into each of next 9 sts, insert hook from front to back into next st, skip next 9 sts, insert hook from front to back into next st, yo and draw through first 2 loops on hook, yo and draw through both loops on hook, *1sc into each of next 10 sts, insert hook from front to back into next st, skip next 9 sts, insert hook from back to front into next st, yo and draw through first 2 loops on hook, yo and draw through both loops on hook, rep from * to end. Fasten off.

Finishing Make the tufted center by cutting 40 lengths of yarn, each 3 inches long, and firmly bind them together around the center with another piece of yarn. Fold the lengths in half and insert the bound section into the center of the flower.

3rd flower

Using size D hook and a Lurex yarn, make 6ch. Join with a sl st into first ch.

1st round 1ch to count as first sc, 17sc into ring.

2nd round 5ch, skip next 2sc, *1sc into next sc, 4ch, skip next 2sc, rep from * to end. Join with a sl st into 2nd of first 5ch. 6ch loops.

3rd round *Into next 4ch loop work 1sc, 1hdc, 5dc, 1hdc and 1sc, rep from * to end. Join with a sl st into first sc.

4th round *5ch, pass this ch length behind next gr of sts and work 1sc in next sc of 2nd round, inserting the hook from behind, rep from * to end.

5th round *Into next 5ch loop work 1sc, 1hdc, 10dc, 1hdc and 1sc, rep from * to end. Join with a sl st into first sc.

6th round *7ch, pass this ch length behind next gr of sts and work 1sc into next sc of 4th round, inserting the hook from behind, rep from * to end.

7th round *Into next 7ch loop work 1sc, 1hdc, 15dc, 1hdc and 1sc, rep from * to end. Join with a sl st into first sc.

8th round *8ch, pass this ch length behind next gr of sts and work 1sc into next sc of 6th round, inserting the hook from behind, rep from * to end.

9th round *Into next 8ch loop work 1sc, 1hdc, 5dc, 10tr, 5dc, 1hdc and 1sc, rep from * to end. Join with a sl st into first ch. Fasten off.

A large pearl bead makes an attractive center to this silver flower.

4th flower

Here is an unusual method of working a chrysanthemum. Using size D hook and a cotton yarn, make 21ch. Skip first ch, sl st into each ch to end, turn.
Skip first st, sl st into each of next 2 sts, inserting hook into back loop only of each st, work 17ch, skip first ch, sl st into loop at back of each ch to end, turn. Rep from * to * until approximately 60 to 70 petals have been completed. Fasten off.

Finishing Beginning at one end of the work, twist the base of all the petals around, until they are placed as desired, then sew together.

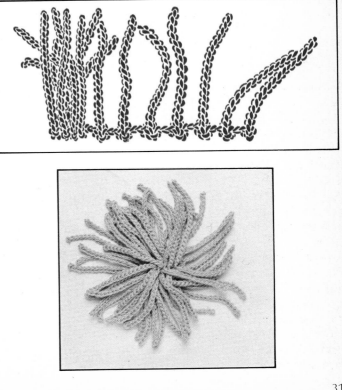

AFGHAN CROCHET
BASIC STEPS

Afghan stitch is a form of work which can look like either crochet or knitting. It is also known as Tunisian crochet. The special tool used for this craft is a single hooked afghan crochet hook. These hooks are extra long to accommodate the large number of stitches in use with this stitch and they come in a size range with the smallest starting at E and then grading up to F, G, H, I, J and K. The fabric produced with this method is very strong and firm and, depending on the stitch used, the finished appearance can resemble crochet or look deceptively like knitting. It is ideal for making fabrics for house furnishings and is also suitable for heavier outer garments where the intricacies of fine detail would be superfluous. Several basic points make this form of crochet different from ordinary crochet, and they should be referred to throughout all afghan stitch instructions.

a) When making an initial length of chain stitches to begin work, you will not require any extra chains for turning, i.e. a chain length of 20 will give you exactly 20 working stitches.

b) The work is not turned at the end of each row, and the right side of the work faces you throughout.

c) afghan stitch is worked in pairs of rows, with the first row worked from right to left and then another row worked from left to right to complete the stitches.

d) Apart from a very small number of exceptions, no turning chains are required at the beginning of each new row.

To work the basic afghan stitch:
Using size G afghan hook and Knitting Worsted, make a length of chain.

1st row Working from right to left, skip first ch, insert hook into 2nd ch from hook, yo and draw through a loop, *insert hook into next ch, yo and draw through a loop, rep from * to end of ch, keeping all loops on hook.

2nd row Working from left to right, yo and draw through first 2 loops on hook, *yo and draw through next 2 loops on hook, rep from * to end until one loop remains on hook.

3rd row Working from right to left, skip first vertical bar on the front of the fabric, insert hook from right to left into next vertical bar, yo and draw through a loop, rep from * to end, keeping all loops on hook.

4th row As 2nd.
The 3rd and 4th rows are repeated throughout.

Note Care should be taken to check the number of stitches at the end of each row as it is very easy to miss the last stitch when working the 3rd row.

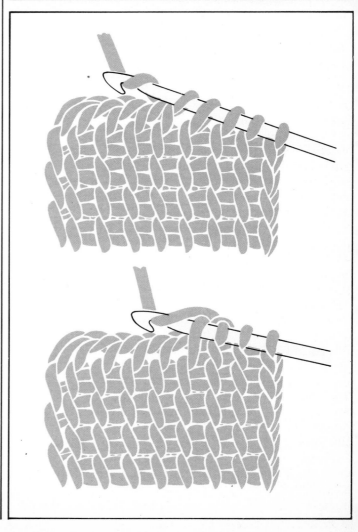

Shaping an afghan stitch

When it is necessary to increase or decrease, this is usually done on the first of the pair of rows you are working.

To increase on the sides of your work fabric: The increased stitch is worked by inserting the hook into the single horizontal loop between two vertical bars.

To increase one stitch at the beginning of a row: This is usually done between the first and second vertical bars.

To increase one stitch at the end of the row: This is usually between the last and next to last vertical bars.

To increase in the middle of a row: One stitch is increased in the middle of a row by inserting the hook into the single horizontal loop between the vertical bars at the point where the increased stitch is required.

To increase more than one stitch at the beginning or end of a row: Remembering that increases are made on the first row of the required pair, to increase several stitches at the beginning of a row, work the extra chain stitches required and go back along these extra chains picking up the working stitches. To increase several stitches at the end of a row complete the row then take a spare length of matching yarn and join this into the last stitch. Work the extra chain stitches required with spare yarn, then continue working into this extra chain length with main yarn.

To decrease on the sides of your work: One stitch is decreased just inside the beginning of a row by inserting the hook into the 2nd and 3rd vertical bars at one time, and then working the stitch in the usual way. At the end of a row the last two stitches before the end stitch are worked together in the same way.

To decrease in the middle of a row: At the required position, decrease one stitch as above.

To decrease more than one stitch at the beginning or end of a row: At the beginning of a row slip stitch over the required number of stitches to be decreased and at the end of a row work until only the required number of stitches to be decreased remains, then work the second of the pair of rows required.

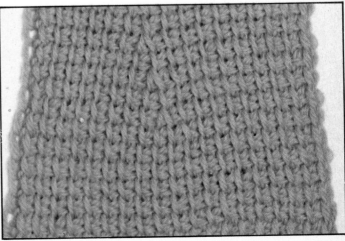

FABRIC STITCHES

An introduction to afghan stitch was made in our last chapter. The stitches may be worked in a variety of ways to give very different patterned effects and textures. These are achieved by different positions of the hook insertion on the first row of the pair necessary for the afghan stitch. For all our samples, it is only the first row which varies, and the second one remains the same throughout.

3rd row *Insert hook into space between vertical bars from front to back, yo and draw through a loop, rep from * to end.
4th row As 2nd.

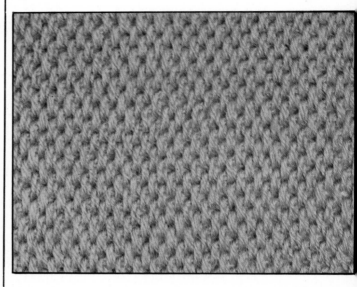

5th row Skip space between first two vertical bars, * insert hook into space between next two vertical bars from front to back, yo and draw through a loop, rep from * to end, inserting hook into last vertical bar.
6th row As 2nd.
The 3rd through 6th rows are repeated throughout.

Sample 2
Using size G afghan hook and Knitting Worsted, make a length of chain.

Sample 1
Using size G afghan hook and Knitting Worsted, make a length of chain.
1st row Insert hook into second ch from hook, yo and draw through a loop, * insert hook into next ch, yo and draw through a loop, rep from * to end.
2nd row Yo and draw through first 2 loops on hook, *yo and draw through next 2 loops on hook, rep from * to end leaving one loop on hook.

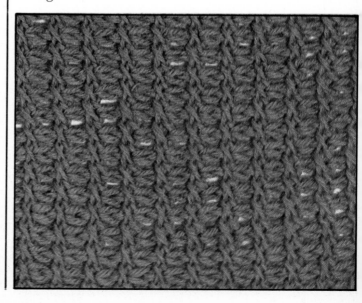

1st-2nd rows As 1st-2nd rows of sample 1.
3rd row Skip first vertical bar, * skip next vertical bar, insert hook from right to left through next vertical bar, yo and draw through a loop, insert hook from right to left through the skipped vertical bar, yo and draw through a loop, rep from * to end, inserting hook in last vertical bar.
4th row As 2nd.
The 3rd and 4th rows are repeated throughout.

Sample 3

Using size G afghan hook and Knitting Worsted, make a length of chain with multiples of 3+2 stitches.
1st-2nd rows As 1st-2nd rows of sample 1.

3rd row Skip first vertical loop, * yarn over hook from front to back, (insert hook into next vertical loop, yo and draw through a loop) 3 times, pass 4th loop from hook from right to left over last 3 loops on the hook, rep from * to end, insert hook into last vertical loop, yo and draw through a loop.
4th row As 2nd.
The 3rd and 4th rows are repeated throughout.

Sample 4

Using size G afghan hook and Knitting Worsted, make a length of chain.
1st-2nd rows As 1st-2nd rows of sample 1.

3rd row Skip first vertical bar, * insert hook directly through center of next vertical bar from front to back

of work, yo and draw through a loop, rep from * to end.
4th row As 2nd.
The 3rd and 4th rows are repeated throughout.

Sample 5

Using size G afghan hook and Knitting Worsted, make a length of chain with multiples of 3+2 stitches.
1st-2nd rows As 1st-2nd rows of sample 1.

3rd row Skip first vertical bar, * insert hook under next three vertical bars, yo and draw through a loop, insert hook under middle loop only of this group of three, yo and draw through a loop, insert hook under first loop only of this group of three, yo and draw through a loop, rep from * to end, then insert hook into last vertical bar, yo and draw through a loop.
4th row As 2nd.
The 3rd and 4th rows are repeated throughout.

DECORATIVE STITCHES

There are so many different patterns to be achieved when working in afghan stitch that we would like to give the instructions for making several more of them for you to practice.

The tension of your work can be gauged in the same way as for other crochet work. Any tendency for the fabric to curl and twist can be overcome by working the stitches more loosely. Always pull the yarn around the hook adequately through the stitch and, when working back along a row from left to right, never pull the first stitch through so tightly that the height of the row is flattened.

Sample 1

This is a variation of the basic afghan stitch. Using size G afghan hook and Knitting Worsted, make a length of chain with multiples of 2 stitches.

1st row Insert hook into second ch from hook, yo and draw through a loop, *insert hook into next ch, yo and draw through a loop, rep from * to end.

2nd row Yo and draw through first 2 loops on hook, *yo and draw through next 2 loops on hook, rep from * to end leaving one loop on hook.

3rd row Skip first vertical bar, *insert hook from right to left through next 2 vertical bars on right side of work, yo and draw through a loop, insert hook from right to left into first of these bars, yo and draw through a loop, rep from * to end, insert hook into last vertical bar, yo and draw through a loop.

4th row As 2nd.

5th row Skip first vertical bar, insert hook into next vertical bar, yo and draw through a loop, *insert hook from right to left through next 2 vertical bars on right side of work, yo and draw through a loop, insert hook from right to left into first of these bars, yo and draw through a loop, rep from * to end.

6th row As 2nd.

The 3rd through 6th rows are repeated throughout.

Sample 2

Here crossed stitches within the pattern give a vertical ribbed effect. Using size G afghan hook and Knitting

Worsted, make a chain with multiples of 2 stitches.

1st-2nd rows As 1st-2nd rows of sample 1.

3rd row 1ch, skip first 2 vertical bars, insert hook from right to left through next vertical bar on right side of work, yo and draw through a loop, insert hook into skipped vertical loop to the right of the one just worked, yo and draw through a loop, and cont in this way, working in groups of 2 and crossing the threads, ending by inserting the hook into the last vertical bar, yo and draw through a loop.

4th row As 2nd.

The 3rd and 4th rows are repeated throughout.

Note If you are using this pattern for a shaped garment where you are increasing and decreasing, take care to see that the crossed stitches come immediately above those on the previous row so that the ribbed effect will not be broken.

Sample 3

Here bobbles are made on a basic afghan background by working extra lengths of 4ch before continuing with the next stitch. Using size G afghan hook and Knitting Worsted, make a length of chain with multiples of 6+1 stitches.

1st-2nd rows As 1st-2nd rows of sample 1.

3rd row 1ch, skip first vertical bar on front of fabric, 1 vertical stitch into next vertical bar, *insert hook into next vertical bar on front of fabric, yo and draw through a loop, 4ch, insert hook into horizontal loop

at base of ch on WS of work, yo and draw through 2 loops on hook—called B1—, work 1 vertical stitch into each of next 2 vertical bars, rep from * to last 2 bars, B1 into next vertical bar, 1 vertical stitch into last vertical bar.

4th-6th rows Work in basic afghan stitch.

7th row 1ch, skip first vertical bar, *B1 in next vertical bar, 1 vertical stitch into each of next 2 vertical bars, rep from * to end of row.

8th row As 2nd.

The 3rd through 8th rows are repeated throughout.

Sample 4

An eyelet stitch gives this sample a simple openwork pattern. Using size G afghan hook and Knitting Worsted, make a chain with multiples of 2+1 stitches.

1st row Yo twice, insert hook into 3rd ch from hook, yo and draw through a loop, yo and draw through first 2 loops on hook, *skip next ch, yo twice, insert hook into next ch, yo and draw through a loop, yo and draw through first 2 loops on hook, rep from * to end.

2nd and 4th rows As 2nd row of sample 1.

3rd row 2ch, *yo twice, insert hook into both next vertical bar and slightly sloping vertical bar to right of it made on the previous row, yo and draw through a loop, yo and draw through first 2 loops on hook, rep from * to end.

The 3rd and 4th rows are repeated throughout.

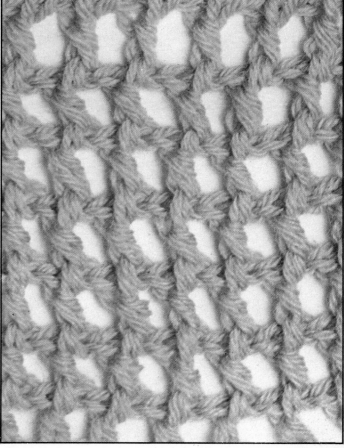

ADVANCED AFGHAN STITCHES

More advanced designs for afghan stitch

Five more interesting afghan stitch patterns are illustrated in this chapter, including two which show the technique of using different colors within the work. As all the samples are worked in a bulky knitting yarn they would be ideal for use in making pillows, rugs and blankets. Reference should be made to the first of these chapters on afghan stitch and checks should always be made during the working of these samples to keep the number of stitches correct.

Sample 1

Using size H hook and bulky yarn, make a length of chain with multiples of 2 stitches.
1st row Insert hook into 2nd ch from hook, yo and draw through a loop, *insert hook into next ch, yo and draw through a loop, rep from * to end.
2nd row *Yo and draw through two loops, rep from * to end, leaving one loop on hook.
3rd row Skip first vertical bar, *yo from front to back, insert hook under next 2 vertical bars, yo and draw through a loop, rep from * to last vertical bar, insert hook into last vertical bar, yo and draw through a loop.
4th row As 2nd.
The 3rd and 4th rows are repeated throughout.

Sample 2

Using size H afghan hook and bulky yarn, make a length of chain with multiples of 2 stitches.
1st-2nd rows As 1st-2nd rows of sample 1.
3rd row Skip first vertical bar, *insert hook into hole under chain st to right of next vertical bar, yo and draw through a loop, insert hook under vertical bar to left of last loop made, yo and draw through a loop, drawing it through one loop on hook, rep from * to last vertical bar, insert hook into last vertical bar, yo and draw through a loop.
4th row As 2nd.
The 3rd and 4th rows are repeated throughout.

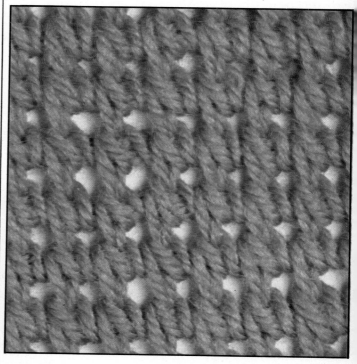

Sample 3

Using size H afghan hook and bulky yarn, make a length of chain with multiples of 2+1 stitches.
1st row (Yo and insert hook into 3rd ch from hook, yo and draw through a loop) twice, yo and draw through 2 loops on hook, yo and draw through 3 loops on hook, *skip next ch, (yo and insert into next ch, yo and draw through a loop) twice, yo and draw through 2 loops on hook, yo and draw through 3 loops on hook, rep from * to end.
2nd row Yo and draw through one loop, *1ch, yo and draw through 2 loops, rep from * to end. One loop remains on hook.
3rd row 2ch, *yo from front to back, insert hook from

front to back into space on right of next st, yo and draw through a loop, yo from front to back and insert into space on left of same st, yo and draw through a loop, yo and draw through 2 loops on hook, yo and draw through 3 loops on hook, rep from * ending with last st worked completely into last space.

4th row As 2nd.

The 3rd and 4th rows are repeated throughout.

Sample 4

For this sample you will need two colors of bulky yarn, coded as A and B. Using size H afghan hook and A, make a length of chain.

1st-2nd rows As 1st-2nd rows of sample 1.

3rd-6th rows Work 4 rows of basic afghan stitch. Do not break off yarn. Join in B.

7th row Using B, 2ch, *yo, insert hook from front to back through work under next horizontal st, yo and draw through a loop extending it to length of 2ch, rep from * ending with last st worked into last horizontal space.

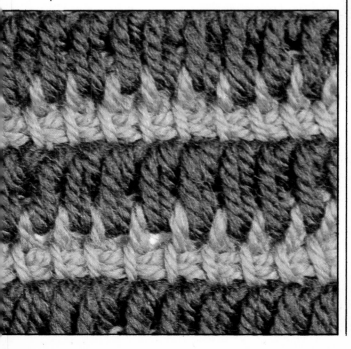

8th row Yo and draw through 2 loops on hook, *yo and draw through 3 loops on hook, rep from * to end.

9th row Draw A through loop on hook, *yo and insert into horizontal loop at back of long st, rep from * to end.

10th-12th rows Work 3 rows basic afghan stitch. Repeat 7th through 12th rows throughout.

Sample 5

Here we have used two colors of Knitting Worsted coded as A and B. Using size F afghan hook and A, make a length of chain with any multiple of 4+7 stitches.

1st-6th rows As 1st-6th rows of sample 4.

7th row Skip first vertical bar, insert hook into next vertical bar, yo and draw through a loop—called one basic tricot st —, one basic tricot st into next bar,

*then using B, (yo and insert in 3rd vertical bar below next st, yo and draw through a loop extending it to meet the working st) 4 times, yo and draw through all loops in B on hook, insert hook in next vertical bar behind bobble, yo and draw through a loop, drawing it through one loop in B on hook—one bobble has been worked—, using A, work one basic tricot st into each of next 3 loops, rep from * to end.

8th-14th rows Using A, work 7 rows of basic afghan stitch.

15th row Skip first vertical bar, *using B, work one bobble into 3rd vertical bar below next st, using A, work one basic tricot st into each of next 3 bars, rep from * to last 2 bars, one bobble in next bar, one basic tricot st into last bar.

16th row Work in basic afghan stitch. Continue in this way, working 7 rows of basic afghan stitch between each bobble row for the required depth of pattern.

319

Clutch bag with woven threads

Size
Width, 14in
Depth, 9in

Gauge
14sts and 14 rows to 4in in basic afghan stitch worked on size J afghan hook.

Materials
3 hanks Lily Sugar 'n Cream yarn
Odds and ends of contrasting color for trim
One size J crochet hook
Lining material, heavy-weight interlining
Velcro for fastening

Bag
Using size J afghan hook make 50ch.
Work in basic afghan stitch until piece measures approx 26 inches from beg.
Fasten off.

Gusset (make 2)
Using size J afghan hook make 14ch.
Work 8 double rows. Dec one st at each end of next and every 4th set of double rows until 6 working sts remain. Work 4 more double rows. Fasten off.

To finish
Cut a piece of interlining the same size as the main part of the bag. Sew the crochet neatly on to the interlining to hold its shape, and steam block.
The gussets are not interlined. Cut out lining material to fit the main part and gussets, allowing $\frac{1}{2}$in for hemming on all sides. Using the same yarn and a tapestry needle sew the gussets to the main part as shown in the illustration, using an overcast st. Finish the lining as given for the bag, sewing in the gussets. Sew the lining on to the crochet. Sew the two pieces of Velcro fastening in position, one to the underside of the flap and one on the corresponding bag section. Follow the diagram and work any desired crochet design on the bag flap.

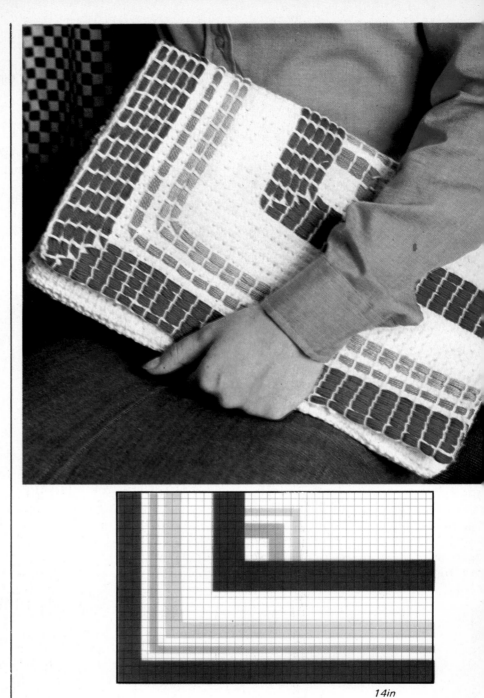

Working the design
You will notice that horizontal and vertical lines of loops are produced on the right side of the crochet fabric. A contrasting colored or textured yarn is then woven over and under these loops or stitches in straight rows. To achieve a good line, it is necessary to use several thicknesses of the yarn for decoration, and an afghan hook in a size smaller than the hook used for the background to draw the threads through the work.

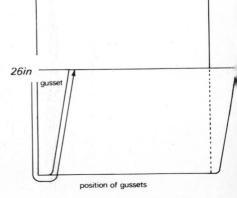

14in

26in

gusset

position of gussets

AN INTRODUCTION TO EMBROIDERY

Anyone who has an interest in needle crafts has a special love for the beautiful art of embroidery. The structure of many different types of fabric, whether bought or hand-made, can be greatly enhanced by this age-old and ever more lovely form of embellishment. It is small wonder that the popularity of this craft has grown in the way that it has through the centuries. Today, actually more people are embroidering things than ever before, although love and appreciation for embroidered decoration have always existed in man, evidenced by the very early origin of the craft.

Even before primitive man had learned to cure skins or weave and knot fabrics, he had already begun the search for some outlet for his creative ability and some way of satisfying his love for beauty. Body painting was, and still is in some remote areas, a form of art which satisfied this very early need. Once he began to clothe himself, this creative urge extended itself to finding some form of decoration with which he could display his own individuality on the warm protective covering he had learned to make for himself.

The art of embroidering with a needle had already reached a high standard in Old Testament days and has since formed a part of the cultural development of almost every nation in the world. Embroidery has evolved into many different forms, and the overall names of some of these categories have a ring of grandeur about them. Groups of stitches which comprise Hardanger, Hedebo and Assisi techniques all evoke memories of past glory and history.

Some stitches, such as cross stitch and chain stitch are so simple that a child can easily master them, while others are so complex that even a small piece could eventually become a prized heirloom. In England, the Victorians had a passion for exquisite embroidery and their way of teaching as many stitches as possible to all who would learn was one that could well be adopted today. A child would be encouraged to begin a sampler of stitches which would be continued throughout his adult life thus forming a unique and lasting record of his achievement. Another popular form of sampler that many children worked was made entirely in cross stitch, depicting a series of pictures and quotations, mostly biblical, and proudly completed with a signature and date.

Many of the most popular stitches today are still very simple ones, for example, the lazy daisy and cross stitches, and French knots, smocking and backstitch. Simple needlepoint too and even some drawn thread work are relatively easy to do.

In this book we have attempted to offer clear and concise instructions, and simple illustrations of the working methods for the basic stitches, as well as for those which call for much more advanced techniques. Our instructions are very easy to follow and the text is presented in a logical way, allowing you to begin with something quite simple but effective, before progressing on to more difficult work. With the aid of this book we hope that you will extend your knowledge of the craft and explore the many possibilities of this beautiful, decorative art form.

Pam Dawson

BASIC SKILLS
EQUIPMENT

The basic tools for embroidery are simple: a pair of good embroidery scissors with fine points; a pair of paper-cutting scissors or blunt, older scissors for making a design of cut paper shapes – embroidery scissors should never be used to cut paper; a thimble; assorted needles, i.e. crewels, betweens, sharps, tapestry, a large chenille needle, or a thick one, such as is used in the joining of heavy knit garments, to take heavy threads through to the back of your work by means of a sling for certain embroidery stitches. The correct needle for particular project will be given in instructions.

Other essentials are beeswax for waxing thread necessary for some types of embroidery; a piece of tailor's chalk or a white dressmaking pencil for use on darker materials; basting thread; pins; embroidery threads; and a frame to hold the fabric firm as you work.

Embroidery fabrics

There are many fabrics suitable for embroidery, providing a constant source of inspiration for both beginner and expert. Linen is a favorite choice and is woven in many weights and colors and in both soft and coarser textures. Suitable cotton materials include such fabrics as poplin, organdy, gingham and glazed cotton. Woolen fabrics are suitable for many stitches, particularly even weave wools, flannels and wool tweeds, both in light and heavy weights. There is also silk in all its varying weights and textures, from thin Chinese silk to raw silk and the heavier silk tweeds. Many man-made home furnishing fabrics make the choice for the needleworker even wider since they serve as excellent backgrounds for stitchery.

A comprehensive reference chart, to help guide you in your choice of fabrics, threads and needles, is given later.

Embroidery hoops

To achieve a really professional finish in embroidery, a hoop is essential. It holds the fabric taut while you are working and helps you to form the stitches evenly and accurately as you go along.

Before starting work, overcast the edges of the fabric to prevent the edges from fraying once the fabric has been placed in the frame.

There are two main types of embroidery hoops – the round, or tambour, frame which is used for small pieces of work with surface or counted embroidery, and the traditional slate frame which is used for large pieces of embroidery.

Round hoops

These are available in different sizes from 3 inches to 12 inches diameter and are usually made from wood, although it is possible to buy aluminum ones which hold the fabric more securely.

A hoop consists of two circles which fit securely one inside the other. The fabric is stretched over the smaller one and the larger one slips on top of it and holds the fabric in place. This second hoop sometimes has a screw which can be adjusted to tighten or slacken the fabric as required. To prevent the fabric from slipping through the hoop when you are mounting it, you can bind the inner hoop with tape or strips of thin cotton fabric first. To mount the fabric, stretch the piece to be embroidered over the inner hoop, keeping the grain of the fabric square, press down the outer hoop and adjust the screw if necessary.

Square frames

Embroidery worked on a stretcher rarely needs pressing before mounting and this is a great advantage when various types of stitchery have been combined, each of which might react differently to heat or dampness.

The frames are available in different sizes from about 18 inches to 30 inches, although it is possible to obtain even larger ones, often combined with a floor stand.

The stretcher consists of two rollers which form the top and bottom of the rectangle and two flat strips which form the side slats of the frame. The side pieces have a series of holes down their length which enables them to be fitted into the rollers at any point with wooden pegs or screws to make a frame the right size for your em-

broidery. Each roller has a strip of tape or webbing nailed along the edge to which the fabric is firmly sewn.

For embroidery which will not be damaged by rolling, such as petit point and other forms of needlepoint, it is possible to buy frames with rotating rollers so the work can be rolled up as it progresses.

A less expensive substitute for the rectangular frame is a canvas painting stretcher, obtainable in various sizes from art suppliers. When this is used the embroidery fabric is attached to it with thumb tacks, care being taken to insure that enough thumb tacks are used and that the fabric is firmly pinned so that it is completely taut.

Preparing a stretcher

Preparing a frame for embroidery is known as dressing the frame.

1 Assemble the stretcher by inserting the side pieces into the rollers at the required height and securing them in place.

2 Mark the centers of the tape or webbing on both rollers with colored thread.

3 If the fabric is likely to fray turn down a $\frac{1}{2}$ inch hem along the top and bottom edges of the fabric and sew them in place. Mark the center points of the edges.

4 Turn under the side edges of the fabric $\frac{1}{2}$ inch around a piece of cord or string to give added strength for attaching it to the side slats. Sew very securely in place.

5 Match the center of the top edge of the fabric to the center of the roller and pin it

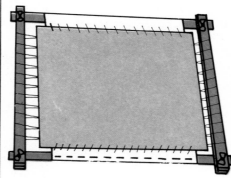

in position, working from the center out to each side. Then sew using strong thread.

6 Repeat on the bottom roller so that the fabric is quite taut between the two rollers.

7 To secure the fabric to the side pieces, use very strong thread or fine string and a heavy needle and lace them together using a diagonal stitch and placing the stitches about 1 inch apart. Leave a fairly

long piece of string at the ends, pull taut, then tie through the last hole at the top and bottom of the slat.

Attaching fine fabrics

If you are mounting a very fine fabric, such as silk or organdy which is likely to tear if it is laced, a different method of attaching the edges to the side slats should be used.

1 Using long pieces of $\frac{3}{4}$ inch wide blanket or bias tape, start at the top and pin the tape to the side edge of the fabric, placing the pin about $\frac{1}{2}$ inch from the edge.

2 Fold the tape back over the pin (to prevent it from pricking you while you work) and take it over and around the side slat. Pin it to the fabric about 1 inch further down, then take it over the side slat again. Continue in this way to the bottom of the fabric and then complete the opposite side in the same way.

Backing the fabric

If you are using a selection of threads of different weights or adding beads to the embroidery which might be too heavy for the fabric, it is advisable to back it for extra strength. The backing can be of washed linen, cotton or muslin – heavy canvas is normally too firmly woven for this purpose.

The embroidery is worked through the double thickness and when it is finished the surplus backing fabric is cut off and trimmed back to the line of embroidery. The method of dressing a frame when using a backing is slightly different.

1 Baste a line down the center of both the backing and the embroidery fabric. Working on a flat surface, place the fabric on the backing, matching the center lines. Pin in position, working out from the center and with the pins pointing inward to avoid puckering. Take care not to stretch either layer. Firmly baste the layers together around the entire outer edge.

2 Turn under the side edges of the backing for $\frac{1}{2}$ inch, enclosing a piece of cord or string to give strength for attaching it to the side slats. Sew very securely in place.

3 Attach the top and bottom edges to the rollers and lace the sides to the slats as for unbacked fabrics.

Backing small pieces of embroidery

If the embroidery fabric is much smaller than the backing fabric, pin it in position on the backing using fine pins or needles to avoid leaving marks. Sew over it by taking the needle from the embroidery fabric, and down into the backing fabric $\frac{3}{8}$ inch above the edge of the embroidery fabric. This pulls the fabric completely taut on the backing.

DESIGN TRANSFERS

There are three main methods of transferring embroidery designs to fabric and usually the type of design and fabric decides which is most suitable. Whichever method you do choose, however, it is normally best to transfer the design after the fabric has been mounted into a frame since it may become rubbed or obliterated if you transfer it before mounting.

For all methods, start by making a tracing of your design – whether it is freely drawn, copied from an illustration, or composed of cut paper shapes – using tracing paper and a non-smudge pencil.

Basting

Use this method for transferring a design onto a fabric with a pile, such as velvet.
1 Pin the tracing in place on the fabric. Using a contrasting thread and small stitches, baste along the lines of the design.
2 Remove the paper by tearing it away from the fabric carefully.

Dressmaker's carbon paper

Use this method on fabrics with very fine and even weave, without irregular slub threads. Do not use it if the design contains any fine detail, as the prick and pounce method is the only reliable one. The carbon paper is available in light colors for use on dark fabrics and vice versa. Simply place the carbon paper under your tracing in the correct position on the fabric and trace over the design with a sharp pencil.

Prick and pounce method

This method is the only reliable one for transferring designs with fine detail or where you are using fabric with irregular slub threads.

Basically, prick holes are made through the tracing paper along the lines of the design and the design is transferred to the fabric underneath by rubbing a mixture of "pounce" over the paper.

"Pounce" was originally a powder made from ground cuttlefish bone used as a wig powder in the eighteenth century, but nowadays it is made from powdered chalk for dark fabrics and powdered charcoal for light fabrics. Some chalks for pouncing can be obtained from a well-stocked notions department or store or alternatively you can use talcum powder. To apply the pounce, you need a felt pad which can be made by rolling up several thicknesses of felt and securing the roll with overcasting.
1 Place the tracing paper onto a folded towel or well-padded ironing board to give a good base for pricking the design.
2 Use a fine needle for smooth fine fabrics or designs with a lot of detail and a larger needle for heavier fabrics. Insert the eye of the needle into a cork to make it easier to handle.
3 Go over the lines of the design, pricking it with holes $\frac{1}{16}$ inch apart on fine fabrics and $\frac{1}{8}$ inch apart on heavier ones.
4 Pin the tracing in position on the embroidery fabric. It is advisable to weight the edges of the tracing with something heavy to prevent it from moving.
5 Using the felt pad, rub the pounce all over the paper. Lift off the paper carefully. When the paper is removed, the design shows up on the fabric as a series of fine dots where the pounce has penetrated the prick holes.
6 Paint in the lines of the design, using a fine brush and white poster paint mixed with a little blue or yellow to make the design clearer on a white or very light fabric. Water color paint can be used instead of poster paint but it does not give as clear an outline and is best for fine transparent fabrics. As you work the embroidery the paint can be flicked off with the point of a needle.

Transferring designs onto sheer fabrics

1 Trace the design onto paper using a hard pencil or non-smudging ink. Check whether the tracing shows through the fabric, and if necessary go over the design again with white poster paint or a light crayon.
2 Place the fabric over the tracing and weight down to prevent it moving. Paint over the lines of the design, using a fine brush and poster or water color paint as in the prick and pounce method.

Transferring designs to canvas

For simple designs use the basting method, and for more complicated designs place the canvas over the tracing and trace the outline with waterproof ink.

Transferring designs using the prick and pounce method.

Making the prick holes through the tracing paper.

Using the felt pad, rub the pounce all over the paper.

Finally, paint in the lines of the design.

Enlarging and reducing designs

Whether you are using your own design or some pattern or illustration which you have copied, you will often need to enlarge or reduce it to fit the size you need. This is easy to do. To enlarge, divide the design into little squares, then copy it onto the same number of larger squares; and to reduce, divide the design in just the same way, then copy it onto smaller squares. The simplest way of doing this in order to avoid marking the original design, and also to save the trouble of drawing out lots of little squares, is to transfer the design onto graph paper. To do this, you can either trace it directly, if the graph paper is thin enough, or use tracing paper and work the following way:

1 Trace the design onto tracing paper.

2 Lay this over graph paper. If you can see the squares clearly through the tracing paper, stick it down with clear tape, taking care that the tracing paper lies flat. This way, you can re-use the graph paper.

3 If, however, you cannot see the squares clearly through the tracing, transfer the design to the graph paper either with carbon paper (dressmaker's carbon is fine) or by shading the back of the tracing paper with a soft pencil and drawing firmly over the design with a ballpoint.

4 Draw a rectangle to enclose the design. This will be divided into a certain number of squares by the graph paper. If you are using plain paper you must, at this point, divide the rectangle by marking off each side and joining up the marks to make a lot of small squares. It is helpful to number

these for reference.

4 Draw, preferably on tracing paper as before, a second rectangle to the size you want the finished design and in the same proportions as the first one. Do this by tracing two adjacent sides of the first rectangle and the diagonal from where they meet. Extend them as much as you need and then draw in the other sides of the second rectangle. Divide this into the same number of squares as the smaller one. A backing sheet of graph paper will make this process easier.

6 Carefully copy the design square by square. If you have to copy a flowing, curved line across several squares, mark the points at which it crosses the squares and then join them up in one flowing movement.

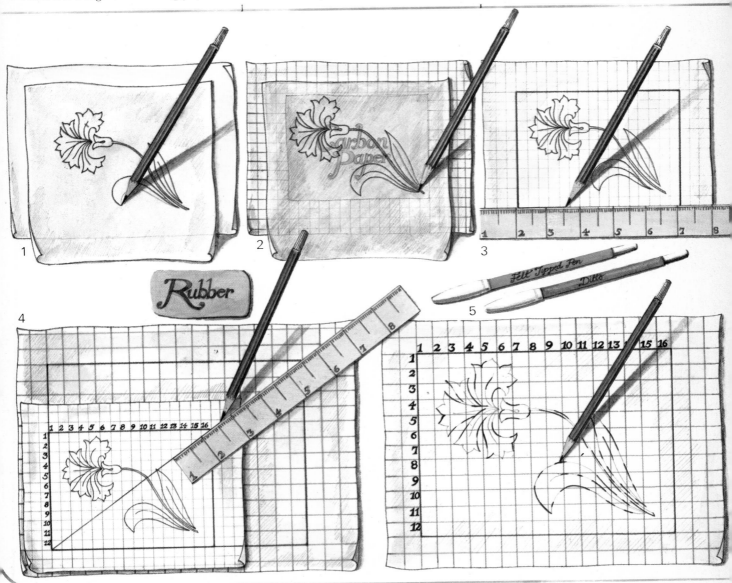

1 *Draw the design onto tracing paper.*
2 *Lay the tracing paper over graph paper.*
3 *Draw a rectangle to enclose the design*

and number the squares in it.
4 *Draw the second rectangle by tracing two sides and a diagonal from the first*

(shown in red). Extend as needed.
5 *Transfer the design square by square until it is completed.*

SIMPLE STITCHES
Line and straight stitches

A knowledge of basic stitchery makes embroidery a creative and stimulating hobby, and it is essential if you intend to create your own individual embroideries. Probably the simplest stitches with which to start are line, or straight, stitches. These are illustrated below and can be used for any of the designs shown, using the tracing overleaf. A basic guide to these elementary stitches can be found for easy reference in the section on the essential stitches.

Basic stitches

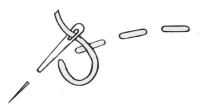

Running stitch
Make the stitches on the right side the same length as those on the wrong side.

Laced running stitch
This can be effective using either the same or contrasting yarn. Use a tapestry needle and thread it in and out of the running stitches without catching in the cloth. This lacing can be used with other stitches.

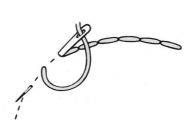

Backstitch
Bring the needle through to the right side of the fabric and make a small stitch backward. Bring the needle through again a little in front of the first stitch and make

another stitch backward to make a continuous line.

Stem stitch
Make a sloping stitch along the line of the design, and then take the needle back and bring it through again about halfway along the previous stitch.

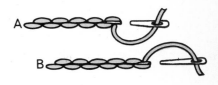

Cable stitch
Work lower stitch A on line of design, as shown; then work upper stitch B in same way with yarn above needle.

All smiles at bedtime with a beaming Mister Moon nightdress

A simple design in a solid color is made demurely pretty with a few motifs

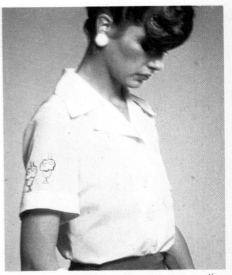

A subtle use of an ice cream cone motif gives this blouse a distinctive look.

Motifs to use on their own or in groups.
Trace the motifs from the page, transfer
them to the fabric, then embroider them
in pretty colors, using any of the straight
stitches illustrated

Satin stitches

Although satin stitch is essentially a simple over-and-over stitch, skill is required to produce the beautiful satiny effect that its name implies. It is a surprisingly versatile stitch and, as it imposes no pattern of its own, it is invaluable for pictures where stitches of varying lengths and shades produce illusions of distance and depth. There are several variations, one of which is padded and gives the effect of an extra dimension. It is shown later in our stitch sample pages.

Satin stitch flower motif

This simple flower motif below is a good example of the effectiveness of the stitch when worked with long and short and split stitch. The motif can be worked in six-strand floss on a table napkin, dress or blouse.

Materials

6-strand floss (used with three strands in the needle) in six or seven colors. Allow 1 skein of yarn in each color for the design, although the exact amount you use will depend on how closely you stitch.

The design

1 Work the motif onto the corner of the napkin, placing it about 1 inch in from the sides.
2 The flowers of the design are worked in long and short stitch, the four upper leaves in satin stitch and the lowest leaf in split stitch. French knots decorate the centers.
3 The dotted line on the tracing pattern indicates the meeting point for stitches and suggests the position of the leaf vein. Transfer the design using tissue paper.
Begin by working the center flower, stitching from the inner line towards the outer edge. Work each half of each leaf in turn. Work flower color 4 first, then color 6, taking the stitches just into the edge of the leaves. Finally, work flower color 5. Make dots with a couple of small satin stitches or French knots at the centers.

▲ *A beautiful example of satin stitch worked in silk for picture making.*

▼ *The motif worked in cotton on a linen napkin.*

A delightful embroidery design "Panier de Fleurs" is featured on this pillow. It is worked in wool on canvas and satin stitch is used throughout. Designed by Jean-Yves Rocher for the D.M.C. "New Tapestry Collection".

Guatemalan motifs

Reversible satin stitch worked in bright colors in geometric patterns is characteristic of Guatemalan peasant embroidery as shown on the poncho and bag in the photograph. A similar motif can also look effective on the flap of a clutch bag and, since it is reversible, it will look as good when the bag is closed as when it is open.

Making a clutch bag

Make the clutch bag from a rectangle of loosely woven fabric, such as coarse linen. The minimum size of fabric for the motif shown is 18 inches × 9 inches.

Working the motif

Draw the motif (right) to scale (see earlier) and trace it onto tissue paper. Place the tracing in position on the top third of the rectangle. Baste over the lines indicating the color areas and then pull away the paper. Start stitching each area, working from the middle outward.

Finishing

Fold up the bottom third of the rectangle with wrong sides together to form the pocket and pin the sides. Trim the edge of the flap to within $\frac{1}{2}$ inch of the stitching. Cover the turnings and raw edge of the flap with a continuous length of bias binding machine stitched on both edges.

Above: Graph pattern for a Guatemalan motif. Work it in bright colors for a bag.

Each square = 1 inch square

Left: This poncho and bag are embroidered with satin stitch in Guatemalan motifs

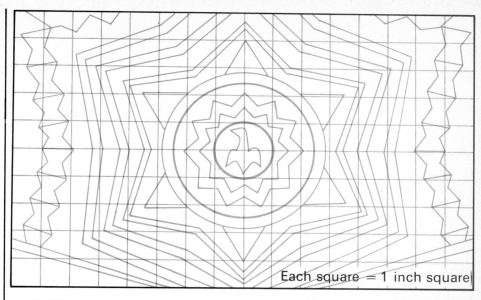

Each square = 1 inch square

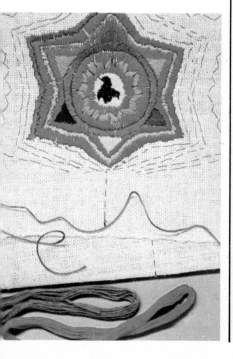

Chain stitches: continuous

Chain stitch has no single origin but can be traced to all parts of the world where ancient fabrics have been found. Chain stitch was found on basket-work from pre-dynastic Egypt (c.350 BC), on the earliest surviving Egyptian textiles, in graves in the Crimea dating from the 4th century BC and on some Chinese and Japanese textiles from the 7th and 8th centuries AD. The Chinese worked chain stitch with silk yarn on silk in a single line technique, widening or tightening the loop with a thread of uniform thickness to produce an effect of variable depths of color and shadow. Some of the finest examples worked with chain stitch alone, using silk thread on satin, have been found on 18th and 19th century Indian garments from Kutch.

In medieval western Europe the richest embroideries used more elaborate stitches and chain stitch appeared only on more humble objects. In 18th century England chain stitch was revived and widely used, often inspired by Chinese motifs to decorate silk coats and satin bedspreads. It appears independently in peasant work throughout the world.

Using chain stitch

Chain stitch worked in lines and curves is very versatile. The stitch can be worked large or small to give a fine or a bold outline. For its usual look the proportions should remain the same; as a rough guide the width should be two-thirds of the length of the stitch.

Chain stitch adapts well to tight curves and can be worked around and around partially to fill in areas.

Chain stitch

When worked, this stitch forms a chain of loops on the right side of the fabric and a line of back stitches at the back. Bring the needle through on the line of the design, hold a loop of the yarn under the left thumb and insert the needle close to where the yarn emerged. Bring the needle through a little further along the line of the design, and, with a loop of the yarn under the point of the needle, draw through. Continue in this way until the required length has been worked (see below).

Suitable yarns

Small stitches worked in a thick yarn give

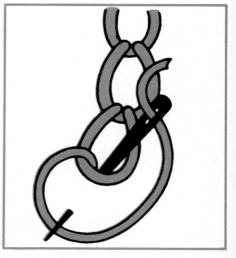

▲ *Working a line of chain stitch.*

These designs are shown about one-third of their actual size, but they may be enlarged to the size you require.

This pretty butterfly picture would be ideal for a girl's bedspread or embroidered onto a dress or apron pocket.

An appropriate design for a beach bag or beach cover-up – a colorful landscape scene with rolling waves.

Brighten up plain table mats with this simple motif. All these designs are worked in Soft Embroidery Cotton.

a solid line, while larger stitches in fine yarn give an open stitch. Use these characteristics to their fullest advantage. Any of the finer yarns and threads previously mentioned are suitable for chain stitch but for quickly worked chain stitch use a thick embroidery yarn such as those shown below, on a large weave backing.

2 ply Crewel yarn: a twisted, matte wool. Use one or, more usually, several strands.
Tapestry yarn: a twisted, matte wool.
Sugar 'n Cream: a knitting and crochet cotton.
Knit-Cro-Sheen: a fine knitting and crochet cotton.
Rug Yarn: a twisted, matte yarn for using on rug canvas.

To work the designs

1 Choose your project – perhaps a T-shirt cotton jacket. Enlarge and transfer the design.

If you plan to use a thick yarn you will need a chenille needle. Do not, however, use heavy yarn for any cotton fabric, including denim. Floss or 1 strand of Crewel is the heaviest you can use to avoid puckering.

2 Follow the lines of the design with closely worked chain stitches until you have covered them all.

Flower bed pillow

Fabric required

Single thread evenweave linen, 26 threads per 1 inch, 14 in × 14 in.

You will also need

Soft Embroidery Cotton, 3 skeins purple, 4 skeins red, 4 skeins mauve, 5 skeins lilac, 6 skeins light green, 6 skeins dark green, 6 skeins orange.
Fabric for back of pillow 14 in × 14 in.
Square pillow 14 in × 14 in.

The design

1 Transfer the pattern on facing page centrally onto the linen.
2 Lightly mark a square ¾ inch in from outer edges with a soft pencil.
3 Work the design in fairly small chain stitch, working over 2 or 3 threads to make stitches uniform in length.
4 Work around the edge of the square in chain stitch and work two more square of chain stitch just inside the first border.
5 Finish the pillow, allowing for ½ inch seams all around.

This flower bed design is set off well by a natural-colored background.

Detached chain stitch

Although chain stitches can be used continuously they can also be used as separate stitches and arranged to form flower or leaf shapes. This is known as lazy daisy or detached chain stitch. The stitches may be worked in any size you desire, but remember, if the stitches are very long they will catch easily and therefore are not suitable for everyday articles of clothing.

Needlework canvas

This is an embroidery fabric woven in even blocks of cotton strands separated by holes through which the needle is drawn. The number of holes per inch vary: 6 holes per inch have been used here and embroidery worked on this scale grows quickly. Penelope Binca and Panama canvas are examples of this type of embroidery fabric. The canvas is also available in smaller gauge for finer work. This is most often used for making pillows, table linen, chairbacks or stool tops.

After care

Wash in warm water and pure soap. Squeeze the fabric gently in the soapy water. Rinse thoroughly in warm water and squeeze gently by hand to remove excess water. Leave the fabric on a towel, lying flat, until it is half-dry. Press on the wrong side, using a moderately hot iron, working from the center outward and not allowing the weight of the iron to rest on the embroidered sections until the fabric is completely dry. If desired, you may also have the fabric dry cleaned.

Basic stitches

Detached chain or lazy daisy stitch

Make a chain stitch and instead of re-inserting the needle inside the loop, make a tiny stitch over the loop to hold it in place (A). Leave a space and bring the needle out again to begin the next stitch. Work the lazy daisy stitch in the same way as for the detached chain but position the stitches to form a flower shape (B).

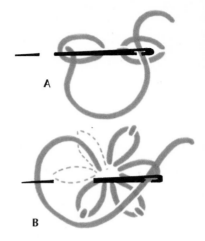

Lazy daisy stitch pillow

The flowers on this design are meant to be worked in a random fashion, therefore embroider the largest flowers first, spacing them out, and then fill the spaces in between with the smaller flowers. In the remaining spaces work the tiny four-petaled flowers and either bunches of, or single, leaves.

Fabric required

14 in square of cotton mesh, 6 holes per inch.

You will also need

11 skeins of embroidery wool in 11 different colors.
Tapestry needle No. 18.
Material for back of pillow cover, 14 inches square.
Pillow form, 13 inches square.

Working the embroidery

1 Work the desired number of flowers over the fabric, leaving a 1 inch border unworked. To define the edge of the pillow work a border of leaves 1 inch in from the edge. Vary the height of the leaves so that they frame the flowers.
Note While working with the wool it is important to twist it to the right to keep the ply tightly twisted, thus being able to get a clean line to the design. Work the larger flowers one at a time.
2 Leave the ends of yarn on the wrong side and, sew them in neatly on the back

This colorful pillow displays a random pattern of flowers in detached chain stitch.

when you are finishing.

3 The detached chain stitches are held in place in two ways; either by bringing the yarn over the loop through the same hole

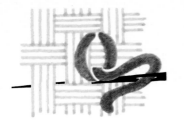

1 *Compact detached chain stitch.*

(Figure 1) or by bringing the yarn over the loop, over one block and through the next hole (Figure 2).

2 *Detached chain stitch with a stem.*

Finishing

1 Fold the edges of the fabric to the wrong side, so that the border of leaves is close to the edge, and pin. Fold the back of the cover to the same size and shape and pin those edges to secure them. Pin the back and front together, wrong sides facing (see below). Slip stitch around three edges,

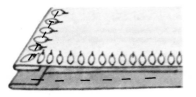

3 *Pin with wrong sides together.*

insert the pillow form and slip stitch neatly along the fourth side to complete the pillow.

2 The motifs show the variety of shapes that can be worked over a similar number of squares.

Each square of the fabric represents the number of blocks to be worked as, for example, if the petal covers three squares there are two holes skipped between the inserting and drawing out of the needle.

Bright and pale colors show up well against either dark brown or cream colored backgrounds. The motifs may be arranged to make a pattern the same as, or similar to, the one opposite, and they are only a sampling of the many you can work.

Chain stitch as a filling stitch

When using chain stitch as a filling stitch it is easiest to start off with designs that are fairly round. With these shapes it is easier to work around and around and to keep the lines of stitches close together. Once you have completed a few such designs you will be ready to go on to more irregular ones. When working a design which is filled in with closely packed stitches choose a medium-weight fabric of some type comparable in weight to that of the stitching. Also choose a color and texture which is suited to the design.

When filling in a shape, work the stitches around the outline of the shape, then, as you return to the starting point, bring the needle point just inside the first round of stitches so that the start of the second round is hardly visible when the work is completed (see below). Keep working around and around, completely covering the background, until the center is reached, then bring the needle over the last loop and draw the yarn through to the back. Fasten off.

Filled chain stitch can be made to look almost three-dimensional if you start along the outline with larger chain stitches and gradually make them smaller and smaller as you progress toward the center. However, if you want the surface of the fabric to be completely covered with embroidery it will be necessary to fill in the center of the outer chain stitches with detached chain stitches.

Yarn

To use chain stitch as a filling stitch it is important to select a yarn of proportionate thickness to the weight of the fabric, which is why 6-stranded floss is most appropriate. Before starting the embroidery, however, work a few stitches to find out how many strands you need to achieve a stitch size that will completely fill your pattern.

Pressing and stretching

When stitches are worked very close together the fabric sometimes becomes puckered because the gauge of the stitching is too tight. All embroidery should be pressed on the wrong side with a warm iron to give it a finished appearance, but if the fabric is distorted it must be pressed and stretched to make it smooth.

To press the embroidery

Pad a large flat surface with a blanket and ironing cloth or use a well-padded ironing board. Place the fabric on the ironing cloth, wrong side uppermost, and press with a damp cloth not allowing the weight of the iron to rest on the embroidery.

To stretch the fabric

Pad a board with clean, damp blotting paper or, if blotting paper is not available, lay the fabric over several thicknesses of damp, white cotton fabric. Place the fabric on the blotting paper, or substitute for it, right side up. Attach one edge of the fabric to the board with thumb tacks, aligning the horizontal strands with the edge of the board. Repeat on the opposite edge and at the sides, aligning the vertical strands with the edge of the board. If the sides of the board are not at right angles, use graph paper or lined blotting paper to obtain accurate stretching.

Leave to dry for at least 24 hours.

To work the iris design

The contrast between the nubbly, dull linen background and the lustrous stranded cotton makes the textural effect of this design very exciting. Note, too, how the narrow spacing between the random, horizontal lines integrates the background cloth with the embroidery; without these lines the embroidery would appear superimposed.

Size

The design should be enlarged from the illustration shown opposite to $6\frac{3}{4}$ inches $\times$ $8\frac{1}{2}$ inches.

Fabric required

A piece of natural colored linen-look fabric, 10 inches $\times$ $10\frac{1}{2}$ inches.

You will also need

6-strand floss, for flowers, 2 skeins of peacock blue and 2 skeins of natural; for leaves, 1 skein dark gray, 1 skein chestnut; for horizontal background lines, 1 skein beige; for buds, 1 skein cinnamon.
1 crewel needle.

Working the design

Transfer and enlarge the design shown on the opposite page. The stitches are all worked with two strands of the floss. While working it is important to remove any kinks from the strands so that they work smoothly together.

To use the design as a picture

Fray the top and bottom edges of the fabric and finish them with an overcast stitch to prevent any further fraying. The sides may be either frayed and overcast or turned under and hemmed. Mount the fabric on a colored cardboard background, leaving about a 1 inch border all around and set the finished piece in a picture frame.

To use the design as a pillow

Center the design on a piece of cloth about 13 inches $\times$ 16 inches and finish into a pillow 12 inches $\times$ 15 inches.

To use the design on a dress

Work the design directly onto the front of a basic woolen dress.

Right: This beautiful piece of embroidery is made up entirely of very small chain stitches, some worked around and around to make up the iris flowers and buds, and others in lines to represent the leaves and the background. Yarn: 6-strand floss. Designed by Shifrah Fram.

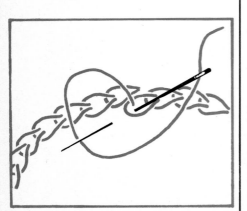

Bring the needle through just inside the first line of embroidery.

French knots and other stitches

For picture making choose a theme with bold and simple shapes. Break down the composition into stitch areas, fitting an appropriate stitch to the type of texture which will best express that portion. As you gain experience, you may want to attempt more detailed subjects with the texture provided by a greater variety of stitches, and most probably some of these invented by your own ingenuity.

Background

To start with choose a finely woven, natural-colored fabric. When you have become more confident you will be able to use more complex backgrounds which will play a part in the composition of the design with textures of the fabric as well as the stitching becoming an integral part of the picture.

Borders

If you wish to embroider a frame around a picture, choose one that is in keeping with the subject – a rose-festooned one as shown here – or a geometric border for a more modern picture. Remember, though, that many pictures look their best when set in the simplest of picture frames.

Yarn quantities

For a small picture, such as the one shown, one skein of each color is usually more than enough. However, if one color predominates, or if the stitches are very closely or thickly worked, an extra skein may be needed.

Apple blossom picture

The apple blossoms on the tree in the picture are superbly shown with the use of French knots. These are also used on the girl's dress and hair band shown. Bold straight stitches which lie flat are used for the trellis in front of the bushes. These add a little perspective and contrast in texture. The colors used are light to medium tones and give the whole picture a pretty, country air.

Trace the design onto tissue paper, being careful not to tear it. Lay the tissue paper over the fabric. Using sewing or basting thread and a fine needle, sew through the tissue paper and fabric with small running stitches around the outline to indicate the position of the areas to be embroidered.

Tear the tissue paper away. The stitches not hidden by the embroidery are removed when the embroidery is complete.

Fabric required

Piece of fabric 15 in × 12 in

You will also need

1 skein each of 6-strand floss in each of the following colors: brown, pale pink, rose pink, light green, mid green, sage green, golden brown, white.
1 ball pearl cotton No. 5 in two shades of brown and pale blue.
Small amount of gold lurex yarn for trellis.

The design

1 Enlarge the picture to measure 13 in × 10 in.
2 Using pearl cotton, work as follows: for the girl's dress, chain stitch and stem stitch.
Bark of tree and branches, stem stitch.
3 Using all strands of floss, work as follows:
for the apple blossom, flowers under tree, girl's hairband and part of her dress: closely worked, loose French knots, with a few knots over the branches of the tree.
Grass and flower leaves, random straight stitches.
Background bush, feather stitch.
Foreground bush, herringbone stitch outlined with stem stitch.
Girl's hair and feet, stem stitch.
Girl's hairband, French knots.
Girl's arms, backstitch.

The trellis

Using all strands of floss together, work a lattice, couching it with the gold lurex yarn. In front of the trellis work the flowers in French knots and the leaves in detached chain stitch.

The border

The border is made of herringbone stitch in floss with stem stitches worked in pearl cotton on each side.
Work the rosettes in stem stitch from the outside toward the center and add one or two French knots at the center of each.
Work leaves in detached chain stitch.
To finish off the picture, lay it right side downward on a well-padded ironing board,

cover. with a damp cloth and press it lightly. When dry, mount the picture.

Basic stitches

French knots (Figure 1)

Bring the thread out at the required position, hold the thread down with the left thumb and wind it around the needle twice as in A. Still holding the thread firmly, twist the needle back to the starting point and insert it as close as possible to where the thread first emerged. Pull the thread through to the wrong side and secure.

Trellis stitch (Figure 2)

Lay threads along the lines of the design and, with another thread, tack down the intersections by making small stitches into the fabric.

Feather stitch (Figure 3)

Work in a vertical line. Bring the needle through to the right of the center line of the design and take a small stitch to the right as shown, catching the thread under the point of the needle. Continue making a series of stitches to the left and right of the design line, catching the thread under the needle.

Herringbone stitch (Figure 4)

Working from left to right, bring the needle through above the center line of the design and insert it below this line to the right, taking a small stitch to the left and keeping the thread above the needle. Insert the needle then on the upper line a little to the right, taking a small stitch to the left with the thread below the needle. Continue alternating these two movements.

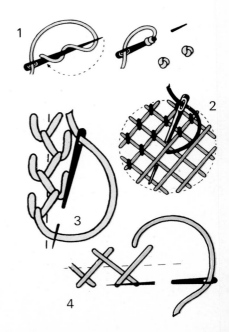

Texture is created in this pretty picture by the use of French knots for blossom and couching for the trellis.

Cross stitch

Cross-stitch is one of the simplest and most ancient of all embroidery stitches. It dates back to the Coptic period and has been a form of peasant art for many centuries, always appearing in one form or another in various parts of the world.

The best examples of this work come from the Slav countries of Eastern Europe where it has been used to adorn national dress. Cross-stitch can be exciting and absorbing to work and in Victorian times in Britain it was a popular pastime to make cross-stitch pictures, often wrongly named "samplers" (true samplers should consist of several stitches).

Many of these pictures were made by young girls and usually consisted of the alphabet, a text, the signature of the artist, her age and the date of working, all in minute cross-stitch.

How to use cross-stitch

Cross-stitch can be used for exciting designs on clothes, such as smocks, blouses, and dresses; as a decoration on bags, belts and slippers; and for the home on rugs, table linen, and curtains. Whether it is worked in an all-over design or simply in a border pattern depends on the size of the item, the background fabric and on the design being worked.

The design

Because of the geometrical nature of the stitch, it looks its best when the design is formal and has a repeating pattern, such as shown on the border in the photograph. The shape of the spaces between the areas is as important as those areas filled with the stitch. Often main areas are left un-worked and the spaces suggest detail – a technique known as "voiding" – which is the main characteristic of another form of cross-stitch, called "Assisi work" (shown later).

The colors

Cross-stitch is usually worked in colors – usually very bright – which contrast with the background fabric, and the interplay of the colors you choose is all-important. It is often more effective to use several tones of one color (as in the design shown in the photograph) rather than introducing completely different colors.

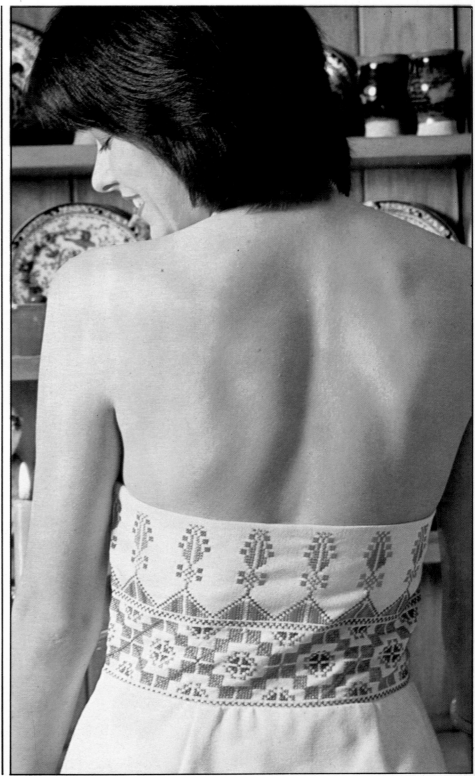

Planning your design

Although it is possible to buy transfers of cross-stitch patterns to print onto fabric, it is much more satisfying to use an evenly woven fabric and make up your own designs.

To plan your design, draw it first onto graph paper, using different colored pencils or different symbols to represent each color, with one square representing one stitch. When working from the graph each square may be considered as consisting of one or more threads, which remains standard throughout the work.

A unit of three threads usually makes a good average size cross, each stitch being made by counting three threads along the fabric and then three threads up.

By reducing or increasing the number of threads in the units – or by using fabric with fewer or more threads to the inch.

It is important in working cross-stitch that the counting of both stitches and threads must be accurate, and that if you are using a transfer it is necessary to be sure that the lines of the crosses lie on the weave of the fabric.

The fabric

Even-weave fabrics with threads which are easy to count are obviously the best to use for cross-stitch and besides the traditional embroidery linens you can also use hopsacking "Hardanger" cotton and many synthetic home furnishings fabrics. Checked fabrics can also be used even if the weave is uneven as the size of the crosses can be determined by the size of the checks.

The threads

Any threads – cotton, silk, linen or wool – can be used provided that they are suitable in weight to the background fabric. A coarse fabric needs a thread of heavier weight, while a fine fabric needs lighter threads.

Variety can be introduced by using threads of different textures for example, a thicker thread can be used to add depth and relief to your design.

The stitches

Cross-stitch is formed by two diagonal stitches, crossing in the center. There are two basic methods in which it can be worked, either by making one complete stitch at a time or by making a row of single diagonal stitches in one direction, then completing the stitch on the return row.

It is important that the upper half of the stitch always lies in the same direction if an even and regular effect is to be achieved. Traditionally the upper stitch should slope from bottom left to top right.

Combining cross-stitch

While there are numerous variations of cross-stitch which are used in other methods of embroidery, the stitch which is most often worked with regular cross-stitch is Holbein, or double running stitch. This is a small line stitch which is used to break up a mass of cross-stitch pattern and to lighten the texture. It produces a light filigree effect and is always worked in two steps.

The first step is worked along the required outline in running stitches which are of equal length to the spaces left between them. The work is then turned for the next step when the spaces left between the first stitches are filled in, thus forming a solid row. To keep the second line of stitches straight and even, bring the needle out of the fabric just below the stitch that was made in the first step, but still using the same hole of the fabric.

The design

The design shown in the photograph is made up of two simple repeat motifs and it can easily be adjusted to make borders for other garments (see chart below).

The top motif is 2 inches wide × $3\frac{1}{4}$ inches high. The border motif is $2\frac{3}{4}$ inches wide × $3\frac{1}{8}$ inches high.

Below: Tracing pattern for the design illustrated opposite.

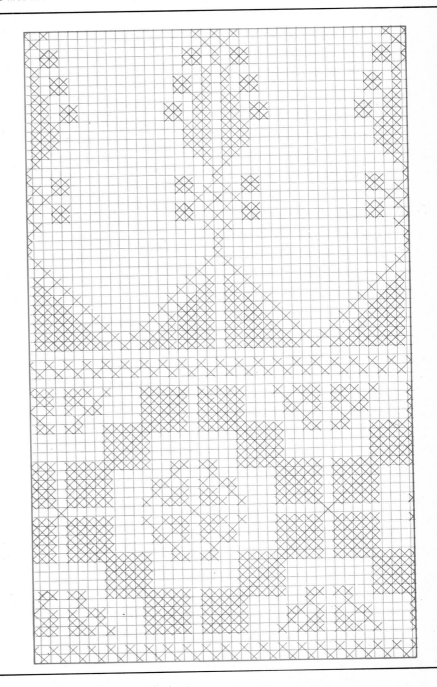

Cross-stitch motif

The photograph opposite shows a charming example of the kind of pictorial "sampler" worked by our forebears when they were children. Notice how the spaces between stitches are used to suggest features. If you do not wish to make a complete item from even-weave fabric, you could work the embroidery only on it, cut round leaving a margin of about ½ inch and apply it as a patch onto the finished item.

Fabric required

The motifs shown worked individually were done in stranded cotton on linen fabric. Alternatively, you could work in wool to brighten up a favorite cardigan or pullover.

You will also need

Remnants of stranded cotton or knitting wool in various colors. Try to match the weight of the yarn to the background using six strands of cotton or a sports yarn on a heavy background.

The design

1 Working over two or three threads of the fabric, work the stitches in the appropriate shades as shown in the charts. Darn all ends neatly through the backs of the stitches on the wrong side.
2 The size of the motif will of course vary, according to the weave of the background.
3 On a fabric with 19 threads per 1 inch for example, the cow motif would be about 4½ inches by 2 inches when each stitch is worked over two threads.
On a knitted background, work over a unit of one or two knitted stitches counted vertically and horizontally.

Basic cross-stitch

To work cross-stitch in two steps, bring the needle through on the lower right line of the cross and insert it at the top left line of the cross. Take a straight stitch along the wrong side of the fabric and bring the needle through on the lower right line of

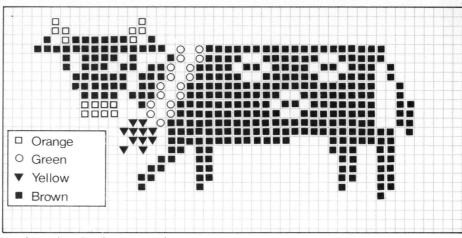

Working chart for the cow. Each square represents one cross-stitch.

Key:
- □ Orange
- ○ Green
- ▼ Yellow
- ■ Brown

The cow worked on linen with 19 threads per inch. Each stitch is over two threads.

the next stitch. Continue to the end of the row in this way (Figure 1a). To complete the stitch, work from left to right now in a similar way (Figure 1b).

Outlines and single stitches

To work cross-stitch individually, start as above but complete the cross each time (Figure 2) before beginning the next stitch. Pass the thread on the wrong side of the fabric to the lower right line of the position of the next and subsequent stitches.

Holbein stitch

Working from right to left, work a row of running stitch, making the stitches and spaces the same length as the crosses. To complete the stitch, work from right to left, filling in the spaces left in the first row (Figure 3).

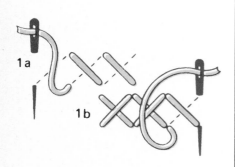

1. Two-step stitch.

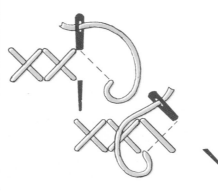

2. Individually worked stitches.

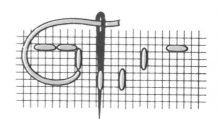

3. Completing Holbein stitch.

Work this charming cross-stitch picture for a nursery or abstract the motifs and use them individually.

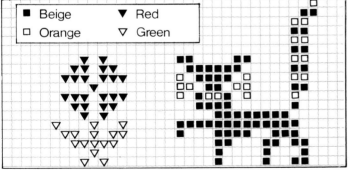

Legend:
- ■ Beige
- □ Orange
- ▼ Red
- ▽ Green

Working chart for the flower and cat.

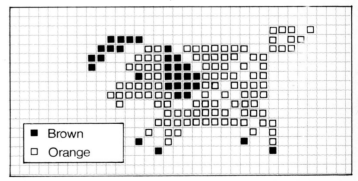

Legend:
- ■ Brown
- □ Orange

Working chart for the pig.

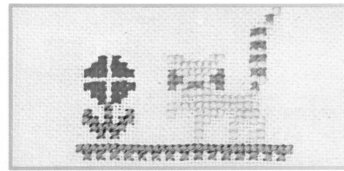

The cat worked on linen as above.

The pig worked on linen as above.

Cross stitch alphabet

Cross-stitch has long been a favorite for embroidered lettering and monograms because it is quick and easy to work. No preliminary outline or transfer is needed when an evenweave fabric is used for the background because the fabric threads can be counted to form each letter. Although cross-stitch designs based on counting threads are necessarily geometric in formation, still they leave plenty of opportunity for embellishment, as shown by the alphabet in the photograph. These letters have been worked in a modern version of the popular Victorian sampler, but you can easily extract the appropriate letters from the chart and use them individually to give a personal finish to your table linen or sheets, or you could combine them to form a monogram to decorate the pocket of a dress or the flap of a bag.

Working the alphabet

1 The alphabet in the photograph is worked on an evenweave cotton with 18 threads to 1 inch in 6-strand embroidery floss, using three strands throughout.
2 Each stitch is worked over one thread of the fabric and the letters are about 1¼ inches high.

Enlarging the letters

If you just want to double the size of the letters – and this means increasing their width too – you can work the stitches over two threads of the fabric.

Alternatively, you can work four stitches for every one stitch indicated on the chart, or if you do not want the increase to be that great, you can work the stitches over two threads but on a finer weave fabric.

Reducing the letters

The only method of reducing the size of the letters in proportion is to use a finer weave fabric.

Monograms

Composite intertwined initials are fun to plan and work. The initials may be arranged so that the base lines are level or you could place them diagonally.

Sketch out your monogram on graph paper before you start work so that you can see how the initials link and where they will have stitches in common.

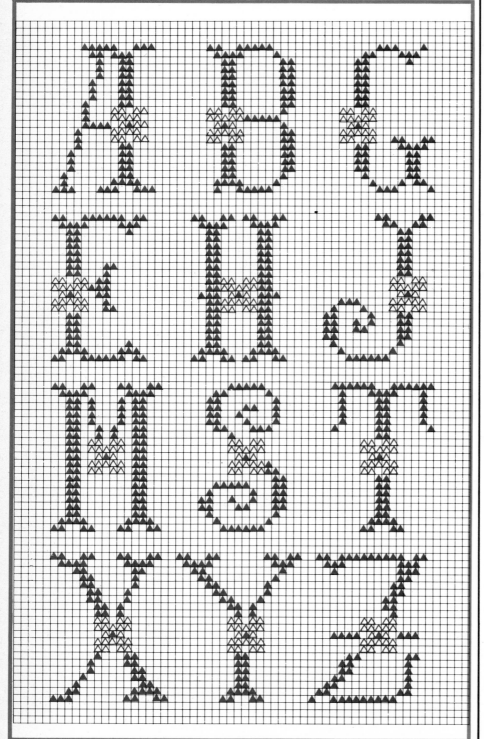

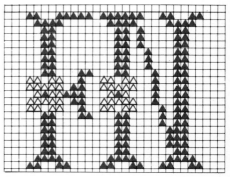

Above: Combined initials for a monogram.
Left: Chart for alphabet.

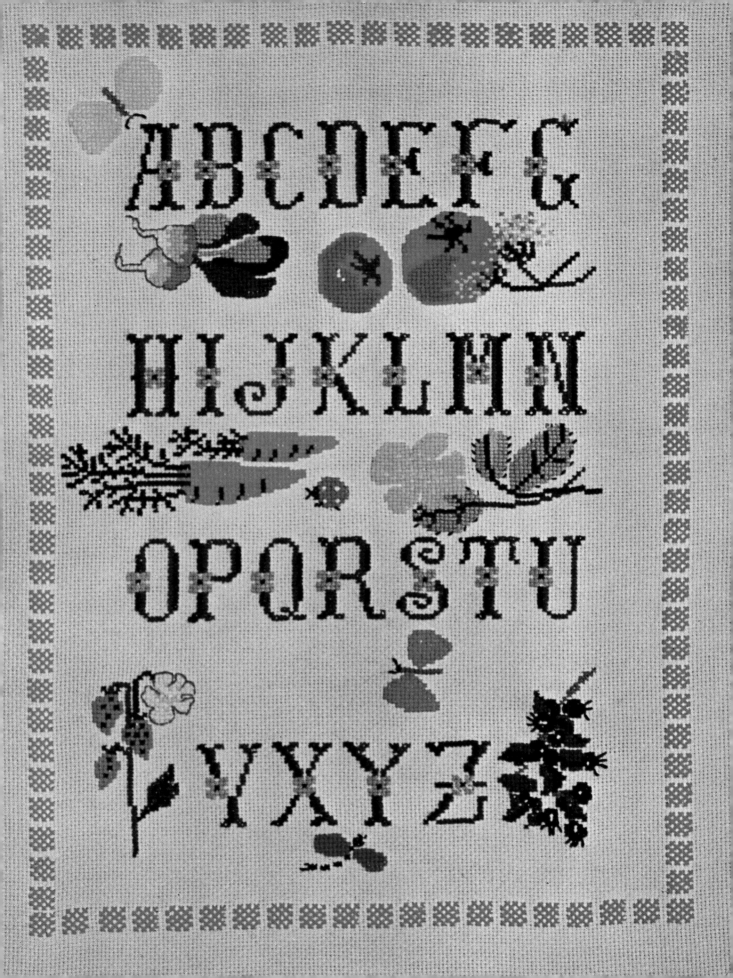

FIRST PROJECTS
Simple peasant design

This beautiful embroidery design is worked with the simplest of stitches. The beginner will be able to work the design after following the previous few chapters – and the experienced embroiderer will have no difficulty at all. The design is suitable for a garment with yoke and sleeves.

To work the embroidery
Materials required

D.M.C. 6-strand floss: 3 skeins each of 666 turkey red, 604 rose pink, 553 violet, 3325 cobalt blue, 986 forest green, 3348 moss green, 972 amber gold.
Crewel needles No. 5 and 7.

Placing the motifs

The tracing pattern gives half the design used on the yoke with the broken lines indicating the fold. The section within the dotted outline gives half the design used on the sleeve.

Mark center-front of the blouse yoke with a line of basting stitches. Placing the fold line to center-front, trace the motif onto the right hand side of the yoke. Reverse and trace onto the left hand side. Trace section given within the dotted outline onto sleeves, approximately 5 inches from cuff. Repeat in reverse to complete the design as shown.

Method of working

Work the embroidery, following diagram 1 and number key. Use 6 strands of floss and No.7 needle for the French knots and 3 strands with No.5 needle for the remainder.

Most of the design is worked in simple satin stitch, stem stitch and French knots, with the centers of the flowers in spider's web filling stitch. Work this as shown in diagram 2. Work nine straight stitches on each side of the fly stitch tail, into the center of the circle. This divides the circle into nine equal sections and separates the spokes from the foundation of the web. Weave over and under the spokes until the circle is filled.

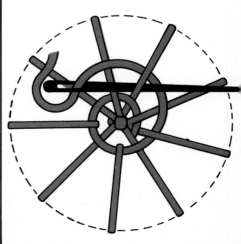

Spider's Web Filling Stitch

KEY TO DIAGRAM

1 — 666

2 — 604

3 — 553

4 — 3325   Satin stitch

5 — 986

6 — 3348

7 — 972

8 — 553

9 — 986   Stem stitch

10 — 3348

11 — 972

12 — 972   Spider's Web Filling Stitch

13 — 972   French Knots

A magnificent dragon

Fabric required
Length of emerald green fabric.

You will also need
D.M.C. 6-stranded floss in the following colors and quantities: 2 skeins each 992 jade and 725 amber gold; 1 skein each 797 cobalt blue; 993 and 991 jade; 704 and 700 grass green; 973 buttercup; 745 gorse yellow; 726 and 781 amber gold; 606 flame.
For alternative thread use D.M.C. Pearl Cotton No. 8 in the same colors.
McCall kimono pattern No. 3738.
Crewel needle No. 8.

The design
1 Lay out the pattern pieces on the fabric as directed in the pattern. Do not cut out the back and pocket pieces, but mark the cutting line on the fabric with either small basting stitches or with a tracing wheel and dressmakers' carbon paper. This is done to prevent the embroidery from pulling and possibly pulling the fabric out of shape.
2 Enlarge the design onto graph paper and transfer it onto the fabric. To do this either use an embroidery transfer pencil or trace the design onto tissue paper and sew it to the fabric with small basting stitches along the lines of the design, tearing the paper away afterwards.
3 Position the dragon on the back of the kimono 3 inches from the neck edge. The bat and pearl should be placed centrally on the pocket.

To work the embroidery
1 Use two strands of floss in the needle throughout. Follow the diagram and stitch key to work the embroidery. All parts similar to the numbered parts are worked in the same color and stitch.
2 To complete the dragon, work a French knot in the center of each eye on top of the satin stitch.

To make the kimono
1 Press the embroidery on the wrong side under a damp cloth.
2 Lay the pattern pieces on the embroidered back and pocket pieces. Check that the outlines of the pattern on the fabric have not been distorted by the embroidery. Adjust if necessary. Finish the kimono as directed by the pattern.

In China the dragon is regarded as the lord of all animals, a rain bringer and symbol of the highest intelligence. This magnificent dragon, embroidered on the back of an emerald green kimono, is chasing a flaming pearl, another popular Chinese symbol which represents the spring moon, herald of the fertile rainy season. A bat, symbol of happiness, is worked on the pocket of the kimono. Either use the design as we have here, or enlarge it and use it for a pillow or wallhanging.

Satin stitch.

Chain stitch.

Stem stitch.

Long and short stitch.

A

B

French knot.

Graph pattern for dragon design

each square = 1 inch square

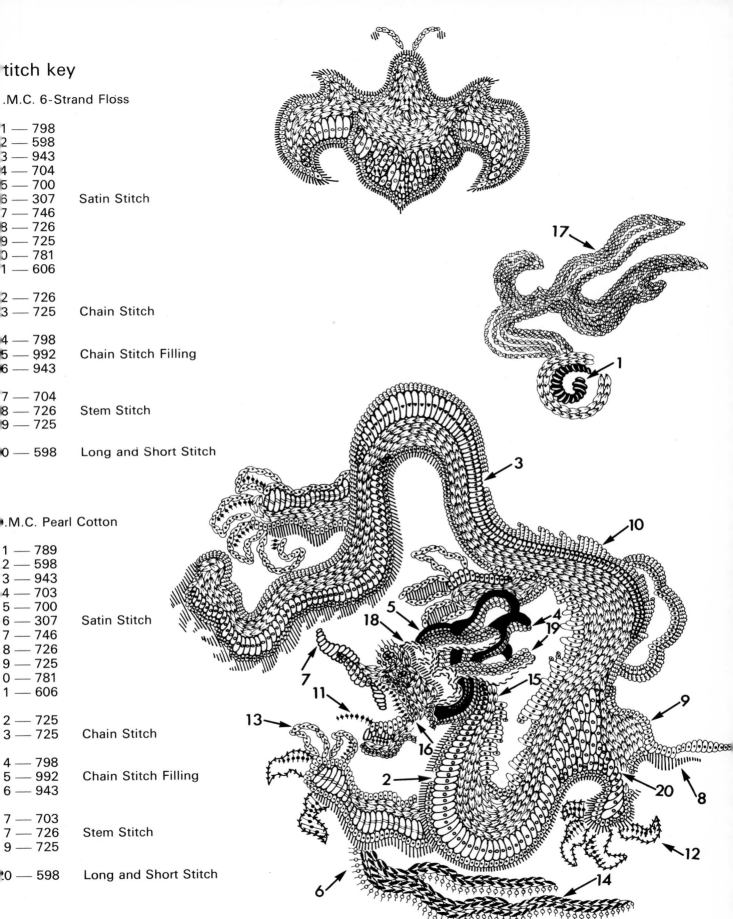

Circles and spirals

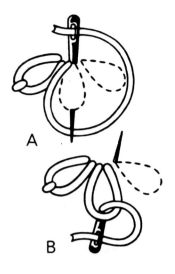

A

B

Detached chain stitch.

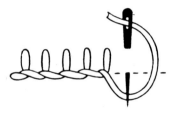

Buttonhole stitch.

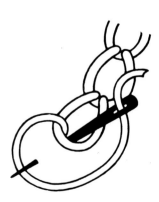

Chain stitch.

The colorful design on this pillow is based on a theme of circles. A vibrant range of colors and a few simple stitches combine to make this attractive pillow. A striking effect could be achieved by matching one embroidered pillow with others in plain fabrics chosen to pick up the embroidery thread colors.

Fabric required
17in squares of heavy cotton.

You will also need
16in square pillow form.
Crewel needles, No. 6 and No. 7.
Contrasting bias binding.

Yarn
D.M.C. 6-strand floss in the following colors and quantities: 1 skein each 796 indigo; 3326 magenta; 553 violet; 611 bark; 793 delphinium; 3024 tawny beige; 778 muted pink; 794 periwinkle; 825 king-fisher.

The design
Work the chain stitch flowers with three strands of floss. Stitch in a spiral from the outer edge to the center. The violet flowers are worked in a long detached chain stitch angled toward the center point. Work a smaller second stitch within each petal. The little flowers in the delphinium are made with closely stitched buttonhole wheels, using four strands in the needle.

To finish the pillow
Press the embroidery face down over a thick pad. Decorate the edges with a bias binding piping. Match it to one of the colors in the embroidery. Pin the two pillow pieces, right sides together, with the folded bias binding between the two layers and the fold of the binding facing into the center. Stitch three sides together through all layers. On the fourth side, stitch the binding to the seam line of the embroidered square. Turn the piece to the right side and press. Insert the pillow form and close with an overcast stitch, with a zipper or with snap fasteners.

Tracing pattern for flower bed pillow

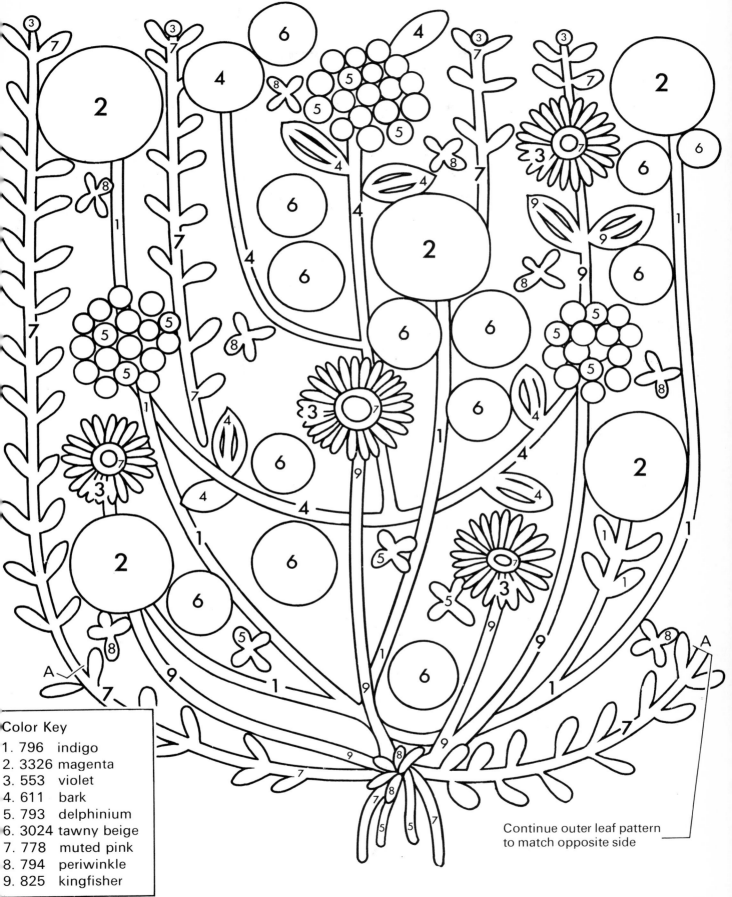

Color Key
1. 796   indigo
2. 3326 magenta
3. 553   violet
4. 611   bark
5. 793   delphinium
6. 3024 tawny beige
7. 778   muted pink
8. 794   periwinkle
9. 825   kingfisher

Continue outer leaf pattern
to match opposite side

357

Working a family tree

Each square =
1 inch square

The design for the family tree shown here is reduced by half. Alter the design to accomodate a larger or smaller family.

One of the best ways of using stitches recently learned is to make up a sampler. This family tree uses four simple stitches, all illustrated on the previous pages and will make a beautiful and very personal addition to your home.

This adaptable embroidered version of a family tree was worked by Mrs Mary Pilcher for her grandson Robin (at the top of the tree), who is the fifth generation of Pilchers shown.

This family tree was worked as a present for Robin's second birthday, but a family tree for your own family would make an equally appropriate wedding or christening gift. The number of branches and sprigs will, of course, vary with the size of the family represented and also with the degree of lineage shown.

For your own tree, choose the fabric and colors that you like, remembering that the more personal the choice, the more your embroidered family tree will mean to you and to those who will, in time, inherit it.

Be sure to date your tree too, as Mrs Pilcher has done, because one day some member of a future generation will regard it with pride as a family heirloom.

Size
10 inches by $15\frac{3}{4}$ inches.
With the dimensions of the mounting board used as a frame, 13 inches by $18\frac{3}{4}$ inches.

Fabric required
$\frac{1}{2}$ yard ivory colored linen
$\frac{1}{2}$ yard of textured linen or similar fabric in contrasting color

You will also need
Anchor Stranded Cotton in the following colors, 0268 medium moss green, 0269 dark moss green, 0280 medium muscat green, 0281 dark muscat green, 0308 amber gold, 0358 medium peat brown, 0359 dark peat brown, 0326 dark orange, 0332 flame.
Shelf paper or similar grease-proof or tracing paper, each sheet measuring approximately 10 inches by 14 inches.
Two pieces heavy cardboard for mounting, one measuring 10 inches by $15\frac{3}{4}$ inches and the other 13 inches by $18\frac{3}{4}$ inches.
2 yards rickrack trim.
Rubber adhesive.
$2\frac{1}{2}$ yards masking tape.

The design
Planning the design
1 Use the design given as a basic pattern for your own family tree, adjusting it as required. Work out whatever changes are necessary on a sheet of shelf paper, doing

this preliminary work in pencil so that changes can be easily made.

2 Fold the sheet of shelf paper in half lengthwise, making a sharp crease. Open it out and use the center, vertical fold as a guide line for the tree trunk. Draw in the tree trunk with a pencil. Make a list of the baby's relations or members of the family to be included, and decide how many branches the tree will need. If working the tree for a baby, the names of his parents and grandparents will be embroidered down the main trunk of the tree and great aunts, uncles and cousins on the side branches.

3 Additional side branches can be worked in if necessary and a strategically placed flower or leaf will balance the design if it becomes asymmetrical. After adjusting the design of the tree, outline it in ink. Underline the names to be worked in ink, but omit the names on this pattern.

Transferring the design

1 Fold the tracing paper vertically as above, open it out and place over the design, matching the center folds. Trace all the lines you will need for the embroidery.

2 Fold the background material in half lengthwise, making certain the fold is along the straight grain of the fabric. Put a few pins along the center fold as a guideline. Place the tracing of the design over the material, matching the folds, then pin and baste them together.

3 With small basting stitches baste along all the lines for embroidery, being careful to start and finish securely so that the basting threads won't pull out. Tear away the paper, leaving the basted design on the background fabric. These basting stitches are removed as the embroidery progresses by snipping the thread and pulling out a short length at a time.

To make the family tree

Follow the working chart and key for stitches and colors to be used in the design. The key also indicates the number of strands to be used in each area.

1 Use two pieces of heavy cardboard to mount the embroidered panel and frame it. The smaller piece measures 10 inches by 15¾ inches and the larger, 13 inches by 18¾ inches.

2 Place the smaller piece of cardboard on a table so that one side extends over the edge by a few inches. Lay the embroidery over it, right side up, centering the work as carefully as possible. Starting at the center of one side, feel the edge of the cardboard through the material with your left thumb and pin at 1 inch intervals. Stick the pins straight through the edge of the card-

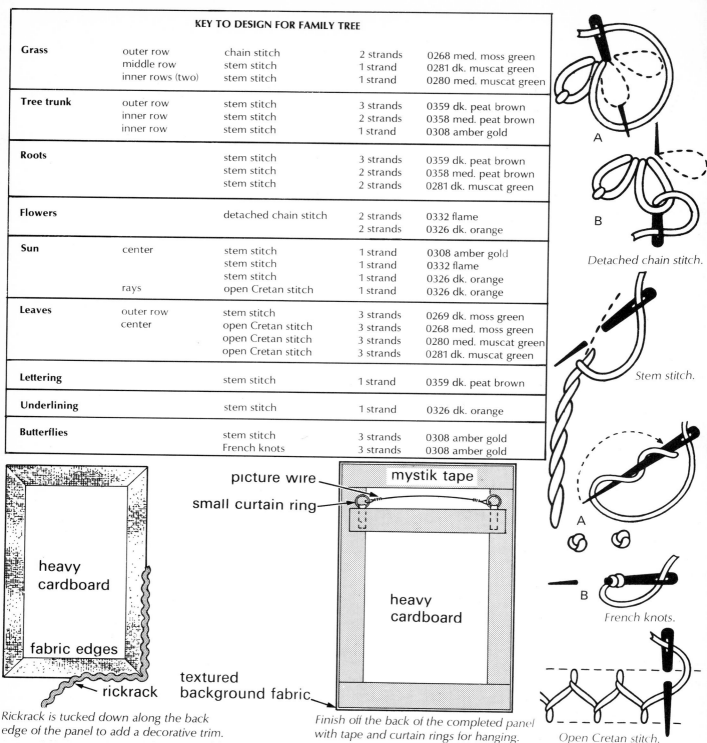

KEY TO DESIGN FOR FAMILY TREE

Grass	outer row	chain stitch	2 strands	0268 med. moss green
	middle row	stem stitch	1 strand	0281 dk. muscat green
	inner rows (two)	stem stitch	1 strand	0280 med. muscat green
Tree trunk	outer row	stem stitch	3 strands	0359 dk. peat brown
	inner row	stem stitch	2 strands	0358 med. peat brown
	inner row	stem stitch	1 strand	0308 amber gold
Roots		stem stitch	3 strands	0359 dk. peat brown
		stem stitch	2 strands	0358 med. peat brown
		stem stitch	2 strands	0281 dk. muscat green
Flowers		detached chain stitch	2 strands	0332 flame
			2 strands	0326 dk. orange
Sun	center	stem stitch	1 strand	0308 amber gold
		stem stitch	1 strand	0332 flame
		stem stitch	1 strand	0326 dk. orange
	rays	open Cretan stitch	1 strand	0326 dk. orange
Leaves	outer row	stem stitch	3 strands	0269 dk. moss green
	center	open Cretan stitch	3 strands	0268 med. moss green
		open Cretan stitch	3 strands	0280 med. muscat green
		open Cretan stitch	3 strands	0281 dk. muscat green
Lettering		stem stitch	1 strand	0359 dk. peat brown
Underlining		stem stitch	1 strand	0326 dk. orange
Butterflies		stem stitch	3 strands	0308 amber gold
		French knots	3 strands	0308 amber gold

Detached chain stitch.

Stem stitch.

French knots.

Open Cretan stitch.

Rickrack is tucked down along the back edge of the panel to add a decorative trim.

Finish off the back of the completed panel with tape and curtain rings for hanging.

board, perpendicular to it. Turn the cardboard around, then pin along the opposite edge, pulling as tight as possible. Check to see that the embroidery is centered on the cardboard and that the grain of the fabric is straight in both directions; take the pins out and adjust if necessary. Now pin the third side and the fourth, so that the fabric is very tight but the embroidery is not distorted.

3 When you are quite certain that the embroidery is positioned correctly, turn the

cardboard over and stick down the edges with rubber cement. Leave the pins in place until the cement is dry, then remove them and trim the corners.

4 Cover the larger piece of cardboard with the textured background fabric in the same way. Spread a small amount of rubber cement in the center of the material to join the two panels.

If rickrack trim is used, stick it down along the back edge of the smaller panel before joining. Glue the rickrack half way down

one side of the panel, adjusting as necessary from the front. Make certain that a loop appears at each corner, stretching or easing the rickrack to make this possible. If you prefer not to frame the finished panel, cover the raw edges of the material on the back with masking tape. Slip a short length of tape through each of two small curtain rings and fix in place with masking tape. A length of picture wire can be extended between the two rings for hanging the panel.

THE ESSENTIAL STITCHES

Stitches can be divided into six main groups, according to their general method of construction, and as you become more expert you will see how they can be adapted to add interest and individuality to your work.

Line stitches
Stem stitch

This stitch is used principally as a line or outline stitch. Work from left to right taking small slanting stitches along the line of the design. The thread should always emerge on the left-hand side of the previous stitch and should be below the needle. Outline stitch is worked in the same way but the thread should be above the needle.

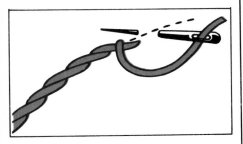

Backstitch

Work from right to left. Bring the thread through the stitch line, take a small stitch back into fabric and bring out the needle the same distance in front of the first stitch. To repeat, insert the needle into the fabric at the point of the first stitch.

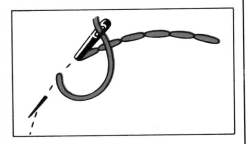

Split stitch

This can be used as a line stitch and a filling stitch when worked closely together. Work from left to right. Bring the thread through the stitch line and make a small stitch with the needle pointing backward.

Bring the needle up piercing the working thread and splitting it.

Running stitch

Work from right to left. Insert the needle into the fabric making stitches of equal length above and below the fabric so that on both sides the stitches and spaces are of equal length.

Pekinese stitch

Work a row of backstitch, then interlace it with a different, preferably heavier thread, for contrast. The bottom part of the interlacing should lie flat, leaving a looped edge on the upper side of the backstitch.

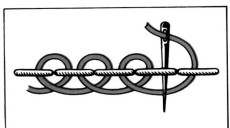

Flat or filling stitches
Satin stitch

This is a close straight stitch which is usually used as a filling stitch. The stitches

should be flat and even on the right side of the work.

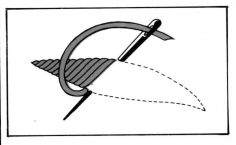

Herringbone stitch

Work from bottom left to upper right. Bring the needle out on the lower line at left and insert at top right, making a small stitch to the left and keeping the thread below the needle. Repeat, making a small stitch at bottom and top as you progress. The stitch can be laced in a variety of ways with ribbon or thread and can be as narrow or as wide as desired.

Encroaching satin stitch

This is another useful way of shading. Work the tops of the stitches in the second and subsequent rows in between the bases of the stitches in the row above.

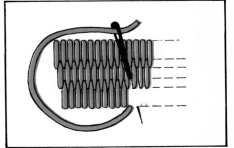

Padded satin stitch

For small surfaces in a design and to give additional texture, some parts may be padded with rows of small running stitches, chain or split stitch before the satin stitch is worked. To make a neat contour you can outline the edge first with split stitch and then work satin stitch over the whole shape.

Raised satin stitch

This is effective for small parts of pictures where you want a three-dimensional effect. Start in the same way as for padded satin stitch across the shape. Then work a second layer at right angles to the first one.

Chevron stitch

Work from bottom left to top right and from top to bottom alternately, making small backstitches. Bring out the needle halfway along each backstitch, keeping the thread alternately above and below the needle as the stitch progresses.

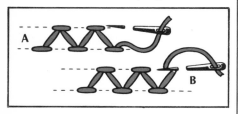

Fishbone stitch

This is a useful filling stitch which should be kept even and compact. Note the small straight stitch at the beginning which is not repeated. Bring the thread through at A and make a small straight vertical stitch along the center line of the shape. Bring the thread through again at B and make a sloping stitch across the center line at the base of the first stitch. Bring the thread through at C and make a similar sloping

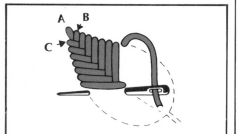

stitch to overlap the previous stitch. Continue working alternately on each side until the shape is filled.

Looped stitches

This group of stitches shows only some of the many which are formed by looping thread around a needle.

Buttonhole stitch

Work from left to right, starting on the bottom line. Insert the needle into the fabric above the line at desired distance, take a straight downward stitch, and bring out the needle with the thread under it. Pull up the stitch to form a loop and repeat the process. Once the basic method of working the stitch is mastered, the variations such as closed, up and down and knotted buttonhole stitch are not difficult.

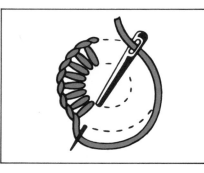

Vandyke stitch

This stitch closely worked will form a thick plaited line but it can also be used as a filling stitch. It must be worked very evenly to form a good plait. Bring the thread through at A. Take a small horizontal stitch at B and insert the needle at C. Bring the thread through at D. Without piercing the fabric, pass the needle under the crossed threads at B and insert at E. Do not pull the stitches too tightly or the regularity of the center plait will be lost.

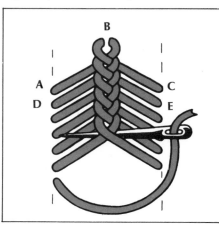

Cretan stitch

A most useful and versatile stitch with a number of uses when worked closely or

openly and irregularly. Work from left to right. Bring the needle through on the left-hand side, take a small stitch on lower line with the needle pointing upward and the thread behind it. Take a stitch on the upper line with the thread under the needle. Repeat movements.

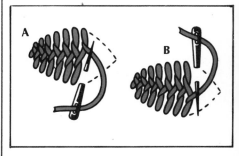

Loop stitch

This is similar to Vandyke stitch but its effect is not so heavy and the two should not be confused. Work from right to left. Start at center of the stitching line, take the thread through at A and insert at B, bring through at C immediately below B. Keep the thread to the left and under the needle, pass the needle under the first stitch without entering the fabric.

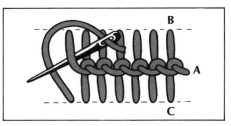

Feather stitch

This stitch gives a feathery effect but must be worked very evenly to prevent it becoming straggly. Bring out the needle at top center, hold the thread down with the left thumb, insert the needle a little to the right on the same level and take a small stitch down to the center, keeping the thread under the needle point.

Insert the needle again, this time a little to the left on the same level as the previous stitch and take a stitch to center, keeping the thread under the needle.

The design is completed by working these two movements alternately

Fly stitch

This can be worked closely as a line and either regularly or sparsely as a filling. Work from the left when using it horizontally and from the top when working on a vertical line. Bring the thread through at top left, hold it down with the left thumb, insert the needle to the right on the same level and take a small stitch down to the center with the thread below the needle. Pull through and insert the needle below the center stitch to hold the loop and bring it through in position to begin the next stitch.

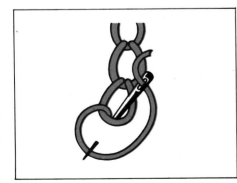

Chain stitches

There are at least nine varieties of chain stitch and the simpler versions, such as ordinary chain, twisted chain and open chain, can be whipped, overcast or threaded.

Chain stitch

This is usually worked from top to bottom vertically and from right to left horizontally. Start by bringing the thread through at the top and inserting the needle again at the same place, forming a loop. (If you are working in the hand, you may find it easier to hold the loop down with your left thumb.) Take a small stitch forward, bringing the needle up through the loop and keeping the thread under the needle. Repeat the stitch, varying its length as desired.

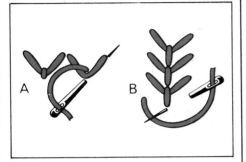

Twisted chain stitch

This most useful stitch should be worked closely and evenly to produce a firm twisted line. Work as for ordinary chain

stitch but insert the needle just outside the last loop and at a slight angle to the stitching line with the thread below the point of the needle, as shown.

Open chain stitch

This must be worked evenly to prevent it from becoming very loose and uneven. Bring the needle through at A, hold down the thread and insert the needle at B, the desired width of the stitch, then bring the needle through at C, the desired depth of the stitch, leaving the loop thus formed slightly loose. Insert the needle now at D and, with the thread under the needle, bring it through for the next stitch. Secure the last loop with a small stitch at each side.

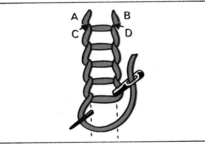

Heavy chain stitch

This makes a very firm close line. Start at the top and work down. Bring out the thread at point A and make a small vertical stitch. Bring the thread through at B and pass the needle under the vertical stitch without penetrating the fabric, using the eye of the needle, rather than the point, since this is easier. Insert the needle again at B and bring it out at C. Pass the needle under the vertical stitch and insert again at C. Continue forming stitches in this way, passing the needle under the two preceding loops.

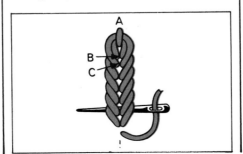

Rosette chain

For this stitch to be effective with either thick or thin threads it must be worked evenly and closely, with no loose top edge. Work from right to left and bring the thread through at the right end of the upper line, then pass it to the left, holding it down with the left thumb. Insert the needle into the upper line a short distance from where it first emerged and bring it out on the lower line with the thread under the needle point. Draw the needle through the loop and, using the eye of the needle, pass it under the top edge of the stitch.

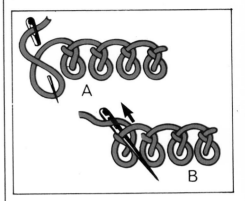

Wheatear

This is a simple stitch which combines straight stitches and a chain stitch. Work two straight stitches at A and B. Bring the thread through below these at C and pass the thread under the two straight stitches without penetrating the fabric. Insert the needle again at C, bring it through at D and repeat.

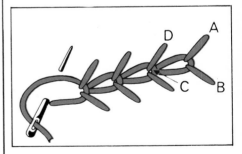

Knotted stitches

Some of the stitches in this group, such as French knots and bullion, are intended to be worked as single stitches while others are more suitable for use as line stitches.

French knots

Bring out the needle at the required position, hold the thread down with the left thumb and encircle the thread with the needle two or three times, depending on the thickness of the thread and the size of knot desired. Still holding the thread firmly, return the needle to the starting point and insert it very close to where the thread emerged. Pull the thread through to the wrong side of the fabric and secure if working a single stitch or pass on to the position of the next stitch if you are working a group. It is a common error to insert the needle too far from the point where the stitch was started, making a loose, untidy knot.

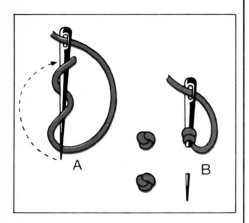

Bullion stitch

The second part of this stitch is taken back over the first part so it is this first part which dictates the finished length of the stitch. Pick up a backstitch of the desired length, bringing the needle point out where it first emerged from the fabric. Wind the thread around the needle point as many times as required to equal the space of the backstitch, hold the wound thread down with your left thumb and pull the needle through. Still holding the wound thread, return the needle to where it was first inserted (see arrow) and pull through until the stitch lies flat.

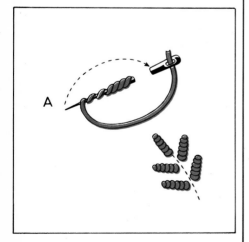

Coral stitch or knot

This is best worked as a firm line as it becomes weak and straggling if the knots are too far apart. Work from right to left or from top to bottom. Bring the thread out at the starting point and lay it along the line to be worked, holding it down with the left thumb. Take a small stitch under

the line where the knot is to be spaced (the thread lies on top of the needle as it enters the fabric) and pull through, taking the needle over the lower loop to form the knot.

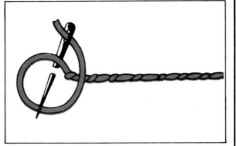

Double knot

This is a slightly more complicated knot stitch. The knots should be spaced evenly and closely to obtain a beaded effect. Bring the thread through at A and take a small stitch across the line to be worked at B. Pass the needle downward under the stitch just made without penetrating the fabric, as at C. With the thread under the needle, pass it under the first stitch again as at D. Pull the thread through to form a knot.

Knotted cable chain

Work from right to left. Bring the thread through at A and place it along the line to be worked. With the thread under the needle, take a stitch at B (which is a coral knot). Pass the needle under the stitch between A and B without penetrating the fabric, as shown at C. With the thread under the needle, make a slanting stitch across the line of stitching at D, close to the coral knot. Pull the thread through to form a chain stitch.

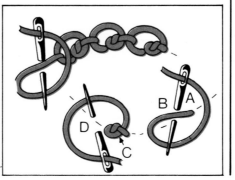

Composite stitches

These form a group which are usually worked on a foundation of satin stitch bars and they can be used as filling or line stitches. The satin stitch bars can be lengthened or shortened as desired.

Portuguese border stitch

Work the desired number of horizontal straight stitches (satin stitch bars). Working from the bottom upward, bring the thread through at the center and below the first bar (point A). Keeping the thread to the left of the needle take the thread over and under the first two bars, over the first two bars again and then under the second bar only without penetrating the fabric. With the thread now at B, work the second pair of stitches in a similar way and continue upward to the top of the row. Return to point A and work the second row of stitches up the foundation bars, keeping the thread to the right of the needle. Do not pull the surface stitches too tightly.

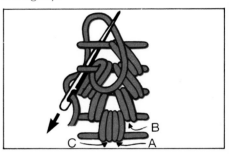

Raised chain band

If worked as a heavy line stitch it is advisable to use a finer thread for the foundation bar, but this should be of suitable weight to carry the chain stitch which can be in a heavier thread (for example 6-strand floss for the bars and soft embroidery cotton for the chain stitches). Work the desired number of satin stitch bars, then, starting at the top and working down, bring the needle through at A in the center of the first bar. Pass the needle up to the left and down to the right under the foundation bar, as shown, then through the chain loop thus formed. Repeat for the following stitches.

Raised stem band

This is worked in a similar way as for raised chain band but substituting stem stitch for chain stitch. The stem stitch can be worked from top to bottom but the effect is more even if worked from the bottom up.

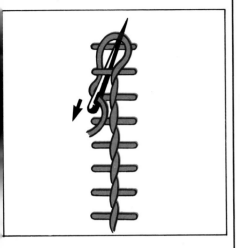

Woven band

This stitch is worked on evenly spaced foundation bars from the top down. You will require two needles with contrasting thread and you will obtain a better effect if one is shiny and the other dull, both in the same color, rather than with two contrasting colors. Bring both threads through at the top of the foundation bars with the lighter or silky thread to the left. Pass this thread under the first bar and leave it there. Take the darker or dull thread over the first bar, under the second bar and under the light thread. Leave the dark thread there and pass the light thread over the second bar, under the third bar and under the dark thread. Continue in this way to the end of the band. Begin each following row at the top. By altering the sequence of the contrasting thread, various patterns can be achieved.

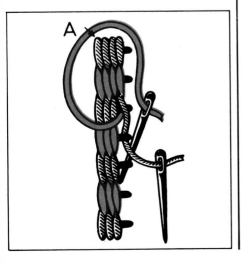

Interlaced band

This stitch is composed of two rows of backstitch with an interlacing band. The distance between the backstitch rows depends on the thickness of the inter-lacing thread, and will be greater when using a thick thread. For the backstitch, the center of the stitches in the bottom row should be directly in line with the end of the stitches in the top row so that the interlacing can be worked evenly. Bring the lacing thread through at A and interlace through every stitch as shown.

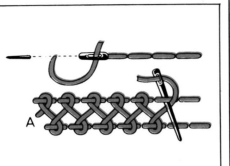

Spider's web

This is a useful and decorative stitch of which there are two varieties.

Spider web, whipped Work an even number of equal or unequal length stitches radiating from a center point — six or eight stitches is the usual number. Bring the needle through the center. Working from right to left as you progress around the spokes of the web, work a backstitch over each spoke. Pass the needle under the next thread before working the backstitch over it. To finish off, take the thread down into the fabric immediately under a spoke and fasten off underneath. The spokes of the web can be completely filled in but a better effect is made by leaving some unworked with the spokes showing.

Woven spider's web or woven wheel

Work an uneven number of stitches radiating from a center point. Bring the needle up in the center and weave the thread over and under the spokes. This can be worked from left to right or vice versa. Finish off as for the backstitched web.

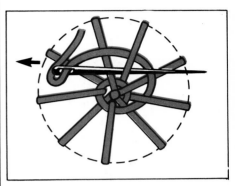

Couching

Couching a line means to lay a line of thread (heavy, light, thick or thin) on the fabric on the line of the design and stitch it down at regular intervals with another thread which may be in a contrasting color. The stitching must be evenly spaced.

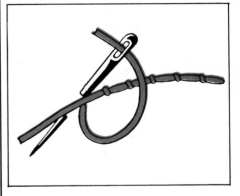

Sheaf stitch

This is a useful stitch which can be used as a filling or as an isolated stitch. It can be worked at spaced intervals or closely grouped. It consists of three vertical satin stitches which are overcast with two horizontal satin stitches, worked with the head of the needle without penetrating the fabric.

ADVANCED STITCHERY
ASSISI WORK

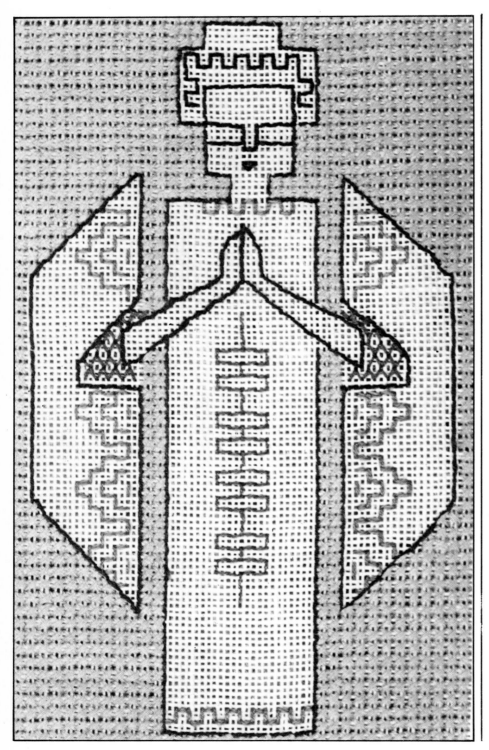

Assisi work is basically a form of cross-stitch embroidery, although the principle of the work is reversed and the stitches form the background of the design while the basic designs are left unworked. (This technique is known as 'voiding'.)

As its name suggests, Assisi work originated in Italy. For centuries it has been used to decorate ecclesiastical linen and vestments, as well as peasant clothing and household linen. Today it can be used to decorate sheets and pillows, place mats and tablecloths, or it can form an unusual embroidery on a child's dress or on an accessory such as a bag or belt.

The designs

Traditionally the designs for Assisi work were formal and generally naturalistic; representing animals, birds or flowers in a stylized manner. Geometric designs were also often used.

Contemporary Assisi work can be inspired by designs from many sources such as mosaics, carvings, wrought iron work, screen walls, architectural details, geometric patterns and lettering.

Abstract shapes or stylized reversed initials can also look effective in a border or on the pocket of a dress.

Making your own design

The simplest way is to draw the design onto a graph, starting by outlining the motif in straight lines, following the lines on the graph and then filling in the background so that you can get an idea of the effect. As with cross-stitch (see earlier), each square on the graph should represent a unit or stitch. The basic stitch is then worked over three or four threads of an even-weave fabric.

The colors

The traditional colors for the embroidery fabric in Assisi work were either white or natural linen with the stitches worked in two colors – usually browns, blues or dark reds, outlined either in a darker tone of the same color or in black.

A contemporary color scheme could be dark blue or navy threads worked on a

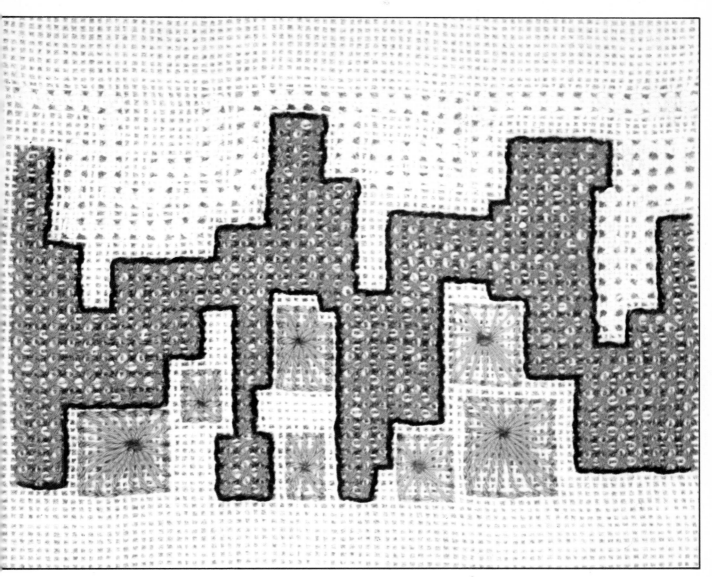

paler blue fabric or orange on yellow, although it is best not to mix colors for the stitchery.

Fabrics
Because all the stitches are worked over a specific number of threads, an even-weave fabric is essential, whether linen, cotton, wool or a synthetic home furnishings fabric.

Threads
Pearl cotton, coton à broder and linen threads of a suitable weight for the fabric can all be used for Assisi work.

Needles
Use tapestry needles of a suitable size for the fabric and thread.

Method
There are only two stitches used for this type of embroidery – cross-stitch for the background and Holbein (or double running) for the outlining of the motif, plus a combination of both stitches for a repeating pattern.

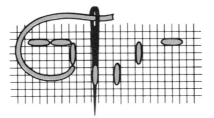

Start by working the Holbein stitch around the outline, counting the threads carefully. Make the stitches about three threads long, with equal spaces. Work around any offshoots of the design, carrying the thread out to the end of the line and back again to the main outline.

On the completion of the first step the design may look rather disjointed and muddled, but with the second step the stitch gaps are filled in and the design begins to take form. When all the outlining is complete the background can be filled in with cross-stitch. Either of the two methods of cross-stitch can be used although for large embroidered areas you may find it quicker to work it in two stages. Make sure that the upper stitch in each cross lies in the same direction and that you take the stitches right up to the outline in order to preserve the character of the work.

Adding a border
When the background is complete the embroidery should have a very solid appearance and quite often needs a small border to soften it slightly. This can be a small geometric repeating pattern in Holbein worked either side of the design.

Finishing the edges
Final hems should be narrow and unobtrusive in order not to detract from the work. On table linen a hemstitched hem usually works well, while on a dress, pocket or belt the work can be finished with an invisible hem.

Assisi work tablecloth

The design in Assisi work is achieved by working over counted threads on an evenweave fabric, with a yarn which should be of a similar thickness to the warp and weft threads of the fabric. The finer the weave, the more attractive the design will be.

The actual motifs are formed by outlining them first in Holbein (double running) stitch and then filling in the background area with cross-stitch. The fabric is thus left showing through the shape of the motifs. As the embroidery is worked over counted threads, the design has a stylized geometric look, and curves can only be indicated by stepped or diagonal stitches. If you wish to make up or adapt your own design, it is best to work it out on graph paper first (10 squares to 1 inch is suitable). Each square on the graph paper should represent one stitch and then, according to the fabric used, you can decide how many threads to work each stitch over. Most designs are repetitive and can be varied to suit the size desired. Figures 1 and 2 show two simple treatments of a flower form and figure 3 shows a stylized bird form.

Assisi work tablecloth
Size
44in square.

Fabric required
1⅓ yards of 54 inch wide cream evenweave fabric, 30 threads to 1 inch.

You will also need
Pearl Cotton No. 8 in the following colors and quantities: 3 balls 797 blue; 1 ball 310 black
Tapestry needle No. 24
Embroidery hoop

Placing the design
1 Trim the fabric to an exact square with 46 inch sides, cutting along the grain lines. Find the center by folding the fabric in half both horizontally and vertically and basting along the creases with a contrasting thread, following the grain. The point where the two lines meet marks the center of the cloth.

2 Turn under ¼ inch all around the edges and baste to prevent the fabric from fraying while you are working.

3 The chart gives just over half of one side of the square design in the center of the cloth. Each square represents one stitch worked over three threads of evenweave fabric. The center is indicated by the white arrow which should coincide with one of the lines of basting stitches. Start the Holbein stitch outline at the small black arrow 213 threads down from the crossed basting stitches, and follow the pattern as shown on the chart.

4 The design is repeated as a mirror image on the other half of the first side. Work the remaining three sides to correspond.

Working the outline
1 Work all the embroidery in a hoop. Embroider the entire outline of the bird and flower design first in Holbein stitch, using black Pearl Cotton. Holbein stitch is worked in two steps. The first row is formed by working running stitch over and under three threads of fabric, following the shape of the design. When this is completed, work back in the opposite direction, filling in the spaces left in the first row. The diagonal stitches are formed by counting three across and three down (or up as desired) and inserting the needle at this point. Work the lines of the pattern inside the motifs, as for example the bird's eye, at the same time as working the outline.

Working the background
1 When the black outline is completed, fill in the background with horizontal lines of cross-stitch, using blue Pearl Cotton. It is important to work all the stitches with the top half of the stitch facing the same way.

2 Continue each row as far as it will go and fill in any separate areas later. Since the back of the cloth should look as perfect as the front, the thread should not be carried over any of the unworked motifs.

3 Where the outline takes a diagonal direction, it may be necessary to use half a cross-stitch only in filling in the background. To finish, work the inner and outer borders in Holbein and cross-stitch as indicated on the chart, using blue Pearl Cotton.

Finishing
Press the embroidery on the wrong side. Turn under a ¾ inch hem all around, mitering the corners as shown in the diagram, and slip stitch in place. A more decorative hem can be worked if desired by withdrawing one or two threads around the edges of the cloth and finishing off with hem stitch.

As a finishing touch, repeat the Holbein and cross-stitch border about 3 inches from the edge of the cloth.

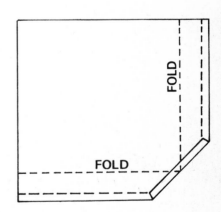

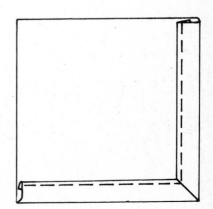

Stitch chart for Assisi work cloth

Figs 1, 2 Two simple treatments of a flower motif.

Fig 3 A basic bird motif is reversed and a simple outline added to create an effective design.

The Holbein stitch outline is worked in black Pearl Cotton and the cross-stitch background and the borders in blue Pearl Cotton.

Center of design

A

B

Cross-stitch.

Holbein or double running stitch

Each square represents one stitch worked over three threads of fabric

BLACKWORK

Blackwork is a monochrome method of embroidery, and relies for effect on the contrasting tone values produced by varying the density of the pattern fillings and the weight of yarn used.

Blackwork became fashionable in England during the reign of Henry VIII when it was used mainly for the decoration of garments. Later it was also used to decorate household articles and home furnishings. Although its name derived from the method of working a geometric pattern in black silk or cotton threads on a white or cream background, any combination which gives a good contrast between dark thread and lighter fabric can be used. In the Tudor period it was frequently worked with a dark red silk on a cream fabric.

The fabric

Since blackwork is a counted thread method of embroidery, choose a fabric which is evenly woven and where the threads can be easily counted.

You could also use a heavy slubbed evenweave linen or cotton which will give a slightly uneven but attractive variation to the stitchery.

The threads and needles

You will need a selection of threads of all weights to provide the depth of tone and contrast in the stitchery. Machine Embroidery cotton No. 30, pure sewing silk, 6-strand floss, pearl cotton Nos. 5 and 8, coton à broder and matte embroidery thread (on a heavier fabric) are all suitable and some of the various types of lurex and metal threads can also be incorporated. You will need tapestry needles in a variety of sizes to suit the fabric and threads.

The stitches

The stitches are simple and mostly variations of backstitch. Holbein or double running stitch can also be used for building up a border pattern incorporating blackwork filling stitches.

The patterns

The basis of all blackwork patterns is a simple geometric design which can be adapted to the depth of tone desired either by using a heavier or lighter thread or by adding and subtracting additional straight stitches. The spacing of the pattern will also enable a lighter or darker tone to be achieved.

The traditional method of working blackwork was to use the patterns as fillings for shapes of flowers, birds or animals, with the shape outlined with a heavier thread. Today these heavy outlines are usually omitted.

If you are experimenting with blackwork, start by using one basic pattern, working it first over four threads of fabric and then altering the tone or size of the pattern by adding or subtracting part of it. Alternatively, you might work the pattern over a different number of threads.

The pattern shown below can be made to appear darker, for example, by working a small cross-stitch in the center of each shape, or lighter in tone if each alternate small cross was omitted.

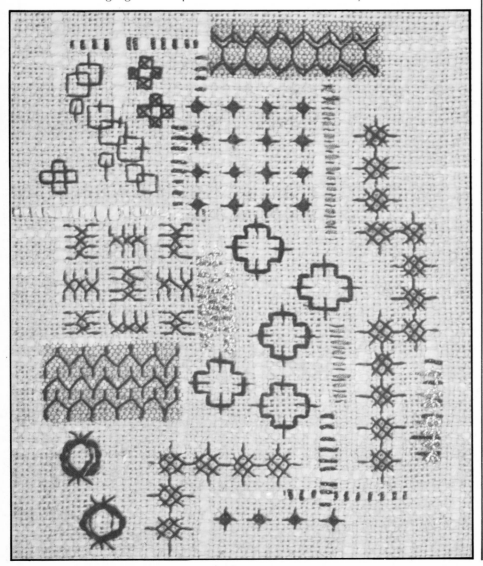

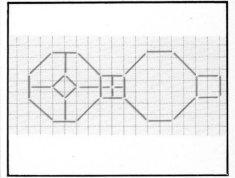

Blackwork chessboard

The chessboard illustrated over, is in fact a blackwork sampler, showing a variety of filling patterns. By working the patterns in alternate squares with blank squares in between, the sampler becomes an attractive and unusual chessboard as well as a permanent reference for the various patterns.

The sampler was stretched over plywood, covered in glass to keep it clean and give a good playing surface for chess, and then framed.

Size

The materials given below are for a chessboard 16 inches square, excluding the border, with 2 inch individual squares.

Right: A simple design in blackwork ideal to form a border.
Below: A complex arrangement of blackwork stitches used to create an abstract design for a wallhanging or picture.

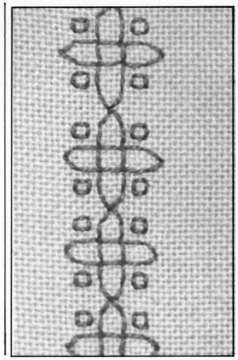

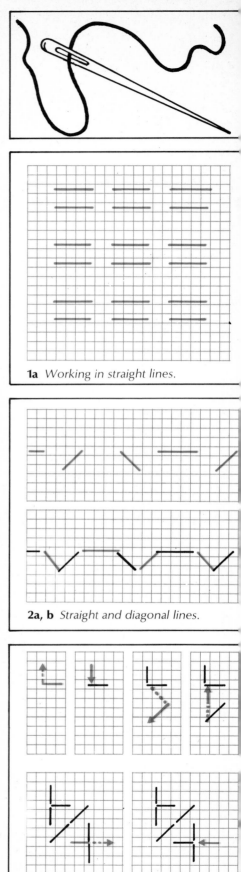

1a *Working in straight lines.*

2a, b *Straight and diagonal lines.*

3a–o *Step by step to building up individual units by working in circular movements. This pattern could be work*

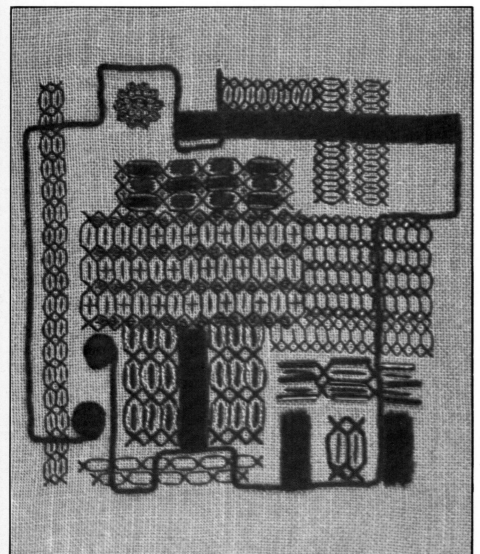

Creating Blackwork patterns

All you need to create your blackwork patterns are graph paper, a ruler and a sharp pointed pencil. Work on the basis of one line on the graph equalling one thread of fabric and draw the patterns using basic geometric shapes from which you can develop intricate and interesting patterns. In order to stitch continuously around the design, so that you do not waste thread, you can work straight lines to form a plain grid or straight lines including diagonals or you can move in continuous circles for complicated patterns.

⊞	Threads of fabric
—	New stitch on right side
----	New stitch on wrong side
→	Direction of stitch
⟳	Back stitch
◯	Detached chain stitch
—	Stitch already worked

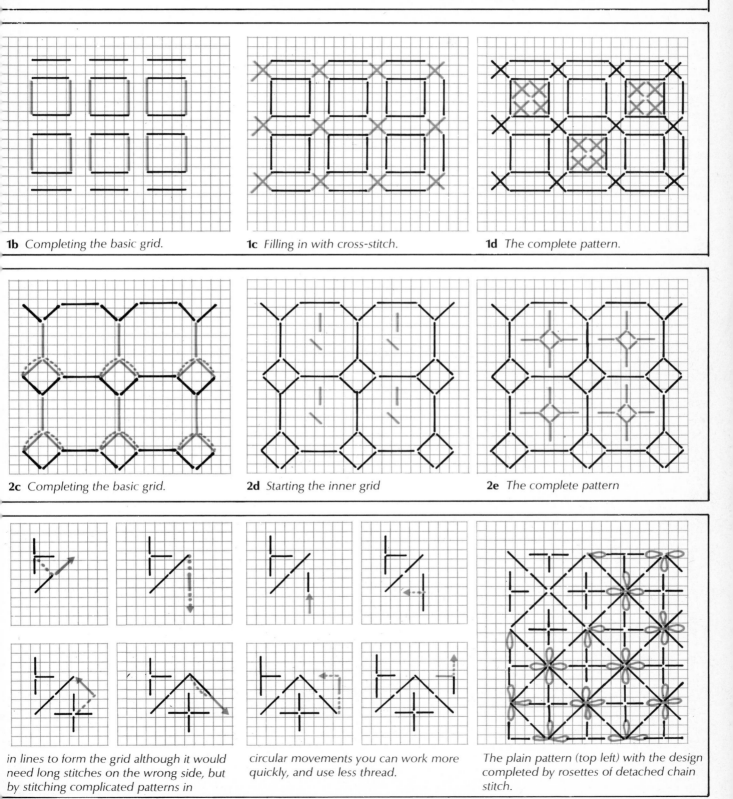

1b Completing the basic grid.

1c Filling in with cross-stitch.

1d The complete pattern.

2c Completing the basic grid.

2d Starting the inner grid

2e The complete pattern

in lines to form the grid although it would need long stitches on the wrong side, but by stitching complicated patterns in

circular movements you can work more quickly, and use less thread.

The plain pattern (top left) with the design completed by rosettes of detached chain stitch.

373

Fabric required

Evenweave embroidery fabric, 24in square, with 18 threads per 1in.

You will also need

Threads, pearl cotton, one 10grm ball No. 5 and two 10grm balls No. 8 in black, seven spools twisted silk.

Tapestry needles, No. 26 for silk thread and No. 22 for pearl cotton.

Plywood 20in square (this can be larger if you want a wide frame).

Staples and staple gun

Glass and framing materials

The design

1 First check that the fabric is cut on the straight grain or straighten if necessary. Find the center of each side of the fabric by folding it in half and marking the fold at each edge with a few basting stitches. Open out the fabric, refold the other way and mark the fold again.

2 Starting at the center, and 4 inches in from the edge on one side, begin by out-lining the shape of the board in backstitch, using the No. 5 pearl cotton and working each stitch over three threads of the fabric. At 2 inch intervals all the way around on the backstitch border, work a single stitch of the same size at right angles and facing inward to indicate the chart for the squares (if you do this there will be no need to recount the threads). Complete the chart by joining up the single stitches in lines across the board.

3 Work the patterns of your choice, using different threads to give variety. Work the border to the size you desire.

Finishing

Press the embroidery on the wrong side. Stretch over the plywood and secure on the wrong side with staples. Cover with glass and frame.

This town scene, designed by Pauline Liu, is a clever example of how blackwork gives contrasting tone values by varying the density of the stitchery.

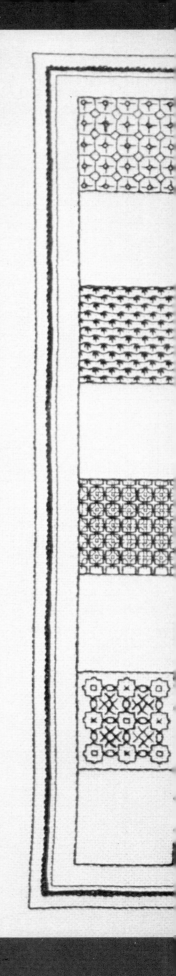

One way of keeping a permanent record of blackwork patterns is to work a sampler, such as this one designed as a chess-board by Pamela Tubby.

DRAWN AND PULLED THREAD WORK
Drawn thread work

Drawn thread work is a method of embroidery which creates a lacy fabric from a plain, closely woven one. It is primarily used for decorative borders for table linen where threads parallel to the edge of the fabric are withdrawn and the remaining threads in the border (those at right angles to the edge) are grouped together by simple stitchery.

The fabric

When choosing a fabric for drawn thread work the most important considerations are that it should be evenweave (with an equal number of warp and weft threads) which can be easily counted and withdrawn.

Linen is the traditional choice for drawn thread work (perhaps because of its durability for table linen), and it is available in an even-weave with a thread count which varies from very fine to the coarser heavier variety.

There are many other suitable evenweave fabrics, including some synthetics, which do not need ironing and are very practical for place mats, table cloths, etcetera. To decide whether a fabric is evenweave, cut a hole 1 inch square in a piece of cardboard, hold it over the fabric and count the threads enclosed in the "window" – there should be the same number in both directions.

The threads

Threads for this type of embroidery need to be strong and hard wearing. It is usually best to choose a matching thread which is slightly heavier than the threads of the fabric for the decorative stitching and a finer one for hem stitching and buttonholing. On a medium-weight linen, for example, a light weight embroidery thread (not 6-strand) is suitable for hem-stitching and buttonholing, with a slightly heavier one for the additional stitchery. However, it is worth experimenting with the thread on a spare piece of fabric since it might do well and be effective to use one thread throughout.

The needles

Tapestry needles of appropriate size should always be used because their blunt points separate the threads of the fabric while a regular sewing needle might split them.

The stitches

The simplest form of drawn thread work is hem-stitching, in which the outer edge of the border is level with the inner edge of the hem so that the stitching can be

Café curtains given a neat but delicate border by the use of drawn thread work.

worked alternately to secure the hem and group the threads in the border. There are numerous decorative ways in which the threads of the border can be stitched, twisted or knotted together. Some of the most commonly used stitches are ladder stitch, coral knot, double knot and herringbone stitch.

Hem-stitched borders

Before starting a major project, it is advisable to work a simple hem-stitched border for a place mat or napkin.

1 Decide on the finished depth of the hem and measure in double this amount plus the depth of the first turning.

2 Using the point of a tapestry needle, pull out the thread immediately above the total depth of the hem and withdraw it across the width of the fabric.

3 Continue to pull out threads of fabric until the border is the desired depth.

4 Turn up the hem to the edge of the border and baste in place.

5 To work the hem-stitching, first knot the end of the thread and run it along the hem so that the knot is securely inside.

6 Starting at the edge of the fabric, wrap the working thread around the first two threads of the border, make a hem stitch into the fold of the hem as for regular hemming, then overcast the next two threads of the border. Continue in this way, overcasting the threads of the border and hemming the fold alternately for the length of the border, always picking up the same number of threads each time.

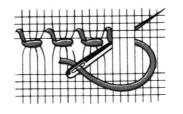

7 To strengthen the opposite edge of the border, work along it in a similar way, overcasting the same pairs of threads and

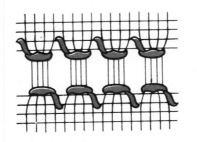

overcasting the edge of the fabric to match the hemmed side.

Four-sided and satin stitch border

When working a border around all four sides of a cloth, the threads are withdrawn in a slightly different way.

1 Calculate the total depth of the hem as for a simple border. Measure in this amount from both directions in each corner and mark the point where they meet with a pin or colored tack to indicate the outer corners of the border. Threads must not be withdrawn beyond this point.

2 Cut the first thread of the border 1 inch away from the marked point at both ends. Pull out the cut ends as far as the point and leave them hanging. Pull out the remaining portion of thread completely from the middle.

3 Continue to withdraw threads in this way all around the border for the required depth.

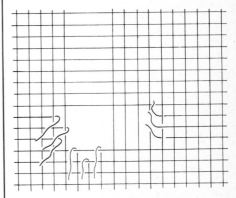

4 The strongest and neatest way of securing the loose threads at the corners is to turn them back into the hem and enclose them when the hem is stitched. Alternatively, on a very fine and firmly woven linen the threads can be cut close to the edge and secured by buttonhole stitch.

5 Turn up the hem, mitering the corners, and stitch the diagonal fold neatly.

6 Work the hem stitching as for a simple border.

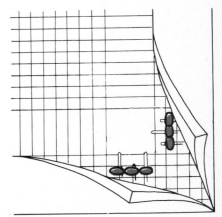

Drawn thread insertions and borders

These insertions can all be used for table linen, to decorate the hems of curtains and, if worked in a heavier thread, for garments. Most drawn thread insertions are first hem stitched along both edges, thus securing the hem if the insertions are used as a border and strengthening the edges when used as plain insertions. They may also be used for tying the threads together for the final decorative stitches.

Twisted border

In this insertion, the tied threads are twisted together into bunches of two or three. For wide insertions, two or three rows of twisting can be worked. Beads can also be picked up on the needle between each twisting to make an attractive variation.

1 Using a heavier or contrasting thread to the one used for hemstitching, anchor it to the middle of the outside edge of the corner square of the border.

2 Pass the needle over the space to form one spoke of the spider's web filling to be completed later.

3 Take the needle over the first two tied groups of threads, then back under the second group and over the first group. Pull

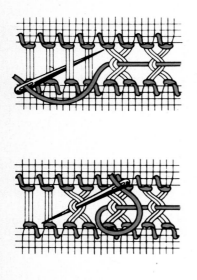

the thread taut so that the groups twist.

4 Repeat this process along the whole border, take the thread across to the opposite side of the corner space and fasten off on the wrong side.

5 Continue in this way on each side of the border.

6 Add four extra crossing threads to the four already formed in each corner space and complete the wheel or web.

Coral stitch twisted border

This is worked in a similar way, but coral stitch is used to tie the groups together.

Lattice border

The groups of threads are drawn together with a binding stitch, by taking the thread alternately above and below the groups.

1 Pass the needle over the first two groups, bring the needle around the second group, pass it over the second and third group, around the third group and over the third and fourth group.

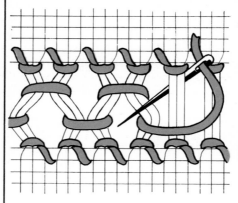

2 Continue in this way, binding the bunches above and below as shown, passing the needle behind the bars from right to left and keeping the working thread above the needle behind the bars from right to left for the lower bars.

Needleweaving border

This can be very effective when worked on a heavy slubbed linen with a combination of self and contrasting threads.

1 Work the hem-stitching along each edge, tying the threads into bunches of four.

2 Run the working threads into the hem or edge above the starting point, leaving about 1 inch to be darned in when the needle weaving is finished.

3 Bring the needle through the hem or edge and pass it over the first four threads to the right, bring the needle up again at the starting point and pass it over and under the first two threads to the left.

4 Working on these four threads, weave over and under until you are halfway down the block of withdrawn threads.

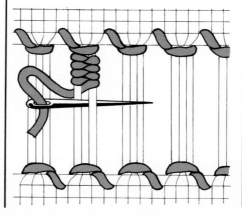

5 Pass the needle to the next four threads to the right and continue weaving over this block until you reach the opposite edge of the insertion.

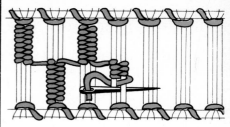

6 Carry the working thread inside this completed block of weaving until you reach the starting point of the block in the middle of the border.

7 Start weaving upward on the next group of four threads to the right, continuing to the top of the border.

8 Continue to weave upward and downward on the groups, carrying the needle through the woven blocks to the next position.

9 When you reach the end of the insertion, return to the beginning and weave on the remaining threads in each block to complete the insertion. Fasten the thread securely and thread it back through the last block of weaving to make the work neat. The weaving should be as neat on the back as on the front of the work.

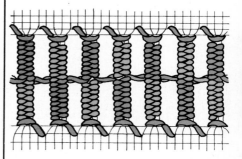

Finishing the corners

Where the withdrawn threads meet at the corners of a border a small square space is formed which should be strengthened and filled with stitchery, such as a woven spider's web. This should be worked after the hem stitching and additional stitchery is worked.

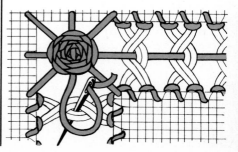

Pulled thread work

Pulled thread work is a method of creating a pattern of holes, spaces or shapes on an even-weave fabric with embroidery stitches which are pulled tightly.

This type of embroidery is ideal for making all kinds of table linen and for lampshades, borders on garments, curtains, bedspreads and pillows.

Sometimes known as drawn fabric work, it is of European peasant origin and started with the use of embroidery on loosely woven muslins and calicos. To prevent the threads from lying loosely over the fabric the stitches were pulled tightly and it was discovered that this could create attractive patterns.

Pulled thread work should not be confused with drawn thread work, in which the pattern is created by actually withdrawing threads from the fabric and stitching on those remaining.

The fabric

Pulled thread work is a form of counted thread embroidery where the stitches are worked over a specific number of threads. For this reason the fabric should be of an even-weave (one with an equal number of warp and weft threads to the same measurement) and the threads should be large enough to count easily.

Several kinds of fabric are suitable, such as linen in various weights, from heavy home furnishing linen to linen scrim used for cleaning; cotton in many weights and colors; evenweave wools; Moygashel dress fabrics and synthetic home furnishing fabrics.

The thread

Generally the thread used for the stitchery should be of equal thickness to a withdrawn thread of the fabric, with the addition of thicker or thinner threads to vary the texture and pattern. If the fabric is a good one and will unravel easily, it is possible to remove threads from an unused end and work the embroidery in these.

Other suitable threads include the pearl and crochet cottons which are available in all weights and in a good range of colors, and although traditionally this type of embroidery was worked in self-color thread, today a contrast color is often used.

Pure silk buttonhole thread is good too, particularly when a fine thread of silky texture is needed. Threads to avoid are stranded embroidery floss, linen threads and mercerized sewing cotton, since these tend to fray and break.

Needles

Always use a tapestry needle for pulled thread work as this will not split the threads of the fabric. Normally the needle should be of a suitable weight for the fabric so it passes between the threads easily. But when you are working a border or edging in a progressive stitch such as three-sided or four-sided stitch, you may find it easier to use a larger needle than that used for the rest of the work.

Frames

Always use a frame for this type of work as it will keep it at an even tension, prevent the fabric from pulling out of shape and enable the threads to be counted easily. The only exception to this rule would be when you are working an edging.

The stitches

The stitches used in pulled thread embroidery are some of the easiest to work and many are based on satin stitch, worked in lines or blocks either at an even tension or pulled tightly. When these two methods are combined, a pattern is produced which can be varied at will. A combination of only two stitches, such as four-sided stitch and satin stitch, can produce a number of patterns when the tension and stitch order are varied. Honeycomb stitch and three-sided stitch are other stitches used. (Border stitches are covered in the next chapter.)

Before you start a project, it is advisable to practice some of the stitches, working each separately and then in combinations, using both thin and thick threads (such as a fine crochet cotton and a heavier pearl cotton).

To begin stitching do not use a knot but bring the thread through the fabric some distance away from the stitching point and make a small backstitch to anchor it. Continue working until the thread is finished then return to the starting point and darn in the surplus thread through the stitching line. Alternatively, hold the end of the thread under the stitching line for a short way and work over it.

To finish stitching darn in the end of the thread to the stitchery on the back of the work, making a small backstitch to secure it. Pulled thread work should be as neat on the back of the fabric as on the front, particularly for table linen and lampshades.

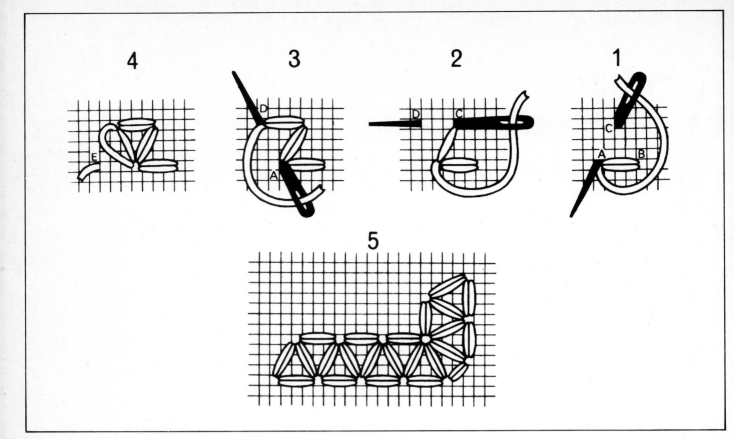

Three-sided stitch (A)

This stitch is worked from right to left. Figure 1: Bring the thread through at A and make two stitches from A to B over four threads of fabric. Bring the needle through at A and take two stitches to C. Figure 2. Bring the needle through at D and take two stitches from D to C. Figure 3. Take two stitches from D to A. Figure 4. Bring the needle through at E. Figure 5. Turning a corner.

Honeycomb filling stitch (B)

This stitch is worked from the top down. Figure 1. Bring the needle through at the arrow and insert at A. Bring through at B and insert at A. Bring through at B and insert at C. Bring through at D, insert again at C and bring through at D. Continue in this way for the row. Figure 2. Where rows connect, the vertical stitches are worked into the same holes.

Four-sided stitch (C)

This stitch is worked from right to left. Figure 1: Bring the thread through at the arrow, insert it at A and bring it through at B. Figure 2: Insert at the arrow and bring it out at D.
Figure 3: Insert at A and bring it out at B. Continue in this way for a row or close the end for a single stitch.

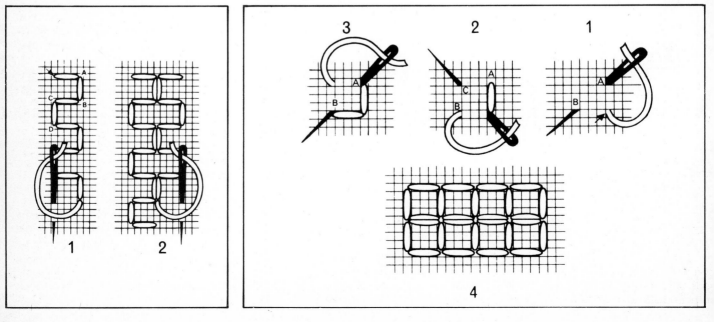

Edgings and borders

One of the most attractive of the various techniques of pulled thread work is to combine them to form simple yet decorative borders on all types of household linen.

Four sided borders

This border is suitable for table linen or to decorate the panels of a lampshade. It combines a repeating pattern of seven satin stitches worked over eight threads with a block of four four-sided stitches worked over four threads. The satin stitch is pulled tightly and the four-sided stitch is worked at normal tension.

1 Using a thread similar in weight to the fabric, work seven satin stitches over eight threads of the fabric. Follow this by four four-sided stitches worked over the center four threads of the eight. Continue in this way to the end of the row.

2 Repeat this row two or three times to form a border of the desired width (you will normally need a wider border for a lampshade than for a place mat, for example).

3 Start the next row with four four-sided stitches worked over the center four threads of a block of eight. Continue with seven satin stitches over all the eight threads. Continue in this way to the end of the row.

4 Repeat this row until you have the same number of rows as the first pattern. The satin stitches should alternate with the four-sided stitches every two or three rows, depending on the width of the pattern desired. The pattern can be varied further by changing the stitch sequence in alternate rows.

Honeycomb and satin stitch border

This border can be worked vertically as shown in the previous chapter to decorate the panels of a lampshade, or it can be worked horizontally for table linen. Follow the diagram for honeycomb stitch, but incorporate eight satin stitches pulled tightly, followed by one backstitch and eight more satin stitches from each backstitch section of honeycomb stitch.

1 Bring the needle through at the arrow.

2 Insert the needle four threads to the right.

3 Bring the needle through four threads down at B.

4 Insert the needle again at A and bring through two threads below.

5 Work eight satin stitches pulled tightly over these two threads.

6 Work one backstitch pulled tightly over four threads and bring the needle through two threads below the first row of satin stitches.

7 Work eight satin stitches pulled tightly below the first row.

8 Proceed to the next honeycomb stitch and repeat as before.

9 When the line of stitching is the desired length, turn the work and repeat the honeycomb and satin stitch combination until the border is complete.

Incorporating beads into the work

The honeycomb and satin stitch border can be made more decorative by adding perhaps a pearl bead of the right size in the center space which is formed between the two rows of honeycomb stitching. Use a strong thread to secure the bead with two stitches before passing on to the next space. Carry the thread from space to space along the back of the work and finish off with a secure overcasting stitch on the back of the work.

Eyelets

These are also simple to work and effective, either singly or in groups. They consist of a number of straight stitches worked into a central hole, usually over a square of eight threads of fabric. They can be arranged in groups to form a pattern, or worked singly as squares or rectangles. Some of the most popular are square eyelet, single cross eyelet and back-stitched eyelet. These can all be worked as rectangles as well as squares, and they can also be grouped irregularly together, leaving part of the eyelet unworked.

Square eyelet

This is worked over a square of eight threads.

1 Begin in the center of one side and take a straight stitch over four threads and into the center hole.

2 Bring the needle up in the next space to the right and take a straight stitch over four threads and into the center hole. Continue in this way around the square until the eyelet is complete.

Single cross eyelet

Work in a similar way over eight threads

as for the square eyelet, but leave one thread free between each quarter.

Backstitched eyelet

This is also worked over eight threads.

1 Begin in the center of one side and work one straight stitch over four threads and into the center hole.

2 Bring the needle out two threads beyond the straight stitch and make a backstitch into it, then work one straight stitch over four threads and into the center hole. Continue around the sides of the square until the eyelet is completed.

Pulled fabric edgings

One of the features of pulled thread embroidery is that it can be worked around the edge of the fabric and incorporated into the hem. The three following edgings are all suitable for most types of table linen.

Edging 1

This is a very simple edging and consists of two rows of four-sided stitch, one of which is worked through a fold or double thickness of fabric.

1 On the right side of the fabric count 10 or 12 threads up from the raw edge and work one row of four-sided stitch over four threads for the desired distance.

2 Fold the fabric to the wrong side so that the fold is level with the outer edge of the stitching. Baste in place.

3 On the right side of the fabric work the second row of four-sided stitch through the double thickness of fabric.

4 Remove the basting and trim the surplus

edge back to the line of stitching.

Edging 2

This is worked in the same way as the first edging with the addition of two rows of buttonhole stitch. Work the buttonhole stitch with a fine and firmly twisted thread to produce a hard-wearing edging and use a slightly larger tapestry needle than usual for the four-sided stitch so that the buttonhole stitch will be easier to work.

1 Count 10 or 12 threads in from the raw edge and work one row of four-sided stitch over four threads as before.

2 Turn the raw edge onto the wrong side and work the second row of four-sided stitch through the double fabric.

3 Using a small tapestry needle, on the right side of the fabric and over the folded edge, work five buttonhole stitches into each hole made by the first row of four-sided stitch.

4 Work a second row of buttonhole stitch into the holes formed by the second row of four-sided stitch.

5 For a deeper border, more rows of four-sided stitch can be worked. The edging will be further defined if you work the

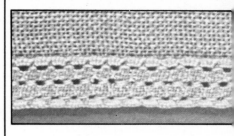

buttonholing in a darker thread.

Edging 3

1 Count 10 threads in from the raw edge of the fabric and fold the fabric over to the wrong side along this thread. Baste in place.

2 Count three threads in from the fold and work a row of three-sided stitch over the next four threads on the right side of the fabric.

3 Work one row of four-sided stitch above the three-sided stitch.

4 Cut the surplus fabric back to the second line of stitching.

5 Work five buttonhole stitches into each stitch hole formed by the four-sided stitch.

6 To finish the edging, work five buttonhole stitches over the three threads along the folded edge and into the holes formed by the three-sided stitch.

Turning corners

To turn a corner using four-sided stitch count the threads and check that the number is divisible by four.

To turn a corner using three-sided stitch count the threads as you near the corner and adjust the fold of the hem so that the stitch can be worked over four threads across the corner.

The corner can also be turned by working one-third of three-sided stitch, known as eyelet filling stitch. The base of the three-sided stitch used for this should come across the corner to be turned.

Pulled fabric runner

This elegant drawn fabric table runner will fit in with any decor, traditional or modern. The three stitches used, satin stitch, ringed backstitch and honeycomb filling are simple to work. Make the runner longer or shorter if you wish, to fit your own furniture.

Size
35 inches by 12 inches

Fabric required
$\frac{3}{8}$ yd off-white evenweave fabric, 21 threads to 1 in, 59 in wide.
D.M.C. 6-strand Floss, 15 skeins 420 snuff brown.
Tapestry needle No. 20.

The design
1 Cut a piece from the fabric measuring $13\frac{1}{2}$ inches by $37\frac{1}{2}$ inches. Mark the center of the fabric lengthwise with a line of stitches. This acts as a guide when placing the design. The working chart shows a section of the design, with the center marked by a blank arrow which should coincide with the line of basting stitches.

2 Each stitch must be pulled firmly, except the satin stitch triangles which are worked with normal tension.

3 Use six strands of thread for satin stitch and three strands for the rest of the embroidery.

4 With the long side of the fabric facing, begin working the design with ringed backstitch, $1\frac{3}{4}$ in from the narrow edge of the fabric. Continue until the embroidery measures 34 inches. Work the rest of the embroidery outward from this central band. Repeat the three outer lines of satin stitch 3 inches from the central band of embroidery.

Ringed backstitch
This stitch is worked from right to left and can be used as a border or as a filling. It is worked in two steps as shown in the diagrams. Figure 1: bring the thread through at the arrow; insert the needle at A (2 threads down), bring it through at B (4 threads up and 2 threads to the left); insert at arrow, bring it through at C (2 threads up and 4 threads to the left); insert the needle at B, bring it through at D (2 threads down and 4 to the left); insert it at C, bring it through at E (4 threads down and 2 to the left). Continue making half rings of backstitch for the required length. Figure 2: turn the fabric around

383

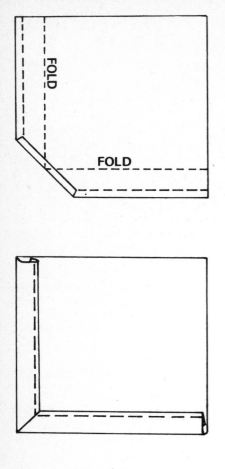

Mitring the corners

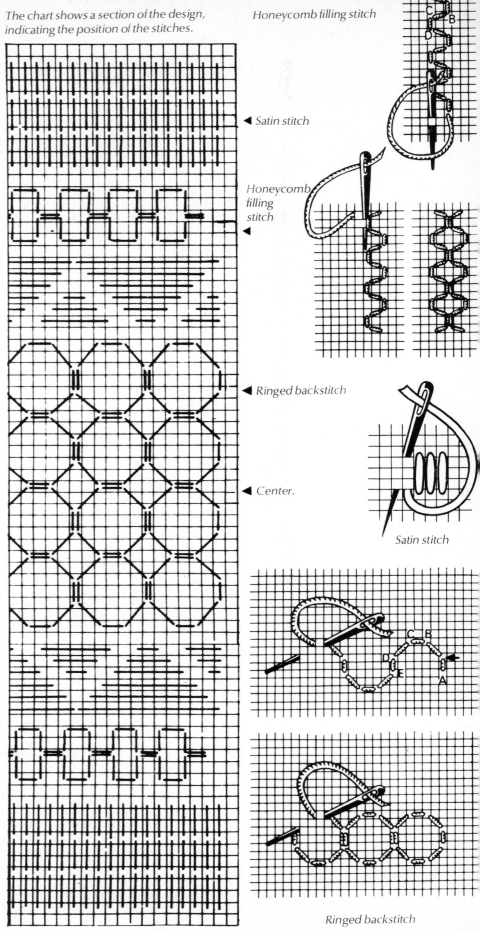

The chart shows a section of the design, indicating the position of the stitches.

◀ *Satin stitch*

Honeycomb filling stitch

◀ *Honeycomb filling stitch*

◀ *Ringed backstitch*

◀ *Center.*

Satin stitch

Ringed backstitch

and work back in the same way to complete the rings. All connecting stitches are worked in the same holes.

Honeycomb filling stitch

This stitch is worked from the top downward again in two stages. Figure 1: bring the thread through at the arrow; insert the needle at A (2 threads to the right), bring it through at B (2 threads down); insert again at A, bring through at B; insert at C (2 threads to the left), bring through at D. Continue in this way for the desired length. Turn the fabric around and work back in the same way. Figure 2 shows the work turned ready for the second row. Figure 3 shows the completed stitch. Pull each stitch firmly.

Finishing

Press the embroidery on the wrong side. Turn back ½ inch hems. Miter the corners and slip stitch. Press the runner again on the wrong side.

HARDANGER WORK

Hardanger work, sometimes called Norwegian embroidery, originated in a district by the same name in western Norway where the local inhabitants were famous for their fine work.

It is a form of drawn thread work which is quick and easy. Geometric in design with an overall heavy openwork appearance, it is very popular in Scandinavia where it is used for adorning traditional dress and household linens.

The main characteristic of this type of embroidery is the rectangular grouping of satin stitch, known as kloster blocks, arranged to outline the spaces and build up the basic portion of the design.

Fabric and threads

Hardanger embroidery requires a fabric with a very regular weave in which the warp and weft threads are equal, or special Hardanger linen or canvas which is woven with double warp and weft threads so that it is extremely strong and does not fray in cutting.

This embroidery is traditionally worked on white or natural linen with self-colored threads although the work can be very effective if a dark thread is used on a light ground or vice versa.

The working threads should be slightly coarser than the threads of the fabric for the satin stitch blocks which form the basis of the design, and slightly finer for the fillings of the open work spaces. Coton à broder and pearl cotton are most suitable for more traditional work.

However, provided the fabrics' are of suitable weight and even weave, you can break with tradition and use synthetic or wool fabrics and threads to create your own exciting and contemporary designs for wall hangings, lampshades, pillow covers, dress insertions and accessories. The only tools required are tapestry needles and a pair of very sharp pointed embroidery scissors.

The design

By its very nature the design has to be geometrical in form, with square, triangle, diamond or oblong shapes.

The main outlines of the design should be kept as simple as possible and the basic shapes and their relationship to each other in forming a pattern can easily be worked out on graph paper. The design can be developed by building up small shapes around and within the larger shapes, and adding surface stitchery.

Working the design

It is essential throughout the work that both the threads and stitches are counted with great accuracy and that the fabric is carefully cut because any irregularity would spoil the general effect. If a frame is used, it is much easier to achieve this and to keep the embroidery at an even tension.

There are four steps in working Hardanger embroidery.

1 Outlining the spaces and design with kloster blocks.

2 Working any surface embroidery.

3 Cutting and drawing the threads for the open spaces.

4 Decorating the bars of the larger spaces and adding the lace stitch fillings.

Kloster blocks

A kloster block is made up of an irregular number of stitches enclosing a regular number of fabric threads. Five stitches to a block is the usual size, but this can vary from nine stitches enclosing eight threads to three stitches enclosing two. The blocks may be grouped vertically or horizontally to outline the space.

To make a vertical line across the fabric to outline a diamond or triangle the blocks should be worked in steps following the weave of the fabric. If you wish to accentuate certain shapes the blocks may be varied in height as well as length. The head of the stitch should always face the cut space to protect the ends of the fabric and to prevent them from fraying.

Surface stitchery

In addition to the outlining blocks, decorative surface stitchery is added to create interest and to enrich the design. This should correspond to the general pattern and principle of following the weave of fabric and a variety of stitches can be used, such as backstitch, star-stitch, herringbone, eyelets, backstitched or woven wheels, four-sided and interlacing stitches.

Cutting the threads

In Hardanger work the embroidery is half complete before the work is cut, unlike other drawn thread work where the threads are removed first and then the decorative stitchery applied.

Using very sharp scissors, cut the threads in the spaces enclosed by the blocks close to the stitches. Complete one motif at a time, removing either all the horizontal threads or the vertical threads, but not both at the same time.

When the cutting is complete it will have created an open mesh of geometric patterns within the outline of the blocks. These now need to be strengthened and decorated.

Decorating the bars

The bars of the threads left in the spaces can be strengthened by overcasting or needleweaving, although it is advisable not to mix the two methods.

At this stage decide whether you want to incorporate lace stitch fillings to add to the delicacy of the work since these are made as a series of twists or loops while the bars are being covered.

On articles not subject to wear, you could leave the bars without weaving or overcasting and just add a filling or interlocking lace stitch. An attractive filling for a larger space can be a backstitched or woven wheel, worked over an even number of anchoring threads.

1 Work the overcasting diagonally across a group of threads, making each stitch firm and covering each bar completely. When one bar is done, carry the thread behind the work to the next bar, leaving a small square of fabric visible between the bars at the intersections.

2 Work the needleweaving over the bars, following the method given in the section on pulled thread work. At this stage if you are not adding a lace stitch filling, you could incorporate small picots.

3 If you do this, place the picots on each side of the bar in the middle, twisting the thread around the needle to make the picot on one side and then moving to the other side and repeating the process.

Hardanger work table cloth

Size
50 inches square

Fabric required
1½ yds of 52 in wide medium weight Hard anger linen with 29 threads to 1 in.

You will also need
D.M.C. Pearl cotton No. 5, 3 × 10 grm balls: white.
D.M.C. Pearl cotton No. 8, 1 × 10 grm balls: white.
Tapestry needles, 1 each No. 20 and No. 24.

Preparing the fabric
Trim the fabric so that it is an exact square. Mark the center in both directions with lines of basting.

The design
This tablecloth uses the techniques of Hardanger embroidery, described in the previous chapter. The layout diagram shows the placing of the design for one quarter of the cloth and this is repeated on the remaining three-quarters. The broken lines correspond to the basted lines across the center of the fabric, the numerals indicate the number of threads, and the shaded area is the section given in figure 1. Figure 1 shows the stitches in a section of the design and how they are arranged on the threads. Follow figure 1 and the number key for the actual embroidery, and the layout diagram for the placing of the design. Work all parts similar to the numbered parts in the same stitch.

Working the embroidery
1 Using the No. 5 Pearl cotton and the

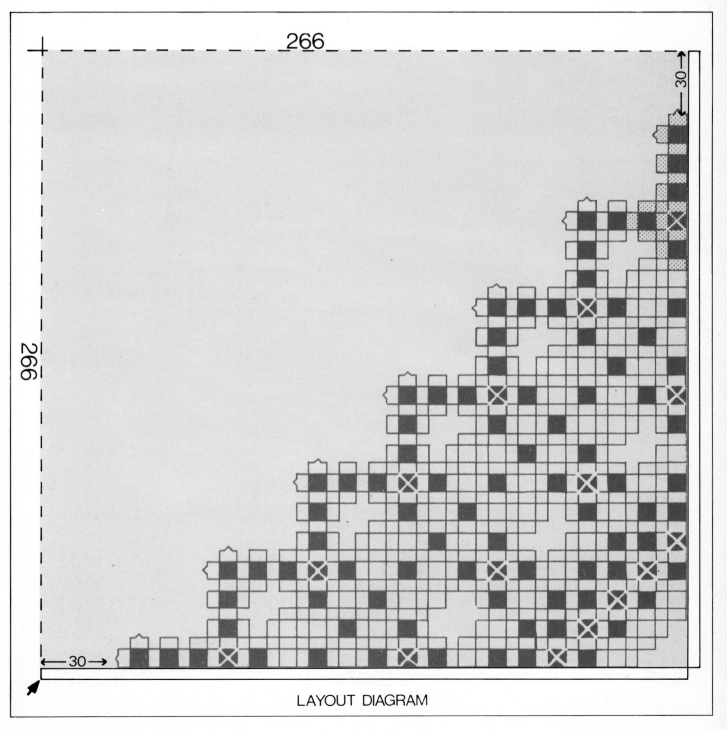

LAYOUT DIAGRAM

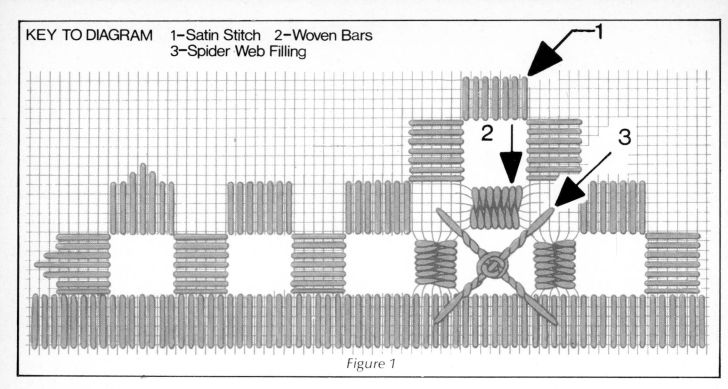

Figure 1

No. 20 tapestry needle, start the embroidery at the black arrow 1 shown in the layout diagram, 266 threads down from the crossed basting threads. Work this part as shown.

2 When all the satin stitch blocks are complete, cut away the threads shown in the black squares on the layout diagram and blank on figure 1.

3 Using the No. 8 Pearl cotton and No. 24 tapestry needle, work the woven bars and fillings (see below) and then complete the remaining sections of the cloth in the same way.

Woven bars

Withdraw an even number of threads from the areas shown in figure 1 and separate the remaining threads into bars with three threads in each by weaving over and under them until the threads are completely covered.

Spider's web filling

1 Work one twisted bar by carrying the thread diagonally across the space. Enter the fabric as shown, twist that thread over the first thread and return to the starting point.

2 Work another twisted bar in the opposite direction but twist the thread back to the center only.

3 Pass the thread over and under the crossed bars twice and then under and over twice. Complete the twisting of the second bar.

Finishing

Press the embroidery on the wrong side. Make 1 inch hems all around, mitering the corners.

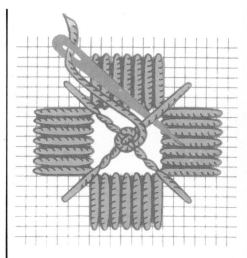

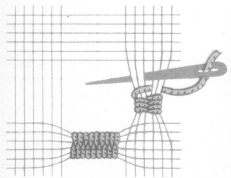

NEEDLEWEAVING

Needleweaving is an ancient craft dating back three thousand years. Most of the early examples are Coptic, and they are known today as loom embroideries since it is thought they were incorporated into the main weaving process of the fabric. Needleweaving is a form of drawn thread work and consists of a decorative pattern worked in weaving or darning stitch upon warp or weft threads after some of the crosswise threads have been withdrawn.

The fabric
Needleweaving is usually worked on a foundation of evenly woven fabric from which threads can be easily removed. Burlap, heavy linen, cottons, woolens and tweed, as well as some acrylic curtain fabrics, are all suitable.

The threads
The choice of threads is limitless provided that they are of a similar weight or slightly heavier than the withdrawn threads of the fabric. If the threads supporting the weaving are sufficiently open and strong, you can incorporate a variety of threads, such as carpet yarn, chenille, straw, heavy nub yarn and even string, leather thongs, ribbon and thin strips of nylon. Beads, rings and metal washers can all be added as the weaving progresses to add interest and texture.

Needles
You will need an assortment of heavy tapestry needles in the right sizes to take the threads you are using. If you are planning to incorporate fine ribbon or thongs, an elastic threader or large, blunt-ended needle is useful.

The design
If you want a fairly free design, the simplest way is to choose a fabric and some interesting threads, and begin work without spending time working out the design first — some of the most exciting results with needleweaving can be created spontaneously.

If the needleweaving is worked for a specific purpose, such as a border with a geometric pattern or in the form of a repeating pattern arranged symmetrically to fill a given space, you should first chart the design on graph paper, showing how the motifs are linked and which colors are to be used.

Preparing the fabric
If the needleweaving is for a border, prepare the fabric by withdrawing the threads in the same way as for drawn thread work. If you are weaving a simple repeating pattern, however, it would be helpful to hem stitch the threads into even groups of threads at the top and bottom of the border as this helps you count the threads during the weaving process. If you are working on a heavy, loosely woven fabric in which the threads are easily counted, this step is not necessary.

The stitch
Weaving or darning stitch is worked by passing the needle over one thread, under the next and so on. If you prefer, you can divide the threads into blocks of two, three or four and pass the needle over and under each block.

To start weaving, insert the needle about an inch above the first block of weaving and pull it through, leaving a length of thread to be darned in later. Begin weaving between the first and second group of threads, working from left to right. Continue weaving between the threads for the desired amount, making sure that each row of stitches lies close to the preceding one and is not pulled too tightly.

To pass to the next block of threads, slip your needle up the side of the block to the top and then work over the next block. You can also pass from one block of weaving to the next by darning the working thread through the back of the work.

If you are using several different types of thread, take care to maintain an even tension.

More open effects

You can vary the solid effect of needleweaving with single bars of overcasting with satin stitch. Work needleweaving over the first blocks of threads for four or six rows then return to the beginning of the block and overcast the first two threads with satin stitch. Slip the needle up the side of the overcast threads and start to weave over the next block. If you wish, the overcast bars can be woven over in the middle of the border.

Needlewoven belt

This belt can be made in wool as shown in the photograph or you can make it in an evenweave cotton or linen, using soft embroidery or pearl cotton.

Size

3 inches wide, to fit any waist size

Fabric required

¼ yd fabric × the length of belt required + 2 in (for buckle), with approximately 14 threads to 1 in.

You will also need

D.M.C. Tapestry Yarn: 4 skeins black; 3 skeins each chestnut 7174, 7176; 1 skein in chestnut 7178.
3 inches × the length of belt of non-woven interfacing.
Buckle.
Tapestry needle No. 18.

The design

The design is a repeating pattern which can be adjusted to make a belt to your own measurements. The diagram below gives a part of the design with the colors used for each area.

Preparing the fabric

With one long side of the fabric facing you, withdraw 26 lengthwise threads through the center 2 inches in from each end. Darn in the ends neatly.

Working the needleweaving

1 With one long side facing, start the needleweaving at the left-hand edge and work the section given following diagram 1 and the letter key for the colors. Diagram 2 shows how the needleweaving is worked over four threads of fabric and how the connecting stitch is worked over and under the start of a new block.
2 Repeat the section until all the loose threads are woven.

Finishing the belt

1 Trim the fabric to within 2½ inches on the long sides of the belt and to within ¾ inch on the short ends.
2 Sew the interfacing lightly in place along the center on the wrong side of the work.
3 Fold one long side of fabric over the interfacing and baste. Turn under the seam allowance of ½ inch on the other side and hem in place along the center of the wrong side of the belt. Turn under the seam allowance at each short end and sew in place. Sew the buckle to one short end of the belt.

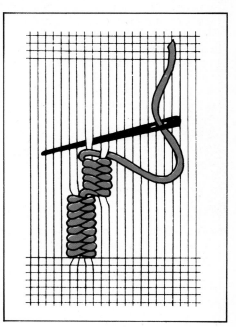

7174

7176

7178

black

CUT WORK
Simple techniques

Cut work is the name given to open-work types of embroidery where portions of the background are cut away and in the more elaborate forms, re-embroidered. Cut work is basically the link between embroidery and needlemade lace and should not be confused with Hardanger and Hedebo, the counted thread methods.

Types of cut work
There are four main types of cut work, varying from simple cut spaces to larger and more elaborately filled spaces.

In simple cut work (see below), the cut spaces are quite small. In Renaissance work they grow larger, while in Richelieu work the addition of bars and picots gives a more decorative appearance. Venetian work has the largest cut spaces with intricate fillings, giving a lace-like quality to the embroidery. These more elaborate and highly decorative methods are covered in later chapters.

Uses of cut work
Cut work is suitable for all types of household linen and can also be successfully used as dress decoration, provided the design is planned as an integral part of the dress and is not just added as an afterthought.

Fabric and threads
As the main interest of cut work lies in the variation of texture produced by the cut spaces – either as open shapes or decorated with bars, picots, spider's web or woven wheels and needlepoint fillings – color is of secondary importance. Most of the charm of cut work lies in it being self-colored although graded shades of color with simple cut work can be effective. It is important to avoid color contrasts with the more elaborate forms.

Only a firm, evenly woven linen or very strong cotton should be used for cut work because other fabrics fray when the spaces are cut. Choose a linen thread or fine pearl floss or coton à broder in a weight to suit the fabric. Linen lace thread may also be used, although this is available in cream shades only. Do not use stranded floss because the strands of this thread are not strong enough when divided and would not withstand friction through wear and laundering.

Needles
Fine crewel needles are suitable for simple cut work although sharps are normally best for working the lace-like fillings of the other forms of cut work. Choose the size according to the weight of the thread being used. You may also need tapestry needles in various sizes to work the hems and finish the edges.

You should also have a pair of very sharp, finely pointed embroidery scissors.

Designs for cut work
Traditional cut work designs are nearly always floral and the more intricate fillings of Venetian work are similar to old lace patterns.

Simple cut work has no bars or picots and consists solely of a design of simple shapes worked in buttonhole stitch with the background area around the motif cut away, thus throwing the main part of the design into relief.

All cut work, however elaborate, may be designed initially by arranging cut paper shapes, either as a repetitive border or as a single motif or design, to fit a given size. Whatever the function, the pattern of the cut shapes should balance with the more solid parts of the design.

When planning or adapting a design, check that all the shapes tie up at vital points of the structure, else they will hang loosely when the background is cut away. Draw all the main outlines of the design in double lines to act as a guide for the running stitch which is worked within them to act as padding for the buttonhole stitch. A design of curved or circular shapes is much easier to work in this method than a geometric design with sharp angles.

When your design has been prepared, transfer it to the fabric using dressmaker's carbon or the prick and pounce method (see the chapter on transferring designs).

The stitches
1 Start by working several rows of running stitch around the motifs inside the double lines. These form a foundation for the buttonholing and enable a firm edge to be worked. The running stitches should lie very evenly on the fabric for if they are pulled too tightly the work will pucker.

2 Work the buttonholing close together with the looped edge of the stitches facing the space which is to be cut away.

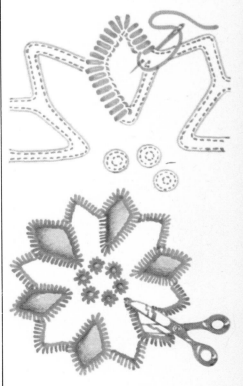

3 Using very sharp scissors, cut away the fabric close to the buttonholing. Cut cleanly, using the points of the scissors so that the edge will not fluff.

Do not be tempted to cut away part of the work before all the stitching is completed or the work will pull out of shape.

Renaissance and Richelieu cut work

Renaissance and Richelieu cut work are more complicated than simple cut work because the cut spaces are larger and need the addition of bars across the spaces to strengthen and hold together the main parts of the design.

The design
As the bars are the most decorative feature of Renaissance cut work, it is important to place them symmetrically. Where there are larger cut spaces than can be filled adequately with a single straight bar, the bar may be branched. These branched bars show to best advantage if they balance the solid parts of the work, although the cut spaces should not be too large and clumsy. Where a number of bars intersect they can be further enriched by a spider's web or woven wheel filling or by a buttonhole ring.

Fabric and threads
Use the same kinds of fabric and thread as for simple cut work and prepare the embroidery in a similar way.

Working the embroidery
1 When the design has been traced or painted onto the fabric, start the embroidery by working an outer row of padding running stitches. When you reach the position of the first bar, take the thread across the space and make a tiny running stitch within the double lines on that side.
Return the thread to the starting point of

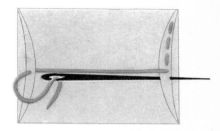

the bar and take another small stitch; then go across the space again.

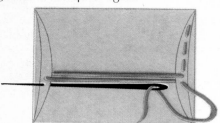

2 Cover the three threads of the bar with close buttonholing, keeping the bar firm and taking care not to let the needle penetrate the fabric below.

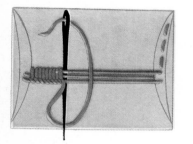

3 Continue with the running stitches around the design until you reach the next bar and work that one in the same way. When all the bars have been worked, complete the second row of padding running stitch.
4 Finish the piece by working close buttonholing over the padding as for simple cut work. Take care not to cut the bars when cutting away the background fabric.

Branched bars

1 Carry the threads across the space in the same way as for a single bar.
2 Work buttonholing over the threads to the point where the bar branches. From this point work the second bar, laying three threads across the space to the point where it joins the double lines. Work the buttonholing over the threads of the second bar back to where it branched from the first bar and then continue working the remaining part of the first bar.

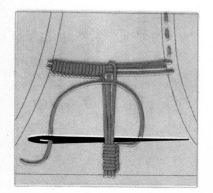

A three or four-branch bar is worked in the same way.

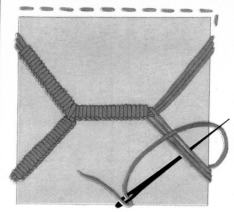

Spider's web filling

If you are filling a large cut space which needs more than a few branched bars, a spider's web filling is a good choice. This filling can be placed in the center or deliberately off-center by altering the angle at which the twists are made.
1 Carry a single thread across the design from top to bottom, then take a tiny stitch between the double lines and take the thread back to the center of the space, twisting the thread around the needle.
2 From the center, take another thread across to the side, twist back to the center and continue in this way, until you have divided the piece into five sections. Before completing the final twist over the last half of the first thread worked, work a woven wheel or spider's web by weaving under and over the five threads. Keep the web or wheel fairly small so that it does not detract from the twisted spokes.

Back-stitched wheel

If the space is large enough, six twists can be worked across it, either at regular or irregular intervals, and then a back-stitched wheel worked over them to complete the design.

Buttonhole ring

This is another decorative filling for a larger cut shape.
1 Wind a fine thread five or six times around a small pencil. Slip the ring off the

pencil, baste it and cover it closely all around with buttonholing.
2 Break off the thread and pin the ring in position on the fabric. To secure the ring to the space, work four or five twisted bars at intervals from the ring to the double lines of the design. To carry the thread to the next twist, work a few running stitches along the double lines to avoid spoiling the ring itself.

Richelieu cut work

This is similar to Renaissance cut work, although the cut spaces are a little larger and the bars are decorated with picots.
Looped picots. Work the buttonholing over the bar to the center from left to right. Insert a pin into the fabric beneath the bar and pass the working thread under the head of the pin from left to right, then up over the bar and out under the bar to the right of the pin. Pass the needle through the loop on the pin and the thread beyond it. Pull the working thread tightly to make the picot and continue buttonholing to the end of the bar.

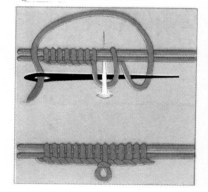

Bullion picots. These are worked on the same principle although they are a little more elaborate. Work close buttonholing to the center of the bar, make a bullion stitch from the looped edge of the last stitch by twisting the thread four or five times around the needle and pulling the thread through the twists to make a firm twisted loop. To secure the picot work the next buttonhole stitch close to the previous stitch.

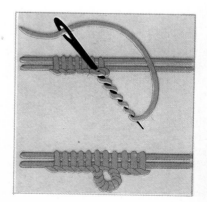

Reticella cut work

This is the most elaborate and lacy form of cut work and bears a strong resemblance to Venetian lace. The types of fabric and working threads are the same as for the other forms of cut work covered in earlier chapters.

The design
The main part of the design for reticella cut work is formed by the stitches worked within the cut squares or geometric shapes. The various fillings are based on a buttonholing or weaving stitch.

While few people today have the time to make large pieces of reticella cut work, small motifs can be made and used to decorate table linens and different kinds of clothing. These motifs are very effective although they do not require the heavy surface stitchery which traditional, examples often contained. A modern pattern or design can be built up by arranging a series of small squares, each containing a different filling. The squares can be cut out completely, or some threads can be left as a base on which to work the filling stitches.

Preparing the squares
1 Start by marking the position of the squares accurately and outlining them with several rows of running stitch to strengthen the cut area. If you are planning to leave threads within the square, count them and check that there is an even number. Leave the threads in pairs both horizontally and vertically. It often helps to tack a piece of firm white paper behind the squares to give a firmer foundation than the fabric alone, although the stitches are not made into the paper.
2 Cut any threads that are to be removed to within three threads of the running stitch. On firm fine fabrics, turn the cut edges to the back of the work. Overcast the edges and cut away the surplus. On heavier fabrics, work buttonholing over the edge to prevent the filling stitches from pulling away.

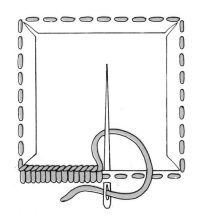

Filling open squares
The fillings in an open square are used to build up small solid shapes such as triangles, arcs and semi-circles within a framework of bars worked in buttonholing.
1 Start at the widest part of the design and take a double thread across from one corner of the square to the other. Work a row of buttonholing on this double thread.
2 Work each following row into the looped edge of the previous row, reducing the number of stitches to form the design, which is anchored to the fabric on the opposite side.

Filling other squares
1 To strengthen the threads left in squares,

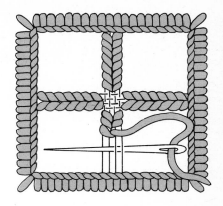

cover them either with weaving or close buttonhole stitch. If you add further decoration with picots, make sure they do not occur at a point where you will be working further bars.
2 To work diagonal lines, take a long stitch from the center to the corner of the square and back again, and fasten off at the back of the center. Cover the diagonal threads by sewing over them or buttonholing to the position of the first bar or arc.
3 To form the bar or arc, take a double thread across for the foundation, cover it with overcast stitch or buttonholing and then complete the diagonal line to the center of the square. The bars or arcs can

be decorated with picots.
4 Alternatively a solid triangular shape can be worked in detached buttonhole stitch from the bar which dissects the diagonal line.
5 On fine fabrics the center of the square can be decorated by working a small back-stitched spider's web over the junction of the threads.

Finishing
Finish off with a simple hemstitch border. For something more elaborate, work several rows of hemstitching and twist the threads into bundles.

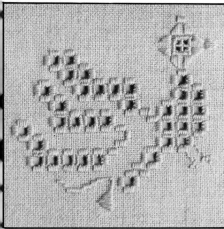

Eyelet embroidery

Eyelet embroidery is a form of embroidery which consists of eyelets of different shapes and sizes, with additional surface embroidery and scalloped edging.

During the 18th and 19th centuries when eyelet embroidery was worked in Britain in its original form it was composed of much elaborate, floral surface stitchery, eyelets and larger cut spaces with needle-made lace or drawn thread fillings.

The intricacy of the work gave it a very delicate appearance which was ideal for the beautiful christening robes and bonnets made in that period. Traditionally it was worked in white thread on white fabric such as cambric, cotton or fine linen, lawn or muslin.

Later the method became simpler, using less surface stitchery with more emphasis on eyelets and cut shapes and it became known at that time as "Madeira work", after the island where it became a cottage industry. It was used to decorate dress, lingerie, baby wear and household linen, as it still is today.

The design

Eyelet embroidery need not be confined to white embroidery, but if color is chosen it is best to use matching or toning threads rather than contrasting ones. Traditional eyelet embroidery was always elaborately floral in design. A contemporary design may be made for a simple border by using a geometric arrangement of circles and ovals of various sizes with a little surface stitchery and scalloping. Both floor and wall tiles can give ideas for this type of design.

The fabrics and threads

Although much eyelet embroidery is made by machine nowadays, it is still worth making your own by hand in order to achieve the beautiful delicate results and the wide range of fabrics, threads and designs which can be used.

Choose a firm and fine fabric which will not fray with washing, and match the working thread in quality, texture and color (it can be a different tone). On cotton or linen, use a cotton or fine linen mercerized thread and on silk fabrics, a fine twisted silk.

Stitches and equipment

Only four basic stitches are used in eyelet embroidery — running, overcasting, button-holing and satin stitch.

To make the eyelets you will need a pair of very sharp embroidery scissors and a sharp pointed instrument for piercing the fabric.

Making eyelets

1 To make round eyelets, outline the circle with small running stitches.

2 If the circles are less than $\frac{1}{4}$ inch in diameter, pierce the center and then cover the edge with fine overcasting.

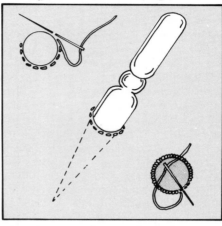

3 For larger circles snip from the center, vertically and horizontally, out to the running stitch. Turn the points of fabric under to the back of the work with the needle and overcast the edge taking the stitches over the folded edge and the running stitch. Cut away the surplus fabric close to the stitching.

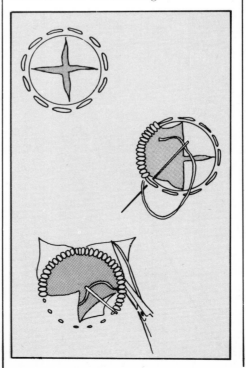

4 If several eyelets run close together so that they almost touch, they should be worked in two steps. First work the running stitch along the lower edge of the first hole, cross to the top of the second hole and continue in this way across the design. Complete the circles in the second step. This helps to prevent the piece from

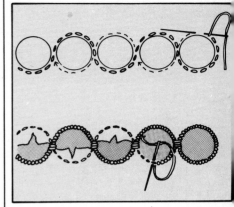

tearing during working and in wear later on.

5 To give a heavier effect, or to make the circles thicker on one side, work several rows of running stitch to pad the area and raise it. Then overcast all around the eyelet, grading the length of the overcasting over the padded area.

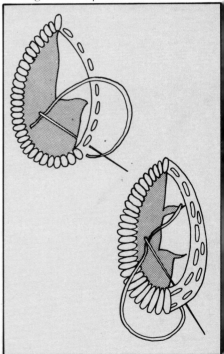

6 To make oval and triangular eyelets work in the same way as for round ones taking care that the shapes are kept accurate and do not become distorted.

7 When making a slot for ribbon, mark the slot and work around it before cutting the opening. This prevents the hole from pulling out of shape while being worked.

The surface embroidery

This is usually worked in satin or stem stitch. If you want solid padded shapes to give emphasis or detail to the design, they should be padded by working horizontal satin stitch across the design just inside the outline, with vertical satin stitch to cover the horizontal ones.

Scalloping

This is one of the main features of eyelet embroidery and is used to decorate and finish the work.

1 To make a simple scalloped edge, draw the shapes around a coin or small saucer, ½ inch from the raw edge, or more if the fabric tends to fray.

2 Pad the edge by working several rows of running stitch along the outline, graduating the distance between the stitches in the points of the scallops.

For a more solid or raised effect, use chain stitch for the padding instead of running stitch.

3 Cover the padding with closely worked buttonholing, working from left to right and with the looped edge of the stitch to the outside. Keep the stitches as even in tension as possible and do not pull the working thread too tight or the work will pucker. Make the stitches quite small in the points of the scallops, increasing in size around the curves to emphasize their symmetry.

4 To finish off a length of thread, take a few running stitches through the padding on the unworked section and fasten off. Join on the new length in a similar way, bringing the needle up through the loop of the last buttonhole stitch.

5 When all the buttonholing is worked, cut away the surplus fabric close to the stitches using very sharp scissors.

6 To make a more elaborate scalloped edge, draw a pattern of the design, including about three repeats and then cut it out of cardboard. You can then use this as a template to draw the shapes along the entire edge.

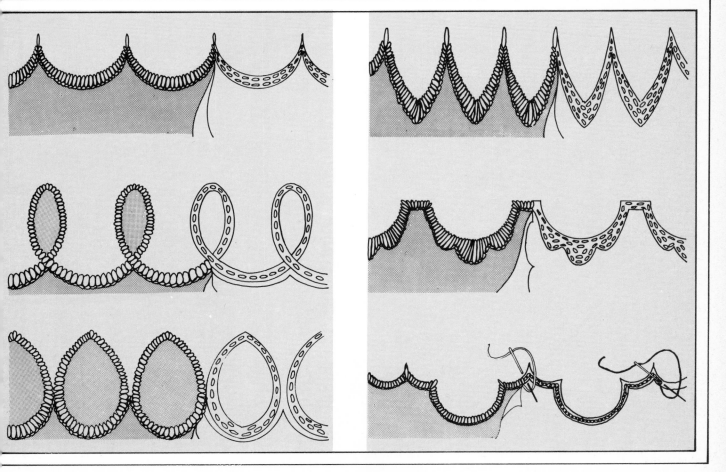

HEDEBO

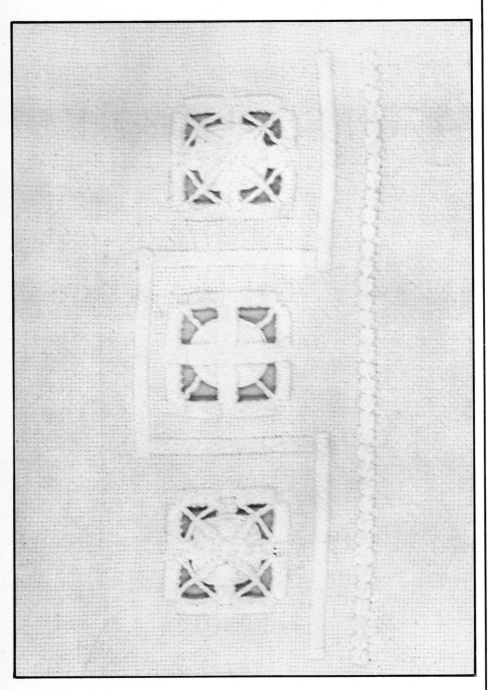

The second type of Hedebo evolved around 1840 when the original floral shapes and cut work were somewhat restrained and the embroidery lost some of its original character. Further cut and drawn thread work was added, usually in squares, making the whole design more formal and geometric.

The third type of Hedebo dates from about 1850 when it became quite popular and gradually lost its peasant-like quality. In modern Hedebo, designs became more conventional and the spaces were cut instead of drawn and cut, and filled in with more elaborate lace stitchery.

Designs for old Hedebo

Old Hedebo is traditionally worked on a close handwoven linen in a medium weight linen thread.

The main open shapes are formed by cutting and leaving two threads alternately, both vertically and horizontally, from the back of the work. The edge of the shape is then made firm by overcasting which is worked in groups of two over the horizontal and vertical bars. The spaces are enriched with more decorative stitches and the shapes are outlined with a double row of small close chain stitches.

The working method for the second form of Hedebo is very similar, with the open drawn squares being arranged in diagonal lines to form a diamond pattern, often interspersed with floral-type surface embroidery.

Designs for modern Hedebo

Designs for modern Hedebo usually consist of an arrangement or pattern of circular, oval or lozenge-shaped cut spaces which are strengthened and then outlined with buttonhole stitch.

Choose a fine, firm linen for the work with a matching linen thread. If a linen thread is unobtainable, use a fine coton à broder or pearl cotton.

The shapes are filled with a variety of lace stitches which are looped, twisted or buttonholed into the foundation row of buttonholing. Buttonholed pyramids are a feature of this type of work and these can be incorporated into the larger shapes or used as edgings to decorate the work. Satin stitch and eyelets, rather like eyelet embroidery, can be added and the work can be finished with a needlepoint lace edging. This form of Hedebo is often used for the decoration of collars and cuffs.

1 Transfer the design onto the fabric either by basting around an arrangement of cut paper shapes or by using a very finely pointed pencil and outlining the shapes with minute dots.

2 Work a double row of running stitches

Hedebo is a form of white embroidery of Danish origin. It dates from the 16th century when the peasant women of Heden, a flat part of Denmark, used to decorate their homespun linens with it.

Types of Hedebo

There are three basic types of Hedebo.

The oldest and most traditional was adapted from wood carvings and usually consisted of formal floral shapes combining surface embroidery with a few open and drawn thread fillings. Most of the surface embroidery was in chain stitch and the finished effect was soft and graceful.

around the outlines.

3 Cut away the fabric within the design, leaving a margin of about ¼ inch to ⅛ inch for smaller spaces.
Clip into this margin and turn it to the wrong side. Outline the space with Hedebo buttonhole stitch (see below), making sure that the fabric is turned under the needle and that the stitch is worked through both layers. Trim away surplus fabric close to the stitches.

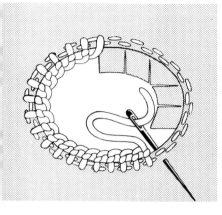

4 Fill the spaces and then add the surface embroidery.
5 Finish the work with a narrow hemstitched edge or with needlepoint lace, constructed of Hedebo buttonholing to form loops, pyramids or small rings.

Hedebo buttonholing

The buttonholing used for outlining the shapes is slightly different from regular buttonholing in that it is worked in two separate steps.
1 Hold the fabric so that the edge to be worked is away from you and insert the needle into the fabric from underneath. Draw the thread through until a small loop remains.
2 Slip the needle through the loop and pull both stitch and loop tight.

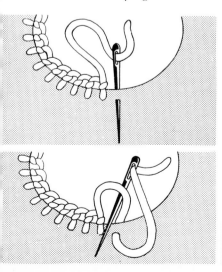

3 To join in a new thread, slip it under the last loop of thread worked and place it alongside the first thread. Work six or seven stitches over both threads and then cut off the remainder of the first thread.

Filling stitches
Circles

1 Work an inner circle of Hedebo buttonholing loosely inside the first circle, placing one stitch into every third stitch of the first circle. To obtain a loose effect, omit the final sharp pull to each stitch.
2 When the inner circle is completed, overcast or whip the looped edges.

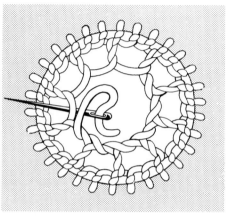

3 Fill the center of the circle by working a woven or backstitched wheel over the four or six threads anchored into the last row of buttonholing.

Circles and lozenge shapes

Fill circles and lozenge shapes by constructing a number of bars with two or three threads across the shape. Cover these with close Hedebo buttonhole stitch.

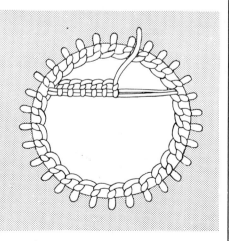

Pyramids

These are a characteristic feature of modern Hedebo and are constructed of Hedebo buttonholing stitches in increasing or decreasing rows. They can be worked singly to fill a small space or in groups of four to fill an oval or pear-shaped space.

1 Prepare the edge with a foundation row of buttonholing.
2 Start the pyramid by working from left to right, working one stitch less at the ends of each row.
3 Continue in this way until the top of the pyramid is reached, then slip the needle down the right side to start the next pyramid.

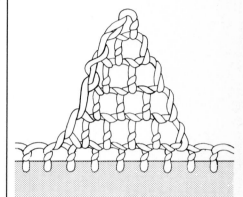

Six-pointed star

This is worked as a separate motif to be used as an insertion.
1 Wrap the thread around a pencil several times and secure the circle with a stitch.
2 Remove the circle from the pencil and buttonhole over it. This forms the foundation circle.
3 Work another round of buttonholing, counting the stitches carefully to make a multiple of six.
4 Work a pyramid onto each multiple number of buttonhole stitches, making six points in all.
5 Secure the shape in position with a single stitch at each point.

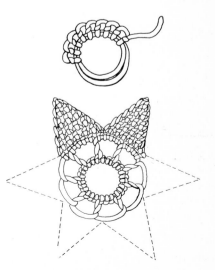

FAGGOTING

Faggoting is an attractive method of joining two pieces of fabric together using an open-work design. It is particularly useful for table linens for which you do not necessarily need the strength of a regular seam and where a seam line would spoil the effect. For example, if you are making a tablecloth from 36 inch wide dress fabric or 48 inch wide home furnishing fabric and you need to join panels to make it the right width for your table, you could join the panels with faggoting. The panels need not be confined to long strips but could be cut to make an attractive added feature. Faggoting can be used on both square and rounded shapes providing the edges to be joined lie along the grain of the fabric. If you work them on the bias, they will not lie flat.

Many of the stitches used in faggoting are common embroidery stitches and they are simple to work. Their success depends however on keeping their size and keeping the spaces between the edges absolutely even. For this reason it is worth mounting the work onto a frame.

Faggoting can be worked in most kinds of embroidery thread of whatever weight will suit the fabric you are working on. You might also use a fine crochet yarn. The instructions given below are for making the mat shown in the photograph, although they can easily be adapted for a tablecloth.

Placemats
Size
$15\frac{3}{4}$ in × $12\frac{1}{2}$ in.

Fabric required
For four mats:
$\frac{3}{4}$ yd firm cotton or linen, 36 in wide (or you can use remnants and cut the panels in sizes to suit the fabric available).

You will also need
Stranded embroidery thread to match the fabric.
Matching sewing thread.
Crewel embroidery needle.
Four strips of firm paper, $12\frac{1}{2}$ in × $1\frac{1}{2}$ in.

Preparing the fabric
1 Cut the fabric across the width to make two pieces $13\frac{1}{2}$ inches × 36 inches. Cut these pieces in half lengthwise to make four pieces each $13\frac{1}{2}$ inches × 18 inches.
2 Cut each of the four pieces into three, with two sections $13\frac{1}{2}$ inches wide and one section 11 inches wide.
3 Turn under $\frac{1}{2}$ inch on the wrong side around the edge of all the pieces and make narrow hems with mitered corners. Hem by hand the two opposite sides of the large sections and one long side and two short sides of the smaller sections. Leave the remaining edges basted in position.
4 For each mat, place the basted hem of one small section on the edge of a strip of firm paper so that it overlaps slightly. Baste in place. Overlap the basted hem of the larger section onto the opposite edge of the paper and baste leaving a gap $\frac{1}{2}$ inch wide. Repeat this procedure on the opposite edge of the larger section and on the second smaller section.

Working the faggoting
1 Mount the fabric into a hoop.
2 Work the faggoting between the basted edges, following one of the stitch patterns shown in the illustration. Make sure that the stitches worked into the edges of the fabric catch the hems securely.
3 When all the faggoting is completed press the finished mats.

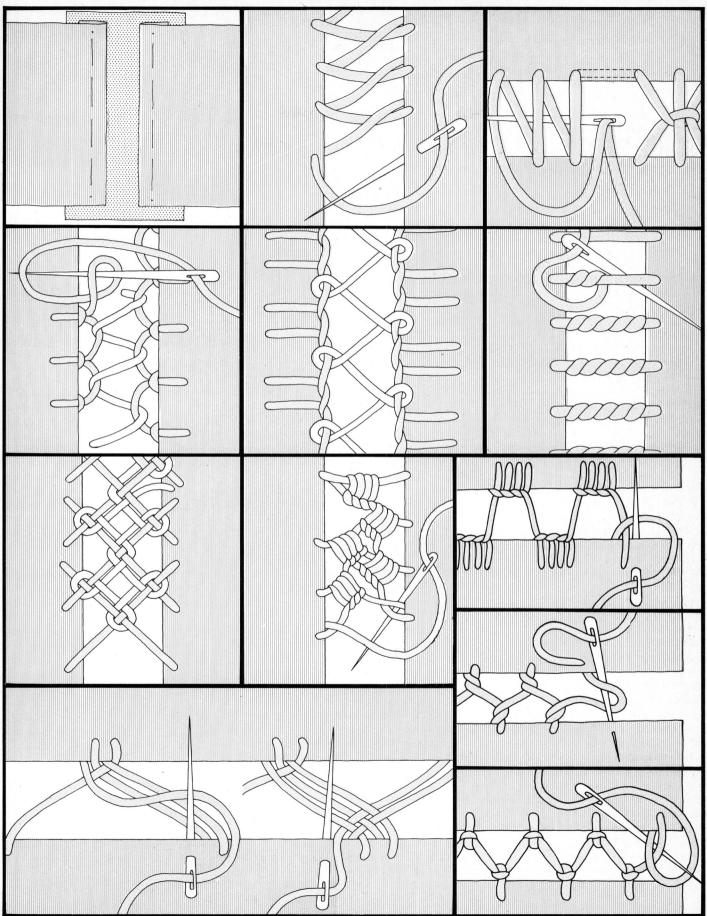

NEEDLEMADE LACE

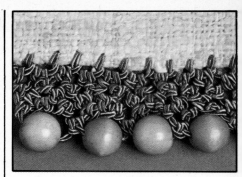

Lace making using a needle is quite different from lace made with an implement, such as a crochet hook or tatting shuttle, and it should not be confused with bobbin lace (sometimes called pillow lace), because it is made on a pillow. Needlemade lace is an old craft which was popular in all European countries in the mid-15th and 16th centuries. It is directly derived from the elaborate cut and drawn work of the 15th century which was often used for ecclesiastical purposes and to decorate the household articles and fashionable garments of the nobility.

The stitches

The Italian name for needlemade lace is "Punto in aria," meaning stitches in the air, and the lace itself is made with nothing more than a foundation, a needle and thread. The stitches used are merely variations of simple embroidery stitches and those most used are buttonhole (or blanket) stitch in one of its various forms, and a number of knotted stitches.

The threads

The thread should be suitable in weight for the fabric on which the edging is to be placed. If you are working on linen, use a linen thread, single-strand embroidery thread or pearlized cotton crochet yarn. If the fabric is heavy, such as tweed, a heavier cord or cotton yarn would be suitable. For working the edgings use a tapestry needle of a suitable size.

First method

This method could be used for narrow borders to decorate table linen, lampshades or perhaps a dress. It is worked directly onto the folded edge of the fabric.
1 Join your thread into the side of the edge to be decorated and take a tiny stitch into the fold about $\frac{3}{8}$ inch further along point A, leaving a small loop.
2 Return to the starting point and make another stitch. Go to point A again, make another stitch, keeping the loops the same size. Return to the starting point again. You now have four equal loops, forming a small scallop.

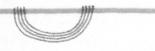

3 Work over the scallop in close buttonhole stitch.
4 Make a second loop in exactly the same way and then lay the threads for a third scallop but work only halfway across them in buttonhole stitch.
5 Make a loop from the center of the third scallop to the center of the second one, and then from the center of the second one to the center of the first one. Repeat this until there are three loops in each of these two scallops thus forming a second row.

6 Work over the first loop and halfway over the second loop in the second row.
7 Make a loop from the middle of the second scallop in the second row into the middle of the first one. Repeat until there are three loops in the scallop and then work over them in buttonhole stitch and over the half loops left in the first and second rows, using a buttonhole stitch.

Second method

This border can be worked into a hem or onto a foundation of buttonholing. Work all rows from left to right and fasten off the thread at the end of each row.
1 Start by working a row of spaced double-knotted buttonhole stitches into the edge of the fabric.
2 For the second row, work the same stitch, putting each one into a loop between the knots of the first row.
3 For the third row, work two double knotted stitches into the first loop, an ordinary single buttonhole stitch into the next loop, and continue alternating in this way to the end of the row.
4 For the last row, work two ordinary buttonhole stitches into the loop on each side of the single stitch on the third row and, with two double knotted stitches, into each space between the double knots.

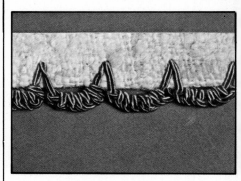

Working a separate strip

If you prefer to make the lace in a separate strip and then sew it on later, a way which is more convenient for a large or heavy item, use a piece of stiff linen or bookbinding cloth as a foundation. The strip should be the same length as the piece of lace required and about 2 inches wider.
1 Draw a line along the strip about $\frac{1}{2}$ inch from the top edge, using a ruler.
2 Couch a double thread of crochet yarn or other firm thread along the line, using a contrasting color for the stitches which hold the thread. This will make it easier to remove.
3 Work the lace onto the couched thread and remove the small stitches holding the thread when the lace is completed.

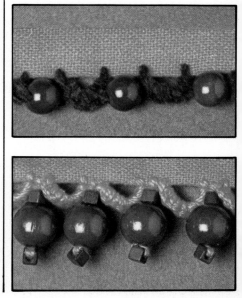

VENETIAN LACE

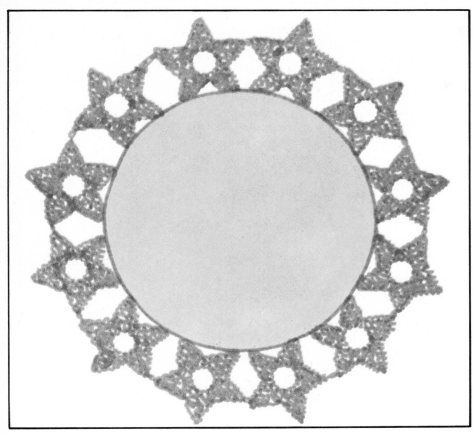

Make a border with stars or buttonholed pyramids to form a circle.

Venetian lace is the oldest type of lace made with a needle. The motifs are geometric in design and, like the narrow edgings described in the previous chapter, they are made with fine, closely worked buttonhole stitches and knotted stitches. They are worked onto couched threads which are held with temporary stitches on a firm foundation while the lace is being made.

The finished motifs, depending on the weight of the thread used, could be sewn onto lingerie, blouses and dresses, and onto sheets, pillowcases and table linen.

The threads and equipment

Linen thread is usually the best for working most types of lace, although fine crochet cotton, pearl cotton, and coton à broder are suitable.

For the couching, use a linen thread or mercerized crochet cotton, and for the final padding, a soft thread such as Sylko Size 5.

You will also need fine tapestry and crewel needles to suit the weight of the thread and a pair of finely pointed embroidery scissors.

For marking the design and for the foundation you will need either white paint and strong black paper with a matte texture, or India ink or a black felt-tipped pen and tracing paper. Both kinds of foundation should be backed with strong muslin or book-binding cloth. Alternatively you can use book binding cloth alone as the foundation.

Marking the design

1 Start by planning a well-balanced geometric design on graph paper, and consider how the lines are to be joined and the spaces filled. One way of doing this is to draw parts of the design in close double lines which separate and.then rejoin them. The spaces can be filled with bars or bridges.

2 Draw the design accurately onto the foundation.

Tracing the design

1 Trace over the design by outlining it with couched threads. Keep the threads as continuous as possible and, where they are used double, insure that they lie evenly side by side.

Where one line branches to another, divide the thread and couch it as far as necessary and then double back to the starting point. Where one line touches another, thread the couching under and back again so that the pattern is joined.

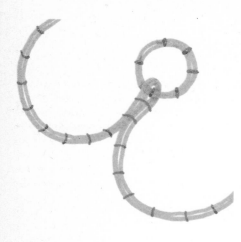

2 Secure the couching to the foundation with small temporary stitches, preferably worked in a contrasting color to make them easier to remove. However, if the lace is being worked in white it is better to use white thread, as the color may leave traces.

Filling in the design

1 Fill in the various spaces of the design by using one of the buttonhole stitches given below. Be as inventive as you like, for it is the variety of the stitches which give reticella lace its character.
2 When the filling is complete, make the final bars or bridges to link those lines which do not touch each other. These can be worked by buttonholing or by oversewing.
3 Start by laying several threads evenly across the space to be filled by taking small stitches in the outline threads on each side. Cover these threads with buttonholing or oversewing.

4 If you want a wider bar, work buttonhole stitches along both edges and decorate the bar with rings, picots or other bars.

Outlining the design
This is the step which gives the final touch to the lace. The whole design is now outlined in close buttonholing, using a fine thread to bring it to life.
To give dimension and emphasis to the various parts, work over a couple of strands of soft padding thread. Where one part appears to pass over another, work the part underneath first.
When joining in and fastening off threads, take a few neat overcast stitches into the part of the outlining nearest to you. These stitches will be worked in with the final outlining, which should cover them completely and also help strengthen the finished lace.

Finishing
The last and most exciting stage is the removal of the lace from the foundation, which is done quite simply by cutting and removing the stitches which hold down the couched thread.

The stitches
Here are just a few of the basic stitches which can be used to create needlemade lace. You can invent numerous patterns with the interplay of the various stitches and the spaces created by them and embellish them further with picots and loops to give greater dexterity to the work. Basic buttonhole stitch, single and double knot stitch and bullion stitch are all described later in the dictionary of stitches.

Knotted buttonhole stitch
1 Work a row of buttonhole stitches from left to right over the couched thread.
2 Work a second row, from right to left, reversing the stitch into the loop made by

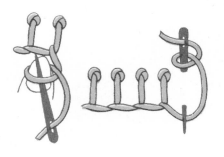

the first stitch. Work each stitch at a slight angle, pulling tight each knot thus formed before continuing to the next stitch. Two or three buttonhole stitches can often be drawn together by working this stitch over a whole group at once.

Corded buttonhole stitch
1 Work a row of spaced buttonhole stitches from right to left.

2 Work a row of overcast stitches from left to right over the loops of the previous row.
3 Repeat these rows alternately for the desired length. When working the third row, be sure that you stitch into the loop of the buttonholing, not into the overcasting.

Twisted stitches
These give a light and airy appearance to the work. It is important to keep the tension as even as possible and the stitches themselves carefully spaced. One method of working this is to overcast the loops, as for corded buttonhole stitch. Alternatively, they can be built up into a pyramid

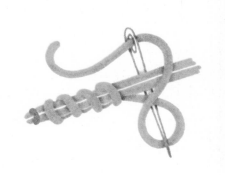

formation, each row having one less twisted stitch than the previous one.

Picots
1 To work a picot, make a second buttonhole stitch into the loop of the last stitch worked and then insert the needle into the loop of this second stitch just made.
2 Twist the working thread around the needle, draw up the knot and pass the needle through the loop of the original buttonhole stitch, ready to continue the row of buttonholing. The knots should twist and form into a small circle.

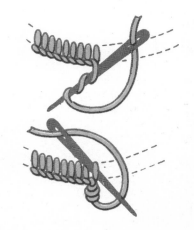

SHADOW WORK

Shadow work is a type of embroidery which relies for effect on a filling stitch, worked on the wrong side of a transparent fabric so that the color of the working thread shows through in a subdued tint to the right side of the work.

It is usually worked on a very fine fabric such as organdy, organza, fine linen lawn, cotton lawn, muslin and crepe de chine in a soft shade.

Until this century it was always worked in white on a white fabric with double back-stitch (a variation of herringbone). The threads of the stitches cross on the back of the work to give an opaque quality on the right side.

In more modern work the introduction of color has changed the effect to produce an opalescent look and this type of work lends itself well to such articles as baby clothes, lingerie, party dresses and aprons as well as on more delicate table linen, lampshades and curtains.

The design

Designs for shadow work should consist of narrow shapes which have simple outlines. Traditionally the work was always floral in design with the addition of a little surface stitchery but nowadays abstract shapes of suitable proportions can be used.

The shapes are nevertheless restricted in width by the double backstitch or herringbone stitch which fills and outlines them. To transfer the design onto the fabric, simply place the fabric over the design with the right side facing down and trace over the lines of the design with a fine pencil.

Threads and needles

Choose a fine thread – either pure silk, 6-strand floss or fine coton à broder – in a color darker or brighter than the fabric so that you can achieve the desired finished effect.

Use fine crewel or between needles.

The working method

When the design has been traced onto the wrong side of the fabric, work all the main areas in close herringbone stitch (or double backstitch). Extra wide shapes can be filled in with two rows of herringbone, but this is best avoided.

Close herringbone stitch is worked in the same way as ordinary herringbone but with the stitches touching each other at the top and bottom, thus building up two parallel lines of backstitch on the front of the work with the opaque area between them.

Form the stitches as evenly as possible, following the outline of the shapes and working into all the corners and points in order to complete the outline accurately on the right side.

Work the stitches slightly smaller and closer together on the inside of curves and slightly larger on the outside. Take care that the stitches do not slope and always remain perpendicular to the base line.

When all the main areas are filled in, any additional stitchery such as linear detail, eyelets and spider's web wheels can be worked on the right side.

Because the fabric is transparent, take care to conceal all ends of threads.

Do not use knots to finish but darn all ends back into the work securely and neatly.

French shadow work

This is extremely easy to work and produces quick and attractive results.

The motif most normally used is the square, which is marked onto the fabric by drawing a thread from side to side to insure an accurate outline.

The squares are first worked one way and then the other, taking up an equal number of threads each time. The threads must be counted carefully so that the blocks of stitches are perfectly even.

Several variations of the square can be developed and the Greek key design is always a good stand-by.

Indian shadow work

This has almost the same effect as traditional shadow work but a slightly different working method is used.

Instead of the stitches crossing on the back of the work they are taken from side to side, picking up a small amount of fabric each time and zig-zagging between the lines of the design.

Take care to pick up a small stitch each time so that the threads will not be too openly spaced on the back of the work, thus spoiling the shadow effect on the front.

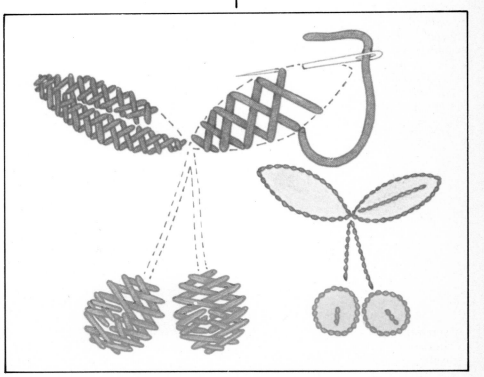

Shadow work for sheers

Light as air and delicate as spring flowers, this curtain with its shadow work motifs has a romantic prettiness far more attractive than any net curtain that can be bought. Only three simple stitches are used: backstitch, satin stitch and double back or closed herringbone stitch.

Fabric required

Length of fine pale green nylon or organdy to fit window, plus 1½ in turnings at top and bottom and ¼ in turnings at side.

You will also need

D.M.C. 6-Strand Floss in the following colors and quantities (to work 8 motifs): 2 skeins each 320 laurel green and white; 1 skein 776 blossom pink.
Alternatively, D.M.C. Pearl Cotton No. 8: one 10 grm ball each 894 carnation, 989 grass green and white.

Embroidery hoop.
Tracing paper.
Crewel needle No. 7.

Transferring the motifs

Two complete motifs are illustrated to size in the tracing pattern. Trace the motifs and transfer them to the fabric either with dressmakers' carbon paper or by outlining with small basting stitches.
Alternate the motifs evenly along the edge of the fabric, placing them above the final hem turning.

The design

1 No special skill is required for shadow work but it is important to work neatly so that the double lines of backstitch lie closely together. This will be easier to do if the work is held in an embroidery hoop.
2 Using 3 strands of floss throughout, follow the working chart as a guide.
3 Double backstitch, or closed herringbone stitch, can be worked either from the right or the wrong side of the fabric. Figure 1 shows how a small backstitch is worked alternately on each side of the traced double lines. The dotted lines on the diagram show the formation of the thread on the wrong side of the fabric, with the color showing delicately through.
4 Figure 2 shows closed herringbone stitch worked on the wrong side of the fabric with no spaces left between the stitches. Both methods achieve the same result. Whichever method you choose, take care that the work is as neat on the back as on the front.
5 To finish off, press the embroidery on the wrong side, turn up the side and bottom hems and make a heading and a casing for the curtain rod at the top.

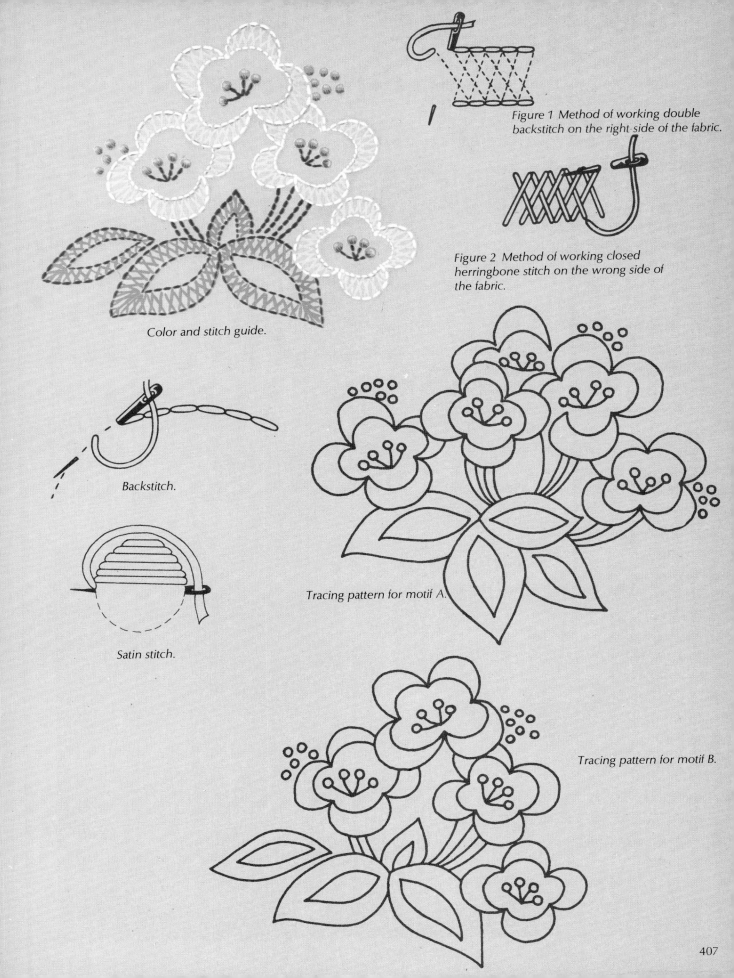

Color and stitch guide.

Figure 1 Method of working double backstitch on the right side of the fabric.

Figure 2 Method of working closed herringbone stitch on the wrong side of the fabric.

Backstitch.

Satin stitch.

Tracing pattern for motif A.

Tracing pattern for motif B.

Organdy apron

Size

The length can be adjusted to fit all sizes.

Fabric required

$1\frac{1}{4}$ yards cotton organdy, 44 inches wide.

You will also need

Matching pure silk thread.
6-strand embroidery floss in a darker and lighter shade of main color.
Pearl cotton embroidery thread in a lighter shade of main color.
Fine crewel needle.
Fine tapestry needle.

Cutting out

Fold the fabric in half lengthwise placing the selvages together. Cut out the pieces as shown in the chart.

Making the apron

1 Place the facing strip along the bottom edge of the main section and baste together all around the edge. This now forms the wrong side of the apron.

2 Using a sharp pencil and a small plate or saucer as a guide, draw a scalloped edge on the wrong side of the fabric along the top edge of the facing. Start from the center-front and work outward to the sides insuring that the scallops are evenly balanced.

	right side		wrong side

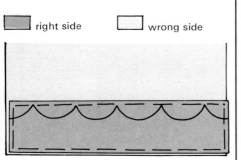

3 With the tapestry needle and pure silk thread, work pin stitching along the scalloped line on the wrong side of the fabric. Use sharp embroidery scissors to trim the excess fabric back to the stitching line.

4 Place the fabric, wrong side facing up, over the motif and trace it, placing one motif above each scallop as shown.

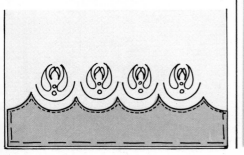

5 Still working on the wrong side, fill in the two inner shapes in herringbone stitch, using the darker shade of stranded floss and the fine crewel needle. Keep the top and bottom of the stitch equal in width so that the work will be even on the right side.

6 Work the two outershapes in the same way, using the lighter shade of the stranded floss.

7 Using the fine pearl cotton complete the surface stitchery on the right side of the work.

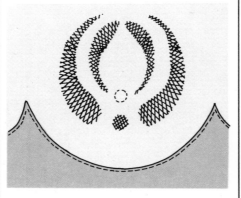

Work a backstitch spider's web in the middle.

8 For the stitching enclosing the bottom of the motif, work a graduating line of fine satin stitch, $\frac{1}{8}$ inch apart, starting with a very small stitch and gradually getting wider then tapering off to a very small stitch at the beginning of the row.

9 On the satin stitch row work a row of raised chain band, making it a double row where the line thickens in the center and tapering it by starting and finishing with several stem or split stitches.

Work a motif onto the pocket in the same way.

The ruffle

10 Finish each side of the apron with a $\frac{1}{2}$ inch hem.

Join the pieces for the ruffle along the narrow edge with a French seam.
Make a narrow hem along the short ends and bottom edge of the ruffle. Work a row of gathering along the top edge.

11 Remove the basting thread from the bottom edge of the apron. With right sides together baste the top edge of the ruffle to the bottom of the apron, arranging the gathers evenly and leaving the edge of of the facing free. Machine stitch, taking $\frac{1}{2}$ inch turnings.

12 Press the turnings upward, turn under the edge of the facing and place the fold to the stitch line. Hem into place.

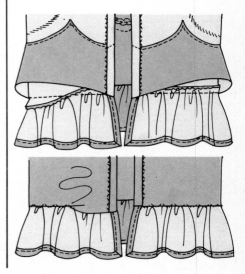

The pocket

13 Prepare the pocket ruffle in the same way as for the main ruffle.

Place the ruffle, wrong side down, on the right side of the pocket so that the raw edges are even along the top. Arrange the gathers evenly and baste in position.

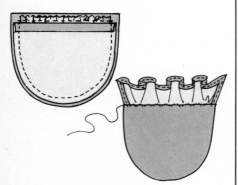

14 Work a very narrow hem along one long edge of the pocket facing. Place the facing on to the top of the pocket so that the raw edges are even along the top and sides. Baste and machine stitch along the top and sides, taking ½ inch turnings. Turn the facing onto the wrong side of the pocket and press.

15 Turn under the remaining sides of the pocket. Place the pocket in position onto the apron. Baste and machine stitch.

The waistband

16 Fold under the short ends of the waistband for ½ inch onto the wrong side and baste. Fold the waistband in half lengthwise.

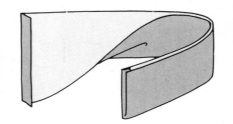

17 Try on the apron for length and adjust it at the top edge if necessary. Work a row of gathering along the top edge. With right sides together, pin the gathered edge to one long side of the waistband, arranging the gathers evenly. Baste in place.

18 Make narrow hems along the two long sides and one short side of the apron ties. Place the fourth side to the ends of the waistband, gathering the fullness as shown below.

19 Stitch, taking ½ inch turnings from the left edge at the top of the tie, across the front and over the tie at the right edge.

Fold under the remaining edges of the waistband and hem neatly but firmly to the stitch line.

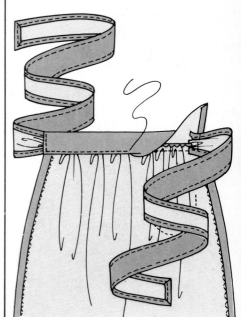

Cutting layout for apron

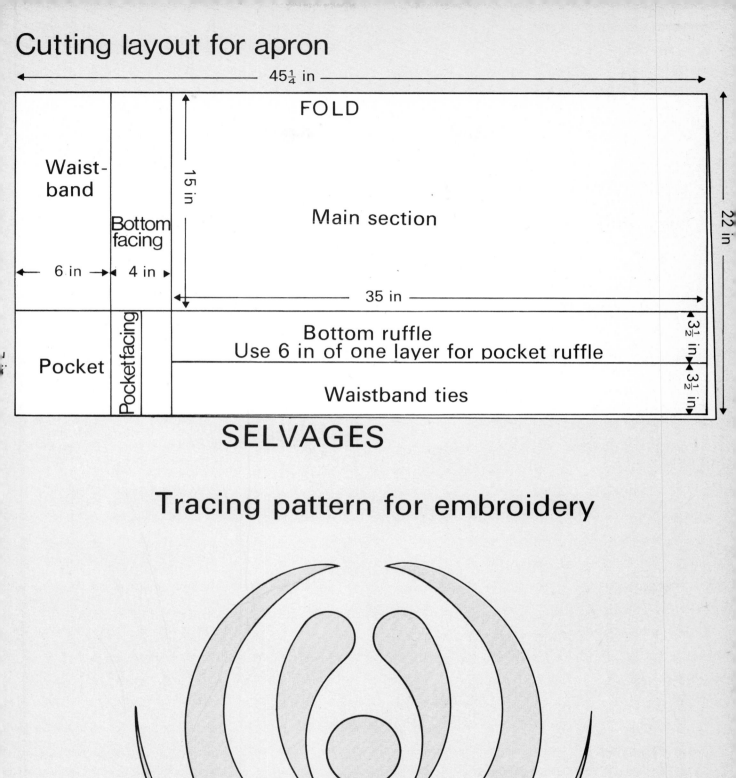

45¼ in

FOLD

Waist-band

Bottom facing

15 in

Main section

6 in

4 in

35 in

22 in

Pocket

Pocketfacing

Bottom ruffle
Use 6 in of one layer for pocket ruffle

Waistband ties

3½ in

3½ in

SELVAGES

Tracing pattern for embroidery

Stitching a sampler

For centuries the sampler was an essential part of every girl's education. Many survive today as beautiful examples of fine needlework. Now you can work your own sampler in the traditional manner. Nearly 20 different stitches, including drawn thread work, are included to make this sampler a technical exercise for the experienced needleworker as well as for the beginner. Add your name and date of completion at top or bottom for a really authentic touch.

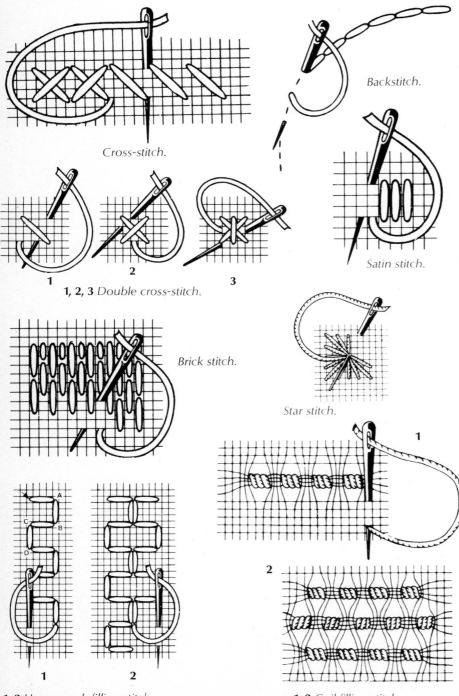

Cross-stitch.

Backstitch.

1, 2, 3 *Double cross-stitch.*

Satin stitch.

Brick stitch.

Star stitch.

1, 2 *Honeycomb filling stitch.*

1, 2 *Coil filling stitch.*

Fabric required

36 in beige medium weight evenweave fabric, 21 threads to 1 in, 59 in wide.

You will also need

D.M.C. 6-strand floss in the following colors and quantities: 3 skeins tapestry shade 610, 2 skeins each tapestry shades 3013, 3012, 3046; 1 skein each tapestry shades 932, 931, 930, ecru, 3045, geranium 948, 352 and 249.
Picture frame with mounting board or cardboard to fit embroidery.
Tapestry needles Nos. 20 and 24 for 6 and 3 strands respectively.

The design

1 Cut a piece from the fabric to measure 36 inches square. Mark the centers both ways with a line of basting stitches.
2 Diagram 1 gives slightly more than half the design with the center indicated by black arrows.
Note It is important to remember when working the design that each background square on the diagram represents 2 threads of the evenweave fabric.
3 Use 6 strands of thread and needle size 20 for Swedish darning, satin stitch, couching and oblique loop stitch. Use 3 strands and needle size 24 for the rest of the embroidery.
4 Diagram 2 shows the Swedish darning and satin stitch tree. The background lines on this diagram indicate the threads of the fabric.
5 Begin working the sampler centrally with four-sided stitch filling, 2 threads down and 6 threads to the right of the crossed basting stitches. Follow Diagram 1 and the stitch and color key for the main part of the design.
Repeat, reversing the design, from the lower black arrow to complete the second half of the sampler.
6 Couching is worked horizontally between satin stitch C9 on the diagram.
7 Once the embroidery for Diagram 1 has been completed, work Diagram 2 in the position indicated, following the key for the design and stitches used. The four drawn thread borders are worked one on each side of the completed design, linked by woven bars and oblique loop stitch as shown in the photograph.

Finishing the sampler

Press the completed sampler on the wrong side. Place it centrally over the mounting board, fold the surplus fabric to the back of the board and secure it all around with pins stuck into the edge of the board. Lace the fabric across the back both ways with strong thread. Remove the pins and mount the sampler in a frame.

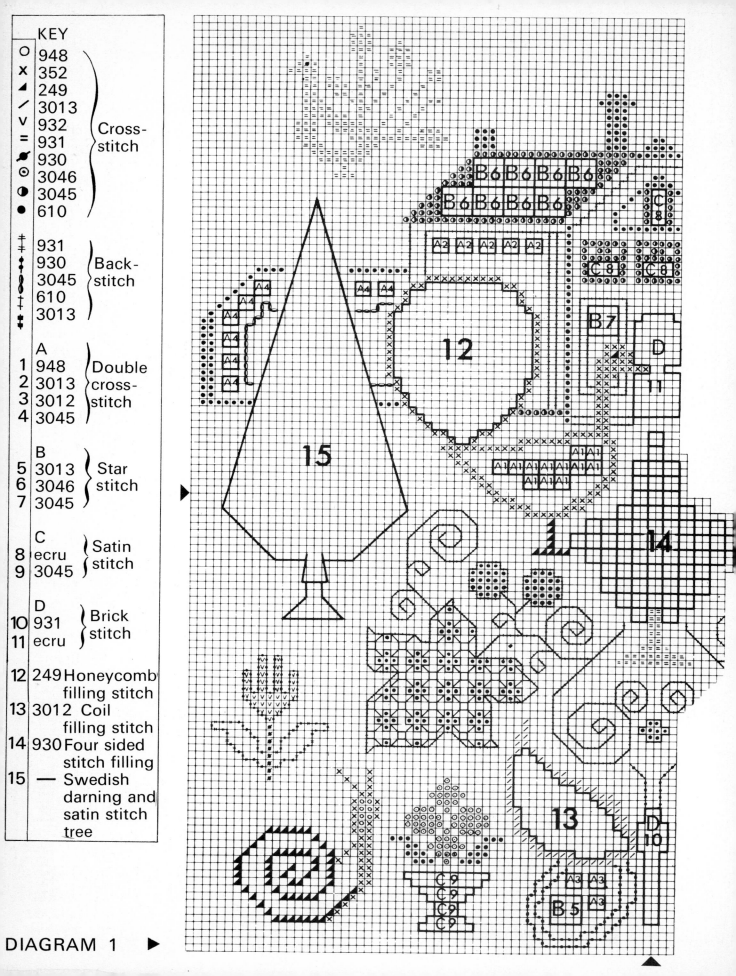

KEY

O	948	
X	352	
▲	249	
/	3013	
V	932	Cross-stitch
=	931	
◣	930	
⊙	3046	
◖	3045	
●	610	

‡	931	
◆	930	
◉	3045	Back-stitch
†	610	
✚	3013	

A		
1	948	Double
2	3013	cross-stitch
3	3012	
4	3045	

B		
5	3013	Star
6	3046	stitch
7	3045	

C		
8	ecru	Satin stitch
9	3045	

D		
10	931	Brick stitch
11	ecru	

12	249	Honeycomb filling stitch
13	3012	Coil filling stitch
14	930	Four sided stitch filling
15	—	Swedish darning and satin stitch tree

DIAGRAM 1 ▶

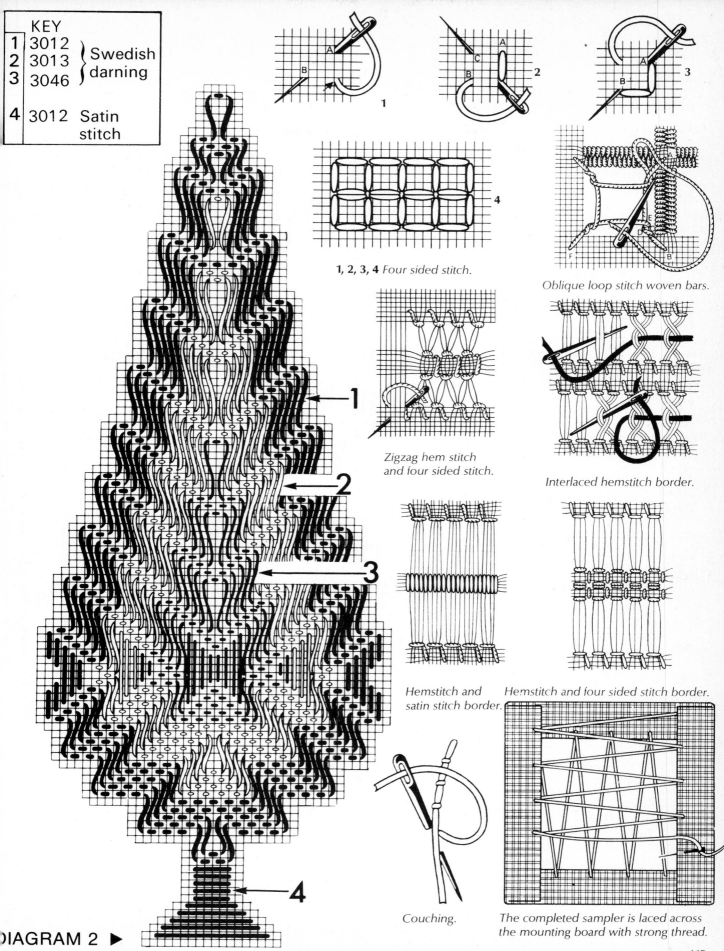

KEY

1	3012	} Swedish
2	3013	darning
3	3046	
4	3012	Satin stitch

1, 2, 3, 4 Four sided stitch.

Oblique loop stitch woven bars.

Zigzag hem stitch
and four sided stitch.

Interlaced hemstitch border.

Hemstitch and
satin stitch border.

Hemstitch and four sided stitch border.

Couching.

The completed sampler is laced across
the mounting board with strong thread.

DIAGRAM 2 ▶

NEEDLEPOINT
Basic equipment

Needlepoint is a relaxing form of embroidery. It requires little mental effort and can be most effective when worked in one stitch. Carried out on a stiff, open-weave fabric, it is hard-wearing for use in the home as chair seat covers, stool tops, pillows, lamp bases, etc. It can also be made into exciting and useful accessories, such as belts, bags and slippers. Its use for clothes, however, is more restricted because of its stiffness although it could be made up into a simple garment such as a vest. Needlepoint is more properly known as canvas work or – mistakenly – tapestry work. Tapestry is the name given to a form of weaving, usually of a pictorial kind and this has led to the canvases sold with the design already painted on also being called tapestries.

The equipment
Needlepoint can be done without a frame if you are able to maintain an even tension throughout, although it frequently does become distorted since the heat of the hands affects the stiffening in the threads of the canvas. This usually results in the work having to be pinned and stretched over layers of damp blotting paper once completed in order to restore it to its former shape.

It is much better to use an embroidery frame or a canvas work frame to prevent this and also to protect the canvas from being creased or crumpled while being worked on as this affects the rigidity that keeps the stitches in place.

Types of canvas frame
There are two types of canvas frame, the flat bar and the screw bar. The flat bar frame is more suitable for large pieces of work using conventional stitches and threads because the canvas is rolled up as the work progresses. It is not so suitable for more adventurous designs using wooden beads, rings, plastic or leather shapes, because these additions prevent the work from rolling smoothly.

The screw bar frame has adjustable side pieces which fit into rollers at both ends. This kind of frame has to be large enough to take the fully extended canvas since it cannot be rolled.

An old picture frame or artist's painting stretcher can sometimes be used success-

fully as a substitute frame. To attach the canvas to it, machine-stitch wide tape over the edge of the canvas to strengthen it and then fix firmly to the frame with thumb tacks or staples placed at $\frac{1}{2}$ inch intervals.

An embroidery hoop is suitable only for small pieces of work where the part of canvas enclosed by the rings will be cut off since it may have become distorted from the pressure.

The canvas
Canvas is made from linen, hemp, cotton or gauze. Single (or mono) canvas has the threads interwoven singly and is the type most often used because any type of stitch can be worked without difficulty. Double canvas has the threads woven in pairs and is normally used when fine detail and small stitching are being used in the design. The stitches are mostly worked over the pair of threads for the background of the design and over one thread of the pair for the detailed sections.

The number of the mesh indicates the number of threads to the inch.

Good quality wide-meshed linen scrim can be used instead of canvas where you want a more pliable effect and this can be worked with all the usual stitches but often with much more exciting results.

Fine wire mesh and wire gauze have also been used for experimental canvas work.

The needles

Tapestry needles, which are blunt-ended with a large eye to enable the thread to be pulled through easily, are sold in a variety of sizes to suit the canvas and thread used. Before threading a needle with yarn, hold the yarn up to the light to see the direction of the fibers (drawing the thread through your fingers will show you if the fibers are lying in the right direction). Thread the yarn into the needle so that the fibers are lying away from the threaded end. In this way, the fibers will be stroked downward when they are pulled through the canvas, thus reducing the tension on the yarn and insuring a smoother finish to the work. You will also need two pairs of good scissors, one for cutting the canvas and paper for designs, and another small sharp-pointed pair for cutting thread. A pair of tweezers will be very useful if you have to unpick any stitches.

The designs

In Victorian times needlepoint was used for elaborate pictorial designs, such as wreaths of full-blown roses, baskets of fruit and other still life scenes, usually worked in tent stitch or cross stitch. Today, however, needlepoint is most attractive when it is used for geometric designs which allow a variety of textures, threads and stitches to be used.

Cut paper shapes arranged in a geometric pattern are perhaps the easiest form of designing for a beginner.

Squared paper or graph paper is best for drawing the final designs for needlepoint, because each square of paper can be used to denote one stitch worked over two threads of the canvas. It is possible to buy graph paper with squares corresponding to those of the canvas. This allows you to work out intricate designs in detail and in advance.

A useful economy is to copy the design onto waxed paper or tracing paper, and to place this over the graph paper to redraw and "square off". In this way the graph paper can be re-used several times.

To transfer the design onto the canvas, tack the tracing to the canvas around the edges and then baste along each line of the design using a colored basting thread and small stitches.

An alternate method is to outline the tracing with black poster paint, India ink or felt-tipped pen. Then center the canvas over the design and trace the outline onto the canvas. It is advisable to mark the center of each edge of both the tracing and the canvas so that they can be matched accurately, and also to secure the tracing with thumb tacks if you are using this method.

The threads

It is extremely important that the yarns and threads used for needlepoint should be right for the mesh of the canvas so that the stitches cover it completely. A large mesh canvas is obviously unsuitable for fine yarn and vice versa.

The type of thread depends largely on the nature of the work and how it will be used. Wool is the traditional thread for needle-point and it is the most durable. Crewel wool is sold especially for needlepoint and it can be used with two or three strands to suit the mesh. Knitting yarn can also be used if crewel yarn is not available. There is an almost unlimited choice of other threads, too – pearl cotton in various weights, stranded thread, twisted silks, tapestry yarn, single-strand embroidery thread, soft thread, lurex and even string.

Needlepoint stitches

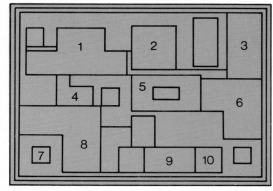

Key to Chart
1 Padded satin stitch
2 Hungarian stitch
3 Large cross stitch worked alternately with Hungarian
4 Long-legged cross stitch
5 Brick stitch
6 Long-legged cross stitch
7 Norwich stitch
8 Large cross stitch and straight cross stitch
9 Paris stitch
10 Eye stitch
Background: tent stitch

There are a great number of needlepoint stitches, many of which are similar to those used in regular embroidery. Here are a few of the most useful.

Smyrna or double cross
This is double cross stitch worked in two directions. Work cross stitch over four threads and then complete each stitch by working another cross stitch vertically

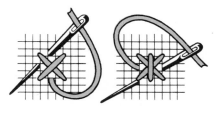

over the first stitch as shown.

Long-legged cross
This is a useful stitch because it can be worked in horizontal rows from left to right and from right to left, or in vertical rows from the top down and from the bottom up. Work as shown in the diagram, always beginning and ending each row with a regular cross stitch. If used to fill in a background, the rows can be worked alternately in each direction. The long-

legged cross stitch can also be combined with the tent stitch worked in alternate rows.

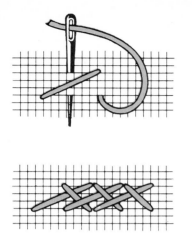

Continental stitch

This looks very much like a half cross-stitch but is worked to give more cover on the back of the canvas. It can be worked from right to left, in vertical rows or diagonal rows. It is a good background stitch and throws more chunky stitches into relief.

Knot stitch

This is another variation of cross stitch with one of the obliques worked over three threads and the other oblique worked over one thread to tie it. A useful filling stitch, it produces a good texture for backgrounds.

Rice stitch

This is a development of cross stitch. Work the crosses in thick yarn over four threads. Then, using a finer thread in a contrasting color or texture, work a single diagonal over each corner. Work these stitches in two horizontal rows, tying down the two upper corners of each cross in the first row and the two lower corners in rhe second row.

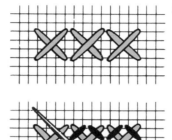

Hungarian stitch

This is a simple stitch which is more effective when worked in two colors or two textures. It consists of straight stitches worked in groups of three. For the first row, work the first stitch over two threads, the second over four threads and the third over two threads. Leave two threads and repeat to the end of the row. Work the second row as for the first, fitting the longer stitches into the spaces left by the previous row as shown.

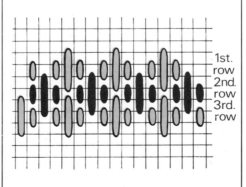

Paris stitch

This is a good background filling stitch made by working alternately over one and then over three threads of the canvas in alternate rows from left to right and right

to left. The short stitches in the second row fit in under the long stitches of the rows on each side.

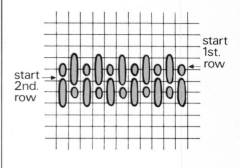

Eye stitch

This consists of 16 stitches worked over eight threads, all radiating from the same center hole.

Norwich stitch

This is not as complicated as it appears. It can be worked over any size square, providing that the square consists of an uneven number of threads. Start at point 1 and take a straight stitch to point 2. Go to the opposite corner and take a stitch from point 3 to point 4. Continue in this way around the square, taking stitches between the points shown on the diagram, giving the effect of a square on the diagonal.

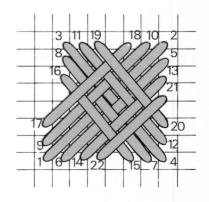

Needlepoint sampler

This pillow can be worked as a sampler to practice many different stitches comprising an interesting collection of textures. The simple use of one color also emphasizes the variation of stitches, although other colors may be used.

Size

17 inches.

Fabric required

$\frac{5}{8}$ yd single thread tapestry canvas, 27 in wide, 18 threads to 1 in.
Cream fabric for backing, 19 in square.

You will also need

D.M.C. Tapestry Yarn: 43 skeins ecru.
Pillow form to fit.
Tapestry frame with 27 inch sides.
Tapestry needle No. 18.

The design

1 Mark the center of the canvas along a line of holes in both directions with basting stitches. Mount the canvas in the frame, with the raw edges to the tapes. When working fern stitch turn the frame on its side to allow the stitches to be worked in the correct direction, as indicated by the black arrows on the working chart. The working chart gives a section of the complete design. Blank arrows indicate the center of the design, which should coincide with the basting stitches.

2 Follow the working chart using the stitch key for the design. Each background square

represents two threads of the canvas. Detailed stitch diagrams are given showing the number of threads over which the stitches are worked. When working cross-stitch it is important that the stitches are crossed in the same direction.

3 Begin the design at the small black arrow 6 threads down and 14 threads to the left of the crossed basting stitches in the center of the canvas, and work the section as given on the working chart. Omit the center section and repeat the stitches in reverse from the blank arrow to complete one quarter of the design. Work the other three quarters to correspond.

Finishing

The completed canvaswork should be dampened, pinned with rustless thumb tacks and stretched to the correct shape on a clean dry board and left to dry naturally.

To work velvet stitch

This stitch resembles the pile of an oriental carpet. It is worked from left to right in rows working from the bottom upward. Follow the stitch diagram, bringing the thread out at the arrow and insert the needle at A (2 threads up and 2 threads to the right), then bring it out again at the arrow. Re-insert the needle at A, leaving a loop of thread at the bottom, bring the needle out at B (2 threads down). Insert at C (2 threads up and 2 threads to the left), bringing the needle out again at B in readiness for the next stitch. To maintain a regular length to the loops they can be worked over a thick knitting needle. After all the rows have been worked, cut the loops and trim them evenly, taking care not to trim the tufts too short.

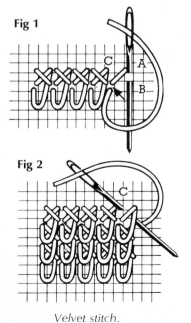

Fig 1

Fig 2

Velvet stitch.

To work brick stitch

This stitch is worked in rows alternately from left to right or from right to left. The first row consists of long and short stitches into which are fitted rows of even satin stitch, giving a "brick" formation. The whole filling must be worked very regularly, making each satin stitch of even length and all exactly parallel.

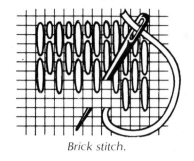

Brick stitch.

To work cross-stitch and upright cross-stitch

Work the required number of cross-stitches over 4 threads, then work upright cross-stitches between each cross-stitch, working diagonally from the lower right to the top left corner in the following way.

Figure 1 – bring the thread out at the arrow; insert the needle at A (2 threads up), then bring it out at B (2 threads to the left). Continue in this way to the end of the row. Figure 2 – after completing the last

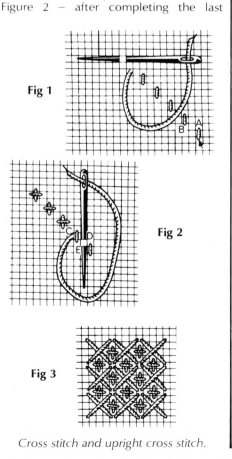

Fig 1

Fig 2

Fig 3

Cross stitch and upright cross stitch.

stitch, bring the needle through as shown at C. Insert the needle at D (2 threads to the right), and bring it through at E. Continue in this way to the end of the row. Figure 3 shows the finished effect.

To work fern stitch

Pull the thread through at the arrow and insert the needle 2 threads down and 4 threads to the right bringing it out 2 threads to the left. Then insert the needle 2 threads up and 4 threads to the right. Bring it out 2 threads down and 4 threads to the left in readiness for the next stitch. The Chart shows the direction of the two rows of fern stitch as they have been worked on the pillow.

Fern stitch.

To work eye stitch

This stitch is worked in the same way as star stitch to form a square over 8 horizontal and 8 vertical threads of canvas. It consists of 16 straight stitches all taken into the same central hole but with their outer ends arranged over a square of eight threads. Finish the square with an outline of backstitch worked over 2 canvas threads, shown in Figure 2.

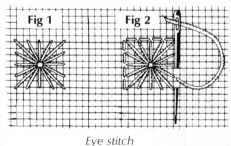

Fig 1 **Fig 2**

Eye stitch

To work straight gobelin stitch

Work a trammed stitch from left to right, then pull the needle through 1 thread down and 1 thread to the left, inserting again 2

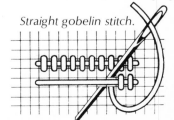

Straight gobelin stitch.

threads above. Pull the needle through 2 threads down and 1 thread to the left in readiness for the next stitch.

To work the cord

Measure off six 15 yard lengths of yarn. With someone to help you, double the pieces of yarn in half to make a length of 7½ yards, then knot the loose ends together and insert a pencil at each end. Pull the threads and, keeping them taut, turn the pencils around in opposite directions following the natural twist of the wool. Continue until the cord is sufficiently tight and begins to curl. Still keeping the cord tight, place another pencil in the center and double the cord over it until both ends meet, making a length of 3¾ yards. Next twist the cord in the opposite direction, until it begins to curl naturally. Set the cord by exerting a steady pull at both ends which will cause it to stretch slightly and so retain its twists permanently.

To make the tassels

For one tassel, wind 2 skeins of yarn evenly around a piece of cardboard 3 inches wide. Tie them together with a piece of matching yarn at one end, cut the yarn at the opposite end, and then remove the cardboard. Now take another ¼ skein of yarn, and wind this around the tied ends near the top to form a head, then fasten off securely. If the yarn does not lie properly when the tassel is completed, hold it for a few minutes over a steaming kettle, or press with a cool iron.

To finish

Trim the canvas, leaving a 1 inch border of unworked canvas all around. Place the canvaswork and backing fabric right sides together and sew them together close to the embroidery around three sides. Turn back to the right sides, insert the pillow, and slip stitch along the opening. Stitch the cord in position around the edge of the pillow and attach the tassels securely to the corners.

KEY

1 Velvet stitch
2 Cross-stitch
3 Satin stitch
3a Satin stitch (horizontal)
4 Brick stitch
5 Cross-stitch and upright cross-stitch (variation)
6 Fern stitch
7 Eye stitch
☐ Petit point
☐ Straight gobelin stitch

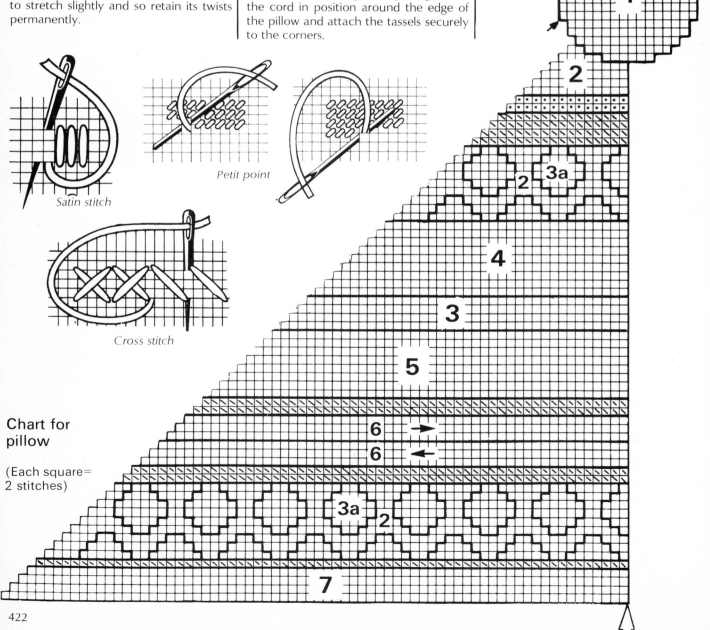

Satin stitch

Petit point

Cross stitch

Chart for pillow

(Each square= 2 stitches)

Quillwork desk set

For your desk

This smart desk set was inspired by the quill work embroidery of North American Indian tribes. The colors – ocher, indigo and rust – are similar to those produced by natural dyes. The embroidery is worked throughout in variations of satin stitch. The simple basic design can easily be adapted to make the pieces of the set larger or smaller if you wish.

Fabric required

$\frac{2}{3}$ yd single thread canvas, 16 threads to 1 in, 23 in wide, $\frac{1}{4}$ yd felt, 72 in wide, to match one of the main colors.

You will also need

Anchor Tapisserie Yarn in the following colors and quantities: 8 skeins 0850 indigo, 7 skeins 0412 rust, 5 skeins 0315 ocher, 4 skeins 0848 light blue.
Hardback address book, 5 in by 8 in.
$10\frac{1}{2}$ oz soup can, 4 in high, for pencil holder.
Piece of heavy cardboard, thin plywood or plastic sheet 16 in by 23 in.
Tapestry needle No. 22.
Sewing needle.
Thread to match felt.

The design

1 Tape the raw edges of the canvas and, following the working charts, work the parts of the desk set. Do not cut the canvas, but leave a 2 inch border of unworked canvas around each piece of embroidery. The embroidery is worked throughout in satin stitch of various lengths.
Note It is important when working the design to remember that each square on the chart represents two stitches.
2 The completed canvaswork should be dampened, then pinned and stretched to the correct shape on a clean dry board, and left to dry naturally.

Pen holder

Trim the unworked canvas to $\frac{3}{4}$ inch all around. Fold the canvas around to form a ring, trim the top layer of unworked canvas down to 4 threads. Work satin stitch, using indigo thread, over the 4 threads as shown, joining the two layers of unworked canvas.
Cut a strip of felt 4 inches by 9 inches and sew the short ends together. Turn under the border of unworked canvas around top and bottom, slip the felt inside the canvas and slip stitch together around top and bottom. Fit the completed cover over the can.

Address book cover

Trim the unworked canvas all around to $\frac{3}{4}$ inch. Miter the corners and fold down the borders of unworked canvas. Cut a

strip of felt 11 inches by $8\frac{1}{4}$ inches. Stitch one short end of the felt to the canvas as shown in the diagram. Cut another piece of felt $4\frac{1}{4}$ inches by $7\frac{1}{4}$ inches; sew this to the remaining three sides of the canvas.
Slide the embroidery onto the front cover of the book, fold the rest of the felt around the book and inside the back cover. Slip stitch at top and bottom.

Blotter

Trim the unworked canvas to $\frac{3}{4}$ inch all around. Cut a piece of felt as shown in the diagram. Turn under the unworked borders of canvas and sew the two embroidered end pieces onto the felt as shown. Lay the board on top of the felt and fold the end pieces around to the front. Fold the excess felt at top and bottom to the back of the board and stitch down. Cut a sheet of blotting paper to size and insert.

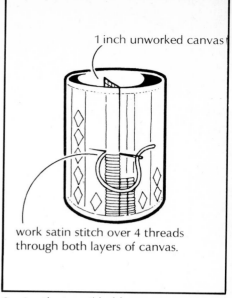

1 inch unworked canvas

work satin stitch over 4 threads through both layers of canvas.

Sewing the pencil holder cover.

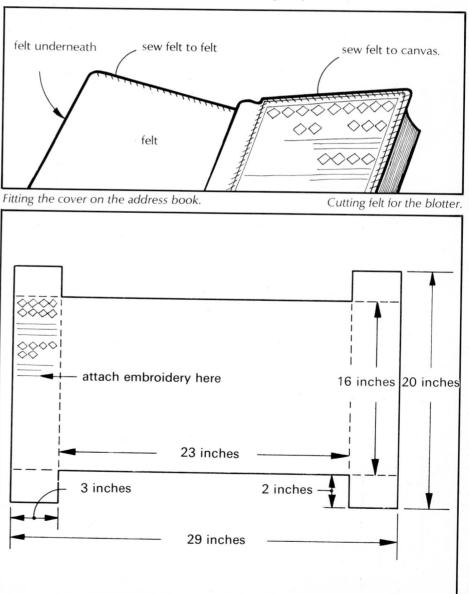

felt underneath   sew felt to felt   sew felt to canvas.

felt

Fitting the cover on the address book.   *Cutting felt for the blotter.*

attach embroidery here

16 inches | 20 inches

23 inches

3 inches   2 inches

29 inches

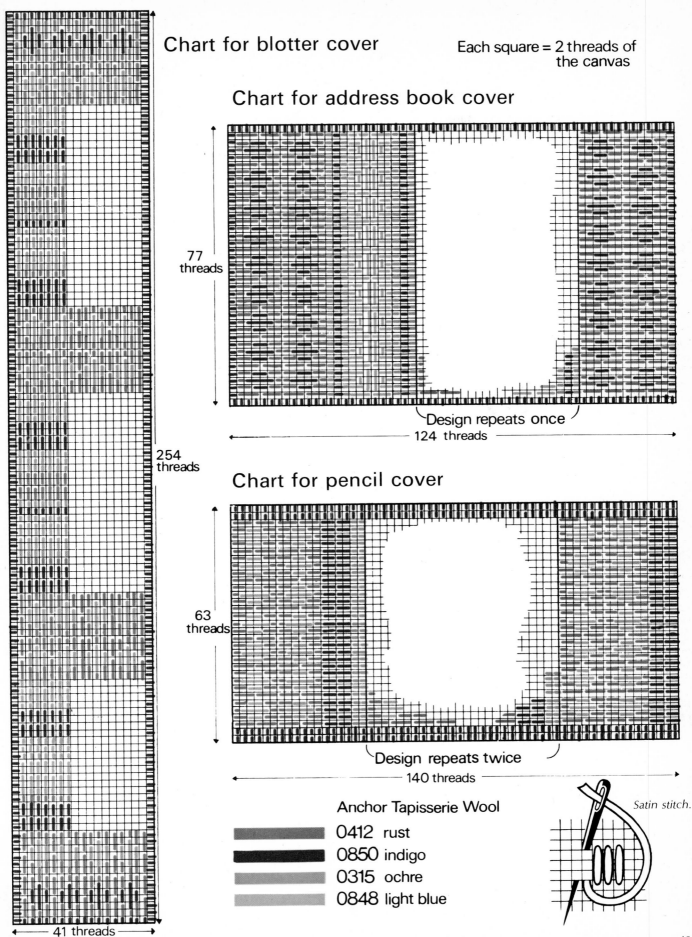

Chart for blotter cover

Each square = 2 threads of the canvas

Chart for address book cover

77 threads

254 threads

Design repeats once
124 threads

Chart for pencil cover

63 threads

Design repeats twice
140 threads

41 threads

Anchor Tapisserie Wool

0412 rust
0850 indigo
0315 ochre
0848 light blue

Satin stitch.

425

FLORENTINE NEEDLEPOINT

Florentine canvas work dates back as far as the 13th century and is thought to be of Hungarian origin.

It is also known as Bargello, which is probably a corruption of Jagiello, the family name of the Polish King Vladislaw who married a young Hungarian princess. She incorporated the arms of Hungary and Poland in a bishop's cope which she worked in the stitch now known as Florentine.

It became known as Florentine work in the 15th century when one of the Medici family married a Hungarian bride who taught the art to the ladies of the Florentine court. Other names for Florentine work include Hungarian point, "Fiamma" or flame stitch.

There is a great difference between the Florentine work of the past and that of today. The main characteristic of the work is the shading and blending of color, but while the early work was subtle with carefully arranged color tints, modern work is bolder and more striking.

Traditionally Florentine work was used for upholstery on stool tops, chair seats and bed drapes, but today it can also be made into stunning accessories, such as the bag shown on the page opposite.

Choosing the colors

As a general rule, it is advisable to use two or three basic colors with as many intermediate shades of these colors as you like. Each successive row is worked in a lighter or darker tint to that of the previous row, so gradually shading from one tone to another. When you are working in shades which are very close, it is advisable to lay all the skeins of yarn on a table and grade them carefully. Number each one with a small tie-on label so that you can always pick up the threads in the correct sequence.

Materials

Use single thread canvas with yarn in the correct thickness to match the mesh and completely cover the canvas. On a 16 or 18 mesh canvas, tapestry and crewel wools (with three strands) are the ones most frequently used because they both have an excellent color range. Knitting wool can also be used and silk threads worked on a fine mesh canvas.

Estimating the amount of yarn

1 Cut a 18 inch length of yarn. Stitch as much of the pattern repeat as this length will allow and then count up the number worked. Multiply by the yarn length to calculate how much you need for a complete row and then multiply that by the number of rows worked in each color.
2 Calculate from the yardage specified by the manufacturer how many skeins of each color you will need.

Needles

Use tapestry needles of a suitable thickness for the canvas and yarn.

Frames

Technically this form of canvas work can be evenly stitched whether held in the hand or mounted in a frame, so whichever method you use is a matter of personal preference.

Preparing the canvas

Baste the center lines both vertically and horizontally on the canvas plus any other guide lines you feel necessary. Count and mark the high points of any pattern where the repeat is the same throughout.

The stitch

Only one type of stitch is used for Florentine work. It is a vertical stitch usually covering an even number of threads, such as four, six or eight, and moving either upward or downward over one or more threads depending on the pattern.

Patterns are constructed by working blocks of stitches side by side, then moving higher or lower to make another block, and so on.

Zig zag stitch

This is the most commonly used Florentine stitch and is worked by passing each stitch over four threads and back under two. The easiest way to vary it is to take it over six threads and back under one. To avoid monotony in the pattern, vary the height

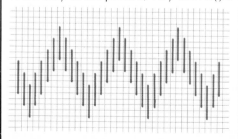

of the pinnacles formed or make the slopes more gradual, perhaps by making two stitches over the same number of threads.

Flame stitch

This is worked over four threads and back under one and produces a flame-like effect. It is important to start in the center of the canvas with the apex of the stitch at the

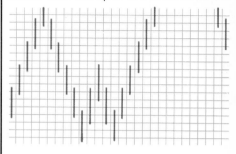

highest point. Both flame stitch and Florentine stitch can be the basis of more complex designs using squares, diamonds or trellises.

Curves

You can form the illusion of a curve by working blocks of stitches over the same

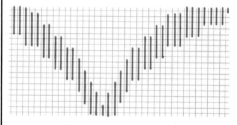

number of threads and varying the rate of progression. Thus stitches or blocks of stitches worked on the 6/1, 5/1 and 4/1 principle will produce steeper curves than those worked on the 6/3 and 4/2 principle.

Medallion pattern

This is a popular repeating pattern where each stitch is taken over four threads and back under two, starting with four single stitches, followed by one block of two stitches, then three blocks of three stitches to form the top of the pattern.

Progress downward, repeating the same number of stitches. This forms the outline of the pattern which can be repeated throughout the work. The spaces formed between the medallions can be filled with contrasting color yarns.

The foundation row

All Florentine patterns depend on an accurate first row and in some patterns the embroidery is worked either above or below this row. In others each section is filled in from one outer foundation row.

When working this foundation row it is extremely important to count the threads accurately – if you make a mistake, cut it out rather than trying to unpick it, since unpicking takes too long and frays the yarn so badly that it is unusable.

Starting and finishing

For patterns where symmetry is important, begin at the marked center line of the canvas and stitch the first row from the center outward. The following rows can be worked from side to side in the usual way, following the pattern established by the first row.

Florentine clutch bag

Use a length of yarn about 15 inches long and knot one end. Thread the needle with the other end and pass the needle through the canvas from the front about 2 inches from the position of the first stitch. Bring the needle up in the position for the first stitch, work several stitches and then cut off the knot, leaving the tail.

Thread the tail through to the back of the canvas and work it in through the back of the stitches. Finish off by working a short length through the stitches on the back in the same way. Always avoid starting and finishing in the same place so that the work will have an even finish and darn in the ends as they occur to avoid matting and tangling on the back of the work.

Size

$7\frac{1}{2}$ in × $11\frac{3}{4}$ in × 2 in.

Fabric required

$\frac{3}{8}$ yd single thread tapestry canvas, 27 in wide, 14 threads to 1 in.
Small skin of suede for back of bag and gussets.
1 felt square, 24 in × 24 in.

You will also need

D.M.C. Tapestry Yarn: 4 skeins Raspberry 7209, 2 skeins each Raspberry 7204, 7205, 7215; 1 skein gray 7618.
D.M.C. 6-Strand Floss: 3 skeins rose pink 819, 2 skeins each white, gray 762. Use six strands throughout.
Tapestry frame with 27 in tapes.
Adhesive.

The design

This design is worked in Florentine canvas embroidery.
The photograph gives a section of the design with the double row of three straight stitches forming the center.

Working the embroidery

1 Mount the canvas into the frame. Mark the center of the canvas widthwise with a line of basting.

2 Start the embroidery in the center of the canvas with the double row of three straight stitches. Work the motifs on each side and repeat to the sides and above and below to the required size. Grade the colors according to the photograph.
Most stitches are worked over six threads of canvas with some stitches over three threads to complete the design.

Finishing

1 Cut out pieces of suede measuring $8\frac{1}{2}$ inches × $12\frac{3}{4}$ inches for the front; 7 inches × $12\frac{3}{4}$ inches for the back, and two pieces, 3 inches × $14\frac{1}{2}$ inches for the gusset.

2 With right sides together stitch the gusset pieces along their short edges making $\frac{1}{2}$ inch turnings. Press the turnings open with your fingers.

3 With right sides together stitch the Florentine flap to one long edge of the suede back. Press the seam open. Working from the right side top-stitch the suede close to the seam line.

4 Cut out pieces of felt the same size as the suede for the front and gusset and $12\frac{3}{4}$ inches × 16 inches for the flap and back. Stitch the gusset sections as for the suede.

5 With right sides together, stitch the felt back and flap piece to the Florentine flap as far as the fold line which is $1\frac{1}{2}$ inches from the seam.
Clip across corners, turn through to the right side and press. Clip seam allowance at the fold line.

6 Place the remaining felt pieces onto the wrong side of the corresponding pieces of suede and treat them as one piece.

7 To finish the top edge of the front, fold the turnings under $\frac{1}{2}$ inch, place together and glue them. Top-stitch close to the edge.

8 With right sides together, stitch the front to the gusset, clipping the gusset turning at the corners. Finish the back in the same way. Trim seams and turn right side out. Topstitch the seams through all thicknesses $\frac{1}{4}$ inch from the edge.

Florentine chair seat

The quantities and instructions are given for a dining chair with a larger than average seat slip but they can easily be adapted to fit your own chairs.

Materials required
Clark's Anchor Tapisserie wool: 5 skeins each Tangerine 0311, 0313, 0315, Chestnut 0350, Black 0403, 2 skeins Flame 0334.
$\frac{3}{4}$ yd single thread tapestry canvas, 18 threads to 1 in, 27 in wide.
Tapestry frame (optional).
Tapestry needle No. 18.
Paper for making template of chair seat.
Upholstery tacks, $\frac{3}{8}$ in long.
Tack hammer.
Wood plane (if necessary).

Making the template
1 Remove the seat from the chair, place it onto the paper and draw around.
2 Draw a second line 1 inch outside the

KEY TO DIAGRAM

▮	Foundation row 0403
2	– 0311
3	– 0313
4	– 0315
5	– 0350
╌●╌	– 0334

TAPISSERIE WOOL

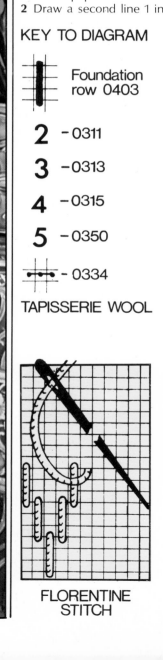

FLORENTINE STITCH

first line to allow for the depth of the padding. Draw 1 inch squares in each corner for mitered corners. The stitching should not be worked in these squares. Cut along the outside line.

3 Pin the template onto the canvas and draw around the edge using a felt-tipped pen. Allow at least 1 inch unworked canvas all around so that it can be attached to the under-side of the seat.

Marking the design

1 Mark the center of the canvas in both directions with basting.

2 Following the chart, mark the pattern onto the canvas starting at the center (indicated by the arrows) and working outward. Repeat the design until you reach the outside edges.

3 Mount the canvas onto a tapestry frame, if you are using one.

Working the design

1 The design is worked in Florentine stitch and satin stitch over four threads of the canvas. Work the foundation row first in the color shown on the chart, starting at the center and going out to the sides in both directions.

2 Work the next row below the foundation row in the color shown on the chart. The tops of the stitches on this row should be worked into the same holes as the bottom of the stitches on the foundation row.

3 Work all following rows in the same way.

4 When the color sequence is completed,

start again with the foundation row and continue as before, working to the outline shape.

5 To complete the design work the horizontal straight stitches.

Attaching the canvas

1 Place the canvas onto the seat and fold the excess onto the underside. Try the seat in position on the chair.

2 If the canvas is too thick for the seat to fit back into the chair, remove the tacks holding the original fabric. Plane the sides of the frame by the required amount and re-tack the fabric.

3 Miter the corners of the canvas and attach the canvas centrally to the seat as for the cover fabric.

4 Replace the seat on the chair.

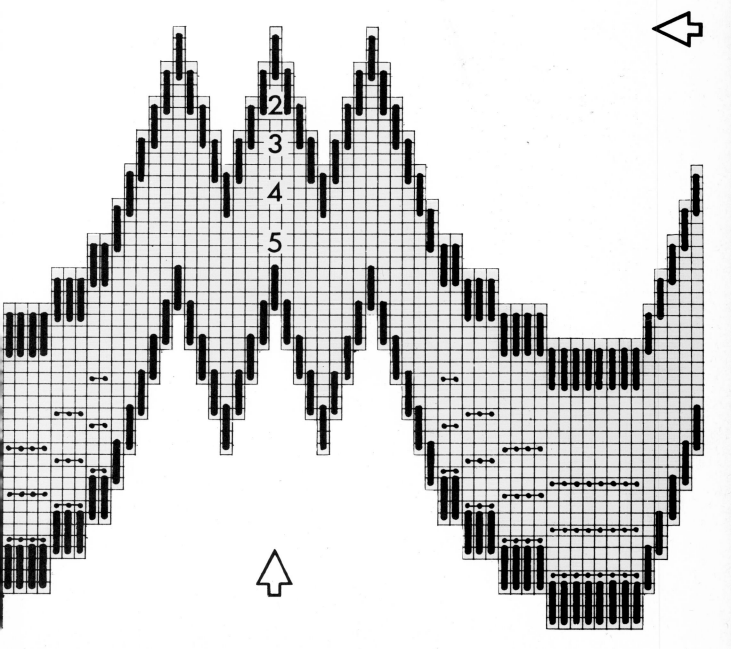

BEADWORK
Simple techniques

Beads have been used as decoration for thousands of years and have been made of many different materials such as pebbles, bone, teeth, seeds, glass and even paper. During the 19th century, embroidery with beads reached its peak when clothes and household articles were often heavily beaded. Berlin woolwork, a form of canvas embroidery incorporating beads, is a good example of this.

Today, beads – wooden, plastic and glass – are used in many ways. They can be combined with stitchery in cut work, needlepoint, smocking, quilting, drawn and pulled fabric embroidery and they can be used without stitchery to decorate any number of things.

Beads

There are wide varieties of beads, sequins and acetate shapes, and they can be obtained in many sizes. Rummage sales and opportunity shops often prove a good source as fragments of old beaded clothes, bags and lampshades will often yield very interesting beads which can be washed and re-used. A bag of "sweepings" from a workroom will often provide sufficient beads and sequins for many pieces of embroidery. When choosing beads for clothes or articles which need to be washed or dry-cleaned, check that they are durable because some acetate shapes will not stand laundering or a hot iron. Most sequins can be washed with care although you should avoid touching them with a hot iron.

Designing with beads

Choose the beads to enhance the background fabric, not necessarily to contrast with it. Often the best effect can be obtained by creating a subtle contrast rather than an obvious one. Always try to avoid crude or over bright effects.

A geometric pattern is probably the easiest way of building up a pattern which can be repeated on a bag, belt or garment, and the simplest starting point is with a square. Start by placing a square bead on a piece of felt and surround it with a row of medium size square or round beads and surround these with a row of flat sequins which might be oval or boat shaped. These could be followed by a small quantity of fine piping cord, securely couched onto the background fabric and covered with succeeding rows of small beads. If you prefer a circular motif, use the same principle but start with a large jewel or circular domed sequin. Another way that beaded and sequinned motifs can be used successfully is to place them on a geometrically patterned fabric, building up a pattern on the design of the fabric.

Whether you decide to build up a geometric pattern or to work out a less formal idea, the design should fill the space intended else it will look thin and meager. Try to insure that different parts of the design balance. A large solid shape should be balanced with several smaller ones. If you are interpreting a design based on cut paper shapes, consider the spaces formed in between the shapes as they are just as important as the shapes themselves.

Frames

It is important to use a square or rectangular frame for bead embroidery. A hoop is not suitable except for an isolated motif since you will often need both hands free and the hoop does not provide sufficient tension on the fabric. When embroidering a section of a garment, mount the whole piece into the frame, complete the bead embroidery, remove from the frame and then finish the garment.

Fabric

Any type of fabric can be enhanced with beads which are suitable for the weight and texture – naturally small glass beads would be unsuitable for a heavy tweed where large wooden or plastic beads would give the best effect.

It is advisable to back the fabric to be embroidered. If it is heavily beaded, a firm non-woven interfacing will support the beads on a bag or a belt. For a garment use a firm lightweight cotton or lawn as a backing for the beaded part only. For this kind of trim, cut away the surplus around the beaded portion before finishing the garment.

Thread

The thread you use will depend on the size and type of fabric and beads. Never use a polyester thread because it stretches too much. The beads should lie on the fabric without being too loose, nor tight enough to pucker it. Pure sewing silk is the most satisfactory thread to use, in a color to match the bead or sequin. Always wax the thread with beeswax to strengthen it and prevent the beads – particularly bugle beads – from cutting into it.

Needles

Use special beading needles which are long and pliable and are available in sizes 12–18. Choose the size to slip through the beads easily.

Attaching beads

Beads, depending on their size, can be attached to fabric in one of four ways.
1 They can be sewn onto the background fabric with a straight stab stitch. The thread is brought through the fabric, the bead is threaded onto the needle and the needle is passed through the fabric again. The bead will then lie on its side.

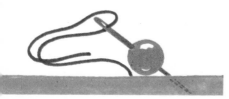

2 The bead, if large enough, can be secured by two or four stitches through the center hole so that it will then lie with the hole upward. Square beads are more effective when used in this way but the use of this method depends on the effect you are trying to produce.

3 Beads can be sewn on with a backstitch or several beads can be threaded onto a needle and couched down to follow the line of the design.

4 A large bead can be sewn on by bringing the threads through the fabric, sliding on the large beads and then one small matching or contrasting bead. The needle and thread then re-enter the large bead and the fabric. This secures the large bead so that it is free-standing.

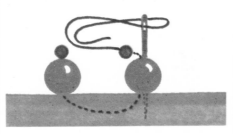

It is advisable to fasten the thread off after sewing on each heavy bead, rather than carry the thread on the back of the work from bead to bead.

Attaching sequins

Sequins are available in flat and cupped shapes in a number of sizes. They can be attached as other beads or jewels when used as isolated units or they can be sewn on in line so that they overlap.
1 Bring the needle up through the fabric and through the hole in the center of the first sequin. Pass the needle back through the fabric at the edge of the sequin and bring it up again immediately next to the point that it entered.
2 Thread on the next sequin making sure that cupped sequins all lie in the same direction with the domed side uppermost. Continue in this way along the entire row. Each sequin should evenly overlap the preceding one.

Sewing beads over cord

Piping cord can be used as a base and can be dyed to show through glass beads.
To attach the cord, place it on the line

of the design and secure it with three over-cast stitches at each end and with three straight stitches from the fabric to the center of the cord alternately on each side.
To cover the cord with beads, bring up the thread at the side of the cord, slide on enough beads to cover the cord from side to side and insert the needle into the fabric on the opposite side of the cord. Repeat this over the entire length of the cord, keeping the beading tightly packed and with the same number of beads for each stitch.

Attaching bugle beads

Bugle beads can be sewn flat, arranged in regular numbers to produce a repeat pattern. For example three or four beads could be placed vertically followed by the same number placed horizontally; or they could be arranged in blocks such as the brick pattern shown.

Some beads are set in metal mounts which have channels through which the thread passes or they might have a hole in the center or at each end. Both kinds can be attached as for heavy beads.

Fastening on and off

Never use a knot for fastening on or off. Work all ends in securely on the back of the work, keeping it as neat as possible.

A touch of luxury

Add a touch of exclusive luxury to your clothes with this spray motif of beads and paillettes. For a very individual look, beading has been worked here onto the patterned velvet bodice of a smock dress. Tiny pearls and beads in shades of brown and gold subtly pick up the colors of the fabric. Paillettes and a feather stitch trim give the dress an exotic air.

To work the embroidery
Beading is worked more easily in an embroidery hoop. If the beading is to be worked on a garment you are making yourself, do your beading before sewing the seams. Outline the shape of the pattern piece, then position and trace the outline of the motif, either with basting stitches or light chalk lines.

Attaching the beads
On a casual dress which will receive more wear than a special occasion dress, the beads should be attached as securely

as possible. Thread used for beading should be the finest and strongest silk or cotton available and should match the background fabric. Use the thread double and draw it across a piece of beeswax for extra strength. Special beading needles, long and very fine, are available in sizes 10–13. To sew the beads on, fasten the thread securely on the underside of the fabric. Bring the beading needle to the front of the work and slide one bead along the needle and onto the thread. Pick up a tiny piece of fabric, the length of the bead along the design line. Draw the needle through the fabric and place the bead in position, then pick up the second bead.

Attaching the paillettes
Use 6-strand floss, either matching or in direct contrast to the color of the paillettes and fabric. The web of stitchery circling the paillette is attractive enough to be a feature of the design. Work with 3 strands of floss in the needle. Hold the

paillette in place with your left thumb and take a stitch across it four times (Figure 1). Then make a small stitch over the crossed threads at each of the corners (Figure 2). Place the needle at right angles to the square of thread and pick up a small piece of fabric just outside the edge of the paillette, keeping the thread to the right and under the point of the needle. Draw the thread through, keeping the stitch flat (Figure 3). Still with the thread to the right, push the needle under the thread forming the square and over the thread emerging from the fabric (Figure 4). Repeat the last two steps, working clockwise around the paillette until the circle is complete and the foundation threads covered.

Ideas for using the motif
Work the spray motif as a bold contrast or as a subtle highlight on a dress bodice, a wide waistband, or on the flap of a velvet bag. Try making up your own motif, perhaps one as simple as this arrangement of curving lines. Experiment with simple flowing shapes, placing beads on a scrap of fabric, moving them around and seeing how they look.

Try not to over-bead. A simple motif has impact, while too many beads, especially on a printed fabric, can produce a confused look.

Chart for position of beads and paillettes

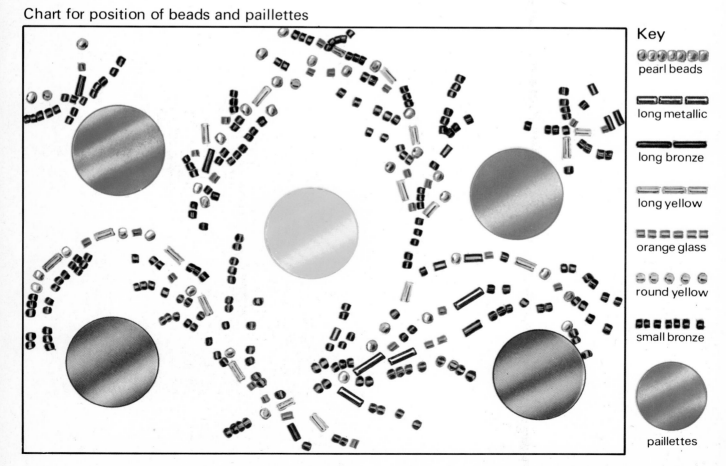

Key
pearl beads
long metallic
long bronze
long yellow
orange glass
round yellow
small bronze
paillettes

Other ideas for using the bead motif

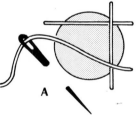

A

B

Attaching the paillettes

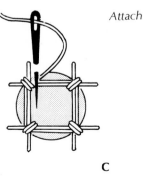

C

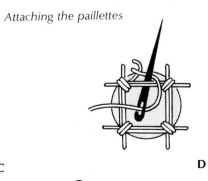

D

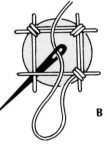

Feather stitch

BEAD WEAVING

Bead weaving is an ancient craft used to make a garment, jewelry or a wall decoration. Traditionally it has been associated with South America, where it is often used as a decoration on parts of some national costumes, and where it has developed into a highly decorative and sophisticated art form. Egyptians also used bead weaving and traces of their version of it have been found in tombs dating back 3,000 years.

The equipment
Little equipment is needed for bead weaving other than a beading loom and beading needles. The looms are inexpensive to buy, although you can easily construct one from a wooden or cardboard box by cutting notches along the edge or by hammering tacks along the edge for small pieces of work. The notches or tacks hold the warp threads and the spaces between them should be equal to the length of the beads.

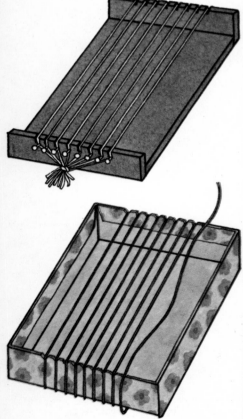

The beads
Any kind of bead can be used, although glass, ceramic, wooden or plastic ones are the easiest to work with. Choose beads of equal size for an even piece of weaving.

Needles and thread
Both the beading needle and the thread must be fine enough to pass twice through the bead. Depending on the size of the beads, pure silk, linen, cotton, or carpet threads can be used. Do not use a synthetic thread, because this tends to stretch. All threads should be waxed with beeswax to strengthen them and allow the beads to slide on easily.

The pattern
The finished bead weaving can be used as a belt, on an evening bag, as cuffs and collar for a dress, or a piece of jewelry such as a bracelet or necklace.
It is easiest to work from a chart, which you can draft out for yourself on graph paper with each square representing one bead of the design. Coloring the chart with ink or crayon in shades to show the colors of the beads makes the chart easy to read while you are working.
A geometric pattern will often produce the most effective pieces of bead weaving, and it is easiest to follow if you intend to build up your own pattern. Alternately, charts for canvas embroidery or cross-stitch can be used and adapted so that one bead represents each stitch marked on the chart.

Setting up the loom
The vertical threads of the design are known as the warp, and these fit into the grooves cut into the combs or bridges on the loom. The beads lie between the warp threads so you must decide how far apart to position the threads and then set up the loom accordingly. There should always be one more warp thread than there are beads in the width of the pattern. To strengthen the weaving when you are using fine threads, make the two outer warp threads double.
To set up the loom:
1 Cut the warp threads to the length of the beading you need plus 6 inches.
2 Knot the warp threads into small equal

bunches, pass them over the roller at the end of the loom and tie them securely to the nail or hook supplied on the roller.
3 Stretch the warp threads tightly across both combs or bridges on the loom, making sure that each warp thread lies in the correct groove. If you are using small beads, the warp threads should lie close together. With larger beads they should be spaced farther apart so that the beads will fit easily between them.
4 Wind the surplus warp thread around the pegs or nails at the opposite end of the loom, making sure that they are evenly taut to give a good tension to the weaving.

Starting to weave
1 Thread the needle with the working thread and attach it securely with a knot to the double thread on the left of the warp threads. If you are using very fine beads, you can give a firm edge to the weaving by working a few rows of darning stitch under and over the warp threads before starting to use the beads.
2 Thread the required number of beads on the needle for the first row of the pattern, working from left to right.
3 Place the string of beads under the warp threads and position each bead between two warp threads. Press the string of beads up between the warp threads with the fingers of your left hand.

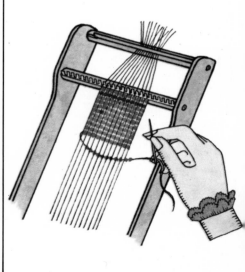

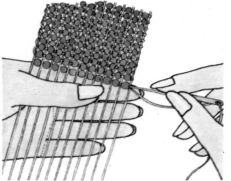

4 Bring the needle out around the last warp threads and pass it back from right to left over the warp threads and through the hole of each bead, thus securing the beads in position. Keep the tension as even as possible to avoid distorting the edge of the weaving.

5 Work the remaining rows of the pattern in the same way.

6 When the work is the required length, work a row, or two of darning stitch if you are using fine small beads, and then take the working thread back through the next to the last row of beads and cut the end. Lift the warp threads from the loom and darn each thread back through the beads or in and out of the thread between the beads. Cut the end, making sure you leave no loose ends.

7 If you are making a long length of weaving, work over the warp threads on the loom, then loosen them, wind the weaving around the roller and stretch the unwoven warp threads into the correct position for weaving. Tighten the roller by re-positioning the pin which secures it.

SMOCKING: Basic techniques

No other form of embroidery is quite so simple or so effective as smocking. Through the combined devices of gathering into pleats and subsequent decorative stitching, the appearance of the surface of a fabric and of a whole garment can be changed in the most attractive way.

The history of smocking

The initial purpose of smocking was utilitarian; it was found to be an effective method of controlling fullness in an English laborer's garment. By the 18th century, the popular "smock frock" had become decorative as well as serviceable and, in the next century, this type of garment reached its peak in elaboration. Ultimately the smocked portions of it were combined with a variety of embroidered patterns, the pattern chosen usually depending on the trade of the wearer. This embroidery usually adorned the "box", an area on either side of the smocking, and sometimes the collar and cuffs. Many surviving smocks are identifiable as having belonged to gardeners, shepherds or milkmaids, by the pattern of flowers, staffs, hearts and other similar forms on each.

The designs worked on these hardwearing linen smock frocks were seldom drawn onto the fabric before working, since the needlewomen who worked them had developed a keen eye for following the thread of the fabric. The most frequently used ground fabric was heavy weight linen, often in a natural unbleached color, with the embroidery worked with a twisted linen thread. Both materials were sturdy enough for a garment which had to accommodate activity and ease of movement.

There were no curves at all in the design of the basic smock. It was, instead, entirely a composition of squares and rectangles. One popular style was reversible, with a square opening for the head, and another had a wide embroidered collar. Although all the working in the smocked area was traditionally a variation of stem or outline stitches, a number of other stitches were often used for other decorative embroidery on a garment. Among these stitches were feather stitch, chain stitch, stem stitch, satin stitch and faggot stitch.

As in smocking today, the success of these garments depended upon accuracy and even tension of the smocking, as well as a carefully executed choice of stitches.

Smocking today

Over the years, the range of uses for smocking has widened to include an attractive variety of clothes for children and adults. Children's dresses, women's nightgowns, blouses and dresses are all particularly suited to the texture and shape which smocking gives.

Fabric

Among the materials suitable for smocking are linen, cotton, nylon, voile and velvet. Any fabric that can be easily gathered is ideal for this purpose. The garment itself will determine the most suitable weight for the fabric to be used. Be sure to allow adequate width for the smocking – about three times the finished width is a general

Surface honeycomb stitch reduces fullness at waist and upper sleeve.

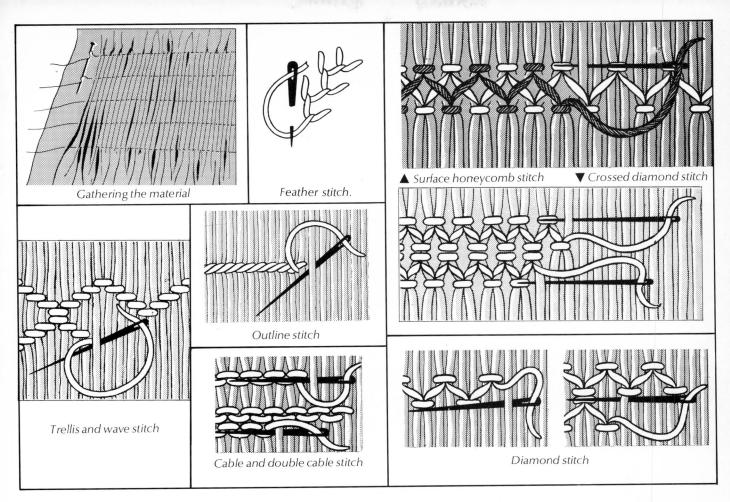

Gathering the material

Feather stitch.

▲ Surface honeycomb stitch   ▼ Crossed diamond stitch

Outline stitch

Trellis and wave stitch

Cable and double cable stitch

Diamond stitch

rule, although this depends upon the tension and elasticity of the stitches, the weight of the fabric used and the depth of the gathers.

Color possibilities

As the decorative value of smocking does not depend on the color – too much color actually detracts from the effect of the stitching – plan your design with a color scheme that is kept simple. There are three possibilities to consider when smocking: you may use threads in the same color as the background fabric, threads in a contrasting color, or threads of various colors. The effectiveness of matching threads is shown on the blouse illustrated. This pink blouse has a little color introduced with some floral embroidery on the bodice, whereas the smocking itself is merely a part of the textured backdrop.

Thread

It is most important that the thread used for the smocking is suitable for the fabric on which it is being worked. Traditionally, a linen thread was used on linen fabric and cotton thread on cotton or similar fabric. In fact, most kinds of embroidery thread are suitable but, for most work, coton à broder or pearl cotton may be

used in a medium sized crewel or embroidery needle. Always work the smocking before a garment is finished. Mark the area to be smocked with a basting stitch following the thread of the material.

Smocking transfers

Ideally, transfers should not be used for smocking, as they are rarely evenly printed and it is difficult to follow the thread of the fabric. If, however, a smocking transfer is used, the spacings between the dots should be determined by the weight of the fabric (a coarse material requires more widely spaced dots than a fine material). Iron the dots onto the wrong side of the material, aligning them with the weave of the material as accurately as possible. An alternative method of using a transfer is to mark the dots on the fabric with a sharp pencil and ruler. This is, in most cases, a more accurate way of aligning the dots on the fabric.

Gathering up the fabric

To gather up each row, use a strong thread with a secure knot at one end. Begin on the right side of the first row of dots and pick up a few threads at each one. At the end of the row, leave the thread unknotted. Then, after running across the

second row of dots, tie the two loose ends together. Continue in this way, tying each pair of threads together along the left hand side of the work. Remember, too, that when it is worked, smocking is flat on the surface but has a certain amount of bulk underneath.

The gathered lines should be pulled up so that the folds in the fabric become a series of close, parallel tubes. After drawing up all the rows of gathers, turn the fabric over and begin to smock.

Smocking stitches

Feather stitch, honeycomb and similar stitches are a modern innovation in smocking, the early smock frocks having been originally worked only in variations of stem or outline stitch. Most smocking stitches are worked from left to right with two notable exceptions, Vandyke stitch and feather stitches, which are worked from right to left. It is particularly important to remember that the only knot in the stitchery should be at the beginning of the row. Remember, therefore, to have enough thread in the needle at the beginning of a row to complete that row. After completing the work, remove the basting threads and check the elasticity of the stitchery on the garment.

Smocking on heavy fabrics

Smocking worked on a heavy cord fabric

Smocking can be just as attractive when worked on heavier fabrics as on traditional fine lawns and cottons.

Many of the same stitches can be used as on lighter materials, although the fabric should be prepared in a slightly different way.

Preparing the fabric

Because of the extra bulk when using heavy fabrics for smocking, allow only twice the required final width before gathering instead of the more usual three widths. If the fabric is dotted, striped or checked, the gathers can be worked using the pattern itself as a guide. If you are working on corduroy the gathers can be worked by picking up alternate ribs, unless it has widely spaced ribs in which case a stitch should be worked on each one. Whether you are buying commercially printed dot transfers or are marking the pattern yourself, be sure that they are fairly widely spaced – approximately $\frac{1}{2}$ inch apart or even more for some of the very heavy fabrics.

If you are unsure, it is advisable to make some trial gathers on a small piece of spare fabric to see how tightly gathered it should be. The fabric should look well pleated and there should be no need to stroke the gathers down as they should lie in flat and even folds.

If you are smocking a definite pattern, count the number of rows and gathers required to complete the pattern accurately, and work the gathering to allow for this. This is particularly important with wide patterns such as open diamond, feather and chevron stitches.

The threads

Use pearl cotton, coton à broder, stranded cotton (use all six strands) or pure silk twist when smocking on heavy fabrics. It is possible to use a fine string or carpet thread on some fabrics such as burlap and linen scrim

The design

Plan the smocking design carefully before you start work as it could be spoiled if a good balance has not been worked out

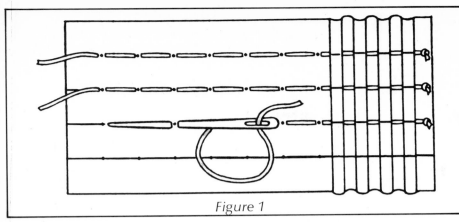

Figure 1

not pull too tightly since the finished garment must have elasticity.

Figure 2 indicates a section of the design repeated across the fabric. The dotted lines at the left hand side indicate the lines of gathers and the placing of stitches in relation to the rows. The vertical broken lines indicate the pleats.

Stem stitch Working from left to right, fasten the thread on the wrong side and bring the needle up through the first pleat. Pick up the top of the next pleat inserting the needle at a slight angle with the thread below the needle. Always work

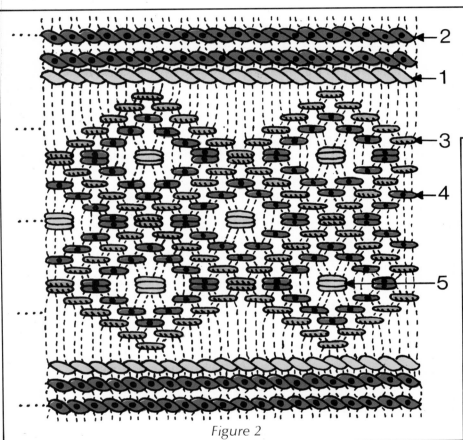

Figure 2

Key

1–0303 **Stem stitch**
2–0352

3–0309 **Wave stitch**
4–0352

5–0303 **3 straight stitches**

the thread over two pleats but pick up only one (figure 3).

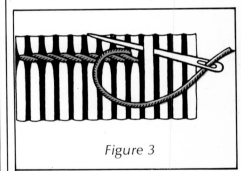

Figure 3

Wave stitch Working from left to right fasten the thread on the wrong side and bring the needle through to the left of the first pleat. Take a stitch through the second pleat on the same level with the thread below the needle, then take a stitch on the third pleat slightly higher than the previous pleat with the thread still below the needle. Continue in this way for five stitches finishing the top stitch with the thread above the needle. This completes the upward slope. Work in the same way on the downward slope except with the thread above the needle (figure 4).

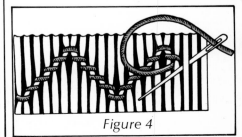

Figure 4

between the various patterns. The basic smocking stitch is stem or outline stitch and this should be used at the beginning of the work along the edges of the border to give it a firm foundation. The modern introductions of feather stitch and herringbone stitch are better used sparingly as they tend to mask the pleated background which is such an important characteristic of smocking.

The pattern shown in the photograph is a simple design using stem stitch and wave stitch and it can easily be adjusted for garments made from heavy fabrics.

Stem stitch and wave stitch pattern

Mark the areas to be embroidered on the wrong side of the pieces to be smocked within the rectangles already marked. Use a soft pencil or tailor's chalk for this and draw fine parallel lines $\frac{1}{2}$ inch apart. Using the horizontal lines as a guide, work five rows of gathering stitches, making sure that the stitches correspond exactly on each line (figure 1). Pick up a small thread only at regular intervals and leave a loose thread at the end of each row.

Pull up the lines of gathering, easing gently to form pleats. Do not pull up too tightly as the pleats must be flexible enough to work the stitches over. Tie the loose ends together in pairs close to the last pleat.

When working the smocking stitches, do

Honeycomb smocked bedspread

Fabric required

Cotton gingham with 1 inch checks. Calculate the amount of fabric you need by measuring the width and length of the bed, allowing $\frac{1}{2}$ inch for turnings and 4 inches for the pillows. Allow the same amount of plain cotton fabric for the backing.

For the ruffle, measure the height of the bed from the floor and to allow for gathering, multiply the length of the bed by 3 and the width by $1\frac{1}{2}$.

You will also need

6–7 skeins 6-strand embroidery floss.
Crewel embroidery needle.
Regular sewing thread.

Finishing this piece

1 Mount each piece of gingham with a plain piece of fabric. Baste all around the edge.

2 Join the pieces for the ruffle, matching the checks of the gingham carefully. Press the turnings open.

Working the smocking

The smocking is different from regular smocking in that the fabric is not gathered first. The stitches are worked on the corners of the gingham squares and form a honeycomb pattern.

1 Working from right to left on the right side of the fabric, leave a complete gingham square along the top and right hand edge of the flounce. Using three strands of embroidery floss, knot the end of the thread and make a small stitch at the bottom right hand corner of the first square.

2 Pass the thread along the front of the fabric and make another small stitch at the bottom right hand corner of the next square. Pull the thread tight, thus drawing the first and second stitches together. Make another half backstitch and pass the needle onto the wrong side of the

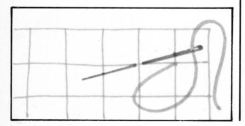

fabric. This completes the first honeycomb stitch.

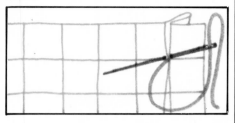

3 Still with the needle on the wrong side, bring it out at the corner of the next square.

4 Keep the fabric flat between the previous stitch and this point and make a small backstitch to secure the thread. Then pass the needle along the front of the fabric and make a small stitch at the corner of the next square.

Pull the thread tight to draw the third and fourth squares together.

5 Continue in this way until six honeycomb stitches have been made.

6 Move to the row below and work five honeycomb stitches in the alternate spaces

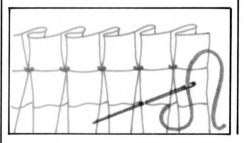

to those on the row above so that you are joining the second square to the third, the fourth to the fifth and so on.

7 Work four honeycomb stitches centrally in the third row, thus omitting the first and sixth stitches of the first row.

8 Work three honeycomb stitches in the fourth row, two stitches in the fifth row and one stitch in the sixth row to complete the V shape.

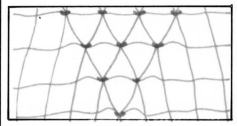

9 Work the next blocks of stitches in the same way all along the length of the flounce. You will now see how the space between the blocks forms an inverted "V" shape.

Attaching the ruffle

1 When all the smocking has been worked, it will form into pleats automatically along the top edge of the ruffle. Pin these down and secure with basting.

2 Make narrow hems along the side edges of the ruffle.

3 Pin the top edge of the ruffle around the edge of the main part of the bedspread and machine stitch taking $\frac{1}{2}$ inch turnings. Make the turnings neat and press them onto the main section.

4 Make a hem along the head edge of the main section.

5 Try the bedspread onto the bed and mark the hem line so that it just clears the floor.

6 Stitch the hem and press the finished bedspread.

Pleated smocked pillow

Sizes

Square pillow: 15 inches square.

Round pillow: 16 inches diameter, 4 inches thick.

Fabric required

For square pillow:
24 in lightweight velvet 48 in wide.

For round pillow:
36 in lightweight velvet 48 in wide.

You will also need

Heavy-duty thread to match velvet.
Graph paper for making pattern.
Basting thread in different colors.
2 button molds, 1 inch in diameter.
Pillow pads in the same size as the finished covers.
Transfer pencil (optional).

The smocking

This sort of smocking is different from conventional smocking. The stitches are all worked on the wrong side of the fabric and do not show on the right side. The fullness is not reduced by gathering, but by drawing points of fabric together to create a decorative pleated finish on the right side.
Although velvet has been used for the pillows in the photograph, this method of smocking is also very attractive on satin or gingham.

The pattern

Each line of smocking is worked over three vertical rows of dots, spaced 1 inch apart. It is possible to buy transfers of the dots which can be ironed on the fabric, but it is quite simple and much less expensive – particularly if you are making several pillows – to draw your own pattern and transfer the dots to the fabric with tailor's tacks. Alternately, you could mark the dots on the pattern with a transfer pencil and then iron it onto the fabric.

Making the pattern

Using graph paper, draw the pattern for the pillow shape you are making to scale. One square = 1 inch. If you are making the square pillow, mark the dots for each line of smocking in different colors as shown so you can easily see where the rows overlap.
Repeat rows two and three until you have ten rows in all.

Cutting out

Cut the fabric in half to make two pieces each 24 inches square. Place the pieces together and pin the pattern centrally to them. Mark the dots with tailor's tacks, using different colored thread for the rows as indicated on the pattern. Unpin the pattern, cut through the tacks and open out the fabric.
Smock each piece separately before making up the pillow.

Working the smocking

To make working easier, the dots are numbered to show the order of the stitches. It may seem very confusing as you start, but after the first few smocked pleats are formed, you will soon find a system.

1 With the wrong side of the fabric facing up, start at dot 1 in the top left hand corner. Using a long length of heavy-duty thread, knot the end and make a small stitch at

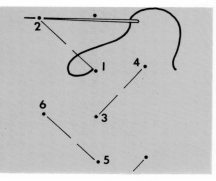

dot 2 in the line of dots to the left.

2 Go back to dot 1, make another small stitch over the one already there and then pull dots 1 and 2 together. Knot them tightly by making a loop of the thread above the stitches and passing the needle under the stitches and through the loop. Be careful not to catch the fabric as you do this or the stitch will show on the right side.

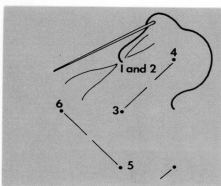

3 Pass the thread along the fabric to dot 3 and make a small stitch. Keep the fabric completely flat between dots 1 and 3, make a loop of the thread above dot 3 and slip the needle under the thread between the dots and above the loop to make another knot. Do not draw up the thread between the dots.

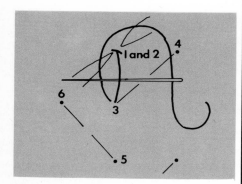

4 Pass the thread along the fabric to dot 4, make a small stitch, go back to dot 3 and make another small stitch. Pull dots 3 and 4 together and knot them as you did for dots 1 and 2.

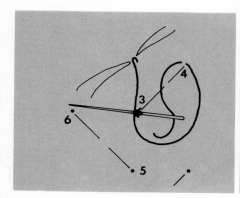

5 Move down to dot 5 and knot the thread keeping the fabric flat, as at dot 3. Pick up a small stitch at dot 6 and join it to dot 5 in the same way as before.

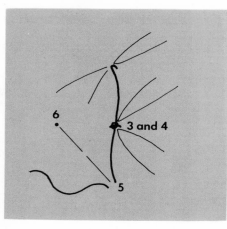

6 Continue down the whole line in this way, picking up a dot on the left, moving down to the next dot in the middle row and then picking up a dot on the right.

7 Work all the lines of smocking in the same way, and then smock the other side of the pillow cover.

Finishing

1 When the smocking is completed, you will find that pleats have formed around all the edges. Pin them down evenly and baste in position, checking that each side of the cover measures 15 inches. Pin the pleats on the other side of the cover in a similar way, having these pleats face the opposite direction so that when the sides of the cover are put together the pleats will match.

2 Place the sides of the cover together, then baste and machine stitch around three sides, making a ½ inch hem.

3 Insert the pillow form, fold under the seam allowance of the opening and slip stitch the folds together.

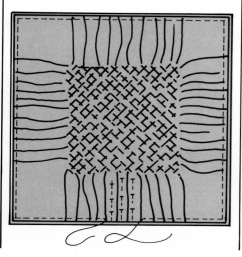

The round pillow
Cutting out

Cut the fabric in half to make two pieces, 36 inches × 24 inches. Join the pieces along the longer edges, making ½ inch seams and making sure that the pile runs the same way on both pieces. Trim the length of the fabric to 70 inches × 21 inches and use the leftover piece to cover the button molds.

Fold the fabric right side out along the seam line. Place on the pattern with the line indicated to the fold. Mark all the dots with tailor's tacks. Unpin the pattern, cut through the tacks and open out the fabric.

Working the smocking

1 Join the short ends of the fabric, making ½ inch seams. The smocking is then worked in a continuous round.

2 Work the smocking in a similar way as for the square pillow. The finished effect will be less tightly pleated than the square pillow because the lines are spaced farther apart.

Finishing

1 Using strong thread, attach the end securely ¼ inch from the edge of the fabric.

2 Form the nearest pleat with your fingers and make a small stitch through the fold. Draw the thread up tightly.

3 Form the next pleat, take a stitch through

the fold and pull it up to meet the first pleat. Work around the pillow in this way.

4 Insert the pillow form. Repeat on the other side.

5 Sew the covered buttons to the center of each side of the pillow.

Graph for square pillow
1 square = 1 inch

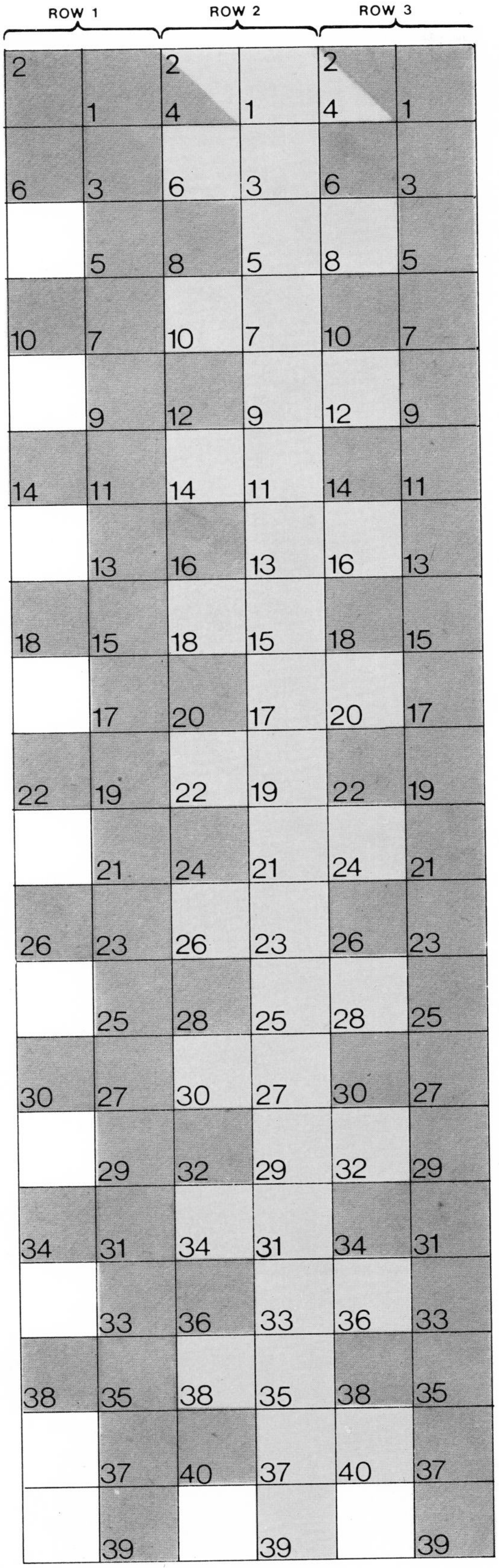
ROW 1
ROW 2
ROW 3

Graph for round pillow
1 square = 1 inch

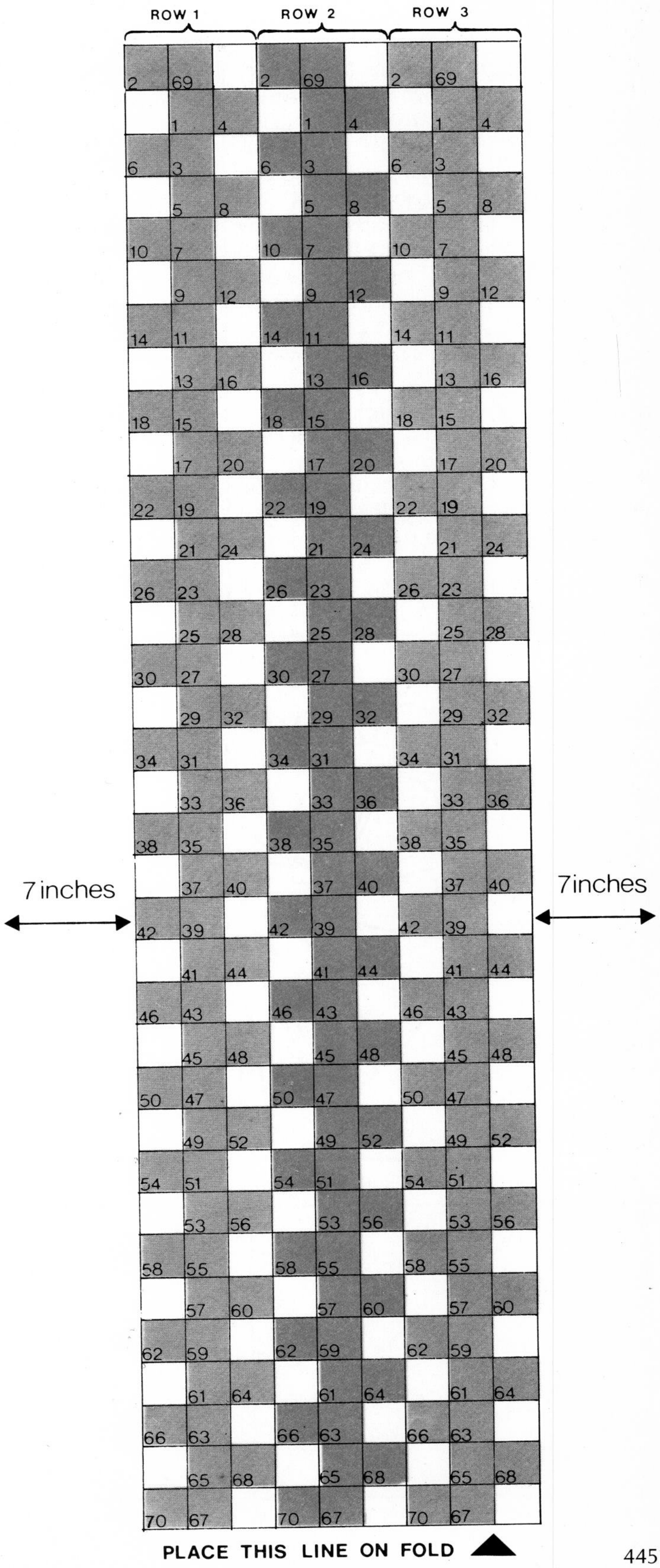
ROW 1
ROW 2
ROW 3
7 inches
7 inches
PLACE THIS LINE ON FOLD

CANDLEWICKING

Candlewick originated in the United States in early Colonial days when, with a severe shortage of sewing materials of all kinds, women settlers used the thick cotton wick intended for candlemaking as an embroidery thread, working it into knotted and tufted designs on bedspreads. For many years the use of candlewick was restricted to bedspreads, but it looks effective in many other forms and can be used for pillows, rugs and bath mats as well as for warm garments such as dressing gowns.

Materials for candlewick

There are two kinds of candlewicking, tufted and smooth, but for both types it is essential that the material on which the embroidery is worked should shrink on the first washing to secure the candlewick in the fabric.

Usually, unbleached muslin is used for candlewick, but linen can also be used.

It is important to choose a weave which will take two thicknesses of the candlewick cotton.

The tracing design given in this chapter is adaptable for almost any use and builds up extremely well, placing the motifs as linking squares. It can be used for both tufted and smooth types of candlewicking and parts of the design might be adapted for a matching border motif.

Yarn

Cotton is used for candlewick and is sold in skeins, available in a variety of colors. Skeins can be cut into 48 inch lengths or, if preferred, wound into a ball and used as desired.

Needles

A special candlewick needle is used. This is a fairly large one with a flattened, curved point and a big eye.

Scissors

It is essential to have scissors which are extremely sharp for cutting the loops. A blunt pair will drag and pull the tufts out of the fabric.

Designs

Designs for candlewick are most effective when based on geometric shapes, but flowing designs can also be used if they are large sized. Small, intricate patterns are difficult to work and the shapes become distorted with the tufting. The candlewick can follow the outlines of the original design, can fill in some areas, or can cover the background completely as an all over design, giving a solid area of pile texture.

Tufted candlewick

In some early examples of candlewick French knots and backstitch were used, but in modern embroidery the stitch mainly used is running stitch worked $\frac{1}{4}$ to $\frac{1}{2}$ inch apart along the line of the design, leaving a small loop between each stitch. To keep the loops at even length place a pencil under the yarn as each loop is made. The candlewick yarn is used double. Cut a length twice as long as is required and thread it through the needle until the ends are even. It is not necessary to finish off the ends when starting or finishing – begin on the right side of the fabric, leaving an end equal to the size of the completed tuft and end in the same way.

When the design is completely worked cut the loops evenly with a very sharp pair of scissors.

Smooth candlewick

This type of candlewick is worked simply in running stitch. One doubled length of yarn is used in the needle as for tufted candlewick and the stitches are worked about $\frac{1}{4}$ inch long and $\frac{1}{4}$ inch apart. This results in a bead-like stitch giving a beautifully raised, sculptured effect. This type of candlewick is at its best worked in geometric designs built up into solid shapes and covering the entire area of the fabric.

Finishing candlewick

The completed work should be washed so that the fabric shrinks to fix the tufts more securely and to fluff them up. If a washing machine is used, wash for at least

A tracing design for working in either tufted or smooth candlewicking

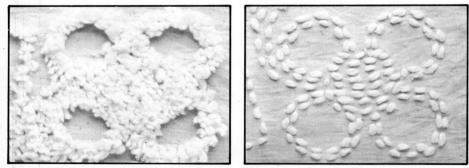

A detail of the design above worked in tufted stitch and showing the reverse side.

Smooth candlewicking in a modern bedspread.

20 minutes in warm soapy water. If washing by hand let the work soak for three to four hours. Do not wring or squeeze, just shake out.

Dry the work outdoors in a strong breeze and shake it frequently while drying to avoid its creasing and to make the tufts fluffier, then finally brush the tufts lightly with a soft brush before they are quite dry to add further fluff.

It is best to avoid ironing candlewick since this will flatten the tufts again.

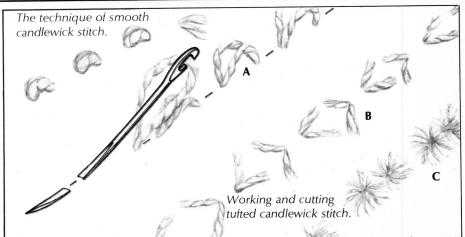

The technique of smooth candlewick stitch.

A

B

C

Working and cutting tufted candlewick stitch.

MACHINE EMBROIDERY
BASIC EQUIPMENT

Although the sewing machine is a standard piece of equipment in so many homes, it is seldom used for embroidery and many people are not even aware of its decorative potential. In these chapters we introduce you to the simpler aspects of machine embroidery and to a whole new range of decorative effects and stitches, many of which can be created with even the simplest straight stitch machine.

Machine embroidery is not only a quick method of decorating clothes and home furnishings. It can be as delicate as traditional hand embroidery or as bold and chunky as a rug or a heavy woven wall hanging. The possibilities are endless. Another important decorative function of the machine is to secure applied fabrics, braids, wool, weaving yarn or even string to the background. In this case the stitching may be nearly invisible or it can be used to supplement the texture of the applied material.

Basic equipment

The only equipment needed for machine embroidery is a sewing machine, fabric, thread, a hoop and tracing paper.

Your machine

It is a common misapprehension that a special sewing machine is needed for machine embroidery. This is not so. There is a great deal you can do on a straight stitch machine and if your machine does even a simple zig-zag you can do a great deal more. The effects that can be achieved with an automatic machine are of course unlimited.

Most modern machines have a drop feed, which is a control to lower the feed for darning and embroidery while others require a plate which will fit over the feed. To adapt a machine, when it is not possible to obtain a plate, the throat plate may be removed and small washers inserted under it before returning the screws. This raises the throat plate to the level of the teeth at their highest point.

Whichever machine you use it is essential that it should be in perfect working order as it receives far more wear during embroidery work than in other sewing, due to the speed at which it is worked. The machine must be cleaned and oiled

regularly. Oil before use rather than after as fine oil tends to evaporate. Run the threaded machine over a spare piece of fabric before starting your work to remove excess oil. Check foot controls and motors occasionally for overheating and should this occur the machine should be serviced.

Fabrics

Many fabrics are suitable for machine embroidery. It is important however that the fabric being worked is firmly woven, so avoid stretch and knitted fabrics such as jersey or crepe which pull out of shape when placed in a hoop. Embroidery will not give with these fabrics. In appliqué work however (described more fully in a later chapter) where the individual shapes are not held in a frame this elasticity is an advantage.

As stitching is so important, and practice is needed to get the fabric into the rings tightly without tearing, the beginner should choose to work on medium weight fabrics such as sailcloth or dress-weight linens. With more experience exciting and varied effects can be achieved using net and fine fabrics such as cotton organdy and even plastic and leather.

Thread

Machine embroidery thread is supplied in two thicknesses, 50 and 30. The 50 is the finer of the two while 30 is comparable in

weight to ordinary machine dressmaking thread. 50 should always be used in the bobbin unless a thicker thread is needed for special effect. 40 and 50 sewing cotton are needed for variety in the weight of stitching and for whip-stitch, while a collection of wool and hand embroidery thread is always useful.

Invisible thread is invaluable to the more experienced embroiderer. It is useful for sewing on fabric pieces when an exact color match cannot be made, and also gives a rich glint to the work when used for free embroidery. It is best used together with machine embroidery thread in the bobbin partly to provide color interest and partly because invisible thread alone will not stand a warm iron. Work using this material should always be pressed from the back.

Glitter threads are also available and handicraft shops will provide a variety of textured threads for appliqué work.

Frames

The hoop comprised of two interlocking rings with an adjustable screw is an essential piece of equipment. An 8 inch to 9 inch hoop is ideal for beginners. The more experienced embroiderer may prefer a 12 inch. A very small hoop is sometimes useful too, for eyelets and working in corners. The most satisfactory hoops are made of wood, are narrow enough in depth to pass under the raised machine needle and have a screw adjustment for extra tightening. Plastic hoops are not as good since they do not grip the fabric as well, particularly if it is a slippery fabric, although covering the inner ring with tape or bias binding may help. Metal hoops have the disadvantage of being too deep to slide easily under the needle on most machines and need complete screw adjustment every time the hoop is moved on the fabric.

Tracing paper

For marking out designs use dressmaker's carbon paper. If the structure of the design is in a straight stitch the main lines may be transferred to the cloth by stitching over the paper with the presser foot down, then tearing the paper away. If the design is heavily drawn on the paper with felt tip

pen, it is possible to trace it directly onto the fabric by taping the paper to a window with the fabric over it. Use a tailor's chalk pencil for a dark fabric and a sharp, hard pencil for a light fabric, making a dotted rather than a solid line.

This striking fish design is an example of machine embroidery used to great effect on the place mats shown above.

STITCHES
Automatic stitches

Automatic stitches can be used for a wide variety of very interesting designs. They can be used to good effect with applied pieces of fabric, braid or ribbon, for border patterns and decorative motifs for casual wear, for children's clothes and to give the most ordinary household linens a luxury look. Automatic stitches must be used selectively to achieve best results, for if too many stitches are combined in one design, the results can be confused and unattractive.

Many machines only make stitches based on the side to side throw of the needle, but some combine this with a backward and forward motion of the feed thus affording a much wider range of stitches. Automatic stitching is normally worked using the press foot in the usual way without placing the fabric in a hoop. Worked freely in the hoop they completely lose their effect unless you have acquired the skill of moving the hoop smoothly with your left hand while operating the stitch lever with your right hand. You can learn this with practice. Free machine embroidery will be described more fully in the following chapter.

The stitching can be done with 30 or 50 machine embroidery thread which gives a smoother and more lustrous effect than sewing cotton or with a thicker thread to give a bolder effect. To prevent the thread from fraying, it is essential that the needle is large enough for the thread to pass easily down the groove and through the eye of the machine. If a very thick thread is used it must be put in the bobbin, a technique which will be more fully described in a later chapter. The stitch to be used should always be tested on spare fabric before you begin your design. The space between the stitches should be adjusted to achieve the desired stitch density according to the thickness of thread.

Some degree of tension is essential on upper and lower threads but swing needle work tends to pull up the fabric more than straight stitching. To counteract this, the upper tension should be slackened as much as possible without affecting the even appearance of the stitching. The lower tension may also be loosened but in

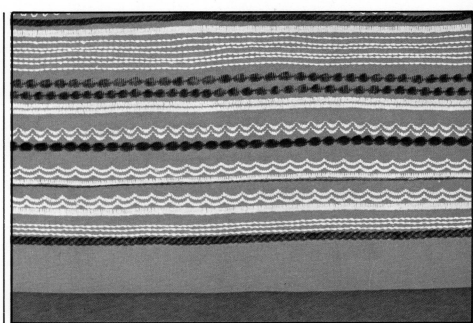

the absence of a numbered dial remember to note the pull of the thread and the position of the screw groove in relation to its socket. In this way the tension may be easily reset for normal sewing. It is often necessary to back the fabric to prevent it from pulling up with the needle swings, or stretching when stitching on the bias. The finer the fabric the more important it is to back it. The ideal backing is vanishing muslin which tears away easily after stitching, although medium weight paper is a good substitute. Pellon should only be used if a permanent stiffness is required. The fabrics should be firmly basted to whatever backing is used.

Automatic patterns need not be limited to straight lines of stitching along the straight grain of the fabric. It is not difficult to follow gently curving lines using the right hand to open and close the stitch width lever to give further variety. It is also possible to put the fabric into an embroidery hoop, replacing the presser foot when the hoop is under the needle. This method is suitable for a series of small shapes or for a design with short lines radiating out from the center. Check that your hoop is small enough in diameter to

pass completely around the needle while resting on the throat plate of your machine. Framing will be described in detail in the following chapter.

The patterns shown may be made even more exciting if shaded threads are used. An interesting effect is sometimes achieved by using different colored threads above and below and tightening the upper tension or loosening the lower tension to give the bobbin stitch colored edges.

The design illustrated above can be worked on most fabrics. It is embroidered in two colors, uses twin needles for the double patterns such as the scallops and a stretch stitch for the heavy lines. The satin stitch is used to stabilize the whole design. Automatic stitches will differ from machine to machine, although similar effects can be achieved on most machines.

This design is worked before the smock is made up. Be sure to cut out the pattern pieces allowing approximately 2 inches all around to make handling easier during embroidery. Allow for extra yardage when buying your fabric. Mark each pattern piece and the design areas with tailor's chalk or basting and work each piece starting at its lowest edge.

Design using free machine embroidery

It is in free machine embroidery that skill and imagination can come fully into play. The sewing machine is a very sensitive drawing instrument and while mastery of this craft takes practice, it can be very rewarding. Even a beginner can soon produce spontaneous designs of great freshness and originality.

Consult your instruction manual to find out how to convert your machine. If it is an old model, the instructions may come under the heading of darning. The feed will either be covered with a special plate or will be retractable (see earlier).

Framing the embroidery

Frame your work carefully. To do this lay the outer hoop on a flat, level surface, lay your fabric right side up across it and fit the inner hoop into the outer one. The screw should now be adjusted so that relatively heavy pressure is required to do this. Tighten the fabric by pulling it up and in to prevent the rings from dislodging and take care not to distort the threads. If there is any tendency for the fabric to slip back when it is pulled, the screw on the frame should be tightened and the pulling up process repeated until the fabric is stretched to its limit. This cannot be overstressed since the success of all kinds of free stitching depends on careful framing. If the work is loose, it will lift up when the needle passes through it, and the machine will miss stitches which may cause the thread to break. The tautness of the work is the only way in which the tension on the machine thread is counteracted. Badly-stretched work will not lie flat when it is removed from the frame and no amount of steam pressing will help to flatten it. When you are correctly set remove the presser foot and with the needle at its highest point slide the hoop under it. Draw the lower thread up through the fabric and lower the presser foot bar to re-set the tension on the upper thread. The stitch length lever should be set at 0. The size of the stitch is decided by the combination of the speed of the motor with the speed at which you move

the frame. Turn the stitch width lever to 0. Hold the hoop and guide the fabric under the needle. With practice you will find the most comfortable position for your hands. Most of the work is done by the right hand which should swing from the shoulder to move the frame. Control will be greater if your thumb and little finger are outside the frame and the rest of your hand inside, although you must be careful not to get your finger too close to the needle. Place your left hand flat on the work now to hold the work down while you steady it. Bracing your little finger against the edge gives greater control. If the hoop measures 8 inches or less it is probably safer to position both hands on the hoop. Rest your left elbow on the table. The fabric should not lift up while you are stitching, although the larger the frame, the more likely it is to do so.

Hold both threads under your left forefinger while you start, to prevent them from getting pulled down and tangled. Run the machine fairly fast and move the frame smoothly. As a safety precaution do not put your foot on the foot control unit until you are ready to stitch and train yourself to remove it every time you stop. Aim to make 20–30 stitches to 1 inch using a large sharp needle. A fine needle is too flexible and may be broken on the edge of the plate. The needle should take up to a 40 sewing thread; with thicker thread, such as buttonhole twist, you will need the largest needle.

The tension

Although you may not have to alter your tension with some threads, if you use machine embroidery thread for instance, it is wise to loosen the tension by a few numbers. If the thread snaps, loosen it until this no longer happens. If this results in a bad stitch, loosen the lower tension as well. However, you may like the effect you get with a tighter top tension, as the bobbin color will show through to the top. If you do loosen the lower tension, be sure to note the normal pull and adjust the screw only by a quarter turn at a time.

When moving from one part of a hoop to another, raise the needle to its highest point, lift the presser foot bar to release the tension from the needle, move the hoop to the new position, dip the needle down, lower the presser foot bar and continue. If, at the end of a line of stitching, you move your frame slowly to make small stitches which won't unravel, the ends can be cut off close to the work. If the back is to be visible, trim it after you do the front but not quite as closely.

In addition to very careful drawing, you can make interesting filling textures by running the machine at top speed and then moving the frame backward and forward or in a small continuous circular movement. If the machine is set for zigzag, a heavy line can be made by moving the frame slowly. When the frame is moved from side to side with the needle swinging, large stitches can be made up to $\frac{1}{2}$ inch in length. These long stitches catch the light, giving quite a different effect to the same movement done with a straight stitch. Always begin and end satin stitch with a few straight stitches or take the ends through and tie them.

The embroidered cloth

The circular linen tablecloth illustrated is 48 inches in diameter and is divided into 8 sections. The motifs are worked using appliquéd fabric and eyelets (described in a later chapter) and a free running stitch. The design for each section was drawn on paper and basted by hand to the wrong side of the tablecloth. The fabric to be appliquéd was basted to the right side and stitched in position from the wrong side using straight stitch and the presser foot. The excess appliqué fabric was then cut away and satin stitch was used around the edges of the designs. The paper was then torn away and the eyelets and free machining were worked from the right side in the hoop. The edges were trimmed with zigzag stitch, then turned to the wrong side and slip stitched in place. Decorative stitching can later be used on the right side to conceal the hem.

Whip stitch

When embroidering by machine, try to forget all the rules for normal sewing. For it is by using different colors and thicknesses of thread through the needle and through the bobbin and experimenting with different tensions that varied and original effects will be discovered.

One of the most effective variations of the free running stitch is the whip stitch. This stitch lends itself well to small curving designs and looks particularly striking when shaded thread is used in the bobbin. Use 50 machine embroidery thread in the bobbin for best results and a 40 cotton on top. Tighten the upper tension 2 or 3 numbers above normal, run the machine fast and move the frame slowly. If the top thread breaks it may be necessary to loosen both tensions.

The top thread should be flat on the fabric pulling the bobbin thread up. The stitches should be close enough together to enclose the top thread, giving a raised, corded appearance. If the frame is moved quickly so that the stitches are separated the top thread is visible. Different colored upper and lower threads produce a speckled line, but if you move the frame slowly again a solid line will result. A most attractive graded line can be obtained by smoothly increasing and decreasing the speed at which you move the frame. If the upper tension is not tightened enough the top thread will appear at uneven intervals producing a pleasing textural line. Side to side and circular textures are very effective using whip stitch settings.

Whip stitch ends should be taken to the back of the work and fastened, so lines will be continuous wherever possible. If the upper tension is set to its tightest and the lower tension very loose or the bobbin spring completely removed, a feather stitch is obtained. This is because the tight upper tension causes a loop of the bobbin thread to be pulled through to the right side with each stitch. This stitch should be worked in a continuous clockwise or counter clockwise movement. If it is worked in a straight line the result is merely a series of untidy loops.

Remember that whenever the upper tension is slightly tighter than the lower tension, the top color will be affected by the color in the bobbin and, in this way, can be

deliberately deepened or lightened. Experiment by using a range of different colors in the bobbin and by varying the length of the stitches. Whenever you change the direction of the hoop movement there will be a concentration of the bobbin color at the point of change and if you run the machine at full speed and move the hoop in a series of pauses and jerks a dotted texture is obtained. This effect can be used to give tinted edges to filled in designs.

With a tighter upper tension and the needle swinging, a satin stitch with bobbin colored edges is obtained. If the hoop is moved from side to side (full speed essential) in a series of pauses and jerks, crisp satin stitch bars will occur. Do not move the frame until each bar is of the required density.

These bars can be used freely or more formally by stopping the machine after each one to position the hoop accurately for the next. If the needle stops on the wrong side to lead on to the next bar, turn the balance wheel by hand.

These bars could be used to make an attractive decoration for the center of a self covered button or the center of an embroidered flower. Being raised they catch the light and give a rich beaded look although they are best worked with a stitch width of 2 or more.

To avoid unravelling never cut the threads between the bars. You may if you wish, conceal the connecting threads with straight free stitching around the bars.

The panel illustrated is worked entirely in whip stitch using shaded thread on the bobbin and moving the hoop slowly so that the needle thread is concealed.

Cable stitch

Cable stitch is a useful means of introducing heavy lines and textures into a design. It is often used with the presser foot for decorative top stitching but can also be used freely in the hoop. The design is worked from the wrong side. Cable stitch is hard wearing and good for articles which will be in constant use.

With cable stitch the top thread is passed around the thick thread with each stitch protecting it from the rubbing it receives if the thread is applied by stitching along its length.

The thick thread must be wound on the bobbin either by hand or on the bobbin winder. You should create slight tension with your fingers to insure that the thread winds evenly. The thread should be smooth enough not to clog the tension spring. The tension should always be loose so that the pull of the thread feels the same as for normal sewing and the stitch appears even. If you are embroidering an article which will receive a lot of wear use 30 machine embroidery thread or ordinary sewing thread on top. Should you have difficulty getting the thick thread through the fabric when you dip the needle, pierce a hole with a blunt-ended needle. Some machines have a separate bobbin case and the tension screw and spring may be completely removed. Without the tension spring, threads the thickness of soft hand embroidery cotton can also be used. Textured yarns can be used provided they are fine enough to pass easily through the hole in the side of the bobbin case. If you have removed the spring be sure you insert the end into the slot in the bobbin case before putting the screw back.

It is a good idea to wind several bobbins at once if you are working a lot of cable stitches since the thick thread runs out quickly. If the bobbin color is being changed frequently you should change the top thread as well so that the shape of each color area can be seen on the wrong side (the side from which you are working). In this way you can produce very rich and varied textures. If the lower tension is released completely and you are using a fairly fine thread it will tend to be released very quickly from the bobbin, this making a pleasing, textural looped line.

Unless you are completely familiar with the way your machine works, be sure to always work a test sample first. Set the upper tension just tight enough to grip the heavy thread firmly. If it is very tight it can pull a fine to medium thickness thread through a loosely woven fabric to the wrong side, giving a moss-like texture which can be used on the right side by reversing your fabric.

With some machines it is possible to get an effect similar to heavy whip stitch by greatly increasing the lower tension and moving the hoop slowly so that the bobbin thread is encased by the top thread. Even if you cannot manage entirely to conceal the thick thread, this is a very interesting way of working the more solid areas of a design and it looks particularly effective if shaded thread is used on top.

Cable stitching and its variations are especially useful for dress embroidery, since these designs may be marked on the wrong side. When the cable stitching is completed it should give enough guidance for free stitching or other work on the right side, without any further mark needed.

The sample shows a freely drawn motif worked in cable stitch and free running stitch. To achieve the bobbled effect on the cable stitch, the tension screw and spring on the bobbin are completely removed. Silky hand embroidery thread is used on the bobbin and sewing thread through the needle. For the free running stitch, machine embroidery thread is used on the bobbin and through the needle. This stitch is worked after the cable stitch from the right side.

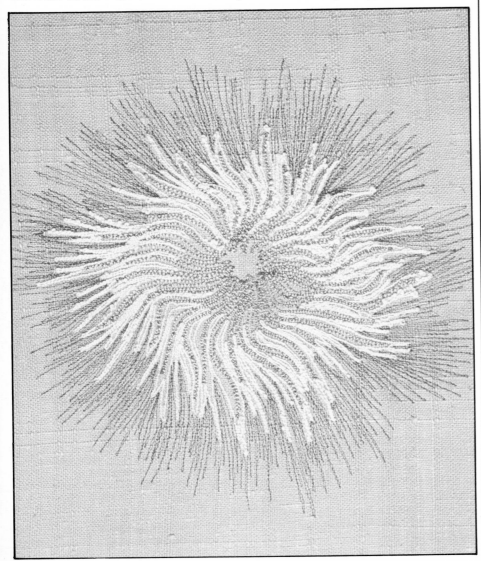

DECORATIVE EFFECTS
Shapes and appliqué

Decorative effects using the presser foot and satin stitch

With a little imagination decorative effects can be worked with the presser foot, without using a hoop. Lines and sharp angles are easily incorporated. Sharp curves are more difficult to make but can be done more easily with the use of the quilting foot with its shorter length, rather than the presser foot, and the shorter than normal stitch length. Geometric designs should be marked out with a series of pencil dots which show on a dark or a light fabric. With more experience you will also be able to stitch straight between dots spaced further apart. Because the threads at each end of a line should be taken through to the back and tied, lines should be continuous wherever possible. Straight stitch effects can be worked on a reasonably firm fabric without a backing.

Heavier effects can be achieved by working a zigzag or satin stitch over an applied thread. There may also be a special hole through the embroidery foot to guide a fine thread under the needle. An Elna foot is designed to apply any number of threads the thickness of pearl cotton side by side which can be held down with the serpentine (multiple zigzag) or other automatic stitch. This foot can be used on some other machines. On a straight stitch machine it is possible with practice to guide a thick thread under the needle so that it is stitched accurately down the center. These suggestions can be used in conjunction with applied braids and ribbons for border patterns too. If using these the ends of ribbons and braids should have their edges turned in unless they go to the edge of the fabric or are enclosed in a seam. Heavy threads must be passed to the back. When a shape rather than a line is to be worked it is wise to take the thread through the back of the fabric before starting to stitch. This will prevent the thread from obscuring your work as you sew and also will help to prevent tangling. Always work the heaviest stitching in a

design first, thus forming the main structure to which finer straight stitching or free machine embroidery may be added. On a fully automatic machine the stretch stitch makes a heavy line which can be used decoratively on the right side of the fabric. The twin needle can be used to make freely shaped pin-tucks either on the background fabric or on fabric to be applied. If a transparent fabric is used a colored wool or embroidery thread can be laid under the needle to give a shadowed effect. Buttonhole twist can be used through the needle (largest size for your machine) to give a thick line on the right side, although thicker threads must be used in the bobbin and the lower tension should be released until it feels the same as for normal sewing. The work must be wrong side uppermost. This is called cable stitch and was described in an earlier chapter.

Always work a sample on the fabric to be used to check tension and stitch length. Only use closely woven fabric or the satin stitch will have irregular edges. Work with tensions as light as possible and take care there is no weight on the fabric passing under the foot which might distort the fabric. If any pulling up of fabric occurs either back the fabric with a thin fabric or stretch the work in a hoop. If a lengthening of the stitch is required as well as variation of width this is best achieved by pulling the work gently through the machine. It is not possible to alter both stitch width and length at the same time. Ends should be taken through to the back and tied.

The panel is worked in satin stitch using the presser foot. 50 machine embroidery thread in shaded colors is used throughout. The area of each square in the design is marked on the background with light pencil dots and the shapes are filled in from the outside toward the center.

Place mats

These place mats were illustrated in the first chapter in this section. They are made of washable linen and heavy cotton fabric. The fish design is worked before the mats are cut out.

The heavy line, designed to be continuous wherever possible, is marked on paper, transferred to the fabric and worked by applying a medium weight embroidery thread with a zigzag stitch and the presser foot. 50 machine embroidery thread is used on the bobbin and through the needle. The design is then placed in a hoop and free machining is worked in different colors to build up areas of texture. The fringed edges of the mats are finished with a machine hemming stitch.

Fine fabrics and nets

One of the great attractions of machine embroidery is that intricate and delicate designs may be completed in a comparatively short time. To achieve anything as complex by hand would take many hours of laborious work.

With a little experience it is possible to place very fine fabrics in a hoop and embroider them although great care must be taken when stretching them in the hoop, since the tension necessary for good results could easily cause the fabric to split. To avoid this adjust the screw on the frame until it is just tight enough to grip the fabric, or tighten the screw and gently pull up the fabric, making sure that you grip it along the width of both palms, spreading the strain as evenly as possible. This needs a lot of patience for if you pull up the fabric between thumb and forefingers it will almost certainly split.

Cotton organdy is a particularly attractive fabric to embroider although it creases easily. It is best used in a design where it will be covered with embroidery. Subtle effects may be obtained by applying pieces of organdy to an organdy background or by placing colored fabric on the wrong side of the background for a shadow effect. Embroidered place mats are particularly lovely when worked on cotton organdy.

Fine fabrics such as organza, cotton organdy or chiffon can be applied to net for evening dresses, or wedding dresses and veils. The fabric to be applied can be mounted on the net and then framed together and tightened securely.

Using free running stitch, outline the edges of all the shapes two or three times. Pull the work clear of the machine, cut away the excess applied fabric and finish the raw edges with further lines of stitching or some fine texture. The shapes should be worked far enough apart to be able to insert the points of the scissors between them.

If the shapes to be applied are very small they may be cut out separately, laid in position and held with the fingers while they are stitched. With more experience you will not be afraid of putting your fingers close to the needle and it is a great advantage to be able to do so. This method is easier to work and there is no danger of damaging the net during the cutting away process. If you are applying pieces of net to net use the second method whatever the size although if the shapes are very large the presser foot should be used.

Do not attempt to do anything other than straight stitch techniques on fragile fabrics. Satin stitch may pull up the fabric so that it is not possible to press your work flat and also fine threads may get dislodged spoiling the effect of the stitch unless its purpose is purely textural.

Embroidery worked on an open fabric gives a completely different effect to that worked on a closely woven fabric since with an open fabric both upper and lower threads are visible so the stitching appears heavier. All weights of net can be embroidered from the heavy net used for ballet tutus to a fine dress net. Shapes may be embroidered on net then cut out and applied to, or inserted into, another fabric. If you are applying net shapes to a solid background either turn the edges under, making a clearly defined edge which can be secured with hemming or zigzag stitch. Alternatively you could leave $\frac{1}{2}$ inch outside the stitching on each shape and attach it with free machine embroidery which will soften the edge and blend it into the background. This method of machine embroidery is very good for decorating clothes since the minimal amount of stitching needed on the background will not impair its draping qualities. Use soft dress net for the embroidered shapes which may be applied with some other shapes in a more closely woven fabric for contrast, overlapping the net shapes on the others for even greater variety.

Use your imagination when choosing your background fabric. Plastic mesh vegetable bags can make interesting backgrounds for panels. Satin stitch can be used but generally straight running stitch is most effective used in a very textural way with contrasting bobbin colors to build up subtle shaded areas. Some cotton vegetable bags have a very open weave and, once washed, are excellent to use. The threads can be dislodged to make large holes and spaces to contrast with heavily worked areas. They are ideal for lampshades when mounted over a fabric fine enough to allow the light to pass through.

The motif illustrated is worked in the frame. The organdy shapes are applied to the background with free running stitch using 50 machine embroidery thread on the bobbin and through the needle. The edges of each shape are trimmed after stitching and emphasized with more running stitch. An eyelet is worked in the center of the motif (see the following chapter), and a free running texture worked around it. The leaves are worked in free running stitch with sewing cotton.

The delicate art of eyelet embroidery and openwork

Eyelets are simple to work and extremely effective when used on their own, or in combination with other free stitching effects and they always make an interesting focal point in a design. The machine attachments for eyelets are "extras" and are usually made in two or three sizes. When working eyelets, the smaller you make your central hole, the wider your stitching can be and vice versa.

The work must be placed in a hoop using a hoop small enough to revolve around the needle completely and the eyelets should be positioned within the frame so that they do not hamper this movement. Follow the machine manufacturer's instructions for fitting the eyelet plate. For best results use 50 machine embroidery thread. When piercing the hole using the awl supplied with the attachment, be careful not to make the hole too large. Set your machine for satin stitch, place the work in position on the eyelet plate, (you may have to remove and replace the needle), position the needle to the left and draw the thread up through the hole. Hold both thread ends when starting and run the machine fast revolving the frame evenly. It is better to turn the frame twice quickly rather than once slowly, although a delicate effect can be achieved by spacing the stitches so that the fabric remains visible between them.

When the eyelet is completed the ends of the stitching should be tied on the wrong side of the fabric. If a number of eyelets are to be worked this can be avoided by having the eyelets touch each other or else designing the work so that the linking threads may be concealed by further textural stitching. Another way of finishing is to position the needle to the right and work another row of small straight stitching around the circumference of the eyelet. The threads can then be cut close to the work and the stitching gives an added finish.

A further textural variation can be given to eyelets by working through the needle with a different color from that on the bobbin and with the upper tension tighter than the lower so that the bobbin color shows around the edges. Loosen the lower tension as well if necessary.

Openwork may be described as a decorative version of darning. It is the technique either of inserting a delicate web-like pattern of machine stitching into specially prepared holes and spaces or working over the spaces so solidly that they become as heavy as the background fabric. If this technique is to be used for dress embroidery the shapes should be well filled if they are large. If the shapes are small, however, they may be left more open but are best worked where there is no likelihood of damage from such things as buckles, handbags or bracelets.

Generally with openwork the same thickness of thread is used through the needle and on the bobbin. It is always important to use a thread that will stand up to wash and wear and therefore choose a thread thicker than 50 machine embroidery cotton. Cable stitch is a good choice of stitch to work as it fills in the space quickly. The tensions for this should always be set as for normal sewing.

For best results use a closely woven fabric of any weight such as linen, sailcloth, cotton lawn or organdy. Place the work in a hoop and outline the shapes with three or four lines of free running stitch which lie either on top of each other or touching. This will prevent the edges of the shape from stretching. Remove the work from the machine and cut out the shapes close to the stitching. Work a few stitches around the edge to secure the threads, then stitch backward and forward across the space carrying the stitching around the edge to the next line if necessary until a framework has been made. The focal points may then be built up by stitching continuously around any area where lines intersect without necessarily continuing the stitching to the edge. If you change colors during your design either secure the ends by close stitching or else take them through to the wrong side and tie them.

The edges of the hole may be finished with satin stitch, either freely if you are sufficiently skilled or else using the presser foot. Whichever method you use the work should remain stretched in a hoop small enough to pass easily around the needle. A softer edge is obtained by working a whipstitch or free running texture over the edge of the hole which blends it into the background. It is a good idea on a swing needle machine to use a throat plate with a needle hole rather than a slit. If it is necessary to move the hoop on the work to complete your design do not let the edge of the hoop cross the stitching if possible. If this cannot be avoided see that the main bulk of stitching is at right angles to the edge of the frame to minimize the risk of damage and tighten the work from the opposite side.

For purely decorative designs, such as wall hangings and panels, holes of any size up to the size of the frame can be filled. The holes should be rounded rather than crescent shaped as the lack of edge tension on the latter causes too many difficulties in working.

Openwork can look particularly exciting if different fabrics such as leather, foil or metallic material are laid underneath the shapes but you should bear in mind the function of the finished article.

For permanent objects such as mobiles, lampshade rings or millinery wire may be used to give the edges of the shape support. Millinery wire should be cut long enough to go around the circumference twice with the ends touching each other. Conceal the join with thread tied over it. To secure each line of stitching as you work wired shapes, you should stop your machine each time you reach the wire and work four stitches backward and forward over it, (finishing the fourth stitch inside), turning the balance wheel by hand. You should also try to make the basic structure of wide angles to prevent the threads of your embroidery from slipping. To also help avoid this, it is a good idea, having completed a horizontal line of stitching in your shape, to work the fourth stitch over the wire so that the stitch finishes inside the wire and above that line of embroidery. This means that when you work the vertical line, the first stitch is worked over the horizontal line thus pulling the stitches over the wire close together, helping to anchor them. Satin stitch can also be worked over the wire or ring to conceal it, using the widest needle throw to lessen the risk of the needle catching on the wire and breaking. Shapes may be worked on stiff wire, which can be bent into more complex shapes. To join the wire, cross the ends and wind an elastic band around them. When the shape is completed it can be laid in position on a background and fastened with a few running stitches inside the wire at each point. Then cut the wire at intervals, carefully remove each section, and further strengthen the points of the shape with stitching or conceal them with satin stitch or applied thread. Never cut the loops which result when the wire is removed.

Several of these shapes can make a pleasing arrangement for a panel but should only be used when the completed work will be stretched, or the effect will be lost. This particular aspect of openwork therefore is unsuitable for dress embroidery.

The sample shows a motif worked with eyelets and a variation of whip stitch. 40 sewing thread is used through the needle and 50 machine embroidery cotton on the bobbin throughout.

Embroidered dress

The dress illustrated has the embroidery worked on the front bodice. This should always be completed before the dress is finished. When you cut out the front bodice piece make sure you allow extra fabric all around to enable you to hoop your work.

The free shapes are worked in the hoop using running and cable stitches. Because you are working across spaces the cable stitch can be worked from the right side. Pure silk thread is used through the needle throughout and silky hand embroidery thread is wound on the bobbin. A free running texture is used around the edge of the shape to conceal the raw edges and soften them into the background.

The front bodice is cut out in lining and basted in position on the wrong side of the front bodice, matching notches. The pattern piece is then treated as one layer during finishing.

QUILTING
Basic techniques

From the small fragments found in early Egyptian tombs, quilting is known to have been used as a means of padding garments and bed covers for warmth and as decoration from the very earliest days. Later, quilting was worn instead of armor in battle and it was also worn under metal armor to prevent chafing.

As well as for bed covers and household furnishings, quilting of garments of all kinds for warmth and decoration was universal during the 16th and mid 19th centuries. In the 19th century, when decorative sewing was at its height, quilting was as popular as patchwork and the two crafts became closely allied. In America, where the latter was an economy measure with the early settlers, it was customary to make patchwork quilt tops during the winter and hold a neighborhood quilting party in the spring to complete the quilts. The two crafts progressed together in this way to an equal degree of technical expertise.

Types of quilting

Today four different types of quilting are practiced in embroidery. These are English quilting, Italian quilting, Trapunto quilting and the delicate shadow quilting.

Of these, English quilting is the most popular and is the only one which provides real extra warmth since it incorporates all-over padding, although the other methods also give added weight and substance to fabrics as well as decoration. All four methods can be used for bedcovers, quilts, pillow tops, tea and coffee pot covers, jackets, housecoats and other similar garments.

English quilting

This is the method of sandwiching padding between a top cover and muslin backing or fabric lining and then securing the three layers together by over-all running stitching. The decoration comes from the patterns worked by the stitching and the attractive texture produced.

Quilting in Britain is particularly associated with North West England and South Wales, and many of the designs have local names, such as the Welsh heart and Weardale chain. Most of them are based on simple motifs of leaves, feathers, circles, scissors, spectacles, and so forth, and it is worth obtaining templates of these basic shapes which can be increased or reduced in size according to the size of the article being made.

Alternatively, some designs used on Continental ceramic tiles might lend ideas for patterns. When planning the design for a piece of English quilting, the pattern should traditionally consist of principal motifs and a background filling pattern which throws into relief the main areas of the design. The filling pattern can be a lattice of squares or diamonds or a series of lozenge shapes.

Italian quilting

This is worked through two thicknesses of fabric only, a top cover and a muslin or lawn backing. The stitching is worked in double lines, $\frac{1}{4}$ inch $-\frac{3}{8}$ inch apart to form channels which are threaded with soft wool, known as quilting 'wool, to give a raised design on the front of the work.

The designs for Italian quilting should be linear and preferably continuous. The scroll patterns on wrought-iron work and the interlaced forms of Celtic decorative lettering are often suitable as the basis for designs.

Trapunto quilting

This is also worked on a top fabric and muslin backing but differs from Italian quilting in that the stitching is worked in single lines which completely encircle shapes which are then raised by padding them with a stuffing of soft wool or wadding.

Shadow quilting

This is a variation of both Italian and Trapunto quilting. The stitching is worked on a transparent fabric such as organdy or organza with a backing of a similar fabric

or muslin. The areas to be raised are stuffed and threaded with a colored quilting yarn or soft thick knitting wool.

Fabrics for all quilting

Because it is the design which is all-important in quilting rather than the stitches which are worked in a color to match the fabric, the top cover fabric should be one which really shows the texture formed. For this reason, if you are using satin, it should be the dull sort rather than the shiny surfaced one. Other suitable fabrics are fine silk, shantung, rayon, glazed cotton, fine wool, Viyella, cotton poplin and closely woven linen.

Thread and needles

Pure silk thread in a color to match the fabric is the most satisfactory, although cotton or fine linen thread can be used. For stitching use a No.7, 8, or 9 betweens needle, according to the weight of the fabric. For marking the design for English quilting, you will also need a yarn or rug needle. For threading the quilting wool in Italian quilting, you will need a large blunt tapestry needle.

The stitches

Running stitch is used for all methods of quilting except corded, where herringbone stitch is used.

Working English quilting

In the past carded sheep's wool or cotton wadding was used for padding, but today it is best to use Dacron or other polyester wadding since these can be washed easily (cotton wadding tends to become

lumpy with wear and washing). The backing fabric can be muslin or soft cotton if you are lining the article separately, or a rayon lining fabric if a separate lining is not required.

1 Baste the layers together, sandwiching the padding berween the top fabric and backing. Work a line of basting across the center of the fabric in both directions.

2 Mount the triple layer of fabric onto a traditional frame, with top fabric facing up.

3 Cut a template of the principal motif, keeping its size in proportion to the article. Place in position on the fabric, using the center basting lines as a guide.

4 To transfer the design to the fabric, mark around the edge of the template with a large needle held at an angle to the work. The point of the needle will leave an impression on the fabric which is easy to follow with running stitch.

5 Work the main areas of the design first in even running stitch. Start the stitching with a small knot on the back of the work which will bury itself in the wadding and finish with a small backstitch.

6 When the main areas have been worked, mark the filling background pattern with a flat ruler and yarn needle. Work along the lines in running stitch.

7 When all the quilting has been worked, take the piece off the frame and finish the article as desired. If you are making something like a bed cover or quilt, one of the best finishes is a piping in the same fabric as the top cover.

8 To attach the piping, make up the casing and enclose the cord in the standard way.

9 If you are using a separate rip out, attach

the piping around the edges of the article on the right side and stitch through all layers. Cut the lining fabric to the required size and place it on the quilting with right sides together and edges matching. Stitch along the piping line, leaving an opening on one side. Turn right side out and close the opening with neat slip-stitching.

10 If the lining is not separate, un-do the basting joining the layers together and stitch the piping to the top cover and wadding only. Turn under the edges of the lining and slip-stitch neatly to the piping line.

Working Italian quilting

Traditionally the design was marked on the muslin backing and the stitching worked on this side. However, you may find it easier to keep the running stitches even if you work on the top fabric, in which case the design should be marked by the prick and pounce method (see earlier) and not by tracing or drawing which would still show when the work is finished.

1 Baste the fabric and backing around the edges and mount them as one onto a frame, with the working side facing up.

2 Trace your design onto the fabric and work along the double lines in running stitch. If you like, some parts of the design can be emphasized by working in chain or back stitch on the right side of the fabric instead of running stitch.

3 Thread a large blunt needle with the quilting yarn and insert it along the channels formed by the double lines of stitching. Where there is an angle, break or intersection in the design, bring the yarn to the surface on the muslin and reinsert the needle leaving a small loop. This allows for an even tension and only a small amount of shrinkage if the quilting is washed or dry cleaned.

Working Trapunto quilting

This is worked in a similar way to Italian quilting, with the main exception that the design is marked in single lines which enclose the area to be raised or padded. The method of padding, however, is different and also applies to shadow quilting.

1 When the stitching is completed make an incision through the muslin into the area to be stuffed. Use a blunt needle to do this, or knitting needle if the area is large.

2 Remove the top skin of wadding and tease the wadding into small .amounts which can easily be inserted through the incision. The amount of stuffing you use depends on the effect you desire.

3 When enough padding is inserted, close the opening with overcasting stitches before moving on to the next area.

Quilted pillow

This simple design for quilting can be modified and used to decorate various objects of home furnishings.

The directions are given for a pillow 16 inches × 12 inches, but the quilting can be adapted for a larger pillow by spacing out the motifs or for a small square pillow by omitting the small leaf shapes.

Fabric required

$\frac{3}{4}$ yd rayon fabric, or a not too shiny pure silk, or a dull satin, 36 in wide.

You will also need

$\frac{1}{2}$ yd thin cotton fabric, 36 in wide for backing the quilting.
$\frac{1}{2}$ yd synthetic wadding.
$1\frac{3}{4}$ yd cotton piping cord, No.2 size.
1 spool pure sewing silk to match the fabric.
1 spool mercerized sewing thread.
Tracing paper.
Thin white cardboard for the templates.
1 large fine-pointed darning needle.
Sewing needles (fine crewels or betweens) for quilting.
Pillow form to fit pillowcase.

Making the templates

1 Trace the heart and leaf motifs for the quilting onto the tracing paper.

2 Place the tracing onto the cardboard; pin or tape in position and cut around.

Working the quilting

1 Cut the quilting fabric to the size of the

finished pillow, plus $\frac{1}{2}$ inch all around for turnings.
Cut the wadding and the cotton backing fabric to the same size.

2 Baste the three layers together, sandwiching the wadding between the fabrics.
3 Mark the center lines of the fabric with basting diagonally from corner to corner.
4 Mount the fabric into the embroidery frame (see earlier).
5 Lay the mounted fabrics (in the frame) right side up on a folded blanket on a firm surface.
6 Position the heart template in the four positions as shown in the diagram. Holding the large needle at an angle, trace around the cardboard shape firmly enough to leave a sharp impression on the fabric. Take care not to cut the fabric with the needle point if your fabric is thin. Trace around the leaf shape at each end of the pillow. Place the smaller shape inside the heart and trace around.
7 Start to quilt the fabric, using the matching silk and working with a small even running stitch.
8 When the main motifs are completed, draw in the background diamond shapes using a ruler and large needle. Draw in the lines, working from each corner and keeping them $\frac{3}{4}$ inch apart. Quilt along the lines.
9 When the quilting is completed, remove it from the frame and fasten off all ends neatly.

Finishing the pillow case

1 From the surplus fabric, cut a piece the same size as the quilting for the back of the pillowcase and then cut bias strips 1½ inches wide for the piping casing. Make up the piping casing.

2 Pin the piping in position around the edge of the quilting and baste. Place the two sides of the pillowcase together with right sides facing. Baste and machine stitch using the mercerized sewing thread along the piping line. Leave one side of the pillowcase open and turn it right side out.

3 Insert a zipper into the open side and then insert the pillow form, or insert the form first and slip-stitch the sides of the opening together.

Traveling slippers and case
Fabric required

½ yd fabric for quilting, 36 in wide.
½ yd cotton fabric, 36 in wide, for the backing.
½ yd rayon lining fabric, 36 in wide.

You will also need

½ yd synthetic wadding.
One pair of foam rubber inner soles in required size.
Felt, to cover foam soles.
Vinyl fabric, to cover bottom of slippers.
Adhesive.
Quilting equipment as for pillowcase.

Working the quilting

1 Trace the shapes for the slipper fronts and case and baste the shapes onto the quilting fabric, allowing at least 1 inch

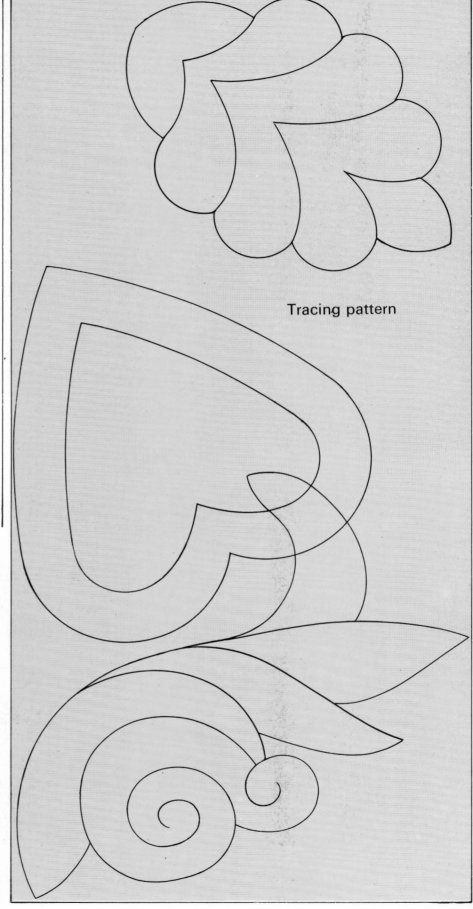

Tracing pattern

between each one.

2 Sandwich the wadding between the quilting fabric and cotton backing and baste the layers together. Mount them into an embroidery frame.

3 Mark the quilting shapes, using the leaf for the slippers and the scroll for the case. Work the quilting.

4 Mark the background diamond pattern, placing the lines $\frac{1}{2}$ inch apart.

Making the slippers

1 Cut around the basted shapes of the slippers, leaving 1 inch for turnings. Cut out linings for the slippers to the same size.

2 Cut bias strips and make piping about 5 inches long for each slipper. Baste in place along each top edge. Place the lining onto the slipper front with right sides

together and stitch close to the piping. Turn right side out and baste the lining and quilting together around the remaining edge.

3 Place the foam inner soles onto the felt and draw around, leaving $\frac{1}{2}$ inch turnings.

4 Clip into the turnings of the felt, place on to the foam inner soles and attach the turnings down on the underside.

5 Place the slipper fronts right side up onto the felt side of the soles, fold the turnings onto the underside and pin in position. Try on the slippers and adjust the size of the turnings if necessary. Secure in position with adhesive.

6 Cut two shapes of the soles from the vinyl fabric and stick in position on the underside to cover the raw edges of the quilting and felt.

Making the slipper case

1 Cut out the lining to the same size as the quilting.

2 Place the quilting and lining together with right sides facing and baste and machine stitch along the top curved edge, taking $\frac{1}{4}$ inch turnings. Clip into the angle and turn right side out.

3 Baste along the top seam so that no lining shows on the quilted side of the case. Press.

4 Fold the case in half so that the curved edges match and the quilted side is inside. Baste and machine stitch down the side and bottom edge, taking $\frac{1}{4}$ inch turnings. Make the edges neat by overcasting or zig-zag stitching. Turn the finished case right side out.

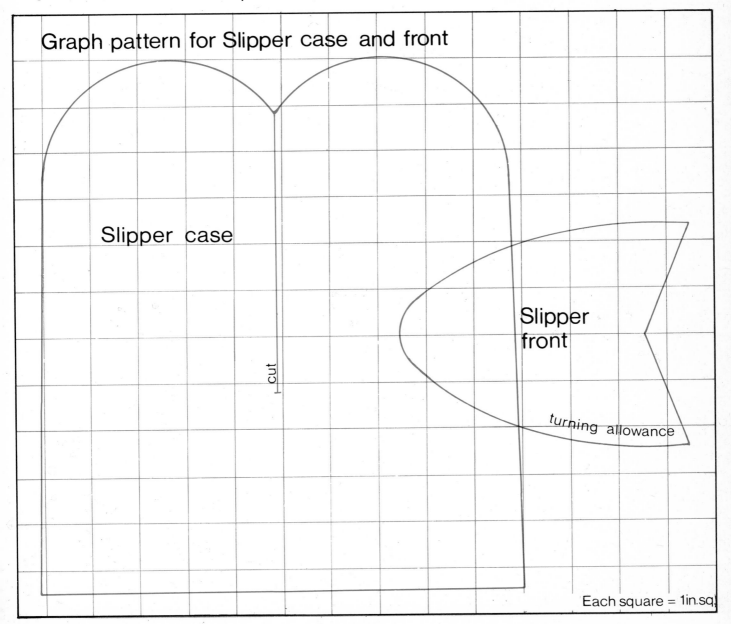

Graph pattern for Slipper case and front

Slipper case

cut

Slipper front

turning allowance

Each square = 1in.sq.

QUILTING BY MACHINE

The cording foot and quilting

Most machines have a cording or braiding foot as an extra attachment. This foot guides a thick thread or cord under the needle. It can be straight stitched down the center, zigzagged or enclosed with satin stitch. This is an effective way of working solid shapes.

The shapes can be worked directly onto the article or on separate pieces of fabric which are then applied to give a more raised effect. The edges of the applied shapes can then be turned under and hemstitched so they are not visible; or the application may become part of the design and can be satin stitched for instance, or concealed with free embroidery. Whichever of these methods you choose the shapes should be worked from the outside toward the center so the shape does not become distorted.

The fabrics and threads

If the fabric is a fine one it will be necessary to back the shape with paper. Iron-on interfacing is excellent for dress embroidery providing the work does not have to drape.

A test sample should always be worked to make sure that the cord used is fine enough to be gripped firmly by the foot. A thicker cord might cause subsequent lines to be uneven and the groove on the underside of the foot, which allows for the passage of the thick thread, may catch on an adjacent line, thus dislodging the work. However, if you wish to use a thicker cord, this difficulty can be overcome by changing to the presser foot after the first round has been completed. To make stitching easier use soft yarns which flatten under the presser foot. Textured yarns may be used and generally look best if a matching thread is used to attach them. If a good match is not available, use transparent thread on top and the nearest color match in the bobbin.

Quilting can be used on its own or combined with areas of free embroidery or any other stitch effects already described. It can be worked in the usual way using the quilting foot and guide, and also in the hoop, making it possible to sew smaller and more intricate shapes. For the best effect the work should not be too tightly stretched in the hoop and only a limited amount of wadding can be used to allow it to fit into the hoop at all. For this reason it is better not to use a hoop with the inner ring bound. If, with the thickness of the work, the machine tends to skip stitches, use the darning foot and work with looser tensions. Quilting by this method could provide a decorative yoke and hem, or collar and cuffs for a dress.

Cotton, Dacron or thin foam make good fillers for quilting and the latter two have the advantage of being washable. Fine soft fabric should be used for the backing. Cotton lawn is excellent. Italian quilting is particularly attractive for garment embroidery. Two parallel lines of stitching are worked holding two fabrics together and thick yarn is inserted by hand from the back between the fabrics. The distance between the two lines is governed by the thickness of the yarn. If a fine fabric is used on top an attractive shadow effect can be achieved. An openweave fabric should be used for the backing to facilitate the wool insertion.

The stitches

Quilting may be worked in cable stitch in which case the design can be marked on tissue paper, basted to and worked from the wrong side, then torn away. Alternatively, the design may be drawn with tailor's chalk and worked from the right side by applying a fine embroidery thread with a zigzag stitch.

Work from the center of a design outward allowing plenty of extra fabric for the seam allowances. Do not trim the edges of cut-out pattern sections until the quilting has been completed.

The flower-shaped motif shown is worked freely in the hoop and the geometric motif is worked with the quilting foot. The design for the floral motif is marked on paper first and basted to the wrong side of the fabric. Cable stitch is worked from the wrong side, using a silky hand embroidery thread on the bobbin and sewing thread through the needle.

Pure silk thread is used for the straight stitching which is worked from the right side. The upper and lower tensions are balanced.

The quilted vest

A vest, such as the one illustrated, is ideal for quilting since the pattern can be worked on both front pieces and there are no buttonholes or buttons to work around. The pattern pieces are cut from 2oz. washable quilting, the dart shapes are cut out and the edges overcast together by hand. The lining is made up and the darts are worked on each remaining pattern piece. The quilting is then basted very firmly on the wrong side of those pieces. The embroidery is worked using the quilting foot. The thread and tensions used are the same as those for the motifs. When the embroidery is completed the vest is made up according to the instructions with the pattern. Hooks and eyes may be sewn at center-front if desired.

A GUIDE TO FABRICS AND THREADS

As more people are experimenting with the ever-increasing number of materials available now, the days when a particular type of embroidery was worked only on one specific type of fabric are past. This chart endeavors to give suggestions for both traditional methods and the more progressive ones and the fabrics and threads appropriate for each.

TYPE OF EMBROIDERY	TRADITIONAL USE		CONTEMPORARY USE	
	Fabrics	**Threads**	**Fabrics**	**Threads**
BASIC STITCHERY	Linen, cotton, rayon, stamped goods	Linen and silk	Any type of material from burlap to organdy	Wool, silk, cotton, nylon, chenille, cords, nylon string
QUILTING (Traditional Padding: carded sheep's wool, cotton wadding, or flannel) (Contemporary Padding: synthetic wadding)				
English	Fine silk, fine linen, dull satin, fine wool	Pure silk, fine linen and silk, silk	Shantung, satin, nylon, glazed cotton, poplin, viyella, fine wool	Pure silk
Italian	As above	As above	As above	As above
Trapunto	As above	As above	As above	As above
DRAWN (OR PULLED FABRIC)	Evenweave linen of various weights	Matching threads	Cotton, wool, linen, synthetic evenweave fabrics	Pearl cotton, Coton à broder, wool, and linen
Drawn thread	As above	As above	As above	As above
Blackwork	As above	As above	As above	As above
Hardanger	Evenweave cotton and linen	As above	As above plus tweed and flannel	Cotton, silk, and wool to contrast in weight and texture

TYPE OF EMBROIDERY	TRADITIONAL USE		CONTEMPORARY USE	
	Fabrics	**Threads**	**Fabrics**	**Threads**
Hedebo	As above	As above	As above	As above
Assisi	As above	As above	As above	As above
Cross-stitch	As above	As above	As above	As above
Needlepoint	Single and double canvas and linen	Crewel	Single and double canvas and linen	Crewel wools, tapestry wools, 6-strand floss, silk and crochet threads
SHADOW WORK	White organdy and muslin	Fine white	White and colored organdy, organza, chiffon, nylon	Pure silk, sewing silk for applied areas. Silk, wool, and 6-strand floss for embroidery
SMOCKING	Fine cotton, georgette, crêpe de chine, silk, fine wools and chiffon, fine linen	Silk, cotton, and linen (threads generally should be slightly heavier than the fabric)	Chiffon, cotton, wool, synthetics, some types of vinyl, corduroy, flannel and dress tweed	Crochet cotton, knitting wools, silk, buttonhole twist, linen embroidery
AYRSHIRE WORK AND EYELET EMBROIDERY (white work)	Fine linen, linen lawn, fine cotton, muslin, organdy (always white)	Matching fine cotton and linen, cotton floche and coton à broder	Cotton, organdy, linen lawn, Swiss cotton and muslin organza	Matching cotton, silk, and linen
CUTWORK				
Simple	White or natural linen	Matching linen, cotton, mercerized	Colored linen, strong cotton, dress tweed, home furnishing fabrics if firm woven	Matching linen and cotton
Renaissance embroidery	As above	As above	As above	As above
Richelieu embroidery	As above	As above	As above	Also fine crochet
Reticella embroidery	As above	As above	As above	As above
NEEDLEWEAVING	Loosely woven linen, linen crash, huckaback, and home furnishing fabrics	Threads should be slightly thicker than withdrawn thread	Burlap, canvas, heavy linens, linen scrim, dress tweeds	Any suitable to the weight and texture of the fabric being woven

A DICTIONARY OF STITCHES

An alphabet of free style embroidery stitches begins here and includes outline, flat, looped, chained, knotted, couching, filling and composite stitches. Diagrams and step-by-step instructions make the alphabet a useful source of reference material for both a beginner and the more experienced embroiderer.

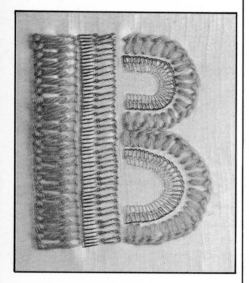

Backstitch

Bring the thread through on the stitch line, then take a small backward stitch through the fabric. Bring the needle through again a little in front of the first stitch and take another stitch, inserting the needle at the point where it first came through.

Blanket stitch and buttonhole stitch

These stitches are worked in the same way – the difference being that in buttonhole stitch the stitches are close together. Bring the thread out on the lower line, insert the needle in position in the upper line, taking a straight downward stitch with the thread under the needle point. Pull up the stitch to form a loop and

repeat. This stitch may also be worked on evenweave fabric.

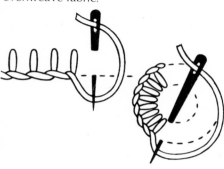

Bokhara couching

This stitch is useful and ornamental for filling in shapes of leaves and petals of flowers. It is worked in the same way as Rumanian stitch, but the small tying stitches are set at regular intervals over the laid thread to form pattern lines across the shape. The tying stitches should be pulled tight, leaving the laid thread slightly loose between.

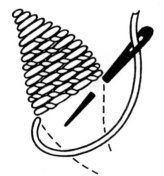

Bullion stitch

Pick up a backstitch, the size of the bullion stitch required, bring the needle point out where it first emerged. Do not pull the needle right through the fabric. Wind the thread around the needle point as many times as required to equal the space of the backstitch. Hold the left thumb on the

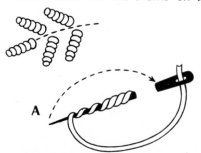

coiled thread and pull the needle through; still holding the coiled thread, turn the needle back to where it was inserted (see arrow) and insert in the same place (A). Pull the thread through until the bullion stitch lies flat. Use a needle with a small eye to allow the thread to pass through the coils easily.

Buttonhole stitch bars and double buttonhole stitch bars

These bars are used in cut-work and Richelieu work. Make a row of running stitch between the double lines of the design as a padding for the buttonhole stitch. Where a single line bar occurs, take a thread across the space and back, securing with a small stitch and buttonhole stitch closely over the loose threads without picking up any of the fabric (A). Buttonhole stitch around the shape, keeping the looped edge of the stitch to the inside, then cut away the fabric from behind the bar and around the inside of the shape. Where a double line or a broad bar is required between shapes or for stems of flowers, when the fabric is to be cut away on each side, make a row of running stitch along one side, spacing the stitches slightly. Buttonhole stitch along the other side into the spaces left by the first row. The fabric is then cut away close to the buttonhole stitch, leaving a strong, broad bar (B).

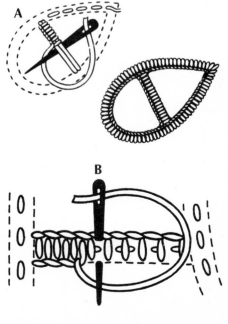

Buttonhole insertion stitch

This insertion stitch consists of groups of four buttonhole stitches worked alternately on each piece of fabric to be joined. The upper row is worked as in ordinary buttonhole stitch. The diagram shows the method of working the groups on the lower row.

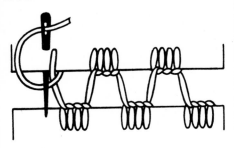

Buttonhole stitch and picot

Work as for ordinary buttonhole stitch until a picot is required, then hold the thread down with the left thumb and wind the needle three times around the thread (A). Still holding the thread securely, pull the working thread until the twisted threads are close to the buttonhole stitch, then make a buttonhole stitch into the last loop (B).

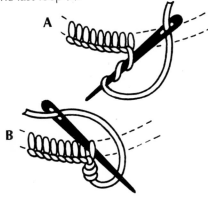

Cable stitch

This stitch is worked from left to right. Bring the thread through on the line of the design. Insert the needle a little to the right on the line and bring the needle out to the left midway between the length of the stitch, with the thread below the needle (Figure A). Work the next stitch in the same way but with the thread above the needle. Continue in this way, alternating the position of the thread. This stitch may also be worked on evenweave fabric (Figure B).

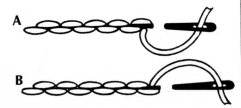

Cable chain stitch

Bring the thread through at A and hold it down with the left thumb. Pass the needle from right to left under the working thread, then twist the needle back over the working thread to the right and, still keeping the thread under the thumb, take a stitch of the required length. Pull the thread through over the loop.

Chain stitch

Bring the thread out at the top of the line and hold down with left thumb. Insert the needle where it last emerged and bring the point out a short distance away. Pull the thread through, keeping the working thread under the needle point.

Chained feather stitch

Working between two parallel lines, bring the thread through at A and make a slanting chain stitch, tying down the stitch at B. Take a second slanting chain stitch from the right at C, tying it down at D. The tying stitches will form a regular zig-zag pattern.

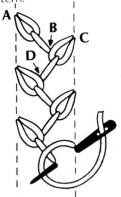

Checkered chain stitch

This stitch is worked in the same way as chain stitch, but with two contrasting threads in the needle at the same time. When making the loops, pass one color under the needle point and let the other color lie on top. Pull through both threads. Work the next loop with the other color under the needle point.

Chevron stitch

Bring the thread through on the lower line at the left side, insert the needle a little to the right on the same line and take a small stitch to the left, emerging halfway between the stitch being made. Next, insert the needle on the upper line a little to the right and take a small stitch to the left as at A. Insert the needle again on the same line a little to the right and take a small stitch to the left, emerging at the center as at B. Work in this way alternately on the upper and lower lines. This stitch may also be worked on evenweave fabric.

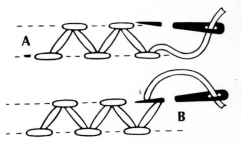

Closed buttonhole stitch

The stitches are made in pairs forming triangles. Bring the thread through at A, insert the needle at B and, with the thread under the needle, bring it through at C. Insert the needle again at B and bring it through at D. This stitch may also be worked on evenweave fabric.

Closed feather stitch

This stitch is worked along two parallel lines. Bring the thread through at A and with the thread under the needle, take a stitch from B to C. Swing the thread over to the left and, with the thread under the needle, take a stitch from D to E. Repeat these two stitches.

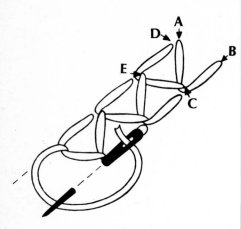

Coral stitch

Bring the thread out at the right side of the line, lay the thread along the line of the design and hold it down with the left thumb. Take a small stitch under the line and the thread and pull through, bringing the needle over the lower thread as in the diagram.

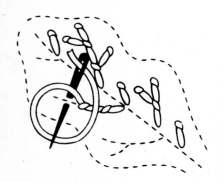

Couching

Lay a thread along the line of the design and, with another thread, tie it down at even intervals with a small stitch into the fabric. The tying stitch can be in a color which contrasts with the laid thread if desired.

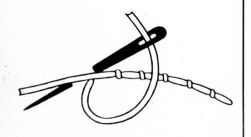

Cretan stitch

Bring the needle through centrally at the left-hand side, taking a small stitch on the lower line, needle pointing inward and with the thread under the needle point, as shown at A. Take a stitch on the upper line and thread under the needle as shown at B. Continue in this way until shape is filled.

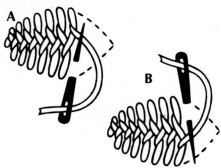

Cross stitch

Bring the needle through on the lower right line of the cross and insert at the top of the same line, taking a stitch through the fabric to the lower left line (Figure A).

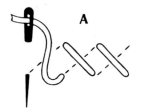

Continue to the end of the row in this way. Complete the other half of the cross (Figure B). It is important that the upper half of each stitch lies in the same direction.

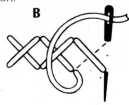

Double backstitch or closed herringbone stitch

This stitch is used for shadow work on fine, transparent fabric and can be worked on the right side of the fabric as at A – a small backstitch worked alternately on each side of the traced double lines (the dotted lines on the diagram show the formation of the thread on the wrong side

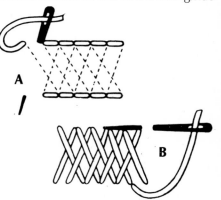

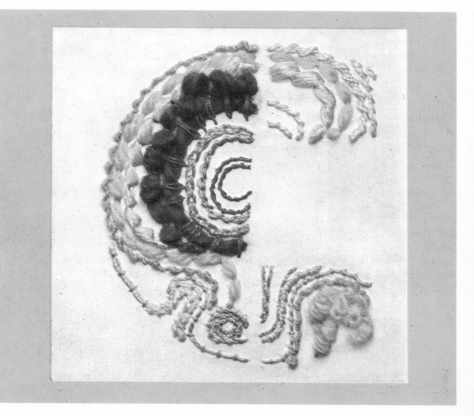

of the fabric). The color of the thread appears delicately through the fabric. Figure B shows the stitch worked on the wrong side of the fabric as a closed herringbone stitch with no spaces left between the stitches. Both methods achieve the same result.

Daisy stitch or detached chain stitch

Work in the same way as chain stitch (A), but fasten each loop at the foot with a small stitch (B). Lazy daisy stitch may be

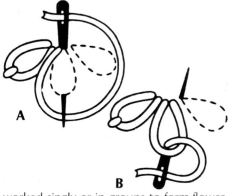

worked singly or in groups to form flower petals.

Double knot stitch

Bring the thread through at A. Take a small stitch across the line at B. Pass the needle downward under the surface stitch just made, without piercing the fabric, as at C. With the thread under the needle, pass

the needle again under the first stitch at D. Pull the thread through to form a knot. The knots should be spaced evenly and closely to obtain a beaded effect.

Eyelet holes

Figure A. Work a row of small running stitches around the circle. Pierce the center with a sharp pointed needle and fold back the ragged edge. Closely overcast the folded edge with running stitch. Trim away any ragged edges at the back. Figure B shows the appearance of the finished eyelet hole. Larger circles or longer eyelet holes may be cut across the center both ways and the cut ends folded back.

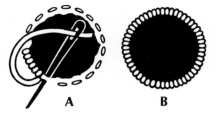

A   B

Feather stitch

Figure A. Bring the needle out at the top center, hold the thread down with the left thumb, insert the needle a little to the right on the same level and take a small stitch down to the center, keeping the thread under the needle point. Next, insert the needle a little to the left on the same level and take a stitch to center, keeping the thread under the needle point. Work these two movements alternately.

Figure B shows double feather stitch, in which two stitches are taken to the right and left alternately.

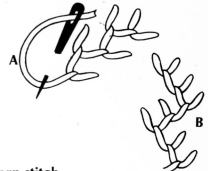

Fern stitch

This stitch consists of three straight stitches of equal length radiating from the same central point A. Bring the thread through at A and make a straight stitch to B. Bring the thread through again at A and make another straight stitch to C. Repeat once more to D and bring the thread through at E to begin the next three radiating stitches. The central stitch follows the line of the design. This stitch may also be worked on evenweave fabric.

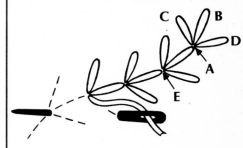

Fishbone stitch

This stitch is useful for filling small shapes. Bring the thread through at A and make a small straight stitch along the center line of the shape. Bring the thread

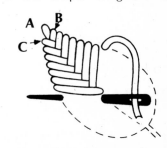

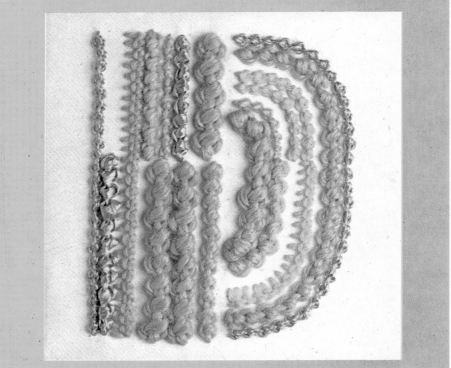

through again at B and make a sloping stitch across the central line at the base of the first stitch. Bring the thread through at C and make a similar sloping stitch to overlap the previous stitch. Continue working alternately on each side until the shape is filled.

Flat stitch
Take a small stitch alternately on each side of the shape to be filled, with the point of the needle always emerging on the outside line of the shape. Two lines may be drawn down the center of the shape as a guide for the size of the stitch. The stitches should be close together and fold into one another.

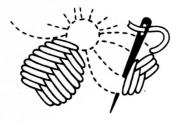

Fly stitch
Bring the thread through at the top left, hold it down with the left thumb, insert the needle to the right on the same level, a little distance from where the thread first emerged and take a small stitch downward to the center with the thread below the needle. Pull through and insert the needle again below the stitch at the center (A) and bring it through in position for the next stitch. This stitch may be worked singly or in horizontal rows (A) or vertically (B).

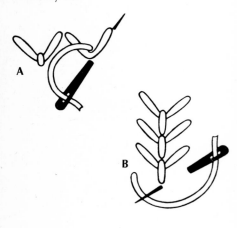

French knots
Bring the thread out at the required position, hold it down with the left thumb and wind the thread twice around the needle as at A. Still holding the thread firmly, twist the needle back to the starting point and insert it close to where the thread first emerged (see arrow). Pull

the thread through to the back and secure for a single French knot or pass on to the position of the next stitch as at B.

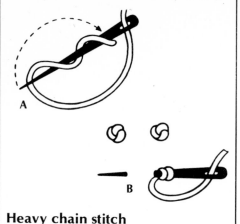

Heavy chain stitch
Bring the thread through at A and make a small vertical stitch. Bring the thread through again at B and pass the needle under the vertical stitch, without piercing the fabric, and insert it again at B. Bring the thread through at C and again pass the needle under the vertical stitch and

insert it at C. The third and all following stitches are made in exactly the same way, except that the needle always passes under the two preceding loops.

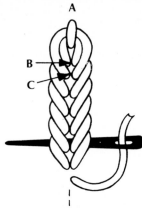

Herringbone stitch
Bring the needle out on the lower line at the left side and insert on the upper line a little to the right, taking a small stitch to the left with the thread below the needle. Next, insert the needle on the lower line

a little to the right and take a small stitch to the left with the thread above the needle. These two movements are worked throughout. For the best effect, the fabric lifted by the needle and the spaces between the stitches should be of equal size. This stitch can be laced with a matching or contrasting thread. Use a tapestry needle for lacing and do not pick up any of the fabric. Herringbone stitch may also be worked on evenweave fabric.

Interlaced band

This stitch is composed of two rows of backstitch with an interlacing. Work two parallel rows of backstitch (as shown at the top of the diagram) having the rows approximately $\frac{1}{2}$ to $\frac{3}{4}$ inch apart, with the stitches worked as on the diagram, i.e., the end of one stitch is directly in line with the center of the opposite stitch. Bring a matching or contrasting thread through at A and, following the diagram, interlace it through every stitch.

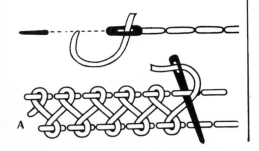

Interlacing stitch

The foundation of the border stitch is a double row of herringbone stitch worked in two steps, with the stitches intertwined in a certain way. The first row of herringbone stitch is shown in medium tone on the diagram. In working the rows of herringbone stitch for the interlacing, there is a slight change in the usual method. In the top stitch the needle is passed under the working thread in each case instead of over it, and attention should be paid to the alternate crossing of the threads when working the second row. Do not work this foundation tightly, as the interlacing thread tends to draw the stitches together. When the rows of herringbone stitch are worked, bring the thread for the surface interlacing through at A and follow the diagram closely. When the end of the row is reached, lace the thread around the last cross in the center and work back in a similar fashion along the lower half of the foundation. The last two crosses on the diagram have been left unlaced so that the construction of the herringbone stitch may be seen clearly.

Jacobean couching or trellis

This stitch makes an attractive filling stitch for the centers of flowers or shapes where an open effect is required. It consists of long evenly spaced stitches (laid threads) taken across the space horizontally and vertically (A) or diagonally (B). The crossed threads are then tied down at all intersecting points. The tying or couching stitch can be a small slanting stitch or cross-stitch.

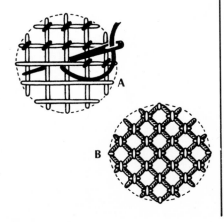

Knot stitch edging or Antwerp edging

Bring the thread through from the back of the fabric and work a single buttonhole stitch. Pass the needle behind the loop of the stitch and over the working thread as shown in the diagram. Space the stitches about $\frac{1}{4}$ inch apart. This edging is very useful for handkerchiefs or lingerie. Several rows, using a different color for each row, make a lacy edging. The stitches of the second and following rows are worked over the loops between the stitches of the previous row.

Knotted buttonhole stitch

Make a loop from right to left over the left thumb. Insert the needle, point upward, under the loop as at A. Slip the loop onto the needle and, with the loop still around the needle, take a stitch into the fabric as at B. Before drawing the needle through, tighten the loop around the head of the needle by pulling the working thread.

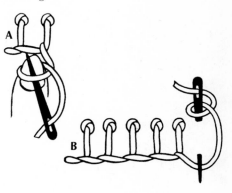

Knotted buttonhole filling stitch

Make an outline of backstitch or close running stitches, then work the detached filling as shown in the diagram. The link with the edging stitches is especially large for clarity.

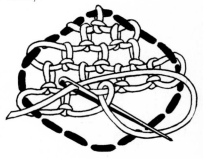

Knotted cable chain stitch

This stitch is worked from right to left. Bring the thread through at A and place it along the line of the design; then, with the thread under the needle, take a stitch at B, which is a coral knot. Then pass the needle under the stitch between A and B without piercing the fabric, as shown at C. With the thread under the needle, take a slanting stitch across the line at D, close to the coral knot. Pull the thread through to form a chain stitch.

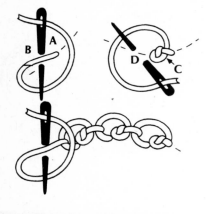

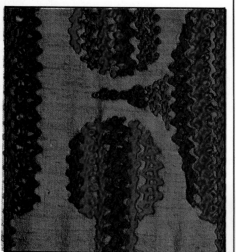

Knotted insertion stitch

This stitch is similar to knot stitch (or Antwerp stitch) edging, except that the stitches are made alternately on each piece of fabric to be joined. A small buttonhole stitch is worked into the edge of the fabric and a second stitch worked over the loops as shown in the figure.

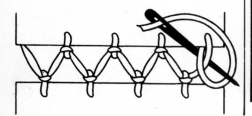

Laced running stitch

Running stitch can be laced with a contrasting color to form a decorative border. Use a tapestry needle for lacing and do not pick up any of the fabric.

Ladder stitch

This stitch may be used to fill shapes of varying widths, but it is shown worked between parallel lines. Bring the thread through at A, insert the needle at B and bring it out at C. Insert the needle again at D and bring out at E. Pass the needle under the first stitch at F and through the double stitch at G. Continue in this way, the needle passing under two stitches at each side to form the braided edge.

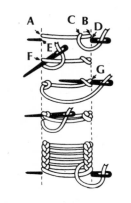

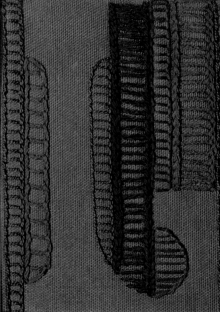

Leaf stitch

Bring the thread through at A and make a sloping stitch to B. Bring the thread through at C and make a sloping stitch to D. Bring the thread through at E, then continue working alternate stitches on each side in this way until the shape is lightly filled. This stitch is generally finished with an outline worked in stem stitch or chain stitch.

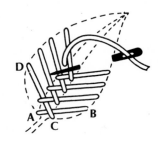

Long and short stitch

This form of satin stitch is so named because all the stitches are of varying lengths. It is often used to fill a shape which is too large or too irregular to be covered by ordinary satin stitch. It is also used to achieve a shaded effect. In the first row the stitches are alternately long and short and closely follow the outline of the shape. The stitches in the following rows are worked to achieve a smooth appearance. The figure shows how a shaded effect may be obtained.

Loop stitch

This stitch is worked from right to left. Bring the thread through at A and insert the needle at B. Bring it through again at C immediately below B. With the thread to the left and under the needle, pass the needle under the first stitch without piercing the fabric.

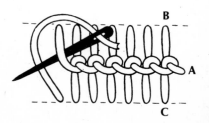

Maltese cross

This decorative motif is worked in a similar way to interlacing stitch. The intertwining of the herringbone stitch must be worked accurately, otherwise the interlacing cannot be achieved. Bring the thread through at A and take a stitch from B to C. Carry the thread from C to D and take a stitch from D to E. Continue in this way following Figure 1 until the foundation is complete. Figure 2 shows the method of interlacing, which begins at F. Figure 3 shows the completed motif.

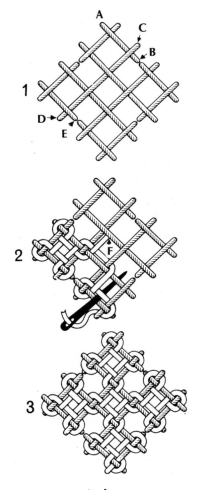

Open chain stitch

This stitch is shown worked on two parallel lines, but it may be used for shapes which vary in width. Bring the thread through at A and, holding the thread

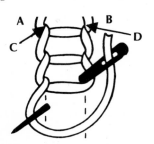

down with the left thumb, insert the needle at B. Bring the needle through at C, the required depth of the stitch. Leave the loop thus formed slightly loose. Insert the needle at D and, with the thread under the needle point, bring it through in readiness for the next stitch. Secure the last loop with a small stitch at each side.

Open Cretan stitch

Bring the thread through at A and, with the thread above the needle, insert the needle at B and bring it through at C. With the thread below the needle, insert the needle at D and bring it through at E. All stitches lie at right angles to the guide lines as shown in the diagram and are spaced at regular intervals. This is a useful stitch for borders.

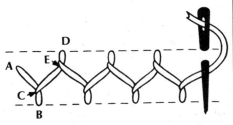

Open fishbone stitch

Bring the thread through at A and make a sloping stitch to B. Bring the thread through again at C and make another sloping stitch to D. Bring the thread through at E, continue in this way until the shape is filled.

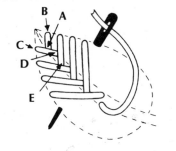

Overcast stitch (or trailing)

Bring the laid threads through at A and hold with the left thumb, then bring through the working thread at A and work small satin stitches closely over the laid threads, following the line of the design.

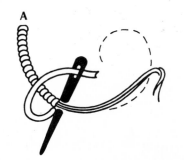

The laid threads are taken through to the back of the fabric to finish. This stitch resembles a fine cord and is useful for embroidering delicate stems and outlines.

Pekinese stitch

Work backstitch in the usual way, then interlace with a thread to tone or a thread of a different color. The stitch is shown open in the diagram but the loops should be pulled slightly tighter when working.

Portuguese border stitch

Work the required number of foundation bars, which are evenly spaced horizontal straight stitches. Bring the thread through at A, with the working thread to the left of the needle. Carry it over and under the first two bars and under the second bar only, without piercing the fabric. The thread is now in position at B to start the second pair of stitches. Continue working in the same way to the top of the row. Bring a new thread through at C and proceed in exactly the same way, but with the working thread to the right of the needle. Do not pull the surface stitches tightly.

Portuguese stem stitch

Figure A, begin as for ordinary stem stitch. Figure B, pull the thread through and pass the needle under the stitch just made, without entering the fabric. Figure C, pass the needle under the same stitch below the first coil. Figure D, make another stem stitch. Figure E, pass the needle twice under the stitch just made and under the previous stitch. Figure F, a section showing the formation of the stitch.

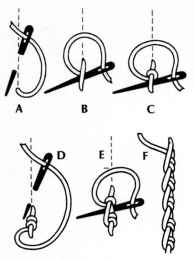

Punch stitch

This stitch can be used as a filling stitch in free embroidery – that is, over a tracing of squares or spots. A punch needle is used for the traced design to make the holes. The stitches are pulled firmly. Bring the thread through and take a stitch directly above, bringing the needle out where the thread first emerged (A). Insert the needle into the same hole above and bring out the same distance to the left on the lower line (B). Work along the row in this way, two stitches into the same place in each case (C). Turn the work upside down for each following row and continue in the same way until all vertical rows are complete (D). Turn the work sideways and repeat the process to complete the squares (E).

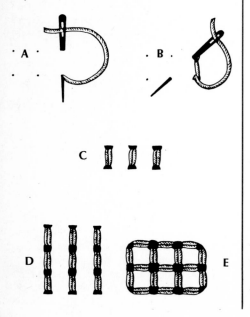

Raised chain band

Work the required number of foundation bars, which are fairly closely spaced horizontal straight stitches. Bring the thread through at A, then pass the needle upward under the center of the first bar and to the left of A. With the thread under the needle, pass the needle downward to the right of A and pull up the chain loop thus formed.

Rosette chain stitch

Bring the thread through at the right end of the upper line, pass the thread across to the left side and hold down with the left thumb. Insert the needle into the upper line a short distance from where the thread emerged and bring it out just above the lower line, passing the thread under the needle point (A). Draw the needle through and then pass the needle under the top thread (B) without picking up any of the fabric. This stitch can be used for small flowers if worked around in a circle or for borders when worked straight.

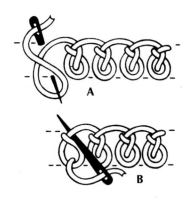

Rumanian couching

This form of couching is useful for filling in large spaces in which a flat, indefinite background is required. Bring the thread through on the left, carry the thread across the space to be filled and take a

small stitch on the right with the thread above the needle (A). Take small stitches along the line at intervals, as in B and C, to the end of the laid thread, emerging in position for the next stitch (D).

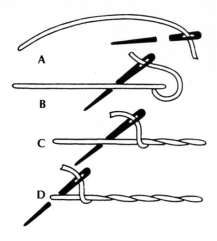

Rumanian stitch

Figure A, bring the thread through at the top left of the shape, carry the thread across and take a stitch on the right side of the shape with the thread below the needle. Figure B, take a stitch at the left side, thread above the needle. These two movements are worked until the shape is filled. Keep the stitches close together. The size of the center crossing stitch can be varied to make a longer diagonal stitch or a small straight stitch.

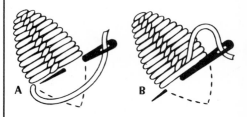

Running stitch

Pass the needle over and under the fabric, making the upper stitches of equal length. The under stitches should also be of equal length, but half the size or less of the upper stitches.

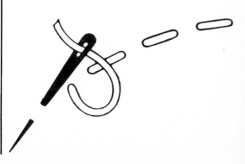

Satin stitch

Work straight stitches worked closely together across the shape, as shown in the diagram. If desired, running stitch or chain stitch may be worked first to form a padding underneath, giving a raised effect. Care must be taken to keep a good edge. Do not make the stitches too long, as this makes them liable to be pulled out of position. To keep a good edge, outline the shape first in chain or split stitch.

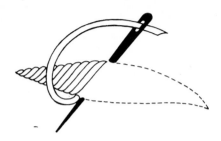

Scroll stitch

This stitch is worked from left to right. The working thread is looped to the right then back to the left on the fabric. Inside this loop the needle takes a small slanting stitch to the left under the line of the design, with the thread of the loop under the needle point. The thread is then pulled through. The stitches should be evenly spaced. This stitch forms an attractive border.

Seeding

This simple filling stitch is composed of small straight stitches of equal length placed at random over the surface, as shown in the figure.

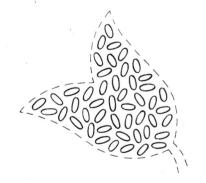

Sheaf stitch

This is an attractive filling stitch consisting of three vertical satin stitches tied across the center with two horizontal overcasting stitches. The overcasting stitches are worked around the satin stitches; the needle only enters the fabric to pass on to the next sheaf. The sheaves may be worked in alternate rows as shown, or in close horizontal rows directly below each other.

Spanish knotted feather stitch

Bring the thread through and hold down to the left with the left thumb. Take a slanting stitch to the left through the fabric under the laid thread and pull through with the needle point over the working thread as shown at A. Pass the thread over to the right and back to the left to form a loop and hold down, then take a slanting stitch to the right under the laid thread and pull through with the needle over the working thread B. Take a stitch in the same way to the left as at C. Repeat B and C to the end of the line, then fasten off with a small stitch as shown at D.

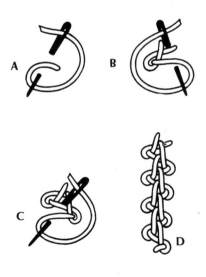

Spider's web filling, woven

Begin with a fly stitch to the center of the circle as shown in A. Then work two straight stitches, one on each side of the fly stitch tail, into the center of the circle. This divides the circle into five equal sections and the "spokes" form the foundation of the web. Weave over and under the "spokes" until the circle is filled as at B. In drawn thread embroidery the "spokes" are not completely covered by the weaving; only half the circle is filled, which gives the filling an open, lacy appearance.

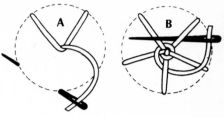

Split stitch

Bring the thread through at A and make a small stitch over the line of the design, piercing the working thread with the needle as shown in the figure. Split stitch may be used as a filling where a fine flat surface is required.

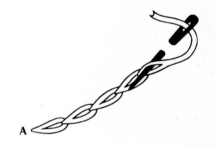

Stem stitch

Work from left to right, taking regular, slightly slanting stitches along the line of the design. The thread always emerges on the left side of the previous stitch. This stitch is used for flower stems, outlines, etc. It can also be used as a filling, where rows of stem stitch are worked closely together within a shape until it is filled completely.

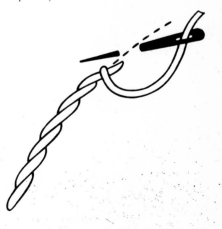

Straight stitch or single satin stitch

This is shown as single spaced stitches worked either in a regular or irregular manner. Sometimes the stitches are of varying size. The stitches should be neither too long nor too loose. This stitch may also be worked on evenweave fabric.

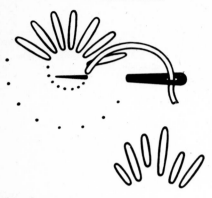

Striped woven band

Work the required number of foundation bars which are evenly spaced horizontal straight stitches. Thread two needles with contrasting threads and bring them through the fabric to lie side by side at A, the light thread on the left side. Pass the light thread under the first straight stitch and leave it lying. Take the dark thread over the first straight stitch and under the second straight stitch and also under the light thread. Leave the dark thread lying and pass the light thread over the second straight stitch, under the third straight stitch and also under the dark thread. Continue to the end of the border. Begin each following row from the top. By altering the sequence of the contrasting threads, various patterns may be achieved.

Twisted chain stitch

Begin as for ordinary chain stitch, but instead of inserting the needle into the place from where it emerged, insert it close to the last loop and take a small slanting stitch, coming out on the line of the design. Pull the thread through. The loops of this stitch should be worked closely together to give the correct effect.

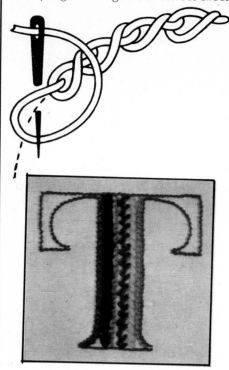

Twisted insertion stitch

A small stitch is taken alternately on each piece of fabric to be joined. The needle always enters the fabric from beneath and is twisted once around the thread before entering the fabric for the opposite stitch.

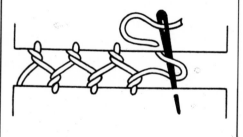

Up and down buttonhole stitch

Figure A. Begin as for ordinary buttonhole stitch and pull thread through. Figure B. Insert the needle on the bottom line and take a straight upward stitch with the thread under the needle point. Pull the thread through first in an upward movement, then downward to continue. This stitch may also be worked on evenweave fabric.

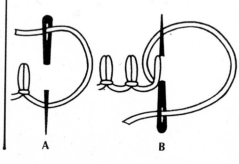

Vandyke stitch

Bring the thread through at A. Take a small horizontal stitch at B and insert the needle at C. Bring the thread through at D. Without piercing the fabric, pass the needle under the crossed threads at B and insert at E. Do not pull the stitches too tightly, otherwise the regularity of the center braid will be lost.

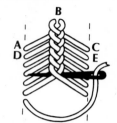

Wheatear stitch

Work two straight stitches at A and B. Bring the thread through below these stitches at C and pass the needle under the two straight stitches without entering the fabric. Insert the needle at C and bring it through at D.

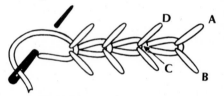

Zigzag cable chain stitch

This stitch is a variation of ordinary cable chain stitch, each stitch being taken at a right angle to the previous stitch. Pull the twisted thread firmly around the needle before drawing the needle through the fabric.

INDEX

Picture credits:
American Museum in Britain 323
Beta pictures 350
Camera Press 168B, 193, 325, 328, 329, 343, 347, 356, 436
Cooper Bridgeman 331
100 Idees de Marie Claire 168T, 332
PAF International 334, 335, 336
Transworld 349
Ulster Folk and Transport Museum 163
Pictures page 3 by courtesy of the Victoria and Albert Museum, London.

Photographers: Steve Bicknell, Stuart Brown, John Carter, Roger Charity, Monty Coles, Richard Dunkley, Alan Duns, David Finch, Jean Paul Froget, John Garrett, Melvin Grey, Peter Heinz, Graham Henderson, Tony Horth, Jeany, Peter Kibbles, Trevor Lawrence, Chris Lewis, Sandra Lousada, Dick Millar, Julian Nieman, Kjell Nilsson, Tony Page, Roger Phillips, Peter Pugh-Cook, Iain Reid, John Ryan, Jill Smyth, John Swannell, Jerry Tubby, Jean Claude Volpeliere, Rupert Watts, Paul Williams.